EMPOWERING ENERGY CONSUMERS IN THE EU

# EMPOWERING ENERGY CONSUMERS IN THE EU

## Legal Pathways for Promoting Renewable Electricity through Demand-Side Management

Ting CHEN

This research was jointly supported by the China Scholarship Council and the Bijzonder Onderzoeksfonds (BOF) of Ghent University

INTERSENTIA
LEFEBVRE GROUP

Intersentia
Lefebvre Belgium SA
Avenue Jean Monnet 4
1348 Louvain-la-Neuve
Belgium
Email: contact@larcier-intersentia.com

*Distribution for the UK, Ireland and*
*Rest of the World (excl. France, Belgium and Luxembourg)*
Ingram Publisher Services UK
1 Deltic Avenue, Rooksley
Milton Keynes MK13 8LD
United Kingdom
Tel: +44 1752 202 301 | Fax: +44 1752 202 331
Email: ipsuk.customercare@ingramcontent.com

*Distribution for France and Rest of the World (excl. Ireland and the UK)*
Interforum Editis
Avenue de France 92
75013 Paris
France

*Distribution for Belgium and Luxembourg*
Larcier-Intersentia
Avenue Jean Monnet 4
1348 Louvain-la-Neuve
Belgium

Empowering Energy Consumers in the EU. Legal Pathways for Promoting Renewable Electricity through Demand-Side Management


ISBN 978-1-83970-617-2
D/2026/06040/0037
NUR 823

British Library Cataloguing in Publication Data. A catalogue record for this book is available from the British Library.

# CONTENTS

# ABSTRACT

Facilitating the uptake of renewable electricity (RES-E) is vital for advancing the sustainable energy transition and mitigating climate change. The early way of deploying RES-E was characterized by a 'supply-side mindset'. It primarily focused on decarbonizing the conventional electricity supply chain, i.e., shifting centralized production from fossil-based to renewables. The role of energy consumers in facilitating the system integration and use of RES-E was largely overlooked. Instead, they were positioned as passive receivers of electricity and prices. Shifts in energy demand or consumer behavior that can favor the use of RES-E were never a central consideration, significantly limiting the electricity system's potential to integrate RES-E. Insufficient focus on the demand side overlooks the fact that transitioning to a low-carbon electricity system is a multifaceted effort requiring a holistic, system-wide approach with comprehensive transformations, including adaptations by energy consumers.

In recent decades, increasing attention has been given to the previously overlooked need for empowering energy consumers to support the high penetration of RES-E. Electricity demand-side management (DSM) mechanisms serve as specific approaches to empowering consumers, which play a pivotal role in accelerating the transition toward an electricity system with high shares of RES-E. To adapt electricity demand to facilitate RES-E uptake, electricity DSM focuses on two key modifications of consumer behavior: (i) making electricity demand flexible to support the system integration of intermittent RES-E, and (ii) increasing the share of RES-E in electricity consumption. Such adjustments imply the need to reshape the roles of energy consumers and address their evolving relationships with traditional players in the energy sector.

Accomplishing these tasks requires a legal framework to define the energy consumers' roles, rights and obligations that are geared toward the goal of facilitating RES-E uptake, and to properly structure these 'proactive' consumers' relationships with other stakeholders (e.g., suppliers, balance responsible parties and system operators) and newly emerging actors (e.g., energy service providers engaged in flexibility provision and energy communities). Additionally, empowering passive consumers to be proactive participants in the energy transition is a complex challenge that requires concrete measures going beyond the mere granting of participation rights.

A legal framework is needed to provide consumers with enabling instruments to solve economic, regulatory and behavioral barriers. The law establishing rules for enabling electricity DSM to adjust electricity consumption is referred to as the 'electricity DSM law'. This book focuses on how the electricity DSM law can operationalize consumer empowerment to facilitate the system integration and use of RES-E.

Since the adoption of the Clean Energy Package, EU energy law has been reoriented to harness consumer engagement as an essential tool for creating a renewables-based electricity system. This makes it a prominent case for studying legal approaches to empowering energy consumers to enable high RES-E uptake. Focusing on EU law on electricity DSM, this book analyzes key elements of a legal framework for empowering consumers to promote RES-E and discusses typical legal challenges.

Through normative analysis and research on the implementation of the law, this book indicates the room for improving the existing EU legal framework for electricity DSM. With the identified gaps, drawing on the CJEU's jurisprudence and existing academic debate, it further explores potential solutions, lessons and implications. These provide useful insights for other jurisdictions with ambitions to increase the penetration level of RES-E.

# LIST OF ABBREVIATIONS

| | |
|---|---|
| ACER | European Agency for the Cooperation of Energy Regulators |
| aFRR | Automatic frequency restoration reserve |
| BRP | Balance responsible party |
| BRUGEL | Brusselse regulerende instantie voor elektriciteit, gas en controle van de waterprijs (Brussels electricity, gas and water price regulator) |
| BSP | Balance service provider |
| CAPEX | Capital expenditure |
| CDSO | Closed distribution system operator |
| CEC | Citizen energy community |
| CEER | Council of European Energy Regulators |
| CEP | Clean energy for all Europeans package |
| CJEU | Court of Justice of the European Union |
| COP | Conference of party |
| CREG | Commission for Electricity and Gas Regulation of Belgium |
| CRU | Commission for Regulation of Utilities |
| CWaPE | Commission wallonne pour l'Energie (Walloon Energy Commission) |
| DA/ID | Day-ahead and intraday |
| DER | Distributed energy resource |
| DG | Distributed generation |
| DR | Demand response |
| DSM | Demand-side management |
| DSO | Distribution system operator |
| EC | European Commission |
| ENTSO-E | European Network of Transmission System Operators for Electricity |

| | |
|---|---|
| EU | European Union |
| EU DSO entity | European Entity for Distribution System Operators |
| FERC | Federal Energy Regulatory Commission |
| FeReSO | FEBEG Reconciliation and Settlement Organisation |
| FCR | Frequency containment reserves |
| FIT | Feed-in tariff |
| FRP | Flexibility request party |
| FRR | Frequency restoration reserves |
| FSP | Flexibility service provider |
| GO | Guarantees of origin |
| GW | Gigawatt |
| GWEC | Global Wind Energy Council |
| ICT | Information and communication technologies |
| IEA | International Energy Agency |
| IFSP | Independent flexibility service provider |
| IRENA | International Renewable Energy Agency |
| LEM | Local electricity market |
| LFC | Load-frequency control |
| LMO | Local market operator |
| LV | Low voltage |
| mFRR | Manual frequency restoration reserve |
| MIIT | Ministry of Industry and Information Technology of China |
| MV | Medium voltage |
| NDRC | National Development and Reform Commission of China |
| NEA | National Energy Administration of China |
| NECP | National energy and climate plan |
| NRA | National regulatory authority |
| OFGEM | Office of Gas and Electricity Markets |
| OPEX | Operational expenditure |
| PAC | Pay-as-clear |

| | |
|---|---|
| PBR | Performance-based regulation |
| PPA | Power purchase agreement |
| PSO | Public service obligation |
| P2P | Peer-to-peer |
| PV | Photovoltaic |
| REC | Renewable energy community |
| REDII | Recast Renewable Energy Directive |
| RES | Renewable energy source |
| RES-E | Renewable energy source electricity |
| RIIO | Revenue = Incentives + Innovation + Outputs |
| RR | Replacement reserves |
| SDP | Service delivery point |
| SME | Small and medium-sized enterprises |
| TEU | Treaty on European Union |
| TFEU | Treaty on the Functioning of the European Union |
| TGC | Tradable green certificate |
| ToE | Transfer of energy |
| TOU | Time-of-use |
| TPA | Third-party access |
| TRDE | Technical Regulations for the Distribution of Electricity |
| TSO | Transmission system operator |
| UNFCCC | United Nations Framework Convention on Climate Change |
| VIU | Vertically integrated undertaking |
| VEKA | Vlaams Energie- en Klimaatagentschap (Flemish Energy and Climate Agency) |
| VME | Vereniging van mede-eigenaars (Association of co-owners) |
| VREG[i] | Vlaamse Regulator van de Elektriciteits- en Gasmarkt (Flemish Regulator of the Electricity and Gas Market) |

[i] As of January 2025, the VREG was renamed the Flemish Utility Regulator (Vlaamse Nutsregulator). However, this book uses 'VREG' throughout, as the referenced documents were issued prior to 2025 under the former name.

# CHAPTER I
# INTRODUCTION

1. This chapter provides the research context as an introduction to how law can use electricity DSM to facilitate the uptake of RES-E. Section 1 sets out the background and explains the conceptual interplay between consumer empowerment, DSM, and RES-E promotion. Section 2 outlines the aim and scope of the research, while Section 3 presents the methodology. The chapter concludes in Section 4 with an overview of the book's structure.

## 1. RESEARCH CONTEXT

2. This section consists of the background of this book and the key concepts referred to in this research. The background, among others, contains the global challenge of the low-carbon energy transition, the importance of decarbonizing the electricity sector, the role of energy consumers and the electricity DSM law in promoting RES-E, and the reasons for focusing on the EU.

### 1.1. BACKGROUND

3. This section provides the background to this research by situating electricity DSM within the context of EU electricity law. It first explains the growing role of energy consumers in promoting the uptake of renewable electricity, particularly as prosumers and flexibility providers. It then introduces the conceptual interplay between consumer empowerment, DSM, and renewable electricity integration: consumer empowerment enables behavioral change, which is realized through DSM measures, and such change is essential for increasing the share of renewable electricity. Finally, the section highlights the role of law in structuring and enabling this process, framing DSM not merely as a technical matter but as a legal and regulatory concept.

#### *1.1.1. The Role of Energy Consumers in Promoting Renewable Electricity*

4. Facing energy security concerns caused by finite fossil fuel sources and the existential threat posed by climate change, the world must switch to sustainable

energy systems (Solomon and Krishna, 2011). Due to its role in providing long-term alternatives to fossil fuels and reducing carbon emissions, renewable energy has been at the heart of the sustainable energy transition (Newbery et al., 2018; Raineau, 2022). Amongst all sectors that make up the energy system, electricity is the most cost-effective to decarbonize (EC, 2016a; Gräper et al., 2021; Newbery et al., 2018). Notably, given the difficulties of decarbonizing transport and heating, the electricity sector will continue to bear a significant burden arising from economy-wide decarbonization (Newbery et al., 2018). As a result, in addition to fostering energy saving in the electricity sector, in the past decades, we have witnessed enhanced actions globally to deploy RES-E, as shown in Figure 1 below. This trend has been reinforced by climate change mitigation ambitions set by the UNFCCC and its follow-up COPs charged with the purpose of finding operational procedures for stabilizing the global climate (*UNFCCC*, 1992; *Kyoto Protocol*, 1997; *Paris Agreement*, 2015; Meyer, 2003; Kahrl et al., 2011).

5. While the energy sector takes a major role in decarbonizing the economy (Meyer, 2003), the above international conventions have invariably left it to their parties to decide on specific approaches to facilitating renewables (*Kyoto Protocol*, 1997; *UNFCCC*, 1992). The Paris Agreement does not even refer to 'energy' (*Paris Agreement*, 2015). In this regard, the high discretion of convention parties echoes that decarbonization of the energy sector is interwoven with sovereignty over natural resources, which is fundamental in international law, and reflects the parties' preference to maintain independent policy control over sectors closely tied to national security (Abraham-Dukuma, 2020; Huhta, 2021). Variations in specific circumstances, energy mix, and capacity to support renewables may place countries at different stages in deploying RES-E, leading to diverse approaches (Haas et al., 2011; Pablo-Romero et al., 2021). Nevertheless, they share common challenges in increasing the penetration of RES-E, which may require significant transformations of the electricity system. In this context, examining specific national or supranational approaches to promoting RES-E is crucial for identifying robust, cost-efficient solutions to the global challenge of the low-carbon energy transition.

6. In terms of facilitating RES-E, a common challenge is which segments of the electricity system should be involved and how to adapt them to enable high penetration of RES-E (Farhangi, 2010; Newbery et al., 2018; Quint et al., 2019). Historically, the electricity sector has been dominated by a supply-side mindset (Michaelis et al., 2024). It leads to a centralized approach to organizing the electricity system with large remote generation mainly based on conventional sources, high-voltage transmission systems serving as 'backbones', low-voltage distribution systems as 'appendages' passing on electricity to the point of final consumption, and the loads (Bouffard and Kirschen, 2008; Goldthau, 2014; Diestelmeier, 2019a). Electricity systems have been envisaged, designed

and operated from the point of view of centralized electricity generation, and have largely focused on the technical and economic aspects of the diverse production technologies as well as on the availability (Fernández et al., 2016). With this perspective, the main objective of the design of electricity systems has always been the adequacy and reliability of supply at the lowest generation cost (Fernández et al., 2016). Correspondingly, energy consumers have long been at the end of the supply chain as largely passive actors and subject to a protective legal framework (Diestelmeier, 2019a). Electricity law was initially tailored to this centrally organized sector and defined the rights and obligations of actors along the 'top-down' supply chain (producers, TSOs and DSOs, suppliers, and consumers), as exemplified in the UK, the EU, the U.S. and China (Ngan, 2010; Kahrl et al., 2011; Joskow, 2008; Lavrijssen, 2017; Diestelmeier, 2019; FERC).

7. The supply-side mindset has long been entrenched, shaping the early way of integrating renewables into the electricity system. The decarbonization of the electricity sector is customarily approached by decarbonizing the conventional electricity supply chain, i.e., shifting centralized production from fossil-based to renewables (Raineau, 2022). The generation capacity of centralized RES-E has increased remarkably over the past decades, especially in several front-runners of developing RES-E, which benefits from massive investments from both the public and private sectors.[1] By contrast, the question of demand has long been left aside: shifts in energy demand or consumer behavior that favor RES-E uptake were never a central consideration (Warren, 2014; Sorrell, 2015; Kuzemko et al., 2017; Raineau, 2022). Consumers remained passive players on the receiving end (Lavrijssen et al., 2023). They were disconnected from the natural origin of energy, from its availability and its production constraints (Raineau, 2022). Nor can they perceive the upstream or downstream effects of their energy consumption on their surrounding environment (Raineau, 2022). To what extent their electricity use could be adapted to unlock the greater potential of integrating RES-E was hardly contemplated.[2]

---

1 For instance, the generation capacity of concentrated solar power increased from 3942 MW in 2013 to 6501 MW in 2022. See IRENA, 2023a.

2 It is interesting to note that there exist a few exceptions. Denmark is an example of enabling and encouraging final customers to engage in renewables DG in the EU. Energy security concerns in the 1970s notably drove measures for engaging consumers in developing a decentralized electricity system. Compared to the highly centralized Danish power infrastructure in 1985, the power infrastructure in 2018 has evolved into a decentralized system with high penetrations of decentralized wind generation and combined heat and power (CHP) plants. Around 2010, international comparisons of the energy security performance of 22 countries within the OECD concluded that Denmark was the most energy secure. The case of Denmark shows that DSM measures have the potential to advance both sustainability and energy security. See Sovacool, 2013; Jin et al., 2020.

8. Little attention to the consumer side indicates the neglect of the fact that transitioning to a low-carbon electricity system is a multifaceted endeavor, affecting various electricity system stakeholders, including rule-makers, producers, investors, and consumers, and necessitating their proactive engagement (Michaelis et al., 2024). When the deployment of renewables is envisioned within the supply-side logic, the due account was not given to a key feature of the electric socio-technical system, which is a complex in which are embedded techniques of production and provision, domestic devices, consumption habits, and lifestyles, and which supports the imaginary (of nature and society) and values on which the system is based (Raineau, 2022). This feature implies that when the socio-technical system adapts to renewables, changes are not only needed in production and provision, but also the relationship between consumers and energy, allowing new practices, routines, and needs of end users to emerge (Raineau, 2022). Hence, a holistic or system-wide approach to developing RES-E is imperative to deliver transitions in behavioral patterns of not only producers and network operators but also final customers (Geels, 2010; Hoggett, 2017; Haley et al., 2020; Raineau, 2022).

9. The absence of such a holistic approach in the nascent stage of developing RES-E has given rise to some problems, which compromise the electricity system's potential to integrate renewables (Raineau, 2022). A leading example is acute RES-E curtailment in China resulting from the widening mismatch between increasing RES-E generation capacity and consumption. RES-E curtailment in China primarily occurs at large, concentrated generation bases for solar and wind electricity located in Northeast and Northwest China (Zhang, 2016; NEA, 2018; Auffhammer et al., 2021). Due to the difficulty of accessing networks and insufficient consumption of RES-E, the renewables generators are compelled to reduce electricity output and thus suffer from a waste of capacity and revenue loss (Zhang, 2016; NEA, 2018). This problem has become severe over the recent decade, when the generation capacities of RES-E started steeply rising in China (Auffhammer et al., 2021). In response to this crisis, from 2017 onward, China's rule-makers started incorporating the missing facet, i.e., adapting the demand side to support RES-E uptake (NDRC, 2017, 2018; MIIT, 2019). Over the same period, other jurisdictions with growing penetration of RES-E also recognized the importance of a system-wide approach to facilitating RES-E, in which final customers have a pivotal role to play (EC, 2016a; Shen et al., 2014; Warren, 2014). Then, in addition to the traditional role of purchasing electricity for their own use, what new roles could be assumed by consumers in the era of developing RES-E?

10. Such roles are closely linked to the potential contributions of an adaptable demand side in supporting high RES-E uptake, primarily on two fronts. First, a flexible electricity load can facilitate system integration of variable

RES-E (Quan et al., 2015; Hoggett, 2017; Barbero et al., 2018). In the past decades, the installed capacity of wind and solar electricity has experienced particularly significant growth worldwide (GWEC, 2022, 2013; IEA, 2023), as shown in Figure 1 below.

**Figure 1. The historical and forecast trend of share of renewable electricity generation by technology, 2000–2028** (IEA, 2023)

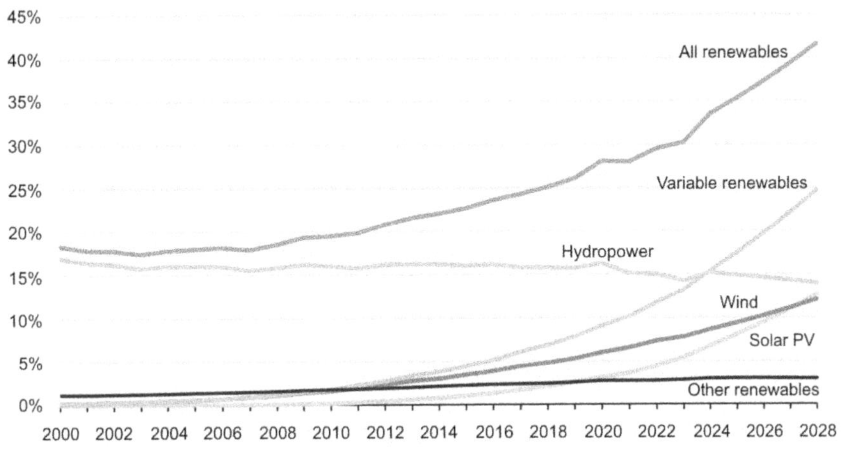


11. The growth trend in solar and wind electricity generation capacity has become even more evident in recent years and is expected to continue in the near future. According to the IRENA, global renewable generation capacity reached 3372 GW by the end of 2022, with solar and wind accounting for a substantial portion of this increase (IRENA, 2023b). That year has seen the largest increase in renewable energy capacity to date – the world added almost 295 GW of renewables (IRENA, 2023a). Solar power alone accounted for almost two-thirds of the renewable additions, with a record 192 GW, while 75 GW of wind energy was added (IRENA, 2023a). The IEA also reports that renewable electricity capacity is expected to rise more than 60% from 2020 levels to over 4800 GW by 2026 (IEA, 2021). This expansion is driven primarily by solar PV, which is forecast to provide more than half of the new capacity, and wind energy (IEA, 2021). Solar and wind sources are 'intermittent', since they are dependent on the weather, which makes electricity output more variable and less predictable (van der Welle and de Joode, 2011). The electricity system requires instantaneous generation-load balance, which is conventionally achieved by adjusting production to fit variable consumer demand (Fernández et al., 2016). With a significant and increasing segment of variable renewable generation that cannot be scheduled on request, system flexibility (provided by flexible power system players by changing their desired energy production

or consumption) is crucial to maintaining system balance and security (Fernández et al., 2016; Lin et al., 2022). One of the key flexibility sources can be provided by final customers by adapting demand to react to variations in the output of RES-E, known as DR or demand flexibility (Paddock and Youngblood, 2012; Papsch, 2020), as defined in Section 1.2 below.

12. While conventional generators or large-scale storage facilities can provide flexibility, it is believed that demand flexibility offers several advantages. Demand flexibility exhibits superior performance in terms of economic efficiency and environmental sustainability (Fernández et al., 2016; Michaelis et al., 2024). This is because it reduces the need for supply-side flexibility provided by conventional power plants, i.e., by keeping fossil-based power plants in operation, and even opening new ones, to meet the demand for electricity in real-time when there is no wind or sun, and thus lowers indirect carbon emissions in integrating variable RES-E (Raineau, 2022). Moreover, demand flexibility does not face public acceptance challenges or protracted administrative approval processes (Michaelis et al., 2024).

13. In addition to the essential role in achieving the flexibility necessary to adapt the electricity system to variable renewable electricity generation, energy consumers could further unlock the potential of RES-E uptake by purchasing and engaging in RES-E prosumption (i.e., producing while consuming renewables). Advances in DG technologies enable consumers to produce RES-E individually or collectively to meet their own energy needs.

14. Efforts to transform formerly passive consumers into proactive actors who are willing and able to provide flexibility and use renewable electricity align closely with the concept of consumer empowerment (Hanke and Lowitzsch, 2020), which has been frequently discussed in contemporary energy policy debates (Lavrijssen, 2017; Ioannidou, 2018; Bedggood et al., 2023).

### *1.1.2. Conceptual Interplay: Consumer Empowerment and Electricity Demand-Side Management*

15. Empowerment refers to the action of empowering someone or something: the granting of the power, right, or authority to perform various acts or duties (Hanke and Lowitzsch, 2020). Achieving empowerment requires addressing the causes of disempowerment and tackling disadvantage arising from the way in which power relations shape choices, opportunities and wellbeing (Luttrell et al., 2009). Its aim is to transform the formerly powerless into capable individuals who are willing and able to take ownership and responsibility for their own choices, decisions, and actions in society or on markets (Hanke and

Lowitzsch, 2020). In policy discourse, empowering consumers is stressed to enable consumers to drive a smart, sustainable and inclusive economy (see e.g., EC, 2012a, 2015a). By establishing a robust framework of safety, information, education, rights, redress, and enforcement, policymakers expect empowered consumers to participate actively in the market, exercise their power of choice, and benefit from the effective protection of their rights (EC, 2012a).

16. In the context of the low-carbon energy transition, consumer empowerment seeks to provide energy users with the rights, tools, and opportunities needed to play a proactive role in advancing the energy transition (EC, 2015b; Lavrijssen, 2017; Hanke and Lowitzsch, 2020). In line with the growing focus on the consumer side, it aims to shift energy consumers from passive recipients of energy into active participants (Lavrijssen, 2017). Realizing this shift, however, depends on specific approaches designed to shape and modify the behavior of energy consumers, collectively referred to as 'demand-side mechanisms'. In a nutshell, DSM provides a concrete set of measures through which the broader concept of consumer empowerment is operationalized in the energy sector.

17. In the electricity sector, in terms of decarbonizing the electricity system, DSM has mainly been about energy efficiency measures since the last century (Didden and D'haeseleer, 2003; Verbong and Geels, 2007; Haley et al., 2020). However, given the consumers' role in supporting RES-E integration and wider use, the task of DSM should extend beyond energy savings to include facilitating the development of a high-renewables electricity system. Electricity DSM serving this goal comprises two groups of mechanisms reflecting the above-mentioned roles of final customers: (i) making electricity load flexible enough to facilitate the system integration of variable RES-E, and (ii) increasing the share of RES-E in electricity consumption. As regards the second mechanism, it should be noted that DSM aims to 'increase the share of RES-E in electricity consumption' rather than simply 'increasing consumption of RES-E'. In this way, the DSM for facilitating RES-E can avoid conflicts with energy-saving purposes. In general, aside from promoting RES-E, energy efficiency is another key pillar for advancing the low-carbon energy transition and enhancing the security of supply.[3] The 'energy efficiency first' principle has been anchored in EU law, which means '*taking utmost account in energy*

[3] Measures in the EU and China are examples in this regard. See NDRC and NEA, 2022; Standing Committee of the National People's Congress, article 1; *Energy and Climate Governance Regulation*, article 2(18).; *European Climate Law*, recitals 9 and 15.

*planning, and in policy and investment decisions, of alternative cost-efficient energy efficiency measures to make energy demand and energy supply more efficient'* (*Energy and Climate Governance Regulation*, 2018; *European Climate Law*, 2021). Thus, to align with energy-saving targets, the second goal of the electricity DSM in question should be formulated as changing electricity consumption patterns to increase the share of RES-E in consumption. In the following text, promoting RES-E use should be understood as increasing its share in electricity consumption. After clarifying the role of electricity DSM, the next question is, why is the law needed to realize the potential of electricity DSM to facilitate RES-E uptake?

### *1.1.3. The Role of Law*

18. The first role of the legislation on electricity DSM is to clearly define the dual role of energy consumers in supporting the uptake of RES-E. The law also needs to empower consumers to undertake activities related to their proactive role by articulating their rights and obligations, which are interwoven with those of other stakeholders in the electricity sector. Enabling the rising role of consumers would cut through those well-defined actor definitions, given their evolving interactions with final customers (Diestelmeier, 2019a). Legal arrangements are necessary to properly structure the relationships between energy consumers and traditional actors (e.g., suppliers, BRPs, and system operators) as well as newly emerging actors (e.g., energy service providers and energy communities). In addition, as highlighted above, consumers have long been passive actors in the traditional energy regime. Prompting them to transition to proactive actors involved in the energy transition is an intractable challenge that requires more actions than simply granting them the right to do so. The law should also provide enabling instruments to address multidimensional barriers to consumer engagement, encompassing both economic and behavioral aspects, as detailed in Chapter II below. The law that creates rules for realizing the role of electricity DSM in adjusting electricity consumption is referred to as the 'electricity DSM law', forming the implementation framework of consumer empowerment. How the electricity DSM law can adapt electricity consumption to facilitate RES-E uptake is the focus of this book.

19. By highlighting sufficient attention to the demand side, this work could contribute to developing a holistic approach to transitioning toward an electricity system with high penetration of RES-E. Figure 2 presents a schematic overview of a systemic approach to developing RES-E encompassing both changes in centralized electricity supply and electricity demand.

**Figure 2. Schematic overview of the system-wide approach to developing RES-E**

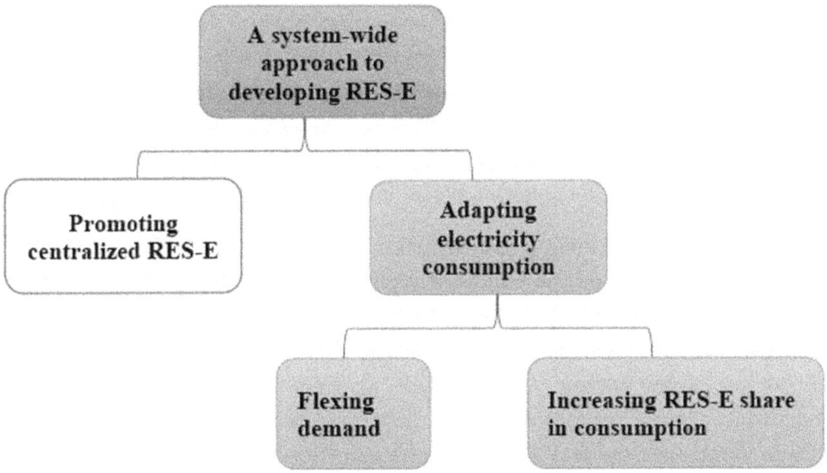


Source: Author's own elaboration.

20. Adopting a system-wide approach implies that the electricity system's transformation is no longer dominated by traditional actors along the electricity supply chain. It represents a significant shift toward polycentric, multi-stakeholder, and collaborative energy transition governance (Määttä, 2021). As a pillar of this whole-system transition, actively engaging consumers to enhance RES-E's integration and use reflects the newly emerging paradigm of the bottom-up energy transition, energy democracy, energy justice,[4] and the distributive economy (Hoggett, 2017; Milčiuvienė et al., 2019; Bjarghov et al., 2021). The EU is also undergoing a paradigm shift, with an increasing role for

[4] A detailed review of doctrines of energy justice is beyond the scope of this book. Yet, as an important concept containing criteria for evaluating energy law and policy, it is also applied in the following chapters. Here in the background, I briefly introduce the context in which this notion was presented. Originally, the purpose of the energy sector was the provision of energy at a reasonable cost and there has been little focus on the merits or value of other directions. In line with this, the regulation of the energy industry served conventional notions of rights and responsibilities for optimal resource exploitation. Amidst reflections on injustices in this field and the climate crisis, there has been increasing discussion for developing a legal and philosophical underpinning for energy law to provide a long-term orientation that enables comprehensive consideration of societal concerns. As a striking example of echoing these evolving notions, the novel concept of energy justice emerged, which contends that energy law should evolve to have justice at its core. It calls for the evolution of legal objectives and principles to embrace a broader mix of principles cutting across energy, environmental, developmental and climate goals. Notably, sustainability and due process, which were traditionally viewed as ancillary issues, have been incorporated in the core principles of energy justice. See Verbong and Geels, 2007; Walker and Day, 2012; Sovacool and Dworkin, 2015; B R. Jones et al., 2015; Walker et al., 2016; Sovacool et al., 2016; Heffron and Talus, 2016; Abraham-Dukuma, 2020; Calver and Simcock, 2021.

consumers in the context of enhanced ambitions to decarbonize the electricity system. The evolution of Union-level energy legislation is illustrative. The first three energy packages provided somewhat limited attention to engaging final customers (*1996 Electricity Directive*; *2003 Electricity Directive*; *2009 Electricity Directive*).[5] Most consumers were merely subject to protective measures, and their role in helping the integration of renewables into the system was not well recognized until the adoption of network codes under the Third Energy Package (*System Operation Guideline*, 2017; *Balancing Regulation*, 2017).

21. Since the fourth energy package (the 'Clean Energy Package (CEP)'), the EU has enhanced its ambition and stepped up climate change mitigation actions to deliver on the implementation of the Paris Agreement (EC, 2016a; *European Climate Law*, 2021). It established a binding Union target of a share of at least 32% of renewable energy (*REDII*, article 3). Under this target, the electricity system faced more profound changes than ever to realize a greater uptake of RES-E. Working in tandem with renewables promotional law, the EU's electricity legislation started searching for solutions on the demand side to further unlock the system's potential to integrate RES-E (Chen and Vandendriessche, 2023a).[6] In line with the vision of an Energy Union with citizens at its core, where citizens take ownership of the energy transition, benefit from new technologies to reduce their bills, and participate actively in the market, and where vulnerable consumers are protected (EC, 2015b), creating a 'customer-centred electricity market' was introduced as a new legislative objective (*Electricity Directive*, article 1). Since then, the EU has been in the process of developing an encompassing legal framework for empowering, enabling and incentivizing consumers to actively support RES-E's system integration and use. Driven by the need to accelerate the phase-out of the Union's dependence on (Russian) fossil fuels, the overall Union renewables target was increased to 42.5% to significantly accelerate the current pace of deployment of renewable energy (*Amendment to the REDII*, 2023, recital 5 and article 1). This move creates an additional driving force for reinforcing measures that engage consumers in contributing to the greater uptake of RES-E.

22. To recap, in the recent decade, EU energy law has been reoriented to harness consumer empowerment as an essential tool for creating a renewables-based electricity system. It is devoted to exploring, innovating and diversifying specific approaches to involving traditionally passive consumers and persistently adjusting regulatory approaches in response to challenges arising in practice. This fact makes the EU a prominent case for examining the legal

[5] For more details about the evolving role of energy consumers in advancing energy efficiency and RES-E development in the context of EU energy law, see Section 1.2.1 below of this Chapter.

[6] See Chapter III also for more details.

pathways through which consumer empowerment supports the promotion of RES-E, justifying this book's focus on EU law. Gains and lessons drawn from the case study of EU law and its implementation can provide useful insights for other jurisdictions with ambitions to further increase RES-E penetration levels.

23. Having introduced the research background and the region focused on by this book, key definitions applied throughout the following discussion will be clarified in the following subsection.

## 1.2. DEFINITION OF KEY CONCEPTS

24. This subsection defines key terms used throughout this book. As addressed above, in the context of developing RES-E, the electricity DSM law needs to facilitate the system integration of RES-E and promote consumers' use of RES-E. Thus, electricity DSM measures cover two subcategories: DR schemes and demand-side mechanisms for promoting RES-E. In the following, the evolving concept of electricity DSM as well as its definition in this book's context will be first dealt with in Section 1.2.1. This will be followed by the definition of 'DR' (Section 1.2.2) and 'demand-side mechanisms for promoting RES-E' (Section 1.2.3). The defining characteristics of demand-side measures, which distinguish them from supply-side measures for developing RES-E, will also become clear through such conceptual clarity. In particular, by highlighting that electricity DSM in this research is limited to adjusting *electricity consumption behavior*, rather than consumer behavior in a broad sense, which includes network use, the scope of this research could be better delimited.

### *1.2.1. Electricity DSM*

25. It has been widely recognized that electricity DSM aims to shape or modify electricity consumption behavior. However, there is a lack of consensus on concrete aspects involved in the adaptations made to electricity consumption and the goals they serve. The following brief review of academic literature and EU legislation suggests that the concept of electricity DSM is context-dependent and has evolved over time, reflecting shifting energy policy objectives.

26. Looking back at the first three energy legislative packages, it is found that the tasks of electricity DSM were initially limited to certain aspects. The 2003 Electricity Directive and the 2009 Electricity Directive imply that DSM is identical to energy efficiency approaches.[7] These directives stressed the DSM's

[7] 'Energy efficiency/demand-side management means '*a global or integrated approach aimed at influencing the amount and timing of electricity consumption in order to reduce primary*

role in reducing primary energy consumption and peak loads. The pivotal role of electricity DSM in adapting electricity consumption to accommodate the need for developing RES-E was largely disregarded. The adoption of the CEP has changed this situation.[8] Before that, network codes and regulations adopted by the EC under the Third Energy Package stress the role of electricity DSM in integrating RES-E, though limited, as mentioned above. A similar trend of extending the role of electricity DSM can also be found in the literature.

27. Over the recent decade, in the context of a broader and more complex range of objectives of the low-carbon energy transition, the multifaceted role of electricity DSM has received much scholarly attention (Strbac, 2008; Warren, 2015; Kuzemko et al., 2017; Haley et al., 2020; Raineau, 2022). Kuzemko et al. note the need to extend definitions of DSM in order to take better account of the complexity and challenges faced in this fast-emerging policy area (Kuzemko et al., 2017). Likewise, Warren proposes an encompassing definition of DSM to better suit all the current policy objectives of emissions reduction, energy security and affordability. He defines DSM as '*technologies, actions and programmes on the demand-side of energy metres that seek to manage or decrease energy consumption, in order to reduce total energy system expenditures or contribute to the achievement of policy objectives such as emissions reduction or balancing supply and demand*' (Warren, 2014). In particular, this definition stresses the role of the low-carbon energy transition target in enriching the concept of DSM. Further, Kuiken and Más view DSM as '*all actions aiming at changing electricity load profiles for optimization of the power system as a whole, from generation to delivery to end-use*' (Kuiken and Más, 2019). This implies that all measures targeting changes in electricity demand could be categorized as DSM, while highlighting the development of DSM in a manner that optimizes the entire electricity system. In line with understanding DSM in a broader sense, it has been widely appreciated that electricity DSM serves a broad spectrum of load-shape objectives, ranging from strategic reduction and load management to strategic load growth (Kuzemko et al., 2017; Warren, 2014; Haley et al., 2020; Gräper et al., 2021).

28. The definition of electricity DSM has developed considerably to go far beyond decreasing load for the sake of energy efficiency, which was historically the primary focus of DSM in the electricity sector (Haley et al., 2020). Promoting renewables DG involved by customers and flexing consumption also

*energy consumption and peak loads by giving precedence to investments in energy efficiency measures, or other measures, such as interruptible supply contracts, over investments to increase generation capacity, if the former are the most effective and economical option, taking into account the positive environmental impact of reduced energy consumption and the security of supply and distribution cost aspects related to it.*' See 2003 Electricity Directive, article 2 (29); 2009 Electricity Directive, article 2 (29).

8 See Chapter III below.

become key components of electricity DSM (Haley et al., 2020; Kuzemko et al., 2017), which is of great relevance in the context of developing RES-E, as explained before (Moura and de Almeida, 2010; Stötzer et al., 2015; Gräper et al., 2021; Raineau, 2022).

29. Furthermore, electricity DSM is widely seen as a portfolio of measures to improve the energy system on the side of consumption (Palensky and Dietrich, 2011). Emphasizing its role in exerting direct influence on the load distinguishes electricity DSM from some supply-side mechanisms, which also have implications for energy consumers' behavior (Palensky and Dietrich, 2011; Stötzer et al., 2015), as will be elaborated later on.

30. Based on the definitions of DSM presented in the literature, some general conclusions can be drawn as follows. Firstly, the concept of electricity DSM serves multiple aims, inter alia, reflecting the need for creating a form of demand that is compatible with the decarbonization of the electricity sector. The objectives of DSM have been extended to include not only energy efficiency and energy reduction but also maintaining electricity system balancing and reliability, as well as facilitating the use of RES-E.

31. Secondly, electricity DSM adapts electricity consumption patterns to facilitate the uptake of RES-E through measures targeting final customers directly. This makes it different from supply-side mechanisms that promote RES-E by providing favorable conditions for or imposing obligations on market players involved in the traditional electricity supply chain, such as subsidizing centralized RES-E projects and obliging suppliers to provide a minimum share of RES-E to their customers (Meyer, 2003; Wüstenhagen and Bilharz, 2006; Verbong and Geels, 2007; Herbes et al., 2020; CEER, 2021a). Admittedly, some of these supply-side schemes, such as subsidizing centralized RES-E production, indirectly influence end customers' acceptance of RES-E; however, they primarily focus on changing the electricity supply industry rather than final customers.[9] By contrast, electricity DSM measures are explicitly geared toward final customers, aiming to empower and encourage consumers to switch from using fossil fuels to RES-E. This is achieved, for instance, by increasing their awareness and mobilizing them to invest in and own renewable DG units, as well as trade self-generated RES-E.[10]

---

9 Granting subsidies to producers of RES-E could compensate for the difference between the production cost of RES-E and the market price of the form of power concerned, enabling RES-E producers to charge competitive prices on the market, which makes RES-E more accepted by consumers. See EC, 2001.

10 In this regard, a striking example is the enabling frameworks for the 'renewable energy community' and the 'renewables self-consumer' in EU law. See *REDII*, 2018, recitals 66 and 72, articles 2 (14)(15), 16, 17, 21 and 22.

32. This book focuses solely on the role of electricity DSM in influencing electricity consumption behavior, rather than all aspects of energy consumers' behavior. This aims to avoid a too broad definition of electricity DSM, contributing to a more detailed analysis. As such, using flexibility from demand-side storage, which is regarded as DSM in some studies (e.g. Jennifer Potter et al., 2018; European Smart Grids Task Force Expert Group 3, 2019) goes beyond the scope of this thesis. Moreover, electricity DSM can also cover measures for adjusting grid use to harness consumers' flexibility in using the electricity grid, via time-differentiated network tariffs or flexibility procurement to keep network utilization within capacity constraints (Neuteleers et al., 2017). Despite their importance in relieving grid congestion, DSM schemes aimed at adjusting consumers' grid use are not the core focus of the electricity DSM discussed in this book. They are mentioned mainly given their role in enabling system operators, especially DSOs, to manage increasing congestion caused by the rising integration of DERs[11] (including DR and renewables from final customers), and in providing economic incentives for consumers involved in DR and renewables self-consumption.[12]

33. Thirdly, electricity DSM could facilitate the uptake of RES-E by shaping electricity consumption on two fronts. One is making the demand flexible. This is realized by DR mechanisms, which play a key role in ensuring system integration of ever-increasing intermittent RES-E. The other is shifting the consumers' preference for types of electricity consumed, i.e., switching from using conventional electricity fueled by fossil fuels to RES-E.

34. Considering the foregoing core elements in the definition of DSM, for the purpose of this book, electricity DSM is defined as '*a portfolio of measures adjusting final customers' electricity consumption behavior for (i) facilitating the system integration of an ever-increasing share of variable RES-E, and (ii) increasing the share of RES-E in electricity consumption*'. It should be noted that this definition does not mean that electricity DSM only concerns the consumer segment. As detailed in Chapter II below, achieving desirable changes in electricity consumption patterns would be impossible without adapting electricity networks. Therefore, adjusting the network segment to accommodate the consumers' proactive role is also a key task of electricity DSM.

35. Two categories of electricity DSM mechanisms that serve the above two goals – DR and demand-side mechanisms for promoting RES-E – are defined below consecutively.

---

11 See Section 1.2.3 of this Chapter below for the definition of DERs.

12 In addition to balancing markets, flexibility procurement organized for congestion management and covering energy loss provides another important way for consumers with flexibility and renewables assets to seek revenues. For more details, see Chapter III below.

### *1.2.2. DR*

36. In EU law, the origin of the term 'DR' can be traced to the 2012 Electricity Efficiency Directive.[13] This legislation merely highlights the task of DR in improving energy efficiency and realizing energy savings in final consumption (*Energy Efficiency Directive*, 2012, recital 44). In recognition of its key role in leveling out large and irregular variations in supply that come along with intermittent renewables, especially solar and wind (*Electricity Directive*, 2019; Pearson, 2020), the rules on DR were moved later on to the existing Electricity Directive, in which the definition of DR was updated and broadened. In the Electricity Directive, DR means *'the change of electricity load by final customers from their normal or current consumption patterns in response to market signals, including in response to time-variable electricity prices or incentive payments, or in response to the acceptance of the final customer's bid to sell demand reduction or increase at a price in an organized market, whether alone or through aggregation'* (*Energy Efficiency Directive*, article 2(20)). This legislation provides a conspicuous example of broadening the definition of DR to cover turning up, turning down, or shifting demand.[14] Different from the 2012 Energy Efficiency Directive, deliberately increasing loads (downward DR) has become a part of DR to match surplus output from renewables and thereby balance the system at any one time (Gellings and Chamberlin, 1993; Bradley et al., 2013; Warren, 2014). Downward DR is necessary in the context of integrating variable RES-E, especially considering that wind tends to provide most energy at night when demand for electricity is at its lowest, and increasing electricity consumption, in this case, is key to drawing down excess electricity on the grid (Paddock and Youngblood, 2012).

37. The legal definition of DR provided by the Electricity Directive is mainly identical to the definition proposed by most existing literature, in which DR represents the flexibility of final customers, i.e., the capability and willingness to modify consumption patterns in reaction to external signals (prices or activation signals) (Lin et al., 2022; Sæle et al., 2023). DR measures are viewed as a set of measures or processes that attempt to deliver such demand flexibility, including increasing, decreasing and temporally shifting end-user electricity consumption in response to external signals (Märkle-Huß et al., 2018; Lockwood et al., 2020; Stede et al., 2020; Calver and Simcock, 2021a).

---

[13] The 2012 Electricity Efficiency Directive was amended in 2018 by a legal instrument of the CEP. See Directive (EU) 2018/2002 of the European Parliament and of the Council of 11 December 2018 amending Directive 2012/27/EU on energy efficiency [2018] OJ L 328/210.

[14] A similar definition is also adopted in other jurisdictions, such as the UK. See Lockwood et al., 2020.

38. These external signals are placed into two categories: (i) price signals and (ii) direct signals from system operators[15] and other market players (Ikäheimo et al., 2010; Li et al., 2011). Based on different ways of reacting to external signals, DR is broadly categorized as (i) implicit DR or price-based DR, and (ii) explicit DR or incentive-based DR (Willems and Zhou, 2020):

- Implicit DR can be organized by an electricity supplier or a system operator via the electricity price per kilowatt-hour and the network tariff, respectively (Weck et al., 2017). Examples of utilizing implicit DR include dynamic pricing, dynamic network tariffs (also known as TOU tariffs or time-differentiated tariffs), and static capacity-based grid tariffs (e.g., capacity tariffs in Flanders). Under dynamic pricing, consumers are exposed to time-varying or real-time electricity prices that reflect the value and cost of electricity in different periods, and adjust their consumption, through automation or personal choices, according to these price signals (Lamprinos et al., 2016; *Electricity Directive*, recital 37; European Smart Grids Task Force Expert Group 3, 2019). Dynamic pricing plays an instrumental role in enabling demand to match variable RES-E output, which is the main implicit DR discussed in this book. Dynamic network tariffs are a type of network tariff that gives incentives to network users to adapt the timing (i.e., peak shifting) and level off their network use (i.e., peak shedding) to keep network utilization within capacity constraints (Neuteleers et al., 2017). As highlighted above, electricity DSM in this book is limited to adjusting electricity consumption behavior. As such, implicit DR responding to network use signals given by dynamic or static network tariffs is not its primary focus.
- Explicit DR is committed and dispatchable DR, meaning customers receive specific rewards or incentives to alter their consumption upon request (Lamprinos et al., 2016; European Smart Grids Task Force Expert Group 3, 2019). This is a kind of flexibility that can be sold as an explicit product in different energy markets, such as wholesale and balancing markets (ACER and CEER, 2021; Sæle et al., 2023).

39. Zooming in on the context of EU law, dynamic pricing is realized by requiring suppliers to offer consumers electricity supply contracts with prices linked dynamically to the wholesale markets, known as 'dynamic price

---

[15] In the context of EU law, DR services provided to system operators can be categorized based on two categories: (i) remotely controlled, including DR active power control, DR reactive power control and DR transmission constraint management; and (ii) autonomously controlled, including DR system frequency control and DR very fast active power control. See *Demand Connection Code*, 2016, article 27 (1).

contracts'.[16] The introduction of dynamic pricing aims to establish a linkage between wholesale prices and retail prices, ensuring that real-time price signals are transmitted from the wholesale to the retail market (Hu et al., 2015; *Electricity Directive*, recital 37; Papsch, 2020). Moreover, dynamic price contracts allow for larger market price spreads between price peaks and the average price, offering greater bill savings for customers who respond to price signals (EC, 2016a). Consumers signing up for electricity supply contracts with prices linked dynamically to wholesale markets could thus be incentivized to match demand with supply, which is affected by variable renewables output, thereby helping maintain system balancing (Hu et al., 2015; EC, 2016; *Electricity Directive*, recital 37 and article 2(15)). For instance, consumers can increase their load to benefit from low prices when there is surplus output from renewables.[17] Apart from implicit DR, EU law also develops explicit DR by mobilizing consumers to react to incentive signals given by TSOs, DSOs and other market players, such as BRPs and suppliers.[18]

40. In existing definitions of DR, another critical element worth noting is that customers are allowed to react to market signals either individually or via intermediaries, such as aggregators (Lamprinos et al., 2016; Stede et al., 2020). As elaborated in Chapter III below, within EU law, customers are entitled to participate in implicit DR and explicit DR on their own. If they need energy services provided by aggregators or energy communities,[19] such as aggregating loads, hedging price risk and accessing market information, they have the right to offer DR to electricity markets through cooperating with these intermediaries.

41. Drawing on the above elements of definitions presented in regulation and academia, in this book, DR refers to '*end users modulating their electricity load to react to price-based or incentive-based signals, directly or through intermediaries.*' DR measures aim to facilitate such adjustments of electricity use and enable DR to be commercialized, to help create a flexible electricity system that accommodates the high-level penetration of RES-E based on variable sources.

---

16 More on dynamic pricing can be found in Section 3 of Chapter III below.

17 For instance, wind tends to provide most energy at night, when electricity demand is at its lowest, and thus increasing electricity consumption in this case by, for instance, charging electric vehicles is key to maintaining system balance. See Paddock and Youngblood, 2012.

18 System operators and market players use DR for different purposes. DR can offer system services, including balancing services and congestion management, to the TSO, while the DSO uses DR for voltage control and congestion management. BRPs and suppliers utilize DR to balance their portfolios and hedge risks. See Koliou et al., 2015; Ramos et al., 2016; Hadush and Meeus, 2018; *Electricity Regulation*, recital 13 and article 7(2)(b); Webster, 2021.

19 See Section 1.2.3 of this Chapter below for definitions of energy communities.

42. Furthermore, in existing studies and legislation, the following concepts relating to DR are worth mentioning. Some of them partially overlap with DR, while others are key concepts associated with the implementation of DR.

- 'Demand flexibility': In some national legislation, rather than DR, the term 'demand flexibility' is used to underline the ability of final customers to make their electricity consumption flexible, accompanied by rules empowering them to do so. For instance, in Belgian law, demand flexibility is defined as '*the ability of a final customer to voluntarily adjust its net offtake upwards or downwards in response to an external signal*' (*Belgian Federal Electricity Law*, art. 2, 66°). It is first evident that the concept of 'demand flexibility' is derived from the broad notion of 'flexibility', which refers to the ability to control and quickly adjust (Fernández et al., 2016). Secondly, demand flexibility emphasizes the ability to adapt to variable electricity production or grid constraints, which are reflected by market signals. In other words, such flexibility is viewed as a capability to make electricity consumption or network use flexible, including shifting electricity use in time, space, and/or intensity in response to external signals (D'hulst et al., 2015; Powells and Fell, 2019; Calver and Simcock, 2021a). Moreover, like DR, demand flexibility could be commercialized or valorized such that it becomes capable of being circulated within markets (*Belgian Federal Electricity Law*, art. 19bis; Powells and Fell, 2019). Since demand flexibility also encompasses the flexible use of the network, it represents a broader range of flexibility than DR defined in this book.
- 'Demand-side flexibility': Compared to demand flexibility, in some academic and non-academic literature, 'demand-side flexibility' is used to represent wider activities of final customers, which contain not only shifting load or consumption but also demand-side storage and distributed generation (European Smart Grids Task Force Expert Group 3, 2019; IRENA, 2019; Forouli et al., 2021). That is to say, demand-side flexibility refers to the flexibility provided by consumers, which is not restricted to DR, since energy storage facilities and decentralized RES-E generation assets owned by consumers could also offer flexibility. Hence, 'demand-side flexibility' is a definition wider than 'DR' or 'demand flexibility'.
- 'Flexibility sources': This term is used to describe sources of flexibility that make the electricity system flexible and maintain system stability and security. Such sources can be provided by generation facilities, storage facilities, zonal interconnections ('ZIC', one of the most important balancing resources, limited by the unused lines capacity), and final customers (Villar et al., 2018; *Electricity Regulation*, recital 22; Leinauer et al., 2022). As shown in Figure 3 below, flexibility sources can be distinguished by different flexibility providers. Due to the pivotal role of adapting electricity

consumption, DR is deemed a subcategory of flexibility sources (e.g. *Electricity Directive*, article 32(1); *Electricity Regulation*, recital 22).

- 'Flexibility services': When flexibility sources are traded on electricity markets, they constitute services that can be acquired by aggregators, system operators, suppliers and BRPs. In the case of offering them to TSOs and DSOs, flexibility services also serve as 'ancillary services' and congestion management services necessary for the operation of a transmission or distribution system.[20] In EU law, DR is treated as a type of 'flexibility service' and can be traded on wholesale markets and participate in flexibility procurement organized by system operators (*Electricity Directive*, articles 32(1) and 40(1)). An overview of the relationship between DR and flexibility services, as well as flexibility sources, is presented in Figure 3.

**Figure 3. DR and flexibility-related concepts**

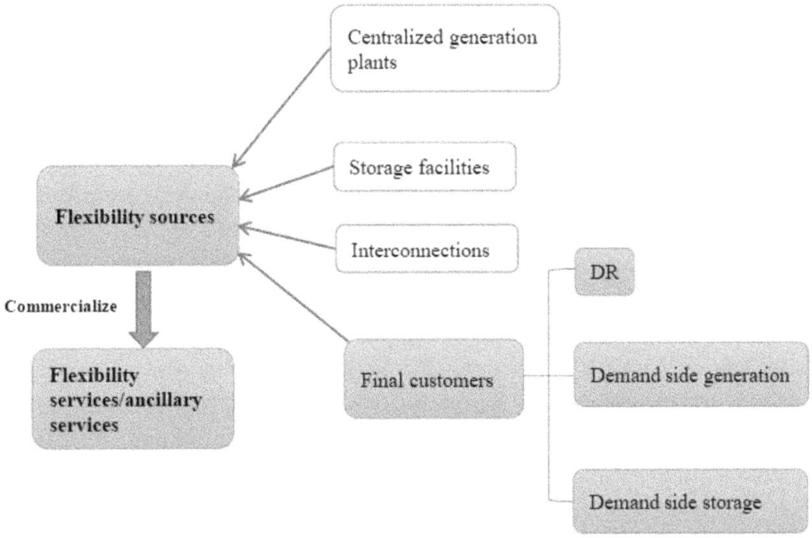


Source: Author's own elaboration.

- 'Flexibility schemes': Measures aimed at increasing system flexibility and promoting the provision of various available flexibility sources, including DR, could be viewed as flexibility schemes. Thus, flexibility schemes are designed

[20] Ancillary services are the resources required by system operators for reliable and secure power system operation, through which important power system characteristics such as frequency, voltage, load and system restart process are maintained. It is important to note that in the context of EU law, ancillary services do not include congestion management. In this thesis, the term 'system services' encompasses ancillary services and congestion management. See (Rebours et al., 2007; Kaushal and Van Hertem, 2019; *Electricity Directive*, article 2(48)).

to develop DR and other flexibility services, which include DR measures defined above.

- 'Flexibility service provider': This term refers to market participants providing flexibility services to one or more off-takers of flexibility.[21] This role can be played by suppliers, energy communities, aggregators, IFSPs and consumers themselves. The IFSP is a third-party market player engaged in trading flexibility who is not affiliated with the customer's supplier and has a separate BRP.[22] Due to its role in aggregating loads and providing balancing services, the IFSP is also referred to as 'independent aggregator' and 'balancing service provider' in the Electricity Directive and the Balancing Regulation.[23] This market actor plays a key role in assisting end users to valorize flexibility and is thus gaining prominence in EU law, as discussed further below in Chapters II and III.

### *1.2.3. Demand-Side Mechanisms for Promoting RES-E*

43. The discussion above indicates that demand or customer-oriented mechanisms for promoting the uptake of RES-E are a key component of electricity DSM. It also demonstrates distinctions between supply-side and demand-side mechanisms for promoting the uptake of RES-E. On this basis, in the context of this research, the term 'demand side mechanisms for promoting RES-E' is defined as '*a range of instruments or mechanisms geared towards final customers to promote the use of RES-E by obligating, mobilizing or incentivizing customers to increase the share of RES-E in their electricity consumption*'. It should be noted that 'mechanisms for promoting RES-E' referred to in this definition only concern 'promotional mechanisms primarily aimed at addressing economic and regulatory barriers specific to RES-E' (Chen and Vandendriessche, 2023a). Thus, EU law, which establishes specific promotional mechanisms centered around obligating or incentivizing consumers, is the focus of this book.[24] By contrast, EU law governing national support schemes,[25] such as state

---

21 See e.g., Flemish Energy Decree, art. 1.1.3, 25°/ 1/2.

22 Flemish Energy Decree, art. 1.1.3, 92°/5. Regarding the reason for defining such a third-party FSP, see Section 2.1.2 of Chapter II below.

23 *Belgian Federal Electricity Law*, art. 2, 64°; CREG, 2016, section V.3; *Balancing Regulation*, art. 18(4)(c); *Electricity Directive*, article 2(18)(19).

24 As will be set out in Section 2 of Chapter III below, energy legislation is a shared competence between Member States and the EU, in light of Article 194 TFEU. As such, while Member States are competent for devising national support schemes for RES-E, EU legislation also provides promotional measures dedicated to addressing economic and non-economic barriers to the deployment of RES-E. See also Chen and Vandendriessche, 2023.

25 In the context of EU law, 'support schemes' refer to the measures adopted by Member States to promote renewables. Although by definition they are also RES-E promotion measures, it is important to note their national character and that they are distinguished from RES-E promotional mechanisms established by EU legislation. See *REDII*, article 2(5); Iliopoulos, 2021.

aid law and articles 4 to 6 of the REDII, is beyond the scope of this research. This is because it aims at creating minimum requirements for the design of national support schemes while not materializing promotional mechanisms for RES-E (Chen and Vandendriessche, 2023a). Table 1 lists major demand-side mechanisms for promoting RES-E.

**Table 1. Demand-side promotional mechanisms for RES-E**

| | | |
|---|---|---|
| **Demand-side promotional mechanisms** | **Information-based mechanisms** | (i) Raising consumers' awareness of purchasing RES-E by disclosing electricity generation attributes; (ii) facilitating access to information about renewables self-consumption; and (iii) delivering market signals and improving access to electricity consumption data |
| | **Facilitating renewables PPA** | Promoting customer choices of RES-E by removing barriers to conclude renewables PPAs |
| | **Enabling frameworks for renewables self-consumption** | Facilitating the use of RES-E by empowering consumers to generate electricity for own use and get remuneration for selling self-generated RES-E, individually or collectively |

Source: Author's own elaboration.[26]

44. These three mechanisms reflect two approaches to increasing the end users' role in facilitating the RES-E uptake: (i) enabling them to shift toward prosumers to generate RES-E for their own use and trade self-generated RES-E; (ii) securing demand for RES-E. These approaches highlight the different roles of consumers. Despite the presence of the former approach, which enables consumers to generate RES-E for their own use, not every consumer will be willing or able to do so. Some consumers may continue playing the traditional consumer role of purchasing electricity from suppliers. Consumers who have already become renewables prosumers still need to withdraw electricity from the grid due to the limited level of energy self-sufficiency resulting from the intermittent output of renewables.[27] Considering the presence of these consumers (partially) preserving the traditional consumer role, changing their purchasing choices to increase the share of RES-E in purchased electricity is still necessary. In this regard, promotional measures include those facilitating renewables PPAs and information-based mechanisms (i.e., the energy sources disclosure obligation and GO mechanisms which enable consumers to track generation attributes of purchased electricity).[28]

---

26 See Chapter III further below for an elaboration of these mechanisms.

27 Regarding the limited level of self-sufficiency in the case of generating renewable electricity based on intermittent renewables, see Section 3 of Chapter III below.

28 For the detailed rationale of the information-based mechanisms, see Section 2.3 of Chapter II below.

45. Among these demand-side mechanisms, particularly, enabling consumers to engage in renewables self-consumption leads to some new concepts. They represent a new category of entities that generate, use and sell RES-E, or a novel approach to collectively engaging in these activities. Further, some concepts associated with decentralized RES-E production participated by consumers become highly relevant, mainly including 'distributed energy resource' and 'distributed generation'. In light of some discrepancies and correlations existing among these concepts, their definitions and relations merit further clarification in the context of this book:

- 'Prosumer' means an energy consumer producing energy to meet (a part of) its own energy demand, while the consumer may also sell self-produced energy (Butenko, 2016; EC, 2016; Parag and Sovacool, 2016; Diestelmeier, 2021). 'Prosumership' or 'prosumption' refers to the new phenomenon of consumers participating in the consumption and production of energy, as well as selling self-produced energy (Hoicka et al., 2021). The term 'prosumer' is constantly used to describe the shift of the consumer's role in the context of developing RES-E because decentralized generation technologies running on renewables notably create opportunities for various consumers, including industrial, commercial and residential users, to generate electricity for their own use (Inês et al., 2020; Diestelmeier, 2021). Prosumers can be broadly classified into two categories: (i) individual prosumers, and (ii) collective prosumers who act together in renewables prosumption (i.e., RECs, CECs and jointly-acting renewable self-consumers) (Ruotsalainen et al., 2017; Frieden et al., 2019; Inês et al., 2020).
- 'Active customer' is a legal definition provided by the EU's Electricity Directive, which means a final customer, or a group of jointly acting final customers, whose activities include inter alia consuming or storing electricity generated within its premises located within confined boundaries or, where permitted by a Member State, within other premises, or selling self-generated electricity while those activities do not constitute its primary commercial or professional activity (*Electricity Directive*, article 2(8)). When generating renewable electricity for private use, active customers constitute renewables prosumers or renewables self-consumers under the EU's REDII.
- 'Renewables self-consumer' is defined by the REDII as a final customer operating within its premises located within confined boundaries or, where permitted by a Member State, within other premises, who generates renewable electricity for its own consumption, and who may store or sell self-generated renewable electricity, while for a non-household renewables self-consumer, those activities do not constitute its primary commercial or professional activity (*REDII*, article 2(14)). Clearly, given its activities of using and selling

self-generated electricity, the renewables self-consumer is a subcategory of the active customer and also constitutes a type of prosumer.

- 'Citizen energy community' is commonly understood as an organization, initiated and managed by actors from civil society and public actors, that aims to educate or facilitate people on energy efficiency, enable the collective procurement of energy, or actually provide (i.e., generate, store or distribute) energy for consumption by inhabitants, participants or members, or sell self-generated energy (Boon and Dieperink, 2014; Kalkbrenner and Roosen, 2016). Under EU law, the 'citizen energy community' is defined as an entity involved in a range of energy activities, which is characterized by voluntary and open participation and effectively controlled by members or shareholders that are natural persons, local authorities, including municipalities, or small enterprises (*Electricity Directive*, article 2(11)). CECs are allowed to engage in wide energy activities, ranging from generation, distribution, supply, consumption, aggregation, energy storage, and energy efficiency services, to providing other energy services to their members or shareholders (*Electricity Directive*, article 2(11)). As these definitions indicate, CECs can be classified as collective renewables prosumers when engaging in RES-E prosumption.
- 'Renewable energy community' refers to an energy community in which private and public actors engage in the energy transition by jointly investing in, producing, selling, distributing and consuming renewable energy (Azarova et al., 2019; Lowitzsch et al., 2020). In the context of EU law, the REC is defined as a legal entity that is based on open and voluntary participation, autonomous, and effectively controlled by shareholders or members that are located in the proximity of the renewable energy projects owned and developed by that legal entity (*REDII*, article 2(16)). The REC could be defined as a category of collective prosumers. In contrast to the CEC, the REC has two features: (i) proximity of participants to a REC's production installations affecting their eligibility to be controlling shareholders (Hicks and Ison, 2018; Hoicka et al., 2021); and (ii) the focus on renewables prosumption (Caramizaru and Uihlein, 2020).
- 'Distributed energy resource' refers to energy resources connected to the distribution grid, including small-scale generation units (e.g., wind turbines and solar panels), storage facilities and DR (Akorede et al., 2010; Poplavskaya and Vries, 2019). These resources provide various distributed energy and flexibility sources, distinct from electrical energy and flexibility connected to the transmission system (Akorede et al., 2010). The renewables DG facilities owned by individual or collective prosumers located at the distribution level fall under the definition of DERs.
- 'Distributed generation' is, in general, defined as an electricity generation source that is connected directly to distribution networks or on the customer

side of the network (Ackermann et al., 2001; Pepermans et al., 2005). It also represents a decentralized way of producing electricity. Departing from the traditional energy regime centered on centralized production based on fossil energy, the advent of DG portends a transition toward a more bottom-up paradigm (Butenko, 2016; Mehigan et al., 2018). The rise of RES-E, usually produced in a more decentralized manner compared to fossil fuels, particularly catalyzes DG (Burke and Stephens, 2018; Butenko, 2016; Mehigan et al., 2018). The generating installations owned by prosumers are a type of DG asset.

## 2. AIM AND SCOPE

46. This book primarily aims at improving the knowledge of how the electricity DSM law empowers energy consumers to facilitate RES-E uptake, using EU law as a case study. Electricity DSM cuts across technical, economic and legal issues. The research aim thus involves an understanding of issues regarding electricity DSM in three dimensions as follows.

47. The first aspect involves core issues and tasks of electricity DSM centered around shaping electricity consumption behavior. The second one is using electricity DSM as a tool for developing RES-E, how EU law incorporates these tasks and solves the multidimensional challenges of steering and shaping electricity consumers' behavior. In other words, this dimension aims to advance the understanding of the elements or building blocks of the electricity DSM law that is dedicated to increasing RES-E uptake. As explained in Section 1.1 above, the increasing role of final customers coming with the application of electricity DSM can induce changes in interactions with other actors in the electricity market and network realms. The role of law lies in defining new roles of energy consumers and properly structuring their relationships with other actors by assigning rights and obligations in a clear and fair manner, while providing enabling frameworks or dedicated support. Third, to fathom how the law could successfully harness electricity DSM as a robust and effective approach to facilitating RES-E, one needs to understand the gains and lessons that can be distilled from the specific case study of EU law. This notably calls for a dedicated focus on practical issues and challenges arising in the application of relevant EU law, as well as legal analyses examining deficiencies or gaps in empowering and incentivizing consumers.

48. A few caveats should be made about the scope of this research. First, as outlined above, DSM law should not be confined to changing customers' behavior toward a more energy-efficient one (Didden and D'haeseleer, 2003). But rather, it should be expanded to include measures aimed at shaping electricity consumption so that the uptake of RES-E can be facilitated. This book only

focuses on the DSM legal framework for increasing the uptake of RES-E. Energy efficiency measures are beyond its scope.

49. Second, DSM measures are also applied in the natural gas and heating sectors. For instance, a natural gas DSM program was launched in British Columbia in 1997 and efficiency obligations were extended to gas suppliers in the UK and Denmark in the 2000s (Rosenow, 2012; Fawcett et al., 2019; IRENA, 2019; Haley et al., 2020). Considering this, it is important to highlight that this book exclusively addresses DSM in the electricity sector.

50. Third, as clarified in the previous section, in this book, both DSM and DR are defined by stressing their aim of shaping consumers' electricity consumption behavior, but not consumer behavior in a broad sense. Thus, legal issues concerning demand-side flexibility from storage facilities owned or operated by consumers are excluded from this research. Moreover, electricity DSM measures that adjust consumers' network utilization, such as dynamic network tariffs that flex network use, are not the primary focus of this research. Admittedly, consumers' network use interacts with their consumption. Their response to dynamic network tariffs also affects their electricity consumption, as charges related to transmission and distribution networks influence the electricity bills of consumers (Weck et al., 2017; ACER, 2023a). As explained above, to respond to economic signals from network tariffs, consumers reduce the strain on the network during peak periods by withdrawing less electricity from the grid. Reducing or shifting network use to other periods indeed results in load shifting as well. However, the primary aim of dynamic network tariffs is to adjust the use of the network by influencing when and how network users utilize the grid (*Electricity Regulation*, article 18(7)). This is exemplified by the nature of the economic signals they send: they shape network use behavior by providing appropriate cost signals regarding the cost of network use (ACER, 2023a). The fact that flexing consumers' network use also leads to consumption adjustment does not change the aim of dynamic tariffs, which is to adjust network use. Similarly, when system operators organize flexibility procurement for congestion management (i.e., purchasing explicit flexibility), they also aim to adjust network use behavior to mitigate grid congestion. Such measures promoting consumers' flexibility in using the grid, either implicit or explicit flexibility, are not the core subject of this book. Yet, they play a key role in shaping network-friendly behavior and enable the grid, especially the distribution grid, to maintain grid stability and efficiency when absorbing large amounts of DR and self-generated RES-E that bring variable generation and bi-directional power flows.[29] Therefore, they will be referred to in Chapters III and IV as one

[29] See Section 3.2 of Chapter II below for challenges faced by DSOs in the era of engaging consumers in supporting RES-E uptake.

of the tools provided to system operators to overcome the challenges associated with greater consumer engagement. In addition, given that consumers can also respond to network use signals and receive remuneration by adjusting their consumption behavior, accessing flexibility markets for adjusting grid use is also relevant to the incentives for adjusting electricity consumption. Market barriers to these markets will thus be mentioned in the following chapters.

51. Lastly, this book examines the binding legislation on electricity DSM taken at the Union level. It mainly involves EU law governing the internal electricity market and promoting renewables, as well as the EU's network codes and regulations. Union-level policies are not the subject of this research. Moreover, the electricity DSM law adopted in Member States will not be reviewed except for some leading examples of national laws and regulations dedicated to transposing and implementing relevant EU law. The given national law examples illustrate typical legal challenges in national transpositions, thereby supporting legal analyses of remaining issues or gaps in existing Union-level legal approaches.

## 3. RESEARCH METHODOLOGY

52. In this section, research questions guiding this book are first listed in Section 3.1, which is followed by approaches to addressing them in Section 3.2.

### 3.1. RESEARCH QUESTIONS

53. This book examines EU legal approaches to using electricity DSM as a means of facilitating the uptake of RES-E. As discussed above, DSM operationalizes consumer empowerment by applying consumer-oriented measures that influence and adapt patterns of electricity consumption. In this sense, the core inquiry of the book is whether EU law provides sufficient and robust DSM mechanisms to enable such behavioral adaptation in support of RES-E integration. This inquiry is structured around the following research questions, the primary one being: *Has EU law adequately addressed the challenges of adapting electricity consumption behavior to facilitate the uptake of RES-E?*

54. Sub-research questions are:

1) *What are the core tasks and challenges of electricity DSM in terms of facilitating RES-E uptake?*
2) *How has EU law addressed these tasks and challenges?*

3) *What are the remaining gaps in the EU law on electricity DSM in adapting electricity consumption behavior to support high RES-E uptake, and what are the potential solutions?*
4) *What lessons or implications can be drawn from the case study of EU law on electricity DSM?*

55. These sub-questions are analyzed in the following chapters. Chapter II answers the first sub-question. It explains the core tasks of electricity DSM by summarizing key prerequisites, barriers and enablers that must be tackled by DSM measures designed to engage various consumers to support greater penetration of RES-E. Moving on to the legal aspect of electricity DSM, Chapter III answers the second sub-question. It is mainly descriptive and outlines the measures taken by EU law to accomplish the central tasks of electricity DSM, i.e., steering electricity consumption in a direction that favors RES-E uptake. Chapter IV analyzes the third question by turning from EU law on paper to its transposition and implementation. It examines the regulatory gaps and issues that emerge during implementation, while also exploring potential solutions to address the remaining challenges. Chapter V compiles the main findings of the chapters and answers the fourth sub-question.

## 3.2. RESEARCH METHOD

56. There are four steps to address the overarching research question, which are guided by the foregoing four sub-questions. To assess whether EU law has adequately addressed the challenges of engaging consumers in supporting the uptake of RES-E, two key questions must be considered: (i) what are the main challenges to empower consumers, or more specifically, to shape electricity consumption behavior that supports RES-E uptake; and (ii) how has existing EU law responded to these challenges?

57. Solving the first question involves a review of academic and non-academic literature, which provides theoretical and empirical insights into general and specific barriers to engaging different customer groups in DR and RES-E use, particularly in the EU context. The research for the second question is conducted using the methodology of doctrinal legal research. This type of research aims primarily 'to give a systematic exposition of the principles, rules and concepts governing a particular legal field or institution and analyze the relationship between these principles, rules and concepts to solve unclarities and gaps in the existing law' (Smits, 2017). With this method, this book addresses the second question by describing and interpreting EU legislation on electricity DSM, to demonstrate how existing EU law addresses challenges faced by traditionally passive consumers in actively supporting the uptake of

RES-E. It distills the building blocks of EU law on electricity DSM. The major legal documents reviewed include Union legislation that empowers and enables consumers to engage in DR and enhances their purchase and self-consumption of RES-E. They involve (i) legislative acts, mainly the existing Electricity Directive, Electricity Regulation and Renewable Energy Directive (covering the REDII and its amendments adopted in 2023), and (ii) network regulations adopted by the EC under delegation (in the form of delegated acts) or to implement a legislative act (in the form of implementing acts). For a detailed explanation of the classification of EU law on electricity DSM, I refer the reader to Section 2.3 of Chapter III.

58. The analysis of EU law on DSM draws on both doctrinal research and empirical data concerning the challenges identified during the transposition and implementation processes. Its approaches are detailed as follows.

59. First, the doctrinal research method is used again to analyze principles and core rules on electricity DSM and evaluate whether they have adequately addressed core enablers and barriers for engaging consumers, which helps reveal unclarities, conflicts and gaps in defining the consumers' role and empowering them. The interpretation of these normative sources is supported by case law of the CJEU and other authoritative sources, such as decisions, guidelines and opinions from EU institutions as well as legal scholarly writings (Hoecke, 2011).

60. Moreover, remaining gaps and problems that were not expected or contemplated by legislators surface in the implementation of the law. Following sociological jurisprudence's conception of focusing on the working of the law (Pound, 1912), the evaluation of the adequacy and effectiveness of EU law on electricity DSM is further approached by drawing on data about its implementation at the national level. Such data are collected from empirical research conducted under this book, the academic and non-academic references that report the existing status of consumer engagement in DR and renewables use (including purchase and renewables self-consumption) and the transposition of relevant EU law in Member States.

61. Before examining the building blocks of the EU legal framework for electricity DSM, a separate national case study is conducted. It aims to elicit more detailed and contextually relevant information on key legal issues and eminent challenges arising in national transposition. So far, national transpositions in the Member States are in various stages of development and are expected to continue for the next few years, despite already being past the required deadline (Hoicka et al., 2021; Fina and Monsberger, 2022; Lavrijssen et al., 2023). In the pending national transposition, the DSM framework is established incrementally and piecemeal. Member States may have parts of legislation for DR in place while other measures engaging consumers in generating and using

RES-E are still under development, or vice versa.[30] This is largely attributed to a typical two-step national transposition process in the electricity law sector: primary legislation incorporates broadly formulated principles or requirements of EU Directives while requiring or empowering governments and NRAs to elaborate or approve specific implementing mechanisms, as shown in Irish,[31] Dutch,[32] Italian (Krug et al., 2023) and Belgian cases.[33] As a result, relevant EU law could not be fully transposed and implemented without more detailed implementing rules developed or approved by national governments and NRAs (ACER, 2023a), which are subject to additional consultation procedures (e.g., CRU, 2023; VREG, 2022, 2022).

62. Given this situation, a mixed approach is adopted, utilizing examples from the ongoing transposition process to examine the implementation of the relevant EU law. First, the case study country is selected from early adopters who have established relatively comprehensive DSM rules for facilitating both DR and the use of RES-E. Belgium stands out as a country that delivers a concrete and relatively complete picture of the implementation of EU law on electricity DSM. This is particularly exemplified by the parallel transpositions of EU law at both the federal and regional levels, due to the allocation of competences.[34] Moreover, in some cases, as set out in Section 2 of Chapter IV, federal law and regional law adopt divergent regulatory approaches to engaging consumers at the transmission and distribution levels, respectively.[35] This also enables the Belgian law case study to reveal different legal challenges arising from the specificities of large, industrial users and small non-household and household consumers, as well as market participants cooperating with them, and how such challenges shape regulatory approaches or instruments.

63. While a single case study allows for a more detailed analysis, it is insufficient to demonstrate the gray areas and regulatory gaps that exist in EU law regarding electricity DSM. Hence, together with the problems revealed by the Belgian

30 A leading example can be found in Ireland. Such fragmentary national transposition also exists in the creation of national frameworks for RECs. See CRU, 2021a, 2021b; Krug et al., 2023.

31 See e.g., *Renewable Energy Regulations 2022*, Regulations 3-10.

32 See e.g., Lavrijssen et al., 2023; Ministerie van Economische Zaken en Klimaat, 2022.

33 See e.g., *Walloon Electricity Decree*, art. 19bis, art. 19quater and art. 19quinquies; *Flemish Energy Decree*, art. 4.1.17/1, art. 4.2.1 and art. 4.8.2; *Belgian Federal Electricity Law*, art. 35duodecies, art. 35terdecies and art. 35quindecies.

34 For instance, both federal law and regional law transpose EU-level legal provisions on enabling active customers, RECs and CECs as well as IFSPs. See e.g. *Decree of 2 APRIL 2021 of amending the Flemish Energy Decree*, 2021, *OCTOBER 23, 2022. – Law amending the Federal Electricity Law*, 2022. See Section 2 of Chapter IV below for more details on competence allocation between the federal authority and regions.

35 A leading example in this respect is the different approaches taken by federal and regional rules to consulting 'all relevant grid users'. See e.g. Sections 2.3.1 and 2.3.3, Chapter IV.

law case, piecemeal implementing rules in other Member States are also used to support an in-depth examination of each element of the EU's electricity DSM framework. In addition to implementing rules that are already in force, those undergoing consultations will also be discussed when the proposals or consultations reveal acute legal issues or gaps.

64. Normative analysis and the research on the implementation of the law demonstrate the potential room for improving the existing EU legal framework for electricity DSM. With the identified gaps, drawing on the CJEU's jurisprudence and existing academic debate, possible solutions, lessons and implications could be further explored. This step aims to realize the research's contribution in a broad sense, namely, furthering the understanding of how the law can harness electricity DSM to advance RES-E uptake and deriving valuable insights for other jurisdictions.

65. Lastly, this book's research was realized over a period spanning from October 2020 to 2024. Thus, relevant legal developments at both the EU and national levels have been followed until 1 July 2024. The 2024 amendments to the Electricity Directive and the Electricity Regulation will be discussed only in Chapter IV.

## 4. BOOK OUTLINE

66. Following this introduction, this book materializes in three chapters plus a conclusion as follows.

67. Chapter II provides an overview of multidimensional factors that have the potential to shape energy consumer behavior or actions and explains the core tasks and challenges that must be addressed by electricity DSM.

68. Chapter III canvasses how EU law adapts electricity consumption to foster the uptake of renewable electricity. It distills the building blocks of the EU legal framework for electricity DSM and analyzes how they respectively address economic and non-economic barriers for passive consumers to change their conventional electricity consumption patterns to support RES-E uptake.

69. Chapter IV examines the legal approaches taken by EU law to engage consumers. The focus will be on whether the empowerment framework is clear, coherent, and pragmatic enough, as well as whether the accompanying enabling frameworks and incentives are robust and targeted to engage different customer groups. After identifying major remaining regulatory gaps and challenges, it also discusses preliminary resolutions to address these issues.

70. Chapter V concludes the merits and remaining challenges of the EU's legal approaches to using electricity DSM to facilitate RES-E uptake. On this basis, it formulates general insights from the EU law case study by summarizing key elements of a legal framework for electricity DSM and typical legal challenges in developing such a framework. It also provides recommendations for further research.

# CHAPTER II

# UNDERSTANDING DSM

## Aims and Core Tasks

## 1. INTRODUCTION

71. The preceding Chapter has indicated that empowering energy consumers to facilitate RES-E uptake requires a twofold shift in electricity consumption behavior: first, enabling DR to support the integration of variable RES-E into the system; and second, increasing the share of RES-E in electricity consumption through greater engagement in its purchase and prosumption. Desirable behavior changes on these two fronts would never be delivered without dedicated DSM mechanisms due to the traditionally passive role of energy consumers. Such consumer inactivity results from cognitive and behavioral constraints, as well as the traditional energy regime, which is oriented toward addressing consumers' sole need for purchasing electricity to meet their own demand. This chapter provides an overview of multidimensional factors that can shape energy consumer actions. This is approached by drawing on academic and non-academic references, which provide theoretical and empirical insights into general and specific barriers to engaging different customer groups in DR and RES-E use, notably in the EU context. By presenting key barriers and enablers of consumer engagement, this chapter further explains the core tasks of DSM measures that aim to facilitate RES-E uptake. It serves as the theoretical foundation for the following chapters, which critically assess whether the EU law on electricity DSM is adequate, suitable, or effective in addressing the identified obstacles.

72. This Chapter unfolds as follows. Section 2 reviews economic and non-economic factors that influence the energy consumers' involvement in DR and RES-E use. In addition, consumers' participation in these energy activities is also contingent upon the performance of the electricity grid. This is rooted in an underlying feature of the electricity sector that the electricity network provides the key infrastructure platform upon which energy exchange or trading relies (Joskow, 2008). Consumers interested in DR and renewables prosuming could be particularly deterred by disproportionate and discriminatory network fees and unsatisfied grid connection requests. Obstacles arising from network operation and obsolete network regulations are the focus of Section 3. This Chapter ends with a

summary of key prerequisites, barriers and enablers that must be tackled by DSM measures to empower various consumers to support greater penetration of RES-E.

## 2. BARRIERS AND ENABLERS OF ENGAGING CONSUMERS

73. Financial benefits are widely considered the major enabler of engaging energy consumers in DR and RES-E use (Biresselioglu et al., 2024; Lashmar et al., 2022; Torriti et al., 2010). Regulated electricity prices and market entry barriers have long been blamed for preventing consumers from adequately benefiting from these energy activities and leading to low levels of consumer engagement. This is the subject of Section 2.1 below. Evidence-based insights from behavioral science or economics demonstrate that insufficient economic incentives alone cannot explain the inaction of energy consumers. There is a set of cognitive and behavioral limits that shape consumers' decisions, hindering them from actively engaging in DR and renewables use and reaping economic benefits. It is interesting to note that not only residential but also non-residential users (notably those from the non-energy-intensive sectors) are vulnerable to such biases or limitations. The situation is even worse for consumers experiencing vulnerability or energy hardship. In an energy poverty or vulnerability context, consumers likely face greater economic and behavioral barriers when making rational economic decisions required to participate in DR and renewables prosuming. The impact of behavioral limitations on the engagement of different customer groups will be discussed in Section 2.2. This is followed by consumers' information access barriers, reviewed in Section 2.3.

### 2.1. ECONOMIC INCENTIVES

74. Financial considerations are essential in changing economic behavior (Biresselioglu et al., 2024; Lennon et al., 2019). Appropriate incentives (or benefits) would be the first logical step in ensuring the uptake and acceptance of new energy technologies, such as DR and renewables DG (Biresselioglu et al., 2024; Devine-Wright, 2013). Despite the existence of non-economic barriers,[36] empirical studies have shown that financial benefits or cost savings are key or even the primary motivation for final customers from residential, industrial and commercial sectors to invest and engage in DR and RES-E use (especially via renewables PPAs and self-consumption) (Ruggiero et al., 2015; Gimeno et al., 2018; Shafie-khah et al., 2019; Wohlfarth et al., 2020; Kotilainen et al., 2021,

[36] See Section 2.2 below of this Chapter.

p 197; Streimikiene et al., 2021; Leinauer et al., 2022; Lashmar et al., 2022). In the EU context, along with out-of-market support, competitive electricity markets play an instrumental role in motivating investments in low-carbon technologies (Chen and Vandendriessche, 2023a). Regulated electricity prices could limit the market's ability to sufficiently remunerate consumers to deliver desirable behavioral changes and maintain required investments in the short and medium terms, as elaborated in Section 2.1.1 below. Furthermore, market entry requirements and conditions in centralized electricity markets, especially wholesale and balancing markets, could also hinder market access for smaller-sized and inexperienced consumers, as shown in Section 2.2.2.

### 2.1.1. *Remuneration*

75. In liberalized electricity markets, incentives to maintain and stimulate both short-term allocation (operations) and long-term allocation (investments) are delivered by price signals (El Gohary et al., 2021; Kara et al., 2022). However, electricity price regulation was common across the EU before 2019, which prevented prices from reflecting the real value of DR and self-generated RES-E and conveying the right incentives to consumers (EC, 2016a; El Gohary et al., 2021). Compared to RES-E purchase, consumers' incentives to carry out DR and renewables prosuming could be affected to a greater extent since profitability, either savings in electricity bills or additional revenues yielded by valorizing DR and using and trading or sharing self-produced RES-E, could be lowered by price caps (Ruggiero et al., 2015). The potential of the competitive market to drive new investment in DR and renewables self-consumption is also undermined by the wide presence of price interventions (EC, 2016a). Moreover, price caps can notably hamper the implementation of implicit DR, which relies on reacting to dynamic prices that reflect the changes in supply (Gurba, 2021). Without dynamic pricing, price peaks either do not occur often or only lead to peak prices slightly higher than the average price, which makes implicit DR not very interesting from a financial point of view (EC, 2016a).

76. As a result, the lack of economic incentives is a frequently-mentioned barrier for consumers to provide flexibility and engage in renewables prosuming (Torriti et al., 2010; Weck et al., 2017; Annala et al., 2018a; Leinauer et al., 2022). Compared to energy-intensive industrial users, it is more difficult to mobilize other customers with low financial rewards. For final customers with small loads, such as users in household, commercial and public sectors, their energy costs are relatively low in comparison to other costs (Cagno et al., 2013; Cardoso et al., 2020). For instance, commercial entities or public organizations represent a group very distinct from energy-intensive industrial consumers (Cardoso et al., 2020). The industrial sector uses energy mostly for productive processes, whilst the commercial and public sectors consume energy in relation to building

occupancy, including lighting, refrigeration and IT services (Cardoso et al., 2020). These consumers with small loads could perceive it economically unattractive to deviate from their conventional consumption patterns, considering both limited gains and potentially high costs (Wohlfarth et al., 2020). Participation in DR and renewables prosuming entails upfront investment, operational costs, and market transaction costs. DR participation costs include initial costs, which refer to the cost of investing in enabling technology (e.g., metering and communication technology) and establishing a response plan, and activation costs, which are the costs incurred when they respond to a DR request (Cardoso et al., 2020; Gruber et al., 2014; Steurer et al., 2015). Renewables self-consumption requires relatively high upfront investments in generation units or battery storage, and this investment tends to have a long pay-off time (Palm, 2018; Kotilainen et al., 2021, p 201).

77. When seeking to reap benefits by trading DR and self-produced RES-E or entering into renewables PPAs, consumers also face market transaction costs, i.e., the costs of gathering information about products and suppliers, managing contracts and administrative procedures for external transactions, which are primarily influenced by the market and therefore by factors outside the consumers' control (Cardoso et al., 2020). Such transaction costs are not non-trivial. Some empirical studies suggest that many industrial and commercial users provide DR resources to balancing markets through aggregators, as they can absorb some of the market transaction costs (Cardoso et al., 2020; Curtis, 2017). There are also other transaction costs involved in choosing an aggregator and in negotiating, managing and monitoring their contracts (Cardoso et al., 2020). The fact that many firms choose to cooperate with aggregators, despite the costs in terms of lost revenue and other transaction costs involved, suggests that market transaction costs of providing flexibility are high (Cardoso et al., 2020).

78. Considering the presence of such costs, the limited financial returns generated by market participation may lead to a negative cost-benefit assessment of adjusting consumption patterns, i.e., the available financial gains or cost savings do not outweigh the costs. Insufficient economic incentives could thus contribute to the low willingness of non-energy-intensive consumers to engage in DR and various activities to increase RES-E use. Such reluctance is further reinforced by another feature of commercial and residential users, that they tend to value comfort over financial reward (Lashmar et al., 2022). In particular, empirical studies have demonstrated that when providing demand flexibility by load shifting or load reduction, the commercial customers' primary concern is the loss of consumer comfort that they must maintain for their core business (Lashmar et al., 2022; Paterakis et al., 2017). Meeting occupant comfort in commercial business, namely maintaining service levels, is a core operational requirement for all commercial businesses (Lashmar et al., 2022). If the expected benefits are not high enough to cover the cost incurred by interrupting or affecting an individual commercial user's core business, it would be challenging

to engage that user in providing flexibility to the electricity system. Similar to insights from behavioral economics mentioned later on, this finding challenges the commonly held assumption that commercial actors generally react to external economic incentives. The case of commercial users suggests that the effectiveness of external incentives in driving behavioral change may be context-specific and vary across individual users, depending largely on their internal cost–benefit structures and priorities.

79. There has been a rife perception that 'ensuring right or sufficient incentives' is a key enabler of adjusting consumer behavior (Poplavskaya and Vries, 2019). It is straightforward to claim this. However, as shown above, it is not easy to make this enabler function in the real world, even though price interventions could be phased out. A key challenge lies in defining the proper or sufficient level of economic incentives, or from whose perspective the adequacy of such incentives can be evaluated. A tricky trade-off is inherent in this challenge. On the one hand, in terms of consumer engagement, market-based remuneration must be financially attractive to energy consumers. On the other hand, however, being attractive to various consumers is not the sole decisive factor, especially considering the significance of cost-efficient flexibility utilization. The overall cost of utilizing flexibility resources from a whole-system perspective also matters, as it largely determines the cost-efficiency of creating a flexible electricity system that accommodates the integration of variable RES-E. This cost will be ultimately passed on to all end users and too high remuneration for (demand-side) flexibility will eventually raise concerns of affordability and public acceptance. The significance of ensuring the low-cost transition toward a high-RES electricity system is reflected in the existing EU law's emphasis on cost-efficient procurement of flexibility used for system operation purposes, as shown in the next Chapter. This illustrates the paradox between providing adequate economic incentives to unlock the flexibility potential from consumers and the need to lower flexibility use costs.

### *2.1.2. Market Entry*

80. Consumers' incentives also depend on whether they can enter electricity markets to trade demand flexibility and self-produced RES-E. Free access to electricity markets is thus a key enabler to engage consumers in relevant energy activities. However, electricity markets were initially designed to allow for market participation of large centralized generators and professional energy undertakings (O'Connell et al., 2014). Their technical rules did not fully account for the characteristics of DR and decentralized RES-E, which led to these resources being ruled out. It is helpful to understand this issue by recalling an inherent feature of electricity markets, notably those aimed at providing ancillary services to system operators (e.g., balancing markets): their rules and requirements are to a large extent mandated by the technical characteristics

of the power system (Poplavskaya and Vries, 2019). An example of entering balancing markets is illustrative. Upon reserving balancing capacity, TSOs procure it from prequalified BSPs (Poplavskaya and Vries, 2019). In other words, the balancing market is not universally accessible; instead, it is restricted to those BSPs that pass the prequalification process (Poplavskaya and Vries, 2019). As such, in case market design does not account for specific characteristics or disadvantages of resources from final customers, *de facto* market entry barriers or biases arise and put customers in a disadvantageous position to compete with traditional actors, such as large and centralized power stations (EC, 2016a). This unfavorable situation is further reinforced by the fact that final customers mostly have little to no understanding of highly formalized electricity markets and their complex technical requirements (Kim and Shcherbakova, 2011; O'Connell et al., 2014; Wohlfarth et al., 2020; Leinauer et al., 2022). The following market design parameters are considered as barriers in particular:

- Minimum resource bid size. Wholesale and ancillary service markets in some Member States were generally criticized for high minimum bid sizes (i.e., the minimum acceptable bidding volume to bid on the market), varying between 1 and 5 MW, blocking medium and small consumers from entering markets (Koliou et al., 2015; Poplavskaya and Vries, 2019; Leinauer et al., 2022). The combination of high capacity requirements and the unavailability of aggregation options excluded residential, commercial and small industrial consumers and limited the flexibility provision option only to large industrial consumers, such as in Denmark (Paterakis et al., 2017). By 2019, in Dutch, German and Austrian balancing markets, the minimum bid size for aFRR and mFRR[37] was considered still too high for DERs (Poplavskaya and Vries, 2019). Yet, it should also be noted that lowering the minimum bid size is not without challenge, since limiting participation to bids above a couple of megawatts aims to keep the computational system tractable and reduce transaction costs (EC, 2016a; IEA, 2016; Inês et al., 2020). Allowing the participation of massive distributed and small bids from consumers could bring challenges to market operations.
- High costs and effort for prequalification. Prequalification is the process of verifying a provider of ancillary services' compliance with the requirements set by the system operators (*Electricity Regulation*, Article 2(18)). Prequalification encompasses complex and strict requirements at the national level and can be lengthy, which is viewed as a barrier for inexperienced consumers to enter the ancillary service markets (Alcázar-Ortega et al., 2015; Paterakis et al., 2017; Annala et al., 2018b; Leinauer et al., 2022).

[37] mFRR and aFRR are two types of FRR with different modes of activation. The former means that the balancing energy is triggered manually by an operator while the latter means that balancing energy is triggered automatically in a closed-loop manner. See Balancing Regulation, article 2 (34).

- Bid direction. Several national markets used to require the bids to be symmetric (Paterakis et al., 2017). This means that resources should provide equal capacity to change in both directions, which, in the case of DR, the loads should be equally able to decrease and increase their consumption (EC, 2016a; Paterakis et al., 2017; Borne et al., 2018). This is a requirement that directly restricts the pool of eligible DR resources since only a few types of load would be equally flexible in both directions (Paterakis et al., 2017). If market products are only symmetrical, FSPs will not be able to provide the optimal amount of available reserve because the same amount of upward reserve and downward reserve may not be available (Borne et al., 2018). In addition, currently, for most DR providers, only downward regulation of their loads is economically viable, and thus symmetrical bidding can undermine their incentives to enter balancing markets (Poplavskaya and Vries, 2019).
- The contracting period, i.e., the period during which flexibility providers must have their power available (SWECO, 2015; Borne et al., 2018). Most markets require the resource to maintain its response from 4 to 12 hours (e.g., Austria and Germany, respectively) during a call (Paterakis et al., 2017). Too long contracting periods could hinder the active participation of consumers providing balancing services with DR or self-produced RES-E (SWECO, 2015; Borne et al., 2018). There are two reasons why long contracting periods are not favorable for the participation of balancing services provided by consumers. First, electricity consumption is characterized by variability, and it is thus often not viable for most individual customers to offer DR many days ahead of the moment when electricity is actually consumed (EC, 2016a). Final customers tend to hesitate to commit to changing their demand for several weeks or months at a time, and a long time in advance (EC, 2016a). Thus, the longer in advance balancing capacity is procured, and the longer the period it needs to be held available, the more challenging it becomes for DR to participate in this market (Papsch, 2020). This is especially the case for small consumers (Koliou et al., 2015). Furthermore, for FSPs aggregating a large number of consumption units in their pool, as the amount of reserves they can provide is highly variable, too long DR duration requirements may also seriously restrict their market participation (Borne et al., 2018). The same problem applies to RES-E prosumers with intermittent electricity output as well. They can only offer balancing services if they can be reasonably sure that their generation capacity is in principle available, and such certainty exists only a short time ahead of delivery (Papsch, 2020).
- The bidding frequency. A bidding frequency that is too low entails an uncertainty that consumers' profits will be lost if the bid is not selected and the waiting time for the next bidding opportunity is considerable (Poplavskaya and Vries, 2019). For instance, the auction frequency for FCR and aFRR in the Netherlands remained remarkably low in 2019, making it impossible even for aggregated sources from consumers to provide balancing capacity

(Poplavskaya and Vries, 2019).[38] The planned introduction of daily auctions for aFRR in Austria and Germany in 2018 is likely to boost the entry of new participants on the demand side, liquidity, competition, and price efficiency accordingly (Poplavskaya and Vries, 2019).

81. Overall, market access is a prerequisite for consumers to fully benefit from DR and renewables self-consumption. However, the traditional electricity market design, originally designed for the participation of large resources, is obsolete in terms of accommodating the participation of consumers with relatively small consumption or generation portfolios. This is why, compared to conventional power plants and large industrial users, in the past decades, consumers from the service and household sectors had few experiences in market participation, notably in commercializing DR and self-generated RES-E (Torriti et al., 2010; Wohlfarth et al., 2020). Despite this, industrial users' participation remains to be further improved since some of them still struggle to handle a high level of complexity and administrative burdens arising from numerous electricity market regulations and associated technical and procedural requirements (Vallés et al., 2016; Wohlfarth et al., 2020; Leinauer et al., 2022). Moreover, in some Member States, even energy-intensive industrial users were subject to distorted incentives, notably those stemming from network fees, as set out in Section 3 below.

82. For medium and small consumers, some of the above unfavorable conditions for entering electricity markets, especially high minimum bid sizes, could be overcome by aggregation. In theory, aggregation services could be provided by suppliers and IFSPs. However, most suppliers do not actively valorize their consumers' flexibility in practice, because many also own generation assets whose rents would be diminished if price peaks were reduced (Pearson, 2020, p 106). The losses that DR would cause to the undertaking's upstream subsidiary may outweigh the savings that DR would bring to the undertaking's supply subsidiary (Pearson, 2020, p 106). There thus exist conflicts of interest for suppliers in terms of offering aggregation services to their consumers. In this case, IFSPs play a pivotal role in providing aggregation services to final customers and enhancing market participation of demand flexibility. Yet, in some national electricity markets, their market entry and engagement with end users were constrained by suppliers and BRPs since activating DR could negatively impact suppliers and BRPs (*CREG 2016 Study*, 2016; Poplavskaya and Vries, 2018; *CREG Decision 1677/3*, 2020). Why they have misaligned interests and suppliers and BRPs have incentives to create barriers for IFSPs' activities is explained in detail below.

83. The supplier of the consumer buys energy in advance on the electricity market to cover the estimated energy offtake of each access point in its portfolio.

---

[38] 'Frequency containment reserves' or 'FCR' means the active power reserves available to contain system frequency after the occurrence of an imbalance. See System Operation Guideline, article 3(6).

Under the contract of valorizing DR between the consumer and the IFSP, the IFSP sells the consumer's flexibility to the BRP of the FRP (i.e., $BRP_{frp}$) or system operators (*TSO 2019 Study*, 2019, section 4). The IFSP then needs to activate flexibility corresponding to the volume sold by asking the consumer to reduce or increase net offtake (*TSO 2019 Study*, 2019, section 4). In the event of upward activation of DR (i.e. reduction of consumption), the IFSP diverts the energy that the supplier uses to cover the expected consumption of its customer (*CREG 2016 Study*, 2016, section V.4.2; *TSO 2019 Study*, 2019, section 4; *CREG Decision 1677/3*, 2020, section 2.2.1). As a consequence of the reduction in net offtake, the supplier can no longer invoice the customer for this activated energy (*CREG 2016 Study*, 2016, section V.4.2; *TSO 2019 Study*, 2019, section 4; *CREG Decision 1677/3*, 2020, section 2.2.1). This could create a distortion in which the IFSP profits from an activation, whereas the risk of financial loss is placed on the supplier (*CREG 2016 Study*, 2016, section V.4.2; *TSO 2019 Study*, 2019, section 4; *CREG Decision 1677/3*, 2020, section 2.2.1). Suppliers thus have incentives to oppose or impede IFSPs' activities (*CREG 2016 Study*, 2016, section V.4.2; *TSO 2019 Study*, 2019, section 4; *CREG Decision 1677/3*, 2020, section 2.2.1). The supplier's BRP, which is responsible for maintaining a balanced portfolio, will face imbalances if it is not informed of DR activation and fails to take action to rebalance its portfolio. In the case of consumption reduction, for instance, the imbalance occurs because the energy injected to cover the demand of the customer is not fully taken from the portfolio of the BRP (*CREG 2016 Study*, 2016, section V.4.2; *TSO 2019 Study*, 2019, section 4; *CREG Decision 1677/3*, 2020, section 2.2.1). This means that the supplier's BRP will face imbalance tariffs due to the IFSP's activity. Thus, in some Member States, suppliers' BRPs used to require IFSPs to gain their consent when IFSPs contract with concerned customers (Stede et al., 2020). Figure 4 overviews the relationship between the IFSP and stakeholders in the activation of DR.

**Figure 4. The relationship between the IFSP and stakeholders in activating DR**[39]

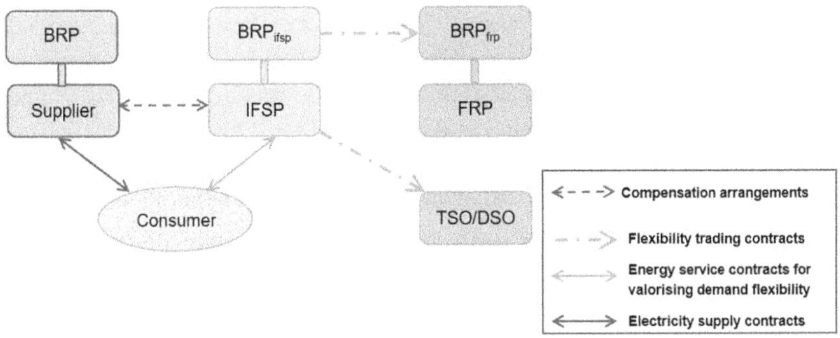


[39] This figure is adapted from *TSO 2019 Study*, 2019.

84. The lack of legal arrangements that regulate the IFSP's relationship with affected market players hindered this entity from widely engaging with customers and valorizing DR in electricity markets (Annala et al., 2018a; Barbero et al., 2018; Poplavskaya and Vries, 2018; Vandorpe and Callaerts, 2018, p 218). In Nordic countries, for instance, IFSPs had difficulty accessing electricity markets, and mainly suppliers and BRPs worked as aggregators, principally to balance their own portfolios (Barbero et al., 2018). This situation significantly limited options for final customers who wish to valorize flexibility.

## 2.2. COGNITIVE AND BEHAVIORAL LIMITATIONS

85. Conventional economics assumes that individuals are entirely rational, have stable and consistent preferences, and make decisions to maximize their wealth or utility (Ghisellini and Chang, 2018, pp 9–26). It is thus believed that the ultimate motivation of people is money (Santos Silva, 2022). Hence, to direct people to comply with rules or encourage behavioral changes, they were given economic incentives (Santos Silva, 2022). The rational actor model of traditional economics has had considerable implications for the design of law and policy in many fields, including the sustainable energy transition (Santos Silva, 2022). Providing economic incentives and information has thus been incorporated into the regulatory toolkit, along with the traditional approach of command and control, to steer desirable behavior (Feldman and Perez, 2009; Santos Silva, 2022). Economic incentives indeed matter to induce behavior change, as indicated in the previous subsection. However, behavioral science or economics built upon evidence-based insights from psychology and other social sciences challenges the claim that people are fully rational in choosing the economically most attractive option (Ghisellini and Chang, 2018, pp 3–4, 26–35 and 37; Ioannidou, 2018; Hanke and Lowitzsch, 2020). Instead, it highlights that under real-world conditions, people tend to make decisions and act in ways that are economically 'irrational' since they are constrained by limited cognitive resources and a range of cognitive and psychological biases.[40] The presence of these restrictions weakens people's responses to economic incentives and could lead to systematic deviations from the conventional model of rational decision-making (Fehr and Rangel, 2011; Yildiz et al., 2015; Ghisellini and Chang, 2018, p 175). Such deviations are also detected in the decision-making of legal persons, especially when external incentives are not linked to essential business, as outlined in Section 2.2.2 below. Failing to identify factors that shape consumer behavior and decision-making beyond economic incentives would eventually render DSM measures ineffective.

---

40 For more details about the definition and taxonomy of decision-making biases, see Kahneman, 2003; Pesendorfer, 2006; Thaler and Sunstein, 2008; Ghisellini and Chang, 2018, pp 96–101.

86. To inform the design of DSM measures, drawing on theoretical and empirical insights from behavioral science and economics, this section examines how cognitive and behavioral limitations affect consumer actions in DR and renewables use (notably prosuming), and outlines behavioral economics-inspired solutions presented in prior studies. As indicated by the existing literature, mainly consumers from the residential, commercial and public sectors suffer from behavioral barriers (Hobman et al., 2016; Cardoso et al., 2020; Hanke and Lowitzsch, 2020). In the industrial sector, distorted economic incentives from regulated prices and network fees were regarded as primary barriers to engaging energy-intensive consumers. While behavioral obstacles are also mentioned in the literature, they are secondary barriers in comparison to economic and regulatory obstacles (Leinauer et al., 2022). Such behavioral obstacles are mainly linked to the risk and inconvenience of energy management activities, such as DR, perceived by employees and management since it differs from the accustomed workflow and may negatively interfere with primary objectives, e.g., faultless production and disruption of operations, of the company and the employees (Olsthoorn et al., 2015; Paterakis et al., 2017; Verpoorten et al., 2016; Leinauer et al., 2022; Lashmar et al., 2022). Similar barriers are also present in commercial users' and public organizations' decision-making, while exhibiting greater complexity linked to their electricity consumption feature (Cardoso et al., 2020). Considering this, for non-residential users, only the 'irrationality' of consumers from the commercial and public sectors is discussed in the following.

87. Different customer groups have unique needs, wants, interests and motivations, and face varying constraints and supports when it comes to using electricity (Hobman et al., 2016). These specificities shape their decision-making and choices on energy consumption. Hence, behavioral barriers of users from residential, commercial and public sectors are discussed separately in Sections 2.2.1 and 2.2.2. Consumers experiencing energy poverty and vulnerability often have limited cognitive capacity and competence and are therefore more susceptible to the impact of cognitive and decision-making biases. Their difficulties in becoming proactive customers involved in DR and renewables use merit specific attention, as elaborated in Section 2.2.3 below. Section 2.2.4 introduces key concepts, especially nudge and boost, which represent behavioral economics-inspired solutions to engage consumers.

### *2.2.1. Household Users*

88. Compared to industrial and commercial users, households are considered more difficult to mobilize for activities favorable to RES-E uptake. This is exemplified by their relatively few experiences in market participation, as noted above, and low interest in energy activities that require active choices beyond mere electricity purchase, especially DR and renewables self-consumption. Their

high level of inertia and passivity is in line with insights from behavioral science or economics, which identify human decision-making biases and irrationality in the real world and explain why people often 'misbehave' in ways that deviate from the rational actor model of traditional economics (Corr and Plagnol, 2019, pp 3–14). The generic theory of behavioral science or economics has been widely applied to explain the inaction of households in the energy sector. This section outlines the general findings and concepts of behavioral economics, focusing on the limited cognitive capabilities of individuals and the resulting barriers to making well-informed and rational decisions. It also looks into residential consumers' behavioral barriers in the specific context of supporting RES-E uptake (notably DR and renewables self-consumption).[41]

89. As noted above, traditional economics assumes that people are able to process information in a cognitively complex, deliberative and unbiased fashion where a choice must be made between alternative courses of action with different expected utility values (Corr and Plagnol, 2019, p 116). This assumption entails two essential competences of rational individuals: deliberately processing (potentially complex and massive) information and reacting to incentives in order to maximize utility. However, the empirical evidence shows that, on the contrary, such rationality is difficult to achieve, as people's cognitive capacity is limited to enable these two competences. Such cognitive constraints stem from human cognitive systems or architecture. People use two cognitive systems for collecting information and making decisions: system 1 (automatic system), a quicker, intuitive, and more impulsive or emotional system; and system 2 (effortful system), a slower, non-emotional, rule-governed system, which demands more reflection and is, therefore, less relied upon in daily life for collecting information and making decisions (Kahneman, 2003b; Hertwig and Grüne-Yanoff, 2017; Santos Silva, 2022). The two systems have respective advantages and flaws. System 1 is an efficient first-response system, but its speed and automatic processes render it susceptible to systematic biases, and it seems ill-equipped for the task of rational and deliberative decision-making (Hertwig and Grüne-Yanoff, 2017; Corr and Plagnol, 2019, pp 114–116). System 2 can support careful and deliberative processing and could, in principle, supervise System 1's mental products and conclusions as well as rectify biases whilst it is inadequate in terms of speed of processing and limited capacity or resources and is also prone to fatigue (Hertwig and Grüne-Yanoff, 2017; Corr and Plagnol, 2019, pp 114–116).

90. The impact of the existence of these two systems makes people's decision-making subject to several cognitive and psychological biases and limited attention

41 In terms of purchasing RES-E, the literature does not mention behavioral barriers. Consumers' decision-making biases or limitations are mainly present when engaging in investment and operation of DR and renewables prosuming.

and cognitive capabilities, contributing to a phenomenon that can also be placed under the theory of 'bounded rationality' (Busch, 2016, p 221; Lavrijssen, 2017; Santos Silva, 2022). Central to the notion of bounded rationality is that given limited knowledge and cognitive capabilities, when facing uncertainty and complex information, and the demands of complex computations, people tend to use simplifying heuristics informed by experience or rules of thumb to make decisions, rather than always optimizing, leading to *'lower-than-optimal utility'* which is called *satisficing* – this is a portmanteau of 'suffice' and 'satisfying' proposed by Herbert Simon in the 1950s (Tversky and Kahneman, 1974; Ghisellini and Chang, 2018, p 175; Corr and Plagnol, 2019, pp 81–82). Simply put, bounded rationality means that individuals are rational but limited in terms of their attention capacity, their knowledge, and their ability to deal with uncertainties and make decisions (Cardoso et al., 2020). It is also found that when lacking time and being overwhelmed by massive information, choices and opportunities, decision-making agents are even more inclined to bounded rationality, namely turning to resort to rules of thumb and aiming for satisfactory rather than optimal outcomes (Simon, 1955; Hobman et al., 2016; Ghisellini and Chang, 2018, p 107; Cardoso et al., 2020). This finding particularly highlights the role of complexity stemming from information and choice overload in inducing sub-optimal economic decisions, which is also highly relevant to other decision-making biases discussed later on.

91. While bounded rationality is a vital notion that explains deviations from the rational agent assumption, it alone cannot cover all decision-making biases resulting from constrained cognitive capabilities and real-world conditions. Based on empirical findings, behavioral economics identifies a set of powerful cognitive biases and psychological anomalies that are likely to influence people's behavior and motivations (Hobman et al., 2016). Some of them interact with each other and reinforce motivational and decision-making deficiencies or irrationality we observe in the energy field, such as the inertia of energy consumers, which is a recurrent barrier to shaping proactive customers in the energy transition context (Hobman et al., 2016). In listing these decision-making principles and resultant biases, non-participating households' behavior in line with these general findings in the DR and renewables prosuming contexts is also discussed as follows:

(1) **Aversion to complexity**: This represents people's tendency to adopt simpler decision rules (and therefore potentially make worse decisions or choices) as the information and stimuli, such as choices or opportunities in one's environment, become more complex (Hobman et al., 2016). Complexity aversion is linked to a cognitive limitation of the human mind mentioned above, namely, attention is a scarce resource, and information overload and the complex decision-making context may consume it (Santos Silva, 2022). The more choices available, the greater the need to gather relevant

information, increasing the complexity of decision-making and the potential for error, resulting in a state referred to as 'choice paralysis' (Hanke and Lowitzsch, 2020). When the cost of processing all necessary information to make the best choice outweighs the benefits of making a choice, consumers choose not to choose (Hanke and Lowitzsch, 2020). In a world where information, choices and opportunities abound and overwhelm, decision-making biases or distortions are easy to arise since people come to rely on simple mental 'short-cuts' or 'heuristics' to guide decision-making, which can alleviate the need for intensive cognitive processing and thereby hasten the speed of decision making (Tversky and Kahneman, 1973, 1974; Gigerenzer and Gaissmaier, 2011; Hobman et al., 2016). Such biases can lead to the outcome of 'lower-than-optimal utility' referred to in bounded rationality mentioned above, and even more irrational choices or actions. It should also be noted that, as a common decision-making bias, complexity aversion could also give rise to or exacerbate other biases mentioned later on, especially trust as a decision heuristic and status quo bias.

Aversion to complexity is present when consumers are empowered and encouraged to engage in relatively novel activities, such as DR and renewables self-consumption. For instance, the inherent complexity of electricity markets and associated regulations is a commonly reported barrier for consumers to valorize their DR and self-produced RES-E (Horstink et al., 2017; Hanke and Lowitzsch, 2020; Streimikiene et al., 2021). This could lower consumers' willingness to seek market-based remuneration and eventually affect their incentives to invest and enroll in these activities. Moreover, a complicated tariff is also a factor responsible for consumers' reluctance to support or choose dynamic tariffs. If the tariff structure itself is too complex, customers are not only unlikely to choose it in the first place, but may also find it challenging to utilize it effectively daily (Hobman et al., 2016). When proposing the CEP, the EC pointed out that consumer inaction in DR is also attributed to the fact that they are ill-informed in terms of the potential room for bill savings (EC, 2016a). This is inter alia because electricity bills were inefficient in providing information that could facilitate effective choices (EC, 2016a). Customer groups reported that end users have difficulties understanding their energy bills (EC, 2016a). The high number of complaints related to billing suggests that there is still scope to improve the comparability, clarity and accuracy of billing information (EC, 2016a).

(2) **Trust as a decision heuristic**: This refers to people's tendency to use perceptions of trust as a decision-making 'heuristic' – i.e., a mental shortcut or rule-of-thumb to speed up information processing, problem-solving and decision-making in complex and cognitively demanding situations (Hobman et al., 2016). This bias is closely linked to complexity aversion noted above. Furthermore, it is found that time and information scarcity can also lead to the use of heuristics or intuition, leading to 'Intuitive

Overconfidence' (IOC) bias, which may result in a flawed assessment of potential risks and encourage more risk-taking that ultimately becomes uncontrolled (Ghisellini and Chang, 2018, p 107).

(3) **Loss aversion**: This means the tendency to focus more heavily on losses than on comparable gains, and to exert far greater effort to avoid a loss as compared to an equivalent-sized gain (Kahneman and Tversky, 1984; Kahneman et al., 1991; Hobman et al., 2016). This persistent tendency is manifest whenever people are weighing up the losses or costs and gains or benefits of different choices, and ultimately reflects the fact that humans tend to experience or 'feel the pain' of losses far more than the pleasure of gains (Ghisellini and Chang, 2018, p 109–110). This bias plays a significant role in shaping the choices and actions of residential consumers regarding DR and renewable energy use (Streimikiene et al., 2021). Notably, in the context of engaging consumers in DR, compared to potential cost savings or financial gains, consumers are more concerned about losses coming with DR, such as inconvenience, loss of comfort and possible economic losses when being unable to shift load away from peak times (Hobman et al., 2016; Nicolson et al., 2017). Their greater focus on avoiding losses explains why households are reluctant to change their behavior, for instance, by adjusting their consumption in exchange for financial returns. Loss aversion is correlated to another prominent cognitive bias listed below, i.e., status quo bias (Samuelson and Zeckhauser, 1988; Hobman et al., 2016; Nicolson et al., 2017; Ghisellini and Chang, 2018, p 109), since consumers are averse to potential loss brought by engaging in new activities and tend to stick with conventional consumption patterns.

(4) **Risk aversion**: People are averse to risk and tend to over-weight certainty and sure gains, favoring a smaller but guaranteed payoff over the gamble of less certain gains of markedly higher value (Kahneman and Tversky, 1979, 1984; Hobman et al., 2016). Uncertain benefits are a vital factor that blocks consumers' participation in implicit DR, either in the form of dynamic price contracts or dynamic tariffs (Faruqui and Palmer, 2011; Hobman et al., 2016). When electricity prices are very variable, it is difficult to predict the bill savings obtained by engaging in DR, especially dynamic pricing connected to wholesale markets, and there is a real or perceived risk that nothing will be gained (Hobman et al., 2016). The same reasoning also applied to dynamic tariffs. Both qualitative and quantitative research indicate that customers often find highly complex, variable pricing schemes less appealing than simpler, more static ones (Paetz et al., 2012; Dütschke and Paetz, 2013; Fell et al., 2015; Hobman et al., 2016). The underlying rationale is households' aversion to uncertainties or risks. Similar to loss aversion, being averse to risk can also contribute to a status quo bias, as elaborated on later.

(5) **Time inconsistency and spatial and temporal discounting**: People tend to discount things that are further away in time (temporal discounting) or space (spatial discounting), and conversely, place disproportionate weight on things that are immediate or nearby, also known as 'present bias' (Thaler, 1981; Loewenstein and Thaler, 1989; Hobman et al., 2016; Lavrijssen, 2017; DellaValle, 2019). This bias leads them to be short-sighted and prefer smaller, immediate rewards (e.g., 5 euros now) over larger future rewards (e.g., 100 euros next year) (Hobman et al., 2016). This is reflected in households' limited capability of making long-term investments in renewables DG (Hanke et al., 2023). Such long-term economic decisions require objective trade-offs built upon accurate identification of short-term and long-term costs and benefits, which can easily be hindered by users' disproportionate emphasis on immediate or nearby costs and benefits (Hobman et al., 2016). In the context of engaging in DR, households can easily perceive several upfront costs that may be immediately salient to them (Hobman et al., 2016). These include 'learning costs' and 'transaction costs', in this case: the time and effort they must invest to learn about new tariff offerings or dynamic price contracts, and about how to modify household energy usage appropriately (Faruqui et al., 2010; Salies, 2013; Hobman et al., 2016). There is also the immediate inconvenience incurred by switching electricity plans, often referred to as 'hassle costs' (Lambrecht and Tucker, 2012; Hobman et al., 2016). Modifying one's energy usage pattern may, in turn, lead to other ongoing costs such as losses in convenience, comfort and cleanliness (Hobman et al., 2016). In contrast, rewards or bill savings obtained by participation in DR might be low and uncertain (given variable electricity prices) and arrive well into the future (Hobman et al., 2016). In this case, households are prone to discount these potential longer-term payoffs by placing a disproportionate weight on the upfront costs (Hobman et al., 2016). The tendency to discount potential longer-term payoffs could also reinforce residential users' preference for the status quo.

(6) **Status quo bias**: People tend to resist change and instead favor the status quo or 'default' setting, which oftentimes means not acting (i.e., inertia) or avoiding making a decision together (Samuelson and Zeckhauser, 1988; Kahneman et al., 1991; Hobman et al., 2016). Such preference to retain the current state of affairs largely results from risks, potential losses, efforts and costs required to deviate from normality, and the inclination to give more weight to these costs or risks than likely gains (Hobman et al., 2016). Moreover, when changing behavior entails processing complex information and making choices among many options, people may also choose to stick to the status quo (Anderson, 2003; Hobman et al., 2016; Good et al., 2017). Hence, the preference for the status quo correlates with several aforementioned biases, including aversion to complexity, risks, losses, and discounting long-term benefits. These factors interplay and

explain why households exhibit inertia when they are mobilized to adapt conventional electricity consumption behavior to participate in DR and renewables prosuming. Empirical research shows that many households demonstrate a deeply entrenched preference for the status quo and are reluctant to either provide explicit DR or shift to dynamic pricing or tariffs (Hobman et al., 2016). This can manifest itself in a focus on the perceived inconvenience of DR participation, and the requirement that interventions 'fit' with current lives (Balta-Ozkan et al., 2013; Good et al., 2017).

(7) **Normative social influence**: People have a tendency to follow the behavior of others, make social comparisons, and adhere to social norms – i.e., people could be heavily influenced by how others think, feel and act; they often care about performance, possessions and wellbeing relative to other people, rather than in absolute terms (Hobman et al., 2016). People tend to do what is socially approved (because it yields social rewards) or popular (because it reflects effective or adaptive behavior), and thus social norms can exert a powerful impact on attitudes and behavior, favoring the sustainable energy transition (Hobman et al., 2016). Numerous studies in the energy domain have found that simply conveying descriptive normative information (e.g., personalized messages comparing one's electricity consumption to a neighborhood norm) can significantly influence customers' energy usage (Nolan et al., 2008; Allcott and Mullainathan, 2010; Allcott, 2011a; Hobman et al., 2016). This finding implies that households' willingness to engage in DR, e.g., shifting to dynamic price contracts, could be affected if they think that many other people are not turning to such pricing (Hobman et al., 2016). Moreover, empirical evidence also shows that social norms are an important determinant of citizens' willingness to participate in energy communities, which represents a collective way of engaging in DR and renewables self-consumption (Yildiz et al., 2015). The impact of social norms is also defined as 'peer effects'. Empirical evidence provided by previous studies highlights that peer effects – the social influence of peers, such as colleagues, neighbors or friends – constitute an important factor for households to invest in renewables DG (Bollinger and Gillingham, 2012; Müller and Rode, 2013a; Graziano and Gillingham, 2015; Palm, 2017).

### 2.2.2. *Commercial Users and Public Organizations*

92. Commercial users and public organizations can be grouped into the service sector since their electricity use is similar: their electricity consumption is mainly related to building occupancy, comprising cross-sectional technologies such as heating, ventilation and air conditioning, lighting, catering and refrigeration (Cardoso et al., 2020). Commercial and public entities have the technical capacity to provide significant amounts of flexibility to the electricity system (Cardoso et al., 2020). In Europe, it has been estimated that the theoretical potential of

this sector is of a similar order of magnitude as that of the residential and industrial sectors (Gils, 2014; Cardoso et al., 2020). Moreover, customers in the service sector consume more electricity than residential users and have greater capital resources to invest in deploying RES-E. They could considerably contribute to the greater penetration of RES-E by actively engaging in renewables procurement and self-consumption. However, such significant potential to provide flexibility and invest in RES-E remained untapped (Paulus and Borggrefe, 2011; Klobasa et al., 2014; Olsthoorn et al., 2015). As mentioned above, a paradox in practice seems to be that commercial users are supposed to respond to price signals and follow economically rational behavior, while a widely reported problem is that they still lack interest in reshaping their electricity consumption to reap economic benefits (Olsthoorn et al., 2015; Shoreh et al., 2016; Good et al., 2017; Annala et al., 2018a; Shafie-khah et al., 2019; Lashmar et al., 2022). Insufficient and uncertain net benefits arising from distorted and variable prices alone cannot fully explain this paradox. Behavior-related factors are inhibiting their investment and engagement in DR and renewables use, which is linked to their small individual electricity loads and complex internal decision-making processes (Cardoso et al., 2020). Interestingly, some of the aforementioned behavioral constraints, such as status quo bias and loss aversion, are also detected in the decision-making of consumers in the service sector (Good et al., 2017; Cardoso et al., 2020).

93. Inactive commercial and public entities' behavioral barriers are rooted in their energy-related decisions taken by individuals within the entities. When these entities' internal decision-making is influenced by their employees' cognitive biases or distortions, they exhibit behavioral barriers to engaging in DR and renewable energy use. The non-essential characteristic of energy matters first induces employees' bounded rationality. In entities where energy is not linked to the core business – either because energy costs are relatively low or energy is not part of the production process – non-essential energy projects are often not considered organizational priorities (Brown, 2001; Schleich and Gruber, 2008; Olsthoorn et al., 2015; Cardoso et al., 2020). Several studies on investment in energy efficiency have shown that in non-energy-intensive entities, investments in energy projects are assessed and treated differently from investments in core business projects (Cooremans, 2011, 2012; Cardoso et al., 2020). Bounded rationality is most relevant for issues perceived as marginal to the core business, including changing electricity consumption via DR and greater RES-E use (Cardoso et al., 2020). That is to say, for these marginal issues, consumers' decisions are not necessarily based on robust assessments of the financial costs and benefits of participation, nor are they made using standard economic appraisal methods (Cardoso et al., 2020). Instead, energy managers of commercial and public entities spend less time considering energy projects, which are often regarded as non-essential business, and consequently, they may

ignore such projects or assess them using heuristics (Cooremans, 2011; Cardoso et al., 2020). There is thus a risk that decisions about DR and renewable energy use are not made on technical or cost-benefit grounds; instead, they are made by people who lack the time or inclination to understand them fully (Cardoso et al., 2020). The absence of a cost-benefit assessment leads relevant decision-makers to overlook the potential financial benefit of changing electricity consumption and also explains why commercial and public entities are not easily mobilized by financial gains brought by behavior change: in this case, pricing plays less of a role, and it is not as much of a determining factor for energy investments as it is in the energy-intensive sector (Schleich, 2009; Cardoso et al., 2020).

94. Moreover, the empirical evidence shows that the use of heuristics (e.g., shortcuts and routines, and unconsciously searching for information to support existing views) is prevalent during the initial phase of the decision-making process,[42] i.e., when companies with little or no experience in altering electricity use first consider a proposal for flexing their electricity demand or investing in renewables self-consumption (Cardoso et al., 2020). A study of aggregators' acquisition process found that during the first two stages of the selling process, a primary reason for commercial sites not taking up DR was a lack of interest (Curtis, 2017; Cardoso et al., 2020). By contrast, during the last two phases of the selling process, if sites chose not to participate in DR, they provided specific reasons for their decision, such as the technical unsuitability of assets (Curtis, 2017; Cardoso et al., 2020). A possible interpretation of these results is that during the initial phases, decisions about DR were taken without carrying out a detailed assessment of the aggregators' proposal, but based on rules of thumb, while formal economic methods of evaluation were applied in the following decision-making phases, especially the selection stage (Cardoso et al., 2020).

95. The irrational decision-making relying on heuristics could be further reinforced by the complex internal decision-making of commercial and public entities. Changing electricity consumption by engaging in DR or using more RES-E can impact different parts of a business and thus require the support of a range of stakeholders within the commercial or public entity (Goulden and Spence, 2015; Cardoso et al., 2020). Especially within large organizations, decision chains can be highly complex, requiring the approval of multiple parties to proceed with a project (Cardoso et al., 2020). Decisions about adjusting electricity use involve multiple decision-makers beyond the energy department, including operational and financial departments, as well as engineers or others in charge of the sites (Cardoso et al., 2020). The complexity and organizational transaction costs of relevant decision-making can be additionally exacerbated by

[42] Decision-making is not a point in time but a process comprising three phases: identification or diagnosis, development (build-up of solutions) and selection, which involves the evaluation of different solutions and choices. See Cardoso et al., 2020.

the fact that these decision-makers have different goals and interests and resultant distinct concerns about new actions in electricity consumption.[43] Even though energy managers are well informed about the costs and financial profitability of engaging in DR and greater RES-E use, persuading other decision-makers and addressing their concerns potentially entails massive time and effort (Sorrell et al., 2004; Cardoso et al., 2020). Another source of organizational transaction costs is the need to collect and coordinate data from different departments, as well as to help negotiate individual site contracts (Cardoso et al., 2020). The complex decision-making context, as highlighted above, can particularly make the individuals involved prone to curtailing rational cost-benefit calculations, leading to inaccurate judgments and decisions that hinder desirable behavior change in the concerned entities. The non-essential nature of energy matters and complex decision-making processes are jointly responsible for decision-makers' tendency to rely on heuristics rather than economic analysis when deciding on involvement in active consumption management.

96. In addition, employees involved in energy-related decisions also perceive risks and losses, which further reinforce resistance to changing the entities' electricity consumption patterns. In particular, as noted above, the fear of reduced service levels or potential risk to core business was one of the most frequently mentioned barriers to DR (Element Energy, 2012; Cardoso et al., 2020; Lashmar et al., 2022). Maintaining a sufficient level of comfort is notably emphasized by commercial users due to its significance to the provision of services, as noted above, which makes them highly averse to the loss of comfort brought by DR. Moreover, similar to other users, when altering electricity consumption, through either DR or renewables self-consumption, commercial and public consumers face several uncertainties, mainly including changes in market regulations and uncertain revenues or savings (Olsthoorn et al., 2015; Cardoso et al., 2020). These uncertainties result in perceptions of shifting to proactive customers being generally risky, and hence reinforcing the status quo bias (Cardoso et al., 2020). The losses and risks perceived by staff members of commercial and public organizations ultimately lead these organizations to exhibit behavioral biases similar to those of individuals, notably resistance to change and loss aversion. The above analysis of internal decision-making and its link to the lack of interest in DR and renewables use explains why inertia and aversion to complexity and losses are also common barriers to engaging energy users from the service sector (Good et al., 2017; Lashmar et al., 2022).

---

43 For instance, operational teams' primary concern is the potential impact of DR on the business core operations, and their interest and knowledge of energy may be very different from that of the energy staff. Site engineers may also be more concerned with the smooth functioning of the equipment than with potential gains from a DR project. See Sorrell et al., 2004; Cardoso et al., 2020.

### 2.2.3. *Energy Poor or Vulnerable Customers*

97. Section 2.2.1 above has demonstrated how cognitive and decision-making biases or distortions hinder individuals from making efficient economic decisions and fully benefiting from new opportunities, notably created by DR and renewables self-consumption. Empirical findings of behavioral economics indicate that such cognitive and behavioral constraints can be reinforced by deprivation and vulnerability, making those relatively novel energy activities inaccessible to energy poor or vulnerable customers (Hanke and Lowitzsch, 2020; Hanke et al., 2023). Failing to recognize the special constraints and disadvantages faced by these consumers can render measures designed for average consumers ineffective in engaging them, which also calls into question the integrity of DSM measures (Hanke and Lowitzsch, 2020; Hanke et al., 2023; Bedggood et al., 2023). Another risk is that energy poor or vulnerable customers will be left behind in the transition toward a high-renewables electricity system. This is a prominent example of demonstrating how distributional injustice arises once recognitional justice is jeopardized:[44] not all final customers are engaged in and access opportunities and benefits coming with the sustainable energy transition; those experiencing deprivation and vulnerability may be even also subject to adverse consequences of being left behind, such as rising costs of the transition socialized among all end users. To alleviate concerns about distributional injustice, an inclusive approach to engaging consumers is necessary. The first step of that approach is to understand how deprivation and vulnerability impact consumers' choices and actions, which informs the design of targeted measures or tools to enable their behavior change.

98. First, energy poor or vulnerable customers could be more prone to be averse to risk and loss, discount long-term benefits, and stick to the status quo, which interacts with their pressing budgetary constraints or financial precarity (Spears, 2011; Hanke and Lowitzsch, 2020). Consumers experiencing deprivation or vulnerability tend to have relatively limited financial room to maneuver and are compelled to make trade-offs in consumption decisions and available resources (Mould and Baker, 2017; Hanke et al., 2023). This situation can exacerbate the tendency to react more strongly to the prospect of further losses, which prevents them from altering behavior and enhances the attraction of the status quo (Adamkovič and Martončik, 2017; DellaValle, 2019). The bias of assigning more weight to immediate costs or benefits than long-term gains could be more

44 Recognitional justice seeks to understand how energy transitions impact various social groups. Assessing distributional and procedural justice must entail understanding and recognizing the prerequisites and capabilities that determine energy transition measures' accessibility and the specific needs of different social groups. Recognitional justice thus constitutes the precondition for realizing procedural and distributional justice. See Hanke et al., 2023; Jones et al., 2015.

serious: energy poor or vulnerable consumers may perceive the financial benefits of renewables self-consumption, which typically materialize over a timespan of several years as irrelevant if confronted with the immediate need to pay overdue electricity bills to avoid electricity cuts (DellaValle, 2019; Hanke and Lowitzsch, 2020). Facing budgetary constraints, high upfront investment costs required for renewables prosuming could be more salient to consumers in vulnerable or poor contexts since they may conflict with other important priorities (Hanke et al., 2023). At the same time, the long investment payback time of renewables prosuming could reinforce individuals' bias of discounting long-term benefits, which could prevent these consumers from grasping the long-term benefits of conducting renewables self-consumption (Spears, 2011; Hanke et al., 2023).

99. Among activities that consumers are encouraged to undertake to support RES-E uptake, DR and renewables self-consumption notably require energy literacy, e.g., know-how regarding the electricity system and markets (Blasch et al., 2019; Hanke et al., 2023). Relevant investments entail rational investment analyses and cost-benefit calculations, including the utilization and assessment of all available information, as well as weighing options and risks (Blasch et al., 2019; Hanke et al., 2023). Satisfying these conditions requires substantial cognitive resources (Hanke et al., 2023). As shown above, the involved complexity is not easily manageable for an average consumer, who may not perform rational calculations but instead rely on heuristics. Those experiencing vulnerability or deprivation who lack mental or cognitive resources due to low education levels and health issues are more likely to find it challenging to deal with such complexity and choose not to take action (Hanke et al., 2023). For example, individual physical and mental disabilities hinder decision-making in that access to information (e.g., internet access, walking to a library, knowledge of ICT infrastructure, utilizing a comparison site) is restrained (Hanke and Lowitzsch, 2020). Economic disabilities such as low income and poverty affect decision-making in similar ways (Hanke and Lowitzsch, 2020).

100. The vulnerability or deprivation context contains a set of structural disadvantages and restrictions (Bouzarovski and Petrova, 2015; Hanke and Lowitzsch, 2020). They not only lead to the lack of awareness, energy and investment literacy mentioned above but also deplete people's available cognitive resources, thus rendering their decisions more susceptible to cognitive biases (DellaValle, 2019). In addition to behavioral economics, an extensive string of social and cognitive psychology investigates the impact of vulnerability and, in particular, different forms of scarcity (e.g., time[45] or financial scarcity) on the

[45] The same economic decisions are more likely to conflict with important priorities for a poor household than they are for a well-off one, the choices involved, for instance, the decision to attend an information meeting for renewables investments rather than working an extra night shift, come at a higher cost. See Spears, 2011; Hanke et al., 2023.

availability and utility of bandwidth (DellaValle, 2019; Hanke and Lowitzsch, 2020). Scarcity captures one's mind and alters the content of cognition and the perception of options by shifting attention and selecting information according to its internal logic to overcome scarcity.[46] As bandwidth-consuming dynamics, different forms of scarcity could cumulatively deplete bandwidth, restraining its availability for more profound cognitive processes, such as those required for efficient economic decision-making (Hanke and Lowitzsch, 2020). Scarcity also adds difficult trade-offs to everyday experiences (Haushofer and Fehr, 2014; Hanke and Lowitzsch, 2020). Living in the context of scarcity requires the constant juggling of pressing tasks, impairing the ability to make (long-term) sound decisions (Shafir, 2017; Shah et al., 2018; Hanke et al., 2023). Hence, diverse forms of scarcity inherent in vulnerability and deprivation could make it hard for energy poor or vulnerable consumers to understand opportunities and expected utility involved in relatively novel activities, such as DR and renewables self-consumption, and promote individual welfare by actively engaging in these activities.

101. Theoretical and empirical insights from behavioral economics indicate that vulnerability and poverty put additional burdens on individuals in the form of time and cognitive constraints (Hanke and Lowitzsch, 2020), hindering energy poor or vulnerable customers from engaging in and benefiting from the sustainable energy transition. An empirical study in Germany exemplifies the low engagement level: surveyed energy-poor households showed little engagement in the energy transition, except for energy savings, and from their perspective, the energy transition is not a concern unless it is somehow linked to reducing costs (Hanke et al., 2023). Understanding the underlying constraints that prevent the involvement of consumers experiencing vulnerability and poverty becomes imperative to shape DSM measures that are empowering rather than patronizing (Hanke et al., 2023). Such behavioral constraints induced by specific vulnerability and scarcity contexts also imply that general approaches to engaging average

---

46 This can be explained by prior experiments. In one set of studies, shoppers at a mall were asked to consider everyday financial scenarios that presented either manageable or highly challenging financial difficulties. One scenario, for example, concerned a car breaking down and needing to be fixed at a cost of either $1500, a serious challenge for many participants, or $150, which most could afford with relative ease. While participants contemplated how they would manage these financial challenges, they were presented with tasks designed to assess their executive control and fluid intelligence. Rich participants did equally well on the cognitive tasks whether they contemplated the manageable or the challenging scenarios. The poor, when entertaining the manageable scenario, did just as well as the rich. However, when they were confronted with the challenging scenario, poor participants did significantly less well on executive control and fluid intelligence tests. The preoccupation with how they would deal with the large expense, with how they would juggle their needs, had a similar effect to what we would have observed had we asked them to retain a seven-digit number in short-term memory. It imposed cognitive load, which left less cognitive capacity for other tasks. See Mani et al., 2013; Hanke and Lowitzsch, 2020.

consumers may not be sufficient to achieve desirable behavior change in energy poor or vulnerable customers.

### *2.2.4. Behavioral Economics-Inspired Solutions*

102. As addressed above, consumers in the residential, commercial, and public sectors notably face behavioral barriers to actively adjusting their electricity consumption. Behavioral economics has developed solutions to address their cognitive and motivational deficiencies, which are distinct from traditionally used monetary incentives and coercive measures (Hertwig and Grüne-Yanoff, 2017). Existing behavioral economics-inspired solutions for consumers' inaction broadly fall into three categories: (1) alleviating consumers' perception of complexity and losses involved in changing consumption behavior, (2) harnessing cognitive deficiencies, and (3) fostering consumers' competence to make well-informed and rational choices and exercise their agency. Given that these solutions and relevant concepts are also applied in the following analysis of this book, it is necessary to introduce them here.

103. The first category solves the barrier to adjusting electricity consumption by reducing perceived complexity and losses. This requires DSM measures to be formulated in a manner that fully considers characteristics of human decision-making and avoids the underlying drivers for decision-making biases or paralysis. As noted above, customers' inaction and inertia in some parts stem from the perceived complexity and losses, as well as their interplay. The corresponding solutions thus naturally prevent or mitigate these unfavorable factors, as shown below.

104. First, to mitigate the impact of complexity aversion and its further implications for reinforcing the reliance on heuristics and status quo, simplicity ('keep it short and simple') is considered to be an overarching principle for the design of consumer engagement measures (Hobman et al., 2016). It is suggested that this principle should be respected when providing information necessary for involving consumers as well as offering consumers choices or options. As explained above, decision-making complexity arises from diverse information and choices, and users often lack the time and cognitive resources or capacity to process such complexity. A high complexity level prevents consumers from conducting a rational or detailed assessment of the economic benefits derived from modifying their electricity consumption, thereby undermining the role of economic incentives in engaging consumers. To lower complexity and the resultant cognitive load, only smaller amounts of the most important information should be presented and in a clear, concise and understandable format while avoiding inundating customers with too many different choices (Hobman et al., 2016; Hertwig and Grüne-Yanoff, 2017). Refraining from placing consumers in complex and cognitively demanding situations, DSM measures could improve consumers' decision-making in seeking economically efficient consumption

patterns and enable them to be more proactive in shaping consumption that benefits both themselves and the electricity system.

105. Second, to mitigate the loss aversion bias, the perceived and actual 'costs' (e.g., loss of time, effort, money, functionality, comfort, etc.) of engaging in DR and renewables use should be reduced (Hobman et al., 2016; Nicolson et al., 2017). This can be realized by simplifying or streamlining the involved application, registration, licensing, grid connection and switching procedures (Hobman et al., 2016; Nicolson et al., 2017). Additionally, automation and the application of ICT could also help reduce consumers' input in efforts and time (Althaher et al., 2015; Good et al., 2017; Nicolson et al., 2017; Michaelis et al., 2024). Ensuring consumers' access to such enabling infrastructure (free of charge or at low cost) (Nicolson et al., 2017) thus matters in terms of reducing losses and bringing about more behavior change. Decreasing relevant costs or losses also helps mitigate another prominent bias: overly focusing on immediate or short-term costs involved in an energy activity that may be economically optimal in the long run.

106. Apart from lowering external factors that contribute to cognitive and decision-making biases, behavioral economics also develops two other groups of non-price-based, behavioral interventions, based on different assumptions, targets and causal pathways through which they affect behavior (Hertwig and Grüne-Yanoff, 2017; Santos Silva, 2022). As shown above, consumers' decision-making flaws are rooted in the limitations of the dual cognitive system. Attempts to change behavior can thus take one of two routes: One is to harness System 1's deficiencies, and the other is to engage System 2 and foster it (Hertwig and Grüne-Yanoff, 2017). Two key concepts representing these two approaches were proposed: 'Nudge' aims to change behavior by harnessing human cognitive biases, whilst 'boost' seeks to empower people by improving their cognitive capacity and decision-making competence (Santos Silva, 2022). Their notions and respective examples in the specific context of engaging consumers in DR and renewables use are elaborated next.

107. In their seminal work on nudging, Richard Thaler and Cass Sunstein defined 'nudge' as '*any aspect of the choice architecture that alters people's behavior in a predictable way without forbidding any options or significantly changing their economic incentives*' (Thaler and Sunstein, 2021; Santos Silva, 2022). The nudge approach is 'bias-preserving', which steers behavior without taking the detour of honing new competences, but instead by exploiting cognitive limitations or biases (Porto and Rangone, 2015, pp 29–59; Jung and Mellers, 2016; Hertwig and Grüne-Yanoff, 2017; Santos Silva, 2022). This approach's starting proposition is that deficits in human decision-making competence are pervasive and robust, and difficult to alter, and thus, de-biasing attempts are often seen as futile (Grüne-Yanoff and Hertwig, 2016; Hertwig and Grüne-Yanoff, 2017).

108. Paradigmatic examples include automatic default enrollment in specific programs unless individuals specifically choose to opt out (Hertwig and Grüne-Yanoff, 2017). To increase consumers' willingness to apply dynamic pricing or tariffs, it is suggested to exploit consumers' preference for the status quo or default and reluctance to choose actively (Hobman et al., 2016). The strategy is to frame dynamic pricing or tariffs as the default option, rather than letting consumers choose them, while offering an opt-out possibility (Hobman et al., 2016; Weck et al., 2017). Moreover, by exploiting the above-mentioned social norm effect, when setting such an opt-out default offer or tariff, suppliers or system operators are also advised to describe it as 'recommended' or 'popular' to improve consumers' acceptance of pricing or tariffs with the effect of flexing energy consumption (Hobman et al., 2016). The solution of harnessing consumers' status quo biases has proven effective in increasing consumers' participation rates in other jurisdictions: dynamic pricing has been carried out in the USA, and results show the opt-out rates are low: for example, results from a study in California revealed that only 2–7% of the default customers opted out before the start of the program and only 4–8% dropped out of the program in the first 2 years (Weck et al., 2017). The bias of overvaluing immediate rewards can also be exploited, and a nudge approach could make the immediate benefits of engaging in DR more salient by communicating consumers' actual bill savings in, or as close to, real-time (Hobman et al., 2016). A similar approach is also suggested to emphasize the costs or losses incurred by maintaining the status quo (flat pricing) and how such losses could be avoided by switching to dynamic pricing (Hobman et al., 2016). The salience of a cost or loss could be maximized by presenting it in isolation by itself (e.g., 'You are currently losing 50 euros per quarter by staying on flat pricing') rather than integrating or embedding it within a larger amount (Hobman et al., 2016). This nudge strategy leverages consumers' aversion to losses to prompt behavioral changes.

109. The above examples appear to show that by putting in place simple nudges with a large scope (e.g., 'mass' default rules, automatic enrollment), rule-makers can realize substantial behavior changes at relatively low costs (Hertwig and Grüne-Yanoff, 2017). However, simple and cost-efficient nudges have raised a concern that they are not transparent and could have a detrimental impact on the autonomy of those being nudged (Hausman and Welch, 2010; Grüne-Yanoff and Hertwig, 2016; Santos Silva, 2022). The concern about individuals' autonomy stems from the nudges' approach to changing or steering behavior: nudges exploit cognitive limitations or biases – unconscious errors of reasoning that distort people's judgment of the world (Ghisellini and Chang, 2018, p 63), and they shape behavior in ways other than rational persuasion that are not always transparent to consumers (Reijula and Hertwig, 2022; Santos Silva, 2022). Not least because of this approach, informing consumers about the non-conscious processes by which the nudge interventions work would affect their effectiveness,

and thus, such interventions are characterized by 'typically working better in the dark' (Bovens, 2010; Reisch et al., 2017; Santos Silva, 2022).

110. In comparison to nudges, boosts are rational-based and de-biasing regulatory strategies (Jolls and Sunstein, 2005; Porto and Rangone, 2015; Santos Silva, 2022). Instead of targeting behavior directly and harnessing cognitive biases, the boost approach targets individual competences to bring about behavior change and exercise agency (Hertwig and Grüne-Yanoff, 2017). It enhances people's capacity to manage emotional responses and adopt deliberately conscious and considerate decisions by overcoming biased thinking and non-deliberative choices (Jolls and Sunstein, 2005). Proponents of boosting believe that people's functional cognitive processes and motivational processes are malleable and worth developing, which determines the approaches to behavior change distinct from nudges (Hertwig and Grüne-Yanoff, 2017). To overcome cognitive biases, decision-making competences developed by boosts can be either specific to a single domain, e.g., financial accounting, or generalized across domains (Drexler et al., 2014; Hertwig and Grüne-Yanoff, 2017). In this sense, boosts are considered to have an encompassing goal of empowering people (Hertwig and Grüne-Yanoff, 2017). Through empowerment, the formerly powerless become capable individuals who are willing and able to take ownership and responsibility for their own choices, decisions, and actions in society or on markets (Hanke and Lowitzsch, 2020). Prominent examples of boosts include (1) risk literacy boosts that establish or foster competence to understand statistical information, (2) uncertainty management boosts that establish or foster procedural rules for making good decisions, predictions and assessments under uncertain conditions, and (3) motivational boosts that foster the competence to autonomously adjust ones' motivation, cognitive capacity, and self-control (Santos Silva, 2022).

111. Overall, boosts contain two elements: (1) preserving people's agency and enabling them to exercise that agency and (2) developing people's decision-making competences and helping overcome cognitive or motivational biases. In practice, concrete approaches fit the concept of boost are broader than information provision and targeted education mentioned above and may contain the provision of enabling conditions or tools to assist rational economic decisions, such as the framework for enabling consumers to trade flexibility with the assistance of intermediaries (e.g. IFSPs and energy communities) discussed in next Chapter.

112. Aside from the underlying assumptions, goals and causal pathways, the distinction between the concepts of boosts and nudges can be further clarified by comparing their differences in the following aspects. First, reversibility is an empirical criterion for distinguishing between boosts and nudges, which means a different degree of reversibility in the behavioral effects induced (Hertwig and Grüne-Yanoff, 2017). If the interventions are nudges, the behavior will revert to

its preintervention state if such interventions are eliminated, while in the case of boosts, behavior persists when interventions are eliminated (Hertwig and Grüne-Yanoff, 2017). The second aspect concerns the normative implications of boosts and nudges. As already noted, nudges are not transparent to consumers and can undermine autonomy. Boosts aiming for fostering competences, in comparison, require the consumers' active cooperation (Hertwig and Grüne-Yanoff, 2017). They therefore need to be explicit, visible, and transparent to consumers, and the requirement of cooperation also implies individual judgment and engagement, which indicates respect for the boosted consumers' autonomy (Hertwig and Grüne-Yanoff, 2017).

## 2.3. INFORMATION ACCESS

113. Final customers tend to suffer from information disadvantages or asymmetries and are not aware of the economic and environmental benefits of different electricity consumption patterns (EC, 2016a; Good et al., 2017; Leinauer et al., 2022). Fully informing them of these benefits is essential to raising their awareness to engage in promoting the system integration, use, and self-production of RES-E, and also prompting them to respond to market incentives (Willems and Zhou, 2020). There are several tools for conveying information necessary to stimulate desirable changes in electricity consumption. Table 2 outlines the respective functions of some commonly used information provision instruments.

**Table 2. Examples of information provision instruments**

| Information provision instruments | Functions |
|---|---|
| Electricity bills | 1. Informing consumers of electricity consumption and costs, making consumers aware of potential room for saving bills, which can stimulate actions in DR, renewables PPAs and renewables self-consumption;<br>2. Disclosing the energy mix in supplied electricity, improving consumers' awareness of using RES-E, e.g., by switching to suppliers that have a higher share of RES-E in their products. |
| GOs | An information disclosure tool for providing evidence to final customers that the share or quantity of electricity was produced from renewable sources, promoting customers to pick a 'green' supplier and contributing to a customer-driven demand for RES-E (Banet, 2012, pp 119 and 127; Raadal et al., 2012) |
| ICT infrastructure | Smart meters, for instance, can measure near-real-time or real-time electricity consumption and communicate this recorded data with end users (Sovacool et al., 2021), notably promoting DR and renewables self-consumption. |

Source: Author's own elaboration.

114. In addition to traditional methods, such as GOs and electricity bills, the advent of ICT has innovated approaches to informing consumers of the opportunities and incentives that are key to adjusting their electricity consumption. However, the theoretical merits of these information provision tools are not easy to achieve, notably because of energy consumers' limited capacity to process complex information, as highlighted above. Inaccurate and excessive information can be counterproductive, preventing the deliberative and unbiased processing of information about the benefits involved in changing electricity consumption. What information items are most important for inducing behavior change, and how to present information that can best engage consumers and prompt the use of information (e.g., accuracy, frequency, timing, and format) are key questions that must be addressed by measures enhancing consumers' information access.

## 3. THE ROLE OF THE ELECTRICITY GRID

115. The electricity industry is a network-bound energy sector, meaning that the electricity network represents an essential facility or bottleneck (Armstrong and Sappington, 2006; Nykamp et al., 2012; Roggenkamp and Diestelmeier, 2020, p 163). Transmission and distribution grids provide the infrastructure platform upon which the competitive segments rely (Joskow, 2008). Their performance thus has important effects on the efficiency of competitive wholesale and retail markets (Joskow, 2008). Historically, in the EU, the prime focus of electricity network regulation was delivering an efficient and non-discriminatory infrastructure platform.[47] Efficient network operation and fair TPA have long been viewed as a cornerstone of the internal electricity market (Joskow, 2008; Edens and Lavrijssen, 2019; Gräper et al., 2021, p 100). However, in the recent decade, the low-carbon energy transition has no longer been an ancillary issue (Abraham-Dukuma, 2020), which considerably challenges the traditional notion and paradigm of regulating network monopolies (de Joode et al., 2009; Frías et al., 2009; Cambini et al., 2014; Edens and Lavrijssen, 2019).

116. During this transition, the need to empower consumers to support high RES-E uptake and the rise of electricity DSM are key drivers for adapting network operation and its regulation. Notably, the advent of DR and renewables self-consumption poses a range of technical challenges for network operation. Network operators must be able to satisfy increasing grid connection requests and cope with congestion and voltage issues that arise from the connection of demand-side resources. As will be shown below, currently, DSOs face greater challenges than TSOs in taking up such technical challenges. Correspondingly,

47 *1996 Electricity Directive*, Articles 10, 16 and 18; *2003 Electricity Directive*, Articles 20 and 23; *2009 Electricity Directive*, Articles 25 and 32 and 37; Joskow, 2008.

distribution network regulation is challenged in several aspects. First, it must ensure that network monopolies are adequately incentivized to deliver the required network service quality in terms of grid connection and operation, and to invest sufficiently in innovation to update the network infrastructure and address relevant technical challenges. Realizing this requires efforts to improve and adapt incentive and performance regulation. Second, it must ensure that consumers interested in DR and renewables self-consumption are not disincentivized by inappropriate network fees. Otherwise, network fees would pose an additional barrier to the diffusion of these relatively novel DSM activities. Combined with considerations in the first aspect, network charges have two goals: being cost-reflective and adequately incentivizing network operators while maintaining fair and proportionate costs for consumers involved in DR and renewables prosumption. Third, system operators' procurement of flexibility for system operational security serves as a key marketplace for consumers to commercialize their flexibility. Network regulation must guarantee that network users have sufficient incentives and capabilities to procure and utilize demand flexibility from DR and renewables DG, and maintain a level playing field of flexibility procurement.

117. Compared to the traditional way of supporting RES-E, i.e., via purchase, electricity networks face more acute challenges in accommodating the development of DR and renewables self-consumption. Thus, challenges to network operation and regulation caused by DR and renewables prosumption are the subject of this section. It will begin with the common problems and difficulties faced by TSOs and DSOs (Section 3.1) and then proceed to the unique challenges faced by DSOs (Section 3.2). Network regulation involves complex economic doctrines that regulate and incentivize natural monopolies. It is also intricately intertwined with the technical aspects of the electricity system. To support a better understanding of the issues surrounding advancing legal and regulatory reforms in this area, relevant economic and technical rationales will also be explained in more detail in the following sections.

## 3.1. COMMON ISSUES ACROSS TRANSMISSION AND DISTRIBUTION LEVELS

118. Due to economies of scale (also rendering duplication uneconomical), electricity network companies, both TSOs and DSOs, exhibit properties of natural monopoly (Shaw et al., 2010). When competition is feasible, the answer to the question of 'what is the optimal quality level and at what price should this be offered to consumers' can be left to the free market (Ajodhia and Hakvoort, 2005). The market more or less automatically converges toward an optimal outcome: prices reflect efficient costs while products are adapted to

the consumers' preferences and expectations (Ajodhia and Hakvoort, 2005). However, the natural monopoly character of network services makes competition impossible in the network segment, leading the network industry to be prone to market failures caused by market power and imperfect information,[48] in particular (Baker and Trémolet, 2000; Giannakis et al., 2005; Correlje and Vries, 2008, p 65). Regulatory interventions are thus justified to induce optimal price and quality outcomes while safeguarding a level playing field supported by non-discriminatory and transparent network access and flexibility procurement (Ajodhia and Hakvoort, 2005; Baldwin et al., 2012, pp 447–448). The common aims of electricity network regulation are generally directed in three areas, which are also crucial to allow grid connection and market participation of consumers involved in DR and renewables self-consumption.

119. Firstly, price or profit regulation for monopolies is intended to protect system users' (including DR providers, renewables self-consumers, energy communities, and IFSPs) interest by keeping prices within acceptable limits while adequately incentivizing system operators to fulfill their tasks (Bauknecht and Brunekreeft, 2008, p 478; Mitchell and Woodman, 2012, p 574). Moreover, network charges should refrain from distorting the incentives of consumers participating in DR and renewables self-consumption. Second, the service quality of network companies is subject to regulation so that stable and reliable functionality can be delivered to grid users involved in DR and renewables self-consumption (Frías et al., 2009; Nolting et al., 2019). Third, promoting market participation of DR and RES-E from consumers calls for close coordination and cooperation between TSOs and DSOs (Soares et al., 2020; Vagropoulos et al., 2022). In the initial stage of developing DR and renewables prosumption, network regulation remained built on the traditional energy regime where large energy undertakings were dominant market players, failing to cater to the greater role of consumers. Its deficiencies in these three aspects will be elaborated on consecutively below.

### *3.1.1. Network Charges*

120. An unregulated monopolist would charge a high price to deliver a monopoly profit (Baldwin et al., 2012, pp 447–448). Privately-owned network undertakings particularly have strong incentives for profit maximization, to the benefit of private shareholders in the monopoly, who will enjoy excess profits,

48 Network regulation typically suffers from serious problems of information asymmetry. In the literature on new institutional economics, relationships between two parties (in this context, i.e., the regulator and the regulated network companies) with asymmetric information are often modeled using the principal-agent theory. Based on the information advantage compared to the regulator, certain scopes of action exist that network companies can use to circumvent regulations, resulting in welfare losses. See Nolting et al., 2019.

whereas system users will suffer (Jamasb et al., 2004; Jamasb and Pollitt, 2007; Joskow, 2008; Baldwin et al., 2012, pp 447–448; Nolting et al., 2019; Johansson et al., 2020). Network services also constitute a substantial portion of the final bill to final customers (Haney and Pollitt, 2011). For the sake of social welfare (Nolting et al., 2019), some form of revenue-cap or price-cap regulation must be in place to prevent the network utilities from charging system use fees at 'monopolistic' levels (Jamasb and Pollitt, 2007; Bauknecht and Brunekreeft, 2008, p 478; de Joode et al., 2009; Baldwin et al., 2012, p 448; Nolting et al., 2019). Network charges are therefore subject to the approval of energy regulators. However, on the other side, the profit control of network companies should be balanced against the need to sufficiently cover investment costs (Ajodhia and Hakvoort, 2005; Shuttleworth, 2005). In EU Member States widely applying revenue-cap regulation, a recurrent issue is that perverse incentives hinder network companies from investing in innovation and new technologies necessary for accommodating the large-scale integration of DR and self-generated RES-E (Jamasb and Pollitt, 2008; McHarg, 2012, pp 324–325; Nykamp et al., 2012). This is especially the case for DSO regulation, as will be further explicated in section 3.2.

121. The lessons drawn from Member States that employ incentive-based revenue regulation[49] demonstrate that the grid operator's investment decisions are sensitive to regulatory settings in the incentive regulation (Huang and Söder, 2017a). As legally regulated monopolies, their inputs and outputs are typically subject to strict economic regulation, making their investment fundamentally directed and steered by incentives from the regulatory framework (Bauknecht and Brunekreeft, 2008, p 480; Oliver et al., 2017; Huang and Söder, 2017b; Johansson et al., 2020). This claim does not suggest that system operators entirely respond to incentives from the regulator, as their profit maximization target often frustrates the attainment of regulatory goals in reality.[50] Instead, it aims

[49] This regulatory approach allows network operators to capture part of the profits resulting from targets met or exceeded, allowing network users to benefit from the efficiency gains through lower network tariffs. In a monopoly environment (i.e., the absence of market mechanisms), incentive regulation attempts to mimic competitive market pressures to reduce costs, innovate, improve service quality and pass efficiency gains on to consumers. Under price or revenue regulation, the incentive to continuously improve productivity arises from the possibility of retaining profits resulting from better than expected performance. Incentive regulation for transmission and distribution systems is usually applied with benchmarking methods as promoted back in the 1980s. The idea is that incentive regulation can imitate the outcome of the markets by setting an external performance standard that represents some average or frontier industry performance (i.e., a benchmark performance) excluding the firm in question. Since the 1990s, the traditional rate-of-return regulation of natural monopoly activities has been progressively replaced by incentive-based regulation. See Shleifer, 1985; Giannakis et al., 2005; Ajodhia and Hakvoort, 2005; Joskow, 2006; Jamasb and Pollitt, 2007; Haney and Pollitt, 2011; Nepal and Jamasb, 2015.

[50] Two typical examples linked to incentive regulation are taken here to illustrate how the attainment of regulatory goals can be frustrated by network companies. The first example concerns the base-year effect. In Germany, before the amendment of the Incentive Regulation

to highlight that incentive regulation dedicated to reducing costs and prices typically forces the regulated entities to mainly focus on allowed revenues rather than proactively take measures to adapt to the energy transition (Bauknecht and Brunekreeft, 2008, p 480; McHarg, 2012, p 325; Edens and Lavrijssen, 2019). At the distribution level, beyond conventional CAPEX,[51] the integration of DERs also incurs new categories of CAPEX, such as ICT infrastructures[52] that support grid monitoring and automation, as well as OPEX arising from the need to utilize flexibility services.[53] However, initially, these additional network costs were not considered or recognized by the revenue cap regulation. Significant uncertainties about the prospects of future cost recovery created disincentives for DSOs to make necessary investments and offer adequate network connection services to actors engaged in DR and renewables prosuming (Shuttleworth, 2005; Bauknecht and Brunekreeft, 2008, pp 469 and 482). This situation would not be reversed until associated changing capital and operational expenditure structures are considered

Ordinance (ARegV) in 2016, investments were only considered in the base year for each regulation period. This means that additional costs of investment during the current period can only be factored into the grid fees for the upcoming period, which can cause a delay of up to five years. Under this regime, DSOs shifted investments to base years in order to maximize their net present values, creating the base-year effect. Postponement of necessary investments, which was within the legal scope of DSOs at that time, is financially beneficial for the operator but socially unfavorable due to possible effects on grid reliability. Such delayed investments can hinder optimal expansion paths and thus indirectly cause grid congestion and increase the need for costly grid stabilizing measures. The second example is the ratchet effect under incentive regulation regimes: regulated firms may underperform to avoid more ambitious regulatory requirements in the following regulation periods. See Freixas et al., 1985; Armstrong and Sappington, 2006; Nykamp et al., 2012; Nolting et al., 2019.

51 The distribution grid tends to be insufficiently large for the transportation of large amounts of energy in the direction of higher voltage levels when local generation exceeds local demand. Although the use of flexibility services can mitigate congestion and voltage problems, a certain degree of gird capacity expansion may be inevitable in some cases to fit the wider integration of DR and DG. See Nykamp et al., 2012; Ruester et al., 2014; Johansson et al., 2020.

52 The ICT is usually used as an instrument to measure the current status in the grid and send appropriate steering signals, enhancing the capability of network operators to efficiently operate networks. Its role is particularly stressed to realize the active network management or 'smart grid' approach to managing distribution networks, deferring or avoiding conventional grid expansion. See Shaw et al., 2010; Nykamp et al., 2012; Ruester et al., 2014.

53 Beyond governmental fees, administration and customer services, and other miscellaneous expenses, electricity grids have two main cost categories. Operating expenditures (OPEX) cover the costs of network operation, including operating and maintenance costs (both variable and fixed), such as energy losses, costs of ancillary services, and operational and maintenance costs of assets. Capital expenditures (CAPEX) generate long-term future benefits. They are incurred when a network company invests in new fixed assets to reinforce the grid, replace the existing old assets or expand the network. In other words, CAPEX refers to spending on long-term assets (e.g., lines, transformers and smart grid infrastructure). The integration of DERs, including DR and self-generated RES-E, can cause additional costs, both operational and capital expenditure. See Giannakis et al., 2005; Bauknecht and Brunekreeft, 2008, p 480; de Joode et al., 2009; Nykamp et al., 2012; Ruester et al., 2014; Nepal and Jamasb, 2015; Edens and Lavrijssen, 2019; Johansson et al., 2020.

in regulation design as thoroughly and timely[54] as possible, and explicit incentives are provided for network companies (Bauknecht and Brunekreeft, 2008, p 488; de Joode et al., 2009; Ruester et al., 2014; Nolting et al., 2019).

122. Furthermore, it is worth noting that capital-intensive, sunk investments and long lifetimes of physical assets characterize the electricity network industry.[55] Potential investors require reassurance that they will be able to recover their reasonable costs over the long term (McHarg, 2012, p 315). Otherwise, they would easily find it unattractive to invest in this industry compared with the returns on offer in other industries (Shuttleworth, 2005). In the case of strict economic regulation, the network industry may face difficulties in attracting or retaining capital for investment (Shuttleworth, 2005), thereby posing a long-term risk of underinvestment in delivering key infrastructure. The regulator thus must avoid creating unnecessary regulatory risk about the prospects of future cost recovery and the consequential underinvestment concerns (Burns and Riechmann, 2004; Shuttleworth, 2005; Bauknecht and Brunekreeft, 2008, p 478).

123. In sum, a general rule for price control of network charges is to balance the interests of investors in network utilities and users of their services (Baldwin et al., 2012, p 450). How to balance investment risk and the risk of monopoly abuse has therefore long been the central problem for the design of network regulatory frameworks at the Union and national level (McHarg, 2012, p 315).

124. Another disincentive for system operators is the problematic trade-off between short-term operating costs and long-term capital expenditures. The experience in some countries has shown that due to the presence of trade-offs between OPEX and CAPEX, it is preferable to use an integrated approach to incentive regulation (Giannakis et al., 2005; Ruester et al., 2014; Edens and Lavrijssen, 2019; Nolting et al., 2019; Pereira et al., 2020). A typical example is the partial approach taken by the UK to review network costs in the 2000s (Shuttleworth, 2005; Bauknecht and Brunekreeft, 2008, p 482). The British energy regulator, the OFGEM, treated Opex and Capex separately, on top of which its incentive regulation focused mostly on achieving greater short-term operational efficiency (Shuttleworth, 2005; Jamasb and Pollitt, 2007). This means that network companies received greater incentives from saving OPEX than from an equal amount of CAPEX reduction (Giannakis et al., 2005; Bauknecht and Brunekreeft, 2008, p 482). They were thus forced to minimize operational costs and shift to adopt the more capital-intensive option, even though the overall costs can be higher (Bauknecht and Brunekreeft, 2008, p 482). This is particularly detrimental to the use of ancillary services and investments in smart

54 The base-year effect mentioned in footnote 50 above suggests the importance of reviewing and recognizing incurred costs timely. See Nolting et al., 2019.

55 Sunk investments mean that as long as network investments are made, they are mostly irreversible and create sunk costs. See Brunekreeft, 2013; Nepal and Jamasb, 2015; Johansson et al., 2020.

technologies necessary to overcome the challenges brought by the emergence of DR and distributed RES-E (Nolting et al., 2019). Furthermore, in an asset-intensive activity such as electricity networks, the cost of capital is particularly relevant to overall costs (Shaw et al., 2010). As such, from the perspective of the overall system cost, the unequal treatment of CAPEX and OPEX prevents system operators from finding the optimal combination between short-term operational and long-term capital inputs (Edens and Lavrijssen, 2019).

125. A similar problem of recognizing CAPEX but neglecting operating costs was also found in German distribution network regulation (Nolting et al., 2019). The resulting distorted incentives equally hindered DSOs from adapting to the growing integration of self-produced RES-E in German distribution networks and aggravated their path dependence on applying the passive network management approaches.[56] The undue emphasis on developing cost-efficient alternatives to grid expansion and reinforcement, however, also carries the risk of undermining long-term investment in network capacity.[57] This may shape the short-sighted investment decisions of network companies.

126. Additionally, in the regulation design, there existed disincentives for system operators to invest in innovation and research and development projects. In the past, it has been expedient not to consider innovation in the network regulation design, because it played only a minor role (McHarg, 2012, p 323; Nykamp et al., 2012). The picture has changed a lot along with the increasing penetration of renewables DG and DR, presenting network companies with various challenges to improve technical and organizational capabilities (Nykamp et al., 2012; Johansson et al., 2020). However, as highlighted above, network monopolies' costs tend to be tightly regulated, leading them to respond to regulatory frameworks that stress cost reduction (Lockwood, 2016; Prettico et al., 2019; Johansson et al., 2020). This can significantly limit their abilities to innovate compared to free enterprises, implying the essential role of regulatory incentives in stimulating innovation (Johansson et al., 2020). Additionally, especially under benchmark-based incentive regulation, speculative returns result in a relatively low incentive to engage in innovation.[58] In some Member States, innovation was

56 The passive network management approach, or 'fit and forget' approach, means that when DERs enter the distribution network, upgrade investments based on their peak output are undertaken, and for the remainder, any electricity production from the unit is taken as given. Under this approach, normally, DSOs would use grid reinforcements, such as laying cables and building transformers, to handle the problem of overloads caused by the integration of DERs. See de Joode et al., 2009; Nykamp et al., 2012; Ruester et al., 2014; Roos, 2017; Edens and Lavrijssen, 2019.

57 Some studies also point out that specific incentive regulation schemes provide substantial incentives for short-term innovation and cost reduction, but the incentives for long-term infrastructure investment are limited. See Armstrong and Sappington, 2006; McHarg, 2012, p 325.

58 Such speculative returns may stem from either the information advantage of the regulated entities vis-à-vis the regulator or unpredictable cost recovery resulting from benchmark-based incentive regulation, as explained above. See McHarg, 2012, 323.

either not adequately considered in incentive regulation or discouraged by short-term cost-cutting incentives.[59] Engagement in innovation projects was thus in the gray area of what TSOs and DSOs are allowed to do under income regulations (Johansson et al., 2020). The grid operators were found to gain profitability by avoiding delivering necessary changes, for instance, implementing 'smart solutions' to operate networks (McHarg, 2012, p 325; Nykamp et al., 2012). Such smart approaches, including the use of ICT technologies, as explained above, are key to enabling the system integration of DR and self-generated RES-E while maintaining system security.

127. The way of charging the network use not only shapes system operators' incentives to accommodate the need for electricity DSM but also affects consumers' incentives to engage in relevant activities. Consumers engaged in DR and renewables self-consumption would be discouraged if they are subject to network charges that are discriminatory and not proportionate to the cost they create for the system.

### 3.1.2. *Quality of Service*

128. Despite the supposed benefits of price-cap regulation in efficiency improvement, in some pioneering countries applying it to system operators, it has been found that this regulatory approach can induce undesired quality effects (Ajodhia and Hakvoort, 2005). Due to the initial priority given to cost efficiency, network utilities faced strong incentives to undertake cost savings (Giannakis et al., 2005). However, at the same time, quality of service, mainly covering system reliability, continuity of supply and connection, comes at a cost and involves both operating and capital costs for the utilities (Giannakis et al., 2005; Jamasb and Pollitt, 2007; Frías et al., 2009; Ruester et al., 2014). There is thus a risk that companies respond to cost-saving incentives by reducing service quality, rather than pursuing genuine efficiency improvements (Giannakis et al., 2005). The fear of deteriorating service quality in the network industry has been confirmed by a range of empirical evidence in the EU and beyond (Ter-Martirosyan, 2003; Giannakis et al., 2005; Jamasb and Pollitt, 2007). Some studies found that cost-efficient firms do not necessarily exhibit high service quality and that efficiency scores of cost-only models do not show a high correlation with those of quality-based models (Giannakis et al., 2005). It has been proved that in the absence of quality controls and explicit incentives, levels of service quality in

---

59 In the UK, for instance, research, development, and demonstration represent areas in which short-term cost savings can be made, and relevant expenditure by the energy network operators has fallen dramatically since privatization. See Bauknecht and Voß, 2009, p 195; McHarg, 2012.

electricity networks tend to decline (Ter-Martirosyan, 2003; Ter-Martirosyan and Kwoka, 2010; Nepal and Jamasb, 2015).

129. In the context of taking DSM actions to facilitate RES-E uptake, quality of service targets should be extended to ensure grid connection for not only consumers but also new entities (e.g., active customers, FSPs, and energy communities).[60] This will incur greater costs, which would exacerbate the problem of degraded service quality if network regulation remains unchanged.[61] The increasing curtailment rate is an example. Load or generation curtailment is one of the measures for securing system reliability in the case of grid congestion,[62] which can occur due to the increasing grid connection of DR and self-generated RES-E, particularly serious at the distribution level.[63] However, frequent reliance on curtailment by system operators would unduly undermine network access for market participants engaged in DR and renewable self-consumption (Edens and Lavrijssen, 2019). An example is that in Germany, facing grid congestion coming with fairly high shares of DG, curtailment had long become a well-established practice of DSOs (Edens and Lavrijssen, 2019). Before the CEP, 82% of German DSOs reported an annual increase in their application of curtailment measures, although they must compensate the curtailed demand-side facilities pursuant to the Renewable Energy Sources Act (EEG) (Edens and Lavrijssen, 2019).[64] The key to addressing relevant problems lies in offering incentives to safeguard adequate service quality levels and governing network service performance based on pre-defined performance indicators (Jamasb and Pollitt, 2007).

130. Additionally, providing sound incentives for network service quality also aims to reduce costs to relevant grid users. As mentioned earlier, in the network segment, the absence of the market makes it hard to achieve the optimal quality

---

60 Quality of service in distribution networks mainly consists of two topics: (i) continuity of supply associated with the frequency and duration of supply interruptions, and (ii) voltage or power quality associated with voltage disturbances such as voltage changes, flicker effect, harmonics, voltage dips, etc. At the transmission level, service quality indicators include system average interruption frequency, system average interruption duration, energy not supplied, average interruption time, as well as overhead lines maintenance cost and substation maintenance cost. See Abdalla et al., 2009; Frías et al., 2009; Llorca et al., 2016.

61 Delayed connection of prosumers was reported in Lithuania, for instance. See Miskinis et al., 2011.

62 Grid congestion is a situation in which the network is not able to fulfill all the desired transactions due to the power system's physical and operational limitations. See Electricity Regulation, art. 2(4); A. Kumar et al., 2004.

63 Although large industrial users connecting to the transmission system also participate in DR and renewables self-consumption, a greater number of users engaged in the two types of DSM activities are located in distribution networks. Moreover, given the relatively small size and distributed ownership of DG and DR, this makes the DSO's local congestion management more complex. See Bauknecht and Brunekreeft, 2008, p 474; Papalexopoulos et al., 2020.

64 See also Renewable Energy Sources Act (EEG 2017), sections 12 and 13, available at <https://www.bmwk.de/Redaktion/EN/Downloads/renewable-energy-sources-act-2017.pdf?__blob=publicationFile&v=3> accessed 16 October 2022.

level, which is realized when the marginal cost of improving quality is equal to the socio-economic value of quality improvement.[65] In the case of lacking incentive regulation, natural monopolies may operate at sub-optimal quality and excessive cost levels (Giannakis et al., 2005). The regulatory framework must avoid the risk that the offered incentives to improve quality are either too low or too high. The former case can lead to under-performance of network companies, while the latter will allow overly expensive quality investments, which push the level of quality above the optimal level (Sioshansi and Pfaffenberger, 2006, p 35; Jamasb and Pollitt, 2007). As presented by existing research, the desirable quality of service should satisfy the criteria as being: (i) importance to grid users, (ii) controllability by network operators, and (iii) measurability by regulators (Giannakis et al., 2005).

131. On these grounds, since the early 2000s,[66] network regulation in some Member States has progressively evolved beyond pure cost-efficiency considerations to extend the application of incentive regulation to network service quality (Giannakis et al., 2005; Mulder, 2016, p 113; Nolting et al., 2019). Moreover, relevant performance indicators have been developed, accompanied by separate incentive schemes, rewards, and penalty schemes, which are known as PBR.[67] Figure 5 depicts the difference between CBR and PBR. As can be seen,

---

65 Assuming that the maximum amount that users would pay for quality equals the total quality-induced costs they incur, the socio-economic optimum occurs at a quality level where the sum of the total cost of quality provision by network operators and the total quality-induced costs faced by grid users is minimized. See Fraser, 1994; Giannakis et al., 2005; Jamasb and Pollitt, 2007; Nepal and Jamasb, 2015.

66 The problem of declining service quality had not gained sufficient attention until around a decade after the adoption of price or revenue cap regulation in European countries. Greater attention to service quality is also partly because of a number of electricity blackouts due to network outages. In the UK, the representative country of applying incentive regulation, quality of service was not incorporated in incentive-based regulation (i.e., linking the quality performance of network operators to the allowed revenue) until 2002. Before that, between 1990 and 2000, quality of service was regulated through guaranteed standards of performance, which entitled consumers to compensation if the firms breached them, and overall standards, which refer to system-level performance. See OFGEM, 2001; Giannakis et al., 2005; Bauknecht and Brunekreeft, 2008, p 478.

67 Quality regulation in PBR is achieved through reward and penalty schemes, which are used to reward the utilities for providing good services and penalize them for providing poor services. As an example, the PBR scheme applied by the OFGEM in the 2000s consists of mechanisms that (i) penalize utilities for not meeting their targets, (ii) reward utilities that exceed targets, and (iii) reward frontier performance by guaranteeing less strict standards for the next control period. Interestingly, the third scheme rewarding frontier performance even considers the need for preventing the ratchet effect, namely, regulated companies may underperform to avoid more ambitious regulatory requirements in the following regulation periods, as mentioned above in footnote 50. The PBR mechanism was further developed by the RIIO (Revenue = Incentives + Innovation + Output) reform introduced in the UK in 2010, where both the intensity of the price control review process and regulatory rewards and penalties will vary according to each company's performance. In Continental Europe, for instance, the PBR regime can be found in §18 and §19 of the Incentive Regulation Ordinance of Germany where surcharges and reductions of the revenue cap are possible

compared to the initial price-cap regulation that focuses on cost efficiency, the link between price and revenue within the PBR mechanism is weaker since the revenue mainly depends on network companies' performance, which is a sequel of an ability to perform cost-efficient investments that improve service quality (Božič and Pantoš, 2013). Apparently, the advent of PBR also implies a transition from input-led (i.e., cost-only approach) toward output-oriented regulation, which underlines the delivery of predetermined quality of service.[68] Performance-based regulation can serve as a vehicle for enabling system operators to properly integrate demand-side resources.

**Figure 5. Difference between CBR and PBR[69]**

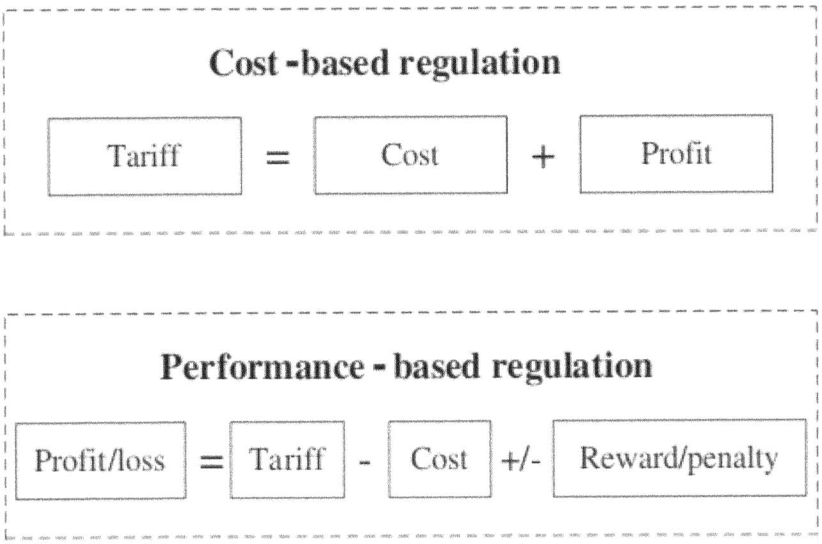


if the grid operator diverges from the given key performance indicators. Since 2000, in addition to the UK, Italy, the Netherlands, Spain, France and Germany have introduced PBR. However, successful implementation of PBR puts high demands on the regulatory body to be able to judge and assess network companies' outputs, which may well require case-by-case assessment. It might thus be difficult to apply this mechanism in countries with many DSOs. See OFGEM, 2001; Billinton and Pan, 2004; Frías et al., 2009; CEER, 2012; McHarg, 2012, p 330; Božič and Pantoš, 2013; Nepal and Jamasb, 2015; Johnston, 2018; Nolting et al., 2019; *ARegV*, 2007, §18 and §19.

68 An output-based incentive regulation approach evaluates the monopoly's performance in terms of the quantity and quality of delivered outputs, such as connection services, and provides incentives to improve quality. Output-based regulation could also contain more output categories apart from quality of service, as exemplified by the aforementioned RIIO regulatory framework. Its outputs are in six categories, relating to customer satisfaction, reliability and availability, safety, connection terms, environmental impact, and social obligations. See Vogelsang, 2005; OFGEM, 2010; McHarg, 2012, pp 324 and 327; Nepal and Jamasb, 2015; Huang and Söder, 2017b; Johansson et al., 2020.

69 This figure is from Božič and Pantoš, 2013.

### 3.1.3. *TSO-DSO Coordination and Cooperation*

132. Vertical unbundling of VIUs shaped the different roles of entities along the electricity supply chain (Barton et al., 2010, p 457). Despite the multiple benefits brought by unbundling, declining collaboration across the supply chain comes to the fore.[70] One of the typical issues in this respect is a lack of cooperation between the TSO and the DSO, which has impeded the adoption of a holistic or 'whole system' approach to the power system operation (Bolton and Foxon, 2011; Roos, 2017; Johansson et al., 2020). The ever-increasing system integration of DR and self-generated RES-E has notably made such coordination problems more acute (Zegers and Brunner, 2014; Yuan and Hesamzadeh, 2017). DR and renewables self-consumption projects could provide flexibility services, including various ancillary services and congestion management services, for both TSOs and DSOs.[71] There may exist tensions between these two entities regarding the activation and access to these system services. These can potentially limit the wider market participation of relevant market actors and affect system reliability. More specifically, the two cases where conflicts between TSO and DSO may take place are detailed hereunder:

- *One entity using flexibility connected to the system of the other entity may cause a violation of the network operational restrictions of the latter* (Hermann et al., 2022). Generally, it does not raise significant problems when DSOs access the system services connected to the transmission system, such as those offered by large final customers. However, existing studies indicate several potential issues arising from the activation of local flexibility services connected to distribution networks. The use of flexibility connected at the distribution level by DSOs for local network management could impact the global system balancing under the responsibility of TSOs.[72] Moreover, when the TSO

---

[70] The network characteristics of the electricity industry and economies of coordination among the different activities led to the creation of vertically integrated structures in many electricity sectors initially. After VIUs were broken apart, in competitive markets, there may be strong disincentives for communication and coordination. Thus, economic efficiency arising from coordination within VIUs is one of the justifications for advocating this structure, from a purely economic point of view. See Sioshansi and Pfaffenberger, 2006, p 37; Jamasb and Pollitt, 2007; Bauknecht and Brunekreeft, 2008, p 485.

[71] DR and self-generated RES-E are able to provide reactive power services helping DSOs and TSOs in the network operation for voltage control and congestion management, and also offer the important sources of balancing services needed by the TSO. See Popelier, 2011; Yousefi et al., 2012; Ruester et al., 2014; Roos, 2017; Poplavskaya and Vries, 2019; Soares et al., 2020.

[72] Typically, TSOs lack visibility over the flexibility sources located in distribution grids, which means they have no information about such resources, such as capacity, type, characteristics, generation and consumption patterns. The activation of such flexibility sources by the DSO could create imbalances, and thus the TSO must be notified of the activation in order to take possible corrective actions to restore the balance in the grid. See Yuan and Hesamzadeh, 2017; Gerard et al., 2018; Hadush and Meeus, 2018; IRENA, 2020; Vagropoulos et al., 2022.

activates any offers from such local flexibility sources, congestion or voltage problems in the distribution network may occur.[73] In this case, the activation can violate the operational constraints of distribution systems, such as nodal voltage or line capacity limits (Verzijlbergh et al., 2014; Vagropoulos et al., 2022; Hermann et al., 2022).

- *Tensions can arise when TSOs and DSOs simultaneously access flexibility services from DR and self-generated RES-E.* To date, the DSO's flexibility needs have not significantly affected the adequacy of flexibility resources available for the TSO. However, by contrast, in some European countries, TSOs have started procuring flexibility services for multiple purposes (i.e., system balancing, voltage control, and congestion management[74]) from grid users located in distribution grids (Hadush and Meeus, 2018; Hermann et al., 2022). The TSOs' need for the volume and diversity of flexible resources is increasing, which could limit the availability of these resources to the DSO (Villar et al., 2018; Hermann et al., 2022). It is especially the case when system balancing or congestion-relieving actions by the TSO and local congestion management by the DSO occur simultaneously, or even when these two entities engage in simultaneous procurement of flexibility services (Ruester et al., 2014; Hadush and Meeus, 2018; Vagropoulos et al., 2022). Conflicts between them could thus arise. Under these circumstances, the DSO may well face misaligned incentives between ensuring adequate flexible resources for its own use and promoting the delivery of such resources to the TSO (Chen and Vandendriessche, 2023b).

133. Apparently, in the above two cases, a lack of communication and coordination between the TSO and the DSO could not only endanger the reliability and security of the electricity system but also undermine the incentives for them to allow each other to use flexibility sources connected to their own systems. This will ultimately prevent them from playing a proactive role in facilitating

---

73 This can take place when, for example, the DSO clears downward offers (e.g., a decrease in production) in a specific location and a few minutes later the TSO clears upwards offers (an increase in production or decrease in consumption) for the same location, for the same market time unit. See Hermann et al., 2022; Vagropoulos et al., 2022.

74 The European DA electricity market uses a simplified representation of transmission constraints. This market solely considers network constraints that limit power exchange among predefined market areas, known as bidding zones. Zonal markets do not account for intra-zonal transmission constraints in the market-clearing process. As a result, market participants within a zone can trade energy at a uniform price. However, the clearing outcomes of zonal electricity markets are not necessarily feasible in the operational stage due to congestion that occurs when electricity exchanges are more than the capacity of transmission network lines. Therefore, in every zone, the corresponding TSO is responsible for restoring feasibility and operating the power system safely at the high-voltage transmission level, while respecting exchange limits between zones. To make the market outcomes feasible, the TSO needs flexibility services to relieve congestion, namely redispatching. See Emami and Sadri, 2012; Hermann et al., 2022.

greater market participation of DR and self-generated RES-E. Tackling these challenges calls for a paradigm shift in the way transmission and distribution systems interact (Givisiez et al., 2020). At the core of the TSO-DSO coordination mechanisms, in the context of utilizing DSM for integrating RES-E, should be facilitating customers to offer flexibility services to TSOs and DSOs without affecting the operational security of respective networks (Givisiez et al., 2020; Hermann et al., 2022). A number of specific dimensions are involved, including network planning, operation, procurement of system services (including market processes and market models),[75] and the establishment of technical requirements for data exchange (CEER, 2015; Roos, 2017; Silva et al., 2018; Lind et al., 2019; Givisiez et al., 2020; Hermann et al., 2022; Vagropoulos et al., 2022).

## 3.2. CHALLENGES FACED BY DSOs

134. In contrast to the transmission system, the emergence and development of DR and renewables self-consumption pose unique technical, organizational, and regulatory challenges for the distribution system (Cossent et al., 2009; Pereira et al., 2020). This situation is jointly caused by the traditional role of the DSO – a passive distributor of power – and the trend that the share of DR and self-generated RES-E connecting to distribution networks is higher than to the transmission system (Bauknecht and Brunekreeft, 2008, p 469; Papalexopoulos et al., 2020). Since the unbundling reform, in most European countries,[76] the statutory tasks of DSOs have become quite streamlined (Bauknecht and Brunekreeft, 2008, p 469; Johansson et al., 2020). Their planning routines and know-how were geared toward running the passive end of central systems, merely for distributing electricity to final customers (Bauknecht and Brunekreeft, 2008, p 488). Simply because of this, distribution networks were not technically and administratively designed to absorb large amounts of DR and self-generated RES-E that bring

[75] The key market processes allowing for optimal access to flexibility by TSOs and DSOs comprise asset qualification, registration, activation and settlement. To enhance coordinated access to flexibility resources, the literature also calls for reforming the existing centralized way of organizing wholesale and system service markets. Some of them propose building electricity markets at the distribution level. See Chapter IV below for a more detailed discussion. See e.g. Hadush and Meeus, 2018; IRENA, 2020; Hartnett et al., 2021, p 279; Vagropoulos et al., 2022.

[76] However, Denmark is an exception, which is a pioneering country in developing new concepts of distribution network management and shifting the traditional role of DSOs. It has fostered the development of distributed production based on renewables since the 2000s; thus, additional tasks have been imposed on DSOs beyond distributing electricity to final customers. Danish electricity distribution companies were legally obligated to finance, construct, and operate the transformer stations and transmission and distribution infrastructure for centralized wind farms and decentralized wind turbines owned by ordinary people. They were even responsible for local balancing. See Lund and Cherian, 2005; Bauknecht and Brunekreeft, 2008, p 478; Sovacool, 2013; Rosen and Madlener, 2016.

variable generation and bi-directional power flows.[77] In this case, how DSOs tackle voltage excursions and capacity issues[78] is found to be highly affected by the traditional 'physical measures' (Edens and Lavrijssen, 2019; Johansson et al., 2020). These measures mainly comprise updating or reinforcing the grid with additional physical components like transformers or cables to reduce the influence of DR and renewables self-consumption on local voltage values and the stress on assets (Nykamp et al., 2012; Roos, 2017; Johansson et al., 2020). The network is typically dimensioned for the 'worst case', which occurs in the case of peak flows or the highest load (Karki et al., 2009; Huang and Söder, 2017b). In some Member States, DSOs were required to resort to this approach to fulfill the obligation of guaranteeing network access stemming from regulated TPA (Edens and Lavrijssen, 2019). However, this is considered economically inefficient as the 'worst case' within the network typically does not last long, especially given that the generation from RES-E prosumers can vary a lot in a short time (Huang and Söder, 2017a; Givisiez et al., 2020). If the network is designed according to the very short-time extreme scenario, the infrastructure investment would be disproportionately high, and the capacity of the network would be redundant most of the time (Zhou and Bialek, 2007; Huang and Söder, 2017a, 2017b). Along with the growing penetration of DR and self-generated RES-E, DSOs have increasingly run into an imbalance between efficient network operation and meeting connection demands as far as possible (Edens and Lavrijssen, 2019).

135. To improve the efficient usage of network assets and avoid wasteful investments, 'active network management' solutions were proposed as alternatives to conventional investments (Overbeeke and Roberts, 2002; Ruester et al., 2014; Colmenar-Santos et al., 2016). They highlight a fundamental shift in DSOs from passive to active network operators, who recognize and can benefit from the network contributions of DR and self-generated RES-E in terms of offering flexibility services (McDonald, 2008; de Joode et al., 2009; Frías et al., 2009; Shaw et al., 2010). In other words, while the integration of these resources

---

77 Historically, electricity was mainly produced in large power stations, such as coal-fired power plants and transported to consumers. Accordingly, physical energy flowed from the plants via the transmission grid and the distribution grid to the end user, in one direction only. A bidirectional flow occurs when distribution grids have more feed-in than consumption, as is the case with RES-E in combination with DG. Then, the transmission grids must take the surplus electricity and transport it to other consumption areas. See Nykamp et al., 2012; Knieps, 2013, p 147; Connolly et al., 2016; Manuel de Villena et al., 2021.

78 The permitted limits for the stress of assets like cables and transformers can be exceeded if too much RES-E is connected, or grid assets are not sufficiently large for these energy flows. This overload damages the assets themselves. Moreover, feed-in can result in exceeding the threshold value for the permitted voltage of the public supply. Exceeding the permissible voltage values may damage connected devices, such as those in households. Especially in rural distribution grid areas with low short-circuit power, RES-E can cause problems in voltage quality and supply security. See Nykamp et al., 2012; Navarro-Espinosa and Ochoa, 2016; Yuan and Hesamzadeh, 2017; Johansson et al., 2020.

poses challenges to distribution network operation, they also have the potential to convert into solutions – though not all[79] – for taking up such challenges. Nevertheless, exploiting these resources requires that the idea of 'active network management' be incorporated into the investment, planning and network operation of DSOs. As already highlighted, since DSOs are regulated entities, this intractable task holds equally for legislators and regulators when adjusting incentive structures and setting out obligations for DSOs (Ruester et al., 2014). Distribution network regulation is thus confronted with the new task of adapting to the evolving notion of distribution network operation.

## 4. INTERIM CONCLUSION

136. This Chapter provides an overview of key tasks of electricity DSM geared toward empowering final customers to support RES-E uptake in the EU context. It demonstrates that, given the feature of the electricity system, apart from offering consumers economic incentives and information and fostering rational economic decisions, adaptations of the network segment are an integral part of electricity DSM. From the end users' perspective, the above literature review highlights the need to take into account behavioral factors that shape energy consumers' choices and actions. Distorted or insufficient economic incentives alone cannot explain the low consumer engagement level. Cognitive and behavioral biases may deter consumers from using standard economic appraisal methods and overlook the potential benefits of shifting from passive to proactive customers. Relevant findings inform the design of fit-for-purpose DSM measures, which should be a toolbox that covers diverse regulatory instruments for addressing economic and behavioral barriers to inducing desirable consumption behavior.

137. Overcoming economic barriers requires the removal of distortions in price signals and market entry barriers, including those faced by individual consumers and intermediaries that cooperate with them (e.g., IFSPs). It should be noted that in a jurisdiction pursuing the completion of market liberalization, steering consumer behavior is not merely about providing economic incentives. The impact on the competitive electricity market is another key consideration (Chen and Vandendriessche, 2023a). Such incentives and measures promoting

[79] As explained in Section 3.1, in terms of addressing the impact on the electricity system created by DR and renewables self-consumption, such as grid congestion, the role of flexibility services is limited and can merely defer or partially replace network reinforcement and expansion. Facing the increasing demand for connection from DR and self-generated RES-E, investments in network capacity are sometimes inevitable to ensure network access. This also explains why network investment faces trade-offs between the efficient use of flexibility and securing long-term capacity adequacy, which requires making optimal decisions in OPEX and CAPEX.

consumers' market entry should be, in principle, compatible with general rules for guaranteeing a level playing field in the electricity market (Chen and Vandendriessche, 2023a). How to maximize the market's role to provide market-based remuneration? In what cases might out-of-market promotional measures be necessary? How to protect consumers lacking experience of market participation from undue administrative burdens while avoiding excessively favoring them and discriminating against other market players? These are core issues faced by a legal framework on electricity DSM.

138. Different customer groups, especially households, commercial and public users, and energy poor or vulnerable consumers, face different behavioral barriers arising from their specificities and electricity use patterns. Their decision-making biases and the underlying mechanisms shape the decision-making process, which must be fully understood and considered when electricity DSM measures seek to provide information and options for them. Moreover, targeted measures can enable an inclusive approach that is able to engage these customer groups plagued by different obstacles, which is necessary to develop robust and effective measures and advance recognitional and distributional justice.

139. Lastly, enabling consumers to collectively act (e.g., via energy communities or cooperatives) and harnessing help from energy service providers could be highly beneficial in mitigating economic and behavioral constraints and achieving greater consumer engagement. However, these approaches are not without challenges. Barriers faced by IFSPs mentioned above are an example. This implies the need for dedicated legal frameworks to recognize the role of these intermediaries and to structure their relationships with consumers and other stakeholders. Their activities could be enabled by identifying and addressing specific barriers shaped by their distinct ways of interacting with consumers and traditional stakeholders. Whether EU law reflects the key tasks of electricity DSM and how it constructs the pillars of electricity DSM, addressing enablers and barriers to empower consumers to foster RES-E uptake, will be elaborated in the next chapter.

# CHAPTER III
# EU LAW ON ELECTRICITY DSM

## 1. INTRODUCTION

140. This Chapter canvasses the specific DSM approaches adopted by EU law to empower energy consumers to actively promote RES-E. As explained in Chapters I and II, facilitating system integration and greater use of RES-E requires final customers to manage their electricity consumption proactively. From earlier discussions, it is also clear that transforming the customers' role from passive takers of price and energy toward active entities that can contribute to a high RES-based electricity system is riddled with challenges. Efforts to tackle these challenges have resulted in a range of measures we see today, cutting across electricity market legislation and renewable energy promotional law at the Union level. They create two frameworks for empowering and prompting end users to (i) actively engage in DR, and (ii) purchase, use and produce RES-E, respectively. These frameworks are supported by four pillars, devoted to addressing challenges and barriers in changing electricity consumption patterns:

- *Defining rights and obligations*: Recognizing the role of final customers and entities cooperating with them (e.g., energy communities and energy service providers), articulating their rights and obligations in flexibility provision and renewables self-consumption, as well as regulating their relationship with traditional market players;
- *Enabling market-based incentives*: Both frameworks include measures that allow consumers to participate in electricity markets by trading their DR and self-generated RES-E, while ensuring the internal market functions properly and fairly rewards participating consumers and supporting actors;
- *Information and communication mechanisms*: To raise consumers' awareness, convey market signals, and enable efficient and secure data exchange in trading DR and self-generated RES-E;
- *Adapting network regulation*: Widely engaging consumers in DR and self-production, use and trading of RES-E requires corresponding adjustments to the obligations of TSOs and DSOs.

141. This Chapter answers Research Question number 2 by analyzing these four pillars consecutively. Before that, it outlines the legal basis that allows the EU to take actions in the area of electricity DSM, providing an overview of the structure of relevant Union-level legal acts. Moreover, the EU's competence in this area and the limitations imposed on such competence, as established in the Treaty framework, are clarified. This constitutes a foundation for the advice proposed in the Conclusion Chapter, which presents potential steps that the EU can take to close the regulatory gaps identified in Chapter IV.

## 2. THE LEGAL BASIS FOR DEVELOPING EU LEGISLATION ON ELECTRICITY DSM

142. This subsection provides an overview of the EU *acquis*, which can be considered relevant in terms of providing the EU with the legal basis for making rules to develop electricity DSM. In what follows, Section 2.1 reviews the EU's competence in the energy sector granted by the Treaty framework, followed by some restrictions imposed on the EU's exercise of this competence, elaborated in Section 2.2. Within these two subsections, contextual elements that exert an influence on the evolution of the relevant acquis are also discussed. In Section 2.3, the categories of legal measures to be discussed in the subsequent sections are distinguished based on different rule-making procedures contained in the *acquis*.

### 2.1. THE EU'S COMPETENCE

143. Within the Treaty framework of the EU, there is no provision specifically authorizing the Union institutions to legislate on electricity DSM. The EU's competence in this field is grounded in its competence in the energy sector, established by both the TEU and TFEU. The EU's competence in the energy sector was, in particular, made explicit and reinforced with the Lisbon Treaty amidst increasingly pronounced challenges of climate change and energy supply (Louis, 2009, p 66; Piris, 2010, p 319). Before the ratification of the Lisbon Treaty in 2009, there was no clear legal basis for a comprehensive EU energy law (Ehricke et al., 2009, p 742). European countries traditionally exercised national sovereignty over the field of energy law and policy (Crossley, 2017; Boasson, 2019). Bound by the principle of limited authority,[80] the EU had

[80] According to the principle of limited authority contained in Article 5 (1) of the TEC, the Community should act within the limits of the powers conferred upon it by this Treaty and of the objectives assigned to it therein. See *Consolidated Versions of the Treaty Establishing the European Community (2002/C 325/01)*, 2002; Ehricke et al., 2009, p 742.

to rely on some general shared competences to exert indirect influence over the energy sector (Piris, 2010, p 318; Crossley, 2017; Huhta, 2021). These mainly concerned environmental protection, the internal market, trans-European networks and difficulties in supply (*TEC*, Articles 95, 100, 155, 156 and 175; Piris, 2010, p 318). With the Lisbon Treaty, for the first time, the Union was conferred an explicit and general competence in the field of energy (Piris, 2010, p318). Article 194 TFEU, acting as a *lex specialis* in this regard, was inserted, and its first paragraph articulates the objectives that EU energy policy should serve (Huhta, 2021).

144. To enable energy consumers to actively engage in DR and the purchase, use, and self-production of RES-E, as mentioned at the beginning of this Chapter, EU law relating to both electricity markets and promoting renewables faces adaptations. Article 194(1) TFEU, which empowers the EU to achieve the objectives of '(a) ensure the functioning of the energy market' and '(c) promote the development of new and renewable forms of energy', is the most relevant legal basis for the EU's DSM legislation.

145. First, developing electricity DSM relies on the EU's competences regarding the internal electricity market. As noted above, the possibility of trading DR and self-generated RES-E is key to incentivizing consumers to shift toward DR providers and renewables prosumers. Moreover, consumers and the energy service providers with whom they cooperate should not be subject to discriminatory, unfair, or disproportionate market conditions. This requires the electricity market design to guarantee that these emerging market participants are provided with (i) effective and undistorted market signals, and (ii) a level playing field. Market rules or conditions originally tailor-made for traditional market actors thus need to be adjusted to correct the disadvantages faced by final customers, energy communities, and other energy service providers engaged in DSM activities. At the same time, the involvement of these new entities in the electricity markets necessitates the articulation of their rights and obligations, as well as their relationship with traditional market actors. This is crucial, not only to provide legal certainty for their broad participation across various electricity segments within the EU but also to prevent latent barriers or constraints imposed by market participants affected by their emergence. The competence of the EU concerning developing the internal energy market and ensuring its functioning, therefore, becomes relevant to promoting electricity DSM. The EU competences in the internal electricity market concern both the general competence for formulating competition rules and the sector-specific competence for ensuring the functioning of the energy market, as elaborated next.

146. Article 3(3) of the TEU enshrines the model of a 'social market economy', which represents a compromise or balance between pure *laissez-faire*

liberalism and a Keynesian interventionist political economy model.[81] This, in large part, determines the EU's approach to completing the internal market,[82] which is characterized by respecting market functioning as the general rule, accompanied by necessary and proportionate public interventions. As such, together with the principal aim of establishing an internal energy market set out in the TEU, Article 3(1)(b) TFEU confers upon the Union an exclusive competence in establishing competition rules necessary for the functioning of the internal market (Piris, 2010, p 308; *TFEU*, 2012, Article 3(1)(b); *TEU*, 2016, Article 3(3)). Since the inception of energy market liberalization, the EU has long made use of competition law to regulate the energy market (Alexiadis and Cave, 2012, p 515; Tews, 2015). The exercise of this competence helps curb exclusionary behavior and ensure a level playing field, which is crucial for offering market-based incentives to market actors involved in DSM.

147. Generic competition law is not sufficient to enable a well-functioning electricity market. It must be accompanied by sector-specific regulation (Alexiadis and Cave, 2012, p 501). This is particularly true for regulating electricity transmission and distribution networks upon which all competitive market actors (including those participating in DSM activities) depend, as mentioned in the previous chapter (Joskow, 2008). In monopoly network industries, fair network access by market players is generally safeguarded by unbundling and continuous market monitoring through sector-specific regulation (Cabau and Kovács, 2021, p 265). This is because, within this regulated segment, competition for the services is completely non-existent or at best very limited (Cabau and Kovács, 2021, p 265). The competence to adopt sector-specific interventions is thus justified, which is set out in Article 194 TFEU.

148. Serving as a *lex specialis*, Article 194(1) TFEU codifies the EU's competence in safeguarding the functioning of the energy market. It serves as the most relevant legal basis for ensuring free market access for market parties involved in electricity DSM and guaranteeing that they are provided with proper incentives. With this sector-specific competence, the EU can establish the rights and obligations for final customers, energy communities and energy service providers involved in the trading of DR and self-generated RES-E. These market

---

81 This economic model was introduced by the Lisbon Treaty. See *TEU*, 2016, Article 3(3); Iliopoulos, 2021.

82 The actions taken at the Union level to complete the internal market date back to the 1980s to facilitate the competitiveness of the European economy. However, energy markets did not originally feature in the package of completing the internal market. In part spurred on by the liberalization reform in the British energy sector, energy was soon added and the Internal Energy Market program was promoted by the Commission at the end of the 1980s. Energy market liberalization was subsequently codified and institutionalized by the consecutive four legislative packages that commenced in the 1990s. See Commission of the European Communities, 1985; Helm, p 559; Leuffen et al., p 116.

parties' relationships with traditional market participants (such as suppliers, BRPs, and network operators) can also be structured, thereby preventing market entry barriers created by the latter.[83] Moreover, the specific competence regarding energy market regulation could also be applied to protect electricity markets against distortive public interventions, notably disproportionate state aid and price regulation imposed by Member States. This is crucial for maintaining a well-functioning electricity market that adequately compensates DR providers and renewable energy prosumers.

149. Aside from necessary adaptations of the internal electricity market, promotional mechanisms for RES-E provided by EU law are crucial to fully empower and encourage final customers to actively purchase, use and produce RES-E. Further realizing the consumers' role in facilitating RES-E uptake primarily hinges upon the employment of the Union's competence granted by Article 194(1)(c) in promoting renewable energy.[84] A variety of promotional measures have already been taken under this competence. They include, for instance, facilitating the provision of information about the benefits of participating in renewables self-consumption and entitling consumers to generate RES-E and get remuneration by selling surplus production (*REDII*, articles 15 to 22). The novel ways of mobilizing the consumers' wider engagement in renewables self-consumption, particularly the community-based approach, were also embedded in EU law (*REDII*, recital 70). The enabling frameworks for RECs constitute new promotional mechanisms for RES-E set out by EU law. Since the energy price crises, the EU has stepped up efforts to increase the penetration level of RES-E, which include reinforced rules for further easing consumers' involvement in renewables self-consumption (*2023 Amendment to the REDII*; *2024 Amendment to the Electricity Directive*). Competence in promoting renewable energy is likely to play a growing role in shaping electricity DSM in the foreseeable future.

## 2.2. THE LIMITS IMPOSED ON THE EU'S COMPETENCE

150. Despite greater clarity made on the Union's competence in the energy sector, the EU still does not have exclusive control of energy legislation and policy but has shared competence with Member States to 'legislate and adopt legally binding acts' in energy matters (*TFEU*, Article 2(2); Crossley, 2017). Article 4(2) TFEU lists energy among the areas in which competences are shared between the EU and the Member States (Piris, 2010, p 318). This

---

83 For more details, see Sections 3 to 5 of this Chapter below.

84 In some occasions, in addition to Article 194, Article 192 TFEU is used as another legal basis for EU-level rules for promoting renewables. See the *2023 Amendment to the REDII*.

shared competence stems from the long-standing tension between the energy sovereignty of Member States and the common approach to energy governance adopted at the Union level. Member States are strongly reluctant to give up sovereignty in the energy sector, especially in terms of determining the energy mix and the general structure of their energy supply (Veum and Bauknecht, 2019). Once conferred energy competence upon the EU, Member States are subject to the principle of the primacy of EU law over national legislation.[85] Further, they must adopt all measures of national law necessary to implement legally binding Union acts adopted under the given competence (*TFEU*, Article 291(1)). The obligations stemming from extending EU competences regarding energy matters can affect the freedom of Member States in this area (Louis, 2009, p 87). Consequently, there have been recurring political debates around the sensitive sovereignty in the area of energy over the past decades (Calliess and Hey, 2013; Resch et al., 2013; Tews, 2015; Boasson, 2021, p 58).

151. Before the Lisbon Treaty, the tension between Member States and the EU in making rules for energy matters had already become apparent. A prominent example is the persistent refusal by Member States to create a Union-wide uniform support scheme for renewable energy (Rowlands, 2005; Lauber and Schenner, 2011; Jacobs, 2012, p 34; Tews, 2015; Crossley, 2017; Jörgens et al., 2017, p 289). During negotiations running up to the Lisbon Treaty, although Member States were aware of the coming imperative of the low-carbon energy transition, there was much hesitation in granting substantial powers to the Union in these fields (Louis, 2009, p 90). The political concerns in the energy sector explain why the EU only has shared competence with Member States in this field.

152. Additionally, the exercise of this shared competence is subject to several caveats laid down in the Treaties. First, under Article 194 TFEU, while specifying that implementing competences relating to paragraph 1 applies the ordinary legislative procedure, paragraph 2 makes clear that the measures fulfilling the aims of paragraph 1 should not '*affect a Member State's right to determine the conditions for exploiting its energy resources, its choice between different energy sources and the general structure of its energy supply.*' A strict grammatical interpretation of this restriction would considerably diminish the practical

[85] The primacy of EU law is a traditional pillar of the Union legal order. It should be noted the distinction between the supremacy that must remain with the Constitution in Member States and the primacy of Union law. The former is based on the 'superior hierarchical character of a norm and, for that reason, that norm is the source for the validity of lower norms, with the natural consequence of the invalidity of the latter where they are incompatible with the binding content of the former.' Primacy, in contrast, is not based on hierarchy but on the principle that the Treaties and the law adopted by the Union on the basis of the Treaties have primacy over the law of Member States. See Louis, p 87–88; *TFEU*, Declaration 17 concerning primacy.

importance of Article 194(1) TFEU, considering that most energy laws and policies will more or less affect the rights of Member States under reference (Iliopoulos, 2021). This is notably the case when the EU takes measures to promote renewable energy, which aims to increase the share of renewables in energy consumption, thereby necessarily affecting the composition of Member States' energy mix (Iliopoulos, 2021). Hence, a teleological contraction is justified: the reservation contained in Article 194(2) indeed restricts the EU's competence in energy, whilst it is not absolute in nature (Haraldsdóttir, 2014; Iliopoulos, 2021). In this context, Article 194(2) can be interpreted as meaning that the measures taken in light of Article 194(1) should limit the impact on the foregoing rights granted to Member States to an appropriate level (Iliopoulos, 2021). This interpretation, to some extent, can be supported by Article 192(2), which provides exceptions to the ordinary legislative procedure in cases where the EU takes action to protect the environment. Under this provision, the TFEU requires the application of a special legislative procedure wherein the Council acts unanimously in case the environmental protection measures *significantly affect a Member State's choice between different energy sources and the general structure of its energy supply* (*TFEU*, Article 192(2)(c)). This suggests that national sovereignty in choosing between different energy sources and the general structure of energy supply is not absolute and untouchable (Iliopoulos, 2021).

153. Finally, the shared competence in energy remains bound by the principles of subsidiarity and proportionality enshrined in Article 5 of the TEU. The former limits the EU's interventions within this area to those where '*Member States are unable to achieve the objectives of a proposed action satisfactorily and added value can be provided if the action is carried out at Union level*' (Ehricke et al., 2009, p 755; *TEU*, Article 5(3); Crossley, 2017). Under the principle of proportionality, the content and form of Union action must not exceed what is necessary to achieve the objectives of the Treaties (*TEU*, Article 5(4)).

## 2.3. RULE-MAKING PROCEDURES

154. Having reviewed the Union's competence in developing rules for electricity DSM, it is worth sketching the rule-making procedures. This allows for a helpful clarification of the body of norms adopted by the co-legislators and the EC in the area of electricity DSM.

155. In accordance with Article 194 TFEU, in principle, legislating on energy matters applies the ordinary legislative procedure set out in Article 294 TFEU. This ordinary legislative procedure reflects the 'Community method' wherein the Commission makes and submits legislative proposals, based on which the legislative acts are adopted jointly by the Parliament and the Council

(Commission of the European Communities, 2001; *TFEU*, Articles 289 and 294). It is important to note that one of the significant institutional reforms made by the Lisbon Treaty is to improve the efficiency of the Union's decision-making process while ensuring democracy and transparency (Bribosia, 2008, p 78). Among other things, this reform involves increasing the number of fields in which the Council decides by a qualified majority and making co-decision between the Parliament and the Council the normal legislative procedure.[86] The competence regarding energy is one of the fields that the Council is subject to qualified majority voting and co-decision with the Parliament (*TFEU*, 2012, Article 294). The Electricity Directive, the Electricity Regulation, the REDII, and the 2023 Amendment to the REDII offer examples of applying the new legislative procedure introduced by the Lisbon Treaty. These legislative acts, as will be explicated in the following sections of this Chapter, take significant steps forward to the development of electricity DSM in the context of enhancing the exploitation of RES-E.

156. Aside from the foregoing legislative procedures for legislative acts, the EC is also empowered to adopt two types of non-legislative acts – delegated acts and implementing acts:

- According to Article 290 TFEU, a legislative act may authorize the EC to adopt non-legislative acts of general application to supplement or amend certain non-essential elements of the legislative act. These acts of the EC are known as 'delegated acts'. Under Article 290 TFEU, the essential elements of an area must be reserved for the legislative act and accordingly must not be the subject of a delegation of power. In delegating the rule-making power to the EC, the objectives, content, scope, and duration of the delegation should be explicitly defined in the legislative acts. Within the framework of the CEP, essential elements for promoting electricity DSM, such as third-party access and secure and efficient data management, have been translated into specific legal provisions. To further supplement the legislative acts, the EC is delegated to adopt network codes and guidelines (*Electricity Directive*, Article 63(9); *Electricity Regulation*, Article 59(2)). For instance, the EC is delegated to adopt delegated acts supplementing the Electricity Regulation concerning the establishment of network codes in certain areas, including network connection of demand side facilities and data exchange (*Electricity Regulation*, Article 59(2)).

[86] In the 1960s, the European Parliament only had, at most, a consultative power. The situation has since changed and the Lisbon Treaty emphasizes this evolution to enable the Parliament to become the co-legislator. Even in the special legislative procedure, the Council acts unanimously after consulting the Parliament. Together with the ordinary legislative procedure, this reform makes the intervention of the Parliament an integral part of the Community decision-making process. See Bribosia, 2008, p 74.

- Under Article 291 TFEU, where uniform conditions for implementing legally binding Union acts are needed, those acts should confer implementing powers on the EC. Under the Electricity Regulation, the implementing powers empowered to the Commission comprise a catalogue of matters about the development of DSM, including DR, aggregation, procurement of balancing services, and cooperation between TSOs and DSOs (*Electricity Regulation*, Articles 58–59).

157. Non-legislative acts adopted by the EC following delegation (delegated acts) or to implement a legislative act (implementing acts) can take the form of either network codes or guidelines, as stated in Article 58 of the Electricity Regulation. All in all, the Union-level legal acts in the field of electricity DSM comprise both legislative acts and non-legislative acts, as shown in Table 3.

**Table 3. The classification of EU law on electricity DSM**

| | Categories | EU institutions and rule-making procedures | Examples |
|---|---|---|---|
| EU-level DSM law | Legislative acts | Adopted by legislative procedure, where the Council is subject to qualified majority voting and co-decision with the Parliament | Electricity Directive, REDII, Electricity Regulation |
| | Non-legislative acts | **Implementing acts:** Adopted by the EC based on implementing powers conferred by legally binding Union acts | Network regulations adopted in light of Article 59(1) of the Electricity Regulation |
| | | **Delegated acts:** Adopted by the EC based on the delegation of legislative acts | Demand Connection Code;[87] Network regulations adopted under Article 59(2) of the Electricity Regulation |

Source: Author's elaboration.

## 3. DEFINING RIGHTS AND OBLIGATIONS

158. The electricity sector is one in which actors' roles are meticulously defined to ensure that the system functions smoothly, and effective competition can take place (Pearson, 2020, p 115). Compared to the purchase of RES-E, final customers' involvement in DR and renewables prosuming notably adds

[87] Recital 22 of this Code states that 'this Regulation has been adopted based on Regulation (EC) No 714/2009 which it supplements and of which it forms an integral part.' Based on this, the Demand Connection Code is used to supplement the 2009 Electricity Regulation, constituting a delegated act. See *Demand Connection Code*, 2016, recital 22.

novel dimensions to their roles. The new roles of final customers also catalyze the emergence of commercial and non-commercial actors who assist them in fulfilling these new roles. This section examines how EU law empowers final customers to engage in flexibility provision and renewables prosuming by defining their role, rights and obligations.

159. The experience before the CEP indicates that in the absence of legal frameworks defining their role, rights and obligations, emerging actors involved in both DR and renewables prosuming were vulnerable to various uncertainties and barriers (Roggenkamp and Diestelmeier, 2020, p 160). As explained in Chapter II above, such obstacles can arise not only from traditional actors but also from pre-existing national laws that were tailored initially for traditional electricity undertakings. Additionally, as shown in the previous chapter, energy consumers, especially those small in size and households, in general, suffer from economic and behavioral constraints, which contribute to their inactivity in optimizing their electricity use. In the traditional energy regime, they have long been regarded and expected to behave as passive takers of energy and price, which also further reinforces such inertia.

160. The previous chapters demonstrate that energy law steers electricity consumption behavior by defining the active role of consumers and specifying the activities they may engage in, along with their associated rights and obligations. Such rights and obligations are also shaped by measures that structure consumers' relationships with traditional and new actors in the electricity sector, ranging from suppliers, BRPs, and system operators to IFSPs and energy communities. Without regulating some of their interactions, it would be difficult to implement the consumers' rights associated with their active role granted by EU law. This section takes a close look at the respective legal frameworks that articulate the rights and obligations of consumers and relevant entities involved in DR and renewables self-consumption in Sections 3.1 and 3.2. Considering that energy communities are used as a common tool for empowering and boosting consumers to engage in DR and renewables use, their rights and obligations are separately analyzed in Section 3.3. Section 3.4 outlines common obligations applicable to consumers and other actors involved in DR and renewables prosumption.

## 3.1. CONSUMERS' RIGHTS TO PROVIDE DR

161. As indicated in Chapter I, existing EU law facilitates the development of both implicit DR and explicit DR. For implicit DR, EU law specifies consumers' rights to access dynamic price contracts. Their rights are supported

by corresponding obligations placed on suppliers. In the case of explicit DR, consumers are entitled to provide such flexibility individually or with the assistance of energy service providers. As mentioned in Section 2 of Chapter II, the latter option serves as a 'boost'. It enhances consumers' participation by reducing the complexity perceived by end users and overcoming their cognitive limitations. Figure 6 gives an overview of the two types of DR that EU law empowers final customers to offer. The two frameworks that entitle consumers to provide implicit and explicit DR are analyzed consecutively in Sections 3.1.1 and 3.1.2 below.

**Figure 6. Two kinds of DR facilitated by EU law**

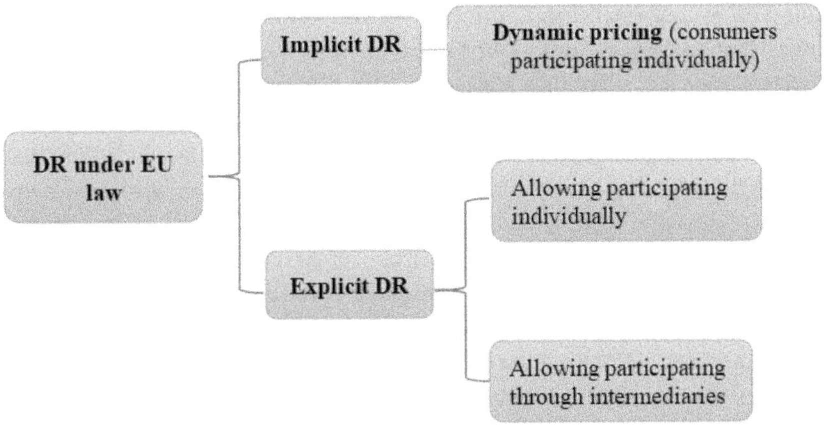


Source: Author's elaboration.

### 3.1.1. *Implicit DR*

162. The rules entitling consumers to access dynamic price contracts are mainly contained in Article 11 of the Electricity Directive. It imposes obligations on both Member States and suppliers. To implement consumers' rights to dynamic price contracts, Member States have the following obligations:

- Ensuring that final customers who have a smart meter[88] installed can request to conclude a dynamic electricity price contract with at least

[88] Although smart meters are critical to enable dynamic pricing, they also facilitate the provision of information to customers which allows for active consumption management and helps promote engagement in other forms of DR. Considering this, deploying the smart metering system is seen as an important component of informational strategies, which is the subject of Section 5 of this Chapter below.

one supplier and with every supplier that has more than 200,000 final customers;[89]

- Ensuring that the national regulatory frameworks enable suppliers to offer such contracts.

163. The scope of final customers entitled to access dynamic price contracts deserves special attention, considering that EU law conditionally allows retail price interventions, as detailed in Section 4 of this Chapter below. To convey robust price signals to drive investments and incentivize DR, existing EU law prohibits interventions in wholesale electricity prices. Once they enter into dynamic price contracts, consumers are directly linked to price changes in wholesale electricity markets. This raises the question whether consumers protected by regulated retail prices[90] are also entitled to such offers, and, under what conditions, this right can be realized. Recital 23 of the Electricity Directive indicates that this legislation also aims to enable beneficiaries of regulated prices to fully benefit from the offers available on the competitive market when they choose to do so. It also states that, to that end, they need to be well informed about offers and savings available in the competitive market, especially relating to dynamic price contracts, and be provided with the necessary assistance to participate in these markets. Article 5 of the Electricity Directive stipulates that household customers and microenterprises, who are neither energy poor nor vulnerable but are beneficiaries of regulated prices, have the right to choose and to be directly informed, at least every quarter, of the availability of dynamic electricity price contracts. For energy poor or vulnerable household customers, although there are no specific provisions that stress their rights to access dynamic price contracts, according to Article 11, where they have installed smart meters, they are also entitled to be offered such contracts. As such, the legislator clarifies that consumers applying regulated prices are also entitled to dynamic price contracts, provided they are willing to switch to such offers. Their right in this respect is supported by measures informing them of potential economic benefits brought by dynamic price contracts.

164. Granting final customers the right to access dynamic price contracts is accompanied by consumer protection measures. While customers on dynamic price contracts can realize additional benefits from shifting their consumption to times of low wholesale prices, they also risk facing higher bills in case they

89 The figure 200,000 is largely a compromise text showing diverging stances of the European Council, which sought to avoid burdening smaller suppliers, and the European Parliament, which advocated for maximizing consumer choice and competition in such offers. See Pearson, 2020, p104.

90 EU law conditionally allows Member States to regulate prices for certain customer groups. See Section 4.1.2 of this Chapter below for more details.

are consuming during peak hours (EC, 2016a). Moreover, suppliers might pass parts of their wholesale price risk on to these consumers (EC, 2016a). Given this, it is crucial to ensure that consumers choose such offers voluntarily and that their choice is based on an understanding of the potential risks. For the sake of consumer protection, Article 11 of the Electricity Directive requires Member States to ensure that final customers are fully informed by the suppliers of the opportunities, costs and risks of such offers. Another relevant obligation is imposed on suppliers, which requires them to obtain the consent of each final customer before switching that customer to a dynamic electricity price contract.

165. In the early stage of promoting dynamic price contracts, the adverse impact of exposing end users to wholesale price fluctuations remains to be seen. There is thus a need for monitoring the impact of implementing dynamic price contracts, and limiting risks of volatile prices to a proper level is necessary (*Electricity Directive*, recital 37). NRAs are thus competent in monitoring the impact of dynamic electricity price contracts and the use of smart metering systems (*Electricity Directive*, Article 59(1)(o)). This competence is further complemented by Article 11 of the Electricity Directive, which lists elements of such monitoring and aims to enhance information disclosure regarding various impacts of dynamic price contracts. It stipulates that Member States or their NRAs should monitor and publish an annual report on the main developments of such contracts, including market offers and the impact on consumers' bills, and specifically the level of price volatility for at least a ten-year period after dynamic electricity price contracts become available.

### *3.1.2. Explicit DR*

166. In the context of EU law, final customers can engage in explicit DR by reacting to market signals sent by market participants and system operators.[91] EU law entitles consumers to offer DR individually (*Electricity Directive*, Article 15(1)(2)), while adapting market design parameters, such as the minimum bid size, to lower market entry barriers for individual customers, as shown in Section 4 of this Chapter below.

---

91 Under EU law, ID markets act as the major tool for market participants to balance themselves as closely as possible to real time in order to accommodate the high penetration of variable RES-E. This is because an increasing penetration of RES-E requires efficient and liquid short-term markets that can operate until very shortly before the time of physical delivery, i.e., the moment when electricity is consumed. Hence, one important adaptation of the market design made by the CEP is to strengthen the short-term markets by bringing them closer to real-time in order to provide maximum opportunity to meet the flexibility needs and balance the market. The closer to real-time electricity is traded (supply and demand matched), the less the need for costly interventions by TSOs to maintain a stable electricity system. See EC, 2016; *Electricity Regulation*, recital 23.

167. However, not every consumer can trade explicit DR on markets on their own. As mentioned in the previous Chapter, despite the potential financial benefits, customers, especially residential users, are typically reluctant to change their consumption to react to market signals (*Electricity Directive*, recital 43; Pearson, 2020, p 102; Stede et al., 2020). Aversion to complexity and losses involved in such energy activities, including the required know-how and capacity, cognitive resources, time, and effort, contributes to their inertia and inactivity (EC, 2016a; Parrish et al., 2020; Leinauer et al., 2022). Moreover, while EU law has taken actions to lower market access barriers for individual customers, some market entry conditions and prequalification requirements are still too demanding for small consumers (Papsch, 2020, p 39). The presence of behavioral and market entry obstacles highlights the importance of energy services that can help consumers engage with the complex and formalized electricity system (EC, 2016a).

168. In this context, EU law improves consumers' participation by providing them with adequate incentives and offering them the tools and new ways to provide explicit DR (*Electricity Directive*, recital 10). Section 4 of this Chapter will specifically address how EU law enables market-based incentives. In this section, the focus is on the approaches to assisting consumers to valorize explicit DR on various electricity markets, by specifying their rights to cooperate with intermediate parties (*Electricity Directive*, recitals 39 and 43; Willems and Zhou, 2020). These intermediaries include independent aggregators, recognized as commercial third-party energy service providers (i.e., IFSPs), and energy communities. As mentioned, the framework empowering consumers to engage in flexibility provision and renewables prosumption collectively via energy communities will be discussed in Section 3.3. The role of IFSPs and how EU law empowers consumers to valorize explicit DR via IFSPs is discussed in more detail hereunder.

169. As a specialized party offering flexibility-related services, the IFSP's roles include inter alia aggregating small loads, providing market information, and hedging risks for final customers (Bruninx et al., 2020; Stede et al., 2020; Willems and Zhou, 2020). At the EU level, their key role was not given adequate attention in the Third Energy Package. The Balancing Regulation merely allows third parties different from customers to access balancing markets, without expressly defining their role (*Balancing Regulation*, Article 18(4)(c)). Before the CEP, two regulatory barriers were frequently named by the literature (Vandorpe and Callaerts, 2017; Poplavskaya and Vries, 2019; Stede et al., 2020), which were also identified by the ACER and NRAs (Autorité de la concurrence, 2013; ACER and CEER, 2015; CREG 2016 Study, 2016; Vandorpe and Callaerts, 2017). First, the role of IFSPs was not recognized and clearly defined in the legislation. Second, their activities could be hindered by suppliers and the

suppliers' BRPs, which are affected by the activation of DR, as explained in Section 2.1.2 of Chapter II.

170. The CEP seeks to tackle these barriers by first recognizing a type of IFSP, the 'independent aggregator', and establishing a framework that entitles consumers to engage with this third-party FSP. The Electricity Directive defines an 'independent aggregator' as *'a market participant engaged in aggregation who is not affiliated to the customer's supplier'* (*Electricity Directive*, Article 2(19)). Based on this, the rights and obligations of this market player around engaging consumers, activating DR, and participating in electricity markets are clarified.

171. First, consumers are granted the right to conclude aggregation contracts, not subject to the consent of or discriminatory technical and administrative requirements, procedures or charges by their electricity suppliers (*Electricity Directive*, Articles 13, 15, 16 and 17). Consumers and IFSPs engaged in aggregation are also entitled to enter all electricity markets without the consent of other market participants (*Electricity Directive*, Article 17). Such rights outlaw barriers or restrictions placed by suppliers and other market players upon consumers that valorize flexibility via IFSPs. In some Member States, the detected constraints include asking the IFSPs to obtain the consent of the suppliers before contracting with the customers or charging the customers who cooperate with the IFSPs (Barbero et al., 2018; Poplavskaya and Vries, 2018).

172. The consumers' right to trade DR via IFSPs is additionally underpinned by legal provisions addressing conflicts of interest between IFSPs and suppliers, as well as BRPs. Article 17 of the Electricity Directive is the most relevant provision for structuring the interactions between IFSPs and suppliers, as well as BRPs, that are directly affected by DR activation. Beyond requiring Member States to assign roles and responsibilities to all market stakeholders involved in aggregating DR in a transparent and non-discriminatory manner, it establishes several key principles that Member States must consider when developing relevant national laws. These principles aim to ensure that when IFSPs are required to compensate suppliers or BRPs for the impact of activating DR, the obligations on them are proportionate and refrain from impeding their market entry.

173. The EU law's solution for addressing the conflicting interests between IFSPs and the affected stakeholders is two-fold. When valorizing DR, IFSPs and consumers are protected against barriers or restrictions imposed by the affected market players, such as the above-mentioned prior consent and discriminatory charges. Nevertheless, the impact of DR activation on stakeholders also needs to be addressed to eliminate the incentives of these stakeholders to hinder DR activities. Requiring IFSPs to compensate affected market

players is one potential solution. EU law grants Member States the flexibility to design such mechanisms (*Electricity Directive*, recital 39 and article 17(4)). However, such compensation schemes – if poorly developed – are liable to be counter-productive for IFSPs' market entry.[92] Cognizant of this, Article 17(4) obligates Member States to ensure that the application of the compensation mechanisms will not hinder the market entry of IFSPs and consumers and that the compensation must not exceed the resulting costs incurred by the suppliers or the suppliers' BRPs during the activation of DR. Additionally, relevant calculation method for the compensation should be subject to approval by NRAs or by another competent national authority.

174. In parallel to widely engaging consumers in DR, a sufficient level of consumer protection is highlighted by EU law, which also determines obligations for IFSPs (*Electricity Directive*, recital 37 and Article 58(g)). Relevant obligations are mainly contained in rules governing aggregation contracts and DR-related data. For instance, IFSPs must comply with the requirements laid down in Article 12 of the Electricity Directive with respect to the customer's right to switch IFSPs. Their obligations include carrying out switching within the shortest possible time, without charging household customers and small enterprises any switching-related fees. Also relevant are the IFSPs' obligations to inform their customers of the terms and conditions of the offered contracts (including termination fees), provide relevant DR data for customers, and ensure the non-discriminatory fulfillment of such obligations (*Electricity Directive*, Article 13(2)(3)(4)). The need for fully protecting commercially sensitive information and customers' data is also emphasized when granting the data access right to IFSPs (*Electricity Directive*, Article 17(3)(c)).

## 3.2. CONSUMERS' ENTITLEMENT TO RENEWABLES SELF-CONSUMPTION

175. To increase the role of final customers in promoting the deployment of RES-E, the CEP introduced a legal framework that clarifies the consumers' rights to engage in renewables prosumption, known as 'renewables self-consumption' in the EU law context. Under this framework, consumers are given two options to engage in renewables self-consumption: acting individually or collectively. In the former case, they are granted the right to act as renewables self-consumers or active customers. To enable the latter choice, they are entitled to be 'jointly-acting active customers' or 'jointly-acting renewables

92 During the negotiations of the proposal of the Electricity Directive, the EC expressed concerns over such compensation given the hurdles to uptake of DR if implemented poorly. See Pearson, 2020, p 109.

self-consumers' or participate in energy communities (*REDII*, recitals 66, 67 and 70). How EU law entitles consumers to become renewables self-consumers or active customers is the focus of this subsection. Section 3.2.1 focuses on the rights of these two entities, while Section 3.2.2 discusses the role of the enabling framework in supporting their exercise.

### 3.2.1. *Empowering Consumers to Act as 'Active Customers' and 'Renewables Self-Consumers'*

176. As Chapter I makes clear, within EU law, the difference between 'active customers' and 'renewables self-consumers' mainly lies in their activities relating to energy prosuming. Electricity generated by the former is not limited to that from renewable sources, whereas the latter's activities primarily revolve around renewable energy; however, self-generated energy encompasses more than just electricity. Both are prosumers entitled to generate RES-E for their own use and store and sell self-generated RES-E, according to the Electricity Directive and the REDII. Therefore, both of the legal frameworks addressing their rights and obligations, which are contained in these two legal acts, are relevant. However, the framework for renewables self-consumers is the major focus of this subsection, as it constitutes lex specialis in defining the rights and obligations of electricity prosumers using renewables and covers broader rules to address the barriers specific to them, as indicated in Table 4. Yet, the legal framework for active customers contains more elaborate principles for network charges applied to electricity prosumers, which are also applied to those based on renewable energy sources. Those principles will also be analyzed.

**Table 4. Comparison between the EU-level frameworks for renewables self-consumers and active customers**

| | Renewables self-consumers (according to the REDII) | Active customers (according to the Electricity Directive) |
|---|---|---|
| (Jointly acting) renewables self-consumption | Article 21(2): '*Member States shall ensure that renewables self-consumers, individually or through aggregators,* ***are entitled*** *(a) to generate renewable energy, including for their own consumption, store and sell their excess production of renewable electricity, including through renewables power purchase agreements, electricity suppliers and peer-to-peer trading arrangements*'<br>Article 21(4): '*Member States shall ensure that renewables self-consumers located in the same building, including multi-apartment blocks,* ***are entitled to engage jointly in activities*** *referred to in paragraph 2*' | Article 15(2): '*Member States shall ensure that active customers are: (a) entitled to operate either directly or through aggregation;*<br>*(b)* ***entitled to*** *sell self-generated electricity, including through power purchase agreements*'<br>Article 15(3): '*Member States* ***may have*** *different provisions applicable to individual and jointly-acting active customers in their national law*' |

*(continued)*

Table 4 *continued*

| | Renewables self-consumers (according to the REDII) | Active customers (according to the Electricity Directive) |
|---|---|---|
| Installation and operation of Electricity storage systems | Article 21(2): '*Member States shall ensure that renewables self-consumers, individually or through aggregators,* ***are entitled*** *(b) to install and operate electricity storage systems combined with installations generating renewable electricity for self-consumption*' | Article 15(5): '*Member States shall ensure that active customers that own an energy storage facility: (a)* ***have the right to*** *a grid connection within a reasonable time after the request …*' |
| Maintaining the role of final customers | Article 21(2): '*Member States shall ensure that renewables self-consumers, individually or through aggregators,* ***are entitled*** *(c) to maintain their rights and obligations as final consumers*' | No clear legal provision |
| Receiving remuneration for the self-generated RES-E fed into the grid | Article 21(2): '*Member States shall ensure that renewables self-consumers, individually or through aggregators,* ***are entitled*** *(d) to receive remuneration, including, where applicable, through support schemes, for the self-generated renewable electricity that they feed into the grid*' | Article 15(2): '*Member States shall ensure that active customers are: (b)* ***entitled to*** *sell self-generated electricity, including through power purchase agreements.*' |
| Barriers that must be addressed by the national enabling framework | Article 21(6): Member States inter alia must address (i) accessibility of renewables self-consumption to all customers, including tenants, vulnerable and energy poor consumers; (ii) unjustified barriers to the financing of projects in the market and measures to facilitate access to finance; (iii) other unjustified regulatory barriers | No obligation for Member States to create an enabling framework |

Source: Author's elaboration.

177. REDII clearly defines the role of renewables self-consumers. Network regulations adopted under the Third Energy Package allow generating facilities using renewable energy sources to offer flexibility services to the TSO (*Balancing Regulation*, Article 18(4)). Final customers with renewables generating installations can benefit from relevant rules, along with other renewables producers. However, the role, rights and obligations of becoming energy prosumers were not explicitly articulated in EU law. Such legal uncertainty inhibited consumers across the EU from engaging in prosuming and participating in various electricity market segments (Roggenkamp and Diestelmeier, 2020, p 165). To further unleash consumers' potential to use RES-E, the REDII officially recognizes the role of 'prosumers' by defining a new entity in EU energy law, i.e., 'renewables self-consumer'. As shown in Section 1.3 of Chapter I above, in defining their role, EU law also clarifies the activities that renewables self-consumers may conduct (including generating RES-E, consuming, storing and selling the self-generated electricity). In addition,

the definition of renewables self-consumers contains eligibility conditions for becoming these actors as follows:

- An entity constituting a renewables self-consumer must first have the status of 'final customer';
- A renewables self-consumer generates renewable electricity for its own consumption;
- For non-household consumers, becoming renewables self-consumers presupposes a condition that those activities do not constitute their primary commercial or professional activity (*REDII*, Article 2(14)).

178. These conditions constitute criteria for assessing when a final customer is considered a renewables self-consumer and eligible for rights contained in the empowerment framework created for this new role. Seen from these conditions, it appears that the EU legislator intends to emphasize the aim of empowering consumers and exclude a situation in which an electricity generation company occasionally using self-produced RES-E also constitutes a renewables self-consumer.[93] They prevent an undertaking engaged in RES-E production from circumventing existing licensing and market rules that govern professional energy activities, thereby ensuring a level playing field. It should also be noted that in the definition of 'active customer', the above last condition, i.e., 'their activities do not constitute primary commercial or professional activity', applies to all final customers, including households (*Electricity Directive*, Article 2(8)). This implies that once final customers' self-consumption activities, such as selling self-produced RES-E, become their primary commercial activity, they are no longer qualified as active customers. However, if they are household consumers, they can still maintain the status of renewables self-consumers.

179. When transposing and applying eligibility conditions contained in definitions of 'active customer' and 'renewables self-consumer', some tricky legal issues arise. They are linked to the difficulty in distinguishing between these two categories of actors and market actors engaged in energy production and supply, which will be discussed in Section 3.1 of Chapter IV.

180. After defining renewables self-consumers, EU law clarifies another option for consumers' involvement in self-consumption by defining the 'jointly

---

93 For instance, on some occasions, energy companies engaged in wind electricity production also use some electricity to kick-start the wind turbines or prevent blades from icing up. With storage facilities, they are also likely to use self-generated electricity and may constitute prosumers. However, they do not constitute renewables self-consumers as defined by EU law, since using self-generated electricity constitutes their primary commercial or professional activity.

acting renewables self-consumers' as a group of at least two jointly acting renewables self-consumers who are located in the same building or multi-apartment block (*REDII*, Article 2(15)).

181. Article 21 of the REDII grants a range of rights for renewables self-consumers and jointly acting renewables self-consumers to generate RES-E while also using, storing and selling such self-generated RES-E. The rationale and legislative intention underlying some of these rights merit further analysis here.

182. First, entitling self-consumers to store and sell self-generated RES-E is key to allowing them to fully reap the economic benefits of renewables self-consumption. Financial gains are considered the primary motivating factor behind consumers' investment in renewables self-consumption (Gamel et al., 2016; Fleiß et al., 2017; Woerter et al., 2017; Curtin et al., 2019). Such gains consist of two parts: (i) energy bill savings enabled by electricity self-sufficiency, and (ii) revenues from selling self-generated electricity. Before the CEP, remuneration schemes, tariffs and network charges applied to prosumers prevented them from fully benefiting from renewables prosumption (Palm, 2018; *Electricity Directive*, recital 42; Diestelmeier, 2021). They faced barriers or unfavorable conditions, especially when storing, feeding self-generated electricity back to the grid, or trading it. This situation is notably disadvantageous for a large number of prosumers with intermittent renewables (i.e., solar and wind), who typically have surplus production since their generation assets' output does not coincide with their demand patterns.[94] When they are unable to sell or store such excess electricity with non-discriminatory conditions, their incentives to engage in renewables self-consumption could be considerably compromised (Diestelmeier, 2021, p 730). Hence, specifying the rights of self-consumers to store and sell self-generated RES-E is essential to enabling a positive cost-benefit ratio for consumers' input in renewables self-consumption.

183. Apart from specifying the renewables self-consumers' right to store self-produced electricity, the REDII concretizes their rights to sell excess production and receive remuneration. Firstly, they are entitled to get market-based remuneration by selling self-generated RES-E (*REDII*, Article 21(2)(a)). Three approaches are highlighted as options: through renewables PPA, electricity suppliers and P2P trading arrangements,[95] drawn out in Section 4 of this Chapter further below. The possibility of trading the surplus electricity

[94] For instance, during the day, when the production of solar panels is at its peak, many renewables self-consumers are away from home, and thus not able to consume. See Khalilpour and Vassallo, 2015; Butenko, 2016.

[95] For the definition and key elements of P2P electricity trading, see Section 4.3 below of this Chapter.

also represents a more economically efficient alternative to electricity storage, which remains technologically limited and expensive so far (Inês et al., 2020). Additionally, the legislation also allows national support schemes to offer remuneration for the self-generated RES-E fed into the grid (*REDII*, Article 21(2)(d)).

184. It is important to highlight the rationale underlying the combination of state-led remuneration and market-based remuneration. Generally, unlike the first three energy legislative packages, the CEP shifts toward promoting RES-E in a market-compatible manner to minimize distortions in electricity markets and further integrate RES-E into competitive markets.[96] In this context, at the EU level, market-based solutions, namely promoting RES-E by maximizing their market revenues, have been strongly preferred to state-led solutions.[97] This is reflected in the market design adaptations centered around integrating RES-E and the rules empowering self-consumers to trade self-generated RES-E (Chen and Vandendriessche, 2023a). Despite this, it is still in the initial stage of promoting distributed RES-E to final customers. The upfront investment cost for renewables generation facilities and the long pay-off time remain significant economic constraints for consumers (Ruggiero et al., 2015; Palm, 2018; Su et al., 2018; Rikkonen et al., 2019; Department of the Environment of Ireland, 2022). Hence, the REDII allows Member States to grant national support and state aid to renewables self-consumers to better secure return on investments and lower the financing cost (*REDII*, Article 21(2)(d) and (7)). This permission can especially help to fill in financial viability gaps associated with installing renewable technologies by consumers from the domestic and SME sectors (Chen and Vandendriessche, 2023a).

185. Such state-led remuneration, as an exception to the overall trend of enhancing the market compatibility of support for RES-E, is not without restrictions. It is bound by newly established minimum requirements for national support schemes and existing state aid rules.[98] Moreover, to ensure

---

[96] EC, 2016; *REDII*, recitals 16 and 19, Article 4(2)(3); *Electricity Regulation*, Article 1(b); *Electricity Directive*, Recital 9; Chen and Vandendriessche, 2023.

[97] *Electricity Directive*, recital 9; *Electricity Regulation*, Article 1(b); Roggenkamp and Diestelmeier, 2020, p 172.

[98] Distinct from previous legislative packages, the CEP intensifies its efforts to regulate national support schemes to avoid conflicts or contradictions with the internal electricity market rules. As general requirements, when designing support schemes, Member States are required to avoid distortions of electricity markets, minimize the overall system cost of RES-E deployment, and maximize the integration of RES-E in the electricity market. To that end, the REDII further elaborates on how to design fit-for-purpose national support schemes. Three elements are involved. Firstly, Member States must provide incentives for such market integration in a market-based and market-responsive way. Secondly, support schemes must ensure that renewable energy producers respond to market price signals and maximize their market revenues. Thirdly, in principle, national support should be applied

small consumers are fully encouraged, small-scale installations are allowed to be exempted from the general principle of adopting market-based and market-responsive national support (*REDII*, Article 4(3)(4)). In the context of phasing out the option for Member States to apply FITs,[99] this exception makes it possible to preserve FITs for small renewables self-consumers, which offer guaranteed revenues and shield them from the risk of variations in electricity market prices.[100] When providing remuneration for the self-generated RES-E fed into the grid through support schemes, apart from the market value of that electricity, its long-term value to the grid, the environment and society is also listed as a factor in determining such remuneration (*REDII*, Article 21(2)(d)). Member States have the discretion to take into account this factor (*REDII*, Article 21(2)(d)).

186. Lastly, when formulating the rights to renewables self-consumption, Article 21 of the REDII imposed restrictions on procedures, charges or fees potentially applied to renewables self-consumers. First, in relation to the electricity that they consume from or feed into the grid, Member States must ensure that they are not subject to discriminatory or disproportionate procedures and charges, and to network charges that are not cost-reflective. Second, as regards their self-generated RES-E remaining within their premises, not only discriminatory or disproportionate procedures, but also any charges or fees are prohibited (*REDII*, Article 21(2)(a)). Moreover, double charging, including network charges, is also prohibited by Article 21 for stored electricity remaining within self-consumers' premises when they install and operate

---

in an open, transparent, competitive, non-discriminatory and cost-effective manner. Apart from these, additional requirements and exemptions are imposed when support for RES-E is granted through direct price support schemes and tendering procedures. See REDII, articles 4 and 21 (7).

99 While Member States are still allowed to apply direct price support schemes, in principle, they should only grant such support in the form of a market premium, namely, granting add-on amounts on top of market-based revenues of RES-E producers. This means that FITs that pay the producers of RES-E the predefined revenues and exempt them from market participation are no longer permissible under EU law. EU law only allows small-scale installations and demonstration projects to be exempted from this principle. See *REDII*, art. 4 (3); Kitzing et al., 2012.

100 In most implementations of FITs, the RES-E producers are exempted from market participation and receive the guaranteed price by delivering the power to an obliged off-taker. The TSO or the DSO is often obliged to offtake the electricity at the guaranteed price, market the electricity, and pass on the cost of the scheme, most commonly to final customers, e.g., via PSO charges added to the electricity bill. This guaranteed price offered to RES-E producers is administratively determined, independently of the market price. Due to the provision of a guarantee for grid connection and revenues, FITs are considered particularly effective in securing sufficient profitability and enabling very low-risk market conditions. This has made it possible for developers to easily obtain bank financing for investments in RES-E, thereby lowering the cost of finance of RES-E and stimulating investment. See *REDII*, recital 17; Meyer, 2003; Haas et al., 2011; Kitzing et al., 2012; Tews, 2015; Kuzemko et al., 2017; Newbery et al., 2018.

electricity storage systems combined with installations generating renewable electricity for self-consumption. These requirements aim to prevent barriers that may be created by stakeholders affected by energy self-consumption and those arising from national legislation and regulations.

187. These requirements play a crucial role in regulating the relationship between renewables self-consumers and traditional stakeholders. Consumers' engagement in renewables self-consumption can lower their dependence on suppliers and public grids. This can lower suppliers' and system operators' revenues. In addition, suppliers' BRPs may face higher imbalance risks due to the increasing difficulty in predicting consumers' behavior after they transition to renewables self-consumers. To counteract these impacts, system operators and suppliers may apply additional charges, procedures or conditions to renewables self-consumers, which could be discriminatory, disproportionate or not cost-reflective. These stakeholders have plenty of chances to impose barriers or unjustified restrictions on renewables self-consumers due to their contractual relationships. Because of the intermittent nature of some renewables, renewables self-consumers are not fully self-sufficient and thus remain dependent on electricity from a supply company for times when not enough electricity is being produced within their premises (EC, 2016; Diestelmeier, 2021, pp 729–730). This also means that they still have a connection to the public grid as a backup (Butenko, 2016). Their contractual relationships with suppliers and system operators enable the latter to influence the cost-benefit ratio of renewables self-consumption. There is thus a need to prohibit discriminatory or disproportionate charges or procedures applied to renewables self-consumption, to avoid discouraging renewables self-consumers.

188. EU law's requirements of proportionate, non-discriminatory and cost-reflective charges or procedures are straightforward on paper. However, ensuring suppliers' and system operators' compliance with them is not an easy task, as pointed out in Sections 2 and 3.4 of Chapter IV.

189. Article 21 of the REDII also stipulates that renewables self-consumers maintain their rights and obligations as final consumers. This means that the whole regulatory framework for empowering and protecting final customers, strengthened by existing electricity market legislation, becomes applicable. It further regulates the self-consumers' relationship with other market actors, especially suppliers, system operators and energy service providers, protecting consumers against unjustified barriers and discriminatory treatment from these market actors when choosing to be renewables self-consumers (Chen and Vandendriessche, 2023a).

190. National legislation and regulations should also align with the above requirements of ensuring proportionate and non-discriminatory procedures, charges and fees for renewables self-consumers. These requirements compel

Member States to evaluate whether existing national laws create legal barriers or unjustified administrative burdens for renewable energy self-consumers. In this respect, Recital 42 of the Electricity Directive views requiring self-consumers selling self-produced RES-E to fulfill the requirements for suppliers as a legal barrier (*Electricity Directive*, recital 42). However, as pointed out in Section 3.2.3 of Chapter IV below, this claim requires verification, as whether subjecting self-consumers to supplier obligations is legitimate is a rather complex legal issue that necessitates thorough proportionality and non-discrimination tests.

### 3.2.2. *Elements of the Enabling Framework*

191. Solely specifying the rights of renewables self-consumers is insufficient to guarantee their implementation. There are both economic and non-economic factors that can influence the exercise of the granted rights by different customer groups. In addition to granting rights, Article 21 of the REDII also lists enablers and barriers that national enabling frameworks must address to promote and facilitate the development of renewables self-consumption.

192. First, the REDII highlights the accessibility of renewables self-consumption to two groups of consumers: tenants and energy poor and vulnerable consumers. The reason for singling out these two customer groups for additional attention lies in the unique challenges confronting them in shifting toward renewables self-consumers. Tenants could have difficulty accessing space for installing RES-E generating installations. Securing their accessibility to self-consumption is notably translated into an obligation for Member States to address incentives for building owners to create opportunities for renewable self-consumption, including for tenants (*REDII*, Article 21(6)(d)). Moreover, energy poor or vulnerable customers can be easily excluded from relevant energy activities due to their inability to make investments in money, time, motivation, and expertise (Karteris and Papadopoulos, 2012; Palm, 2018; Roggenkamp and Diestelmeier, 2020, p 166; Diestelmeier, 2021b). One of the reinforced efforts taken by the CEP to address energy poverty and protect vulnerable customers is 'protection via empowerment' (Roggenkamp and Diestelmeier, 2020, p 176), namely, to stress the involvement of consumers who might otherwise not be able to participate in renewables self-consumption (*REDII*, recital 67). This effort is also reflected in Article 21(6)(a), which obligates Member States to ensure accessibility of renewables self-consumption to all final customers, including those with low-income or vulnerable households.

193. In addition, the difficulty in getting financing is widely detected as one of the economic obstacles for final customers to invest in renewables self-consumption, especially for smaller consumers (Balcombe et al., 2014; Ruggiero et al., 2015; Varho et al., 2016; Mehigan et al., 2018; Palm, 2018;

Su et al., 2018; Rikkonen et al., 2019; Curtin et al., 2019). In setting the minimum requirements for national enabling frameworks, Article 21 of the REDII requires Member States to address unjustified barriers to the financing of projects in the market and measures to facilitate access to finance.

194. Apart from economic factors, many studies have indicated that economic motivations and 'rational' economic behavior may not adequately explain consumer investment decisions (Wüstenhagen and Menichetti, 2012; Masini and Menichetti, 2013; Mehigan et al., 2018; Curtin et al., 2019). A variety of non-economic or regulatory barriers are considered to significantly affect consumers' investments in renewables prosumption (Horbach and Jacob, 2018; Horbach and Rammer, 2018; Palm, 2018). In this respect, various administrative burdens become relevant, which are linked to the permit-granting process, grid connection, and subsidy application (*REDII*, recital 51; Ruggiero et al., 2015; Inês et al., 2020). Such administrative procedures tend to be lengthy, complex, and vary across regions within a Member State and are disproportionate to the size and potential impact of the producers (Ruggiero et al., 2015; Inês et al., 2020; *Electricity Directive*, recital 79). Compared to traditional power producers, medium and small final customers are far less able to deal with lengthy and complex administrative procedures, and their engagement is prone to be affected by the increase in necessary efforts and costs.[101]

195. In recognition of the impact of administrative burdens or institutional complexity on consumer engagement, the CEP strives to avoid unnecessary burdens and delays (*REDII*, recital 51). This effort is first translated into a requirement for the national enabling framework for renewables self-consumption. The above-cited Article 21(6) requires Member States to address unjustified regulatory barriers to renewables self-consumption. The REDII additionally sets out specific measures to streamline permit-granting and grid connection procedures for self-consumers, which were subsequently reinforced by Council Regulation (EU) 2022/2577 and the 2023 Amendment to the REDII. Member States are obligated to set up contact points, which ease permit application by improving information provision, as elaborated in Section 5 of this Chapter below (*REDII*, recital 50 and Article 16).

196. Final customers could also benefit from the requirement for avoiding disproportionately lengthy permit applications, which establishes that, in principle, the permit-granting process must not exceed six months for

[101] Small actors tend to lack sufficient capabilities to deal with a great deal of administrative work, and their market access is more likely to be blocked by institutional complexity. The same reasoning also applies to customers, especially SMEs and households. This is why, in terms of increasing market participation of customers, apart from providing appropriate economic incentives, the EC also considered how to minimize the active efforts required from final customers. See Baldwin et al., 2012, p 214; EC, 2016.

installations with an electrical capacity of less than 150 kW. Member States are allowed to extend the six-month period by up to three months, where duly justified on the grounds of extraordinary circumstances, such as on grounds of overriding safety reasons, where the repowering project has a substantial impact on the grid or the original capacity, size or performance of the installation (*REDII*, Article 16a). In this case, Member States must inform the project developer clearly about the extraordinary circumstances that justify such an extension (*REDII*, Article 16a). Council Regulation (EU) 2022/2577 introduced additional urgent and targeted measures to streamline permitting for small solar systems.[102] Article 4 of the Regulation mandates automatic permit approval for solar energy equipment with a capacity of ≤50 kW, including that used by self-consumers. If the relevant authorities do not respond within one month of receiving the application, the permit is automatically granted, provided that the equipment's capacity does not exceed the current grid connection capacity. If applying the 50 kW threshold would create significant administrative or grid-related challenges, Member States may lower the threshold, provided it remains above 10.8 kW.

197. Additionally, an obligation is imposed on Member States to establish a simple notification procedure for grid connections for renewables self-consumption projects with an electrical capacity of 10,8 kW or less (*REDII*, Article 17(1)).

198. The last minimum requirement for the national enabling framework for renewables self-consumption relates to the sharing of grid use costs. EU law requires Member States to ensure that '*renewables self-consumers contribute in an adequate and balanced way to the overall cost sharing of the system when electricity is fed into the grid*'. Renewables self-consumers could also constitute active customers when they use, store or sell self-produced RES-E and apply rules for active customers set out by the Electricity Directive. As noted above, in terms of network charges, Article 15 of the Electricity Directive imposes an additional requirement. Aside from ensuring their adequate and balanced contribution to the overall cost-sharing of the system, Member States must also ensure that network charges account separately for the electricity fed into the grid and the electricity consumed from the grid. These requirements aim to address some pre-existing issues associated with tariffs applied to prosumers, which have raised concerns and debates regarding the unfair cost sharing of grid use, as detailed below.

---

[102] As a response to the energy price crisis, the aim is to accelerate the permit granting of specific technologies and types of renewables projects (e.g., building-integrated solar installations and rooftop solar energy equipment) which have the highest potential for quick deployment and immediate effect on the objectives of reducing price volatility and lowering the demand for natural gas without constraining the overall energy demand. See Council Regulation (EU) 2022/2577, recitals 5 and 12.

199. There are complicated trade-offs involved in determining the proper contribution of prosumers to the network. Generating electricity for private use could indeed reduce electricity taken from the grid and thus lower grid use, helping to avoid further network expansion. However, this raises additional concerns that prosumers, especially those with storage facilities, could lead to the possibility of grid defection, namely, their reduced use of networks lowers their fixed network cost contributions (Mehigan et al., 2018; Newbery et al., 2018; ACER and CEER, 2021). Fewer paying network charges by these prosumers increase system costs that must be shared by other consumers still connected to the grid, which can, in turn, lead more customers to opt for self-generation (Kantamneni et al., 2016; Mehigan et al., 2018; Peng and Poudineh, 2019). Despite the benefits coming with the increased self-consumption rate, a concern about network development is that it can end up resulting in spiraling network charges and stranded network assets, known as a '*utility death spiral*' (Khalilpour and Vassallo, 2015; Laws et al., 2017; Mehigan et al., 2018). Moreover, the rising uptake of self-generated RES-E does not entirely lower the need for the extension and reinforcement of the existing grid infrastructure.[103] An increase in connections of self-generated RES-E assets, especially those that would require network reinforcements (e.g., due to the electricity fed into the grid), may negatively affect non-prosuming customers if relevant network costs are socialized (Anaya and Pollitt, 2017). These fears point to the emerging tricky task of tariff setting, which needs to ensure not only the fair sharing of system costs between prosumers and non-prosuming consumers but also provide sufficient incentives for DSOs to ensure that they can cope with the potential loss of utility revenues or the new investment in grid infrastructure (Woodman and Baker, 2008; ACER and CEER, 2021).

200. Before the CEP, the reality was that grid tariff setting was prone to swing between two extremes. It either discouraged renewables prosumers or created advantages for them and requires other system users to socialize the grid technical adaptation costs required to integrate decentralized RES-E. This situation arises from the failure to comprehend the complex nature of determining appropriate tariffs for prosumers and fully account for both the benefits and costs associated with their network access. An example of the second extreme is net metering applicable to prosumers, which uses surplus electricity generated to offset metered electricity consumption (Eid et al., 2014; Newbery et al., 2018). Net metering refers to a situation where the meter only measures gross consumption less the amount generated on the premises, usually without distinguishing times and different values for importing and exporting power (Newbery et al., 2018). Existing studies have shown that the increasing number of prosumers combined with net metering results in reduced incomes

103 For the mixed network impact of self-generated RES-E assets, see Section 6 of this Chapter below.

for many network utilities worldwide (Eid et al., 2014; Newbery et al., 2018). This situation pushes network companies to increase charges per kWh in order to recover costs (Eid et al., 2014; Newbery et al., 2018). Non-prosumers must pay higher charges for the electricity they consume to offset the netted costs of prosumers, creating potential cross subsidies between prosumers and non-prosumers (Eid et al., 2014; Newbery et al., 2018). Substantial wealth transfers and consequential inequity issues between these customer groups can be more pronounced in countries with high domestic RES-E penetration and high distribution system costs (Eid et al., 2014; Simshauser, 2016; Newbery et al., 2018).

201. The tariff method needs to be adjusted to address the complex trade-offs involved in facilitating renewables self-consumption. Renewables self-consumers need to bear the costs they impose on the network in a fair and balanced manner (Newbery et al., 2018). In other words, their engagement in self-consumption should not be affected negatively by disproportionate and unjustified network charges, while they should also contribute adequately to the network based on the system cost incurred by their activities (*REDII*, recital 68). This is crucial to ensure that other customer groups will not bear additional costs incurred by the emergence and growth of self-consumers, avoiding cross-subsidization. It is also highly relevant to sufficiently incentivize DSOs to take up challenges that come with the increasing network connection of consumer-owned DG.[104]

202. On these grounds, although the exact tariff setting is left to Member States, on top of Article 18 of the Electricity Regulation, the REDII and the Electricity Directive further elaborate on requirements for ensuring fair, proportionate and cost-reflective network charges in the specific context of facilitating renewables self-consumption. In particular, the Electricity Directive reacts to the problem caused by the net-metering method by obligating Member States to adopt separate accounting of the electricity offtaken from and fed into the grid. Such separate accounting, as explained in Section 5 of this Chapter below, relies on smart meters. However, as will be detailed therein, the requirement of deploying smart meters is not absolute under EU law. A problem arises regarding how to guarantee the implementation of the above separate accounting and fair system cost-sharing without that technical precondition.

---

[104] The increasing share of DG and new loads (e.g., heat pumps and electric vehicles) is connected directly to the distribution grid. The CEP aims to shift the DSOs' role from passively transporting power from transmission networks to final consumers to actively and effectively managing their networks by utilizing DERs. The legislation places particular emphasis on providing incentives for DSOs to enable them to actively manage their networks, including addressing local congestion. See *Electricity Directive*, recital 61, articles 31 and 32; Woodman and Baker, 2008; CEER, 2020. See Section 6 of this Chapter for more details of the transition of the DSO.

## 3.3. ENERGY COMMUNITIES

203. Empowering final customers to participate in energy communities is another key approach of the CEP to boost customers' participation in renewables self-consumption and DR, known as 'community-based solutions'. The EU legislation advances the development of energy communities, notably given its advantages in engaging certain groups of customers, who otherwise might not have been willing or able to do so, and broadening options for customers to engage in flexibility provision and RES-E use (*Electricity Directive*, recital 43; Inês et al., 2020; Roggenkamp and Diestelmeier, 2020, p 166). This is of particular significance to create a path for energy poor or vulnerable consumers to engage in these activities. In what follows, Section 3.3.1 explains the legislative background of facilitating the development of energy communities. It mainly covers (i) the role of the community-based approach in mitigating economic and behavioral barriers for final customers to actively provide demand flexibility and conduct RES-E prosumption, and (ii) key legal issues to be addressed when promoting energy communities' development. Section 3.3.2 then looks at the specific empowerment and enabling frameworks for two energy communities recognized by EU law. This is followed by Section 3.3.3, which examines how EU law entitles consumers to participate in these two entities.

### *3.3.1. Community-Based Solutions*

204. Energy communities provide additional boosts for consumers utilizing their particular membership structure and composition. With membership in energy communities, consumers could avoid fully investing in expertise, technologies and financial resources but engage in and benefit nevertheless from DR and renewables self-consumption by having a stake in producing, consuming and sharing energy.[105] This helps to lower the capital and cognitive resources required to devote to these energy activities, mitigating economic and behavioral obstacles mentioned in Chapter II.

205. Final customers involved in energy communities could participate in DR and renewables use (including self-consumption) in a more cost-efficient way than individual investments, which is especially conducive to small, vulnerable and energy poor customers. This is because energy communities allow the participation of both private and public actors (Creamer et al., 2018), including not only various customer groups but also local authorities

---

105 The benefit of sharing energy is tangible even for those who, for lack of space or economic issues, cannot install privately owned PV systems. See Di Silvestre et al., 2021; *Electricity Directive*, recital 43.

and municipalities (*REDII*, recital 70 and Article 2 (16)(b)). The involvement of multiple investors could help to share investment risks and lower upfront investment costs (Jager et al., 2008). Moreover, participating public agencies may offer loan guarantees, which can also contribute to lowering the financing cost of renewables production and flexibility assets.[106] Further, energy communities could stimulate a transition toward sustainable electricity consumption patterns by harnessing the 'peer effects'. As mentioned in Chapter II, empirical evidence highlights that peer effects – the social influence of peers, such as colleagues, neighbors or friends – constitute an important factor for households to invest in decentralized RES-E (Bollinger and Gillingham, 2012; Müller and Rode, 2013b; Graziano and Gillingham, 2014; Palm, 2017; Mehigan et al., 2018). Energy communities have a proactive role in expanding the participation of local households due to their advantages in harnessing such peer effects and engaging entrusted actors, such as neighbors (Kalkbrenner and Roosen, 2016; *REDII*, recital 70; Parrish et al., 2020).

206. Apart from engaging consumers, the energy community approach exhibits some added values, including inter alia improving local acceptance of decentralized RES-E (*REDII*, recital 70). In recent decades, there has been increasing local opposition against new energy projects because of environmental concerns and the 'Not-in-My-Backyard' motives ('NIMBY').[107] Developing decentralized RES-E projects based on solar and wind can particularly face additional local resistance as they require supportive infrastructure, such as additional power lines, storage technologies or backup generation (Friedl and Reichl, 2016; Azarova et al., 2019). A vast number of studies show that local ownership of DG and active citizen participation in all stages of developing decentralized RES-E could help counteract this problem (Schively, 2007; Wolsink, 2007; Schmid et al., 2016; Gamel et al., 2016; Kuzemko et al., 2017). In this regard, energy communities serve as a promising solution.[108]

---

106 Governments can offer loan guarantees for certain projects. In that case, the government guarantees debt repayment to the lending bank, thereby reducing risk and, consequently, the interest rate (e.g., 1 to 2%), the debt term, and the debt service conditions of the loan. See Jager et al., 2008.

107 'Not-in-My-Backyard' refers to a phenomenon whereby the public perceives infrastructure projects as necessary but opposes them in their own neighborhoods. See Meyer, 2003; Schively, 2007; Wolsink, 2007; Azarova et al., 2019; Raineau, 2022.

108 In Germany, for example, over the past decades, energy community projects have been increasingly based on wind and solar energy, reaching 25% of total community-owned wind energy capacity in 2012 and 50% of community-owned photovoltaic production in 2014. In the Netherlands, 74.5 MW of solar energy and 159 MW of wind energy were owned by 484 RECs distributed in the country in 2018. See Cohen et al., 2016; Azarova et al., 2019; Di Silvestre et al., 2021.

207. Before the CEP, energy communities already emerged within the EU, while diverse community initiatives were fragmented amid scattered legal provisions (Capellán-Pérez et al., 2018; Diestelmeier, 2021b). Moreover, electricity markets had not been fully open to them, but were still *de facto* controlled by traditional electrical companies, making the operation of these novel entities difficult (Huybrechts, 2013, p 113; Capellán-Pérez et al., 2018). To build up a shared understanding of energy communities and enhance their potential role in engaging final customers in flexibility provision and renewables use, the CEP recognizes two categories of energy communities and provides them with a catalogue of rights and obligations (*Electricity Directive*, recital 43; Inês et al., 2020).

208. Realizing the various benefits of energy communities mentioned above requires a specific governance framework because they constitute an entity with a new membership structure, governance requirements and purposes (*Electricity Directive*, recital 46). Notably, several relationships, both within and outside the energy communities, need to be expressly structured. The aim is to ensure that consumers genuinely benefit from the energy activities of such entities, while the entities' composition is conducive to improving their economic viability. Figure 7 depicts the core relationships that must be considered by legal frameworks that empower energy communities and participating consumers.

**Figure 7. Key relationships to be structured when empowering energy communities**

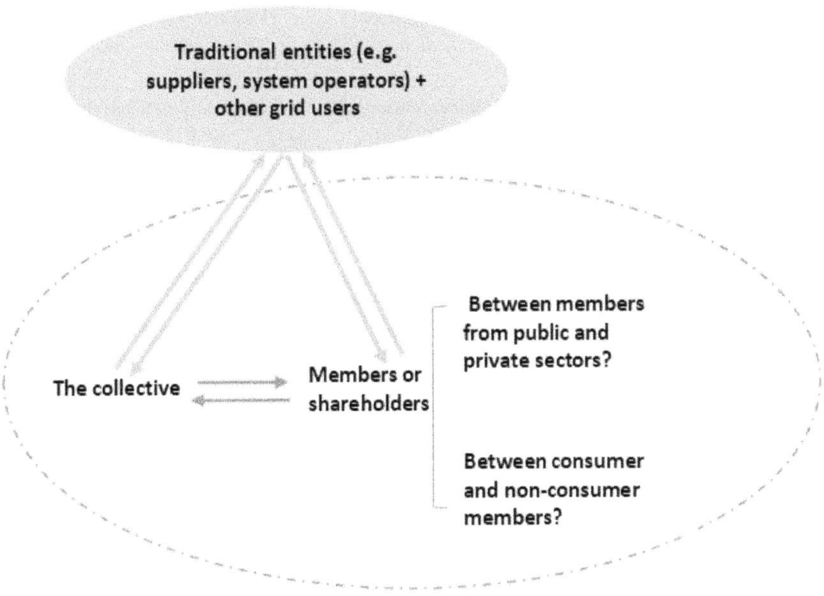


Source: Author's elaboration.

209. In accordance with the Electricity Directive, although CECs are allowed to carry out broader activities than RECs and are not restricted to a specific location, they are also envisaged to involve various consumers in DR and RES-E self-consumption (*Electricity Directive*, recital 43 and Article 2(11)).[109] As such, both CECs and RECs could provide a community-based approach to engaging wider final customers in facilitating RES-E uptake. The respective frameworks for CECs and RECs share some common elements (E Caramizaru and Uihlein, 2020), as Table 5 shows. For the purposes of this book, the following subsection focuses on the framework for RECs. The legal arrangements for CECs are discussed when it comes to the possibility of managing the community's distribution grid and the energy community's relationship with participating consumers.

**Table 5. Comparisons between the two Union-level frameworks for RECs and CECs**

| | RECs (according to the REDII) | CECs (according to the Electricity Directive) |
|---|---|---|
| Energy self-consumption | Article 22(2)(a) '***Member States shall ensure that RECs are entitled*** *to produce, consume, store and sell renewable energy*' | Article 16(3) '***Member States shall ensure that CECs*** (d) *with regard to consumption of self-generated electricity, CECs are treated like active customers*' |
| Energy sharing within energy communities | Article 22(2)(b) '***Member States shall ensure that RECs are entitled to*** *share, within the renewable energy community, renewable energy that is produced by the production units owned by that REC*' | Article 16(3) '***Member States shall ensure that CECs (e) are entitled to*** *arrange within the CEC the sharing of electricity that is produced by the production units owned by the community*' |
| Market access | Article 22(2)(c) '***Member States shall ensure that RECs are entitled to*** *access all suitable energy markets both directly or through aggregation in a non-discriminatory manner*' | Article 16(3) '***Member States shall ensure that CECs: (a) are able to*** *access all electricity markets, either directly or through aggregation, in a non-discriminatory manner*' |
| Distribution system operation | Article 22(4) ***the national enabling framework for facilitating the development of RECs*** shall ensure '(e) *RECs are not subject to discriminatory treatment with regard to their activities, rights and obligations as final customers, producers, suppliers,* ***DSOs****, or as other market participants*' | Article 16(2) '***Member States may provide in the enabling regulatory framework*** *that CECs: b) are entitled to own, establish, purchase or lease distribution networks and to autonomously manage them subject to conditions set out in paragraph 4 of this Article*' |

Source: Author's elaboration.

[109] For different definitions of CECs and RECs, see Section 1.2 of Chapter I.

### 3.3.2. *Empowering RECs and Facilitating their Development*

210. Like empowering renewables self-consumers, the REDII requires Member States to not only grant a range of rights to RECs but also create a national enabling framework to promote and facilitate their development. Their rights, obligations and enabling frameworks are analyzed consecutively next.

#### 3.3.2.1. Rights and Obligations

211. Firstly, RECs are entitled or allowed to carry out several energy activities. Similar to renewables self-consumers, RECs have a set of rights around renewables self-consumption, ranging from producing, consuming, to selling self-generated electricity via renewables PPA and electricity markets (*REDII*, article 22(2)(a)(c)). In addition, RECs are entitled to share self-produced RES-E within the entities.[110] Moreover, unlike renewables self-consumers, EU law does not specify that the activities of RECs cannot constitute a primary commercial or professional activity (Inês et al., 2020).[111] By contrast, the REDII allows them to offer commercial energy services, such as supplying energy or providing aggregation (*REDII*, Article 22(4)(b)). However, RECs are subject to an eligibility requirement regarding their primary purposes, which must be providing environmental, economic or social community benefits for its shareholders or members or for the local areas where it operates, rather than financial profits (*REDII*, Article 2(16)(c)) and must respect provisions applicable to relevant commercial activities (*REDII*, Articles 2(16)(c) and 22(4)(b)).

212. In fact, EU law does not confer rights to support other energy activities that energy communities may potentially carry out, such as aggregation and supply. It is essential to distinguish between activities that EU law expressly entitles energy communities to carry out and those that are merely permitted under EU law but left to the discretion of Member States in deciding whether to grant the relevant rights. Table 5 above also gives the wording used by EU law for different energy activities in which RECs and CECs can engage. As it indicates, energy activities of self-consumption, energy sharing, and market access are rights granted by EU law and must be secured by Member States. By contrast, under Article 16(2) of the Electricity Directive, it is left to Member States to decide whether CECs can operate distribution networks. The REDII does not

---

110 This right to energy sharing has been expanded to individual active customers by the 2024 Amendment to the Electricity Directive. As explained in the Introduction, the 2024 Amendments to the Electricity Directive and the Electricity Regulation entered into force after the data collection period of this book. They are not the primary focus here.

111 Yet, the requirement of self-consumption activities not constituting does not constitute the primary commercial or professional activity applies to the participation of private undertakings in RECs, as set out above.

explicitly allow RECs to do so, but merely stresses non-discriminatory treatment with regard to their activities, rights, and obligations as DSOs.[112] Despite a broad leeway given to Member States, EU law still establishes several principles applicable when Member States allow CECs to own or manage distribution networks, which merit further examination.

213. Indeed, in addition to cooperating with the DSO (*REDII*, Article 22(4)(c); *Electricity Directive*, Article 16(1)(d)), operating its own distribution grid is also conducive to implementing physical energy sharing[113] or energy transfers within the energy communities.[114] However, when doing so, such entities may constitute VIUs, thereby raising concerns about discrimination. Before the adoption of the CEP, in Germany, for instance, some energy cooperatives had already become 'local integrated utilities' that were both the owners of the local network and responsible for electricity supply (Eid et al., 2016). This can affect consumer choices of retailers as well as retail competition (Jones and Kettlewell, 2021, p 217). Switching suppliers contradicts the interests of such communities, and so they have strong incentives to discriminate against other suppliers in terms of network access (Jones and Kettlewell, 2021, p 217). To exclude discriminatory conduct, Article 16(4) of the Electricity Directive stipulates that when Member States decide to allow CECs to manage distribution networks in their area of operation, Chapter IV and other rules applied to DSOs must be respected (*Electricity Directive*, Articles 16(2) and (4)). This requirement implies that once a CEC is granted the status of a DSO, it should be treated

---

112 In its original legislative proposal, the EC suggested providing CECs with the right to set up, own, and operate local power networks, called 'community networks'. However, this proposal was met with strong pushback from Member States, such as France, where distribution is still under monopoly control. See Roberts, 2020.

113 EU law does not clearly define electricity or energy sharing. Recital 46 of the Electricity Directive states that '*energy sharing enables members or shareholders to be supplied with electricity from generating installations within the community without being in direct physical proximity to the generating installation and without being behind a single metering point.*' Energy sharing within the REC potentially enables a high level of energy self-sufficiency for participating consumers. An example is a community based on PV modules in Austria, where the distribution of the energy produced occurs according to a dynamic model, through which instantaneous production is conveyed to users who need it at that moment. See *REDII*, Article 22 (2)(b); *Electricity Directive*, recital 46; Battisti, 2019; Di Silvestre et al., 2021.

114 Before the adoption of the CEP, within the EU, it was found that energy communities were more likely to distribute electricity in those countries where the electric network is publicly owned and privately operated after a public tender. For example, by 2015, energy communities had acquired management of 90 local distribution networks across Germany, alongside a wave of re-municipalization of energy networks and supply. In Austria, allowing the community to co-own the distribution grid is one of the actions that eases the operation of energy communities and the sharing of electricity within the community. With an amendment to the national energy law in 2017, the electricity grids in condominiums were defined as the property of the users, opening up the possibility to produce PV electricity and then distribute it to the users of the condominium itself. See Wagner and Berlo, 2015, p 559; Capellán-Pérez et al., 2018; Julian, 2021; Di Silvestre et al., 2021; Haji Bashi et al., 2023.

as, and be subject to the same obligations as, a DSO (*Electricity Directive*, recital 47). These obligations mainly include non-discriminatory third-party access, legal unbundling and flexibility procurement. CECs are also bound by the same surveillance by NRAs as other DSOs (Jones and Kettlewell, 2021, p 245).[115] In this case, electricity sharing within CECs can still benefit from the distribution grid infrastructure owned, established, leased and managed by the energy communities, provided that distribution system operation activities remain independent from other activities in terms of legal form, organization and decision-making (*Electricity Directive*, Article 35(1)). Based on Member States' decisions, CECs can also be exempted from obligations stemming from legal unbundling if they constitute a certain type of small DSOs provided in Article 35(4) of the Electricity Directive.

214. To mitigate discrimination concerns that cannot be fully addressed by legal unbundling (Buchmann, 2020) and may arise from the possibility of exempting CECs from legal unbundling, Article 16 (4) sets out another principle. That is, Member States must ensure that customers who remain connected to the distribution system will not be discriminated or harmed. Given the risk that energy communities may discriminate against participating consumers who switch suppliers, both the REDII and the Electricity Directive provide that those customers maintain their rights or obligations as final customers (*REDII*, Article 22(1); *Electricity Directive*, Article 16(1)(c)). In this case, legal provisions dedicated to securing consumers' rights to contract with a supplier of their choice and to switch suppliers become applicable to consumers who participate in energy communities.

215. Overall, paragraphs 2 and 4 of Article 16 of the Electricity Directive reflect the efforts to strike a balance between the CEC's rights and obligations. While paragraph 2 reduces the legal uncertainty of allowing CECs to operate physical grid infrastructure, paragraph 4 seeks to mitigate potential discrimination concerns and avoid granting CECs extra advantages in terms of grid operation over other market participants.

216. When Member States decide to grant CECs the right to manage distribution networks, the last principle set out by EU law aims to address the relationship between the community's grid and the distribution and transmission grids. CECs in this case are entitled to conclude an agreement on the operation of their network with the relevant DSO or TSO to which their network is connected (*Electricity Directive*, Article 16(4)(a)).

217. As already noted, the REDII does not explicitly address whether Member States are allowed to entitle RECs to operate distribution networks

---

115 For the definition of legal unbundling and distinction with ownership unbundling, see Section 6 of this Chapter further below.

but highlights RECs are not subject to discriminatory treatment '*with regard to their activities, rights and obligations as DSOs*'. This implies that when RECs act as DSOs, they must comply equally with obligations applicable to DSOs, while also being subject to exemptions provided for certain types of small DSOs. Similar to CECs, RECs are not granted any extra advantages that allow them to bypass obligations imposed on DSOs.

### 3.3.2.2. Elements of the Enabling Framework

218. Energy communities may face various barriers to performing activities relating to renewables self-consumption and flexibility. Such barriers may arise from the regulatory regime and stakeholders affected by energy community activities, and also relate to the characteristics of energy communities. To enable energy communities to perform the activities necessary to fulfill their role in widely engaging consumers, these barriers must be addressed. This task is largely left to Member States to accomplish via national enabling frameworks, while the REDII merely sets out minimum requirements.

219. Under Article 22 of REDII, disproportionate and unfair procedures, including registration and licensing procedures, and discriminatory treatment are prohibited. This requirement implies the removal or prevention of discriminatory conditions contained in national law. Moreover, it also acts as a principle dealing with the relationship between the REC and traditional electricity undertakings affected by community activities, such as suppliers and the DSO. The REC's relationship with the DSO is additionally subject to another element of the national enabling framework: the relevant DSO cooperates with RECs to facilitate energy transfers within the entities.

220. Similar to renewables self-consumers, Member States must ensure RECs are also subject to fair and cost-reflective network charges (*REDII*, Article 22(4)(d)). This requirement aims to deal with the relationship between energy communities and other grid users to prevent cross-subsidization, as discussed in the previous subsection. The fair allocation of network use costs is also applicable to the case of sharing self-generated RES-E within a CEC (*Electricity Directive*, recital 46 and Article 16(2)(e)).

221. In addition, the specificities of RECs in terms of size, ownership structure and the number of projects may affect their capacity to perform energy activities and compete on an equal footing with energy undertakings (*REDII*, recital 71). As elaborated later, the eligibility criteria for RECs impose several limitations on the participation of energy undertakings. Despite some benefits, they also limit access by RECs to expertise or financing from energy professionals (Roberts, 2020). RECs are likely plagued with a lack of capacity to deal with regulatory requirements and organizational and technical aspects

of operating communities and participating in electricity markets (*REDII*, recital 71; Watson et al., 2020; Hoicka et al., 2021). Interestingly, the EU's approach to addressing RECs' capacity issues does not require Member States to directly offer capacity-building support to the energy communities. Instead, it requires such support to be made available to public authorities in enabling and setting up RECs, and in helping authorities to participate directly (*REDII*, Article 22(4)(h)). To address the obstacles to financing, Member States are required to make available tools to facilitate RECs' access to finance (*REDII*, Article 22(4)(g)).

222. The remaining elements of the national enabling framework specifically support consumers' rights to participate in the REC, which will be detailed in the following subsection.

### *3.3.3. Entitling Consumers to Participate in Energy Communities*

223. Apart from addressing the rights and obligations of energy communities, another key task of the EU's legal framework for energy communities is granting final customers the right to participate in these entities (*REDII*, Article 22(1)). The energy community's promising role in widely engaging consumers cannot be realized without clearly structuring several relationships between (i) participating consumers and the energy community, (ii) different categories of members, as well as (iii) participating consumers and actors outside the energy community, as indicated in Figure 7 above. Definitions of RECs and RECs govern the first two relations. They contain criteria for qualifying as these two energy communities, regarding the energy communities' primary purpose, membership, and decision-making (in short, 'eligibility criteria' hereunder). They are analyzed in Section 3.3.3.1. Rules governing interactions between consumers participating in energy communities and other actors potentially affected by such participation are the subject of Section 3.3.3.2.

#### 3.3.3.1. Governing Relationships within Energy Communities

224. In terms of governing relationships within the energy community, two dimensions are crucial. One is a process dimension, which determines who is involved and who exercises influence, and the other is an outcome dimension, which determines how outcomes of a community initiative are spatially and socially distributed, essentially organizing who benefits in economic and social terms (Walker and Devine-Wright, 2008; Hicks and Ison, 2018; Diestelmeier, 2021b; Hoicka et al., 2021).

225. Several eligibility criteria listed in the definitions of CECs and RECs address these two dimensions. Serving as the conditions for determining whether an entity constitutes a CEC or a REC that has a range of rights under

EU law, these criteria play a key role in ensuring that consumers can benefit from participation in energy communities. Based on them, the rights of participating consumers with respect to membership and decision-making can be better materialized by Member States. Some of these criteria are further underpinned by Article 22 of the REDII, which lists minimum elements of the national enabling framework. The eligibility criteria that pertain to energy communities' relationships with their members are detailed as follows. As elaborated in Section 3.1.3 of Chapter IV below, implementing these general requirements entails many legal issues or challenges.

(i) Primary Purposes

226. EU law sets out identical requirements regarding the primary purpose of CECs and RECs. A legal entity constituting a CEC or a REC must have the primary purpose of providing environmental, economic or social community benefits to its members or shareholders or to the local areas where it operates rather than to generate financial profits (*REDII*, Article 2(16); *Electricity Directive*, Article 2(11)). Four elements can be distilled from this eligibility condition. First, the provision of 'community benefits' must be the primary purpose. Second, such community benefits could be provided for either the energy community's members or shareholders, or to the local areas where it operates. Third, such community benefits include environmental, economic or social dimensions. Fourth, EU law merely emphasizes that pursuing financial profits should not be the primary purpose, rather than prohibiting energy communities from seeking profits. As highlighted in Section 3.1 of the next Chapter, allowing profit-seeking is crucial for incentivizing energy communities and maintaining their economic viability, particularly in attracting investment from commercial actors.

(ii) Membership

227. Both CECs and RECs are based on voluntary participation (*REDII*, Article 2(16)(a)). There typically exists an asymmetry of power between the collective and the individual participant. This asymmetry makes it possible for the collective to impose disproportionate restrictions on participants' freedom to join or leave, which can easily compromise the individual participant's interests. Clarifying voluntary participation is thus important to properly structure the energy communities' relationships with consumers. The legal framework for CECs further clarifies that members or shareholders of a CEC have the right to exit from the community, and in this case, the legal provisions on the right to switch suppliers and switching-related fees apply (*Electricity Directive*, Article 16(1)(b)).

228. The Electricity Directive does not limit membership of CECs. The CEC is open to all actors, although there are restrictions on members entitled to exercise effective control, as will be explained later. Under the REDII, the first restriction is that membership in RECs is open to natural persons, SMEs or local authorities, including municipalities (*REDII*, Article 2(16)(b)). In addition, Article 22 imposes a limitation on the entitlement to be members of RECs. That is, private undertakings are only allowed to be members when their participation does not constitute their primary commercial or professional activity (*REDII*, Article 22(1)). This limitation aims to address a fear that, by being a member of energy communities, private undertakings might abuse the REC to serve their own interests. It also helps to mitigate the risk that electricity undertakings somehow find a legal loophole that enables them to benefit from the rights accorded to RECs to bypass unbundling requirements (Pearson, 2020, p 116). Furthermore, RECs promise to deliver a bottom-up or decentralized approach to the energy transition, which represents a shift from an energy system dominated by large, centralized production companies and system operators toward decentral, local initiatives that involve different stakeholders from both the public and the private sector (Kunze and Becker, 2015; Capellán-Pérez et al., 2018; Gui and MacGill, 2018; Diestelmeier, 2021b). The exclusion of private companies whose participation constitutes primary commercial or professional energy activity, therefore, avoids a reconcentration of political power and wealth in the hands of a small number of energy companies (Hoicka et al., 2021). This arrangement helps ensure the role of energy communities in engaging consumers. Moreover, Article 22 places a particular emphasis on the accessibility to all final customers, in particular household customers, including low-income or vulnerable households (*REDII*, Article 22(1) and (4)(f)).

### (iii) Decision-Making

229. An entity wishing to be a CEC or a REC must also satisfy requirements regarding decision-making mechanisms. These requirements primarily aim to prevent the risk that energy incumbents or large companies predominate in the energy community's decision-making, while other members, notably consumers from the residential and SME sectors, are marginalized and underrepresented. Among others, they take into account power asymmetry (arising from capital resources, information and expertise) between potential participants from different sectors and seek to avoid its impacts on due process[116] and distributional justice within an energy community.

---

[116] The principle of due process suggests that all those affected by energy projects must be involved in all stages of decision-making about those projects, from agenda setting and design through

230. The RECs' decision-making is subject to more restrictions than CECs. The only requirement for the CEC's decision-making is that it is effectively controlled by certain groups of members or shareholders, which are natural persons, local authorities, including municipalities, or small enterprises. As noted above, the CEC is open to all actors to enter, while medium or large enterprises are not eligible for membership that confers effective control (*Electricity Directive*, recital 44). Different from the CEC, the REC must be '*effectively controlled by shareholders or members that are located in the proximity of the renewable energy projects that are owned and developed by that legal entity*' (*REDII*, Article 2(16)(a)). In conjunction with restrictions on the membership of the REC, it can be established that actors entitled to effective control cover *natural persons, SMEs (excluding private SMEs whose participation constitutes their primary commercial or professional activity) or local authorities, including municipalities*. The REC's effective control criterion is additionally based on the proximity condition. Only members or shareholders located adjacent to the renewables projects owned and developed by the REC can exercise effective control.[117] This criterion is not explicitly defined in EU law, but is left to Member States to determine (Roberts, 2020).

231. To safeguard democratic and impartial decision-making, another condition for constituting RECs is autonomy (*REDII*, Article 2(16)(a)). The aim is to shield the collective interest of the members from being compromised due to the investment or decision-making by one or a small group of individual members, or outside business partners (E Caramizaru and Uihlein, 2020; Roberts, 2020). This condition is of significance not only for the decision-making process but also for the outcome dimension related to the distribution of community benefits. Due to uneven capital resources, information, and expertise held by different members, power asymmetry can exist between members from the public and private sectors, as well as between different customer groups participating in energy communities. This asymmetry can lead to both procedural and substantive concerns. Participating consumers with comparatively unfavorable conditions can be vulnerable to a decision-making process lacking inclusiveness, where more organized shareholders could be 'representatives' dominating the decision-making process (Popelier, 2011). Not only is this a form of injustice in itself, but it also has a direct influence

to implementation and use, and give fair and informed consent for involvement throughout. See Sovacool and Dworkin, 2015.

117 The EC has indicated that it is for Member States to define effective control, consistent with their existing statutes on corporate governance (i.e., company law) or tax law. This suggests that effective control will 'vary between each Member State, ranging between, for example, a standard that requires majority control of the board or 51 percent of shares or voting power in the decision-making body of the energy community, to a standard that allows only a blocking minority.' See Roberts, 2020.

on distributional justice (Calver and Simcock, 2021b). Unfair distribution of community benefits can especially compromise the interests of smaller-sized or energy poor or vulnerable consumers participating in energy communities. The unfair process and outcomes stemming from such power asymmetry could eventually undermine the community-based approach's potential to widely engage final customers.

232. In addition, in laying down minimum requirements for the national enabling framework for developing RECs, Article 22(4)(i) requires Member States to '*secure the equal and non-discriminatory treatment of consumers that participate in RECs*'. Apart from preventing traditional actors (e.g., suppliers or system operators) from discriminating against consumers participating in RECs, this requirement can also underpin the autonomy criterion or due process. That is, it also implies that different members or consumer groups within energy communities must not be subject to unfair treatment in both the process dimension (i.e., participation and decision-making) and the outcome dimension (e.g., distribution of community benefits).

#### 3.3.3.2. Preventing Barriers from Other Stakeholders

233. Aside from governing interactions within energy communities, enabling consumers to exercise the right to participate in CECs and RECs smoothly also hinges upon clearly structuring their relationship with other stakeholders. There are two general requirements governing their relationships. First, Member States must ensure that consumers are not subject to unjustified or discriminatory conditions or procedures that would prevent their participation in a REC (*REDII*, Article 22(1)). Similar to the case of renewables self-consumers, this aims to shield consumers from barriers created by traditional actors who are affected by the consumers' decisions to rely on the REC to meet their energy demand. Second, members or shareholders of CECs and RECs maintain their rights and obligations as final customers (*REDII*, Article 22(1); *Electricity Directive*, Article 16(1)(c)). It implies that after customers participate in CECs or RECs, their suppliers, energy service providers and system operators are still bound by obligations that correspond to the final customers' rights relating to supply and energy service contracts as well as network connection.

## 3.4. GENERAL OBLIGATIONS ON GRID CONNECTION

234. Along with consumers increasingly offering flexibility services to the TSO, the Demand Connection Code establishes minimum technical design and operational requirements for grid connection for demand facilities (including

offering DR and RES-E).[118] They constitute an integral part of the framework empowering consumers for several reasons. First, they create obligations to ensure grid security and the stability of offered system services, which are key to ensuring that consumers, IFSPs and energy communities can properly exercise the right to access the grid and offer flexibility services to the TSO. Second, aside from rights, obligations also shape the costs and benefits of participating in DR and renewables self-consumption. Clear and proportionate obligations help improve economic viability and mitigate legal uncertainties, which have long been considered key challenges for consumers' involvement in electricity DSM, as already noted. Third, by harmonizing common requirements for connecting to the transmission system upon which competitive segments rely (Joskow, 2008), the entitlement of consumers and other parties cooperating with them to a level playing field can be further secured (*Demand Connection Code*, Article 1(2)).

235. At the Union level, connection to distribution networks has not been harmonized, and the connection requirements contained in the Demand Connection Code apply to entities involved in electricity DSM activities connected to transmission networks (*Demand Connection Code*, recital 8 and Article 34), such as large industrial users, IFSPs and CECs. Four categories of facilities are subject to the Demand Connection Code: (i) transmission-connected demand facilities, (ii) transmission-connected distribution facilities, (iii) distribution systems, including closed distribution systems, and (iv) demand units used by a demand facility or a closed distribution system to provide DR services to TSOs (*Demand Connection Code*, Article 1(1)). The connection

---

118 The distinction between network access and connection is noteworthy. In 2008, the CJEU's ruling in the case of *Sabatauskas* emphasized that Union law on the internal electricity market distinguishes between the terms 'access' and 'connection'. The term 'access' is linked to the supply of electricity, including inter alia the quality, regularity and cost of the service, and is often used in the context of guaranteeing non-discriminatory tariffs and ensuring a level playing field for market actors to access the electricity system to trade electricity. In contrast, the term 'connection' is used, particularly in a technical context, and refers to a physical connection to the system. Thus, the Court concluded that 'access' to the system includes the right to use electricity systems in general, while 'connection' corresponds to physical connection to the system. Regulated third-party access concerns obligations imposed on Member States only in respect of access to the system, not in respect of connections thereto. Subsequently, the 2009 Electricity Directive required Member States to ensure that objective and non-discriminatory technical rules are developed to establish minimum technical design and operational requirements for the connection to the system. Hence, there were no specific Union-level rules on connection to the transmission system until the adoption of the Demand Connection Code in 2016. The EC adopted this network code to establish a common understanding of the requirements for grid connection applicable to demand facilities and distribution systems connected to transmission systems in order to facilitate Union-wide trade and allow for the provision of system services in the context of facilitating system integration of RES-E. See (*2009 Electricity Directive*, Article 37 (6); *Judgment of the Court of 9 October 2008, Sabatauskas and Others, C-239/07*, 2008; *Demand Connection Code*, recitals 1 and 2; Gräper et al., 2021, p 102.

rules for all four categories are relevant in the context of developing DR and renewables prosuming, especially considering that CECs are allowed to operate the distribution system.

236. The technical requirements are largely straightforward and relate to the grid system's technical parameters and do not merit being reproduced here in full. Nevertheless, several warrant mention on a thematic basis. Connection requirements set out for demand facilities and demand units are taken as examples.[119]

237. Firstly, entities involved in DSM activities are bound by some general obligations with respect to ensuring system security:

- Demand facilities should comply with technical parameters such as frequency, voltage, short-circuit and reactive power defined for demand facilities (*Demand Connection Code*, Articles 12, 13, 14 and 15, Annexes I and II). For instance, transmission-connected demand facilities must be capable of remaining connected to the network and operating at the frequency ranges, voltage ranges, and periods specified in Annex I and Annex II, respectively.
- Avoid grid connections that endanger system security. Relevant requirements inter alia include: (i) connection to the network does not result in a determined level of distortion or fluctuation of the supply voltage on the network, at the connection point (*Demand Connection Code*, Article 20); (ii) the level of distortion should not exceed that allocated to them by the relevant TSO (*Demand Connection Code*, Article 20); (iii) respect the priority ranking with respect to protection and control determined under this network regulation.[120]

238. Additionally, there are specific technical requirements in place to ensure the reliability of DR services. Two sets of rules are respectively set for remotely controlled DR and autonomously controlled DR under the Demand

119 'Transmission-connected demand facility' means a demand facility that has a connection point to a transmission system. 'Demand unit' means an indivisible set of installations containing equipment that can be actively controlled by a demand facility owner or by a CDSO, either individually or commonly as part of demand aggregation through a third party. See Demand Connection Code, Article 2 (2)(4).

120 Transmission network protection is prioritized, which is followed by transmission-connected demand facility protection, and then operational controls, including frequency control and power restriction. As regards electrical protection of the transmission-connected demand facility, the transmission-connected demand facility owner and the relevant TSO are obliged to agree on relevant protection schemes and settings. An agreement should also be achieved to determine the schemes and settings of the different control devices of the transmission-connected demand facility. See Demand Connection Code, articles 16 (1)(2) and 17 (1)(4).

Connection Code (*Demand Connection Code*, Article 27(1)). In the case of providing autonomously controlled DR, the requirements mainly relate to various technical parameters of frequency control (*Demand Connection Code*, Article 29). For remotely controlled DR, relevant requirements reflect obligations for demand units stemming from the contract between the DR provider and the TSO. The obligations cover, for instance, being capable of controlling power consumption from the network in a range equal to the range contracted, adjusting its power consumption within a period specified by the relevant TSO and full execution of an instruction issued by the relevant TSO to modify its power consumption to the limits of the electrical protection safeguards (*Demand Connection Code*, Article 28(2)).

239. Actors providing DR have a range of obligations to notify the TSO and exchange information. Transmission-connected demand facilities should be equipped according to the standards specified by the relevant TSO to exchange information between the relevant TSO and the demand facility, with the specified time stamping (*Demand Connection Code*, Article 18(1)). In providing remotely controlled DR services, demand units should be equipped to receive instructions, directly or indirectly through a third party, from the TSO to modify their demand and to transfer the necessary information (*Demand Connection Code*, Article 28(2)(e)). These obligations aim to ensure the reliability and safety of DR services while enhancing the visibility and monitoring of the TSO on the capabilities of relevant DR facilities.

240. To ensure compliance with these technical requirements, DR providers are also required to carry out compliance testing for information exchange and for the capability of providing system services (*Demand Connection Code*, Articles 36, 40 and 41). Furthermore, given the need to provide regulatory certainty, in principle, the requirements of the Demand Connection Code only apply to new facilities (*Demand Connection Code*, recital 7). For existing facilities, relevant requirements only apply where Member States decide otherwise based on the evolution of system requirements and a full cost-benefit analysis, or a substantial modernization or replacement of equipment impacts their technical capabilities, for instance (*Demand Connection Code*, Article 4).

## 4. ENABLING MARKET-BASED INCENTIVES

241. As set out in Chapter II above, one of the widely recognized barriers to motivating consumers to support the use of RES-E and facilitate its system integration is the lack of economic incentives. When engaging in DR and renewables self-consumption, consumers might find that expected benefits are financially unattractive, especially compared to required input, including

investment costs, time, and active efforts. Member States commonly use state aid or support schemes to stimulate consumers' engagement in DR and the purchase, use and self-generation of RES-E. Typical incentives include financial support (e.g., subsidies, loans and grants), exemption from or reduction of tax, charges or tariffs, and granting advantages in network access or dispatch (EC, 2014a; Newbery et al., 2018). Existing EU law, in comparison, puts weight on a market-based approach to providing incentives. The role of a well-functioning internal electricity market is highlighted to adequately reward consumers and other entities involved in DR and renewables self-consumption (*Electricity Directive*, recital 9; *Electricity Regulation*, Article 1(a)). The adaptations introduced by the CEP to that end also reflect its newly built legal objective: creating a consumer-centred electricity market (*Electricity Directive*, Article 3). This ambitious goal, among others, implies that the internal market framework should fully take into account the characteristics of final customers so that their market participation can be eased and facilitated (*Electricity Directive*, recitals 4, 5 and 37).

242. Market-based incentives for consumers are enabled by market principles for securing the market participation of consumers and actors cooperating with them and adapting the electricity market design to the market participation of DR and self-generated RES-E, elaborated in Sections 4.1 and 4.2 below. The efforts to offer market-based incentives also include broadening consumers' approaches to participating in electricity markets, addressed in Section 4.3.

## 4.1. GENERAL PRINCIPLES FOR MARKET PARTICIPATION

243. Within the Union legislation relating to the internal electricity market, two groups of principles are especially relevant to offering proper incentives for DR and renewables self-consumption. One highlights the fair market access of actors involved in these two energy activities (Section 4.1.1). The other guarantees that on this basis of fair market access, proper market-based remuneration is made available to them (Section 4.1.2).

### *4.1.1. Fair Market Access*

244. A fundamental idea presented throughout the current electricity market design is ensuring fair market access for final customers and other market participants involved in DR and renewables self-consumption (*Electricity Regulation*, Article 3). Although ensuring free market entry is a general principle of operating the internal electricity market, the Union's electricity market legislation places particular emphasis on market participation of

DR and self-generated RES-E (*Electricity Directive*, Article 3; *Electricity Regulation*, Article 3(c)(e)(j)). The significance of such emphasis lies in two aspects. One is aiming to remove market entry barriers (*Electricity Directive*, recital 42; Palm, 2018; Diestelmeier, 2021a, p 729), which can stem from established market rules (EC, 2016a; Poplavskaya and Vries, 2018), traditional market players (mainly suppliers, BRPs and system operators) and market incumbents already engaged in DSM activities (EC, 2016a; Chen and Vandendriessche, 2023b).[121]

245. The other reflects the consideration of promoting DR and renewables self-consumption in a market-compatible way. That is to say, facilitating market integration of DR providers and renewables prosumers, reducing the need for dedicated support, which can compromise market functioning (EC, 2016a; Chen and Vandendriessche, 2023a).

246. To fully engage consumers in electricity markets to trade their flexibility and self-generated RES-E, there are two relevant general principles. Firstly, under the Electricity Directive, for securing free market entry, Member States are under a general obligation to address undue market entry barriers and ensure that national law does not unduly hamper consumer participation (*Electricity Directive*, Article 3(1)(3)). The Electricity Regulation further elaborates on this by establishing the principle for market entry by consumers through aggregation. It states that market participation of final customers and small enterprises should be enabled by aggregation of generation from multiple power-generating facilities or load from multiple DR facilities to provide joint offers on the electricity market (*Electricity Regulation*, Article 3(e)).

247. The second important principle is creating a level playing field for all market actors, as unfair conditions or distorted competition can hinder new market entry. Member States are thus subject to a general requirement to set out transparent, proportionate and non-discriminatory rules, fees and treatment for electricity undertakings (*Electricity Directive*, Article 3(4)). The Electricity Regulation complements this by providing that the electricity market must be operated in a way that flexibility sources, including DR, should be able to participate on equal footing in the market (*Electricity Regulation*, Article 3(j)). Furthermore, non-discrimination also acts as an important principle for organizing balancing markets and setting prequalification processes (*Electricity Regulation*, Article 6). This aims to avoid TSOs discriminating against consumers and other entities providing demand flexibility in the procurement

121 For instance, market entry of IFSPs could also be deterred by incumbent IFSPs since the incumbents sign long-term contracts or contracts with tacit renewal with their customers. This was detected in Belgian electricity markets. See CREG 2016 Study, Section IV.

of balancing services[122] and in establishing relevant technical requirements for participation in balancing markets (*Electricity Directive*, Article 40(4)).

248. Market principles with respect to fair market access have a dual nature.[123] Indeed, stressing market participation of DR and self-generated RES-E aims to remove unjustified barriers or restrictions faced by consumers, IFSPs and energy communities, enabling them to compete on an equal footing with other market players. However, this does not imply granting market entry priority to participants offering DR or self-generated renewable electricity over other competitors. Instead, another important aspect of fair market access lies in non-discriminatory treatment in terms of rights and obligations, to guarantee a level playing field. In principle, actors involved in DR and renewables self-consumption are subject to obligations, ranging from balance responsibility[124] to those that must be respected in grid connection and balancing service provision,[125] as well as general market rules (e.g., market-based dispatch)[126] commonly applicable to all market players. Exceptions to these obligations and general market rules are only permitted in very limited cases and are clearly defined to support demonstration projects or small-scale RES-E generating facilities (Electricity Regulation, Articles 5(2) and 12.[127]

249. Lastly, based on the principles for securing fair market access, the market design must avoid market conditions that are not neutral in their treatment of DR and self-generated RES-E (Mitchell and Woodman, 2012, p 582).

122 Balancing services are used to avoid frequency deviation and a blackout caused by the imbalance between production and consumption (which can be common when integrating large-scale intermittent renewable generation). In the EU, balancing services procured by TSOs include balancing capacity and balancing energy. TSOs commonly first reserve the capacity in the balancing capacity market and then activate it as balancing energy when actual system imbalances occur. See Balancing Regulation, article 2 (3)(4)(5). For more details about balancing capacity and balancing energy, as well as their procurement and activation, see Schittekatte et al., 2020; Poplavskaya et al., 2021.

123 Regarding the trade-off between supporting certain technologies to deliver sustainable energy transition and maintaining fair market conditions, see Mitchell and Woodman, 2012, p 582.

124 All market participants shall be responsible for the imbalances they cause in the system. EU law provides two possible means to fulfill this responsibility: market players must either be BRPs or contractually delegate their responsibility to a BRP of their choice. Moreover, each BRP must be financially responsible for its imbalances and strive to be balanced or help the electricity system to be balanced. See *Electricity Regulation*, article 5; *Electricity Directive*, articles 15 (2)(f) and 16 (3)(c).

125 For obligations set for connecting to the transmission grid, see Section 3.4 of this Chapter above. When offering balancing services to the TSO, entities involved in DR and renewables self-consumption also have a range of obligations arising from minimum technical requirements for prequalification, offering balancing capacity and activating balancing energy bids. See *Balancing Regulation*, Articles 16 and 18; *System Operation Guideline*, Articles 154, 156, 158 and 161.

126 The general criteria for dispatch are based on the economic order of bids and due regard to network constraints. See *Electricity Regulation*, articles 2 (20) and 12 (1).

127 For why such exceptions matter, see Chen and Vandendriessche, 2023a.

As indicated in Chapter II, the original market framework was regarded as one factor contributing to the low market participation level of DR and decentralized RES-E, since it was designed for and befit large-scale, centralized power stations, primarily fired by fossil fuels (EC, 2016a). By giving examples, Chapter II shows that before the CEP, technical rules of the market (i.e., products, bid sizes, gate closure times) were often not defined with renewables and DR and the increased role of consumers in such activities in mind (EC, 2016a). Such an oversight notably leads to unequal opportunities for small consumers and FSPs to access electricity markets. The general requirement for fair market access also drives ongoing adjustments and optimization of market design within the respective competences of the EU and Member States to correct biased conditions faced by market actors involved in DR and renewables self-consumption.

### *4.1.2. Free Price Formation*

250. Securing entry to electricity markets alone cannot offer adequate incentives for consumers to engage in DR and renewables self-consumption. Such incentives are delivered by price signals. Chapter II indicated that before the CEP, price interventions lowered or distorted incentives for consumers to actively carry out these activities. To enable market prices to sufficiently remunerate consumers and encourage desirable consumption behavior, the CEP expressly states that free price formation is the general rule, while monitoring and marginalizing the role of state interventions (Huhta, 2020a). The Electricity Directive establishes a general requirement for Member States to ensure that electricity prices reflect actual demand and supply (*Electricity Directive*, Article 3(1)).[128] This means that the different electricity markets,

[128] However, market-based prices do not come without risks. Historical experience shows that market power is a significant potential problem in electricity markets, especially in wholesale markets and balancing markets. In wholesale markets, price manipulation is to be expected in tight markets. A very clear lesson from the California electricity price crisis in 2000–2001 is that the scarcity price of electricity can reach extremely high levels when supply is tight. There is abundant evidence that some suppliers exploited opportunities to engage in strategic behavior to jack up market prices. At least in the summer of 2000, some generators were taking advantage of a tight supply situation and withholding supplies to exercise market power. This demonstrates the importance of regulatory oversight of competitive and liberalized electricity markets to ensure that markets are not manipulated or that market power is abused. In the EU, the REMIT has been put in place to avoid unreasonable price increases in wholesale markets driven up by manipulation. Nevertheless, in practice, for energy regulators, it is not an easy task to make a distinction between price manipulation, namely 'securing the price of one or several wholesale energy products at an artificial level', and rising prices driven up by scarcity. To prevent the risk of market manipulation, NRAs might warn suppliers who increase prices about the suspicion of such an increase constituting market manipulation, based on some arbitrary criteria. This situation demonstrates the practical difficulty in realizing free price formation while deterring market abuse on wholesale markets. In balancing markets across

ranging from wholesale markets to balancing markets and retail markets, should, in principle, not be subject to price caps.

251. Together with the Electricity Directive, the Electricity Regulation elaborates the principle of market-based price formation in different electricity market segments as follows.

252. For wholesale markets, there is an overall prohibition of a maximum and a minimum limit to the wholesale electricity price (*Electricity Regulation*, Articles 7 and 10; Huhta, 2020). This means that the requirement to remove caps on wholesale prices is absolute (Huhta, 2020a).

253. For balancing markets, the principles include (i) ensuring efficient and non-distortive price formation in the procurement of balancing capacity and balancing energy (*Electricity Regulation*, recital 11); (ii) prohibiting the price of balancing energy from being pre-determined in contracts for balancing capacity (*Balancing Regulation*, Article 16 (6); *Electricity Regulation*, Article 6(2)); (iii) the imbalances should also be settled at a price that reflects the real-time value of energy (*Electricity Regulation*, Article 6(5)). Article 16 of the Balancing Regulation allows a deviation from the second principle, which has also been incorporated by the Electricity Regulation (*Electricity Regulation*, Article 6(14)). Under Article 26 of the Balancing Regulation, derogation is only justified when standard balancing products are insufficient to ensure operational security or when some balancing resources cannot participate in the balancing market through standard balancing products. The TSO is allowed to propose, and the regulatory authorities may approve the predetermination of prices for specific balancing products that are activated locally without exchanging them with other TSOs (*Balancing Regulation*, Article 26(3)(b)). The Balancing Regulation also requires that the triggering of this exemption should be accompanied by a justification demonstrating higher economic efficiency (*Balancing Regulation*, Article 16(6)).

254. For retail markets, the general rule of free price formation is also applicable (*Electricity Regulation*, Article 3(b)). Thus, suppliers are entitled to freely determine the price at which they supply electricity to customers

---

the EU, the concentrated nature of balancing markets has long raised concerns about the high risk of strategic bidding and market power. At times unaffected by scarcities, there is the repeated presence of unrealistically high prices for the balancing service. Some studies have shown that, unlike largely competitive DA markets, balancing markets offer different options for strategic behavior, such as the orientation of bid prices to the highest bid in pay-as-bid auctions rather than to one's actual costs. To avoid market power driving up prices, in parallel to deregulating prices, increasing competition and liquidity in balancing markets is considered essential. See *REMIT*, recital 13, Articles 2 (2)(3) and 5; Joskow and Kahn, 2001; Newbery, 2002; Borenstein et al., 2002; Joskow, 2008; Weber and Just, 2012; Ocker, 2017; Poplavskaya et al., 2020, 2021.

(*Electricity Directive*, Article 5(1)). However, due to the politically sensitive nature of price issues and the need to grant Member States discretion to protect certain energy customers, respecting this general rule is not absolute (*Electricity Regulation*, recital 22). A trade-off involved is worth mentioning. On the one hand, free price formation on the retail markets is particularly pivotal to sufficiently remunerate renewables self-consumers and DR. On the other hand, certain consumer groups, especially energy poor or vulnerable consumers, need to be protected from high prices.[129] Put in another way, the task of retail price regulation has become enabling those who want to be active market participants to become so, whilst protecting those who are unable to do so (Hoggett, 2017).

255. Seeking an acceptable balance between stimulating market participation of consumers and consumer protection is uncontroversial. However, what matters is how to realize such a balance without disproportionately compromising market functioning. In the following, before looking into the specific approaches taken by existing EU law, the rationale behind preserving regulated retail prices for specific consumers and problems caused by the previously wide national discretion in this field are outlined.

256. In the retail segment, the reason for precluding a free-wheeling approach to regulation lies in the need to protect vulnerable and energy poor customers, and smaller customers, particularly households and SMEs (*Electricity Directive*, recital 58 and Article 27(1); Pearson, 2020, p 65). In the case of severely constrained supply, significantly higher electricity prices than normal arise, which would disproportionately affect households, particularly vulnerable customers who typically expend a higher share of their disposable income on energy bills compared to high-income consumers (*Electricity Directive*, recitals 23 and 58). Relying entirely on the market-based logic, in this case, may sometimes result in suboptimal results (Talus, 2016, p 29). To ensure the affordability of electricity supply to these customer groups, which are vulnerable to suffering from acute price increases, Member States intervene in retail price setting, mostly through imposing PSOs on electricity undertakings. PSOs serve the objectives of general economic interest, namely delivering outcomes for the overall public good (e.g., affordable energy), which would not be supplied by the market without public intervention (*Electricity Directive*, recital 22; Gurba, 2021, pp 541–542). Thus, in the field of price regulation, PSOs have long been used as an essential justification for deviating from market-based prices. For the same reason, in EU legislation on energy markets and relevant Court jurisprudence, price

[129] The EC highlighted that rising energy poverty as well as a lack of clarity on the most appropriate means of tackling consumer vulnerability and energy poverty can hamper the further deepening of the internal energy market. See EC, 2016a, 2016b, *Electricity Directive*, recital 4, Articles 1 and 5.

setting in the form of PSOs to protect certain vulnerable consumer groups has traditionally been accepted.[130] In particular, the 2009 Electricity Directive granted broad powers to Member States to impose PSOs to protect small customers and vulnerable customers (*2009 Electricity Directive*, Article 3). However, it did so without setting out adequate conditions to regulate the application of PSOs, nor did it provide additional measures to mitigate the detrimental impacts of these PSOs on market functioning. Whilst well-intentioned, wide national discretion over applying PSOs led to excessive state interventions in retail price setting. In 2016, almost ten years after the opening of retail markets,[131] 13 Member States still practiced some form of retail price regulation for electricity.[132]

257. Furthermore, such a wide margin of discretion stemming from the Third Energy Package also contributed to increased poorly-designed PSOs, which could hinder the functioning of the internal electricity market and distort competition (Gurba, 2021, p 539). Before the adoption of the CEP, PSOs in the form of price setting for the supply of electricity have constituted a fundamentally distortive measure, giving rise to a host of adverse impacts

---

130 The imposition of PSOs to ensure security of supply and consumer protection has been allowed at the Union level since the first Electricity Directive. The first three Energy Packages left significant discretion to Member States on imposing PSOs to regulate retail prices for electricity and gas. In the absence of applicable measures reducing contradictions of PSOs with the internal energy market, case law plays a crucial role in guiding the design of PSOs with respect to price regulation and narrowing the scope of wide interpretation of such exceptional state intervention. Notably, in the *Federutility* case, the CJEU considered that while state intervention in the gas price is not in violation of EU law per se, it would be compatible with the Gas Directive only provided that several conditions are met. Some of these conditions notably relate to the principle of proportionality, and the ruling clarifies that several requirements must be met cumulatively to comply with this principle. Although the *Federutility* judgment is about PSOs in the field of natural gas, these standards with respect to the principle of proportionality have subsequently been incorporated by the Electricity Directive in Article 5. Moreover, case law relating to state intervention also makes clear that, considering that the market-based approaches are the rule and primary approach, while state intervention should remain the exception, exceptions should always be interpreted narrowly to avoid undermining the objectives of the rules themselves. See *1996 Electricity Directive*, Article 3; *2003 Electricity Directive*, recital 50 and Article 3; *2009 Electricity Directive*, Article 3; *C-265/08 Federutility and Others v Autorità per l'energia elettrica e il gas*, 2010; *C-121/15 Association nationale des opérateurs détaillants en énergie (ANODE) v Premier ministre and Others*, 2016; Hancher and Larouche, 2011, p 575; Talus, 2016, pp 29–32; Huhta, 2020; Marinova, 2021, pp 774–775.

131 The initial focus of the electricity market liberalization reform in the EU was on 'market opening' for retail customers rather than comprehensive reforms in wholesale markets, network access and price institutions. For relevant comparisons between the EU model and the liberalization models adopted in other countries, especially the so-called 'textbook' model of electricity market liberalization, see Joskow, 2008.

132 The number of Member States regulating retail electricity prices fluctuated over the recent decade, which was 18 in 2012, 13 in 2016 and 15 in 2021. Amidst the COVID-19 pandemic and the EU energy price crisis from 2021, there is a growing trend of intervening in retail prices at the national level. See EC, 2014b; Pearson, 2020, p 68; ACER and CEER, 2021.

(*Electricity Directive*, recital 22). These include inter alia the accumulation of tariff deficits, the restriction of competition and lower levels of consumer engagement and satisfaction (*Electricity Directive*, recital 22). To counter this, PSOs – the key instruments for intervening retail prices, which were applied largely unhindered – became a prime focus of the reform introduced by the CEP.

258. The CEP confirms that the importance of ensuring affordability and consumer protection is, in itself, uncontroversial, while the pre-existing policy instruments and legal approaches used to pursue that aim are problematic (Huhta, 2020a). The widespread presence of retail price regulation is also not suited to the trend of engaging consumers in actively managing their consumption and participating in electricity markets, as noted above. The Electricity Directive thus seeks to reconcile the approaches to delivering affordability with those aimed at creating a well-functioning retail electricity market that encourages the broad participation of customers.[133]

259. First, this legislation highlights that other policy tools, in particular targeted social policy measures, are preferred in fulfilling the goal of safeguarding the affordability of electricity supply to citizens (*Electricity Directive*, recital 15 and Article 5(2)).[134] In other words, PSOs in the form of regulating retail prices should act as the last resort to complement the role of the electricity market (EC, 2015b). To achieve this, the necessity of price regulation and its rule compliance comes under scrutiny by the EC (*Electricity Directive*, Article 5(8)(9)). Member States must notify the EC of the measures taken concerning price intervention and explain why other instruments were insufficient to achieve the pursued objective. This could prompt Member States to thoroughly consider alternative policy instruments before resorting to price regulation.

260. The Electricity Directive further harmonizes Union-wide criteria for legalizing price interventions via PSOs to minimize their impact on the internal electricity market (Huhta, 2020a). The experience of implementing the Third Energy Package demonstrates that views on the limits of legitimate regulatory interventions in retail prices may vary radically depending on the Member State (Pearson, 2020, p 65). With the growing interdependence between the Member States, the public interventions in one Member State yield more direct

---

133 According to Recital 15 of the Electricity Directive, the possibility for Member States to impose PSOs in the general economic interest and the principle of safeguarding market functioning are not incompatible. However, the tricky issue lies in reconciling the respective instruments used for achieving the two purposes and phasing out the way of applying PSOs that could be mutually incompatible with the internal electricity market. See *Electricity Directive*, recital 15; Gurba, 2021, p 541.

134 A combination of measures is available to address energy poverty and protect vulnerable customers, including mechanisms provided through the general welfare system and the energy market. See EC, 2015.

and stronger effects on the neighboring Member States (Gurba, 2021, p 540). A lack of Union-level criteria for relevant state interventions makes cross-border competition liable to be distorted, undermining the functioning of the internal electricity market. Hence, the Electricity Directive introduced a control mechanism to regulate Member States' discretion over price regulation and enable well-targeted PSOs (Pearson, 2020, p 65). Under this Directive, the role of PSOs in protecting certain customer groups is still recognized (*Electricity Directive*, recital 22). Nevertheless, they are only allowed in limited cases and must be adopted in a manner that diminishes the distortions deriving from regulated prices as far as possible.

261. Specifically, regulating retail prices through the imposition of PSOs is subject to the provisions contained in Articles 5 and 9 of the Electricity Directive. Article 9 preserves general principles for imposing PSOs set out in previous Electricity Directives, including that the obligations imposed on electricity undertakings should be clearly defined, transparent, non-discriminatory and verifiable. PSOs also need to guarantee equality of access for electricity undertakings of the Union to national consumers, avoiding impeding cross-border competition. Article 5, acting as *lex specialis*, further defines a series of restrictions, conditions and criteria. Only in case they are fulfilled, PSOs in the form of regulating retail prices can be justified. Two groups of customers could be beneficiaries of such public interventions permitted by Article 5.

262. Firstly, free price formation can be derogated to protect energy poor or vulnerable household customers,[135] subject to various conditions (*Electricity Directive*, Article 5(3)). These conditions notably reflect the principle of proportionality and seek to mitigate impacts upon market functioning (*Electricity Directive*, Article 5(4)): (i) such retail price regulation is required not to go beyond what is necessary to achieve that general economic interest; (ii) it should be limited in time and proportionate as regards their beneficiaries; and (iii) applying such public interventions should also avoid resulting in additional costs for market participants in a discriminatory way. Moreover, Member States that regulate retail prices in this context are also subject to the provisions addressing energy poverty contained in the Energy and Climate Governance Regulation. Article 5 makes specific references to point (d) of Article 3(3) and Article 24 of the Energy and Climate Governance Regulation.

[135] Given that the protection of energy poor customers and vulnerable customers can trigger state interventions in market-based pricing, clearly defining the two customer groups is also crucial to enable more targeted PSOs. The Electricity Directive requires Member States to define the concept of vulnerable customers, which may refer to energy poverty. This concept may be established by referring to income levels, the share of energy expenditure of disposable income, the energy efficiency of homes, critical dependence on electrical equipment for health reasons, age or other criteria. See *Electricity Directive*, article 28.

These provisions aim to ensure that the interests of households in energy poverty are taken into account in the low-carbon energy transition.[136]

263. The second group of consumers is household customers and microenterprises, which are neither energy poor nor vulnerable customers (*Electricity Directive*, Article 5(6)). Offering them regulated prices is only justified for '*a transition period purpose*', i.e., a transition period to establish effective competition for electricity supply contracts between suppliers, and to achieve fully effective market-based retail pricing of electricity (*Electricity Directive*, Article 5(6)). This also suggests that price intervention for those customers is a transitory regime. The Electricity Directive provides definitions for all these beneficiaries of such price regulation. In contrast to the 2009 Electricity Directive, the definition of 'microenterprise' was newly introduced.[137] Equally, such public interventions should also be clearly defined and fulfill the proportionality and non-discrimination requirements mentioned above. Additionally, there are specific conditions that must be met to mitigate impacts on fair competition as well as customer engagement and protection. For the former purpose, there are three primary requirements:

- Price regulation in this context must be accompanied by a set of measures to achieve effective competition and a methodology for assessing progress with regard to those measures;
- Despite being regulated, the price should be set at a price that is above cost, at a level where effective price competition can occur;
- Its design must minimize any negative impact on the wholesale electricity market and ensure non-discriminatory treatment of suppliers.

264. To ensure customer choice and entitlement to access electricity markets, Article 5(7) of the Electricity Directive imposes additional obligations

---

136 Article 3 (3) of the Energy and Climate Governance Regulation requires Member States to assess the number of households in energy poverty. In the event that there is a significant number of households in energy poverty on the basis of this assessment, the concerned Member States should contain a national indicative objective to reduce energy poverty and the policies and measures for addressing energy poverty in their integrated national energy and climate plans. Article 24 of this Regulation complements this by listing relevant information with respect to progress toward reducing energy poverty that should be contained in national integrated national energy and climate progress reports. Such information includes (a) information on progress toward the national indicative objective to reduce the number of households in energy poverty; and (b) quantitative information on the number of households in energy poverty, and, where available, information on policies and measures addressing energy poverty. See EC, 2015; *Energy and Climate Governance Regulation*, recital 5 and Article 24.

137 'Microenterprise' means an enterprise which employs fewer than 10 persons and whose annual turnover and/or annual balance sheet total does not exceed EUR 2 million. See *Electricity Directive*, article 2 (6).

on Member States that apply price regulation for the purpose of the above transition period. First, Member States must ensure that the possibility of accessing competitive market offers is created for the beneficiaries of regulated prices. Second, they should ensure that it is possible for these beneficiaries to choose competitive market offers, and they are directly informed at least every quarter of the availability of offers and savings in the competitive market (*Electricity Directive*, Article 5(7)). When wishing to switch to a market-based offer, these beneficiaries should be provided with assistance. Their access to dynamic electricity price contracts and smart meters is particularly mentioned, as discussed in more detail in Section 5 below. Finally, to prevent public intervention from harming other customer groups, direct cross-subsidization between customers supplied at free market prices and those supplied at regulated supply prices is prohibited. This means that such regulated price regimes must not explicitly lead specific categories of customers to bear the cost of price interventions that affect other categories of customers (*Electricity Directive*, recital 25).

265. Furthermore, Member States have a set of reporting obligations. For example, they should notify the EC of how the requirements set out for price regulation are fulfilled and of the effects of the notified measures on competition. To increase transparency of such price setting and demonstrate rule compliance, this notification also needs to describe the scope of the beneficiaries, the duration of the measures and the number of household customers affected by the measures, and to explain how the regulated prices have been determined. For price regulation for the transition period purpose, Member States have obligations to report on the compliance with relevant conditions, including on compliance by suppliers that are required to apply such interventions, as well as on the impact of regulated prices on the finances of those suppliers.

266. The last paragraph of Article 5 specifies the responsibility of the EC to report the implementation of Article 5 to the European Council and the European Parliament. This provision implies the possibility of a future complete phase-out of regulated prices in the EU, as it mentions that the EC may submit a legislative proposal that includes an end date for regulated prices.

## 4.2. ADJUSTING ELECTRICITY MARKET DESIGN PARAMETERS

267. Before the CEP, the design of electricity markets across the EU was considered not fit for actors involved in DR and renewables self-consumption but for traditional market players (EC, 2016a; Inês et al., 2020). This situation can compromise equal market access opportunities for consumers and

other market actors involved in these two DSM activities, as detailed in Section 2.1.2 of Chapter II above. The CEP adjusts market design parameters of wholesale and balancing markets, as shown below consecutively. Given the technical nature of these parameters, this subsection merely gives several examples to demonstrate how existing EU law facilitates equal market access opportunities by adapting the market design parameters.

### *4.2.1. Adapting Wholesale Market Design*

268. To further open the wholesale market to DR and self-generated RES-E, the major adjustments of wholesale markets include increasing the role of short-term wholesale markets and harmonizing the imbalance settlement period and the minimum bid size.

269. First, the short-term markets are strengthened to reduce the risks and costs of RES-E producers (including prosumers) induced by forecasting errors. Before the CEP, ID markets were not efficiently organized to accommodate the increasing penetration of variable RES-E, including the newly installed capacity based on intermittent renewables on the demand side (EC, 2016a). Existing EU law highlights the essential role of efficient and liquid ID markets in maximizing the ability of market participants to manage imbalances as closely as possible in real time, thereby enabling the system to better deal with variations in RES-E output (EC, 2016a; *Electricity Regulation*, recital 13; Papsch, 2020, pp 28 and 30). For renewables self-consumers and DR providers, adjusting the ID market design can lower their risks and better price the value of the flexibility they offer (EC, 2016a). The Electricity Regulation provides that NEMOs should allow market participants to trade energy as close to real-time as possible (*Electricity Regulation*, Article 8(1)). This is highly relevant to mitigating imbalance risks faced by renewables prosumers based on intermittent wind and solar power. The production from such weather-dependent RES-E can only be predicted with acceptable accuracy within hours (EC, 2016a). In the absence of short-term markets near real-time, renewables prosumers with intermittent renewables are exposed to imbalance risks and costs caused by possible deviation from their plans due to forecasting errors (EC, 2016a). Such risks and costs can be even more pronounced than before since EU law no longer remains silent on a wide range of exemptions from balance responsibility previously granted by Member States, including those made for RES-E generation facilities (EC, 2016a; Peng and Poudineh, 2019). Along with the CEP expressly restricting exceptions to the balance responsibility, other than demonstration projects and a certain type of small renewables generating installation, renewables prosumers are subject to balance responsibility, as mentioned in Section 4.1. In this context, short-term markets, which allow for trading closer to real-time, help reduce imbalance risks, encouraging their market participation.

270. Second, the imbalance settlement period is harmonized to improve wholesale market participation of DR and self-generated RES-E. The 'imbalance settlement period' is the time unit for which the BRP's energy imbalances, i.e., the difference between the BRP's contracted positions and what is delivered or consumed in real time, are calculated (*Electricity Regulation*, Article 2(15); SWECO, 2015). In the EU, countries used to apply 60, 30, or 15 minutes as the standard imbalance settlement period (Schittekatte et al., 2020). Existing EU law harmonizes the imbalance settlement period, stipulating that by 1 January 2021, the imbalance settlement period should be 15 minutes in all scheduling areas, and derogations granted by NRAs are only allowed before 31 December 2024 (*Electricity Regulation*, Article 8(4)). This means that every 15 minutes, the TSO determines which market party was in positive (more generation than consumption) or negative (more consumption than generation) imbalance and proceeds to imbalance settlement, paying[138] or demanding payment of the imbalance costs (Papsch, 2020, p 29). From 1 January 2025, exceptions to this requirement are only possible if all the regulatory authorities within a synchronous area agree, but in such cases, the imbalance settlement period is not allowed to exceed 30 minutes (*Electricity Regulation*, Article 8(4)).

271. A short balance settlement period allows renewables prosumers to more precisely indicate when they will be available and when this will not be the case, making their market participation less risky while also allowing other generation assets to fill the remaining gaps (Papsch, 2020, p 30). The length of imbalance settlement periods also matters to reveal the value of flexibility, which can vary significantly both on a geographical level and across time (SWECO, 2015). The hourly prices hide some of the value of flexibility, whilst shortening the imbalance settlement period could contribute to revealing more of the true value (SWECO, 2015). Sufficiently short imbalance settlement periods allow DR providers to more exactly price the value of flexibility and get remuneration (SWECO, 2015; Papsch, 2020, p 30).

272. Lastly, a high minimum bid size is considered a critical barrier for DR and self-generated RES-E to enter electricity markets since they are typically small bids and cannot meet the bid threshold without aggregation (Koliou et al., 2015; SWECO, 2015; Papsch, 2020). It thus deters medium and small customers from bidding on electricity markets individually and could also block the market entry of small-scale aggregators.[139] To mitigate this market entry barrier, the

[138] The TSO pays when passive balancing services are provided by a BRP when it indirectly assists the TSO in reducing system imbalances. This service occurs when a BRP's deviations counteract the system imbalance. In such scenarios, the BRP is compensated because its actions are interpreted as providing service to the TSO. See Alonso Pedrero and Crespo del Granado, 2023.

[139] The minimum bid size also defines the minimum level of aggregation necessary to deliver reserves and is thus also a key parameter for the participation of IFSPs or aggregators. If the

Electricity Regulation has capped the minimum bid sizes of DA/ID markets to 500 kW (*Electricity Regulation*, Article 8(3)).

### 4.2.2. *Changes in Balancing Market Design*

273. The balancing market is another important marketplace for actors involved in DR and renewables self-consumption to seek revenues. However, these actors are blocked from doing so due to market entry barriers stemming from bid requirements or procurement rules. Some of them constitute obstacles specific to DR, while others impede the market participation of both DR and self-generated RES-E. As a result, before the CEP, the ACER detected high levels of concentration within some national balancing markets due to the low involvement level of balancing services from consumers (EC, 2016a; Roos, 2017). Chapter II provides examples to illustrate how consumers' entry into balancing markets was hindered. How the EU law adjusted the balancing market design parameters is outlined next.

274. First, to address barriers created by the requirement for 'symmetric bids', the Electricity Regulation updates relevant requirements previously contained in the Balancing Regulation by requiring that the procurement of upward balancing capacity and downward balancing capacity should be carried out separately (*Electricity Regulation*, Article 6(9)). Under the Balancing Regulation, the separate procurement of upward and downward products is only mandatory for standard products, namely FRR and RR.[140] However, under Article 6(9) of the Electricity Regulation, this requirement has been extended to apply to all balancing products as a principle for organizing balancing markets. The regulatory authority can only approve a derogation on the basis that respecting that requirement would result in higher economic efficiency as demonstrated by an evaluation performed by the TSO (*Electricity Regulation*, Article 6(9)).

275. Second, to mitigate barriers linked to the contract duration and contracting period for balancing capacity, the Electricity Regulation provides that, in principle, contracts for balancing capacity should not be concluded more than one day before the provision of the balancing capacity, and the

---

minimum bid is set too high, it will be difficult for aggregators to participate, as it would require managing an overly cumbersome number of small flexibility sources. See Borne et al., 2018; Schittekatte et al., 2020.

[140] 'FRR' means the active power reserves available to restore the system frequency to the nominal frequency. 'RR' means the active power reserves available to restore or support the required level of FRR to be prepared for additional system imbalances, including generation reserves. Balancing Regulation provides that the procurement of upward and downward balancing capacity for at least the FRR and the RR shall be carried out separately. See *Balancing Regulation*, article 32 (3); *System Operation Guideline*, article 2 (6)(7).

contracting period shall be no longer than one day (*Electricity Regulation*, Article 6(9)). As an exception, the regulatory authority is permitted to approve earlier contracting or longer contracting periods to ensure the security of supply or to improve economic efficiency. Yet, this Regulation sets out two additional requirements when the derogation is granted (*Electricity Regulation*, Article 6(9)(10)(11)).

## 4.3. BROADENING APPROACHES TO ACCESSING ELECTRICITY MARKETS

276. As set out above, with the adapted electricity market framework, the EU legislature aims to create an electricity market that enables consumers to actively participate in various market segments to valorize DR and self-produced RES-E (*REDII*, Articles 21(6)(e) and 22(2)(c); *Electricity Directive*, Articles 3, 31(8) and 40(3); *Electricity Regulation*, Articles (1)(b) and 3(j)). The REDII additionally indicates the routes to competitive markets for self-generated electricity. It works in parallel with Union law relating to the electricity market, furthering the common goal of promoting RES-E in a market-based way, i.e., enabling RES-E to get market-based remuneration (Chen and Vandendriessche, 2023a). Moreover, as explained in the previous subsections, facilitating the selling of (surplus) self-produced electricity is a key enabler for incentivizing renewables self-consumption. In addition to the above principles ensuring fair market access, the REDII provides additional routes to sell self-produced RES-E, including through renewables PPAs, suppliers and P2P trading arrangements, which are elaborated consecutively below. It should also be noted that electricity sharing could also be an approach to selling self-produced RES-E if it is defined as the sale of electricity by national law.

### *4.3.1. Through Renewables PPAs*

277. Renewables PPAs refer to bilateral power purchase agreements wherein an end customer agrees to buy RES-E directly from a RES-E generator (or a prosumer) at an agreed-upon fixed price outside of the wholesale spot electricity market, with a typical duration of 10 to 15 years (Mendicino et al., 2019; Ghiassi-Farrokhfal et al., 2021; Kobus et al., 2021; Gabrielli et al., 2022). Traditionally, the vast majority of PPAs were signed with utility companies as buyers (Kobus et al., 2021). In recent years, there has been an emerging trend that customers have been entering into PPAs directly with renewable developers of onshore wind and solar generation assets (Bruck et al., 2018; Kobus et al., 2021; Gabrielli et al., 2022). Some large consumers sign renewables PPAs to improve the 'green and social brand' of their products and services as well as protect against future high or volatile wholesale prices (Mendicino et al., 2019;

Ghiassi-Farrokhfal et al., 2021; Kobus et al., 2021; ACER, 2022). They may also be willing to pay a premium for the general risk reduction that stems from locking in a fixed price (Kobus et al., 2021). The risk-mitigating role of renewables PPAs is even more crucial for customers to adapt to the electricity system with increasingly dominant shares of variable RES-E, in which price volatility is bound to rise.[141] As such, compared to wholesale markets, PPAs help consumers mitigate price risks while also offering a guaranteed revenue stream to RES-E generators and reducing financing costs for RES-E projects (Jager et al., 2008; Neuhoff et al., 2016; Kobus et al., 2021). Among them, long-term or multi-year renewables PPAs are a commonly used means to secure long-term financing for RES-E producers, as the price is set long into the future.[142] This is why renewables PPAs are viewed as an important commercially-driven approach to promoting RES-E, either derived from centralized producers or renewables prosumers (ACER, 2022; Gabrielli et al., 2022).

278. This approach has been incorporated into the Union framework for enabling renewables self-consumption, acting as one of the key approaches to selling self-generated RES-E. Both renewables self-consumers and RECs are entitled to choose to use this approach and reap economic benefits (*REDII*, Articles 21(2)(a) and 22(2)(a)). At first sight, it seems that PPAs may overlap with contracts that sell surplus RES-E to suppliers, other peers or end users. This is because the Union-level definition does not limit buyers under PPAs to suppliers or end users (*REDII*, Article 2(17)). The defining characteristic of renewables PPAs, according to that definition, is that they are concluded directly between electricity producers and purchasers (*REDII*, article 2(17)). In practice, such direct contract negotiation typically implies a tailor-made nature of such contracts, which allows the assignment of risks and costs according to the wishes and needs of those contractual partners.[143] This highly customizable feature distinguishes renewables PPAs from other ways of selling self-produced RES-E, i.e., contracts with suppliers[144] and P2P electricity contracts.

---

141 The following elements will likely push volatility upwards: (i) numerous market entries and exits; (ii) the impact of intermittent generation on the system; and (iii) volatility of other underlying market fundamentals. See ACER, 2022.

142 A renewables PPA with corporate buyers' involvement is typically structured as a long-term agreement, usually as a 10-year contract or more, according to renewable power plant technology; otherwise, it may not see a return on the capital costs and may not satisfy the requirements of lenders. See Mendicino et al., 2019; ACER, 2022.

143 Regarding the tailor-made nature of PPAs, see ACER and CEER, 2023.

144 In the Flemish Region, for instance, renewables self-consumers and active customers with digital meters are entitled to sell self-produced RES-E to suppliers. They can enter into a feed-in contract with their own suppliers or with other suppliers. The pricing in this feed-in contract is usually in line with their existing electricity purchase contract, i.e., a fixed, variable,

279. The right to sell self-produced RES-E via PPAs is additionally underpinned by measures facilitating the uptake of long-term renewables PPAs. Member States are under an obligation to assess regulatory and administrative barriers to long-term renewables PPAs, and to remove unjustified barriers to, and facilitate the uptake of, such agreements (*REDII*, Article 15(8)). The barriers that must be overcome, inter alia, include disproportionate or discriminatory procedures or charges (*REDII*, Article 15(8)).

280. Facilitating access to renewables PPAs could not only facilitate the purchase of RES-E but also enable prosumers to sell self-generated RES-E. As such, renewables PPAs are used as an approach to realizing the two-fold role of final customers, i.e., as off-takers and prosumers, in facilitating the uptake of RES-E.

#### *4.3.2. Enabling Trading with Suppliers and Peers*

281. Apart from renewables PPAs, the REDII empowers self-consumers to sell self-generated RES-E through two other means: electricity suppliers and P2P trading arrangements.[145] In the former case, suppliers remain the party responsible for selling, including reselling, electricity to customers. In the case of P2P trading, self-consumers can offer electricity to other customers without the involvement of suppliers or other intermediaries. In this case, self-consumers in fact play the role of suppliers. This is why, before the CEP, some Member States required prosumers wishing to engage in P2P electricity trading to have the status of suppliers, implying subjecting them to obligations set for suppliers (*Electricity Directive*, recital 42; Inês et al., 2020). Other Member States even prohibited prosumers from exchanging self-produced electricity directly via P2P trading (Inês et al., 2020).

282. There is a thorny dilemma when allowing prosumers to engage in P2P trading. On the one hand, requiring them to comply with the licensing regime and technical rules designed for suppliers may yield obligations or administrative burdens disproportionate to the size and potential impact of the prosumers. On the other hand, given that they indeed offer electricity to other consumers, a certain level of regulation and monitoring is necessary to uphold a sufficient level of consumer protection and retail competition. Member States need to ensure that the requirements applied to prosumers selling

---

or dynamic energy price. In principle, such pricing is commonly applied to consumers, and the contracts are not highly tailored. See *Electricity and gas market report 2022*, 2023, section 2.1.1.8.

145 P2P electricity trading is a business model, first proposed in 2007, based on an interconnected platform that serves as an online marketplace where consumers and producers 'meet' to trade electricity directly, without the need for an intermediary. See Parag and Sovacool, 2016; Sousa et al., 2019; Dudjak et al., 2021.

self-produced electricity are proportionate and also adequate to protect the interests of buyers. Another question is whether treating them and suppliers differently is compatible with the principle of non-discrimination. These legal issues may explain the reluctance of some Member States to permit prosumers to engage in P2P electricity trading.

283. The REDII requires Member States to ensure that renewables self-consumers are entitled to participate in P2P trading, thereby outlawing previous bans imposed by Member States. It also clearly defines P2P electricity trading, which recognizes its several elements: (i) relying on a contract with pre-determined conditions governing the automated execution and settlement of the transaction; (ii) taking place either directly between market participants or indirectly through a certified third-party market participant, such as an aggregator; and (iii) the right to conduct such trading should be without prejudice to the rights and obligations of the parties involved as final customers, producers, suppliers or aggregators.

284. However, the REDII does not further address a key issue, i.e., in the case of P2P trading, whether self-consumers should be subject to rules governing electricity supply. Neither the REDII nor the Union legislation relating to the electricity market sets out any principles for addressing the above-mentioned dilemma arising from engaging renewables self-consumers in P2P electricity trading. This leaves a series of legal issues unresolved, linked to creating a proportionate and non-discriminatory regulatory regime that enables self-consumers to engage in P2P electricity trading, which Member States must address. How Member States deal with these issues and the remaining challenges will be examined in Section 3.2 of Chapter IV.

## 5. INFORMATION AND COMMUNICATION MECHANISMS

285. Chapter II indicated that consumers must be provided with sufficient information on the economic and environmental benefits of engaging in DR and RES-E use. It also highlighted that when making information available, care should be taken to consider consumers' limited capacity to process complex information and the reinforced reliance on heuristics and the status quo in complex decision-making contexts. The way EU law enhances consumers' access to information while avoiding complexity is outlined in Section 5.1.

286. Aside from mechanisms that overcome information asymmetry, a data-management framework is pivotal for communicating the data required to trade DR and self-generated RES-E. In the context of engaging final customers, data exchange can take place between multiple market players (i.e., consumers,

suppliers, IFSPs, BRPs and system operators), raising considerable data privacy and security concerns (Chen and Vandendriessche, 2023b). As will be explained, properly addressing data security issues is also highly relevant to enabling consumer participation in fully reaping the benefits brought by the emerging ICT. Section 5.2 will look into how the data-management framework contained in existing EU law seeks to facilitate efficient and secure data exchange in relevant market processes.

## 5.1. APPROACHES TO IMPROVING INFORMATION ACCESS

287. EU law establishes four groups of measures to enhance consumers' access to information, working in parallel with other measures to facilitate the active management of electricity consumption, thereby promoting the greater uptake of RES-E. They are (i) adapting billing information; (ii) building minimum requirements for smart meter rollout; (iii) GO mechanisms; and (iv) improving consumers' know-how in engaging in renewables self-consumption. The first two sets of actions aim to make information on electricity consumption and market signals accessible to consumers, contained in Sections 5.1.1 and 5.1.2. Through them, consumers are informed of the room for savings on electricity bills and the possibility of getting revenues, which is essential to driving consumers to actively manage electricity use through either DR or renewables procurement and self-consumption. Furthermore, the framework for bills and billing information also contains general rules for disclosing the energy mix of electricity supplied to final customers. Together with the GO mechanisms elaborated in Section 5.1.3, it discloses the generation attributes of grid-supplied electricity (i.e., derived from fossil fuels or renewable sources) to consumers. By reminding consumers of RES-E's benefits, notably its impact on climate change and the environment, these information-based mechanisms can prompt them to purchase RES-E or choose suppliers offering a higher share of RES-E. Lastly, the Union framework for promoting renewables self-consumption also contains measures that offer consumers information to facilitate their understanding of permit-granting procedures, as addressed in Section 5.1.4.

### *5.1.1. Billing Information Governance*

288. By informing final customers about electricity consumption and costs, electricity bills present them with the potential to optimize electricity consumption through participating in DR and the purchase and self-consumption of RES-E. Facing energy price spikes or volatility, for instance, sufficient information on electricity consumption can prompt consumers to consider DR, contracting renewables PPA, or shifting to renewables self-consumption as

a possible means to save energy costs and hedge price risks. Notably, because the PAC pricing mechanism is subject to volatile natural gas prices,[146] the role of electricity consumption information in triggering more active consumption management is evident.

289. EU-level provisions on billing information were previously contained in the 2012 Energy Efficiency Directive. In bringing forward the legislative proposal for the Electricity Directive, as mentioned in Chapter II, the EC identified that final customers had difficulties understanding their electricity bills, and there was a broad divergence in national requirements around billing (EC, 2016a). Low efficiency in providing information to customers contributed to the persistently low levels of consumer satisfaction and engagement in the electricity sector (*Electricity Directive*, recital 48). To make the approaches to displaying billing information fit for facilitating active electricity consumption management, relevant provisions have been moved to the Electricity Directive and updated and streamlined (*Electricity Directive*, recital 50).

290. The Electricity Directive emphasizes that bills should be clearer and easier to understand. Moreover, information overload should be avoided, and only a limited number of important items of information should be displayed on the bill. Hence, Article 18 and Annex I of this legislation address the following issues: (i) which items of information are defined as the most important, (ii) how other items of information should be provided, and (iii) the way to display such information, described as follows.

#### 5.1.1.1. Prioritizing Diverse Items of Information

291. As highlighted in Chapter II, there is a crucial trade-off between providing useful information for final customers and avoiding information overload. When seeking to remedy an absence of information, a pervasive

---

146 The EU applies the PAC mechanism on wholesale markets. The price of the last producer from which electricity was bought determines the uniform, market-clearing price that other successful sellers of power obtain at a given moment. In theory, this pricing regime does not necessarily assign a decisive role to gas power plants. The existing strong correlation between electricity prices and gas prices is due to the fact that, within the EU, around 37% of electricity is still generated from fossil fuels, and gas power plants continue to play a key role in providing backup capacity to meet demand when there is insufficient output from solar and wind-based electricity. As a result, gas power plants typically become the last generating unit to be turned off to meet demand, and in turn, determine the uniform, market-clearing price received by other bidders who supply electricity. These gas generators have a high marginal generation cost due to fuel costs. In the high gas price situation, other bidders, including renewable producers and nuclear power plants, obtain high market-clearing prices accordingly. This explains why natural gas price spikes drive up electricity prices as a whole in the EU. See Kahn et al., 2001; Tierney et al., 2010; Levin and Botterud, 2015; ACER, 2022.

problem with information strategies is letting consumers treat a large amount of information (Sunstein, 2002, pp 260–262). Existing studies warn that given the limited ability of people to process information, such a way of providing numerous information can be ineffectual or even counterproductive – equivalent to no information at all (Sunstein, 2002, pp 260–262). These concerns have already been considered by EU law. The Electricity Directive prioritizes information items by importance, which determines their placement on the bill. The Directive's Annex I first lists the most important information, which should be provided to final customers by showing on the bill and in the billing information. The key information includes, inter alia, the price and electricity consumption for the billing period, the availability and benefits of switching, and the final customer's rights regarding out-of-court dispute settlement. While most of the requirements on billing information seem to be designed for suppliers, some of them, especially those concerned with switching and dispute settlement, also apply to (I)FSPs who contract with end customers (Pearson, 2020, p 91). This enables final customers to be informed of their rights to switch energy service providers and settle disputes through out-of-court means.[147]

292. For bills based on actual consumption or remote reading by the operator, the minimum information contains comparisons of the final customer's current electricity consumption with the customer's consumption for the same period in the previous year in graphic form (*Electricity Directive*, annex I, paragraph 1.3). Exposing consumers to the past and present consumption levels and allowing for comparison can stimulate customers to seek potential bill savings by engaging in DR or shifting to renewables PPAs or self-consumption. Moreover, Annex I of the Electricity Directive makes it clear that, at the request of the final customer, complementary information on historical consumption should be made available to service providers designated by the final customer, such as the IFSPs. It also lists the information that must be provided in this context.[148]

---

147 The diverging stances of EU institutions toward the trade-off involved in informational strategies, largely relating to their composition and competences, are worth mentioning. In the legislative negotiations, the European Council and EC sought to limit the number of items of information that must be displayed on bills or in the billing information. The reason lies in the need to avoid providing too prescriptive details, which can be counterproductive to improving customers' attention to and understanding of key information, as already explained. However, the European Parliament advocated the addition of three elements to the list of essential information items, including the one relating to switching as a result of intense lobbying of the European Consumer Organisation. Unlike the other two EU institutions, the Members of the European Parliament sit in political groups, which explains why they have closer links with citizens and NGOs and emphasize the interests of final customers more than the EC and the European Council. See Pearson, 2020, pp 93 and 98; Sunstein, 2002.

148 These information covers (1) cumulative data for at least the three previous years or the period since the start of the electricity supply contract, if that period is shorter, and (2) detailed data

#### 5.1.1.2. How to Display Information

293. The general requirements for displaying billing information are mainly contained in Article 18 of the Electricity Directive. Firstly, bills and billing information must be accurate, easy to understand, clear, concise, user-friendly, and presented in a manner that facilitates comparison by final customers (*Electricity Directive*, Article 18(1)). Moreover, final customers are entitled to receive all their bills and billing information free of charge. Member States are obliged to consult consumer organizations when they consider changes to the requirements for the content of bills.

294. Annex I of this Directive further elaborates on the way to display the aforementioned key information and complementary information, as well as the frequency of billing and the provision of billing information:

- Key information, such as the price to be paid and electricity consumption for the billing period, must be prominently displayed in final customers' bills and billing information, distinctly separate from other parts of the bill and billing information.
- Where bills are based on actual consumption or remote reading by the operator, Annex I applies relatively flexible wording, namely allowing such information to be made available to final customers in, with or signposted to within their bills and periodic settlement bills.
- The provision of complementary information on historical consumption is based on the request of final customers. Where the final customer has a meter that allows remote reading by the operator installed, the provision of complementary information on historical consumption must ensure the final customer's easy access to such information and allow detailed self-checks.

295. Paragraph 2 of Annex I specifies the frequency of providing billing information for different meters and types of information. Billing based on actual consumption is required to take place at least once a year. In the case of making available accurate billing information based on actual consumption, the minimum requirements vary according to whether remote reading is available.

---

according to the time of use for any day, week, month and year, which is made available to the final customer without undue delay via the internet or the meter interface, covering the period of at least the previous 24 months or the period since the start of the electricity supply contract, if that period is shorter. See *Electricity Directive*, annex I, paragraph 4.

#### 5.1.1.3. Disclosing the Energy Mix in Supplied Electricity

296. As already noted in Section 2.3 of Chapter II, measures that disclose electricity generation attributes are crucial to creating consumption patterns that favor the purchase of electricity generated from renewables. Within EU law governing the information provided by electricity bills, a general energy sources disclosure obligation is created, i.e., disclosing the energy mix of supplied electricity. Under Annex I of the Electricity Directive, suppliers are required to specify in bills the supplied energy sources. Two pieces of information over the preceding year must be offered: (i) the contribution of each energy source to the overall energy mix of the supplier, and (ii) information on the environmental impact, in at least terms of $CO_2$ emissions and the radioactive waste resulting from the electricity produced by the overall energy mix of the supplier. An additional requirement for disclosing the contribution of different energy sources to the supplier's product is to provide relevant information in a comprehensible and comparable manner. These measures could enhance customer choice in purchasing electricity and thus create opportunities for them to shift toward favoring the use of RES-E, for example, by switching to suppliers with a higher share of RES-E in their products.

### *5.1.2. Facilitating Smart Meter Roll-Out*

297. Smart meters can be defined as devices that measure near-real-time or real-time electricity consumption and communicate this recorded data to end users (*Electricity Directive*, Article 2(23); Sovacool et al., 2021). As a type of ICT infrastructure, they enable final customers to be more aware of the electricity flows imported from and exported to the grid, as well as their various consumption data (*Electricity Directive*, recitals 52 and 55; ACER and CEER, 2021). Based on these data, consumers could actively participate in trading self-generated RES-E and DR, thereby benefiting from these energy activities. It constitutes a particular technical prerequisite for implementing implicit DR (EC, 2016a). Moreover, as mentioned above in Section 3 of this Chapter, the Electricity Directive requires actors engaged in (RES-E) self-consumption, including active customers and CECs, to be subject to network charges that account separately for the electricity fed into the grid and the electricity consumed from the grid (*Electricity Directive*, Article 15(2)(e) and 16(4)(b)). Separate accounting is crucial to ensuring that these prosumers share system costs fairly and adequately. Its implementation relies on one of the functionalities provided by smart

meters, namely measuring the electricity fed into the grid or the electricity consumed from the grid.[149]

298. Prior to the CEP, a lack of fit-for-purpose smart metering systems prevented the attainment of the above benefits. Without defining the functionalities of smart meters, the 2009 Electricity Directive merely required that where the roll-out of smart meters is assessed positively, at least 80 % of consumers shall be equipped with intelligent metering systems by 2020 (*2009 Electricity Directive*, annex I). Consequently, even in Member States where smart meters were rolled out, they did not always have the functionalities necessary to allow consumers to take active control of their consumption (EC, 2016a; Sovacool et al., 2017). Moreover, most Member States failed to accomplish the timeline established in the 2009 Electricity Directive, which also limits the accessibility of such smart infrastructure across the EU (Pearson, 2020).

299. The existing Electricity Directive aims to address this situation by harmonizing minimum requirements for the rollout of smart meters. Most of the provisions in this regard are straightforward. Yet, the following three elements merit mention for their significance in ensuring consumers' access to such infrastructure within the EU and the deployment of fit-for-purpose communication infrastructure: (i) deployment based on cost-benefit assessments; (ii) the right to access smart meters in different cases; and (iii) functionalities of smart meters. They are detailed consecutively below.

#### 5.1.2.1. Deployment Based on Cost-Benefit Assessments

300. Smart-meter deployment is not an absolute requirement for Member States. The Electricity Directive allows Member States to determine whether to progress the roll-out of smart metering systems nationwide based on a cost-benefit assessment. Considering that this assessment can significantly affect the rollout of these enabling infrastructures within the EU, Member States are subject to some principles when conducting it, contained in Article 19 and Annex II:

- This assessment should take into account: (1) the methodology for the cost-benefit analysis and the minimum functionalities for smart metering systems provided for in the EC Recommendation on preparations for the roll-out of smart metering systems[150] and (2) the best available

[149] For the functionalities of smart meters defined by EU law, see Section 5.1.2.3 of this Chapter below.

[150] According to Article 288 TFEU, recommendations and opinions should have no binding force. Such instruments issued by the EC are deemed as soft law. Yet, the Electricity Directive

techniques[151] for ensuring the highest level of cybersecurity and data protection.[152]

- Subject to that assessment, Member States or the designated competent authority should prepare a timetable with a target of up to ten years for the deployment of smart metering systems.
- In case of a negative cost-benefit analysis, Member States must reconsider the introduction of smart metering systems based on technological and market developments (*Electricity Directive*, Article 19(5)). Thus, they must ensure that this assessment is revised at least every four years, or more frequently, in response to significant changes in the underlying assumptions and to technological and market developments. Union-level scrutiny is put on Member States by obligating them to notify the EC of the outcome of their updated cost-benefit assessment.

301. Regarding the cost-benefit assessment, Annex II complements Article 19 by listing factors that this economic assessment may take into consideration, providing more guidance to Member States. They include (1) the long-term costs and benefits to the market and the individual consumer, or (2) which form of smart metering is economically reasonable and cost-effective, and which time frame is feasible for their distribution. By combining minimum requirements and guidance, EU law prevents disproportionate interventions in facilitating the rollout of smart meters. On the one hand, it creates sufficient flexibility for Member States, which allows for due regard to diverging costs and benefits in different national contexts, especially considering the need for data security techniques. On the other hand, through setting requirements for conducting the cost-benefit assessment and offering guidance, EU law also provides the necessary impetus for the deployment of this key ICT infrastructure.

302. Although Member States were given discretion in deploying smart meters, the regulatory authority must strongly recommend that electricity undertakings and other market participants optimize the use of electricity by introducing smart metering systems that are interoperable, to optimize the use of electricity (*Electricity Directive*, Articles 19(1) and 59(1)(o)).

---

integrates the functional requirements contained in the Recommendation and makes them binding for Member States. See *TFEU*, Article 288; EC, 2012; Robilant, 2006.

151 In the context of data protection and security in a smart metering environment, 'best available techniques' refer to the most effective, advanced and practically suitable techniques for providing, in principle, the basis for complying with the Union data protection and security rules. See *Electricity Directive*, Article 2 (27) and Annex II (2).

152 As the number of connection points to the network increases and an enormous quantity of energy information is now exchanged, it is important to prepare for cybersecurity threats and personal information leakage. This issue has already arisen in the Netherlands, one of the first adopters of the smart metering system. See Park and Heo, 2020; Hampton et al., 2022.

Article 19 of the Electricity Directive also gives discretion to Member States in determining specific means to recover the costs of installing smart meters. Yet, this cost recovery is subject to a requirement that final customers should contribute to the associated costs of the deployment in a transparent and non-discriminatory manner, while taking into account the long-term benefits to the whole value chain (*Electricity Directive*, Article 19(4)). Where the cost-benefit assessment of rolling out smart metering systems in a specific Member State is negative, final customers who request a smart meter are required to bear the associated costs. In this case, Member States or relevant authorities need to review these costs regularly, and at least every two years, make them publicly available and trace the evolution of those costs as a result of technology developments and potential metering system upgrades (*Electricity Directive*, Article 21(2)(c)).

#### 5.1.2.2. Consumers' Rights Concerning Smart Meters

303. The Electricity Directive particularly stipulates the right to access smart meters in two cases. One of these is ensuring access for beneficiaries of regulated prices to smart meters, provided by its Article 5(7) that governs the utilization of regulated pricing for the supply of electricity to household customers and to microenterprises who are neither energy poor nor vulnerable customers, as discussed in Section 4 of this Chapter above. In the case of introducing price interventions for these two groups of customers, Member States must ensure that they are entitled to, and are offered, smart meters installed at no extra upfront cost. These customers should also be directly informed of the possibility of installing smart meters and provided with necessary assistance.

304. The other situation relates to the circumstances where the nationwide deployment of smart metering systems has been negatively assessed and where smart metering systems are not systematically deployed. Article 21 of the Electricity Directive lays down a set of requirements for Member States to meet the demand of final customers for accessing or having an upgraded smart meter. In the context of this legal provision, Member States only need to make available smart meters upon the customers' requests, and associated costs should be borne by the customers requesting the smart meter, as already noted (*Electricity Directive*, Article 21).

305. Lastly, Article 20(e) of the Directive provides that, if final customers request it, data on their electricity consumption shall be made available to them or a third party they nominate, such as IFSPs.[153] The provision of

153 This provision should be read with the second paragraph of Article 20, which grants customers the right to retrieve their metering data or transmit it to another party at no additional cost.

such data should be done through a standardized communication interface or remote access and in an easily understandable format that allows final customers to compare offers.

#### 5.1.2.3. Defining Functionalities

306. To address deficiencies of smart metering systems operating in Member States, the Electricity Directive highlights that the deployed smart metering systems should be equipped with fit-for-purpose functionalities defined in this legislation (*Electricity Directive*, recital 55). When proceeding with the deployment of smart metering systems in their territories, Member States should adopt and publish the minimum functional and technical requirements for the smart metering systems to be deployed. The setting of these requirements should align with the minimum requirements for smart meters' functionalities contained in Article 20 and Annex II.[154]

307. Furthermore, relevant definitions also clarify the binding minimum functional requirements for smart metering systems. The Electricity Directive defines the smart meter by stressing its superior capabilities in enabling consumer engagement compared to a conventional meter. Its capabilities include, but are not limited to, measuring electricity fed into the grid or electricity consumed from the grid, transmitting and receiving data for information, monitoring and control purposes, and using a form of electronic communication (*Electricity Directive*, Article 2(23)). These are further elaborated in Article 20, which is dedicated to dealing with functionalities of smart metering systems. In principle, the functional requirements must be fully complied with when the deployment of smart metering systems is positively assessed as a result of the cost-benefit analysis or when smart metering systems are systematically deployed.

308. In accordance with the first subparagraph of Article 20, requirements on functionalities vary according to three types of consumption data, as illustrated in Table 6 below. As can be seen, these functionalities aim to facilitate changes in consumption decisions by updating readings frequently and enabling comparisons between historical and current consumption and costs. Moreover, some of them are notably pivotal in assisting the uptake of dynamic electricity price contracts and explicit DR. In particular, according to Article 11 of the Electricity Directive, installing a smart meter constitutes the technological prerequisite for a consumer to conclude a dynamic electricity price contract. This implies that such meters must be able to inform customers fully of

[154] Article 20 of the Electricity Directive builds upon the 2012 Commission Recommendation on functionalities for smart metering systems. See EC, 2012; Pearson, 2020, p 124.

the impact of dynamic changes in supply on their electricity consumption and costs, thereby encouraging customers to adjust their consumption. Providing real-time or near-real-time billing data based on electricity consumption could make this possible. On these grounds, the legislation specifically harmonizes functionalities of smart metering systems in making available actual and near real-time consumption data, and sets out respective standards.[155] As shown in Table 6, for actual electricity consumption, the provision of relevant data is mandatory, whether customers request it or not. Less strict requirements apply to non-validated near real-time consumption data, which should be provided at the customer's request. Furthermore, making a comparison of consumption data possible is another important goal served by smart metering systems. Hence, there are additional requirements for visualizing validated historical consumption data.

**Table 6. Functionalities regarding the measuring and provision of various consumption data under Article 20**

| Data | Functionalities of smart metering systems |
|---|---|
| Actual electricity consumption | ➢ Accurately measuring;<br>➢ Providing final customers with information on the actual time of use. |
| Validated historical consumption | ➢ Making the data easily and securely available to final customers;<br>➢ Making the data visualized to final customers;<br>➢ Providing upon customers' request and no additional cost charged. |
| Non-validated near real-time consumption | ➢ Making the data easily and securely available to final customers;<br>➢ No additional cost is charged;<br>➢ Through a standardized interface or remote access. |

Source: Author's elaboration.

309. In addition, the harmonized standards contained in Article 20 also aim to raise customers' awareness of both the use of smart infrastructure and private data protection. Firstly, Member States must provide appropriate advice and information to final customers before or at the time of smart meter installation. Consumers often have scarce knowledge of how to use smart meters to offer DR. Experience in some countries that have deployed smart meters shows that many customers are either unaware that a smart meter has been installed or are hesitant to respond to the price signals (Kowalska-Pyzalska, 2018; Hampton et al., 2022). This demonstrates that merely installing smart meters cannot guarantee the realization of the full benefits of such infrastructure. To fully reap the advantages of smart meters, Article 20 prescribes that the

[155] In the context of deploying smart metering, 'near real-time' means a short time period, usually down to seconds or up to the imbalance settlement period in the national market. See *Electricity Directive*, Article 2 (26).

advice and information offered to final customers should, in particular, cover the full potential of smart meters with regard to managing meter readings and monitoring energy consumption. Secondly, to safeguard rights relating to personal data, customers should be informed about the collection and processing of personal data in accordance with the applicable Union data protection rules.

310. Another functional and technical requirement concerns the interoperability of the smart metering systems, as outlined in Article 19.[156] Member States are required to deliver smart metering systems that are interoperable and able to provide output for consumer energy management systems (*Electricity Directive*, Article 19(3)). In doing so, they need to take into account the use of relevant available standards, including those enabling interoperability, best practices, and the importance of developing smart grids and the development of the internal electricity market.

#### 5.1.2.4. Requirements for Conventional Meters

311. As already noted, the systematic deployment of smart metering systems in Member States depends on the result of the cost-benefit assessment undertaken at the national level. In a Member State where the smart metering system is not systematically deployed, individual customers have the right to request the installation of a smart meter. Nevertheless, a question remains as to how final customers who do not do so are provided with information on their actual consumption, which is at a minimum necessary for adjusting consumption. Article 22 of the Electricity Directive addresses this by setting out minimum requirements for conventional meters. Even though such meters are not capable of both transmitting and receiving data,[157] Member States are required to ensure that final customers are provided with individual conventional meters that accurately measure their actual consumption. In addition, they must ensure that final customers can easily read their conventional meters, either directly or indirectly through an online interface or another appropriate interface.

### *5.1.3. Guarantees of Origin*

312. Alongside the general rules imposing the energy source disclosure obligation on suppliers, EU law also creates a specific legal framework for GOs

---

156 Interoperability means the ability of two or more energy or communication networks, systems, devices, applications or components to interwork to exchange and use information in order to perform required functions. See *Electricity Directive*, Article 2 (24).

157 The 'conventional meter' means an analogue or electronic meter with no capability to transmit and receive data. See *Electricity Directive*, Article 2 (22).

to help trace the origin of RES-E. It is impossible to track power flows through the grid, making it challenging to promote RES-E to consumers (Hamburger, 2019). GOs are thus utilized as an information disclosure tool for providing evidence to final customers that the share or quantity of electricity was produced from renewable sources.[158] They are electronic documents that are recorded in a centralized electronic registry, and issued, transferred and canceled electronically (*REDII*, Articles 2(12) and 19(6); Ragwitz et al., 2009). This tracking instrument can improve the quality and transparency of the information to consumers when suppliers market RES-E to them, also contributing to consumer protection (Banet, 2012, pp 118–119). Through showing generation attributes of renewable electricity, GOs further promote customers to pick a 'green' supplier, thereby contributing to a customer-driven demand for RES-E (Banet, 2012, pp 119 and 127; Raadal et al., 2012; *REDII*, recital 56). Some Member States have also utilized GOs to enhance the implementation of the aforementioned energy sources disclosure obligation (Hamburger, 2019). This has been allowed by the REDII by stating that 'Member States may arrange for guarantees of origin to be issued for energy from nonrenewable sources' (*REDII*, Article 19(2)).

313. As early as 2001, the GO mechanism was introduced in EU law and subsequently developed in the 2009 RED (*2001 Renewable Electricity Directive*, recital 10 and Article 5; *2009 RED*, Article 15). Since 2009, EU law has defined a clear delimitation between GOs and green certificates used as a national support scheme. It does so by strictly limiting the function of GOs to information disclosure, namely proving that certain electricity supplied is of renewable origin (Hamburger, 2019), and stating that they do not by themselves confer a right to benefit from national support schemes (*2009 RED*, recitals 52 and 56; *REDII*, recital 55 and Article 2(12)). The reason underlying this distinction is to avoid affecting the exercise of national competences regarding the devising of support schemes, notably given that green certificates applied in some Member States also allow for the tracking of electricity generation attributes.[159] Moreover, restricting the purpose of GOs is also intended to respond

---

158 In the 2001 Renewable Electricity Directive, the GO was merely used to guarantee the origin of electricity produced from renewable energy sources. Since 2009, the GO system has been extended to cover other forms of energy produced from renewable sources, such as renewable gas. This book only focuses on its function allowing the tracing of the source of renewable electricity. See *2001 Renewable Electricity Directive*, Article 5; *2009 RED*, Article 15; *REDII*, recitals 55, 56 and 59, Articles 2 and 19.

159 In an early leaked draft of the 2009 RED, the EC attempted again to push forward a harmonized approach to the regulatory support schemes across all Member States by proposing unrestricted certificate trading in GOs. Like previous attempts to build an EU-wide support scheme, this was strongly opposed by a number of countries, particularly those with FIT schemes. The struggle between the EU and Member States over regulatory harmonization of RES-E support schemes ended with Member States fending off the supranational pressure for top-down

to the potential shortcomings arising from the divergent use of GOs in Member States.[160] The limited function of GOs is further materialized in Article 19(2) of the REDII by firstly preventing GOs from being used for compliance with binding overall Union targets for renewables. Secondly, the EU legislator recognizes that GOs are the object of intensive trading both together with and separately from electricity (Banet, 2012, p 134). Such trading may enhance compliance with the energy sources disclosure obligation and contribute to the overall objective of facilitating trade in RES-E (Banet, 2012, p 134). For such reasons, transfers of GOs are permissible but must refrain from affecting the decisions of Member States relating to cooperation mechanisms aiming at promoting cross-border renewables support, namely statistical transfers, joint projects or joint support schemes for compliance with the Union's renewables targets. Thirdly, the calculation of the gross final consumption of renewables would not be affected by the transfer of GOs.

314. Despite the failed attempts to harmonize an EU-wide support scheme based on GOs, EU law seeks to build a uniform EU-wide GO system to ensure the reliability and accuracy of this information disclosure tool. The major requirements relating to the issuance, utilization, transfer, and supervision of GOs are worth mentioning here:

- Mandatory issuance on request of RES-E generators: The REDII specifies that Member States must issue in response to a request from a producer of RES-E. In other words, the use of GOs as a tracking instrument for disclosure is not absolute, and Member States are merely required to ensure that RES-E generators can obtain GOs on demand (Banet, 2012, p 128).
- The minimum content of GOs includes information on generating installations and the national support schemes applied to those installations.[161]

harmonization. This led to the national competence in applying different support schemes being formally entrenched in the 2009 RED. In this context, since then, EU law has sought to avoid affecting the exercise of relevant national rule-making competences by making a clear distinction between promotional measures applied at the Union level and support schemes at the Member State level. A leading example is emphasizing the distinction between the GO and green certificates. The fundamental distinction between green certificates or TGCs and GOs lies in the TGC system representing a mandatory market, which is created by the quota obligation, while GOs represent voluntary support from final customers. See Ragwitz et al., 2009; Howes et al., 2010, pp 110–111; Banet, 2012, pp 19, 21 and 133; Tews, 2015; Gkarakis and Dagoumas, 2016; Crossley, 2017.

160 Existing research argues that a lack of harmonization between countries can result in unreliable information for consumers in the case of international GO trade. See Banet, 2012, p 133; Hamburger, 2019.

161 This is intended to provide information on how supported electricity is allocated to final customers. See *REDII*, recital 57.

- Each GO should be of the standard size of 1 MWh and correspond strictly to one unit of energy, to avoid double counting of any electricity amount.[162]
- GOs are only valid for 12 months after the production of the relevant energy unit (*REDII*, Article 19(3)). This aims to prevent the national energy mix from being based on old data when GOs are taken into account, as this would misinform final customers as to the real volume of RES-E produced (Howes et al., 2010, p 111).
- To allow cross-border trade of GOs, mutual recognition of GOs among Member States is mandatory, and limited exceptions are made clear. Member States must mutually recognize GOs, while refusals are only justified where the Member States have well-founded doubts about the concerned GOs' accuracy, reliability, or veracity (Banet, 2012, p 134; *REDII*, Article 19(9)). Such refusals and justification should also be notified to the EC, which retains the power to change relevant national decisions.
- Member States or designated competent bodies are responsible for supervising the issuance, transfer and cancellation of GOs, and guaranteeing that GOs are accurate, reliable and fraud-resistant (*REDII*, Article 19(5)(6)). To ensure the reliability of GOs, conflicts of interest should be avoided, and thus the designated competent bodies should be independent of production, trade and supply activities (*REDII*, Article 19(5)).

315. Another issue worth noting is whether TGCs applied in Member States and GOs could be issued concomitantly. As explained above, EU law draws a clear distinction between these two certificate schemes. Their coexistence raises the question of how to coordinate them to fulfill their respective roles in supporting RES-E and disclosing energy sources while avoiding overcompensation. Under EU law, it is left to Member States to decide whether a RES-E producer will receive a TGC in addition to a GO for the same unit of electricity generated, to allow Member States to retain control over national support schemes.[163] In this

---

162 Double counting may occur because when GOs are not issued for every MWh of electricity produced, the disclosure obligation of suppliers refers to all electricity consumed. Hence, disclosure statements are partly based on statistical energy generation mix data besides GOs. If a supplier uses GOs to verify the origin of an electricity amount, this amount should be subtracted from energy statistics. Otherwise, one amount of RES-E would be taken into account twice: once with GOs and once in the statistics. See *REDII*, Article 19 (2); Raadal et al., 2009; Banet, 2012, p 131; Hamburger, 2019.

163 The REDII allows an exception to the general requirement of issuing GOs on demand of RES-E producers: Member States may decide, for the purposes of accounting for the market value of the GO, not to issue such a GO to a producer that receives financial support from a support scheme. This implies that under EU law, Member States may allow a combination of the GO and the TGC or choose not to do so. See *REDII*, Article 19 (2); Banet, 2012, p 142.

context, relevant national law has shown significant differences with respect to the possible bundling of TGCs and GOs.[164]

### 5.1.4. *Information Provision in Facilitating Renewables Self-Consumption*

316. As elucidated above in Section 3, final customers are entitled to engage in renewables self-consumption by becoming active customers, renewables self-consumers, and members of energy communities. Some consumers, especially residential customers interested in renewables prosuming, however, could not exercise this right well because of the lack of information (Palm, 2018). Against this background, in REDII, how to exercise relevant rights and reap subsequent benefits is listed as an element of the rules for offering information (*REDII*, recitals 26 and 39, Article 18). Furthermore, consumers are faced with fragmented information as well as confusing bureaucratic processes regarding installation (Ruggiero et al., 2015). To address this problem, providing relevant information is also incorporated in legal provisions for streamlining and facilitating the entire permit-granting procedure. The REDII confers on Member States a duty to set up or designate one or more contact points, which are intended to guide permit applicants (*REDII*, Article 16(1)). The rules governing the establishment of contact points and their tasks were subsequently reinforced by the 2023 Amendment to the RED II. These arrangements aim to further reduce the costs and efforts required by actors involved in renewables self-consumption when applying for administrative permits to build or operate renewables production assets.

317. Under Article 16 of the REDII, one of the tasks of such contact points is to provide all necessary information for consumers wishing to invest in renewables DG to facilitate their understanding of procedures (*REDII*, recital 51). This should be implemented by making available a manual of procedures for developers of renewable energy plants and providing that information online, addressing distinctly also small-scale renewable energy projects, renewables self-consumers projects and RECs. In addition, contact points are also tasked to guide and facilitate the applicant during the entire administrative permit application and permit-granting procedure upon the request of the applicant. At the end of the permit-granting procedure, they must

---

164 By way of example, in the Flemish Region of Belgium, the GO and the TGC are required to be issued and traded together at the wholesale level, while the two certificates can be used separately and be unbundled to fulfill a quota obligation and an energy-mix disclosure obligation at the retail level. However, in the Wallonia Region of Belgium, GOs and TGCs are issued concomitantly for the same units of RES-E, while they are not bundled and can be traded separately. Issuing both a GO and a TGC to the same generated MW h is also allowed in Sweden. See Raadal et al., 2009; Banet, 2012, pp 142–143.

provide the applicant with all necessary information and, where appropriate, involve other administrative authorities.

318. The REDII also takes measures to mitigate potential complexity when individual or collective prosumers engage with the contact points. First, the applicant should not be required to contact more than one contact point during the entire procedure. Second, when providing information on procedures for developers of renewable energy plants online, the online information should indicate the contact point relevant to the application in question. If a Member State has more than one contact point, the online information should also indicate the contact point relevant to the specific application.

## 5.2. CONSUMER DATA MANAGEMENT

319. In the context of engaging consumers in electricity markets, the market process is, inter alia, challenged with effective data exchange, as data is collected from a large number of smaller, distributed consumers. Relevant challenges are especially pronounced when consumers trade explicit DR and self-generated RES-E through a third party (e.g., in the case of using aggregation services). This is because data collection, processing, and communication will take place between consumers and multiple entities, including the TSO, the DSO, IFSPs (or aggregators), and affected suppliers and BRPs.

320. Another key issue that makes data management highly demanding and thereby increases transaction costs is data security and privacy concerns (Nolan and O'Malley, 2015; Good et al., 2017). Such concerns from industrial, commercial and residential users even constitute one of the major barriers for them to actively participate in electricity markets to trade DR and self-generated RES-E (EC, 2016a; Good et al., 2017; Paterakis et al., 2017; Annala et al., 2018a; Stede et al., 2020; Leinauer et al., 2022). In addition, data security concerns could also hinder the rollout of smart meters (Schallehn and Valogianni, 2022). The foregoing literature review in Chapter II highlights, aside from economic benefits, how inconvenience and the active efforts required to react to market signals can affect consumers' willingness to trade DR and self-generated RES-E. ICT infrastructure is one of the linchpins to increasing automation and minimizing disruption to comfort and convenience (EC, 2016a; Powells and Fell, 2019). Data safety issues, if poorly resolved, can substantially hinder the widespread deployment of ICT infrastructure and consumer market participation.

321. Additionally, other stakeholders have diverse interests in data security. For instance, suppliers and IFSPs may require the protection of different commercially sensitive data when exchanging data for implementing the

above-mentioned compensation in the activation of explicit DR.[165] This leads to additional tasks to process data before communicating it to relevant stakeholders. In this case, several key issues arise (i) which data should be protected and how, (ii) who is entitled to the concerned data, and (iii) who will be in charge of data processing and coordinating data communication. The EU-level framework for data management sets out principles for Member States to elaborate on rules for addressing these issues.

322. EU law develops this framework by defining the rights of customers and other eligible parties to access data required to trade DR and self-generated RES-E, among other services (Section 5.2.1). On this basis of enabling the correct information to be made available to the right parties, fair access to relevant data is highlighted, which can impact the level playing field (Section 5.2.2). While facilitating efficient data exchange, this framework bears in mind the Union's legal framework for data management (Section 5.2.3) (Pearson, 2020, p 126).[166] Lastly, it also establishes some principles for recovering costs incurred in data management (Section 5.2.4).

### 5.2.1. *Defining Rights to Access Data*

323. Article 23 of the Electricity Directive specifically deals with how the management and exchange of data should be organized. In that provision, the determination of eligible parties is left to Member States to establish, which is largely context-dependent.[167] Nevertheless, Article 13 and Article 17 complement Article 23 to further clarify which parties have a legitimate interest in accessing DR-related data in the context of DR through aggregation. The entitled parties include final customers concluding aggregation contracts, market participants engaged in aggregation, such as CECs and IFSPs, and other electricity undertakings affected by DR activation, such as suppliers and BRPs (*Electricity Directive*, Article 17(3)(c)). Article 20 and Annex I also specify the rights of consumers and third parties acting on their behalf to access data provided by smart meters and electricity bills, as summarized in Section 5.1 above.

---

165 National law in this respect, see e.g. *ToE Rules*, 2021, Sections 14 and 16. For more details, see the case study of Belgian law in Chapter IV below.

166 For relevant EU law for data management, see e.g., *General Data Protection Regulation*, 2016; *Regulation (EU) 2018/1725 of the European Parliament and of the Council of 23 October 2018 on the protection of natural persons with regard to the processing of personal data by the Union institutions, bodies, offices and agencies and on the free movement of such data, and repealing Regulation (EC) No 45/2001 and Decision No 1247/2002/EC [2018] OJ L 295/39*, 2018.

167 For national law defining eligible parties in the context of explicit DR, see Chapter IV below.

324. The above-cited Article 23 sets out the right of these eligible parties to enjoy effective data flow. It provides that access to data must be made easily for eligible parties, and the relevant procedures for obtaining access to data should be made publicly available. In particular, the Electricity Directive highlights the role of facilitating better access for customers to their metering data, consumption data and DR-related data in making the market more contestable and fostering customer switching (*Electricity Directive*, recital 56 and Article 58(h)). The rationale behind this is that, based on adequate data on consumption, prices and service costs associated with their consumption, customers are enabled to invite competitors to make offers based on that information (*Electricity Directive*, recital 56). Moreover, enabling customers to easily access their consumption data is one of the prerequisites for engaging them to actively manage their electricity consumption, as stressed at the beginning of this section. To realize these benefits, aside from the aforementioned provisions on DR, billing information and smart meters, Article 23 forbids additional costs charged to final customers for access to their data or for a request to make their data available (*Electricity Directive*, Article 23(5)).

### *5.2.2. Fair Data Access*

325. Under Article 3 of the Electricity Directive, data access is highlighted as an aspect of ensuring a level playing field (*Electricity Directive*, Article 3(4)). Member States have a general obligation to put in place transparent, proportionate, and non-discriminatory rules concerning data access. Article 13, Article 17 and Article 23 of the Directive stress that Member States must ensure customers and eligible parties participating in DR have access to DR-related data on equal and non-discriminatory terms. Furthermore, the Electricity Directive enhances the neutrality of the data management parties nominated by Member States in two ways.

- Member States are allowed to decide whether to require parties responsible for data management to appoint compliance officers. EU law highlights the task of such compliance officers concerning ensuring non-discriminatory access to data (*Electricity Directive*, Article 23(4)).
- Under Article 34, where DSOs are nominated to manage data from smart metering systems, there is a risk that vertically integrated DSOs have privileged access to data and discriminate against eligible parties. To mitigate this risk, this Article specifies that specific measures for preventing discriminatory access to data should be contained in the compliance programs for unbundling.

### 5.2.3. *Efficient and Secure Data Access and Exchange*

326. Member States are given the freedom to develop various models for data management (*Electricity Directive*, recital 57 and Article 23(2)). Even so, Article 23 of the Electricity Directive creates minimum criteria that relevant national law should respect. Above all, the management of data serves the goal of ensuring efficient data access and exchange, as well as data protection and data security. To this end, the parties responsible for data management nominated[168] in Member States must provide access to the data of the final customer to any eligible party (*Electricity Directive*, Article 23(2)). Increased efficiency in using consumption data also hinges upon national actions to adopt an easily understandable, harmonized format for consumption data. NRAs have thus been granted duties to deliver this and ensure prompt access for all customers to their consumption data (*Electricity Directive*, Article 59(1)(t)).

327. Moreover, the efforts to achieve optimal data access and exchange are also reflected in provisions on promoting the full interoperability of energy services within the EU. Unlike actions taken at the national level, interoperability is beneficial for increasing the overall efficiency of data communication across the EU, and realizing its benefits largely relies on coordinated efforts at the Union level. Interoperability has the potential to make metering data, consumption data and data required for DR easily usable by a wide range of eligible parties (Pearson, 2020, p 131). This also promises to avoid excessive administrative costs for market players active in multiple European countries, who would otherwise have to adapt to the different data management models of each of the national markets they operate (Pearson, 2020, p 131). For these reasons, Article 24 empowers the EC to adopt implementing acts concerning interoperability requirements.

328. The remaining provisions contained in Article 23 seek to guarantee the security and privacy of data by first referring to Union law on data management (*Electricity Directive*, Article 23(1)(3)(4)). For instance, the General Data Protection Regulation is referred to in this Article to provide applicable rules for the processing of personal data. Furthermore, Member States must supervise the compliance of the national parties responsible for data management with the relevant requirements of this Directive. In this respect, Member States

---

168 Under EU law, it is left to Member States to entrust the tasks of data management to the TSO, the DSO or a centralized data platform managed by another party (sometimes known as a data hub), for instance. See Pearson, 2020, p 127. For examples of nominating the TSO and the independent market operator as the DR data managers, see *Belgian Federal Electricity Law*, art. 19ter; CEER, 2019.

have leeway to decide whether to require data management parties to appoint compliance officers to monitor their rule compliance.

### *5.2.4. Data Management Cost Recovery*

329. The experience from Member States suggests that communicating data among eligible parties while safeguarding data confidentiality can involve a complex set of procedures and create high transaction costs (*ToE Rules*, 2021).[169] This points to a trade-off between incentivizing high-quality data management and reducing financial burdens on consumers and other market participants involved in exchanging DR and self-generated RES-E. Hence, the nominated parties responsible for data management, either network operators or independent data hubs, need to get adequate remuneration for their provided services. Article 23 of the Electricity Directive addresses this by obliging Member States to set the relevant charges for access to data by eligible parties (*Electricity Directive*, Article 23(5)). At the same time, such data management costs should be regulated to a reasonable and duly justified level to avoid overly burdening stakeholders (*Electricity Directive*, Article 23(5)). This is particularly relevant in cases where Member States allow such costs to be socialized through network tariffs or PSOs imposed on network operators, which may lead to increased energy bills for customers.[170]

## 6. ADAPTING NETWORK REGULATION

330. Section 3 of Chapter II elaborates that the need for involving final customers in facilitating RES-E uptake has posed new challenges to electricity grids and their regulation. The technical and societal context of the TSO and the DSO has been in flux with the advent of new technologies and the involvement of new market players engaged in DR and renewables self-consumption (Ruester et al., 2014; Edens and Lavrijssen, 2019). Beyond efficient, secure, and non-discriminatory network operation, the regulatory focus has shifted to encompass broader network performance that favors the sustainable

[169] See also the case study of Belgian law in Chapter IV below.

[170] In the Flemish Region of Belgium, for example, its Energy Decree delegates the Flemish Government to impose PSOs on DSOs to provide metering services to various market participants involved in DR, such as customers, IFSPs and FRPs. However, imposing PSOs raises concerns about increasing the distribution system tariffs. The significant increase in Flemish distribution system tariffs is linked to the higher costs of PSOs. The net costs associated with these obligations are recovered in the PSO tariff in the distribution system tariff. In the Flemish Region, compared to 2007, the distribution system tariff rose on average by 137.21% (€58.50/MWh). 73.85% of this increase is due to the increase in the tariff for PSOs. See *Flemish Energy Decree*, Article 4.1.8/2; CREG, 2021.

low-carbon energy transition (Shaw et al., 2010; Pollitt and Haney, 2013; Nepal and Jamasb, 2015).

331. So far, the EU's legal framework for the electricity grid has evolved to essentially rest on three pillars: (i) economic regulation of revenues or profits, (ii) vertical unbundling[171] and regulated TPA,[172] and (iii) active network management to integrate flexibility and RES-E (*Electricity Directive*, recitals 61, 65, 81 and 83; Bauknecht and Brunekreeft, 2008, p 470). For the purpose of this book, the main focus will be on how the goal of shifting the consumer's role to facilitate the uptake of RES-E reinvents economic regulation, access arrangements for electricity networks, and network operation tasks.

332. As mentioned above, one of the overriding goals of the existing electricity market design is to create a customer-centered market wherein final customers are adequately mobilized to contribute to enhancing system flexibility and the uptake of RES-E (*Electricity Directive*, recitals 9, 10, 39 and 42, Article 1). Alongside the regulatory reform of competitive segments, adapting the electric network and corresponding regulatory frameworks is also underway with a view to supporting the final customers' increasing role in facilitating the RES-E's uptake (*Electricity Directive*, recitals 51, 52, 61 and 83). Among others, the core activities of electricity transmission and distribution are being updated around the system operators' interactions with consumers and other entities involved in DR and renewables self-consumption, ranging from investment, planning, to operation, as well as remuneration schemes (Ruester et al., 2014; Nepal and Jamasb, 2015; Pereira et al., 2018; Edens and Lavrijssen, 2019; Pereira et al., 2020).

333. Due to the distinct natures and objectives of the transmission and distribution systems,[173] the challenges faced by the TSO and the DSO, as well

---

171 Vertical unbundling aims to prevent the VIU from having incentives to take advantage of its own network platform to benefit its generation, supply or energy service departments by deterring third-party access and using other subtle methods to limit competition in competitive segments. See *Electricity Directive*, recitals 68 and 69; Cabau and Sandberg, 2021, pp 113–114.

172 Regulated TPA means that TSOs and DSOs provide services under regulated conditions. It covers (i) regulated tariffs (objective, transparent and subject to regulatory view), (ii) guaranteeing network users access to the network in an objective and non-discriminatory manner, coupled with a set of rules applicable to the refusal of access, and (iii) limited and clearly defined exemptions from non-discriminatory access. These essential elements of regulated TPA are also entrenched throughout economic regulation, service quality regulation and requirements on non-discrimination and transparency, as will be discussed respectively in the following subsections focusing on the three aspects. See *Electricity Directive*, Article 6; Kuiken and Más, 2019.

173 In existing electricity systems, the distribution system and the transmission system differ in a number of dimensions. Firstly, transmission involves long-distance transportation of electricity at high voltage. Distribution is the transportation of low-voltage electricity through local networks, which consists of overhead lines, cables, switchgear, transformers,

as the requirements imposed on them to support relevant DSM activities, differ in several ways. Nevertheless, their regulation shares similar mechanisms based on the theory of regulating network monopolies,[174] which equally matters for enabling a greater role of consumers in promoting RES-E. Given this, before examining their respective regulatory frameworks in sections 6.2 and 6.3, this section begins with the common rules applied to transmission and distribution networks.

## 6.1. COMMON RULES FOR TRANSMISSION AND DISTRIBUTION NETWORKS

334. Section 3.1 of Chapter II describes common problems or challenges that must be addressed by network regulation in the context of engaging consumers in supporting system integration and the use of RES-E. This subsection focuses on how existing EU law adapts network regulation to consumer engagement.

### *6.1.1. Economic Regulation of Networks*

335. EU law only establishes generic principles for the economic regulation of network companies, which are contained in legal provisions regulating network charges and tariffs. Member States are given significant discretion over the specific approaches to carrying out cost regulation accordingly. Such specific approaches include, for example, the methods of calculating the revenue cap or price cap, the price review period, as well as the specific rewards and penalties for over- or under-delivering on cost-efficiency targets.[175] Despite this, EU law seeks to steer necessary reform of economic regulation to enable

---

and meters to transfer electricity from the transmission system to customers' premises. Distribution networks were originally neither used nor equipped to handle large amounts of generation (such as self-generated RES-E) on their network. Secondly, transmission systems are highly meshed, whereas distribution systems are characterized by a radial or looped grid architecture. Thirdly, the high-voltage lines of transmission systems have a lower resistance than the lower-voltage lines in the distribution system. Therefore, if a generator gets connected to the low-voltage distribution system, this can more easily affect the voltage levels. Fourthly, in distribution systems, and especially the low-voltage ends, there are usually no control systems available that are standard on the transmission level. As a consequence, it is difficult for DSOs to influence the operation of generators and maintain system stability. See Cardell and Tabors, 1997; Jamasb and Pollitt, 2007; Bauknecht and Brunekreeft, 2008, pp 473–474; *Electricity Directive*, Article 2 (28)(29).

174 For the tasks of network regulation and the relevant rationale, see Section 3 of Chapter II above.

175 Pertinent examples from Member States in these aspects, see e.g., Shuttleworth, 2005; Jamasb and Pollitt, 2007; Nolting et al., 2019; Johansson et al., 2020.

the network segment to sufficiently support the increasing role of consumers in facilitating the uptake of RES-E.

336. The Union-level principles first include empowering NRAs to fix or approve tariffs, or the methodologies underlying the calculation of the tariffs, based on a proposal by TSOs or DSOs, or based on a proposal agreed between those operators and the network users (*Electricity Directive*, recital 81, Articles 6(1) and 59(1)(a)). This has been an integral component of regulated TPA (*Electricity Directive*, Article 6(1)). In regulating grid tariffs and charges, a more specific requirement is that the regulator must ensure transmission and distribution tariffs and charges[176] are cost-reflective and transparent (*Electricity Regulation*, Article 18(1)). The key question arises as to how to determine the efficient cost level for regulated network companies. Article 18 of the Electricity Regulation addresses this issue by prescribing that actual costs incurred should be incorporated in network charges, *insofar as they correspond to those of an efficient and structurally comparable network operator and are applied in a non-discriminatory manner.*'

337. Interestingly, this provision implies that the EU has begun to shape the benchmarking method for determining a proper remuneration level. A specific reference to the charges of '*an efficient and structurally comparable network operator*' appears to aim to help decouple the allowed revenues of a network utility from its own underlying costs, through which the regulated revenue cap for the regulated entity can be determined (Nepal and Jamasb, 2015). This is well in line with the idea of benchmarking, which helps ascertain the efficient cost level by enabling a comparison of the actual efficiency performance against a reference or benchmark performance.[177] At the national

[176] Compared to its predecessors, the CEP provides greater clarity on what costs should be taken into account and what should be excluded. It specifies that charges applied by network operators for access to networks, including charges for connection to the networks, charges for use of networks, and, where applicable, charges for related network reinforcements. Unrelated costs supporting unrelated policy objectives are expressly excluded. See *Electricity Regulation*, article 18 (1).

[177] More specifically, benchmarking estimates a target for the costs of each company by using information about the costs of other companies. As widely discussed in the literature, the optimal design of the price regulation scheme is severely hindered by the asymmetry of information between the network company and its regulator. As described in the principal-agent relationship, the regulated agent holds superior information on its own cost and demand structures than the principal (the regulator in the network regulation case). It is generally challenging for regulators to determine whether planned investments are justified or not. Benchmarking was thus proposed to identify 'efficient costs' or 'the costs of an efficient company' by allowing comparative regulation and using outside information beyond what is revealed by the regulated company itself. In this way, the allowed revenue of the given regulated company can be estimated, which denies unnecessary costs caused by inefficient management, thereby helping to eliminate or reduce informational disadvantages of the regulator. Moreover, it is also conducive to reducing regulatory burden. Checking whether the regulated company's costs are reasonable would normally require a detailed review of

level, prior to the CEP, Member States primarily employed average or frontier-oriented benchmarking techniques.[178] However, using these two methods to set revenue allowances inevitably excludes some actual costs incurred in operating electricity networks, given the heterogeneity in the costs of network companies.[179] They are thus criticized for exposing regulated companies to a substantial risk that cost recovery will be denied for unpredictable and subjective reasons, also raising concerns over unfair administrative procedures in network regulation.[180] Against this background, the introduction of the

---

each company's past expenditure (or, for some price cap plans, of each company's future expenditure plans). When the regulator has a number of network operators to review at the same time, this task becomes very time-consuming. This drives regulators in some countries to turn to benchmarking, in an attempt to simplify the task and exploit information available from data sets containing cost information on several companies. See Giannakis et al., 2005; Shuttleworth, 2005; Haney and Pollitt, 2011; Nepal and Jamasb, 2015.

178 The main benchmarking methods can be classified as either average or frontier-oriented. Average-based approaches to benchmarking are best suited for introducing yardstick competition between relatively efficient firms, which means that the financial income of each firm depends on its performance relative to others, typically the average performance of the industry. This approach has been adopted in the Netherlands to regulate DSOs. In comparison, frontier methods can be used to close larger performance gaps. Using the frontier performance benchmark, an efficiency value for each grid operator is identified and compared to the most efficient operator, which has been applied to German DSOs. The discrepancy between the efficiency value of the considered operator and the most efficient one represents individual inefficiency. See Ajodhia and Hakvoort, 2005; Giannakis et al., 2005; Shuttleworth, 2005; Jamasb and Pollitt, 2007; Nolting et al., 2019; Edens and Lavrijssen, 2019.

179 Networks are complex constructions offering multiple outputs whose costs depend on many individual factors, including geographical conditions in each part of their service territory, the load characteristics of their customers and the history of load growth over the years. Taking geographical conditions as an example, specific local cost drivers might include the proportion of the terrain covered by mountains (significant in Austria), or whether the companies have to serve offshore islands (which affects some companies in the Netherlands), or problems with boggy acidic sub-soils or have to pay more for delivery of plant and materials, or higher than average staff costs, or rural or sparsely populated areas. See Ajodhia and Hakvoort, 2005; Shuttleworth, 2005; Nykamp et al., 2012.

180 As already noted, the costs of network companies can be highly case-specific or unique. The literature thus points out that in reality, no benchmarking model, whether based on an average or frontier performance, can ever hope to capture all factors affecting costs in the model specification. Thus, there inevitably exists the residual (i.e., the gap between observed costs and benchmarked costs) representing the costs that the model has 'failed to explain'. Ascribing this residual to 'inefficiency', or describing the benchmark as a measure of 'efficient costs' is unjustified, since it may be due to any combination of omitted or even unique factors. From the perspective of administrative procedural law, when the regulator uses the results of benchmarking as a reason to disallow the company-specific costs, they are, in fact, acting on an arbitrary basis without proper evidence. The deficiencies inherent in average and frontier benchmarking techniques imply their limited role in helping determine revenue or profit cap for regulated network companies. Since the 2000s, however, NRAs in a number of Member States (e.g., the Netherlands, the UK, and Germany) have used them as the major means to set allowed revenues, creating unduly significant room for subjective judgment of cost review. From the energy law point of view, the application of the two techniques would therefore offer average returns to exceptional performance delivered by certain network operators with special cost drivers. The exclusion of a proportion of actual costs incurred undermines

twofold benchmarking, 'an efficient and structurally comparable network operator', implies that the EU legislator seeks to mitigate relevant concerns. In particular, the standard of a 'structurally comparable network operator' reflects due attention to case-specific costs and the specificities of individual network companies when seeking benchmark performance, as opposed to simply employing average or frontier levels. This contributes to capturing more factors that influence the costs of regulated entities and narrowing the unexplained gap between observed costs and the referred benchmarks, which creates undesired room for arbitrary decisions in recognizing actual costs (Shuttleworth, 2005). Nevertheless, this new standard could raise additional problems and challenges in terms of implementation, as discussed in Chapter IV.

338. In addition to benchmarking, another noteworthy aspect of cost-reflective charges is that profits are not necessarily required to be limited to low levels of return (Gräper et al., 2021, p 70). By contrast, it suggests that network charges must be able to cover the necessary costs required to achieve objectives with regard to empowering final customers and enhancing system flexibility. This is demonstrated by a set of criteria for designing network tariffs contained in Article 18 of the Electricity Regulation. An overall requirement is that network charges should take into account the need for network security and flexibility. 'Network security' referred to here can be understood as encompassing the conventional elements of supply security, such as short-run operational reliability, commercial reliability and long-run resource adequacy (Joskow, 2007; Nepal and Jamasb, 2015). In conjunction with this concept, this provision recognizes two categories of costs incurred by integrating flexibility. One is the operating cost for procuring flexibility services. The other is the spending on long-term assets for expanding and reinforcing the grid and smart grid infrastructure required to cater to the increasing connection demands due to the development of DR and renewables self-consumption, while securing network reliability.

339. Another criterion sets minimum requirements for Member States when devising incentive regulation to enable system operators to actively accommodate and facilitate system integration of DR and self-generated RES-E. It highlights the need for designing appropriate incentives to effectuate a

the assurance of cost recovery, and thereby weakens the incentives offered by the regulatory framework. From the perspective of procedural law, procedural fairness requires an accurate finding of fact and the proper application of statutory criteria to it. To make this possible, procedures are needed to provide the necessary information and evidence, and to facilitate a sound and impartial judgement. In the case of average or frontier-based benchmark, the criteria used to assess cost efficiency overlook some cost categories and the regulator relying on such criteria fails to conduct a cost review based on accurate findings of fact and impartial judgement, leading to detriments to procedural fairness. See Galligan, 1996, p 53; Shuttleworth, 2005.

balance between short-term operating and long-term capital expenditures. Section 3.1.1 of Chapter II took some examples from Member States to demonstrate how previous tariff regulation failed to attain proper trade-offs between OPEX and CAPEX and the negative impacts on the system operators' incentives to use flexibility and ensure long-term network capacity adequacy (Giannakis et al., 2005; Ruester et al., 2014; Nolting et al., 2019; Edens and Lavrijssen, 2019; Pereira et al., 2020). To ensure correct trade-offs between short-term and long-term incentives, Article 18 of the Electricity Regulation stipulates that TSOs and DSOs should be properly incentivized over both the short and long run.

340. As mentioned in Section 3.1.1 of Chapter II, in some Member States, there were disincentives for investments in innovation and research and development projects in the regulation design. To reverse the system operators' reluctance to innovate, Article 18 explicitly mandates that, through tariff methodologies, network companies must be provided incentives to engage in innovation and research projects in the interest of consumers in areas such as digitization and flexibility services.

### *6.1.2. Quality of Service*

341. Section 3.1.2 of Chapter II indicated that price-cap regulation of electricity grids can lead to undesired effects on system operators' service quality. In the context of taking electricity DSM measures, achieving quality of service targets can incur greater costs. The system operators may lower service quality if tariffs do not fully recover these additional costs, or there are no clear requirements or mechanisms for monitoring the system operators' performance in delivering proper levels of service quality.

342. At the Union level, ensuring the service quality of electricity networks has progressively gained attention since the second Energy Package.[181] The CEP, for facilitating DSM measures in the context of developing RES-E, consolidates and updates requirements for service quality performance. These consist of three fronts as follows.

343. Firstly, grid users are entitled to access the transmission and distribution network under regulated TPA (*Electricity Directive*, Article 6(1)).

[181] The 2003 Energy Directive already required NRAs to monitor service quality, mainly concerning the time taken by transmission and distribution system undertakings to make connections and repairs. Within the 2009 Electricity Directive, under provisions specifying NRAs' general objectives and duties, performance-based regulation was introduced to link system performance with incentives and mandate the regulator to set or approve standards and requirements for quality of service. See *2003 Electricity Directive*, Article 23 (1)(f); *2009 Electricity Directive*, Articles 36 (f) and 37 (1)(h).

To ensure the realization of this right, both the TSO and the DSO are subject to the general obligation of maintaining an adequate level of service quality necessary for fulfilling their respective tasks. Ensuring adequate transmission capacity and system reliability is under the TSO's responsibility (*Electricity Directive*, Article 40(1)(c)). The DSO must be able to ensure the long-term ability of the system to meet reasonable demands for the distribution of electricity, for operating, maintaining, and developing a secure, reliable and efficient electricity distribution system in its area (*Electricity Directive*, Article 31(1)). These, inter alia, aim to accommodate the rising network connection demands driven by consumers' growing involvement in supporting the uptake of RES-E.

344. Secondly, additional costs incurred by connecting DR and decentralized RES-E and relevant incentives should be reflected in regulated network charges and tariffs, as elaborated above. Seen in conjunction with Article 58(f) of the Electricity Directive, such costs, inter alia, encompass the costs of maintaining system performance to connect market participants involved in these two DSM activities while ensuring system reliability.[182] This clarity further helps avoid service quality being undermined by economic regulation of the network, which may not fully consider the cost of guaranteeing adequate quality levels. The parallel requirement of considering cost efficiency goals helps avoid unduly expensive quality investments, thereby contributing to maintaining service quality at an optimal level (*Electricity Directive*, Article 31(1)).

345. Thirdly, the Electricity Directive reinforces the competence of NRAs in terms of monitoring and improving the performance of TSOs and DSOs in delivering network services. Compared to the 2009 Electricity Directive, it preserves the task conferred on NRAs of monitoring the time taken by TSOs and DSOs to make connections and repairs (*Electricity Directive*, Article 59(1)(q)). It additionally elaborates on requirements for the use of performance-based regulation. NRAs are obligated to monitor and assess the performance of TSOs and DSOs about the development of a smart grid that promotes the integration of renewable electricity, based on a limited set of indicators (*Electricity Directive*, Article 59(1)(l)). This competence can be better understood by examining Recital 83 of the Electricity Directive, which provides further clarity on the common performance indicators that should be incorporated in the context of building a flexible and renewables-based electricity system. By taking examples, Recital 83 specifies that such indicators include the capability of TSOs and DSOs to operate lines under dynamic line rating, the development of remote monitoring and real-time control of

182 Article 58 (f) of the Electricity Directive specifies that one of the general objectives of the regulatory authority is 'ensuring that system operators and system users are granted appropriate incentives, in both the short and the long term, to increase efficiencies, especially energy efficiency, in system performance and to foster market integration'.

substations, the reduction of grid losses, and the frequency and duration of power interruptions. These are crucial to enable TSOs and DSOs to manage active power flows in their networks and meet the network connection demands of DR and self-generated RES-E.

346. The last aspect refers to the introduction of a group of rules governing curtailment.[183] To force network operators to take proper measures to provide connection services and minimize curtailment, the Electricity Directive reiterates fundamental principles anchored in regulated TPA.[184] As mentioned, the right to network access must be safeguarded, in principle. In the case of lacking the necessary network capacity, the TSO or DSO may refuse access. Even so, such refusal is subject to a number of requirements, for instance, duly substantiated reasons and the NRA's scrutiny of necessary measures to reinforce the network (*Electricity Directive*, Article 6(2)). The Electricity Regulation supports the implementation of these requirements by stipulating the priority ranking with respect to congestion management. In accordance with this legal act, in principle, market-based redispatching[185] must be performed by system operators by procuring flexibility sources (*Electricity Directive*, Article 32(1); *Electricity Regulation*, Article 13(1); Hadush and Meeus, 2018). Non-market-based downward redispatching (or curtailment) only acts as the last resort, which should be used only in emergency situations, while subject to strict conditions or restrictions[186] and financial compensation (Edens and Lavrijssen, 2019; *Electricity Regulation*, Article 13(7)). Moreover, in terms of curtailment, self-generated RES-E can benefit from additional specific requirements for guaranteeing the network connection of RES-E. Consumers and energy communities generating RES-E are only subject to downward redispatching if no other alternative exists or if other solutions would result in significantly disproportionate costs or severe risks to network security (*Electricity Regulation*,

[183] Unlike market-based redispatching, which modifies the dispatch schedule through a trade, curtailment is a non-market-based congestion management solution that reduces the feed-in from generators or the intake by loads. See Hadush and Meeus, 2018.

[184] These principles governing access and refusal of access are enshrined in the EU's regulated TPA, representing their essential role in the legal order of the internal electricity market. They have been significantly developed since the 2003 Electricity Directive. See *2003 Electricity Directive*, Article 20 (2); *2009 Electricity Directive*, Article 32 (2); *Electricity Directive*, Article 6.

[185] In the context of EU law, 'redispatching' means a measure, including curtailment, that is activated by one or more TSOs or DSOs by altering the generation, load pattern, or both, in order to change physical flows in the electricity system and relieve a physical congestion or otherwise ensure system security. See *Electricity Regulation*, article 2 (26).

[186] The conditions mainly concern the case of unavailability of market-based solutions, including for instance (a) no market-based alternative available; (b) all available market-based resources having been used; (c) the number of available power generating, energy storage or DR facilities being too low to ensure effective competition in the area where suitable facilities for the provision of the service are located. See *Electricity Regulation*, Articles 13 (3) and 16 (2).

Article 13(6)). When their self-generated RES-E is not fed into the transmission or distribution network, they will not be subject to downward redispatching unless no other solution would resolve network security issues (*Electricity Regulation*, Article 13(6)).

### *6.1.3. Non-Discriminatory Treatment*

347. The non-discrimination principle is of fundamental importance for engaging consumers in DSM activities, as well as the overall effectiveness of competition in the market (Correlje and Vries, 2008, p 72; Papsch, 2020, p 26). Non-discrimination requirements laid down by the framework for enabling DR and renewables self-consumption have been explicated above.[187] This subsection further elaborates on the significance of the general principle of non-discriminatory treatment of system users – framed within the rationale for monopoly regulation – for the development of DSM. Firstly, different levels of network unbundling have been applied to the TSO and the DSO to address the incentive of network companies as a part of VIUs to discriminate against competitors as regards network access and flexibility procurement, as noted earlier (*Electricity Directive*, recital 68; Correlje and Vries, 2008, p 76). On top of this, under regulated TPA, providing equal conditions for all network users is emphasized throughout network charges, dispatch, and connection, also constituting a key pillar for accomplishing the internal electricity market (Bohne, 2011; Talus, 2013, p 275; *Electricity Regulation*, recital 39 and Article 12(1); *Electricity Directive*, Article 6(1)). By doing so, all interested parties are further secured to equally benefit from the key infrastructure required to participate in electricity markets for trading DR and self-generated RES-E (Gräper et al., 2021, p 75). This was particularly crucial before the EU introduced more stringent unbundling rules for the TSO, considering the residual incentives for TSOs to misuse network assets (*Electricity Directive*, recitals 68 and 69). Currently, under the CEP, DSOs are only bound by legal unbundling, rather than full ownership unbundling.[188] This makes the requirement of equally treating market actors still rather important to prevent potential anti-competitive behavior by DSOs.

---

[187] See Sections 3 and 4 of this Chapter above.

[188] Ownership unbundling implies the appointment of the network owner as the system operator and its independence from any supply and production interests, which means that a system operator cannot be part of a group of companies that also comprise energy producers, suppliers or traders. This represents the most extensive form of unbundling. In contrast to ownership unbundling, legal unbundling is less stringent, which requires the system operator to be independent at least in terms of their legal form, organization, and decision-making from other activities not relating to distribution, while the DSO can still belong to a larger VIU with a business portfolio comprising other activities than electricity distribution. The Electricity Directive does not impose more stringent unbundling requirements for DSOs than the previous Directive. See *Electricity Directive*, recitals 68 and 69, Article 35; Edens and Lavrijssen, 2019; Kuiken and Más, 2019.

This is especially the case when discrimination concerns stemming from limited unbundling of the DSO are detected in the context of operating local electricity markets (including those running within energy communities), as will be discussed in Chapter IV.

### 6.1.4. *TSO-DSO Coordination and Cooperation*

348. Before the CEP, the EC had already established coordination mechanisms for the TSOs' use of balancing services. Given the possibility of the TSO using balancing services from reserves connected to the distribution network, together with the System Operation Guideline, the Balancing Regulation elaborates on the specific dimensions of coordination between the TSO and the relevant DSO (*Balancing Regulation*, Article 15). In addition to the necessary information sharing and exchange (*Balancing Regulation*, Article 15(2)), worth-mentioning elements are cost allocation schemes and the measures ensuring distribution network constraints are respected. The need to avoid activating balancing services threatening the distribution system operation has been integrated into the prequalification process. This is achieved by firstly specifying that the prequalification process should rely on the agreed timeline and rules concerning information exchanges and the delivery of balancing reserves between the TSO, the reserve connecting DSO, and the intermediate DSOs (*System Operation Guideline*, Article 182(3)). Second, the DSO is explicitly granted the right to participate in setting limits to or excluding the delivery of balancing reserves located in its network (*System Operation Guideline*, Article 182(4)). This enables its network restrictions to be properly considered by the TSO and prevents balancing service activation from harming the distribution system. These tasks necessarily come at a cost, which requires additional coordination to allocate relevant costs between the involved TSOs and DSOs. The Balancing Regulation allows the concerned system operators to jointly elaborate a methodology for allocating costs resulting from actions of DSOs, with an emphasis on a fair allocation of costs, taking into account the responsibilities of the parties involved (*Balancing Regulation*, Article 15(3)).

349. The CEP also pursues maximum system flexibility, with a particular emphasis on market participation by demand-side flexibility sources. Thus, a more comprehensive set of principles is specified for closer interaction between TSOs and DSOs, in parallel to the above two network codes. Greater TSO-DSO coordination is envisioned to contribute to the attainment of two goals under the CEP: (i) achieving coordinated access to flexibility services, and (ii) facilitating market participants connected to distribution networks to participate in retail, wholesale and balancing markets (*Electricity Directive*, Article 31(9); *Electricity Regulation*, Article 57(2)). Hence, their collaboration is now beyond solely avoiding the aforementioned tensions in accessing

flexibility services, but should be conducive to fostering market participation of DR and self-generated RES-E connected to the distribution grid. In the following dimensions, existing EU law defines general principles of TSO-DSO coordination:

1) *Network planning and operation*: TSOs and DSOs should cooperate with each other in planning and operating their networks (*Electricity Regulation*, Article 57(1)). This general requirement can apply to all activities associated with accessing flexibility sources for system operation purposes and promoting their participation in various market segments. Moreover, network planning is underlined not least because the set of tasks for DSOs expands under the CEP in terms of using and promoting market participation of flexibility (Ruester et al., 2014). Power flows managed at the distribution level in this case should not conflict with the overall system planning at the transmission layer, and therefore, the new DSO activities, from planning to operation, have to be aligned with existing TSO procedures (Ruester et al., 2014). This reading can be further supported by Article 32(4) of the Electricity Directive, which imposes additional obligations on DSOs to consult the relevant TSOs when developing their network development plans.
2) *Establishing technical requirements*: TSOs and DSOs should act in close cooperation with market participants and final customers, and establish the technical requirements for participation of DR and decentralized RES-E in all electricity markets (*Electricity Directive*, Articles 17(4), 31(8) and 40(4)). As explained above, the TSO using the resources connected to the distribution system may violate the operation regulations of DSOs, and vice versa. This justifies the requirement for efficient coordination in developing relevant technical requirements so that each other's network constraints and regulations can be respected when TSOs and DSOs activate flexibility, preventing threatening transmission and distribution network operation (Vagropoulos et al., 2022).
3) *Information exchange*: The integration of demand-side flexibility has increased the complexity of system operation and dispatch, and can easily create conflicts between the TSO and the DSO when they activate these resources.[189] Efficient coordination between these two entities relies on accurate network information (CEER, 2015; Givisiez et al., 2020). Sharing network information can significantly contribute to enhancing the visibility of both the transmission network and distribution network,

[189] By way of example, the particular case of the German 'Redispatch 2.0' highlights that integration of DERs into existing congestion management processes causes very high efforts for both DSOs and TSOs, and gives rise to new platforms supporting grid operator collaboration. See Givisiez et al., 2020; Ringelstein et al., 2022.

thereby minimizing the system impacts of flexibility activation.[190] Additionally, improving the information flow between the two entities also has the potential to mitigate the tension resulting from engaging in the simultaneous procurement of certain flexibility sources.

350. Apart from the above, the principle of seeking enhanced collaboration between TSOs and DSOs is also integrated into the framework for the ENTSO-E and the EU DSO entity, the newly built Union-level entities that are tasked to promote coordination within TSOs and DSOs respectively (*Electricity Regulation*, recitals 42 and 60, Articles 30(1)(g) and 52(1)). Cooperating with the ENTSO-E is emphasized in the monitoring of the implementation of the network codes and guidelines adopted relating to the coordinated operation of the transmission and distribution networks (*Electricity Regulation*, Article 55(2)(a)). In particular, more detailed requirements are imposed on the EU DSO entity to support the better implementation of several of the above-mentioned coordination mechanisms. A prime example is that, among others, this entity is responsible for adopting best practices for the coordinated operation of transmission and distribution systems (*Electricity Regulation*, Article 55(2)(b)). Clearly assigning a task of disseminating best practices harnesses a bottom-up governance approach, with a view to encouraging mutual learning and sharing of experiences regarding the advancement of TSO-DSO coordination in the new market environment.[191] Considering that the development and practice of detailed TSO-DSO coordination mechanisms are in their infancy (Papalexopoulos et al., 2020), this action particularly promises to foster the development of national laws transposing and implementing relevant EU law. Moreover, the establishment of the EU DSO entity and ENTSO-E embodies the application of a relatively networked approach, which leverages their role at the center of elaborate networks of exchanging information and perspectives in the area of network operation.[192] In parallel to current generic Union-level rules for TSO-DSO coordination, this serves as a supplement to help the EU steer DSOs' and

---

190 For instance, in Portugal, there has been an Inter Control Centre Protocol (ICCP) link which enables the TSO and the DSO to share network information. Another example can be found in Belgium, where a new cooperation agreement is being discussed between the TSO and DSOs regarding flexibility services, which further addresses models of data exchange and the roles and responsibilities of the TSO and DSOs. See N. Silva et al., 2012; Yuan and Hesamzadeh, 2017; Samenwerkingsovereenkomst Elia – DNB, 2021.

191 The role of mutual learning and best practice dissemination is also underlined in the new governance approach developed within the EU – 'Open Method of Coordination' – serving as a complement to the prevalent top-down steering approach. See Scott, 2009; Zhou et al., 2019.

192 The establishment of ACER also reflects a similar approach. See Scott, 2009; Maher and Stefan, 2019.

TSOs' behavior toward facilitating the development of DR and renewables self-consumption.[193]

351. Overall, in terms of intensifying interactions between TSOs and DSOs, EU law only defines general principles and key elements. Concrete means and procedures for materializing TSO-DSO synergy are left to Member States and governmental and non-governmental entities, opening up the room for diverse regulatory innovation and best practices (Ruester et al., 2014).

## 6.2. TRANSMISSION NETWORK REGULATION

352. Beyond the above common requirements, TSOs have their own specific obligations with respect to supporting DSM activities for facilitating the uptake of RES-E. In particular, the need to engage consumers in DR and renewables self-consumption, as well as to ensure the market participation of relevant DSM participants, reshapes the tasks of the TSO. TSOs are expressly required and incentivized to use flexibility services, including those provided by DR and self-generated RES-E, to ensure operational security (*Electricity Directive*, Article 40(1)(d)(i), (4) and (6); *Electricity Regulation*, Article 13(1)). This reduces legal uncertainty and disincentives faced by the TSO in procuring and using these services. As elaborated in Section 4 of this Chapter, the TSO also has obligations to ensure the non-discriminatory participation of actors involved in DR and renewables self-consumption in balancing markets and other flexibility procurement.

353. In this subsection, the residual tasks assigned to the TSO in fostering the development of DR and renewables self-consumption, which are incorporated in network plans (section 6.2.1) and market information disclosure (section 6.2.2), are described.

### 6.2.1. *Network Planning*

354. Article 59 of the Electricity Directive confers the competence on NRAs to monitor the investment plans of TSOs and allows them to present recommendations for amending those plans. Combined with the NRAs' general objectives and other duties in promoting DR and renewables self-consumption, this competence strengthens scrutiny of TSO investment decisions to ensure they fully consider the goal of developing a flexible and renewables-based electricity system.

---

193 This networked approach is also an instrument contained in 'Open Method of Coordination', complementing the exercise of formal power of the EU in steering legislation and its implementation at the Member State level. See Scott, 2009.

355. Beyond investment plans, the relatively long-term planning of the transmission system has also been adapted. As discussed in the previous subsection, system integration of DR and self-generated RES-E requires both short-term investment to execute procurement and the investment in network capacity, smart infrastructure and innovation over the long-term horizon. Existing EU law explicitly incorporates DR and self-generated RES-E into the long-term planning of the transmission system.[194] To ensure the long-term ability of the transmission network to meet reasonable demands for their development, TSOs and NRAs are required to ensure the involvement of relevant system users in the consultation process when developing and reviewing the ten-year network development plan (*Electricity Directive*, Article 51(1)(4)). Network planning is a forward-looking process, which typically faces uncertainties about the future need for grid infrastructure and therefore requires information about new generation and load (Bauknecht and Brunekreeft, p 495). This process has become more challenging due to a lack of coordination between the TSO and generation and energy trading segments following vertical unbundling. There is a need to involve relevant stakeholders (including those engaged in DR and renewables self-consumption) in the process of elaborating the network development plan, to mirror the required investment and an evolving network management philosophy. However, a common problem confronting network planning is how to give effect to the standard of involving all 'relevant system users' in the consultation process. This problem is even more pronounced in distribution network planning, given that relevant stakeholders are smaller and more distributed in nature. As will be discussed in Chapter IV, in the context of engaging consumers in the transition toward a high RES electricity system, decision-making processes, including network planning, are increasingly struggling with a two-fold challenge. On the one hand, they are challenged with safeguarding due process, especially in terms of inclusiveness, when facing a large number of medium and small system users, which entails the risk of a democratic deficit and compromises the interests of small actors. On the other hand, ensuring a large diversity of perspectives can fragment and complicate energy decision-making (Sovacool, 2013).

356. The ten-year network plan is also subject to regulatory review by the NRA, which, inter alia, examines whether it has covered all investment needs identified during the consultation process (*Electricity Directive*, Article 51(5)). Moreover, in elaborating the plan, the TSO is required to fully take into account the potential for the use of flexibility as an alternative to system expansion (*Electricity Directive*, Article 51(3)). Among others, this requirement

[194] The ten-year network development plan was introduced by the 2009 Electricity Directive, while relevant provisions therein did not stress DR and decentralized RES-E. See *2009 Electricity Directive*, article 22.

enables the TSO to create demand and develop markets for flexibility derived from DR and self-generated RES-E.

357. It is also important to note that NRAs are not responsible for approving and examining all arrangements contained in the network plan. Instead, in terms of adequacy of investment, EU law only empowers NRAs to examine whether the plan covers investment needs identified by stakeholders. Thus, investment decisions are left to TSOs who are always in possession of private information about making optimal investments while reinforcing scrutiny of planning on the basis of relevant system users' opinions (Agrell et al., 2013; Nolting et al., 2019). Doing so helps to avoid welfare loss caused by overly strict examination or approval of investment decisions, which typically suffer from imperfect information held by regulators (Agrell et al., 2013; Nolting et al., 2019). Moreover, by involving stakeholders, EU law enables NRAs to access outside information beyond what is provided by the regulated TSO, which is key to conducting robust regulation. NRAs are thus offered a regulatory instrument to remedy their informational disadvantages relative to the regulated network company.

### 6.2.2. *Promoting Information Access*

358. An asymmetry in accessing commercial information between incumbents and potential market entrants acts as a market entry barrier for market participants engaged in DSM (Ruester et al., 2014; EC, 2016a). In terms of procuring flexibility services, requiring TSOs to publish ex-post procurement-related data can help counter this problem. The resulting improved market transparency could also contribute to preventing TSOs from discriminating against flexibility services from DR and self-generated RES-E. Under existing EU law, the TSO's obligations in this regard have not applied to all system service procurement, except for balancing markets.

359. To improve the transparency of balancing markets and encourage market entry, in light of the Balancing Regulation, each TSO must publish certain information about balancing energy procurement in a timely manner (*Balancing Regulation*, Article 12). Article 12 of the Regulation lists a range of information items that the TSO is supposed to publish. These mainly include information on, for instance, the current system balance of its scheduling area or scheduling areas, all balancing energy bids, offered volumes, as well as offered prices of procured balancing capacity. In terms of the information on all balancing energy bids from its scheduling area or scheduling areas, detailed information items are required to be published, ranging from the type of product, validity period, and offered volumes to offered prices (*Balancing Regulation*, Article 12(3)(b)). These can help potential market participants evaluate the potential economic benefits derived from balancing markets, thereby mitigating

their informational disadvantages compared to incumbent actors. Further, in performing these tasks, due regard to data security is stressed, and thus some data must be published anonymized where necessary or in an aggregated manner (*Balancing Regulation*, Article 12(3)(b)(e)).

## 6.3. DISTRIBUTION NETWORK REGULATION

360. Within the EU, unlike transmission network regulation, distribution network regulation used to have a relatively low degree of harmonization. Substantial differences existed regarding the scope of activities, the level of unbundling, and applied regulatory formulas at the Member State level (CEER, 2013; Edens and Lavrijssen, 2019; Pereira et al., 2020). The CEP strengthens uniform legal arrangements to enable the increased role of DSOs and steer regulatory changes toward fostering DSM activities required for a high-RES electricity system. This subsection canvasses how existing EU law approaches this. Key components to be analyzed include network planning (section 6.3.1), the increased role of DSOs (section 6.3.2), and dynamic tariffs (section 6.3.3).

### *6.3.1. Medium and Long-Term Network Planning*

361. The recent decade has seen a steady increase in the number of low-voltage level customers participating in DR and renewables self-consumption. In Germany, for instance, with the involvement of individual consumers and energy communities (Fernandez, 2021), around 2012, the DG output of distribution networks already exceeded the local load sometimes multiple times (Eurelectric, 2013; Ruester et al., 2014). In the years ahead, much of renewable electricity generation will be connected at the distribution level.[195] In the context of empowering and encouraging final customers to offer flexibility and produce RES-E themselves, the future path of distribution systems must adapt to this trend while promoting the use of flexibility services by DSOs. In doing so, distribution network planning may encounter a number of special challenges. First, TSOs may have a good notion of the potential for large-scale plants, but for DSOs, the situation of network planning changes drastically, as DG and DR are decentralized and small-scale (Bauknecht and Brunekreeft, 2008, p 495). Further, as pointed out above in Section 3 of this Chapter, the potential of DR from medium and small consumers connected at the distribution level remains largely untapped. Significant uncertainty confronts the DSO over how electricity demand patterns and mix of electricity production will change, and how much

---

195 Two-thirds of the installed renewable capacity in Europe is expected to be connected to the distribution grid. See EC, 2016c; Lind et al., 2019.

generation will be on distribution networks (Shaw et al., 2010). These must be considered in measures governing network planning.

362. The measures for distribution network planning are contained in Article 32 of the Electricity Directive. A requirement similar to transmission network planning is transparency and consulting all relevant system users, enabling a network plan that better fits future needs. As already noted, distribution network planning faces more acute challenges in terms of involving relevant stakeholders. This issue will be further examined in Chapter IV below.

363. To remove disincentives for DSOs identified before in using flexibility, the Directive explicitly recognizes the role of flexibility from DR and self-generated RES-E in assisting efficient network operation and providing alternative solutions to system expansion (*Electricity Directive*, recital 61 and Articles 31(5)(6) and 32(3)). The use of these resources must be enshrined in the network plan in accordance with Article 32. Moreover, this provision requires the network development plan to set out the planned investments for the next five to ten years, with a particular emphasis on the main distribution infrastructure, which is required in order to connect new generation capacity and new loads (*Electricity Directive*, Article 32(3)). The emphasis on both flexibility procurement and infrastructure investment in network planning, again, reflects the importance of balancing these two considerations in network investment and development.

364. Integrating DR and self-produced RES-E, and utilizing the flexibility services they offer, requires new types of infrastructure, such as smart grids, which enable advanced system monitoring and control capabilities, and the employment of ICT.[196] However, as noted above, in distribution systems, and especially the low-voltage ends, there are usually no control systems available that are standard on the transmission level (Bauknecht and Brunekreeft, 2008, p 474). The lack of key technical prerequisites (i.e., observability and controllability of assets offering demand flexibility) acts as one of the major factors hindering DSOs from using these resources.[197] Equipping DSOs with new assets that address such technical prerequisites alters the cost structure and the use of inputs, which must be considered in the investment plan and remuneration

196 'Smart grid' or 'smart electricity system' approaches are in line with the concept of active network management. They stress the use of new types of appliances and ICT to ensure peak shaving and avoid or defer conventional grid expansion. See *Electricity Directive*, recital 51; Shaw et al., 2010; Nykamp et al., 2012; Knieps, 2013; Diestelmeier, 2019.

197 Both sufficient observability and controllability are key technical prerequisites for leveraging flexibility sources. Observability means that DSO knows where the problems are, including actual state and forecasts of the network. Controllability concerns activation, confirmation and verification of procured flexibility. See Frías et al., 2009; Givisiez et al., 2020; Johansson et al., 2020; CEER, 2020.

schemes.[198] The above-cited Article 32 thus clearly permits expenditures for new infrastructure and mandates due attention to them in network planning, serving as an initial step in a process of adaptation (*Electricity Directive*, Article 32(2)(3); Pereira et al., 2020).

365. Additionally, unlike transmission network planning, the medium- and long-term plan, i.e., for the next five to ten years, is only emphasized in the case of planning distribution grid development. Another requirement is that the DSO must publish this plan at least every two years (*Electricity Directive*, Article 32(3)). The rapidly changing picture of consumer participation at the distribution level and the resulting huge uncertainty about predicting the investment need may explain the reason for doing so. A biennial frequency can help DSOs to keep pace with the development of DR and renewables self-consumption in their networks by adjusting investments in a relatively timely manner. In addition, as noted above, unlike TSOs, DSOs are not bound by full ownership unbundling under EU law. Recital 67 of the Electricity Directive states concerns over the impact of lacking effective unbundling on incentives for VIUs to invest adequately in their networks.[199] Improving the potentially poor performance of DSOs on investment may be translated into the requirement of developing network plans relatively frequently.

366. In accordance with the above-cited Article 32, DSOs must submit the network development plan to NRAs. While the Electricity Directive does not expressly mandate NRAs to monitor or examine such plans as it does in the case of transmission network planning, it allows NRAs to request amendments to the plan. This enables the regulator to provide guidance to DSOs. Such guidance has been empirically confirmed necessary for smaller-sized DSOs, especially those who have difficulty in tackling challenges in transitioning toward active network operators featured by properly managing DR and self-generated RES-E and utilizing flexibility (Johansson et al., 2020).

### *6.3.2. Increased Role of DSOs*

367. The CEP reformulates the role of DSOs on two fronts: (i) actively managing their networks, and (ii) being a neutral market facilitator of DR and

[198] It is expected that installing these new network assets requires large-scale new types of CAPEX. The investment needs in Europe's distribution grid are estimated to be around 520 billion euros by 2035 in the transition toward a low-carbon economy. See Nepal and Jamasb, 2015.

[199] Recital 67 points out that without effective separation of networks from activities of generation and supply (effective unbundling), there is an inherent risk of discrimination not only in the operation of the network but also in the incentives for VIUs to invest adequately in their networks.

renewables self-consumption. It creates corresponding statutory obligations for DSOs, which are crucial to foster DR and renewables self-consumption. The Third Energy Package failed to align the role and responsibilities of DSOs with the need for a low-carbon energy transition. At the national level, the focus of the regulatory regimes was very much on safeguarding the availability and affordability of the distribution network, rather than on sustainability (Edens and Lavrijssen, 2019). Tightly regulated DSOs were not granted leeway and incentives to apply the flexibility services offered by consumers (Edens and Lavrijssen, 2019; Nolting et al., 2019). Instead, they were bound by the obligation to expand the network to fulfill regulated TPA as well as to compensate for curtailed demand-side facilities, as illustrated by German and Dutch cases (Edens and Lavrijssen, 2019). We have seen in Section 6.1 that DSOs were forced to opt for conventional network expansion and curtailment to fulfill their obligations and ensure that relevant costs are recognized by price-cap regulation. This prevents DSOs from responding to the radically changing environment in which they operate, which is marked by the emergence of new technologies and the shifting role of consumers (Edens and Lavrijssen, 2019). The CEP aims to change this by enabling DSOs to expand beyond their traditional role. Aside from the adjusted rules on tariffs or charges reviewed above, the increased role of DSOs is reflected in the assignment of additional tasks to them to procure flexibility services for day-to-day network operations and congestion management.[200] Such tasks could only deviate when the regulatory authorities have established that the procurement of such services is not economically efficient or that such procurement would lead to severe market distortions or higher congestion (*Electricity Directive*, Article 32(1)).

368. In terms of relieving local congestion, their use of DERs, such as DR and DG, is underlined as a solution to support the efficient and secure operation of the distribution system and alleviate the need to upgrade or replace electricity capacity (*Electricity Directive*, Article 32(3)). This has significant legal consequences. Firstly, DSOs are permitted to increase network flexibility, without having to expand the network itself as required by some previous national law (Edens and Lavrijssen, 2019). Secondly, they are granted more leeway to use a wider set of instruments available to efficiently execute their traditional tasks of distributing electricity and new ones of connecting DR and self-generated RES-E (Edens and Lavrijssen, 2019).

---

200 Although both Article 31 and Article 32 require the DSO to procure flexibility services, they serve different purposes. Article 31 stresses the use of a certain type of flexibility services, namely non-frequency ancillary services, in the day-to-day network operation, such as for steady state voltage control and fast reactive current injections. Article 32 especially concerns the role of flexibility services in congestion management. See *Electricity Directive*, Articles 31 (7) and 32 (1); Pearson, 2020, p 137.

369. Furthermore, DSOs have a key role in facilitating market participation of DR and self-generated RES-E connected to their networks (Mateo et al., 2017; Zehir et al., 2017; Johansson et al., 2020). This is because their procurement of flexibility services has implications for the market entry of relevant market actors. Whether actors involved in DR and renewables self-consumption connected to their networks could widely participate in wholesale, retail and balancing markets also depends on their performance. The CEP defines the DSO's role and obligations in this regard as a neutral market facilitator. The concept of such a neutral market facilitator is further concretized by obligating the DSO to (i) ensure the level playing field and transparency of procurement and the effective participation of all qualified market participants, and (ii) facilitate wider involvement of market actors connected to its grid in various market segments (*Electricity Directive*, Articles 31(2)(5)–(9) and 32(1)(2)). This role is also reflected in a more specific requirement of considering the capabilities of all market participants in establishing the technical requirements for participation in the procurement of flexibility sources (*Electricity Directive*, Articles 31(8) and 32(2)).

370. Once again, it is also important to note that, compared to TSOs, EU law places additional emphasis on the neutral role of DSOs, which may be due to their limited degree of unbundling. No explicit 'unbundling' rules (or other equivalent prohibitions) are provided for by the CEP concerning aggregation and the provision of flexibility services by DSOs (Jones and Kettlewell, 2021, p 251). Within EU law, DSOs are thus not expressly forbidden from acting as aggregators or providing flexibility services (Jones and Kettlewell, 2021, p 253). In this case, the risk of market distortion remains: the DSO could discriminate between system users to favor its business units or affiliated companies engaged in flexibility service provision when procuring flexibility services, and frustrate the development of a new market (Edens and Lavrijssen, 2019). This justifies additional requirements regarding, for instance, transparency and neutrality in the procurement of flexibility for distribution system operations (Ruester et al., 2014).

371. However, merely defining the role and tasks of DSOs is insufficient to enable necessary changes in distribution network operation. DSOs are found to be prone to path dependence because of their traditionally passive role following market restructuring (Johansson et al., 2020). This characteristic contributes to their clear preference for relying on technological practices characterized by direct control over components in their systems and a reluctance to exploit system services from consumers (Johansson et al., 2020). DSOs within some Member States have previously shown little interest in acquiring demand flexibility, and only a small fraction of DSOs have started using demand

flexibility.[201] DERs were seen by some DSOs, both large and small ones, as a potential source of problems rather than a help for network management and quality improvement.[202] Indeed, compared to other available options for operating networks (e.g., traditional grid expansion and dynamic tariffs),[203] procuring flexibility services, either through contracts or organizing local markets, requires more technological adaptations and regulatory changes (Johansson et al., 2020). Moreover, from the DSO's perspective, investing in reinforcing network assets (available more reliably) is the lower-risk solution than relying on third-party actors offering flexibility services, given their frequent disconnections in case of network disturbances (Frías et al., 2009; Shaw et al., 2010; Johansson et al., 2020). The latter solution also requires more efforts from DSOs than ever before in terms of interacting with multiple parties, including active customers and FSPs involved in DR and renewables self-consumption (Bauknecht and Brunekreeft, 2008, p 484; Edens and Lavrijssen, 2019; Johansson et al., 2020). For these reasons, DSOs easily perceive additional burdens and risks. This situation also explains why some of them expressed concerns over the new regulatory focus on the distribution level and suggested deflecting the responsibility of managing technological issues stemming from the changing DERs to other levels in the electricity system (Johansson et al., 2020). The herculean task of enabling the DSOs' increased role demonstrates the particular importance of providing them with positive incentives, among others. In view of this, the CEP takes a significant step forward to harmonize specific rules that offer incentives to DSOs.

372. Under Article 32 of the Electricity Directive, specifically addressing DSOs' incentives, Member States are responsible for providing the necessary regulatory framework to enable and provide incentives to DSOs to procure flexibility services. This implies both removing existing disincentives that penalize DSOs for utilizing flexibility services and providing positive incentives to support the application of these relatively novel solutions. Illustrative of such disincentives is that in Germany, curtailment was deemed cost-neutral by incentive regulation, making it a prevalent tool for DSOs to cope with grid congestion (Edens and Lavrijssen, 2019). By contrast, DSOs searching for more efficient alternatives faced significant uncertainties around cost approval and recovery, and the risk

201 In Sweden, for example, by 2020, 57% of the surveyed DSOs had no engagement with flexibility programs. See Johansson et al., 2020.

202 Among them, the small DSOs expressed that they were too small to be early adopters and take the risk of testing new technologies. The larger-sized DSOs, on the other hand, stated that they were too big and had too many customers who would be affected if they tested new technologies and something went wrong. See Frías et al., 2009; Hansson and Carlsson, 2012; Johansson et al., 2020.

203 See Section 6.3.4 below for more details about dynamic tariffs.

of under-delivering on efficiency outputs (Edens and Lavrijssen, 2019). These perverse incentives must be corrected. Otherwise, DSOs would keep resisting the usage of flexibility services and a necessary shift to support a renewables-based electricity system (Bauknecht and Brunekreeft, 2008, p 488).

373. In this context, in addition to the common adjustments of tariff-setting, the changed cost structures of DSOs are recognized by Article 32. Member States are under the obligation to ensure that DSOs are adequately remunerated for the procurement of flexibility services to allow them to recover at least their reasonable relevant costs, including the necessary ICT expenses and infrastructure costs (*Electricity Directive*, Article 32(2)). The Electricity Regulation further complements this principle. Article 18 specifies that distribution tariff methodologies should provide incentives to DSOs for the most cost-efficient operation and development of their networks, including through the procurement of services (*Electricity Regulation*, Article 18(8)). To support the implementation of incentive-based regulation, NRAs are given additional options of applying specific performance indicators in respect of applying smart grid solutions, including greater use of flexibility services (*Electricity Regulation*, Article 18(8)).

### *6.3.3. Differentiated Obligations on DSOs*

374. While significant, a fundamental transformation to actively manage networks by using flexibility sources is not a distribution system-wide change, in light of existing EU law. Continuing with a relatively passive network approach may be more cost-effective for some areas, and also avoid an unnecessary administrative burden for certain types of DSOs (*Electricity Directive*, recital 66; Shaw et al., 2010). The Electricity Directive explicitly defines two types of DSOs that can be exempted from the above-mentioned measures governing network planning or the increased role of DSOs:

- For certain small DSOs: Member States may decide not to apply the obligation with regard to network planning to DSOs which serve less than 100,000 connected customers or which serve small isolated systems (*Electricity Directive*, Article 32(5)).
- For CDSOs: given the particular nature of the relationship between such DSOs and their system users in certain conditions,[204] Member States may

[204] Where a closed distribution system is used to ensure the optimal efficiency of an integrated supply that requires specific operational standards, or where a closed distribution system is maintained primarily for the use of the owner of the system, such as supplying electricity for industrial sites, commercial sites or airports, such special relation between CDSOs and the system users may well exist. See *Electricity Directive*, recital 66.

allow the exemption from (i) the requirements with respect to procuring the energy it uses to cover energy losses and the non-frequency ancillary services in its system in accordance with transparent, non-discriminatory and market-based procedures; (ii) the requirements to procure flexibility services to address congestion and to develop the operator's system based on network development plans (*Electricity Directive*, Article 38(2)).

### 6.3.4. *Distribution Tariffs*

375. The integration of DR and self-generated RES-E creates 'deep' network impacts due to their system use patterns and location within the distribution network.[205] In this context, some present that distribution tariffs should be able to internalize such effects at least partly (Bauknecht and Brunekreeft, 2008, p 494). First, grid congestion and voltage problems within the distribution network can be mitigated by time-variable tariffs, other than the procurement of flexibility services (Schleicher-Tappeser, 2012; Funcke and Bauknecht, 2016; Roos, 2017; Edens and Lavrijssen, 2019). The rationale is that DSOs put a price on scarce network capacity as a signal to guide system users to reduce or reschedule their network usage, through which congestion risk would be diminished (Edens and Lavrijssen, 2019; Manuel de Villena et al., 2021).

376. Moreover, dynamic tariffs could also be designed to send locational signals to DR and self-generation projects for the sake of optimizing network efficiency.[206] For the distribution system, the exact locations of DERs can substantially influence the grid-related costs or benefits (Bauknecht and Brunekreeft, 2008, p 485). More generation units close to the consumption points can decrease losses in the network (Huang and Söder, 2017b). Certain facility locations may reduce grid congestion, whereas others may pose grid capacity problems (Bauknecht and Brunekreeft, 2008, p 485). From the perspective of DSOs, these demand-side facilities should be connected to the grid at points where the costs for upgrading the grid are minimized or the benefits are maximized (Bauknecht and Brunekreeft, 2008, p 485). Again, unbundling makes it difficult for DSOs to coordinate with energy communities and vastly distributed and small end users participating in DR and renewables

205 A new notion, the 'deep connection charge', is related to such deep network impacts, which means that market participants engaged in DG and DR are obliged to pay for the connection line and the grid upgrade and reinforcement. By contrast, shallow connection charges mean that relevant system users only pay for the connection line regardless of other costs they incur. See Bauknecht and Brunekreeft, 2008, p 493; Frías et al., 2009; Huang and Söder, 2017.

206 The locational signals discussed here should be distinguished from the 'locational signals provided at Union level' referred to in Article 18 (3) of the Electricity Regulation. The latter only explicitly concerns cross-border electricity exchanges. See Frías et al., 2009; Schoser and Sandberg, 2021, pp 503–506.

self-consumption to steer their optimal and cost-reflective sitting (Bauknecht and Brunekreeft, 2008, pp 484–485). The potential tension between the site selection of individual DR and DG projects and the overall network efficiency is becoming increasingly pronounced with the greater involvement of energy communities and active customers (Bauknecht and Brunekreeft, 2008, pp 484–485).

377. For the above theoretical merits, dynamic tariff structures with time or location-dependent components have been proposed to reflect system integration costs of DR and self-generated RES-E, challenging the long-term domination of fixed or average tariffs (Sotkiewicz and Vignolo, 2007; Edens and Lavrijssen, 2019; Johansson et al., 2020; Manuel de Villena et al., 2021). Applying dynamic tariffs, especially time-of-use tariffs, requires smart meters to work (Manuel de Villena et al., 2021). The wider diffusion of smart meters within some Member States has made it possible to send improved cost-reflective signals to system users engaged in DR and renewables self-consumption.[207] The Electricity Regulation introduced dynamic tariffs at the distribution level for the first time, serving as additional measures to reinforce the cost reflectivity of tariffs. Article 18(7) of the Regulation clearly states that distribution tariffs should take into account the use of the distribution network by system users, including active customers. This implies that distribution tariffs should consider various impacts on distribution networks brought about by consumers engaged in DR and renewables self-consumption. The same legal provision further stipulates that distribution tariffs may include network connection capacity elements and may be differentiated based on the system users' consumption or generation profiles. This creates large discretion for Member States to determine cost-causation tariff structures that are contingent upon a variety of factors affecting system users' impacts on networks (Manuel de Villena et al., 2021). These may include the foregoing means of relying on time and location to determine the charges.

378. In addition, this clause imposes another duty on NRAs to consider time-differentiated tariffs when fixing or approving distribution tariffs where Member States concerned have deployed smart metering systems. It also states that, where necessary, time-differentiated network tariffs may be introduced to reflect the use of the network in a transparent, cost-efficient, and foreseeable way for the final customer. The accompanying requirements of transparency, cost efficiency, and predictability appear to aim at mitigating the potential risks posed by such time-dependent tariffs.

---

[207] In Sweden, dynamic tariffs are used to replace fixed grid fees and reduce arbitrary grid fee limits with dynamic grid fees based on local grid conditions. See Johansson et al., 2020.

# 7. INTERIM CONCLUSION

379. This chapter elaborates on how EU law empowers energy consumers by translating core tasks of electricity DSM (i.e., adapting electricity consumption behavior to facilitate RES-E uptake) into legal measures. Specifically, consumer empowerment is operationalized through four building blocks of EU law on electricity DSM. These elements represent actions in defining rights and obligations, providing economic incentives, enabling information access and data exchange, as well as adapting system operation and regulation, aiming to steer consumer behavior changes in both DR and renewables use. Hence, the two DSM frameworks for DR and promoting RES-E use share general approaches to adjusting electricity consumption behavior. Table 7 summarizes the components of the two DSM frameworks. As can be observed, existing EU law makes relatively elaborate rules for promoting DR and renewables self-consumption.

**Table 7. Components of two electricity DSM frameworks**

| | | **Rights and obligations** | **Economic incentives** | **Information access and data exchange** | **Network operation and regulation** |
|---|---|---|---|---|---|
| DR | | ✓ | ✓ | ✓ | ✓ |
| Promoting RES-E use | Purchase | × | × | ✓ | × |
| | Self-consumption | ✓ | ✓ | ✓ | ✓ |

✓: with specific arrangements
×: no specific arrangements
Source: Author's own elaboration.

380. There are several findings worth highlighting. The first finding relates to the essential role of structuring the increased role of energy consumers. Within the EU's competence under Article 194 TFEU, EU law has taken action to overcome economic and non-economic barriers that prevent consumers from modifying their electricity consumption. These actions are first and foremost built upon a legal framework that recognizes and defines the consumers' roles in participating in energy activities that favor RES-E uptake and specifies their rights and obligations. This framework is a prime characteristic of developing electricity DSM through law, which differs from other approaches, such as those via policies. This implies that when solving the core tasks of electricity DSM listed in Chapter II, the legal framework for electricity DSM per se could induce new problems or challenges. They are associated with gaps in fulfilling clarity, certainty and coherence of law and complying with

fundamental legal principles, especially non-discrimination and proportionality. Bearing this in mind is key to understanding the legal nature of this book's research, as well as regulatory gaps and legal challenges discussed in Chapter IV later on.

381. The rights and obligations evolve with a particular actor's role shift. As noted above in Chapter II, in the traditional energy regime, energy consumers were mostly passive actors and subject to protective frameworks. With the legislation seeking to change their role, this Chapter shows that the previous rights centered around consumer protection were reshaped to transcend consumer protection and cover consumer empowerment. Furthermore, the rights of energy consumers are supported by obligations imposed on other actors with whom they have contractual relationships, notably suppliers and system operators. This holds in both traditional and contemporary energy regimes. Thus, the evolution of consumers' rights, under the overarching aim of empowering them to favor RES-E uptake, is naturally accompanied by changes in the obligations of other stakeholders. These stakeholders' tasks transition from ensuring service quality and consumer protection to refraining from hindering and even supporting the consumers' greater role in providing flexibility and engaging in renewables use. In addition, during the energy transition, it is inevitable that there are 'winners' and 'losers' (Kelsey and Meckling, 2018). As shown above, suppliers and BRPs can be negatively impacted by consumers' engagement in explicit DR, which leads them to hinder the activities of IFSPs and consumers. Realigning their interests is a key approach taken by the law to realize a smooth transformation of the consumer's role.

382. Role clarification and right granting serve as the cornerstone of other empowerment arrangements that incentivize consumers and address their barriers to market entry, information access, and engagement with system operators. First, following the articulation of the consumer's proactive role in DR and renewables use, a set of changes to the electricity system, especially electricity market rules and network operation, have been made to accommodate that role transformation. In this regard, EU law serves as a representative example showing that consumer empowerment encompasses two-way actions: consumers are empowered and enabled to adjust their electricity consumption patterns while the whole electricity system is also reformed or even overhauled to enable active actions of small, inexperienced and traditionally passive consumers. The existence of such a two-way interactive approach refutes criticism of 'consumer empowerment', which asserts that *maintaining a consumer empowerment paradigm is unfair to consumers as it abrogates the responsibilities of the electricity sector on to them* (Bedggood et al., 2023). This general criticism is not tenable, as the fairness of responsibility allocation between the electricity system and consumers hinges on specific

legal approaches to consumer empowerment, which are tasked with making trade-offs and balancing interests in assigning rights and obligations, as explained above.

383. Specific enabling tools for consumer empowerment are also shaped by the role and rights of consumers concerning DR and renewables use. This is exemplified by measures that improve the provision of information, which can stimulate consumers' actions to deviate from conventional electricity consumption. Hence, in a legal framework for electricity DSM, the clarification of the role and rights of consumers plays an essential role.

384. The second finding concerns the pivotal role of the other three pillars in enabling energy consumers to exercise their rights. It has been highlighted in this chapter that relying solely on the granted role and rights cannot deliver the desired changes in electricity consumption behavior. A metaphor of 'picking up carrots' can demonstrate the relationship between the granted rights and the other three pillars of the legal framework for electricity DSM. The carrots are ready in the basket; whether anyone will pick them up is another question (Sokołowski, 2020). Similarly, the rights structured around the proactive role of energy consumers have been granted; now, the follow-up question is whether consumers will be willing and capable of exercising them. The above review of EU law indicates that the EU legislator has made some arrangements to enable consumers to exercise their rights to renewables self-consumption and DR provision. This is reflected in the provision of (i) enabling frameworks addressing barriers or disadvantages, as exemplified by enabling frameworks for renewables self-consumers and RECs, (ii) the information-related tools, and (iii) companion arrangements concerning data exchange and network operation.

385. The third worth-noting finding concerns the role of competitive electricity markets. The EU's legal framework for electricity DSM seeks to achieve the role of competitive electricity markets in empowering and incentivizing consumers. Electricity market rules have been adapted and reinforced to ensure that competitive markets can provide proper incentives for consumers, while at a minimum, avoiding distorted incentives or even penalizing consumers interested in DR and renewables use. In general, the EU legislation on the internal electricity market develops a market-competitive way of incentivizing consumers to engage in relevant energy activities, by addressing biased market conditions, safeguarding free price formation, and expanding routes to electricity markets (Chen and Vandendriessche, 2023a).

386. The fourth finding is linked to the key question of whether EU law has given due consideration to behavioral constraints hindering consumer behavior change and how it addresses relevant behavioral barriers. The analysis conducted in this Chapter reveals that EU law has considered factors shaping

and influencing consumer behavior and choices, as well as common decision-making biases, notably those linked to complexity aversion and normative social influence. This is indicated by measures governing billing information with a view to avoiding information overload while highlighting information that is most likely to induce changes in electricity consumption, as well as measures facilitating the deployment of ICT infrastructure to lower perceived inconvenience and efforts in engaging in energy activities. Through mitigating complexity, EU law has the potential to alleviate other behavioral constraints, such as inertia, reliance on heuristics, loss aversion, and excessive attention to short-term costs. Furthermore, given the role of peer effects or social influence in motivating consumers, they are empowered to act collectively by becoming jointly acting renewables self-consumers or participating in energy communities. Empowerment frameworks for energy communities are specifically developed to better harness the entities' role in engaging consumers in DR and renewables use, who may be reluctant to act individually.

387. Aside from measures to lower complexity in taking actions to favor RES-E uptake, EU law adopts another approach informed by behavioral economics. Its empowerment framework could, in large part, be defined as 'boosts' instead of 'nudges' since they grant the power, right, or authority to consumers to enable them to perform various acts or choices, which is in line with the essence of boosts, which aim at preserving personal agency and enabling individuals to exercise that agency.[208] Moreover, consumers are not obliged but empowered and incentivized to conduct activities that favor the uptake of RES-E, which is more respectful of autonomy, as highlighted by the boosts. The above analysis demonstrates that EU law explicitly envisions a proactive role of energy consumers and takes measures to equip them with competences, approaches, and information to carry out new energy activities (notably DR and renewables self-consumption). Yet, such competence enhancement is not approached by targeted education, but by harnessing the greater competences of energy service providers and energy communities. Making these actors assume the role of intermediaries between consumers and the formalized electricity system or market, EU law provides a relatively pragmatic way of implementing consumer empowerment. The concrete mechanisms employed by EU law to address economic incentives and behavioral obstacles reveal its underlying assumptions. It is not entirely informed by traditional economic thought, but also draws upon the findings of behavioral science and economics.

388. However, energy consumers' behavioral barriers are not entirely overcome by the Union's legal framework, due to limitations on two fronts.

[208] See Chapter II for features of boosts and their differences from nudges.

First, the EU's rule-making competence in the electricity DSM area, as set out in Section 2 of this Chapter, is limited by Article 194 (2) TFEU and principles of subsidiarity and proportionality. Restrictions stemming from these provisions prevent the EU from fully harmonizing various actions to address diverse behavioral and cognitive constraints of different customer groups. Member States, instead, have the right or are better placed to contemplate more granular behavioral science-inspired solutions. Second, one should also note the limitations of the law in improving consumers' decision-making competences and helping overcome cognitive or motivational biases. Indeed, the legal framework on electricity DSM provides pivotal norms for steering desirable consumer behavior. However, on some occasions, soft laws and policies are better positioned to provide other awareness-raising and behavior-changing strategies.

389. Overall, existing EU law is ambitious in terms of empowering consumers to enable high penetration of RES-E. Its legal objective of creating a consumer-centric electricity market is an indication. Increasing the role of energy consumers, or even placing them at the heart of the electricity system or market, is forward-looking and provides a heuristic for discussing how the evolution of electricity systems might unfold in the following decades. A question ahead of us is to what extent the existing legal framework has attained this vision, which is the focus of the next chapter.

# CHAPTER IV
# REGULATORY CHALLENGES AND GAPS

## 1. INTRODUCTION

390. The previous chapter demonstrates how EU law is designed to adapt electricity consumption to facilitate the uptake of RES-E. A brief overview of legislative history therein also indicates that the building blocks of a comprehensive DSM framework for promoting DR and the use of RES-E were not established until the CEP. On paper, in terms of empowering consumers to support the transition to a high-RES electricity system, the CEP is indeed a game-changer (Roberts, 2020). However, whether this is also the case in reality hinges upon its implementation. Following sociological jurisprudence's conception of focusing on the working of the law beyond its abstract content (Pound, 1912), in this Chapter, we turn from EU law on paper to its transposition and implementation and examine what regulatory gaps and gray areas surface during implementation.

391. Additionally, the present legislative package is not an end but rather just the beginning of a larger process to ensure that consumers are brought along in the transition toward a high-RES electricity system (Roberts, 2020). Considering this, examining potential regulatory gaps and 'gray areas' – that have not been noticed during the process of creating the novel legislation and occur naturally once practical implementation is actually conducted (Fina and Monsberger, 2022) – is of significance to bring to light specific areas for improvement. Existing EU law on electricity DSM is examined, inter alia, by looking at detailed mechanisms for transposing and implementing EU law at the national level. As detailed in the Introduction, Belgian law will be taken as an example to indicate how national law concretizes the four elements of EU law on electricity DSM. This choice is based on the fact that, compared to other Member States with fragmented and scattered measures, the Belgian framework is relatively comprehensive. When reviewing each element, examples of national implementing mechanisms from other countries will be used to discuss legal challenges or problems encountered in national transpositions.

392. This Chapter is organized as follows. Section 2 looks into the Belgian transposition and implementation of EU DSM law on facilitating DR and the

use of RES-E. It unfolds along the building blocks distilled in the previous Chapter. This is followed by a systematic examination of the EU legal framework for DSM in Section 3. This chapter ends with conclusions on the legal challenges and gaps identified.

## 2. TRANSPOSITION AND IMPLEMENTATION: A CASE STUDY OF BELGIUM

393. In Belgium, the regulatory framework for DSM consists of federal rules and regional rules due to a legal division of competences between the federal authority and the regions (*Belgian Constitution*, art. 39; *Special Law of 8 August 1980*, art. 6, §1, VII; Graaf et al., 2019). Article 6 of the Special Law of 8 August 1980 on Institutional Reform provides a general framework for allocating competences in the energy sector. However, it does not contain explicit guidance on how to define the federal and regional competences in setting rules for electricity DSM. Rule-making competences in this area must therefore be determined by interpreting the respective powers assigned to the federal authority and the regions under the Special Law on Institutional Reform.[209]

394. So far, both federal and regional legislation have been amended to transpose EU law on electricity DSM, ranging from enabling consumers to conduct DR and renewables self-consumption and enter markets, developing correlative information and data management mechanisms, to adapting network regulation. For instance, federal law empowers active customers connected to the transmission grid and enables free market participation of DR and self-generated RES-E in electricity markets at the transmission level (*Belgian Federal Electricity Law*, arts. 19bis, 19ter, 19quater and 19quinquies). Regional law makes rules to promote the use of flexibility by the DSO and local TSO,[210] empower and regulate active customers and energy communities

---

209 This issue was first met by the federal legislator when trying to introduce a specific framework to promote demand flexibility through IFSPs. The federal legislator specified federal competence on demand flexibility by invoking a judgment of the Constitutional Court of 28 April 2016, which ruled that the commercialization of commercial flexibility, notably for the TSO, is a federal competence. See *Arrest nr. 56/2016*, B.5.4, B.6.2 and A.9.2; Vandorpe and Callaerts, 189.

210 The local transmission grid is the set of electric lines with a nominal voltage up to and including 70 kilovolts and the associated installations, located in the Flemish Region, used primarily to enable the transport of electricity to distribution networks. A list of local transmission lines is determined by the independent regulator, the VREG. That set of electrical lines and installations constitutes the local transport network of electricity. The local TSO is a legal entity appointed by the VREG to be responsible for managing the local electricity transmission grid in the Flemish Region. Only the manager of the local electricity transmission network may construct and manage electrical lines with a nominal voltage of

whose members or shareholders are connected to the local transmission system, the distribution system, or the closed distribution system.[211] Seen from respective measures, in the electricity DSM area, the federal rule-making competence mainly stems from federal competence concerning the transmission of energy and property rights,[212] while regional actions are based on the regional energy competences regarding renewables and local transmission and distribution of electricity.

395. Given that electricity DSM measures are implemented at both the federal and regional levels, the Belgian law case study encompasses relevant federal and regional laws. Flemish rules are taken as an example of regional law, given that among the three regions, the Flemish Region was the frontrunner in transposing relevant EU law and elaborating implementing mechanisms.[213]

less than or equal to 70 kilovolts, which are used for the transport of electricity to distribution networks. See *Flemish Energy Decree*, art. 1.1.3, 100° and art. 4.1.2.

211 See e.g., *Flemish Energy Decree*, art. 1.1.3, 8° /4, art. 4.1.17/1, art. 4.8.1, art. 4.8.2 and art. 4.8.4.

212 The link with the federal competence concerning property rights is reflected in the federal framework for RECs. In the context of the Federal Electricity Law, RECs are defined as energy communities carrying out activities exclusively in the territorial sea and the exclusive economic zone. It implies that Federal law bases its competence in making rules for RECs on its property right to the territorial sea and the exclusive economic zone. See *Belgian Federal Electricity Law*, art. 19quinquies; Vandorpe and Callaerts, 189; Vandendriessche and Bogaert, 17.

213 Flanders has transposed EU law on DSM since 2020, while the Wallonia Region and the Brussels-Capital Region started the transposition in 2022. See *17 JULY 2020. – Decree of the Flemish Government amending the Energy Decree of 19 November 2010, regarding the maximum roll-out of digital meters [17 JULI 2020. – Besluit van de Vlaamse Regering tot wijziging van het Energiebesluit van 19 november 2010, wat betreft de maximale uitrol van digitale meters]*, 2020; *Decree of 2 APRIL 2021 of amending the Flemish Energy Decree*, 2021; *MARCH 17, 2022. – Ordinance amending the ordinance of 19 July 2001 on the organization of the electricity market in the Brussels-Capital Region, the ordinance of 1 April 2004 on the organization of the gas market in the Brussels-Capital Region, on road charges for gas and electricity and amending the ordinance of 19 July 2001 on the organization of the electricity market in the Brussels-Capital Region and the ordinance of 12 December 1991 establishing budget funds with a view to the transposition of Directive 2018/2001 and Directive 2019/944 [17 MAART 2022. – Ordonnantie tot wijziging van de ordonnantie van 19 juli 2001 betreffende de organisatie van de elektriciteitsmarkt in het Brussels Hoofdstedelijk Gewest, de ordonnantie van 1 april 2004 betreffende de organisatie van de gasmarkt in het Brussels Hoofdstedelijk Gewest, betreffende wegenisretributies inzake gas en elektriciteit en houdende wijziging van de ordonnantie van 19 juli 2001 betreffende de organisatie van de elektriciteitsmarkt in het Brussels Hoofdstedelijk Gewest en de ordonnantie van 12 december 1991 houdende oprichting van begrotingsfondsen met het oog op de omzetting van richtlijn 2018/2001 en richtlijn 2019/944]*, 2022; *MAY 5, 2022. – Decree amending several provisions on energy as part of the partial transposition of Directives 2019/944/EU of 5 June 2019 on common rules for the internal market in electricity and 2018/2001/EU of 11 December 2018 on the promotion of the use of energy from renewable sources and with a view to adapting the principles on tariff methodology [5 MEI 2022. – Decreet tot wijziging van verscheidene bepalingen inzake energie in het kader van de gedeeltelijke omzetting van richtlijnen 2019/944/EU van 5 juni 2019 betreffende gemeenschappelijke regels voor de interne markt voor elektriciteit en 2018/2001/EU van 11 december 2018 ter bevordering van het gebruik van energie uit hernieuwbare bronnen en met het oog op de aanpassing van de beginselen betreffende de tariefmethodologie]*, 2022.

In what follows, Section 2.1 analyzes the legal framework defining the role, rights and obligations of actors engaged in electricity DSM. This framework also enables market-based incentives by structuring the relationships between these actors and traditional market participants, and clarifying their rights and obligations in newly established routes to electricity markets, such as P2P trading. Section 2.2 then proceeds to explain how Belgian law enhances consumer engagement by improving access to information and developing data management mechanisms to support relevant energy activities. Section 2.3 discusses adaptations to network regulation.

## 2.1. CONCRETIZING RIGHTS AND OBLIGATIONS

396. In the following, Sections 2.1.1 and 2.1.2 examine how federal and regional legislation and implementing rules facilitate DR and renewables self-consumption by concretizing the role, rights and obligations of involved consumers and other market participants. Given the instrumental role of the governance framework of energy communities in enabling final customers to widely engage consumers in DR and renewables prosuming, Belgian law addressing their governance aspects will be analyzed separately in Section 2.1.3. Before this, the energy activities that energy communities are entitled to carry out are elaborated in the respective frameworks for DR and renewables self-consumption.

### *2.1.1. Entities Involved in DR*

397. Compared to implicit DR, the framework for empowering consumers to engage in explicit DR is more elaborate due to the need to reconcile the interests of several parties when consumers commercialize explicit DR with IFSPs. Section 2.1.1.1 focuses on the Belgian framework that entitles consumers to access dynamic price contracts. Section 2.1.1.2 then analyzes how Belgian law materializes the consumers' rights to valorize explicit DR via IFSPs.

#### 2.1.1.1. Implicit DR

398. Both federal law and regional law grant final customers with smart meters the right to access dynamic electricity price contracts from suppliers who have more than 200,000 end customers.[214] They have incorporated Union-level requirements concerning dynamic price contracts, including informing consumers of the possibilities, benefits, costs, and potential price

---

[214] *Belgian Federal Electricity Law*, art. 20quinquies; *Flemish Energy Decree*, art. 4.4.1.

risks associated with such contracts, as well as the need to install appropriate electricity meters.[215] Flemish law takes a step further to reinforce suppliers' obligations to enhance the consumers' access to dynamic price contracts while ensuring consumer protection. On the one hand, it requires suppliers to inform customers at least annually about the possibility of concluding dynamic price contracts.[216] Informing consumers of their rights to access such offers annually could encourage customers to adjust their electricity demand.

399. On the other hand, given the potential risk of exposure to high and volatile electricity prices, the promotion of dynamic price contracts is accompanied by measures to protect consumers. As highlighted in Chapter III above, despite the advantage of offering DR automatically, in a dynamic contract, the customer takes part of the price risk from the supplier. The size of the price advantage or price risk depends on the consumption pattern of the customer, and also on the volatility of day-ahead hourly prices (VREG, 2024). If one fails to shift electricity use during hours of high general electricity demand, the bill could be more expensive than with a fixed or variable energy price contract (VREG, 2024). Given this, it is crucial to safeguard the customer's right to freely enter into dynamic price contracts while ensuring their access to information about risks. Under Flemish law, customers are clearly protected from being unwillingly shifted to dynamic price contracts. This is reflected in suppliers' obligations to offer consumers information, which were adapted with the diffusion of dynamic price contracts. Under Art. 3.2.18, 8° /6 of the Government Decision on Energy Policy, suppliers must inform consumers of the costs and risks associated with dynamic price contracts. That provision clearly states that a switch to a contract based on a dynamic electricity price is only possible after explicit and written permission from customers, and prior information about possible price fluctuations and their implications has been provided to them.

#### 2.1.1.2. Explicit DR

400. In terms of explicit DR, consumers are entitled to valorize flexibility or participate in aggregation as active customers.[217] In federal law and Flemish law, both CECs and RECs are entitled to either become FSPs or participate in flexibility provision by contracting with an FSP, while they are also subject to balance responsibility.[218] Federal law further supports the rights

---

215 Ibid.

216 *Government Decision on Energy Policy*, art. 3.2.18, 8° /6.

217 *Belgian Federal Electricity Law*, art. 19quater; *Flemish Energy Decree*, art. 4.1.17/3 and art. 4.4.2.

218 As mentioned above, federal law and Flemish law develop enabling frameworks for RECs and CECs based on different competences, which also leads to some differences in their

of active customers and energy communities to engage in DR by stating that if any contracts or contractual clauses between active customers or energy communities and electricity companies affect the former's right to buy or sell flexibility services or to enter into contracts with FSPs, they shall be null and void.[219] In comparison to specifying consumers' rights to provide explicit DR individually, more elaborate rules have been put in place to enable them to valorize such flexibility with IFSPs' services. There are two parallel frameworks that safeguard consumers' entitlements to cooperate with IFSPs at the federal and regional levels, which are the primary focus of this subsection.

(i) Federal Law

401. As explained in Section 3.1.2 of the preceding Chapter, IFSPs play a key role in assisting consumers in offering explicit DR and benefiting from valorizing such flexibility. Crucial to enabling DR through IFSP is to properly regulate the relationship between IFSPs cooperating with consumers and the affected suppliers and BRPs. To address this problem, Federal law introduced the ToE regime, even before the CEP, making Belgium a pioneering country in opening markets to explicit DR and IFSPs.[220] As indicated later on in Figure 8, through the ToE regime and its alternatives, federal law seeks to ensure consumers, either from the transmission or distribution grid, can valorize their DR via IFSPs on wholesale and balancing markets.

402. Since 2017, the ToE regime has been under development, which aims to facilitate final customers to valorize their demand flexibility through IFSPs (also acting as independent aggregators) they choose independently of their suppliers (*Belgian Federal Electricity Law*, art. 19bis). To enable consumers to do so without being subject to barriers or restrictions from suppliers and BRPs, the ToE regime seeks to address adverse impacts created by IFSPs on suppliers and BRPs.[221] It does so by establishing three legal arrangements: (i) a fallback financial and contractual framework for addressing the relationship between suppliers and IFSPs in the absence of successful commercial negotiations between them, (ii) balancing perimeter correction measures

definitions and governance aspects. Their distinctions in the contexts of federal and Flemish law will be addressed in Section 2.1.3 of this Chapter. See *Belgian Federal Electricity Law*, art. 2, 107° and art. 19quinquies; *Flemish Energy Decree*, art. 4.8.4 and art. 4.1.17/3.

219 *Belgian Federal Electricity Law*, art. 19quater, §2 and art. 19quinquies, §3.

220 From 2014 onwards, Belgium has been considered by SEDC – the European Industry Association of DR operators – as one of the highest-scoring European countries in terms of the market design and environment allowing IFSPs to access balancing markets and thus making demand flexibility commercially viable. See SEDC, 2014, 2017; smartEn Map, 2018; Barbero et al., 2018; Delta-EE and smartEn, 2019, 2020.

221 For the interactions between IFSPs and the affected suppliers and $BRP_{source}$ and how the latter parties are affected in activation of DR, see Section 2 of Chapter II.

aimed at countering impacts upon BRPs, and (iii) data exchange mechanisms necessary for accomplishing compensation and balancing perimeter correction. These are mainly elaborated by two legal instruments adopted by the federal energy regulator, CREG, under the delegation of the Federal Electricity Law. Table 8 depicts the general structure of the ToE regime and the issues addressed by these two instruments, respectively, in accordance with the ToE provisions contained in the Federal Electricity Law.

**Table 8. Overview of the federal ToE regime**

<table>
<tr><td rowspan="8">The ToE regime</td><td colspan="3">Federal Electricity Law, Article 19bis and Article 19ter</td></tr>
<tr><td rowspan="4">ToE Rules</td><td rowspan="4">Implementing Art. 19bis, §2</td><td>Principles for the determination of the delivered volume</td></tr>
<tr><td>Principles for correcting the quarter-hourly imbalances arising from the activation of demand flexibility by an IFSP</td></tr>
<tr><td>Mechanisms for sharing and exchanging data required for implementing the ToE</td></tr>
<tr><td>Phased implementation of the ToE in different market segments[222]</td></tr>
<tr><td rowspan="3">CREG Decision 1677/3</td><td rowspan="3">Implementing Art. 19bis, §3, §4 and §5</td><td>A standard formula for determining the price of transferred energy is used to address financial compensation between IFSPs and suppliers</td></tr>
<tr><td>Financial guarantee mechanisms</td></tr>
<tr><td>Standard clauses for the contractual relationship between IFSPs and suppliers</td></tr>
</table>

Source: Author's own elaboration.

403. As noted in Section 3.1.2.1 of the previous Chapter, suppliers may have incentives to impede activities and market entry of IFSPs when DR leads to a reduction in consumption. Addressing financial implications for suppliers is key to facilitating DR through IFSPs. To that end, the ToE regime adopts the financial compensation regime, i.e., requiring the IFSP to financially compensate

222 Federal law specifies market segments applying the ToE regime, covering the DA market, the ID market, the strategic reserve market, and the market for compensating quarter-hourly imbalances (i.e., the balancing market). The ToE regime has been applied in the FRR balancing market segment and the strategic demand reserve (SDR) market in 2018 and 2019, respectively. In 2021, the application of the ToE regime was extended to the DA/ID markets. See *Belgian Federal Electricity Law*, art. 19bis, §2, *Decision (B) 2195 on the proposal of the Elia Transmission Belgium SA/NV concerning the rules organizing the transfer of energy Article 19bis, §2 of the Law of 29 April 1999 on the organization of the electricity market [Beslissing (B) 2195 over het voorstel van de nv Elia Transmission Belgium betreffende de regels die de energieoverdracht organiseren Artikel 19bis, §2 van de wet van 29 april 1999 betreffende de organisatie van de elektriciteitsmarkt]*, section 2.

the affected supplier (*CREG Decision 1677/3*, section 2.2.1). It offers fallback solutions for addressing compensation and the contractual relationship between suppliers and IFSPs. Here, it should be noted that the federal legislation only aims at regulating the relationship between IFSPs and suppliers in the absence of bilaterally negotiated solutions. This is exemplified by Article 19bis, §4, which provides that in case no agreement can be reached between a specific supplier and an IFSP through commercial negotiation, CREG applies the formula for determining the price of the transfer between these parties. Therefore, this standard formula designed by CREG is only intended to play a residual role, i.e., to provide a last resort.[223] In other words, the aim of the formula is only to prevent the absence of an agreement on determining the compensation from being a barrier for IFSPs to enter the market (CREG 2016 Study, section V.4.7.3). The supplier and the IFSP are allowed to deviate from these standard arrangements at any time by mutual agreement and notifying CREG as required.[224]

404. The significant trade-offs contained in the fallback compensation mechanism merit further examination. The design of the formula particularly takes into account the impact of the transfer price on the profitability of both the supplier and the IFSP. It thus seeks to prevent disadvantaging IFSPs and creating detriments to suppliers (CREG 2016 Study, 2016), which aligns with the requirements of the CEP. Taking upward activation as an example, on the one hand, a transfer price that is too low could penalize the affected supplier, leaving opposition from the supplier unresolved. On the other hand, a too-high price would make the participation of the IFSP unprofitable, deterring its market entry.[225] The CREG noticed the fact that the margin taken on the ToE is the only source of remuneration of the IFSP on 'energy only' markets (CREG 2016 Study, section V.4.7.3). On these grounds, the CREG Decision 1677/3 determines the indexes and corresponding weighting used in the formula in a way that IFSPs will not be disadvantaged, while suppliers could be fairly compensated.[226] Further, to encourage negotiated solutions for

---

223 The explanatory memorandum to the Amendment of 13 July 2017 to the Federal Electricity Law shows that the legislator prefers the negotiated contractual arrangement for the financial compensation between the IFSP and the supplier of the final customer. See *CREG Decision 1677/3*, section 1; Chen and Vandendriessche, 2023.

224 In the event of a later agreement reached between the two parties about compensation, after jointly communicating with the CREG, the decision to apply the standard formula will be suspended for the duration of this agreement. See *CREG Decision 1677/3*, art. 14.

225 Such unduly high compensation to suppliers existed in some European countries. For instance, the literature reports that in France, 90% of the aggregator's profit is handed back to retailers, holding back their further participation and commercialization of DR. See Barbero et al., 2018; Sousa and Soares, 2023.

226 For more technical details with regard to selecting and determining indexes and weighting, see CREG Decision 1677/3, section 2.2.3.

determining the transfer price, the formula is also designed to be, in a certain way, unattractive for both the IFSP and the supplier. The problem of gaming arises if the result of the standard price formula is predictable during the negotiation. There is a risk that the party favored by this 'predictable' price wants to make the bilateral negotiation fail so as to enjoy the standard price (*CREG Decision 1677/3*, section 2.2.3). It is particularly problematic where there are more upward than downward activations in practice, and suppliers are more likely to take advantage of the formula to exaggerate the transfer price in an upward direction, disadvantaging the IFSP (*CREG Decision 1677/3*, section 2.2.3). The CREG Decision 1677/3 thus added some uncertain components into the formula, for both encouraging the pursuit of negotiated solutions and mitigating the risk of gaming.

405. Additionally, to better guarantee the implementation of compensation offered by IFSPs to suppliers, bank guarantee requirements are set out in Decision 1677/3.[227] For example, each IFSP is required to provide a single bank guarantee for all suppliers in whose portfolios the IFSP is active and to ensure that the amount of the bank guarantee does not fall below the required minimum threshold. The TSO is appointed to regularly monitor whether the IFSP meets the bank guarantee requirements. In case of non-compliance, the TSO is required to refuse activation of flexibility at the request of the concerned IFSP until the relevant requirements of the bank guarantee have been met.

406. The ToE regime also puts in place applicable standard clauses for the contractual relationship between IFSPs and suppliers in the absence of an agreement on the modalities of their contractual relationship (*Belgian Federal Electricity Law*, art. 19bis, §5). Annex 1 to the CREG Decision 1677/3 sets out the standard clauses that can be applied in full or in part, which address force majeure, suspending the application of the standard clauses, and enforced execution, for instance.

407. In the case of activation of DR, not only does the supplier suffer losses, but the $BRP_{source}$ will be out of balance when an IFSP delivers a volume of flexibility by means of a net-offtake reduction or increase of one delivery point located in the perimeter of the $BRP_{source}$ (CREG 2016 Study, section V.4.2). If the balancing perimeter of the $BRP_{source}$ is not corrected, it suffers imbalance tariffs, as explained in Section 2.1.2 of Chapter II above. To avoid these BRPs' potential loss, the ToE Rules present a range of provisions to correct their balancing perimeters for each quarter hour of the activation period

[227] Given that the preparatory work for the Amendment of 13 July 2017 to the Federal Electricity Law did not contain any clarification of the contractual guarantees, CREG mainly elaborated the financial guarantee mechanisms in Decision 1677/3. Moreover, CREG inferred from §3 of Article 19bis that the financial guarantee only needs to be provided by the IFSP so that the compensation to the supplier could be ensured. See CREG Decision 1677/3, section 3.1.

in different circumstances (*ToE Rules*, section 13). A set of obligations is placed on the IFSP to notify the characteristics of each activation to the TSO, as elaborated in Section 2.2 further below (*ToE Rules*, section 14.2). The TSO then informs the $BRP_{source}$ of relevant information, including, for example, the total activated flexibility volume per quarter-hour in its portfolio (*ToE Rules*, section 14.3).

408. Beyond the ToE regime, two alternative mechanisms – 'Opt-out' and 'Pass-through' – are available to structure the relationship between IFSPs and the affected suppliers and BRPs. The ToE mechanism provides the most comprehensive framework for addressing the rights and obligations of involved parties, while the other two alternatives can be applied where there is no need to invoke the complete ToE mechanism. An Opt-out agreement allows the IFSP and other stakeholders to enter into an agreement within which the issues that the ToE mechanism intends to deal with (e.g., transfer price, contractual modalities, and financial guarantees) are jointly settled (*ToE Rules*, section 8.2). In the case of a Pass-through mechanism, the $BRP_{source}$ and the supplier are not impacted by the changes in the customer's normal consumption as a result of DR activation, since they have already financially passed their imbalance or loss to the customer with a pass-through contract in advance (*ToE Rules*, section 8.2). The Pass-through mechanism enables a simplified pattern for the participation of the IFSP since additional negotiations with the customer's supplier and $BRP_{source}$ to address compensation and perimeter correction are no longer needed. As Figure 8 shows, the 'Opt-out' mechanism and the 'Pass-through' mechanism apply to balancing markets (both mFRR and aFRR markets), DA/ID markets, and strategic reserve markets (*ToE Rules*, section 4). They apply to all types of flexibility delivery points.

**Figure 8. Three available mechanisms under the federal regime for IFSPs**

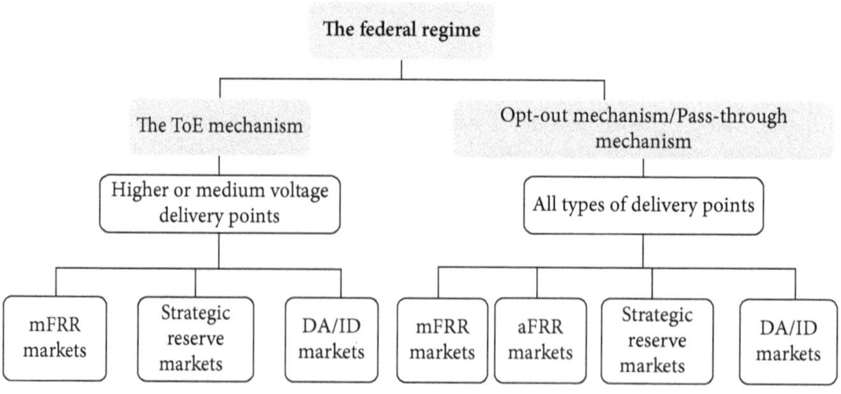


Source: Author's own elaboration based on the ToE Rules.

409. For examining the effectiveness of federal law for enabling DR through IFSPs, market actors involved in DR and independent regulators at the federal

and regional levels[228] were surveyed. Stakeholders active in Belgian electricity markets and regulators were sent questionnaires to gather their feedback on deficiencies and positive developments of the concerned framework. The questionnaires aimed to examine (i) whether previously identified barriers for IFSPs have been effectively removed, (ii) whether the ToE regime creates unfair obligations and disproportionate burdens on IFSPs and other stakeholders, (iii) the potential risks to final customers, and (iv) remaining challenges to market entry for IFSPs. The respondents include IFSPs, the association representing suppliers and BRPs, the federation representing Belgian industrial energy customers, and the VREG.

410. Results from the questionnaires suggest, firstly, that not all problems named in the literature are relevant to the Belgian framework for DR. For instance, in Belgium, there are no significant problems with the automatic activation of customers' flexibility by IFSPs, and thus the risk of causing damage to customers remains low.[229] Importantly, it was observed that significant advances have been made in overcoming previously identified barriers from suppliers and BRPs, as well as in empowering customers. Despite these gains, regulatory gaps and the paradoxes of regulation remain, which may deter market entry for DR.

411. Firstly, the case of the federal ToE regime suggests that design parameters of balancing markets still play a key role in promoting market participation of DR. Surveyed IFSPs and the organization representing industrial consumers view strict technical requirements and lengthy prequalification procedures as typical barriers for DR in the context of the Belgian balancing market. This aligns with the findings of existing academic literature that focuses on recurring problems in the EU's balancing markets (Poplavskaya et al., 2021). To be more specific, in Belgium, the prequalification processes are perceived as *de facto* barriers for small and new market entrants. According to the

228 The DSO has an important role in enabling consumers connected to the distribution grid to trade DR in transmission-level markets, and thus ensuring the DSO fulfills its role in this process is also relevant to the implementation of the federal regime for facilitating explicit DR through IFSPs. However, regulating the DSO is beyond the federal competence. The regional regulator, the VREG, was thus surveyed to examine the fulfillment of the DSO's role in assisting DR from the distribution level to participate in transmission-level electricity markets. Relevant responses from the VREG and legal arrangements in Flanders will be reviewed below.

229 In other countries, there have been examples of problematic activation where DR technology went wrong and did not perform as intended or required, and thus final customers suffered financial damages. However, according to the information received via questionnaires, due to thorough pretesting and a set of safety measures taken by customers, such as imposing restrictions on the amount of automatic activation, in Belgium, no relevant concerns call for regulatory interventions. Regarding risks caused by the automatic activation of IFSPs, see e.g., Nyborg and Røpke, 2013; Friis and Haunstrup Christensen, 2016; Calver and Simcock, 2021.

existing prequalification test requirements adopted by the TSO in balancing service procurement, the IFSP (in its role of BSP) is required to perform a new prequalification test in case it wishes to add new delivery point(s) to its pool of flexibility.[230] However, in reality, it takes one or two months to accomplish the new test, making IFSPs face considerable costs to add new flexibility delivery points.[231] At the same time, this prequalification process also implies that the customer is not allowed to perform a prequalification test with a new IFSP while they are under contract with another one (TSO 2019 Study, annex 2). Therefore, when changing the IFSP, the customer would face a loss of income stemming from performing a new prequalification test, which impedes switching of IFSPs and competition among IFSPs.

412. Secondly, the regulatory framework structuring the relationship between IFSPs and affected suppliers and BRPs is likely to create heavy administrative burdens and institutional complexity. Although the respondents have varying evaluations of the ToE mechanism, a common view is that it involves complex and lengthy procedures, placing administrative burdens on relevant market actors. In particular, the IFSP is subject to more than ten requirements, including those relating to data exchange (*ToE Rules*, sections 7 and 14). This implies potentially high costs to implement this mechanism and the risk of hindering market entry for potential entrants.

413. When seeking to address barriers created by the behavior of other market players, the highly elaborate ToE mechanism may create new market entry barriers for IFSPs. It raises a concern that the dedicated framework, intended to promote market entry for IFSPs, could paradoxically bring about precisely the opposite of its intended purpose over the long run.[232] So far, there is no adequate evidence that the complexity of the ToE regime has affected market entry for IFSPs.[233] However, potentially high transaction costs and heavy

---

230 Adding a new delivery point in the pool of the IFSP means that the IFSP contracts with a new customer to use its flexibility. See Terms and Conditions for balancing service providers for manual Frequency Restoration Reserve (mFRR), art. II.1 and annex 6. C.

231 According to EU network regulations, completing prequalification and being ensured by the connecting TSO is a prerequisite for the successful completion of the qualification process to become qualified flexibility providing units and BSPs. Thus, in the implementation of the new qualification procedure, participating customers and IFSPs cannot provide balancing services and receive remuneration. See *System Operation Guideline*, art. 159; *Balancing Regulation*, art. 16; Terms and Conditions for balancing service providers for manual Frequency Restoration Reserve (mFRR), art. II.7.10.

232 Regarding paradoxes of regulation in which the regulatory strategies defeat the goal of the law, see Sunstein, 74.

233 A survey conducted to review the implementation of the ToE regime in 2019 shows that the introduction of the ToE regime had not led to additional flexibility volumes on electricity markets, and the number of active IFSPs decreased. However, no available data indicate that this correlation between the ToE regime and active IFSPs and demand flexibility volumes still exists after 2019. See TSO 2019 Study, section 8.2 and annex 4.

compliance burdens stemming from applying the ToE regime can increase the risk of deterring potential market entrants and burdening small IFSPs.[234] Concerns arise that market liquidity may be adversely affected.

414. Thirdly, market entry barriers from incumbent IFSPs have not been adequately addressed within federal legislation. As early as 2016, the CREG had received feedback that incumbent IFSPs held back competition by signing long-term contracts or contracts with tacit renewal with their customers (CREG 2016 Study, section IV). Restricted customer switching has long been regarded as a strong barrier to entry for new market players and to effective market opening.[235] However, respondents pointed out that this problem remains unsolved, indicating that there may be several regulatory loopholes in the federal regime. Firstly, federal law has not yet transposed the EU-level requirements on switching aggregators or IFSPs set out in Article 12 of the Electricity Directive. Furthermore, as already mentioned, the lengthy prequalification procedure also represents a barrier to switching IFSPs, making it difficult or impossible for a new IFSP to compete against an incumbent. This could further increase market concentration in balancing markets and lead to a high risk of strategic bidding and market power.[236] In addition to the impact on market entry and competition, the benefits of the ToE mechanism in improving the negotiation power of customers could also be straitjacketed if the liberal switching of IFSPs is hindered.

### (ii) Flemish Law

415. In Flanders, the Flemish Energy Decree has transposed EU law by defining the rights of customers and IFSPs to enter electricity markets (including the local congestion market) in a non-discriminatory manner,[237] and access data related to DR.[238] The rights and obligations of consumers and IFSPs are further materialized in the context of concluding a contract of valorizing flexibility and governing the relationship with suppliers and their BRPs.

---

234 In this regard, for example, studies in emission trading schemes show that small and medium enterprises may suffer competitively because they are far less able than large companies to deal with the extensive administrative and informational burdens. See Barzantny et al., 2004; Baldwin et al., 214.

235 It is an important lesson learned from switching suppliers. See Jones, 62.

236 The concentrated nature of balancing markets in the EU has long raised concerns over strategic bidding and market power. See Poplavskaya et al., 2020, 2021.

237 'Local congestion' means a situation where an element of the electricity distribution system, the local electricity transmission system or the interconnection point with the local electricity transmission system or the transmission system cannot accommodate all physical flows without endangering operational security. See *Flemish Energy Decree*, art. 1.1.3, 79°/0.

238 *Flemish Energy Decree*, art. 4.1.17/1, art. 4.1.17/3 and art. 4.1.17/8.

416. Each IFSP should enter into an agreement with customers based on prior commercial negotiations. In the absence of this agreement on the commercial modalities, the Energy Decree delegates the Flemish Government, after consulting the VREG, to determine the basic elements of an applicable standard agreement.[239] This distinguishes the regional rules from the relevant federal regime because the latter only deals with the standard agreement between the supplier and the IFSP. Moreover, different from federal law, this Decree has transposed Union-level requirements concerning switching energy service providers. It states that consumers are entitled to choose and switch IFSPs freely, and to support this right, IFSPs must ensure that customers can do so without discriminatory treatment with regard to costs, effort and time.[240]

417. For the same purpose of neutralizing the impact on the supplier and the BRP caused by the activation of DR, Article 4.1.17/2 of the Flemish Energy Decree also introduced a compensation mechanism. The VREG is allowed to set out rules for determining the calculation method for the financial compensation under which the IFSP compensates the supplier of the participating customer or the BRP of the supplier.[241] Under art. 4.1.17/2, the compensation must be determined in such a way that it cannot create obstacles to the market access of IFSPs, as required by EU law. Concerned market participants are permitted to voluntarily deviate from this calculation method, provided they notify the DSO. The VREG may evaluate that process. At the time of writing (October 2024), the VREG has not exercised this power to create such standardized mechanisms for addressing the impact on suppliers and BRPs.[242]

418. Article 2.3.22 of the TRDE requires the DSO to contain a methodology for neutralization or compensation of the impact on the BRP and supplier,[243] if applicable, in the specifications for the market-based purchase of flexibility services for the management of local congestion within its coverage area or for redispatching.[244] So far (October 2024), this methodology has not been in place. In the most recent specifications submitted for approval, the DSO misinterpreted Article 4.1.17/2 of the Flemish Energy Decree and stated that no compensation is provided, with the possibility of adjusting this position after

---

[239] *Flemish Energy Decree*, art. 4.1.17/1, §3.

[240] *Flemish Energy Decree*, art. 4.1.17/1, §1 and art. 4.1.17/3, §3.

[241] *Flemish Energy Decree*, art. 4.1.17/2.

[242] This is based on the search results of the VREG Document database with the keyword 'flexibility'.

[243] Regarding legal issues of the DSO's fulfillment of obligations for making rules for flexibility procurement, see Section 2.3.3.2 below.

[244] Article 2.3.23 of the TRDE specifies the elements that must be contained in the specifications for procuring non-frequency ancillary services, which do not contain mechanisms for addressing the impact of IFSPs' activation of flexibility on suppliers and BRPs.

the first market tests.[245] The consultation responses from market players, including the TSO and FEBEG, show a strong demand for substantiated provisions regarding perimeter correction of BRPs.[246] The VREG refused to approve the procurement specifications for many substantive deficiencies and non-compliance with the Energy Decree and the TRDE. One of the problems is the absence of a method for addressing the impact on suppliers and BRPs created by IFSP's flexibility activation. It highlighted that the intention of Art. 4.1.17/2, as further explained in the explanatory memorandum, is to provide a fallback mechanism if market parties cannot agree among themselves on the financial compensation.[247] That provision in no way imposes a general principle that there is no need to develop mechanisms for neutralizing the impact on suppliers and BRPs.[248]

419. Flemish law also contains measures for supporting the federal ToE regime. Among the three regions, the Flemish Region is an early adopter of defining the role of the DSO in allowing consumers connected to the distribution system to bid in transmission-level markets applying the ToE. Article 4.1.8/2 of the Flemish Energy Decree clearly states that the DSO's obligations regarding flexibility data management serve inter alia the valorization of flexibility involved in a ToE and meeting the needs of the TSO. This suggests that the relevant obligations of the DSO are not only set to achieve the goal of distribution network management but also to facilitate the implementation of the ToE. The role and responsibilities of the DSO in assisting the implementation of the ToE are further materialized by the TRDE. First, the exchange of data for facilitating market participation of flexibility has been listed as a key aspect that the DSO should seek cooperation with the TSO (*TRDE*, Article 6.1.3). Moreover, to clarify the roles and responsibilities of the DSO and the TSO within the TSO-DSO cooperation framework, the TRDE requires an agreement between the TSO and the DSO on the calculations and exchange of data regarding flexibility connected to the distribution network (*TRDE*, Article 6.1.6, §2). This agreement should contain the procedures for the exchange of data, the respective responsibilities for the quality, the periodicity of the data provision, and the reliability of this data, as well as the confidentiality of the data exchanged (*TRDE*, Article 6.1.6, §1). Second, the DSO is tasked with timely calculations for flexibility-related data at the delivery points in its distribution network as well as timely data provision to the TSO within the framework of the tasks assigned to it by Art. 4.1.8/2 of the Flemish Energy Decree (*TRDE*, Article 6.1.11, §2).

245 *VREG 2024 Decision on the specifications for flexibility procurement for local congestion management*, section II.3.

246 Ibid.

247 Ibid.

248 Ibid.

420. Despite these arrangements, a potential issue arises regarding the performance of the DSO. Whether the DSO can fulfill its obligation to support the implementation of the ToE regime remains to be seen after it begins procuring flexibility. As indicated in Section 6 of Chapter III, with DR connected to the distribution grid increasingly bidding in wholesale and balancing markets, the tension between the TSO and the DSO in accessing flexibility may arise. The DSO may perceive limited availability of these local flexibility sources and thus face misaligned incentives between ensuring adequate flexible resources for distribution network management and assisting the delivery of such resources to the TSO (Chen and Vandendriessche, 2023b). This situation could thereby affect the performance of the DSO to fulfill its role in managing and exchanging data necessary for proceeding with the ToE regime when IFSPs activate flexibility connected to its system. This risk was also confirmed by the VREG in the above-mentioned survey of examining federal law.

### *2.1.2. Entities Involved in Renewables Self-Consumption*

421. Federal law has already granted consumers and energy communities the right to conduct self-consumption (including using, storing and selling self-generated electricity) while incorporating EU-level requirements for qualifying as active customers, CECs and RECs.[249] However, as shown later, substantiating the rights to renewables self-consumption, especially regarding electricity sharing and P2P electricity trading, raises complex legal issues. Federal law has not created further implementing rules beyond incorporating the general requirements of EU law. By contrast, the Flemish framework is relatively elaborate, primarily developed by the Flemish Energy Decree and implementing measures contained in the TRDE and the Protocol on Sharing and Selling Self-generated RES-E.[250] Aside from incorporating the general requirements of EU law,[251] Flemish rules provide further clarification on the concept and forms of electricity sharing and P2P trading. Additionally, the Flemish law created a framework for enable the association of co-owners ('vereniging van mede-eigenaars') to conduct 'VME sales'.[252] This framework could specifically increase the involvement of landlords and tenants in renewables self-generation and use.

422. Considering this, this subsection mainly focuses on Flemish law for empowering consumers and energy communities to engage in renewables

---

[249] *Belgian Federal Electricity Law*, art. 2, 104°, 106° and 107°, art. 19quater and art. 19quinquies.

[250] *TRDE*, art. 4.3.65 and art. 4.3.66; *Protocol on Sharing and Selling Self-generated RES-E*, 2024; Decision of the VREG regarding the approval of Protocol on Sharing and Selling Self-generated RES-E – version 3.2, 2024.

[251] *Flemish Energy Decree*, art. 4.4.2, §1, arts. 4.8.1 to 4.8.4, arts. 7.2.1 and 7.2.2.

[252] See Section 2.1.2.2 below.

self-consumption. It begins with how Flemish law concretizes the role, rights, and obligations of consumers, the association of co-owners, and energy communities in different self-consumption activities (from Sections 2.1.2.1 to 2.1.2.3). This is followed by a detailed examination of common rules in Section 2.1.2.4. These rules address common obligations for all consumers involved in sharing and selling self-produced RES-E as well as their relationships with traditional actors, mainly the DSO and suppliers, and with the new entity (i.e., the delegated intermediary).

### 2.1.2.1. Active Customers

423. Similar to federal law, Flemish legislation does not develop a separate framework for renewables self-consumers. Instead, their rights and obligations are specified in legal provisions relating to active customers and the sharing and selling of self-generated RES-E. In terms of energy sharing, active customers are entitled to engage in two forms of sharing of RES-E: (i) 'sharing with oneself', i.e., sharing RES-E between access points with the same access holder, and (ii) sharing of RES-E jointly produced in or on the apartment building or multipurpose building with a group of active customers in the same apartment building or multipurpose building.[253] Aside from electricity sharing, active customers are entitled to sell self-generated RES-E through suppliers and P2P trading. Their specific role, rights and obligations within the context of these energy activities are analyzed consecutively below.

424. For 'sharing with oneself', the Protocol on Sharing and Selling Self-generated RES-E further clarifies that sharing between two or multiple access points is possible, provided they have the same access holder.[254] With the Protocol defining such a possibility and specifying implementing mechanisms, consumers with two or multiple residences or venues can benefit from investing in renewables self-consumption as much as possible, further increasing their incentives.[255] As an example, Figure 9 visually outlines how energy sharing

---

253 Flemish law defines the apartment building or multipurpose building in this context as a building or building complex consisting of one or more buildings on a private site with at least two residential units or other units per building, which meets the following conditions: 1° the building or building complex has one or more common connection points to an electricity distribution network, the local transmission network of electricity or a closed distribution network of electricity; 2° in the case of a building complex, the buildings that are part of the building complex have common appurtenances. See *Flemish Energy Decree*, art. 7.2.1; *2022 Report on energy communities, energy sharing and P2P trading*, section 1.1.2.

254 An example of electricity sharing with multiple access points is a municipality that has installed solar panels on the roofs of the town hall and the sports hall, and wants to share its self-generated RES-E with other municipal buildings, such as the library and the school. See *Protocol on Sharing and Selling Self-generated RES-E*, section 5.3.

255 Since July 2022, in Flanders, the forms of 'sharing energy with oneself' and P2P have been on the rise. See *2022 Report on energy communities, energy sharing and P2P trading*, section 3.2.

between two access points with the same access holder takes place and the interactions of involved active customers and other stakeholders, mainly suppliers and the DSO.

**Figure 9. Electricity sharing between access points with the same access holder**[256]

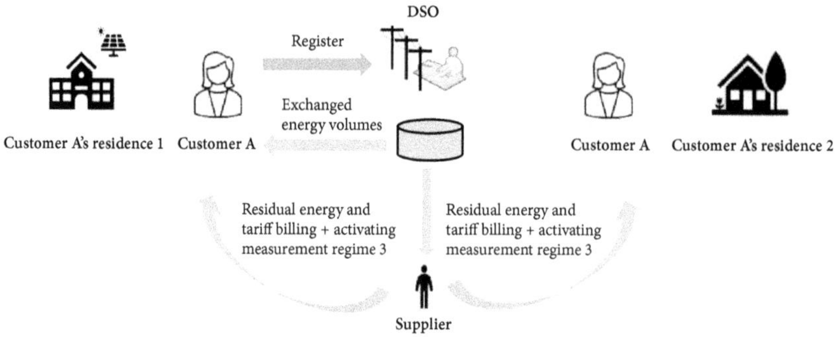


425. A customer wishing to share self-generated RES-E from one residence to the other must register the energy sharing with the DSO, with both residences having installed digital meters with metering regime 3 activated with the energy supplier.[257] The same requirements also apply to electricity sharing between multiple access points with the same access holder. Moreover, as is the case for enabling explicit DR, smoothly implementing electricity sharing relies on properly structuring the active customers' relationship with affected traditional actors, especially the DSO and suppliers. In this respect, the Protocol establishes some common requirements that must be fulfilled by the parties involved in sharing and selling self-generated RES-E, which will be addressed later.

426. For sharing RES-E produced in or on the building or its appurtenances, Figure 10 gives an example of how five active customers jointly investing in solar panels on the roof of their apartment building share the self-generated RES-E among themselves. Equally, the involved active customers must have digital meters with metering regime 3 activated by their suppliers. In light of the Protocol, they must jointly appoint one authorized representative, the sharing 'community manager',[258] which will act on their behalf to interact with the

---

[256] This figure is adapted from the *Protocol on Sharing and Selling Self-generated RES-E*, 2024.

[257] *Protocol on Sharing and Selling Self-generated RES-E*, section 5.3.

[258] The community in the context of the Protocol on Sharing and Selling Self-generated RES-E refers to 'the totality of participants who share or sell energy within a specific group'. It is different from the CEC and the REC defined by the Flemish Energy Decree. See Section 2.1.2.4 of this Chapter below for more details about the community manager.

DSO and suppliers. The community manager, acting as an intermediary, plays a pivotal role in easing the sharing and selling of self-generated RES-E. How Flemish law defines this entity's role and relationship with other stakeholders will be discussed further below in Section 2.1.2.4.

**Figure 10. Electricity sharing within a building**[259]

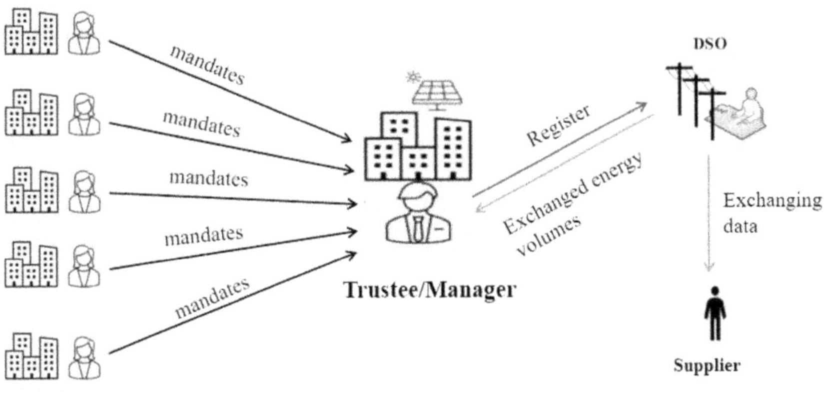


427. Another worth-mentioning aspect of the Flemish framework for electricity sharing is that it clearly distinguishes electricity sharing from trading activities, such as P2P sales. This distinction affects not only the obligations of active customers but also those of energy communities engaged in energy sharing, as discussed later in Section 2.1.2.3. Before the 2024 Amendment to the Electricity Directive,[260] EU law did not define energy sharing, and it was unclear whether energy sharing involves energy transactions. The 2024 Amendment defines energy sharing as the exchange of energy for a price or free of charge. In some technical literature, P2P trading is also regarded as a way of realizing energy sharing (Morstyn et al., 2018; REScoop.eu and ClientEarth, 2020; Lee and Zhang, 2023; Bukar et al., 2023). Flemish legislation defines 'energy sharing' as '*the free allocation over one imbalance settlement period of all or part of the self-generated, and where appropriate stored, energy injected into an electricity distribution grid, the local transmission grid, a closed distribution grid, between customers in the cases referred to in Article 7.2.1, §1*'.[261] It makes clear that electricity sharing is a free exchange of energy. During electricity sharing, unlike P2P trading, active customers are not allowed to ask each other for a price or remuneration for the energy they share.[262] Given that electricity sharing is

259 This figure is adapted from the *Protocol on Sharing and Selling Self-generated RES-E*, 2024.
260 *2024 Amendment to the Electricity Directive*, Article 2.
261 *Flemish Energy Decree*, art.1.1.3, 38°/1.
262 *Electricity and gas market report 2022*, section 4.2.2.

not considered energy sales, active customers or energy communities sharing electricity do not constitute suppliers and, therefore, are not subject to the obligations imposed on suppliers.[263]

428. However, this does not mean that active customers sharing electricity are not subject to any obligations, especially toward recipients of the shared electricity. Art. 7.2.1 of the Flemish Energy Decree allows the Flemish Government, after consulting the VREG, to impose obligations on active customers and energy communities in the context of energy sharing in the following aspects: (i) the provision of information; (ii) the handling of complaints; (iii) measures of a social nature; and (iv) measures to promote rational use of energy and renewable energy sources. This delegation, among others, creates flexibility for the government to take measures to protect energy consumers as recipients of shared electricity. This legal provision highlights an important legal issue concerning the potential need for adjusting consumer rights as consumers increasingly engage in sharing and selling self-generated electricity. As will be elaborated shortly in the P2P trading case, a high level of energy consumer protection in EU energy law has traditionally stemmed from the consumers' contractual relationship with suppliers. However, consumer rights supported by corresponding obligations imposed on suppliers become inapplicable in electricity sharing, as entities sharing electricity, whether active customers or energy communities, are not bound by supplier obligations in the Flemish law context. Potential risks or disadvantages of consumers as recipients of shared self-generated electricity remain to be identified in the practical implementation of electricity sharing. Where necessary, consumer rights should be specified within the specific relationships between them and entities sharing or selling self-generated electricity. These will, in turn, shape the obligations of individuals or collectives sharing or selling their self-produced RES-E, which deserves continuous attention.

429. In addition to electricity sharing, active customers are entitled to sell self-generated RES-E in two ways: through suppliers and P2P trading. To give effect to the right of renewables self-consumers to sell self-generated electricity through suppliers granted by Article 21(2)(a) of the REDII, suppliers in Flanders must offer 'Feed-in contracts' ('terugleveringscontract') at the request of active customers, but are free to determine the remuneration for the electricity injected into the grid by the active customers.[264] Alternatively, an active customer can sell self-generated RES-E through a P2P sale agreement in accordance with Art. 7.2.2 of the Flemish Energy Decree. It is worth mentioning that the Protocol

[263] Suppliers' activities are characterized by the sale of energy. See *Flemish Energy Decree*, art. 1.1.3, 78°.

[264] *Government Decision on Energy Policy*, art. 7.13.2.

explicitly provides for the possibility of 'multiple person-to-person sales' in the P2P trading context, as shown in Figure 11.[265]

Figure 11. Multiple person-to-person sales[266]

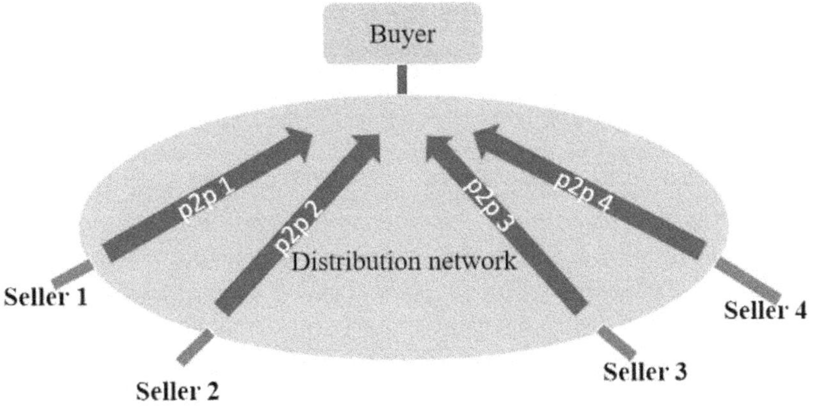


430. As a form of P2P trading, multiple person-to-person sales amount to a situation where one active customer buys from several other active customers the RES-E that the latter have each individually produced and injected into the distribution grid.[267] Although the comments from the consulted stakeholders on this form of P2P are quite divided, the DSO established that the above-cited Article 7.2.2 does not exclude this possibility, which was confirmed by the VREG when approving the Protocol.[268] The justification is based on the fact that Art. 7.2.2 only requires that P2P trading must concern sales 'to one other active customer' and be 'up to a maximum of the purchase of that active customer at its access point.' It is clear, based on the provision, that the limitation 'to one active customer' applies to the buyer rather than the seller. In multiple P2P sales, although there exist multiple P2P trading contracts, they are concluded between one buyer and several sellers separately.[269] That is to say, these contracts remain completely separate from one another, and the selling parties have no contractual relationships with each other in the context of peer-to-peer green electricity trading.[270] In this sense, the multiple P2P sales between several separate sellers and one buyer are in line with Art. 7.2.2, which stresses that there is only one buyer.

265 *Protocol on Sharing and Selling Self-generated RES-E*, section 5.3.
266 This figure is adapted from the *Protocol on Sharing and Selling Self-generated RES-E*, 2024.
267 *Protocol on Sharing and Selling Self-generated RES-E*, section 5.3.
268 *VREG Decision on the approval of the third protocol version*, section II.1.3.
269 Ibid.
270 Ibid.

431. Once P2P constitutes a sale of energy, a key legal issue, as stressed in the previous Chapter, is whether the active customer acting as the seller should be defined as a supplier and comply with the corresponding obligations for suppliers. Art. 7.2.2, §2 of the Flemish Energy Decree addresses this issue by clarifying that by jointly meeting the following conditions, the active customer as a seller is not subject to the suppliers' obligations: (i) selling self-generated electricity to one other active customer and it does not constitute its primary commercial or professional activity, (ii) the traded electricity is green electricity (i.e. generated from renewables)[271] and has been injected into the distribution grid at the seller's residence or place of establishment, per imbalance settlement period, (ii) the injected volume is up to the amount of offtake by that other active customer at its access point. The exempted obligations include those created by or pursuant to legal provisions on supply permits and PSOs imposed on suppliers, ranging from billing, information provision, and customer complaints handling to encouraging the rational use of energy and the use of renewables.[272]

432. However, Art. 7.2.2, §1 also stipulates that '*the right to engage in P2P trading does not affect the rights and obligations of the parties involved as final customers, producers, suppliers or aggregators*', as stressed by the REDII in defining P2P trading. A follow-up question is, in the case of exempting the selling parties from supply permit obligations and other PSOs applied to suppliers, would it deprive buyers in P2P trading of their rights as final customers? Member States can easily encounter a dilemma in national transpositions. Selling self-produced RES-E also falls under the definition of 'supply' given by the Electricity Directive, while that legislation does not distinguish actors engaged in electricity supply. EU law neither delimits 'suppliers' to energy undertakings engaged in electricity supply. Nor does it expressly state that supplier obligations, which are shaped based on consumers' rights under supply contracts (mainly granted by Articles 10, 12 and 18 and Annex I), only apply to supply companies. This situation implies that under EU law, all actors involved in the sale of electricity, including active customers selling self-produced RES-E via P2P trading, are subject to supplier obligations aimed at supporting corresponding consumer rights. A similar situation exists in Flemish law, which defines 'supplier' as '*any natural person or legal entity that sells electricity or natural gas to customers, except if the sale takes place via a direct line, a direct pipeline or a private distribution network*'. When P2P electricity trading among active customers occurs via the public distribution grid in most cases, the selling party can easily constitute a supplier within the Flemish law context, and should, in principle, apply provisions setting out obligations for suppliers.

---

271 *Flemish Energy Decree*, art. 1.1.3, 58°.
272 *Flemish Energy Decree*, art. 7.2.2, §2, art. 4.3.1, art. 4.3.2 and art. 7.5.1.

433. Exempting these active customers from supplier obligations makes it impossible to safeguard final customers' rights granted in the context of consumer empowerment and protection.[273] This also seems to violate the above Union-level general requirement that entitlement to P2P electricity trading does not affect the rights of the involved parties as final customers.

434. However, on the other hand, applying supplier obligations could raise concerns of creating disproportionate and discriminatory obligations for consumers selling surplus self-produced RES-E, given their small size and unprofessional nature. Moreover, burdensome obligations could make it difficult for consumers to financially benefit from selling surplus self-generated RES-E, which could significantly undermine their incentives to engage in renewables self-consumption. This dilemma and relevant legal issues will be discussed in more detail in Section 3.2.3 of this Chapter below.

435. Another issue unresolved by Flemish law is, 'from which moment on the consumer does not qualify as an active consumer anymore' (Lavrijssen et al., 2023). As rightly pointed out by the literature, that issue is acute especially given the potentially varying status of prosumers: this is for example the case if a person is no longer working, i.e., does not carry out any, or hardly any, economic activities; In this case, the generation of electricity will soon be considered as the only economic activity of the consumer (Lavrijssen et al., 2023). This situation may challenge their legal qualification as an active customer and trigger heavier obligations when they sell electricity to other active customers, given that the prosumer-to-prosumer relationship is not applicable. Within Flemish law, the existing criteria for defining active customers are too obscure, considering the possibility of changing customer statuses.

#### 2.1.2.2. Association of Co-Owners (VME)

436. Aside from empowering active customers, Art. 7.2.3 of the Flemish Energy Decree defines the role of the association of co-owners ('vereniging van mede-eigenaars'). It enables them to sell the RES-E produced in or on an apartment building or multifunctional building, or the appurtenances of that building, to the occupants or customers in that building. In addition to sales by an association of co-owners, this legal provision applies mutatis mutandis to the other two cases: (i) apartment buildings or multifunctional buildings that have only one owner (for which no association of co-owners is required), or (ii) where an owner of the association of co-owners (or of the other co-owners in joint

273 For a more detailed discussion of the nature and purposes of consumer rights granted by EU energy law, see Section 3.2.3.2 of this Chapter below.

ownership) has been given the right to use the common parts privately (e.g., for a private solar panel installation on the roof).[274]

437. Buyers in such VME sales could be co-owners who live in or use part of the building themselves, as well as tenants.[275] By enabling this energy activity, Flemish law can notably engage a certain consumer group, namely landlords and tenants, in renewables self-generation and use, going beyond the minimum requirements of EU law. It also expands the approaches to selling self-generated RES-E, which is of significance in the context of gradually increasing market integration of RES-E (Chen and Vandendriessche, 2023a). Moreover, such transactions address a particular dilemma in enabling tenants to benefit from renewables self-consumption. Tenants may have a possessory interest in the renewables generation assets, but not the authority to decide to install them on the landlord's property (Almeida et al., 2021). In addition to barriers arising from property rights, they may also lack incentives to invest in generation installations since their occupancy is generally too short to reap the gains on any investment in installations such as rooftop solar PV (Almeida et al., 2021). In contrast, landlords have the authority to make decisions and the time to reap a return on any investment, but they lack incentives to invest in such energy projects because they do not bear energy consumption costs (Almeida et al., 2021). Empowering owners or the association of co-owners to sell RES-E generated in their buildings to occupants helps to address this dilemma. It creates economic incentives for landlords to invest in renewables while protecting tenants from the long payback period and high upfront costs of installing generation facilities.

438. Similar to P2P electricity trading, VME sales of RES-E also occur on a per-imbalance settlement period basis (quarter-hourly), up to a maximum of the purchase amount for each resident or user involved. When jointly meeting these conditions, there is also an exemption from supply permit obligations and certain other PSOs that normally apply to suppliers under the Flemish Energy Decree.[276] Despite this, the association of co-owners may be subject to additional obligations set by the Flemish Government within the framework of the VME sale activity, including providing information, handling complaints, and promoting the rational use of energy and renewables.[277] These are similar to PSOs that can be imposed on suppliers under Articles 4.3.2 and 7.5.1 of

274 *Flemish Energy Decree*, art. 7.2.3, §2; *Electricity and gas market report 2022*, section 4.2.2.1.

275 *Electricity and gas market report 2022*, section 4.2.2.1.

276 *Flemish Energy Decree*, art. 7.2.3, §2.

277 The legislation states that the Flemish Government may, after an opinion from the VREG, impose obligations on the association of co-owners within the framework of the activity of VME sales with respect to the following aspects: (i) the provision of information; (ii) the handling of complaints; (iii) measures of a social nature; and (iv) measures to promote rational use of energy and renewable energy sources. See *Flemish Energy Decree*, art. 7.2.3, §2.

the Flemish Energy Decree. As such, while the association of co-owners is exempted from Articles 4.3.2 and 7.5.1, consumers in VME sales might also have consumer rights stemming from rules specifically governing their relationships with the association of co-owners. This is different from the foregoing case of P2P electricity trading. This difference may be attributed to the fact that the contractual counterparty of a buyer in VME sales is not an individual active customer but an association. Another contributing factor is that the legislation does not prohibit the trading activity of the association of co-owners from becoming its primary commercial or professional activity. The legislator tends to create room for protecting energy consumers from potential disadvantages in their contractual relationships with associations or organizations, as is the case for the rules governing energy communities.

#### 2.1.2.3. Energy Communities

439. Both CECs and RECs are entitled to produce RES-E from installations directly connected or indirectly connected via the connection of their members or shareholders to the local transmission grid, distribution grid, or closed distribution grid.[278] They also have the right to consume and sell such self-generated RES-E, including through PPAs.[279] Apart from restrictions placed on composition, governance and proximity discussed in the next subsection, under Flemish law, RECs are subject to additional preconditions for carrying out these activities. These are that (i) the self-produced electricity must be generated from renewables,[280] and (ii) RECs are always the owners of the generation facilities.[281] By contrast, CECs can use and sell self-produced electricity, regardless of energy sources, even though they only have user rights to the production installation.[282] Together with Art. 7.2.1, Art. 4.8.4 of the Flemish Energy Decree empowers CECs and RECs to share RES-E produced within the energy communities with members or shareholders up to the amount of offtake at members' or shareholders' access points. Flemish law does not grant RECs and CECs the right to own or operate the distribution grid.

440. To transpose EU-level requirements of ensuring that energy communities contribute to the overall cost-sharing of the system in an adequate, fair, and balanced way when using, selling, and sharing self-generated RES-E, members or shareholders of RECs and CECs must have meters that measure

---

278 *Flemish Energy Decree*, art. 4.8.4, §1.

279 Ibid.

280 Art. 4.8.2, §1 of the Flemish Energy Decree requires that the REC's activities on energy production, self-consumption, energy sales and energy shares relate only to energy from renewable sources.

281 *Flemish Energy Decree*, art. 4.8.4, §1.

282 Ibid.

separately the energy purchased and the energy injected into the distribution grid.[283] Flemish legislation particularly requires separate metering, given that so far some consumers still have meters with reversing counters, which are unable to make tariffs depend on actual offtake and could lead to insufficient and unfair grid cost sharing.[284]

441. In the Flemish Energy Decree, the legal provisions empowering CECs and RECs do not expressly specify their obligations toward the recipients of electricity sold or shared. The energy communities' obligations and the corresponding rights of consumers receiving electricity from them need to be determined by their specific relationships in different energy activities, as emphasized in the previous subsections. Section 2.1.2.1 above indicates that Flemish legislation has established that electricity sharing is not an energy transaction. The free nature of electricity sharing implies that when sharing electricity with members or shareholders, energy communities do not constitute suppliers and are not subject to the obligations created for suppliers accordingly. However, energy communities might have obligations toward consumers receiving the shared electricity, as Article 7.2.1 of the Energy Decree allows the Flemish Government to set obligations for energy communities sharing electricity, mainly regarding consumer protection and sustainable use of energy.

442. In terms of selling self-generated RES-E to non-members, Flemish law does not clarify whether energy communities are subject to supplier obligations. But it indeed requires '*the supply of electricity through the electricity distribution network or local transmission network, to customers, is subject to the prior granting of a supply license by the VREG.*' Based on this, the VREG holds that if the energy community sells electricity to customers via the distribution grid or local transmission grid, it must have a supply license.[285] A controversial issue, however, is whether applying supply obligations to energy communities is compatible with principles of non-discrimination and proportionality. The key to solving this issue lies in the application and interpretation of these two principles. However, while referring to these principles frequently, including in legal frameworks for energy communities,[286] EU energy legislation has not elaborated on their specific connotation and application criteria. As noted by the recent literature, how to apply the principle of non-discrimination in the

283 *Flemish Energy Decree*, art. 4.8.4, §2.

284 For tariffs adapted to the emergence of active customers and energy communities in the Belgian case, see Section 2.3 below of this Chapter.

285 *2022 Report on energy communities, energy sharing and P2P trading*, section 2.3.5.

286 EU law requires Member States to ensure that energy communities are treated in a non-discriminatory and proportionate manner with regard to their rights and obligations in conducting different energy activities. See *REDII*, Article 22 (4)(d); *Electricity Directive*, Article 16 (3)(b) and recital 46.

energy sector in practice remains an unanswered legal question (Rumpf and Bjørnebye, 2019; Rumpf and Hancher, 2021), especially when determining network charges or obligations applied to new entities carrying out renewables self-consumption (Lavrijssen et al., 2023).

443. One may consider that requiring energy communities to have a supply license is problematic from the perspective of the principle of proportionality. This is because there is a set of legal consequences of becoming 'the holder of a supply license'. Under Flemish law, the licensees must meet stringent requirements in terms of financial, administrative and technical capacity (Lavrijssen et al., 2023), professional reliability and sufficient capacity to meet the customers' needs.[287] They are also subject to a complex set of obligations regarding billing, information provision (toward both the regulator and consumers) and encouraging the rational use of energy and the use of renewables.[288] As mentioned in the previous Chapter, due to the specific characteristics of energy communities, especially relatively small scale, non-profit structure, and reliance on informal and voluntary labor, they are liable to lack the capacity to deal with administrative requirements and sustain operations in a highly formalized and competitive energy system (Almeida et al., 2021; Laes and Bombaerts, 2022). EU legislators have clearly realized these disadvantages, while it is left to Member States to determine detailed obligations applicable to energy communities. At the initial stage of developing energy communities, many of them have not yet grown beyond the level of a niche (Laes and Bombaerts, 2022). A concern is that requiring energy communities, regardless of their size and capacity, to obtain supply permits could easily create disproportionate administrative burdens and costs, thereby failing the *stricto sensu* proportionality test.[289]

444. However, assessing whether existing supplier obligations are proportionate for renewables self-consumers and energy communities in principle requires separate proportionality tests of each obligation set for suppliers. Moreover, there are debates over elements of the principle of proportionality, which increases the difficulty of proportionality tests, as indicated in Section 3.2 of this Chapter below. The CJEU, for instance, did not conduct the aforementioned *stricto sensu* proportionality test in some rulings assessing the proportionality of a measure or action. The regulator may also have different interpretations of the principle of proportionality referred to in EU energy law. An example is when approving the DSO's rules for

287 *Government Decision on Energy Policy*, arts. 3.2.1 to 3.2.6.

288 *Flemish Energy Decree*, art. 4.3.2 and art. 4.3.2/1, art. 7.4.1, art. 7.5.1; *Government Decision on Energy Policy*, arts. 3.2.16 to 3.2.18, arts. 6.3.1 to 6.3.3, art. 6.4.23.

289 The *stricto sensu* proportionality test examines whether the burden placed on the individuals' interests is proportionate to the benefits secured, which has received some judicial support from the CJEU. See Takis Tridimas, 1999, 65; Paul Craig, 2006, 670–671.

procuring flexibility, the VREG adopted a three-fold standard for conducting the proportionality test.[290] First, the exercise of power must be useful and relevant, i.e., it must help achieve the objective for which it is given.[291] Second, it must be necessary and indispensable, in the sense that if the power can be used in different ways that are all equally useful to (help) achieve the stated objective, that form of exercise of power should be preferred that causes the least harm to another protectable objective or interest.[292] Lastly, the exercise of power must be proportional; that is, the harm caused to another worthy of protection must not be disproportionate to the benefit to the objective it pursues.[293] In the public law doctrine employed by the VREG,[294] the *stricto sensu* proportionality test is embedded in the proportionality principle's application. The nuanced differences in criteria for assessing proportionality will be further examined in Section 3.2 of this Chapter further below.

445. Moreover, the energy communities' activity of supplying electricity to consumers beyond their communities also raises legal issues regarding the consistent interpretation and application of the non-discrimination principle. The present EU law indeed requires treating RECs and CECs in a non-discriminatory manner with regard to their activities, rights and obligations as producers, suppliers, or other market participants.[295] However, it does not necessarily mean applying the same rules governing other market players to energy communities. The CJEU, for over 50 years, has consistently defined discrimination as the application of different rules to comparable situations or the application of the same rule to different situations unless there are objective reasons to do so.[296] Some may argue that, due to the above-mentioned specificities of energy communities, they are in circumstances different from those of suppliers. Such distinct circumstances faced by energy communities are highlighted by EU law. This is exemplified by Article 22 (7) of the REDII, which requires Member States to give due account to the specificities of RECs when designing support schemes, to enable them to compete equally with other market

290 See e.g. VREG 2023 Decision on the rules for the purchase of non-frequency-related ancillary services and grid losses, section II.1.2; VREG 2024 Decision on the specifications for flexibility procurement for local congestion management," section II.3.

291 *VREG 2023 Decision on the rules for the purchase of non-frequency-related ancillary services and grid losses*, section II.1.2.

292 Ibid.

293 Ibid.

294 The VREG cited W. VAN GERVEN, 'De beginselen, subsidiariteit, evenredigheid en samenwerking, in het Europese gemeenschapsrecht', RW 1991–1992- nr. 36- 9 mei 1992.

295 *REDII*, article 22(4)(e); *Electricity Directive*, art. 16(3)(b).

296 It is settled law that the prohibition of discrimination is a specific expression of the general principle of equality, which is one of the fundamental principles of EU law and which requires that '*comparable situations must not be treated differently and different situations must not be treated in the same way unless such treatment is objectively justified*'. See Hannah Kruimer, 2011; De Vos, 2020. See also Section 3.2 of this Chapter below.

participants. Considering the different situations, a conclusion might be that it is in line with the non-discrimination principle to grant energy communities different treatment, such as exempting them from obligations applied to suppliers, although they are also supplying electricity.

446. However, as will be detailed later in Section 3.2 of this Chapter, in a discrimination test, assessing the comparability of two actors is a rather complex issue. Such complexity first stems from the fact that the CJEU has applied different general standards for this comparability analysis in different fields, as shown later. Second, the court, in some rulings, clearly refused to use general characteristics of the concerned actor (e.g., the specificities of energy communities listed above) to determine whether it is in an analogous situation with the comparison object. Not all aspects are relevant for the concerned comparability analysis. In a particular context, those features may be completely irrelevant and could not shape the result of the discrimination test. In addition, the criteria for applying the non-discrimination principle also include those for assessing justifications that can legitimize different treatment of comparable situations and identical treatment of different situations. Given this, it is far from straightforward to conclude that, based on features of energy communities, treating them and suppliers differently in terms of their obligations is compatible with the non-discrimination principle.

447. Last, there exist potential tensions between safeguarding the principles of proportionality and non-discrimination. To align with the principle of proportionality, the national legislator needs to thoroughly examine whether forcing them to comply with general rules for various energy activities, such as electricity supply, would induce disproportionate outcomes. Doing so may lead to the conclusion that setting separate rules for such emerging actors is a proportionate approach. However, such different rules may risk violating the principle of non-discrimination if energy communities and suppliers are parties in analogous situations according to criteria developed by the CJEU.

448. To sum up, the connotations and application standards of the fundamental principles of EU energy law, especially non-discrimination and proportionality, warrant dedicated examination in the specific context of engaging consumers and energy communities in energy trading activities. Relevant legal challenges will be discussed in more detail in Section 3 of this Chapter, combined with examples from other Member States.

#### 2.1.2.4. Common Rules

449. Under the delegation of the Flemish Energy Decree, the TRDE develops a set of common rules for participants and other stakeholders involved in sharing and selling RES-E (*TRDE*, arts. 4.3.64 to 4.3.66). These rules address

conditions and requirements for enabling various forms of electricity sharing, P2P trading and VME sales. They are further elaborated by the Protocol on Sharing and Selling Self-generated RES-E. Among other things, the protocol addresses how the sharing and sale of self-produced RES-E can be initiated, based on which distribution keys this can occur, how participants can be added and removed, and how measurement data and other information are exchanged between the DSO and energy suppliers. In addition, this protocol is supplemented by a separate agreement between market parties to address the settlement impact on suppliers through ex-post financial reconciliation, which is soft law in nature, as elaborated later.

450. These common rules cover technical and procedural arrangements. Their legal aspect is the major focus of this subsection. They contain more detailed obligations for involved consumers, structure their relationship with other key stakeholders affected by RES-E sharing and selling, and define a new actor that helps mitigate institutional complexity. This subsection will first analyze the common requirements for defining the suppliers' role and dealing with the impact on them. It will then look into the Flemish approach to mitigating the complexity involved in consumers' participation in electricity sharing and trading.

#### (i) Interactions with Suppliers

451. Each consumer participating in all forms of energy sharing, P2P trading and VME sales is mainly subject to the following common requirements:[297]

- Having an individual connection to the grid, each with an individual meter;
- Having a contract with a commercial energy supplier and reporting its participation to the relevant energy supplier, and checking whether the supplier has specific conditions in the context of sharing or selling energy;
- Having an automatic meter reading meter or a communicating digital meter with metering regime 3 (quarter-hourly data in the allocation) activated by the relevant energy supplier;
- Only participating in one specific group of sharing or selling RES-E with each access point and direction (offtake or injection).

452. These requirements are largely straightforward, whereas several merit further examination, as they highlight the role of suppliers in an era of rising renewables self-consumption. There is no shortage of literature adapting market models to wider consumer engagement, which marginalizes or even ignores the role of suppliers (Bray and Woodman, 2018; Capper et al., 2022). Conversely, the fact is that for now and the near future, due to technical, economic, and even

[297] *Protocol on Sharing and Selling Self-generated RES-E*, sections 3.3.2 and 5.4.

regulatory barriers to fully realizing energy self-sufficiency,[298] self-consumption cannot fully meet energy demand. Thereby, the commercial supplier will continue to supply the residual energy demand of most consumers. Suppliers thus still have many interactions with active customers and consumers involved in energy communities. At the same time, they are also subject to a series of impacts brought by consumers' involvement in sharing and selling their self-produced RES-E, especially on profits and balance responsibility (Pedrero and Del Granado, 2023; *Electricity and gas market report 2022*, section 4.2.2.2). Their contractual relationship with consumers enables them to exert influence on the realization and cost-benefit ratio of various activities involved in renewable self-consumption. Such impacts, in the form of extra costs or conditions imposed on involved consumers, as will be discussed later, provided that they are transparent and justified, might be allowed by national law. This situation has implications for the legal framework empowering consumers. It must be able to properly reconcile conflicting interests between concerned consumers and their suppliers and enable suppliers to contribute to fostering renewables self-consumption.

453. Serving as a prominent example, the above common requirements for consumers wishing to engage in electricity sharing, P2P and VME sales reveal the role and potential impact of suppliers in these activities. Having contracts with suppliers and having the specific metering regime activated by suppliers are two preconditions. The former helps ensure an energy supply, as noted, since self-consumption (including electricity sharing and sales) only partially covers energy demand. The latter indicates that the supplier plays a role in assisting consumers to meet a metering condition required to align the sharing and selling of self-produced RES-E with the existing regimes of balance settlement and allocation. Moreover, another precondition is that a final customer must check whether its supplier applies specific conditions for sharing and selling self-produced RES-E. This requirement is supported by the VREG's view of allowing suppliers to impose extra costs or conditions on consumers wishing to conduct energy sharing or sales. In March 2023, the regulator surveyed suppliers in Flanders on extra conditions or costs they had already applied to their consumers and on what account. Supplies reported that they are subject to additional burdens in the following aspects (*Electricity and gas market report 2022*, section 4.2.2.2):

- Decreasing revenues since customers who engage in energy sharing, P2P, or VME sales buy less electricity from their suppliers when their renewables output is available for consumption, sharing and sales;

298 One challenge is costly storage facilities. See e.g. Department of the Environment of Ireland, 2022.

- Rising imbalance costs induced by increasingly unpredictable offtake and injection behavior of consumers, since the supplier remains the access holder in some cases[299] and has to take care of the imbalance of a customer's full offtake and injection;
- Extra costs in the processing of the data regarding energy sharing, P2P and VME sales received via the DSO;[300]
- Additional costs in developing a separate reconciliation process devoted to addressing the impact of energy sharing, P2P and VME sales;[301]
- Increasing costs incurred by the collection of all other costs (including levies and network tariffs) of shared and sold self-produced RES-E.

454. Such implications can be further summarized into (i) the adverse impact on retail revenues, (ii) increasing imbalance risks, and (iii) extra coordination and administrative costs incurred by allowing sharing and sales of self-produced RES-E. Given such implications and underlying causes, the VREG takes the view that the choice of whether or not to charge additional costs for energy sharing, P2P, and VME sales or to impose additional conditions, in principle, falls within the commercial freedom of the supplier (*Electricity and Gas Market*

---

299 The legislation specifies that for electricity sharing and P2P trading, the access holders cannot, under any circumstances, be the system operator, while in the VME sales, the association of co-owners cannot be the access holder unless it has applied for a supply license. Art. 4.2.1 of the TRDE specifies which actors are allowed to perform the role of access holders. At allocation points to which only injection is allocated, connected to access points on the electricity distribution network: the access holder is either the electricity distribution network user (producer) itself, or a mandated third party, depending on which party has requested and obtained access to the network. At the allocation points to which offtake is (also) allocated connected to an access point on the electricity distribution network: the access holder is either the customer himself (the same natural or legal person), provided that the customer has a connection capacity for offtake greater than or equal to 56kVA, or the supplier, depending on which party has requested and obtained network access for that access point. See *Flemish Energy Decree*, art. 7.2.1, §1, art. 7.2.2, §2 and art. 7.2.3, §2; *TRDE*, art. 4.2.1.

300 Surveys sent out by VREG to all electricity suppliers in March 2023 and February 2024 revealed that the fact that sharing and sales of self-produced RES-E are not yet embedded in regular market processes is a complaint by most suppliers. They indicated that processing the data supplied by Fluvius (the Flemish DSO) via parallel data streams requires manual work for the time being, which is one of the reasons suppliers mention charging an additional cost. The VREG, therefore, urged Fluvius to conduct serious market negotiations on the structural integration of energy sharing and energy sales into the market processes in 2024. Once this step is accomplished, the impact on suppliers could be partially mitigated. See *VREG 2024 Report on Energy Communities, Energy Sharing and Sales*, section 3.3.

301 Reconciliation refers to a mutual settlement between market participants based on the difference between the allocated and actually metered energy quantities. By means of the reconciliation process, suppliers get 'assigned' ultimately the energy volumes as read on their customers' meters. See *Flemish Energy Decree*, art. 1.1.3, 107°. The separate reconciliation process developed in the context of sharing and selling self-generated RES-E will be elaborated on later.

*Report 2022*, section 4.2.2.4).[302] According to the surveyed suppliers, examples of such extra conditions include only allowing energy sharing in combination with a dynamic price,[303] or in combination with monthly billing, or reporting the start-up of energy sharing in a timely manner.[304] The extra costs take the form of, for instance, a fixed cost per connection and per year, varying between 24 and 150 euros, or a cost depending on the volume of shared electricity.[305] On the other hand, via calculations, the VREG also noted that the additional costs charged by some suppliers limit and can even offset the potential benefits of energy sharing and P2P for households.[306] In 2024, based on a study on the costs and benefits of households and SMEs, the VREG drew a similar conclusion.[307] It found that by sharing or selling energy, buyers and sellers can save money, but the savings may not be enough to cover the additional charges from suppliers. Additional charges and conditions applied by suppliers make energy sharing and selling not financially interesting, especially for households. They could only recover costs by sharing a great volume of electricity. For the SMEs studied, it seems easier to recoup costs, thanks to the higher volumes they can share or sell. It seems that, as of 2024, in Flanders, due to conditions or charges imposed by suppliers, it is still hard for renewables self-consumers from the residential sector to obtain market-based incentives to sell or share surplus RES-E. This situation could also affect their overall incentives to engage in renewables self-consumption.

455. By October 2024, the regulator has not stepped in to regulate such extra conditions and charges. Yet, this does not mean that suppliers can set them without restrictions. They are subject to relevant rules on contract law, market practices, and consumer protection rules, including the (federal) rules on contracts with consumers in the Code of Economic Law, the Consumer Agreement and the recent Code of Conduct.[308] In light of these rules, additional conditions and costs for customers engaged in energy sharing, P2P and VME sales must always be clearly described in the general conditions, the special conditions, or the rate card accompanying the supply contracts.[309] In addition, the VREG views ensuring sufficient transparency about the extra conditions and costs imposed

---

302 The VREG drew similar conclusions based on another survey in 2022. See *2022 Report on energy communities, energy sharing and P2P trading*, section 3.3.1.

303 By March 2024, two suppliers still maintained the condition that allows energy sharing and energy selling only in combination with a dynamic contract. See *VREG 2024 Report on Energy Communities, Energy Sharing and Sales*, section 3.4.1.

304 *Electricity and Gas Market Report 2022*, section 4.2.2.2.

305 *Electricity and Gas Market Report 2022*, section 4.2.2.2; *VREG 2024 Report on Energy Communities, Energy Sharing and Sales*, section 3.4.1.

306 *Electricity and gas market report 2022*, sections 4.2.2.3 and 4.2.2.4.

307 *VREG 2024 Report on Energy Communities, Energy Sharing and Sales*, section 3.4.2.5.

308 *Akkoord 'De consument in de vrije elektriciteits- en gasmarkt,'* 2022; *Gedragscode voor de bescherming van de zelfstandigen en de kmo's in de elektriciteits- en gasmarkt*, 2023.

309 *Electricity and Gas Market Report 2022*, section 4.2.2.4.

by suppliers as the key to balancing suppliers' interests against consumers' rights and incentives to engage in RES-E sharing and selling. Since March 2023, the VREG has provided more information for consumers in this regard via a price comparison tool developed by itself.[310] Such information, together with that displayed in supply offers, can help consumers choose or switch to suppliers with lower costs and less restrictive conditions, thereby prompting suppliers to apply only extra costs and conditions that reflect their actual impacts or costs.

456. With this information-based approach, the regulator adopts a less intrusive way than regularly monitoring additional charges and conditions applied by suppliers. Moreover, this approach also helps to overcome informational disadvantages faced by both consumers and the regulator vis-à-vis suppliers. First, it avoids placing the burden on consumers to assess whether individual suppliers' additional requirements are justified, as this can be too demanding for many. Being informed of the charges and conditions applied by suppliers, along with using the comparison tool, consumers can switch to suppliers whose conditions are less restrictive or more conducive to electricity sharing or selling. Second, this approach also helps the regulator circumvent the tricky issue of monitoring extra fees charged by suppliers, which requires assessments of whether they are proportionate to the costs incurred by electricity sharing and selling. Informational asymmetry exists not only between consumers but also between the regulator and suppliers. The regulator may also lack sufficient information about the actual costs of suppliers caused by their consumers' involvement in renewables self-consumption. This disadvantage can be countered by information disclosure and market mechanisms, which lead suppliers to set cost-reflective charges. Despite these merits, this approach might not be sufficient to protect consumers. It only works well under certain preconditions. It is also questionable whether it can be broadly applied in other Member States, as elaborated next.

457. First, relying on disclosing suppliers' extra conditions or costs may not be sufficient to safeguard consumers' rights to renewables self-consumption. This approach heavily relies on robust national efforts to facilitate switching suppliers, including the required time to handle requests and switching-related fees. The Flemish approach is advisable only when consumers can switch suppliers who apply unjustified conditions or charges with minimal transaction costs, i.e., within the shortest time (e.g., no longer than 24 hours on working days)[311] and

---

310 *VREG 2024 Report on Energy Communities, Energy Sharing and Sales*, section 3.4.1.

311 Article 12 of the Electricity Directive stipulates that '*Switching supplier or market participant engaged in aggregation shall be carried out within the shortest possible time ... By no later than 2026, the technical process of switching supplier shall take no longer than 24 hours and shall be possible on any working day.*'

without additional costs. Household customers and small enterprises could be protected from unjustified conditions or fees for electricity sharing or trading, since they are entitled to switch suppliers without switching-related fees.[312] This might not be the case for other customer groups, as it is left to Member States to decide whether to prohibit switching-related fees for other final customers (*Electricity Directive*, article 12(2)). In Member States that allow suppliers to charge other customer groups for switching suppliers, these consumers cannot switch to suppliers with less restrictive conditions at minimal costs.

458. Another customer group liable to unfavorable conditions is those entering fixed-term, fixed-price electricity supply contracts. Article 12 of the Electricity Directive allows suppliers to charge customers contract termination fees where those customers voluntarily terminate fixed-term, fixed-price supply contracts before their maturity. This implies that customers with fixed-term, fixed-price supply contracts are subject to additional costs when terminating contracts with suppliers that hinder their participation in electricity sharing or trading. The same problem may also exist for consumers having separate contracts for offtake and injection. Article 4 of the Electricity Directive entitles all customers to have more than one electricity supply contract at the same time, provided that the required connection and metering points are established. Yet, that legislation does not grant consumers with multiple contracts a particular right to switch suppliers freely. For instance, when they have separate offtake and injection contracts with the same supplier and wish to terminate the offtake one, the supplier may renegotiate the injection one with extra conditions or charges, implying high transaction costs for such consumers.

459. Overall, customer groups subject to switching-related fees are not adequately protected from unjustified restrictions or barriers to renewables self-consumption potentially imposed by suppliers. They are subject to either unfavorable conditions imposed by their suppliers or economic loss when protecting themselves from barriers created by suppliers. For these consumers, additional regular oversight of conditions and charges applied by suppliers is still needed to prevent them from disproportionately obstructing the sale and sharing of self-produced RES-E.

460. In addition, the VREG's information-based approach to preventing disproportionate charges or conditions also includes the use of the comparison tool. Whether the comparison tool is user-friendly and capable of properly providing sufficient information for offer comparison, as enshrined in Article 14 of the Electricity Directive, matters in terms of ensuring the effectiveness of that regulatory approach. However, the most recent data shows that although

312 Article 12 of the Electricity Directive requires Member States to ensure that at least household customers and small enterprises are not charged any switching-related fees.

a large number of comparison tools are available to energy consumers, very few consumers have access to a comparison tool that meets the requirements of Article 14 and can therefore be considered reliable (ACER and CEER, 2023b). The information-based regulatory approach presented by the VREG may not function effectively in Member States without the full transposition of Article 14 of the Electricity Directive. Moreover, the comparison tool does not provide all the necessary information to compare offers, such as promotions offered by suppliers, which also affects consumers' decisions to switch to suppliers that provide more favorable conditions for renewables self-consumption.

461. Among the implications listed above, another aspect worth noting is the ex-post financial reconciliation process for dealing with the settlement impact created by sharing and selling self-generated RES-E.[313] As the general precondition that all parties involved must have a supply contract with the same commercial energy supplier each time (i.e., have the same access holder) is no longer applied, there is a need to introduce a separate reconciliation process.[314] This reconciliation process ensures that impacted suppliers mutually settle the difference between allocated and actually measured energy volumes, which results from the sharing and sales of self-generated RES-E.[315] Figure 12 provides an example to illustrate how the sharing or sales of RES-E lead to ex-post financial reconciliation. The supplier at the offtake point must be compensated for the volume of electricity that it has already sourced based on the existing supply contract, but can no longer bill to its consumer, i.e., Customer B.[316] Conversely, the supplier at the injection point must reimburse the supplier at the offtake point for the share of electricity that its consumer, i.e., Customer A, offered to Customer B, since it has marketed the same amount of electricity based on the feed-in contract with Customer A.[317]

---

313 *Protocol on Sharing and Selling Self-generated RES-E*, section 6.3.

314 An important precondition in the first and second versions of the Protocol on Sharing and Selling Self-generated RES-E is that all active customers involved in energy sharing or P2P must always have a supply contract with the same commercial energy supplier. For example, for energy sharing in a building, all active customers who participate in energy sharing must have a contract with the same energy supplier, and for 'energy sharing with oneself', the active customer must have a contract with the same energy supplier in all their residences/business locations. As a result of this precondition, the VREG determined that the DSO had not fully implemented P2P trading of renewable electricity and the four forms of energy sharing. In July 2022, for that reason, the VREG initiated an enforcement process against ten Flemish electricity DSOs for which Fluvius acts as an operating company. Under these decisions, the administrative fine will be imposed on electricity distribution system operators from 1 February 2023, if the implementation of energy sharing and P2P is still incomplete by then. See *2022 Report on energy communities, energy sharing and P2P trading*, section 3.2; VREG, 2022a, 2022b, 2022c, 2022d, 2022e, 2022f, 2022g, 2022h, 2022i, 2022j.

315 *Protocol on Sharing and Selling Self-generated RES-E*, section 6.3.1.

316 Ibid.

317 Ibid.

**Figure 12. An example of financial reconciliation resulted from consumers' RES-E sharing or selling**

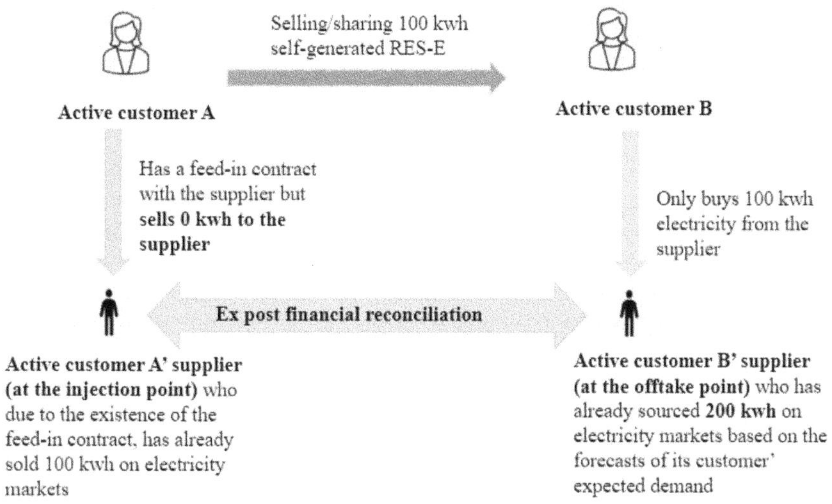


Source: Author's own elaboration.

462. The suppliers who are access holders and have customers in their portfolio who share or sell electricity are obliged to participate in the ex-post financial reconciliation.[318] To support the financial reconciliation, the DSO must offer suppliers relevant data concerning changes in allocation points involved in energy sharing, P2P sales, or VME sales of RES-E.[319] Relevant data exchange mechanisms will be addressed in Section 2.2 of this Chapter below.

463. Based on the data communicated by the DSO, FeReSO, acting as a joint appointee of suppliers and DSOs, takes up the role of the financial reconciliation body in the context of energy sharing or sales.[320] This financial reconciliation is not regulated in the Protocol on Sharing and Selling Self-generated RES-E itself, but in a separate agreement between the market parties involved.[321] The market parties within FeReSO have already revised the financial reconciliation of energy sharing, whereby the frequency of the financial reconciliation has been adjusted to half-yearly, instead of quarterly.[322] Version 3.2 of the Protocol

318 *Protocol on Sharing and Selling Self-generated RES-E*, section 5.4.
319 *TRDE*, art. 4.3.64, §1 and §2, art. 4.3.65, §1, *Protocol on Sharing and Selling Self-generated RES-E*, section 6.4.
320 *Protocol on Sharing and Selling Self-generated RES-E*, section 6.3.3.
321 *Decision of the VREG regarding the approval of Protocol on Sharing and Selling Self-generated RES-E – version 3.2*, section II.1.
322 Ibid.

was adopted in July 2024 to bring the protocol in line with the current market agreement regarding the financial reconciliation.[323]

(ii) Efforts to Mitigate Complexity

464. The Protocol on Sharing and Selling Self-generated RES-E defines an entity communicating the required data to the DSO for the above reconciliation purposes on behalf of participating consumers. In fact, its role goes beyond interacting with the DSO. It represents a key actor in mitigating complexity and transaction costs faced by consumers in engaging in various forms of electricity sharing and trading.

465. The Protocol defines this authorized representative as the 'community manager' ('Beheerder van de Gemeenschap').[324] It should be highlighted that the 'community' in the context of the Protocol on Sharing and Selling Self-generated RES-E refers to '*the totality of participants who share or sell energy within a specific group*',[325] which is distinct from CECs or RECs defined by the Flemish Energy Decree. The community manager is an entity jointly appointed by grid users wishing to share or trade electricity, acting on their behalf vis-à-vis the DSO.[326] It can be a natural or legal person, or one of the participants in energy sharing or selling, or a third party.[327] The rule of appointing a manager applies to all forms of electricity sharing, P2P and VME sales. For instance, in the case of sharing electricity with oneself, an active customer with multiple access points can register as a manager. Alternatively, it can delegate the management of generation installations, which are necessary to carry out energy sharing activities, to a third party, including with regard to installation, operation, data processing and maintenance, where the third party is not considered an active customer.[328] In situations with multiple participants, such as P2P and VME sales, jointly appointing a community manager is required, as Figure 10 above shows. With the authorization, the participants give permission to the manager to act as a community manager, as well as permission to make available the relevant data to that manager.[329] These data, in accordance with the TRDE, are used to address impacts on suppliers and BRPs, as noted above. With the authorization, the major tasks of the community manager can be broadly divided into two groups, as listed in Table 9.[330]

---

323 *Protocol on Sharing and Selling Self-generated RES-E.*
324 *Protocol on Sharing and Selling Self-generated RES-E*, section 6.1.2.
325 *Protocol on Sharing and Selling Self-generated RES-E*, section 5.1.
326 *Protocol on Sharing and Selling Self-generated RES-E*, section 6.1.2.
327 Ibid.
328 *Flemish Energy Decree*, art.4.4.2, §3.
329 *Protocol on Sharing and Selling Self-generated RES-E*, section 6.1.2.
330 *Protocol on Sharing and Selling Self-generated RES-E*, sections 5.4 and 6.1.

**Table 9. Tasks of the community manager**

| | |
|---|---|
| Registering and managing the community | • Choosing a community type: choosing from the four forms of electricity sharing or selling (including VME sales, P2P and multiple P2P sales);<br>• Notifying the relevant energy supplier of each consumer's participation and checking in advance whether specific conditions are applied by the relevant supplier in the context of sharing or selling energy, and informing the participant of those conditions;<br>• Dividing large communities into groups of a maximum of 100 participants and registering them separately;[331]<br>• Configuring participating points: determining the role for each participating point: 'offtake', 'injection' or 'offtake and injection';<br>• Configuring distribution key for offtake points:[332] choosing which type of distribution key to use to distribute the injection between the different participants in the case of electricity sharing and VME sales.[333] |
| Providing data | Communicating all changes in the community (changes in the parameters of the community or its participants)[334] to the DSO as soon as possible, given the impact on the calculation of shared or sold energy volumes and the financial reconciliation. |

Source: Author's own elaboration.

466. The presence of the community manager prevents consumers from exchanging data required for the ex-post reconciliation with the DSO. Moreover, managing electricity sharing or transactions according to the implementing rules, such as setting up participation points and distribution keys, requires technical and administrative capacity. The lack of expertise in understanding and complying with relevant technical requirements is another factor deterring consumers from engaging in self-consumption activities, as mentioned in the previous Chapter. The possibility of delegating these tasks to a third party, such as an energy service provider, could reduce additional input required from consumers, especially time, active efforts and expertise, facilitating consumer engagement.

467. Aside from potential benefits for consumers, the introduction of the community manager is also conducive to addressing the challenges of shifting

331 This does not mean that a separate legal entity must be established for each group. See *Protocol on Sharing and Selling Self-generated RES-E*, 2024.

332 The total of the injection to be distributed is 100%, and the community manager chooses how the total of 100% is distributed among participants. The manager enters a distribution key value per participant. Three distribution keys are possible: the fixed, relative and optimal distribution key, representing different ways of distributing the available injected electricity among participants. Regardless of the type of allocation key, the sharing or selling of energy is limited to the offtake of the recipient. See *Protocol on Sharing and Selling Self-generated RES-E*, sections 2.4 and 6.2.

333 For P2P sales and multiple person-to-person sales, there is no need to set up the distribution key. See *Protocol on Sharing and Selling Self-generated RES-E*, sections 6.1.1 and 6.5.3.

334 See more details about the data exchange in Section 2.2 of this Chapter below.

the role of the DSO. Empirical evidence cited in the previous Chapter indicates that compared to the TSO, a major challenge encountered by the DSO in the energy transition is coordinating a large number of smaller and vastly distributed consumers.[335] Lowering transaction costs and complexity thus not only helps engage consumers but also eases the fulfillment of the more active role of the DSO in facilitating renewables self-consumption. Introducing an entity acting on behalf of multiple consumers is a typical solution in this respect. The Protocol additionally takes proactive actions to enable the smooth management of large communities and limit the number of calculations and rectifications for the actors involved.[336] This is reflected in the measure requiring the community manager to divide large communities into groups and register them separately.[337]

### *2.1.3. Governance Aspects of Energy Communities*

468. Energy communities are envisioned as a promising vehicle for engaging consumers in flexibility provision and renewables self-consumption in EU energy law. As explained in the previous Chapter, their advantages in this respect are realized by enabling multiple consumers to collectively engage in these energy activities and offering them social, economic and environmental community benefits. Because of this, aside from granting the collective the right to conduct relevant energy activities, crucial to the success of such collective solutions lies in governing the relationship between the participating consumers and the collective.[338] The relationship must be structured in a way that enables consumers to benefit from collective involvement in sustainable energy activities, as entrenched in eligibility requirements contained in EU-level definitions of CECs and RECs. Having reviewed the rights granted to CECs and CECs in the Belgian legal context, this subsection focuses on how Belgian law has transposed those eligibility requirements.

#### 2.1.3.1. Federal Approach

469. At the federal level, the Federal Electricity Law incorporates EU-level eligibility conditions regarding membership, composition and purpose in the

---

335 See Section 6.3 of Chapter III.

336 *Protocol on Sharing and Selling Self-generated RES-E*, sections 5.4.

337 The protocol currently limits the number of participants of a group doing energy sharing or energy selling to a maximum of 100. That limit aims to avoid more difficult manageability of larger groups and a greater impact on settlements. Ibid. See also *VREG 2024 Report on Energy Communities, Energy Sharing and Sales*, section 3.3.

338 See Section 3.3 of the previous Chapter for the link between governing this relationship and EU-level requirements for the purpose, membership, composition and decision making of energy communities.

definition of the CEC.[339] However, it does not provide further specification of those general requirements, such as 'effective control by shareholders or members', the autonomy, and proximity of the REC.[340] Due to the division of competence, federal law delimits the REC to those carrying out activities within Belgium but exclusively in the territorial sea and the exclusive economic zone. An objective standard for assessing the proximity of members or shareholders toward the renewable energy projects owned by the energy community remains absent. Moreover, the Federal Electricity Law does not set out rules for the registration and recognition of CECs and RECs. Art. 19quinquies, §2 of that legislation allows the federal government to develop further rules regarding the conditions for the recognition and participation in RECs.

470. By October 2024, when searching the Belgian law database 'Justel' with keywords 'hernieuwbare-energiegemeenschappen' ('renewable energy community) and 'erkenning' (recognition), a Royal Decree adopted on 3 June 2024 is the only federal legal act containing these two terms.[341] Yet, this legal act mainly aims to fulfill an obligation imposed by Article 6/3, §3 of the Federal Electricity Law[342] instead of making specific rules under the empowerment of the above Art. 19quinquies, §2. Despite this, the conditions for 'direct citizen participation' partially overlap with the eligibility criteria for RECs. This legal instrument, to some extent, helps to concretize the REC's eligibility conditions, especially for membership and primary purposes. Given this, the Royal Decree of 3 June 2024 merits further examination.

471. More specifically, the Royal Decree lays down the competitive tender procedure, the conditions and the procedure for awarding the domain concessions and the general conditions for the use of the plots for the construction and operation of an installation for the production of RES-E in the maritime areas under the jurisdiction of Belgium. Among others, to implement Article 6/3, §3, 9° of the Federal Electricity Law, the Decree specifies criteria for assessing citizen participation, which is a mandatory criterion in a competitive bidding process for a domain concession in the North Sea.[343]

339 *Belgian Federal Electricity Law*, art. 2, 106°.

340 *Belgian Federal Electricity Law*, art. 2, 107°.

341 *Royal Decree of 3 June 2024*, 2024.

342 Article 6/3, §3 of the Federal Electricity Law requires the federal government to determine the course of the competitive tender procedure, the conditions and procedure for awarding the domain concessions and the general conditions for the use of the plots for the construction and operation of a plant for the production of electricity from renewable energy sources in the sea areas under the jurisdiction of Belgium.

343 Article 6/3, §3 of the Federal Electricity Law stipulates that '*By decision, taken after consultation in the Council of Ministers, following advice from the Commission, the King shall determine the course of the competitive tender procedure, the conditions and procedure for awarding the*

It provides that citizens, and possibly together with SMEs and local authorities (including municipalities, educational institutions, and associations), can engage in 'direct citizen participation' through a REC.[344] The rule-maker further explains how this community-based approach operates: '*Citizens, and possibly together with SMEs and local authorities, including municipalities, educational institutions and associations can participate in the capital of the project through a renewable energy community (legal entity).*' Art. 21, §3 of that Royal Decree lays down a set of conditions for such direct citizen participation, ranging from open and voluntary participation, democratic control and ownership to autonomy and independence, which (partially) overlap with eligibility criteria for RECs. Such overlap is confirmed by the rule-maker: It states that '*through the energy community vehicle, all the criteria of direct citizen participation can then be met*'[345] and highlights that the profit allocation of the energy community must respect conditions regarding '*Economic participation of participating citizens*' listed below.[346] Table 10 below compares the general requirements for qualifying as RECs and conditions for direct citizen participation set out by the Royal Decree.

---

*domain concessions and the general conditions for the use of the plots, and in particular: ... 9° the extent and manner in which citizen participation can be provided for and renewable energy communities can be involved by the holder of a domain concession, as well as the minimum percentage of citizen participation to be achieved.*' See also *Royal Decree of 3 June 2024*, arts. 7, 9° and 21, §3.

344 Royal Decree of 3 June 2024, Art. 21, §3(f). When explaining Art. 21, the rule-maker states that '*Article 21 §3 sets out the conditions that direct civic participation should meet. These are six conditions, namely: (1) open and voluntary participation, (2) democratic control and ownership, (3) creation of support, (4) economic participation of the participating citizens, (5) autonomy and independence, and (6) direct citizens' participation can also be provided by a partnership between several citizens' initiatives for renewable energy to which the citizens can directly join .... This sixth condition could include participation by SMEs, local authorities, including municipalities, educational institutions and associations. This should be understood in the same sense as its mention in the definition of 'renewable energy community' as provided for in Article 2, 107° Electricity Law.*'

345 However, this claim is problematic. So far, federal law has not created detailed criteria for assessing compliance with those broadly worded eligibility requirements contained in energy communities' definitions. In this context, how could the rule-maker ensure the involvement of energy communities amounts to the satisfaction of all the criteria of direct citizen participation? See Royal Decree of 3 June 2024, Preamble.

346 The rule-maker stresses that '*first, the profits of the energy community should be used to realize social added value. This includes strengthening local energy transition initiatives such as awareness raising, energy delivery, electrification programs, energy demand management and addressing energy poverty. If compensation, for the contribution of capital, to members of the energy community is decided upon, it should be modest.*' See Royal Decree of 3 June 2024, Preamble.

**Table 10. Comparisons between respective conditions for constituting RECs and direct citizen participation**

| Eligibility criteria for RECs | Conditions for direct citizen participation |
|---|---|
| Membership:<br>Open and voluntary participation;<br>Members are natural persons, SMEs or local authorities, including municipalities, while private undertakings' participation does not constitute their primary commercial or professional activity | *Open and voluntary participation*:<br>(1) Should be open to all citizens who wish to take responsibility for this, without any discrimination based on gender, social origin, race, political preference or religion;<br>(2) Should allow citizens or end users to participate as much as possible in the production of electricity from renewable energy sources in the maritime areas under the jurisdiction of Belgium, through low entry costs and limited contributions per person;<br>(3) The participation of citizens cannot constitute their main commercial or professional activity. |
| Decision-making:<br>Autonomy;<br>Effectively control: by shareholders or members that are located in the proximity of the renewable energy projects that are owned and developed by the REC | *Democratic control and ownership*:<br>It is the participating citizens who have control (say in rights and facts) over the part that is realized through direct citizen participation and the production that this yields;<br>*Autonomy and independence*:<br>Direct citizen participation is designed in such a way that it is autonomous and self-reliant, and is supervised by the participating citizens;<br>*Economic participation of participating citizens*:<br>Participating citizens contribute equitably to the share of capital needed for the part of the project realized through direct citizen participation, and they have democratic control over it. |
| Primary purposes:<br>Provide community benefits instead of financial profits | *Economic participation of participating citizens*:<br>(1) Economic participation is through shares in the project's capital. If participating citizens receive compensation for the capital they contribute, this is a modest compensation, and the profits are mainly used to realize social added value, including strengthening local functioning around energy transition through initiatives such as sensitization, energy supply, electrification, and demand-side management programs and measures to combat energy poverty.<br>(2) Participating citizens can, for example, dispose of part of the electricity produced in the form of an electricity supply contract concluded with the citizens' initiative that unites the citizens. |

Source: Author's own elaboration.

472. As can be seen, in the context of allowing RECs' involvement in a competitive bidding process for a domain concession in the North Sea and relevant support schemes financing offshore renewables projects, two general eligibility requirements contained in the definition of the REC are translated into more detailed criteria:

- Open participation is secured by 'low entry costs and limited contributions per person';
- To ensure the primary purpose of providing community benefits and the secondary role of profit-making, the use of profits is subject to two conditions: (i) compensation received by community members for the capital they contribute must be modest, and (ii) the majority of profits must be used for social added value defined by the Royal Decree.

473. However, the remaining eligibility conditions remain obscure:

- Voluntary participation: it remains unclear (i) whether members can leave the REC without any restrictions, and (ii) how to solve the potential impact of membership termination on the financial stability and autonomy of the REC;[347]
- Decision-making mechanisms: (i) the specific criteria for assessing the autonomy of the REC are missing, and (ii) democratic control does not entirely amount to effective control,[348] and how to assess the REC's compliance with effective control and the proximity element remains unclear.

474. Moreover, Art. 54 of the Royal Decree empowers the CREG to periodically monitor the concessionaire's compliance with the above conditions for direct citizen participation and penalize non-compliance.[349] When direct

---

[347] For a more detailed discussion about key legal problems involved in voluntary participation, see Section 3.1.3.2 below.

[348] For elements that should be contained in defining 'effective control', see Section 3.1.3.3 below.

[349] Art. 54 of the *Royal Decree of 3 June 2024* stipulates that '*After one year from the commissioning of the first production installation of a concessionaire, the Commission checks whether the concessionaire has achieved the minimum percentage of one percent citizen participation. If this is not the case, the Commission may impose an administrative fine on the concessionaire equal to a maximum percentage of the total investment costs corresponding to the part of the minimum percentage not achieved, unless the concessionaire can demonstrate force majeure. When determining the amount of the administrative fine, the Commission may take into account the circumstances and the efforts made. After three years from the commissioning of the first production unit of a concessionaire, the commission checks:*

*1° whether the concessionaire complies with its commitments regarding the percentage of citizen participation promised in its application above the minimum percentage;*

*2° whether it complies with its citizen participation plan as referred to in Articles 7, 9° and 21, §2.*

citizen participation is achieved through the involvement of a REC, compliance with the REC's definition and relevant eligibility conditions is subject to ex-post oversight conducted by the CREG. Federal law thus represents an example of monitoring the REC's compliance with eligibility requirements after awarding concession and public support, instead of building ex-ante oversight via recognition procedures. This is different from the Flemish approach and its alternatives proposed by the VREG, as detailed later on.

475. In conclusion, in the federal context, specific rules detailing the eligibility criteria for energy communities have not been established. Some conditions for qualifying as RECs have been further clarified when domain concession applicants in the North Sea choose to involve RECs to meet the mandatory requirement for direct citizen participation. Yet, eligibility criteria regarding membership and decision-making of RECs remain incomplete and obscure. Concrete legal issues ignored by Member States when transposing general eligibility requirements for CECs and RECs will be discussed in detail in Section 3.1 of this Chapter below. The next subsection examines to what extent Flemish law has materialized those requirements.

#### 2.1.3.2. Flemish Approach

476. Compared to federal law, Flemish law provides more clarification on conditions and requirements for qualifying as CECs and RECs, as shown in Table 11 below. It first clarifies that the non-profit motive is not absolute, as EU law only prohibits pursuing profits as the primary purpose of energy communities. While Flemish law does not clearly define 'effective control by members or shareholders', it defines 'control' in this context. EU law indeed introduced a general definition of control, but it does not specify that this definition is

---

*If the concessionaire has not achieved the percentage(s) of citizen participation promised in its application above the minimum percentage but has respected its action plan, the concessionaire has an additional period of one year from the determination of the insufficient citizen participation by the commission to achieve the promised percentage(s). If, even after this additional period of one year, the concessionaire fails to achieve the percentage(s) promised in its application for citizen participation, or if, after the initial period of three years, it fails to achieve this percentage(s) and is also unable to demonstrate that it has respected its action plan, the Commission may impose on the concessionaire the sanctions provided for in the Act of 29 April 1999, unless the concessionaire can demonstrate force majeure. When determining the amount of the administrative fine, the Commission may take into account the circumstances and the efforts made.*
*Following the five-yearly reporting referred to in Article 53, paragraph 1, 17°, the Commission shall check whether the concessionaire continues to comply with its obligations regarding citizen participation and its financing plan in this regard in accordance with Article 17, §1, 1°. If this is not the case, the Commission may impose a fine in accordance with the second and fifth, unless the reason for not following the obligations is due to a reason in the citizen participation itself. The Commission shall submit each five-yearly audit report to the Minister.'*

intended to define 'effective control' for energy communities (Almeida et al., 2021). The Flemish Energy Decree adopts the EU law's definition of 'control' in the legal provision for energy communities.[350] The legislation leaves the implementation of member control in both CECs and RECs to their respective statutes. As noted in Chapter III, under EU law, effective control of the REC is additionally limited by the proximity requirement. The Flemish Energy Decree provides the REC with two options to define their proximity, i.e., technical proximity and geographical proximity (*Belgian Federal Electricity Law*, art. 4.8.2). It does not define these two alternatives but instead allows the Flemish Government to determine specific criteria for them. As of October 2024, the government has not taken action.[351]

477. The absence of clear criteria or guidance has led to difficulty in applying the technical proximity in practice.[352] In a report, the VREG states that technical proximity represents electrical proximity, e.g., coupling shareholders or members on the same asset of the distribution grid, such as one feeder or LV/MV transformer), while the geographical one can be based on municipal or provincial boundaries, a radius of x number of kilometers around a production installation of the REC, taking into account the objectives or activities that the REC wants to achieve.[353] Nevertheless, this is not a legal definition of technical proximity, which cannot entirely address the uncertainties of applying it and assessing its compliance. By 2022, only 15% of established RECs described their proximity in a technical way.[354]

478. By contrast, the absence of applicable criteria for defining geographical proximity leads to diverse interpretations in practice, with different orders of magnitude of areas where the reported organizations are active. These range

---

350 Flemish Energy Decree art. 4.8.1, §1 states that 'control means rights, contracts or any other means which, either separately or in combination and having regard to the considerations of fact or law involved, confer the possibility of exercising decisive influence on the activities of an undertaking, namely: 1° rights of ownership or use of all or parts of the assets of an undertaking; 2° rights or agreements which confer a decisive influence on the composition, voting or decisions of the bodies of a company.' This is almost identical to the definition of 'control' stated in Article 2 (56) of the Electricity Directive.

351 This is based on the search results using the keyword 'geografische nabijheid' in the Belgian law database Justel on 10 October 2024.

352 Based on reports of CECs and RECs, the VREG found that the organizations that choose a demarcation based on technical proximity do not seem to fill this in correctly at all. They seem more in line with 'sharing energy within a building' or 'sharing energy with themselves'. See *2022 Report on energy communities, energy sharing and P2P trading*, section 2.3.4.

353 *2022 Report on energy communities, energy sharing and P2P trading*, section 2.1.

354 15% of the organizations reporting to the VREG indicate that they fill in the proximity requirement in a technical way, 85% indicate that they fill it in a geographical way. See 2022 Report on energy communities, energy sharing and P2P trading, section 2.3.4.

from being active throughout Belgium, over only Flanders, a specific province, or a few municipalities, to a school community with its employees.[355]

479. In terms of the autonomy of the REC, the Flemish legislation specifies that the REC should be autonomous from its individual members or shareholders or other market participants who participate in it through other means, such as investment (*Flemish Energy Decree*, art. 4.8.2, §1).

**Table 11. Conditions for qualifying as two types of energy communities under Flemish law (*Flemish Energy Decree*, arts. 4.8.1 and 4.8.2)**

<table>
<tr><th></th><th>CEC</th><th>REC</th></tr>
<tr><td>Legal form</td><td colspan="2">Legal entity (company, association)</td></tr>
<tr><td>Main purposes</td><td colspan="2">• Environmental, economic, or social benefits to its associates or members or the environment in which it operates;<br>• No profit motive, unless subordinate to the primary purposes.</td></tr>
<tr><td>Members/ shareholders</td><td>Anyone can become a member or shareholder</td><td rowspan="2">• Natural persons, local governments, or SMEs whose participation in the energy community does not constitute the main commercial or professional activity;<br>• Members or shareholders are located in proximity (technical or geographical proximity) to the renewable energy projects of the REC.</td></tr>
<tr><td>Control</td><td>• Natural persons, local authorities, or small enterprises that are not involved in large-scale commercial activities and for whom the energy sector is not the main economic activity;<br>• Integrating EU law's definition of 'control' in the context of defining energy communities.</td></tr>
<tr><td>Statutes</td><td>Each CEC should determine in its statutes the rules around the control of its members or shareholders</td><td>Each REC should determine in its statutes the rules on the control of its members or shareholders and the autonomy of the REC</td></tr>
<tr><td>Agreements between energy communities and members</td><td colspan="2">• Members or shareholders should each conclude an agreement with the concerned energy communities about their rights and obligations;<br>• If energy sharing is done within the energy community, the agreement should contain the rights and obligations of the members or shareholders for the applicable energy sharing key;<br>• The Flemish Government may determine the minimum content of that agreement.</td></tr>
</table>

480. Based on principles of effective control and autonomy, Flemish law grants rather broad freedom to energy communities and their members or

355 *2022 Report on energy communities, energy sharing and P2P trading*, section 2.3.4.

shareholders to structure their relationship through a mutual agreement that addresses their rights and obligations, including those related to energy sharing. The legislation delegates to the Flemish Government the task of determining the minimum elements of such agreements. The government has exercised this power by introducing Art. 3.3.1 to the Government Decision on Energy Policy. This provision specifies fifteen elements that the agreement between members or shareholders and the CEC or the REC should cover. This provision also provides that this agreement is entered into on an entirely voluntary basis and cannot be made mandatory by any other agreement binding the parties. The content contained by the agreement can be broadly classified into five aspects as follows:

- Membership: (i) provisions on the life span and dissolution of the energy community; (ii) the conditions for joining and exiting the energy community.
- Decision making: (i) the provisions on the effective control or control of the energy community's activities and the voting modalities within the energy community's bodies; (ii) in the case of a REC, the way in which its autonomy is guaranteed and the production facilities it owns and uses to carry out its activities.
- Energy activities and profits allocation: (i) the activities that the energy community will carry out based on the empowerment of the Flemish Energy Decree; (ii) the provisions on the costs of the community and the allocation of any profits generated by the activities of the energy community; (iii) if applicable, pursuant to the TRDE, the determination of the applicable allocation key and any financial consequences in the context of energy sharing and the conditions and procedures under which the allocation key can be changed; (iv) if applicable, and in accordance with the TRDE, the method for reporting errors relating to the distribution key applied; (v) if applicable, the conditions for joining and exiting energy sharing in accordance with the TRDE.
- Information provision and data exchange: (i) if applicable, the provisions on the management of green certificates and GOs; (ii) the provisions on the rights and obligations of the energy community and its members or shareholders with respect to privacy and the protection of personal data.
- Complaint and dispute settlement: (i) the method for submitting a complaint to the energy community; (ii) the method for initiating dispute settlement procedures with the energy community.

481. Among these, Art. 3.3.1 particularly stresses fairness, transparency, proportionality, and non-discrimination for clauses with respect to joining, exiting, and implementing energy sharing as well as joining and exiting the energy community. Another aspect worth noting is the rights of consumers

involved in energy communities with respect to information access, data protection, complaint and dispute settlement. As noted above, in the context of energy sharing, energy communities do not constitute suppliers and accordingly are not subject to obligations stemming from the suppliers' relationship with consumers. However, consumers' rights arising from the relationships that they may have with energy communities, especially as investors and recipients of shared electricity, are granted as contractual rights. The above-cited Art. 3.3.1 only clarifies in what aspects such contractual rights should be created. In large part, the determination of specific rights and obligations is left to energy communities and their members or shareholders, which is subject to some minimum requirements. It appears that the Flemish legislation endeavors to avoid overly intervening in the governance of energy communities. However, doing so might fall into another pitfall of lacking robust measures to safeguard the conformity of energy communities with the obligations and conditions set out by EU law.

482. This risk is evident, firstly, considering the absence of application or recognition procedures for CECs and RECs. In such application or recognition procedures, an energy community applicant is required to submit an application to an appointed authority, which assesses the application for conformity with the conditions for establishing an energy community and, in the affirmative, recognizes the applicant as a CEC or a REC.[356] Instead, Flemish legislation only imposes a notification obligation upon energy communities. Within 30 days of its establishment, a CEC or a REC is obligated to report to the VREG mainly regarding (i) its name, type, legal form and address, (ii) the activities it carries out, (iii) the way in which it is composed,[357] and (iv) where applicable, how it elaborates the concept of technical or geographical proximity.[358] Any changes in these reported data should be reported annually.[359] The only legal consequence of this notification procedure is that the VREG publishes the received information on its website.[360]

483. Admittedly, disclosing reported information can, to some extent, enhance transparency and public scrutiny of the operation of RECs and CECs. However, such monitoring is very limited. An unresolved problem is that neither the reporting nor the information disclosure can ensure compliance with the

356 *2022 Report on energy communities, energy sharing and P2P trading*, section 2.3.

357 Art. 3.3.2 of the Government Decision on Energy Policy adds a requirement for reporting the composition: an overview showing to what extent the shareholders or members of the energy community are, proportionally, natural persons, local authorities, small enterprises, medium-sized enterprises or large enterprises.

358 *Flemish Energy Decree*, art. 4.8.3; *Government Decision on Energy Policy*, art. 3.3.2.

359 *Government Decision on Energy Policy*, art. 3.3.2.

360 *Flemish Energy Decree*, art. 4.8.3.

eligibility conditions for the CEC or the REC, which range from membership and primary objectives to effective control. An organization's reporting does not exert any influence over its establishment as an energy community, because, in light of Flemish legislation, it takes place after the establishment of a CEC or a REC.[361] Moreover, the legislation does not empower the VREG or other authorities to verify whether an entity claiming to be a CEC or REC has met the qualification conditions of these two energy communities as laid down by law. In this case, the VREG only monitors the notification by addressing the two most common problems: the notification that does not correspond to an existing legal entity, and the notification of a form of energy sales or energy sharing that does not require an energy community.[362] The absence of regulatory oversight of energy communities' establishment can lead to a situation in which some energy communities that have not met eligibility conditions are likely to operate as CECs or RECs. Based on the reported data, the VREG indeed found some organizations, for instance, with members consisting of medium-sized companies,[363] misrepresent themselves as energy communities. In this case, the VREG could only remove those non-compliant entities from the list of reported energy communities based on its information disclosure task.[364]

484. On the other hand, the fact that an energy community has been published on the VREG's website does not mean that it has been qualified as a CEC or a REC defined by EU law. The reasons are twofold. First, as already noted, within the current notification procedure, the VREG is not empowered to conduct a detailed review of the reported data and decide on the eligibility of the reported entities for being CECs or RECs.[365] Second, because of this, the regulator also lacks the competence to verify the integrity and authenticity of the reported data, which cannot be secured solely by relying on the reporting obligation.

485. Indeed, Art. 3.1.4, §2 of the Flemish Energy Decree confers power on the VREG to impose administrative sanctions for breaches of the provisions of the Decree and their implementing provisions, which cover those for energy communities. The VREG can thus exercise this ex-post power to regulate those organizations operating as CECs or RECs but violating the conditions and obligations set for these two entities. Despite this, ex-ante oversight of the establishment of CECs and RECs, approached by a recognition framework,

361 *Government Decision on Energy Policy*, art. 3.3.2.

362 *VREG 2024 Report on Energy Communities, Energy Sharing and Sales*, section 2.1.1.

363 There is an organization that has registered as an energy community but indicates that its members are 100% medium-sized companies. This contradicts the condition concerning effective control. See *2022 Report on energy communities, energy sharing and P2P trading*, section 2.3.3.

364 *2022 Report on energy communities, energy sharing and P2P trading*, section 2.4.

365 *2022 Report on energy communities, energy sharing and P2P trading*, section 2.3.

for instance, seems imperative for several reasons. The first consideration is to protect consumers. In particular, households typically lack the capacity to verify energy communities' qualifications, especially whether their primary purpose and decision-making mechanisms could go against the participants' legitimate interests. When participation in energy communities requires a minimum investment, the lack of ex-ante verification entails an investment risk. Second, as highlighted, CECs and RECs have a range of rights substantiated by national law and are eligible to access state aid and national support schemes.[366] Ex-ante monitoring of their establishment ensures that these rights and public support are only granted to entities that have satisfied the conditions for constituting CECs and RECs.

486. Despite the advantages of introducing an approval procedure, as rightly pointed out by the VREG, it should be borne in mind that a recognition or application procedure represents a significant additional administrative burden for both the applicant energy communities and the evaluating authority.[367] Section 3.1.3 of this Chapter will analyze possible advantages and disadvantages of different ex-ante and ex-post regulatory approaches (including the above federal approach) and formulate preliminary legal advice.

487. The existing notification procedure is not the only factor leading to inadequate monitoring of compliance with energy communities' eligibility requirements. Specific criteria for assessing whether an entity qualifies as a CEC or REC have not been fully established. As noted above, Flemish law has added further details to EU-level requirements for constituting these two energy communities. However, requirements with respect to their membership, primary purposes, effective control (including proximity in the case of RECs), and autonomy still contain some broadly formulated and ambiguous elements. These obscure requirements make it difficult to assess the rule compliance of an energy community.

488. The first prominent example concerns the primary purpose of energy communities. In line with EU law, Flemish law stresses the correlation between the primary purpose of energy communities and the fulfillment of required community benefits. However, ascertaining whether the former does serve the latter requires further criteria for assessing whether the primary purpose stated

---

366 For the renewables support schemes covering CECs and RECs, see e.g. *17 FEBRUARY 2023. – Ministerial decree organising calls for the year 2023 for the submission of aid applications for medium-sized solar installations and small and medium-sized wind turbines [17 FEBRUARI 2023. – Ministerieel besluit houdende de organisatie van calls voor het jaar 2023 voor het indienen van steunaanvragen voor middelgrote installaties op basis van zonne-energie en kleine en middelgrote windturbines]*, 2023.

367 *VREG 2024 Report on Energy Communities, Energy Sharing and Sales*, section 2.2.

in the statutes of an energy community actually amounts to the provision of social, environmental or economic benefits to its members, shareholders or the area in which it operates.[368]

489. Additionally, there are no applicable criteria to help evaluate in what cases the profit motive of an energy community is considered secondary to its primary objective. This assessment becomes highly relevant given that energy communities are empowered to participate in electricity markets alongside other market participants under EU law. When an energy community becomes increasingly involved in commercial activities, such as supplying electricity to a third party or trading flexibility, a question arises as to how to assess whether its profit motive remains subordinate to its main purposes over time.[369] The true aim of an energy community could be identified by its use of expenditure on investment, operating costs or salaries, and by the allocation of return on investment (including both the produced electricity and the profits made by trading electricity or flexibility) (Almeida et al., 2021).[370] Moreover, the ratio of revenue to expenditure may be useful as a threshold to reflect the priority given to the community benefits required by law. Clearly, the implementation of the requirement regarding primary purposes and community benefits must be secured by specific criteria. To date, the specific indicators used to reveal the primary purposes of energy communities have not been developed by Flemish law and its implementing regulations.

490. Another example of the obscure principle is, in defining effective control, Flemish law provides that the CEC should be effectively controlled by natural persons, local authorities or small enterprises that are not involved in large-scale commercial activities and the energy sector is not the main economic activity. Standards for defining 'large-scale commercial activities' and 'main economic activity' also remain to be clarified.[371]

491. Overall, Flemish legislation refrains from playing a leading role in the governance of energy communities, instead providing an enabling framework. However, this prudent approach raises other concerns, including the lack of robust monitoring of energy community qualifications and the difficulty in identifying breaches of their eligibility requirements. These issues could ultimately undermine the role of energy communities as a vehicle for engaging consumers.

---

368 *2022 Report on energy communities, energy sharing and P2P trading*, section 2.4.

369 *2022 Report on energy communities, energy sharing and P2P trading*, section 2.3.5.

370 For a more detailed analysis of criteria for assessing the primary purpose of CECs and RECs, see Section 3.1.3.1 of this Chapter below.

371 *2022 Report on energy communities, energy sharing and P2P trading*, section 2.3.

## 2.2. ENHANCING INFORMATION PROVISION AND DATA MANAGEMENT

492. This section begins by examining federal and Flemish measures that enhance information provision for consumers in Section 2.2.1. It then describes data exchange mechanisms in the context of trading DR and self-generated RES-E in Section 2.2.2.

### *2.2.1. Facilitating Consumers' Access to Information*

493. As shown in previous chapters, information on electricity consumption and energy sources is crucial for raising consumers' awareness and engaging them in supporting system integration and the use of RES-E. Such information is delivered by electricity bills and billing information, smart meters and GOs. How federal and Flemish law transposes EU law on facilitating the provision of this information is the subject of this subsection.

#### 2.2.1.1. Suppliers' Obligations to Provide Information

494. At the federal level, the Federal Electricity Law requires the federal government to determine the minimum requirements to be met by bills and billing information, at least reflecting the requirements of the Electricity Directive (*Belgian Federal Electricity Law*, art. 18). A Royal Decree was adopted in 2021 to specify suppliers' obligations to make available information most relevant to trigger active consumption management and raise awareness of using renewables, among others. These include providing information on actual consumption, historical consumption, comparisons between current consumption and historical consumption, energy mix of both supplied electricity and the overall energy mix of the supplier,[372] accompanied by frequency and specific ways of providing this information.[373] Relevant provisions merely incorporate the minimum requirements for information that must be displayed in bills and billing information, as set out in Annex I to the Electricity Directive. In terms of disclosing energy mix, the Decree obligates the CREG to verify that information provided by suppliers for final customers regarding energy mix is reliable and provided in a clearly comparable manner at the national level.[374]

---

372 The overall energy mix disclosure in the context of federal law refers to providing information on the share of each energy source in the total energy mix that the supplier used in the previous year for the electricity supply contracts concluded in Belgium, as well as at the level of the supplier if it is active in several Member States. See *Royal Decree on electricity and gas bills and billing information*, art. 12.

373 *Royal Decree on electricity and gas bills and billing information*, arts. 3, 7 to 10, 11 to 12.

374 *Royal Decree on electricity and gas bills and billing information*, art. 13.

495. In comparison, Flemish law takes more proactive measures to implement relevant requirements of EU law. The Flemish Energy Decree does not elaborate on suppliers' obligations in respect of offering consumers information necessary to encourage active consumption management, but empowers the Flemish Government to impose PSOs in this respect.[375] The Government Decision on Energy Policy specifies suppliers' obligations to provide consumption information for different consumer groups, as shown in Table 12 below. Such obligations are contained in the general provisions for licensed suppliers and PSOs imposed on suppliers specifically for facilitating rational energy use.[376] Beyond the minimum requirements of EU law, they are established by distinguishing households, non-households, and consumers with digital meters. As can be seen from Table 12, suppliers are subject to additional requirements to provide information to households and consumers with digital meters. This reflects particular efforts to engage household customers who are more reluctant to modify consumption patterns than industrial and commercial users.[377]

**Table 12. Suppliers' obligations regarding information provision**

| Consumer groups | Information offered by suppliers and frequency |
|---|---|
| Non-household customers | A total settlement bill for the sale and transport of electricity based on actual consumption, offered at least annually |
| Household customers | A total settlement bill for the sale and the transport of electricity based on actual consumption, offered annually, or at the explicit request of the customer more than once a year |
| Customers with digital meters | • Accurate consumption information based on actual consumption, offered on a monthly basis, without charging additional costs;<br>• From 1 July 2024: the charged monthly offtake and monthly injection, which shall be based on the actually measured monthly values by 1 April 2024, provided that the supplier has received the necessary metering data from the data manager (not applicable for customers with dynamic price contracts). |
| All consumers | • Reliable and accurate consumption information based on actual consumption is made available at least twice a year or, if the customer has opted for electronic invoicing or at his request, at least four times a year, without charging additional costs;<br>• On each bill based on new offtake data or on an accompanying document or in the billing information, providing (1) the annual offtake of electricity during the last three years, presented in a clear manner and in graph form; (2) comparisons with an average normalized or benchmarked customer of the same consumer category. |

Source: Author's own elaboration.

375 *Flemish Energy Decree*, art. 4.3.2.

376 *Government Decision on Energy Policy*, art. 3.2.18 and art. 6.4.23.

377 See Section 3 of Chapter III and Section 2 of Chapter II above.

496. Moreover, the additional information provided to consumers with smart meters also enables the maximization of benefits delivered by this key information infrastructure, facilitating more informed electricity consumption management. Aside from the information displayed on bills and billing information, suppliers are required to provide information through other channels. From 2024, customers with digital meters can find the information on the charged monthly offtake and injection in the online customer zone after the settlement or final bill has been sent.[378] Information on monthly metered offtake and injection not only informs consumers of actual electricity consumption and facilitates DR but also is relevant to fostering selling or sharing surplus self-produced RES-E. To support the fulfillment of these obligations, the metered data is communicated to suppliers by the DSO,[379] which is appointed as the data manager by Art. 4.1.8/2 of the Flemish Energy Decree and is responsible for reading smart meters at the access points of the distribution network.

497. Art. 7.4.1 of the Flemish Energy Decree sets out general obligations for suppliers to disclose the energy mix (of their total fuel mix used and of products sold in Flanders) and relevant environmental consequences in their bills and all printed and electronic promotional material. It provides that in bills and promotional materials, suppliers must also state that GOs have been submitted to the VREG for electricity supplied from renewable energy, as required by EU law. The VREG is responsible for verifying the reliability of the information provided by suppliers to their customers. Art. 7.4.1 also requires the Flemish Government to develop detailed rules to support the application of this obligation. These are contained in the Government Decision on Energy Policy. In accordance with this Decision, first, suppliers must state the origin of the electricity supplied along the required categories, ranging from renewables, fossil fuels, and nuclear to other energy sources.[380]

498. In addition, the supplier's energy mix disclosure is subject to monitoring to ensure the authenticity and reliability of the relevant information displayed to consumers. This is realized by materializing EU-level requirements for substantiating the share of renewable electricity in a supplier's fuel mix by using GOs.[381] Together with implementing the rules of the VREG (*VREG Decision on GOs*, 2011), the Government Decision on Energy Policy develops two groups of rules to respectively oversee the disclosure of the share of RES-E in a supplier's total energy mix and that share in its specific products.

378 *Government Decision on Energy Policy*, art. 3.2.18.

379 Ibid.

380 *Government Decision on Energy Policy*, art. 6.3.1.

381 *Government Decision on Energy Policy*, arts. 6.3.1 to 6.3.3.

499. First, the share of RES-E in a supplier's total energy mix is determined based on the ratio of the number of GOs (expressed in MWh) that the supplier has submitted for deliveries in the previous calendar year, compared to the amount of electricity that the supplier concerned has supplied to customers in the Flemish Region via the distribution network, the local electricity transport network or the transmission network.[382] Suppliers must submit GOs to the VREG to prove the share of RES-E in the electricity delivered in the previous calendar year, no later than March 31 of the current year.[383] The VREG then assesses and publishes the result of its inspection on its website, together with the percentages for the origin of the electricity that suppliers supply and use.[384] Under the delegation of Art. 6.3.2 of the Government Decision on Energy Policy, the VREG has laid down further rules for determining the fuel mix of all deliveries from an electricity supplier (*VREG Decision on GOs*, 2011). To determine the amount of electricity supplied from all products in this calendar year, the VREG uses the allocation figures submitted to the VREG by the grid operator (*VREG Decision on GOs*, art. 7).

500. Second, the disclosure of the share of RES-E in a supplier's products is subject to monthly monitoring. The supplier must report to the VREG an overview of access points at which the supplier supplied electricity from renewables to its customers during the previous month, indicating the reference of the electricity product supplied.[385] The VREG provides each local TSO or DSO with the data of all access points on its grid at which suppliers supplied RES-E to their customers over the same month.[386] The local TSO or the DSO then offers offtake data of the concerned customers, based on which the VREG informs each supplier of the total number of GOs to be submitted for each electricity product.[387] The supplier must provide a number of GOs as required via the central database, which is managed and monitored by the VREG.[388] The VREG then checks whether the supplier has submitted the correct number of GOs.[389] For a certain product, if a supplier fails to provide sufficient GOs, the VREG will deduct the share of electricity from renewables corresponding to the missing number of GOs.[390] Subsequently, it publishes the share of electricity from renewables for each product from each supplier for the previous month, which

382 *Government Decision on Energy Policy*, art. 6.3.1, §2.
383 Ibid.
384 *Government Decision on Energy Policy*, art. 6.3.3.
385 *Government Decision on Energy Policy*, art. 6.2/3.26, §2; *VREG Decision on GOs*, art. 1.
386 Ibid.
387 *Government Decision on Energy Policy*, art. 6.2/3.26, §3; *VREG Decision on GOs*, art. 2.
388 *Flemish Energy Decree*, art. 7.1/1.1, §3 and art. 6.2/3.18, §1; *Government Decision on Energy Policy*, art. 6.2/3.25 and art. 6.2/3.26.
389 *Government Decision on Energy Policy*, art. 6.2/3.26, §4; *VREG Decision on GOs*, arts. 1 to 5.
390 *VREG Decision on GOs*, art. 5.

is calculated based on the submitted GOs.[391] The VREG's monthly inspection enables a functionality called 'green check', i.e., on the VREG's website, customers can verify whether, and to what extent, their suppliers have supplied them RES-E.[392]

501. In line with EU law, these rules harness GOs to ensure transparency and reliability of green power marketing, facilitating consumers' choices favoring suppliers and products that deliver higher shares of RES-E. Measures governing GOs' application, issuance, trading, and submission are elaborated next.

#### 2.2.1.2. GOs

502. Similar to the case of governing suppliers' information provision, federal law mainly incorporates minimum requirements of EU law on GOs (only for offshore renewables projects).[393] As the competent authority for granting and monitoring the use of GOs (*Royal Decree on the establishment of a system for granting GOs for RES-E*, arts. 2 to 7), the CREG has not developed further implementing rules by October 2024.[394] By contrast, Flemish rules in this area consist of the Flemish Energy Decree and implementing rules adopted by the Flemish Government and the VREG pursuant to the requirements and empowerment of the Energy Decree.[395] Beyond embedding the minimum requirements of the REDII,[396] they put in place more elaborate implementing rules, especially in GOs' granting and monitoring, as well as recognizing GOs from other Member States. Considering this, Flemish law is the main focus of this subsection.

503. The precondition for supplying a quantity of electricity from renewables in the Flemish Region is that the quantity of electricity supplied amounts to the corresponding number of MWh of the GOs for RES-E, which have been submitted to the central database.[397] That is to say, green power marketing is subject to submitting GOs for demonstrating the origin of a corresponding amount of energy from renewables.[398] This requirement creates demand for GOs.

391 *VREG Decision on GOs*, art. 4.

392 *Government Decision on Energy Policy*, art. 6.2/3.26, §5.

393 *Belgian Federal Electricity Law*, art. 7; *Royal Decree on promoting RES-E*, arts. 2–6; *Royal Decree on the establishment of a system for granting GOs for RES-E*, 2013.

394 This is based on the search results of the CREG's publication database with the keyword 'Garanties van oorsprong'.

395 *Flemish Energy Decree*, art. 7.1/1.1, art. 7.1/1.3 and art. 7.1/1.5; *Government Decision on Energy Policy*, arts. 6.2/3.1 to 6.2/3.27; *VREG Decision on GOs*, 2011; *Decision of the VREG of 3/12/2019*, 2019.

396 *Flemish Energy Decree*, art. 7.1/1.4; *Government Decision on Energy Policy*, art. 6.2/3.3 and art. 6.2/3.21.

397 *Flemish Energy Decree*, art. 7.1/1.2.

398 *Flemish Energy Decree*, art. 7.1/1.4; *Government Decision on Energy Policy*, art. 6.2/3.25.

In Flanders, in addition to electricity generated from qualitative cogeneration, GOs are only granted to generating facilities located in the Flemish Region producing energy (including electricity, gas, heat and cold) from renewable energy sources.[399] The legislator thus does not choose to use GOs to demonstrate the origin of energy produced from other non-renewable sources, though this is allowed by Article 19(2) of the REDII. GOs are only granted to the owner of these generating facilities or the natural or legal person designated by the owner, in response to their application.[400] As such, if suppliers selling the share of RES-E to consumers do not own renewables generation installations, they must buy GOs to fulfill the above green power marketing requirement.[401]

504. Undoubtedly, the obligation of submitting GOs has traditionally applied to suppliers. However, with consumers, associations of co-owners and energy communities also selling RES-E, a question arises as to whether that obligation is equally applied to them. Legal provisions empowering these entities do not explicitly address this issue. As set out above, when selling self-produced RES-E via the public grid, active customers, associations of co-owners and energy communities can be regarded as suppliers defined by Flemish law. In P2P trading and VME sales, when cumulatively meeting some conditions, active customers and associations of co-owners are exempted from supply permit obligations and PSOs set by or under Articles 4.3.1, 4.3.2 and 7.5.1 of the Flemish Energy Decree, which do not contain obligations to submit GOs. As such, when selling RES-E, active customers and associations of co-owners are generally subject to obligations regarding the submission of GOs. However, a key issue is whether imposing these obligations aligns with the principles of proportionality and non-discrimination. Addressing this legal question depends on establishing clear criteria for applying these fundamental principles, which presents another legal challenge, as discussed in Section 3 of this chapter.

505. Flemish law does not clearly exempt energy communities from obligations relating to GOs. The applicability of such obligations differs in two scenarios. First, when supplying RES-E to third parties via the public grid, they are, in principle, subject to the general rules for submitting GOs and relevant PSOs contained in the Flemish Energy Decree and the Government Decision on Energy Policy. As mentioned above, pursuant to Art. 3.3.1 of the Government Decision on Energy Policy, where applicable, the provisions on the management of GOs should be contained in the agreement between energy communities and their members or shareholders.[402] This requirement also confirms the possibility that CECs and RECs are involved in the application and submission of GOs.

399 *Flemish Energy Decree*, art. 7.1/1.1.

400 *Flemish Energy Decree*, art. 7.1/1.1; *Government Decision on Energy Policy*, art. 6.2/3.1, §1.

401 *Government Decision on Energy Policy*, art. 6.2/3.1 and art. 6.2/3.24.

402 See Section 2.1.3 of this Chapter above.

Second, since electricity sharing is not defined as supply under Flemish law, it can be concluded that the obligation to submit GOs does not apply to CECs and RECs sharing RES-E with their members or shareholders.

506. The next important aspect reviewed here is the granting and mutual recognition of GOs. The VREG is responsible for supervising the granting, trade, import and export, submission, expiry and cancellation of GOs in the Flemish Region.[403] It grants GOs to RES-E producers when the following conditions are met:

- Eligible installations generating electricity from renewables must have a rated electrical capacity of more than 10 kW;[404]
- Electricity has been injected into a distribution network, a local transmission network, a transmission network or a closed distribution network with a free choice of suppliers;[405]
- A valid inspection report of the production installation, drawn up by an accredited independent inspection body, has been submitted to the production registrar.[406]

507. Notably, the requirement for the issuance of tradable GOs is worth noting. In Flanders, GOs that can be traded are not granted for electricity not injected into the grid.[407] For RES-E consumed on-site or allocated to a specified user immediately upon production, at the applicant's request, GOs can be granted while they cannot be traded, exported or submitted for monitoring.[408] The restriction imposed on the issuance of tradable GOs aims to safeguard the function of GOs, which is devoted to demonstrating to consumers the share of RES-E in an energy supplier's energy mix and in the electricity supplied to them, as required by Article 19 of the REDII. The electricity consumed at the site of the generation plant is not included in a supplier's energy mix and is not supplied by a supplier to consumers.[409] If tradable GOs are granted to such onsite consumption, it is possible to claim the same amount of RES-E elsewhere.[410] It causes double counting of the same amount of RES-E and therefore compromises the reliability and credibility of the relevant GOs.[411] The requirement of not granting GOs to electricity consumed at the location of production installations

403 *Government Decision on Energy Policy*, art. 6.2/3.18.
404 *Government Decision on Energy Policy*, art. 6.2/3.10.
405 *Government Decision on Energy Policy*, art. 6.2/3.10.
406 *Government Decision on Energy Policy*, art. 6.2/3.3.
407 *Government Decision on Energy Policy*, art. 6.2/3.4.
408 *Government Decision on Energy Policy*, art. 6.2/3.20.
409 *VREG Decision on refusing Swedish GOs*, 2019.
410 Ibid.
411 Ibid.

equally applies to GOs from other regions or countries.[412] Based on this, the VREG has decided to refuse to recognize GOs issued for energy consumed on site from Sweden by employing Article 19(9) of the REDII, which allows for such refusal where the regulator has well-founded doubts about GOs' accuracy, reliability or veracity.[413]

508. In addition, Flemish law provides an example of allowing for the coexistence of TGCs and GOs. Flemish law allows granting both GOs and TGCs to the same unit of generated RES-E, which is also the case under federal law (*Royal Decree on promoting RES-E*, art. 7). It specifies that the granting of GOs for electricity generated from renewables starts at the same time as the granting of TGCs.[414] This also implies that RES-E producers benefiting from national support schemes can also obtain GOs. Some Member States, such as Germany, utilize the option permitted by the REDII to refrain from issuing a GO to a producer who receives financial support from a support scheme (Lavrijssen et al., 2023).

509. Another significant issue with the Flemish GO mechanisms pertains to the granting of GOs to self-generated RES-E. As shown above, generating facilities with a rated electrical capacity of less than 10 kW are not eligible to receive GOs. Given that green power marketing is subject to the obligation of submitting GOs, small prosumers ineligible for GOs cannot sell their electricity as 'green electricity' but as 'gray electricity'. Moreover, when such electricity is sold to suppliers, these suppliers cannot resell it as RES-E in electricity markets unless they buy additional GOs to certify its renewable source. This creates a paradox: consumers have the right to sell RES-E and obtain market incentives, whilst those with small generation capacity are not granted GOs, and thereby the RES-E from them cannot be labeled as RES-E. As a result, such self-produced RES-E would lose its competitive advantages derived from the low-carbon nature of RES-E production, which could hinder its market integration.

510. According to Art. 4.1.22/2 of the Energy Decree, consumers with new decentralized production installations with a maximum AC capacity of 10 kVA can request the DSO to install the 'production meter' ('productiemeter'), also called 'green energy meter',[415] which can be linked to digital meters.

---

412 *Government Decision on Energy Policy*, art. 6.2/3.22.

413 *VREG Decision on refusing Swedish GOs*, 2019.

414 *Government Decision on Energy Policy*, art. 6.2/3.9.

415 For more information about the green energy meter, see <https://www.fluvius.be/nl/groene-energie/grote-productie-installatie/plaatsen-groenestroomteller?app-refresh=1733851569772> accessed 10 December 2024.

Existing Flemish law has not defined the production meter[416] while the DSO's website shows that to obtain GOs, renewables self-consumers need to install such production meters, apart from digital meters (Fluvius, 2023a). However, associated installation costs may not outweigh the benefits. Some self-consumers may thus not choose to install this meter to obtain GOs. This also leads to the above perverse result that they could only sell self-produced RES-E as electricity from non-renewable sources. The barrier to accessing GOs and associated costs constitutes an additional obstacle to selling RES-E, which has not yet received sufficient attention.

2.2.1.3. Smart Meter Rollout

511. As explained in the previous chapter, smart meters serve as key infrastructure for communicating consumption data and enabling metering required for sharing and selling self-produced RES-E. They are thus pivotal to engage consumers in DR and renewables self-consumption. At the transmission level, the digitization of meters has been accomplished. Thus, federal law does not introduce specific measures to deploy smart meters. In the legal provision for dynamic price contracts, the term 'suitable meter' instead of 'smart meter' is used to describe the ICT infrastructure that a consumer entitled to a dynamic price contract must have.[417] Flemish law facilitates smart meter deployment by imposing obligations on the DSO to install smart meters and fully inform consumers of the full potential that the meter has, the use of the data from the meter, and the possibility of monitoring their energy consumption.[418]

512. Within Flemish law, smart meters are referred to as 'digital meters', which fulfill functionalities of smart meters, especially in measuring electricity fed into the grid or electricity consumed from the grid, transmitting and receiving data for information, monitoring and control purposes, two-way electronic communications, as well as local and remote reading.[419] In 2019, under the requirement of the Flemish Energy Decree, the implementing rules of the Flemish Government specified the timetable for the digital meter system rollout

---

416 This is based on a review of the search results of the Belgian law database with the term 'productiemeter' on 10 December 2024. See <https://www.ejustice.just.fgov.be/cgi/list.pl?language=nl&sum_date=2024-12-11&page=1&text1=productiemeter&fr=f&nl=n&du=d>. Annex II of the TRDE sets out standards for production meter, while it does not clarify their role in granting GOs.

417 *Belgian Federal Electricity Law*, art. 20quinquies, §1.

418 *Flemish Energy Decree*, art. 4.1.22/2 and art. 4.1.22/13; *Government Decision on Energy Policy*, art. 3.1.53.

419 *Flemish Energy Decree*, art. 1.1.3, 25° /2.

in Flanders.[420] The DSO must install at least 80% of the total number of digital meters to be installed by 31 December 2024.[421] Monitoring for this purpose is imposed, including requiring the DSO to make general and specific roll-out schedules publicly available and report to the energy minister and the VREG annually the actual roll-out of digital meters.[422] Such reporting particularly includes an overview of the number of digital meters whose installation was delayed and the reason. Based on such annual reporting, the VEKA is responsible for assessing the roll-out biennially and on this basis, the Flemish minister responsible for energy policy may submit a proposal to the Flemish Government to adjust the speed of the roll-out or define new target groups having priority to install digital meters.[423]

513. Having decided on the systematic deployment of the digital meter system, Flemish law addresses the technical capabilities of these meters and the entitlement to them. It embeds EU law's requirements on smart meters' functionalities, which are further elaborated by rules adopted by the government.[424] Consumers with a low-voltage connection < 56 kV are entitled to digital meters.[425] Given that the deployment of digital meters has progressed stepwise and for different grid users, the cost-benefit analysis varies. The Flemish Energy Decree clarifies in what cases grid users can have priority to install smart meters. These, inter alia, include the installation of new DG facilities with a maximum AC power of 10 kVa.[426] Based on the cost-benefit analysis, the Flemish Government is allowed to determine additional cases in which the DSO installs a digital meter on a priority basis.[427] Under this delegation, the Government Decision on Energy Policy further specifies the timing of installing digital meters for different grid users. For new DG installations with an AC capacity of more than 10 kVa, a mandatory meter replacement started in January 2021.[428] The costs of installing and commissioning digital meters

420 *Flemish Energy Decree*, art. 4.1.22/2; *Government Decision on Energy Policy*, arts. 3.1.52 and 3.1.53.

421 *Government Decision on Energy Policy*, art. 3.1.53.

422 *Government Decision on Energy Policy*, arts. 3.1.53 and 3.1.56.

423 *Government Decision on Energy Policy*, art. 3.1.56.

424 *Flemish Energy Decree*, art. 4.1.22/3; *Government Decision on Energy Policy*, art. 3.1.45.

425 *Flemish Energy Decree*, art. 4.1.22/2.

426 Ibid.

427 Ibid.

428 If the installation of a digital meter proves to be technically impossible or economically unfeasible due to poor or no wireless communication capability with the meter, the DSO is allowed to postpone the installation until the technical impossibility or economic unfeasibility has been remedied, either by a new tender for the digital meter in which the distribution network operator will include these situations, or by physical intervention by the network user, whichever is earlier. In any case, the installation of a digital meter will take place before 1 July 2029. See *Government Decision on Energy Policy*, 2010, art. 3.1.52.

are borne by the DSO.[429] As will be noted in Section 2.3 below, such costs have been covered by tariffs. However, if a grid user opts to install a digital meter that communicates with the DSO via cabling, the user is responsible for the additional cost of the meter compared to the standard digital meter, as well as for the relevant installation and commissioning costs.[430]

514. Along with the above-mentioned consumption data provided by suppliers, the DSO must also make available data to consumers with digital meters to maximize the potential of such information infrastructure in conducting desirable electricity consumption behavior. The metered data provided by the DSO primarily includes additional information on consumption history, specifically detailed consumption data for each day, week, month, and year, categorized by tariff period.[431]

### *2.2.2. Data Management*

515. Data management is another key enabler in facilitating market participation of DR and self-generated RES-E, as elaborated in the previous Chapter. In the following section, Section 2.2.2.1 reviews how Belgian law specifies the rights of consumers and FSPs to access their metered data while ensuring data protection. This is followed by Section 2.2.2.2, which focuses on data exchange mechanisms within the context of trading DR and exchanging self-generated RES-E.

#### 2.2.2.1. Data Access and Protection

516. Federal and Flemish rules have defined the right of grid users, including consumers and energy communities, to access their metered data and processed data.[432] The right of energy service providers (including IFSPs) to access data necessary to carry out their activities based on the explicit and informed consent of consumers is also specified, while the processing of relevant data is subject to the GDPR.[433]

---

429 *Government Decision on Energy Policy*, art. 3.1.52.

430 Ibid.

431 This obligation entered into force from 1 April 2020. Such data shall be made available without delay, for at least the previous twenty-four months or for the period since the customer has had a digital meter, whichever is shorter. See *Government Decision on Energy Policy*, 2010, art. 3.1.58.

432 *Belgian Federal Electricity Law*, art. 19bis, §1; *Flemish Energy Decree*, art. 4.1.17/8 and art. 4.1.22/4 and art. 4.1.22/5.

433 *Belgian Federal Electricity Law*, art. 8, §3; *Flemish Energy Decree*, art. 4.1.17/8, art. 4.1.22/5 and art. 4.1.22/8; *Government Decision on Energy Policy*, art. 3.1.58 and art. 3.2.18; *Royal Decree on electricity and gas bills and billing information*, art. 10.

517. What is worth mentioning is that the data protection rules in Flanders go beyond the minimum requirements of the Electricity Directive and the GDPR. While systematically deploying smart meters, Flemish law also transposes EU law regarding ensuring the security of smart metering systems and data communication.[434] Thus, when granting access to metered data to (I)FSPs or aggregators cooperating with consumers, the DSO must ensure such access is limited to the data that is strictly necessary to perform their tasks.[435] To protect personal data, the DSO and eligible parties processing customers' data are also subject to additional obligations. These mainly include: (i) pseudonymizing and encrypting personal data processed, and (ii) establishing a continuous risk management system with regard to the probability and severity of the various risks to the rights and freedoms of natural persons.[436]

518. Under the requirements of the Flemish Energy Decree, the Flemish Government has established uniform conditions for this risk management system and specified procedures and modalities to ensure transparency in the processing of customers' data and prevent misuse of such data.[437] To increase transparency toward final customers regarding the processing of their data, customers must be informed about the data processing activities prior to such activities, and they are entitled to obtain additional information from the DSO on the processing of their personal data.[438]

519. Additionally, implementing rules adopted by the Flemish Government establish the above risk management system, consisting of a prior data protection impact assessment and follow-up risk monitoring. In line with Article 35 of the GDPR, eligible parties, including (I)FSPs or aggregators, must conduct a data protection impact assessment to assess the impact of the envisaged processing activities on the protection of personal data and establish security requirements.[439] A continuous risk follow-up is required afterwards to reanalyze the risks identified during the prior data protection impact assessment, while analyzing the new risks.[440] The Flemish Government further elaborates on the situations where an additional data protection impact assessment is needed in the context of applying smart meters. These include significant changes in the application, technical organization and measurement regime of digital meters, such as changes in the use of personal data beyond the purposes initially envisaged or changes in the processing activity.[441] Such an impact assessment

434 *Flemish Energy Decree*, art. 4.1.22/13.
435 *Flemish Energy Decree*, art. 4.1.22/5.
436 *Flemish Energy Decree*, art. 4.1.22/13; *Government Decision on Energy Policy*, art. 3.1.61.
437 *Flemish Energy Decree*, art. 4.1.22/13.
438 *Government Decision on Energy Policy*, arts. 3.1.58 and 3.1.59.
439 *Government Decision on Energy Policy*, art. 3.1.61.
440 Ibid.
441 Ibid.

must be conducted by a multidisciplinary team with expertise in information security and relevant laws and regulations, among other areas. Based on the GDPR, the tasks of the data protection officer appointed by the DSO are also specified, including advising the multidisciplinary team and monitoring the implementation of the concerned impact assessment.[442]

#### 2.2.2.2. Data Exchange Mechanisms

520. This subsection consecutively outlines data exchange mechanisms in the respective contexts of explicit DR and renewables self-consumption.

##### (i) Valorizing Explicit DR

521. In the context of trading DR via IFSPs, data exchange is necessary to address the impact on suppliers and BRPs. To ensure efficient and secure data exchange, the Federal Electricity Law assigns an additional role to the TSO as a neutral flexibility data manager, performing central management of data required for proceeding compensation between IFSPs and suppliers, and correcting the BRPs' balancing perimeter. Its data management tasks are monitored by the CREG, given that suppliers and BRPs cannot verify whether the communicated data is correct.[443] The costs incurred in data management are allowed to be recovered through tariffs, which are subject to the applicable tariff methodology.[444]

522. A range of notification procedures is then developed to communicate necessary data to the supplier and $BRP_{source}$, with due regard to confidentiality, while specific obligations are imposed on IFSPs and the TSO. For example, Section 14.2 of the ToE Rules establishes notification obligations for IFSPs in the context of providing ancillary services and DA/ID flexibility services, respectively. They must inform the TSO of the characteristics of each activation, such as expected and actual activated volumes, the activation period, and the final list of delivery points within the specified timescale (*ToE Rules*, section 14). Certain conditions are laid down in Section 16.1 of the ToE Rules to guarantee the confidentiality of commercially sensitive data. For example, for the $BRP_{source}$, the perimeter correction is made per quarter hour at the portfolio level and the impacts on its portfolio created by different delivery points are only presented in an aggregated manner.

523. The survey for IFSPs mentioned in Section 2.1.1.1 above shows that, while the ToE regime helps address barriers from suppliers and their BRPs, it

---

442 Ibid.

443 *Belgian Federal Electricity Law*, art. 23, §2, 13°.

444 *Belgian Federal Electricity Law*, arts. 12 and 19ter, §3.

creates complex procedures and administrative burdens. Such complexity and burdens partially arise from data exchange mechanisms, which must deliver integral data required to proceed with compensation and balancing perimeter correction.

524. Within Flemish law, as mentioned above, the DSO is appointed as the data manager, responsible for the collection, calculation, processing and delivery of data to the relevant market participants. The delivered data includes the information necessary to calculate the flexibility volume and the delivered flexibility volume per access point or allocation point, among others.[445] These data are used for DR through IFSPs, flexibility products defined by the DSO, and the needs of the TSO.[446] Art. 4.3.63 of the TRDE requires the DSO to develop flexibility market processes to address data exchange mechanisms between market participants for valorizing flexibility on the low-voltage distribution grid. As shown by the approved Flexibility Market Processes, such data exchange is first conducted between the (I)FSP and the data manager, the DSO. In the DSO prequalification process, these two parties have the most intensive interactions if the final customer mandates the (I)FSP to accomplish delivery points prequalification. The Flexibility Market Processes specify the information that should be communicated between the (I)FSP and the DSO when performing connection contract checks, the network flexibility study that determines prequalified capacity,[447] and delivery point identification.[448] In the prequalification process, the (I)FSP should also set up and test real-time and ex-post exchange of metering data with the DSO.[449]

525. During the settlement stage, under the Flexibility Market Processes, the DSO communicates data necessary to address the impact on suppliers and BRPs caused by the activities of IFSPs, in coordination with the TSO. More detailed tasks of the DSO are contained in the Data Exchange Mechanisms for ToE, developed by Synergrid.[450] Although Flemish law allows market participation of IFSPs in the local congestion market, so far, the data exchange tasks for the DSO are designed to support the implementation of the federal ToE regime.[451] When flexibility located in the distribution grid participates in federal markets applying the ToE regime, the DSO verifies the completeness of the

---

445 *Flemish Energy Decree*, art. 4.1.8/2.

446 Ibid.

447 Prequalified capacity is the result of the Network Flex Study and is the maximum flexibility power that the Service Delivery Point Flex can contract for a flexibility product. It ensures that the operational security of the distribution grid is not violated in trading DR, which affects the bids in the tendering process. See *Flexibility Market Processes 2.0*, sections 2.2 and 4.2.

448 *Flexibility Market Processes 2.0*, sections 4.2.2 to 4.2.4.

449 *Flexibility Market Processes 2.0*, section 4.2.5.

450 *Data Exchange Mechanisms for ToE*, 2018.

451 *Data Exchange Mechanisms for ToE*, sections 1 and 2.

energy transferred volumes, aggregates ToE volumes per IFSP and supplier, and communicates to the TSO, which compares and confirms total ToE volumes per BRP, IFSP, and supplier.[452] Based on the TSO's confirmation, the DSO delivers aggregated ToE volumes per IFSP and supplier to the TSO/DSO Flex Data Hub platform, a common IT platform managed by all Belgian electricity system operators, where IFSPs and suppliers can receive aggregated ToE volumes.[453]

526. The specific data exchange procedures are rather straightforward and do not merit being reproduced here in full. However, the role of the association representing Belgian TSOs and DSOs, i.e., the Synergrid, in developing technical measures and supporting platforms for data exchange deserves special attention.

527. In the Belgian context, the division of competences with respect to regulating transmission and distribution networks may hinder systematic arrangements for TSO-DSO cooperation. This is reflected in the amendment to the TRDE adopted in 2023. The VREG revised the original wording of requiring mutual cooperation between the TSO and the DSO since imposing an obligation on the TSO is beyond regional competence.[454] Art. 6.1.2 of the amended TRDE only requires the Flemish DSO to provide necessary cooperation for the operator of the grid to which its grid is connected, in the performance of the tasks to which both parties are legally or contractually obliged. Similar wording can also be found in federal law, which requires the TSO to '*provide the operator of any other network connected to its network with the necessary information to ensure the safe and efficient operation, coordinated development and interoperability of the connected network*'.[455] Moreover, the federal regulator and the Flemish regulator respectively regulate the agreement dealing with cooperation between the TSO and the DSO in respect of its minimum content and approval.[456] Yet, the establishment of detailed cooperation mechanisms serving specific purposes, such as applying the ToE, may require a holistic view instead of being determined solely from the perspective of either federal or regional regulators. Before federal and regional rule-makers take steps, Synergrid has harnessed its role at the center of elaborate networks of exchanging information and perspectives[457] in the area of grid

452 *Flexibility Market Processes 2.0*, section 7.1.3.

453 *Data Exchange Mechanisms for ToE*, section 4; *Flexibility Market Processes 2.0*, section 7.1.3.

454 The original Art. 6.1.2 prescribes '*the electricity distribution system operator and the operator of the system to which its system is connected shall provide each other with the necessary cooperation in carrying out the tasks to which both parties are legally or contractually obliged to do*.' See *Explanatory note of the TRDE*, section 2; *TRDE*, art. 6.1.2.

455 *Belgian Federal Electricity Law*, art. 8, §1.

456 *Federal Grid Code, arts. 316 and 319, §2*; *Electricity code of conduct*, arts. 3 and 209; *TRDE*, art. 6.1.6.

457 Regarding the role of the organization in the networks of exchanging information and perspectives in promoting best practices and developing non-state norms, see Scott, 2009.

operation to advance cooperation between the TSO and the DSO in establishing data exchange platforms and relevant technical rules. This serves as a prominent example of demonstrating the role of non-state norms in complementing state norms, with which the implementation of the law can benefit from resources possessed by regulatees (Scott, 2001). It highlights the multiplicity of actors who do, or have the potential to, participate in rule-making, and the dispersed nature of public policy power because of the fragmented possession of key resources (Scott, 2001). As an interest group representing system operators, the Synergrid possesses no formal authority (Scott, 2001). Yet, its possession of organizational resources and expertise in grid operation could permit it to play a proactive role in rule formation in the case of incomplete regulations on TSO-DSO cooperation.[458]

528. As mentioned in Section 6 of the previous Chapter, the establishment of ENTSO-E and the EU DSO Entity also embodies a similar approach to utilizing the resources of grid operator organizations to ensure compliance with EU law. The Belgian case study demonstrates the role of non-state actors in improving the effectiveness of regulation. They do so by developing relevant standards, platforms and technical rules underpinning the relevant enabling framework built by law and regulations.

#### (ii) Sharing and Trading of Self-Produced RES-E

529. In the context of sharing and trading self-generated RES-E, data exchange is required to deal with the settlement impact through an additional financial reconciliation process.[459] Flemish rules in this respect are the primary focus here since federal law has not put in place implementing rules for P2P and electricity sharing, as noted in Section 2.1.2. The DSO is responsible for processing and exchanging data with community managers, access holders and the FeReSO.[460] Once a month, the DSO provides the access holder with the (re)calculated metering data relating to the sharing or selling of RES-E via P2P and VME sales, including:[461]

- Volumes of the settled offtake and injection per quarter hour and per participant in the access holder's portfolio, as well as the (re)calculated volumes aggregated on a monthly basis;

458 Regarding why non-state actors can play an active role in rule-making and their resources enabling them to do so, see Scott, 2001.
459 *Protocol on Sharing and Selling Self-generated RES-E*, section 6.3.1.
460 *TRDE*, art. 4.3.64, §2; *Protocol on Sharing and Selling Self-generated RES-E*, section 6.3.2.
461 *Protocol on Sharing and Selling Self-generated RES-E*, section 6.4.3.

- Net volumes per quarter hour and per participant in the portfolio of the access holder, as well as the (re)calculated net volumes aggregated on a monthly basis.

530. The access holder of offtake points thus receives the volume allocated as a result of sharing or selling RES-E, which must be deducted from the participant's purchase. The access holder of injection points receives the volume allocated as a result of sharing or selling RES-E, which must be deducted from the participant's injection.[462] To support suppliers' ex-post financial reconciliation, the DSO is responsible for ex-post calculation. Such calculation is first performed at the level of the individual communities engaged in RES-E sharing or sales, based on which the totals of the volumes exchanged per individual market combination, i.e., the combination of parameters, such as suppliers, BRPs, grid operators, energy direction (injection or offtake), are calculated.[463] These volumes are then communicated to the FeReSo, which makes the settlement between suppliers based on a reconciliation price.[464]

531. Under Art. 4.3.64, §2 of the TRDE, in the event of any change in the parameters of the registered community or its participants, the access holder of each respective participant must be notified.[465] At the participant level, such changes include adding or removing a participant and changing the role or distribution key of a participant. At the community level, the change that should inform the access holder is the modification of the type of distribution key.[466]

## 2.3. ADAPTING NETWORK REGULATION

532. As shown in previous sections, enabling energy consumers' involvement in energy activities conducive to the system integration and use of RES-E is highly interwoven with specific tasks entrusted to the TSO and the DSO. Such tasks especially involve two respects: (i) providing network access to support trading of DR and exchange (including sales and sharing) of self-generated RES-E, and (ii) offering and managing data to raise consumers' awareness and address impacts of DR and renewables self-consumption on traditional players and facilitate market processes.

533. As set out in Section 6 of the preceding Chapter, compared to the TSO, the DSO faces a relatively radical transition under the CEP, which extends far

462 Ibid.
463 *Protocol on Sharing and Selling Self-generated RES-E*, section 6.3.2.
464 *Protocol on Sharing and Selling Self-generated RES-E*, section 6.4.4.
465 *Protocol on Sharing and Selling Self-generated RES-E*, section 6.4.3.
466 Ibid.

beyond its traditional role of distributing electricity. As seen from the foregoing sections, the Flemish DSO is adapting to its new role as a neutral market facilitator. This is reflected in its ongoing fulfillment of obligations with respect to deploying the smart meter system and making rules for the trading of DR and the exchange of self-generated RES-E. Such rules must not only provide the physical grid layer, the information and communication layer necessary for these energy activities, but also create market platforms for flexibility resources from consumers. As expected, the DSO indeed encounters challenges when developing rules or specifications for implementing the sharing and sales of self-produced RES-E and procuring flexibility. In this process, the role of the independent regulator is worth noting. In Flanders, the VREG has consistently urged and forced the DSO to improve the Protocol on Sharing and Selling Self-generated RES-E to minimize barriers to electricity sharing and sales of RES-E and adapt to legislative developments (e.g., the introduction of VME sales).[467] It also forced the DSO to redesign flexibility procurement rules, which failed to satisfy the substantive and procedural requirements of Flemish law and regulations, as mentioned later on. Although some procurement rules have not been approved by the VREG by 2024,[468] the DSO has been gradually adapting to its rule-making tasks in the context of integrating DR and self-generated RES-E.

534. The role and obligations of the TSO and the DSO in specific DSM contexts have been described in the previous sections. In this section, the focus will be on relevant adaptations made to the regulation of network planning, tariff regulation, and specific regulatory requirements for flexibility procurement, which require separate examination.

### *2.3.1. Network Planning*

535. Network planning must be able to cover investment needs for integrating DR and self-generated RES-E and adapt network development to the high-RES electricity system, where consumers play a pivotal role, as elaborated in Section 6 of Chapter III. In Belgium, federal and regional laws transpose EU law by addressing typical challenges in drawing up grid development plans, namely, a lack of information to accurately forecast investment needs. As noted in the previous Chapter, profound uncertainties faced by network planning inter alia stem from a lack of coordination between grid users and system operators after unbundling. In Flanders, the DSO is bound by ownership unbundling. Thus, in terms of lacking coordination with market participants and fully considering

---

467 *VREG Decision on Approving the Protocol Version 3.1*, section 1; *Protocol on Sharing and Selling Self-generated RES-E*, section 2.

468 See Section 2.3.3.2 below for more details about the approval of flexibility procurement rules.

their future grid use needs, it faces similar challenges to the TSO. Yet, the nature of consumers connected to the distribution grid is different from that of consumers in the transmission grid. They are vastly distributed, small in size, and large in number, confronting the DSO with relatively unique challenges in considering their grid use needs and involving them in the planning process. How federal and Flemish legislation tackles these problems will be examined consecutively in Sections 2.3.1.1 and 2.3.1.2 next.

#### 2.3.1.1. Federal Approach

536. Within federal law, enhanced coordination is first sought at the government and independent regulator levels. Art. 13 of the Federal Electricity Law stipulates that when the TSO draws up the ten-year transmission grid development plan, it must cooperate with the Directorate-General for Energy ('Algemene Directie Energie') and the Federal Planning Bureau.[469] In particular, the former agency is, among others, responsible for collecting, processing, analyzing and using energy data, serving a better understanding of energy markets and better energy decision-making. Cooperation with this agency enables the TSO to access data that informs the evolving market environment and potential needs for grid infrastructure. Moreover, the transmission grid plan is subject to the opinion of the CREG and then the approval of the Minister for Energy.[470] If the CREG, after consulting the grid operator, determines that the investments provided for in the development plan do not enable the TSO to adequately and effectively meet the capacity requirements, the Minister may require the TSO to adapt the development plan in order to remedy this situation.[471] According to Art. 13 of the Federal Electricity Law, the adaptations are also subject to the above requirements on coordination.

537. Moreover, the Minister may ask the CREG to express an opinion on whether it is necessary to review tariff methodologies adopted under Article 12 of the Federal Electricity Law to guarantee the means of financing the investments under consideration.[472] The reasoning for reconciling the tariff methodology and transmission grid plan is noteworthy. By providing examples, Section 6 of Chapter III illustrates how tariff regulation significantly influences system operators' economic incentives to facilitate the low-carbon system transition. The tariff structure can also affect the design, implementation and adaptation of the network plan. For instance, how the plan copes with complex trade-offs between using flexibility as an alternative to system expansion and ensuring

469 *Belgian Federal Electricity Law*, art. 13, §1.
470 *Belgian Federal Electricity Law*, art. 13, §1; *Royal Decree on the transmission grid development plan*, arts. 3 and 4.
471 *Belgian Federal Electricity Law*, art. 13, §3.
472 Ibid.

sufficient investment in grid capacity is largely shaped by the CAPEX and OPEX approved by the regulator.[473]

538. The above-cited Art. 12 requires the tariff methodology to allow the balanced development of the transmission network, in accordance with the development plan of the TSO and the investment plans as approved. The regulator, however, may not be fully aware of the future need for flexibility or grid expansion and reinforcement when determining the tariff methodology for a certain tariff period. This is especially the case considering that the tariff period does not coincide with the cycle of elaborating and adapting the ten-year network plan, while changes made to the tariff methodology during the existing tariff period could apply only from the following tariff period.[474] For instance, in 2022, the CREG issued the tariff methodology for the upcoming regulatory period 2024–2027 (CREG, 2022a), based on which the TSO submitted a tariff proposal for approval for that period in 2023.[475] The CREG will decide on the new tariff methodology afterward in 2026. The Transmission Development Plan 2024–2034 was approved by the Minister in 2023[476] and will be adapted first in 2027 as required.[477] As a result, when the CREG determined the tariff methodology for the 2024–2027 tariff period, the Transmission Development Plan 2024–2034 was not available for the regulator to consider. Similarly, the regulator cannot consider the investment needs potentially proposed in the first adjustment of the ten-year network plan when elaborating the tariff methodology for the tariff period 2028–2031. The fact that tariff methodology is determined prior to the approval and adaptation of the network plan can lead to gaps between the approved tariffs and the needed expenses to finance the investments covered by the network development plan. In this case, stressing the potential cooperation between the Minister and the CREG helps to enhance alignment between network planning and permitted expenses, ensuring adequate incentives for the TSO.

539. Overall, engaging the most relevant authorities can help ensure a relatively holistic view of investment needs and strike a balance between ensuring adequate infrastructure investment and utilizing flexible services as alternatives to system expansion.

540. In addition, federal law takes further actions to enhance the TSO's access to necessary data, thereby improving its estimate of future grid capacity needs

---

473 For more details, see Section 6.1.1 of Chapter III above.

474 *Belgian Federal Electricity Law*, art. 12, §4.

475 *Belgian Federal Electricity Law*, art. 12, §6 and §7.

476 *Ministerial Decree approving the 2024–2034 federal development plan of the electricity transmission network*, 2023.

477 The ten-year transmission grid plan must be adapted every four years, starting from the date of the minister's approval of the previous plan. See *Belgian Federal Electricity Law*, art. 13, §1; *Royal Decree on the transmission grid development plan*, art. 2, §2.

and other grid development trends. First, the Federal Electricity Law requires the ten-year network plan to be updated every four years, and this adjustment must take place within 12 months of the publication of the prospective study.[478] This study inter alia estimates the evolution of the demand for and the supply of electricity in the medium and long term and identifies the resultant need for new resources.[479] Adjusting the network plan after its publication enables the TSO to fully take into account and exploit data and recommendations provided by the prospective study. The network plan can especially benefit from the prospective study because the legislation takes particular measures to ensure the reliability and sufficiency of data for conducting that study. To fulfill duties regarding that study, the Directorate-General for Energy is granted powers to require electricity companies operating on the Belgian market to provide all the information it requires.[480] Such powers also include conducting a site visit during which it may consult all the information and documents needed to carry out the duties assigned to it and, if necessary, copy them, in the event of a refusal to provide the information requested within thirty days.[481]

541. Second, to implement the above-cited Art. 13 of the Federal Electricity Law, the Federal Grid Code prescribes the TSO's interactions with transmission grid users to access planning-related data. Transmission grid users are under the obligation to provide complete and accurate planning data to the TSO annually to enable it to fully take into account adequate reserve capacity and projects of common interest in the domain of trans-European networks, among others, in network planning.[482] The offered planning data cover those relating to the seven years following the current year.[483] The TSO should also inform the transmission system user when an evolution need of the transmission network with potential consequences for this transmission system user is identified in the context of transmission network planning.[484]

542. The transmission network planning can also benefit from data communicated by DSOs under the Federal Grid Code. As noted above, regulating the distribution of electricity is a regional competence. Still, DSOs have some obligations under the Federal Grid Code due to their role as transmission grid users. This Code creates obligations for DSOs merely as conditions that must be respected to obtain the right to connect and access the transmission grid.[485] Thus, the aforementioned obligation regarding the annual provision of planning data

478 *Belgian Federal Electricity Law*, art. 13, §1.
479 *Belgian Federal Electricity Law*, art. 3, §2.
480 *Belgian Federal Electricity Law*, art. 3, §4.
481 Ibid.
482 *Federal Grid Code*, arts. 23, 24, 26 to 29, 362 and 363.
483 *Federal Grid Code*, art. 24.
484 Ibid.
485 *Federal Grid Code*, art. 313.

also applies to DSOs.[486] Moreover, when communicating to the TSO their new connection requests annually, DSOs also should inform the TSO of their best estimates of the power trends in offtake and injection in the distribution system, as well as any adaptations of their networks to meet, in particular, the evolution of their customers.[487] The TSO must also consult with all DSOs to determine, in their cooperation agreements with DSOs, inter alia, the capacity that it should make available to the concerned DSOs at each connection point between their respective systems.[488] The annual interactions, which help determine new connections or adapt existing ones, also increase the TSO's visibility into evolving situations at the distribution level. In the context of DG and DR increasingly connected to the distribution grid, being regularly informed of the evolution in the distribution grid and considering it in transmission network planning helps ensure due account is taken of available flexibility resources and evaluates the adequacy of grid capacity.

543. To sum up, federal law implements the TSO's obligation under EU law of 'consulting all the relevant stakeholders' in network planning by requiring those stakeholders to provide planning data for the TSO. Despite this, federal law has not fully transposed EU law on the ten-year transmission network development plan. First, at the time of writing (October 2024), the Federal Electricity Law has not been revised to update the frequency of adapting the ten-year network plan to align with EU law, which requires the TSO to submit this plan every two years. Furthermore, under the Federal Electricity Law, the minimum content of such plans contains (i) a detailed estimate of the transmission capacity needs, and (ii) the investment program that the TSO undertakes to carry out to meet these needs.[489] It must also take into consideration the need for adequate reserve capacity and the trans-European network projects.[490] The legislation does not explicitly stress due account to the potential for the use of flexibility, including DR, as alternatives to grid expansion, as required by Article 51 of the Electricity Directive.

#### 2.3.1.2. Flemish Approach

544. In Flanders, the rules for the distribution network development plan go beyond the minimum requirements of EU law in terms of the time horizon of planning, the frequency of submitting for approval and elements of network investment plans. The DSO must base the development of the distribution grid on a transparent investment plan for the next three to ten years and submit it

486 *Federal Grid Code*, art. 313, 3°.
487 *Federal Grid Code*, art. 319.
488 *Federal Grid Code*, art. 320.
489 *Belgian Federal Electricity Law*, art. 13, §2.
490 Ibid.

annually to the VREG for approval.[491] The Flemish Energy Decree elaborates elements and requirements for this investment plan. The elements can be broadly divided into three aspects as follows:[492]

- Estimates of grid capacity needs: a detailed estimate of the grid capacity needs and future expectations in relation to DG, indicating the underlying assumptions;
- An investment program for upgrade and expansion of the network that the DSO implements to meet the capacity needs, which includes (i) the concrete planned investments for a three-year period and the planned investments for the long-term development of the grid for a ten-year period; (ii) the main infrastructure required to connect new generation capacity and new load; (iii) forecasts of long-term trends;
- Plans and measures for supporting the DSO's use of flexibility resources, including DR, as alternatives to system expansion: (i) a transparent quantitative and qualitative description of the flexibility services or other resources (in the form of non-frequency ancillary services and local congestion management) within the DSO's coverage area required for a three-year period and ten-year period, which includes the underlying parameters, assumptions and locations where such services are required; (ii) a transparent description of applying the methodology provided in the TRDE of procuring flexibility and energy for local congestion management, efficient network operation and covering grid losses; (iii) the results of considering a trade-off between procuring flexibility and grid investment based on that methodology; (iv) the development of services and measures that increase the use of flexibility on the distribution grid.

545. Among these, how the EU-level requirement for integrating the use of flexibility sources in network planning is implemented is worth noting. As can be seen above, instead of copying and pasting this requirement, Flemish law obligates the DSO to elaborate on the flexibility sources that may be used during the planning period. By doing so, it forces the DSO to understand the role of different kinds of flexibility sources in addressing potential network issues in the planning stage and make reasonable investments to support their use in practice. Furthermore, it also requires the DSO to consider how to seek a balance between flexibility use and investment in grid expansion and reinforcement. It is pivotal to consider this balance in the investment plan, as its attainment hinges on an optimal combination of short-term operations and long-term capital inputs, as explicated in Section 6 of Chapter III above. To enable this balance,

491 *Flemish Energy Decree*, art. 4.1.19, §1 and §3.
492 *Flemish Energy Decree*, art. 4.1.19, §1.

the DSO's investment plan must contain an assessment framework to weigh the cost of grid investment against that of using commercial flexibility.[493] The assessment criterion, pursuant to the TRDE, is to compare the total expected remuneration for market-based flexibility, each time on an annual basis, with the avoided accounting cost of the deferred or avoided grid investment.[494] If the assessment shows that network investment is the cheapest solution, but if, for example, it cannot yet be carried out operationally, this case can be interpreted as 'exceptional circumstances' that allow the temporary application of reserved technical flexibility pending the grid investment.[495]

546. Regarding access to planning data, Art. 4.1.19, §2 of the Flemish Energy Decree stipulates a general principle of consulting all relevant network users and the TSO regarding the investment plan. Under its delegation, the TRDE further clarifies additional data that can be requested by the DSO for developing the above investment plan and the provision of this data. Similar to the federal approach, the consultation is implemented by imposing obligations on grid users to provide data for the DSO (*TRDE*, arts. 2.1.3 to 2.1.5 and 2.1.8). Yet, differences exist in several respects. First, the implementation of such obligations depends on the DSO's written request. Second, an overview of the data that the DSO could request is subject to the VREG's monitoring, which verifies the proportionality of that request, i.e., whether such data are adequate, relevant, and not excessive in relation to the purposes for which they will be used (*TRDE*, art. 2.1.6). Third, the TRDE divides 'all relevant stakeholders' to be consulted into different groups of grid users. It respectively determines their data provision obligations as follows:

- Grid users with offtake or injection capacity greater than 1,000 kVA provide data, e.g., the outlook on the maximum power to be purchased (kW, kvar) on an annual basis, indicating the expected trend breaks (*TRDE*, art. 2.1.3);
- Grid users whose installations include or will include generation units with a total rated capacity per access point of at least 400 kVA provide data, including, for instance, the maximum rated power, description of the expected production profile, technical data, operational limits, and control behavior of the various generation units commissioned (*TRDE*, art. 2.1.4);

493 *Flemish Energy Decree*, art. 4.1.17/5, §1; *TRDE*, art. 2.3.22 /1; *Explanatory note of the TRDE*, section 1.1.2.2.

494 *TRDE*, art. 2.3.22 /1; *Explanatory note of the TRDE*, section 1.1.2.2.

495 Under exceptional circumstances of the distribution grid operation, the DSO may require grid users to participate in the provision of flexibility. Such mandatory flexibility is referred to as reserved technical flexibility. See Flemish Energy Decree, art. 1.1.3, 56° /1/2 and art, 4.1.17/5. See also Explanatory note of the TRDE, section 1.1.2.2.

- For other grid users, their access holders inform the DSO of two sets of data: (i) the outlook on the maximum power to be offtaken or injected (kW, kvar) on an annual basis, indicating the expected trend breaks, and (ii) the description of the annual usage profile of the active power to be offtaken (*TRDE*, art. 2.1.5);
- Future distribution grid users are also subject to the obligations set for the first and second groups of grid users when submitting their applications for connection (*TRDE*, art. 2.1.8).

547. In this way, the TRDE responds to the specific challenges faced by the DSO in engaging with a large number of widely distributed grid users at the distribution level. As can be seen, the DSO only directly interacts with relatively large grid users defined by their offtake or injection profiles or their generation capacity. For those with smaller consumption or generation profiles, their access holders, such as suppliers, are designated to communicate planning data to the DSO on their behalf. In doing so, the DSO is protected from the high costs of coordinating with a multitude of small consumers. At the same time, it also reduces the active efforts and technical capacity that small consumers must devote to engaging in DR and renewables self-consumption. Similar arrangements aimed at reducing complexity and administrative burdens that hinder consumer engagement can also be found in the aforementioned Flemish framework for enabling the sharing and sale of self-produced RES-E. Taken as a whole, Flemish law represents an example of helping the DSO adapt to its increased role in fostering DR and renewables self-consumption, while taking actions to mitigate institutional complexity that typically impede consumers' engagement in such activities.

### *2.3.2. Tariff Regulation*

548. Regulated tariffs determine the inputs required for realizing low-carbon transitions within the network segment. Not least because of this, they significantly shape the output and performance of system operators in network planning, investment and service quality necessary for accommodating the consumers' greater role in supporting high RES-E penetrations. Moreover, such tariffs may differentiate between grid user groups, although this distinction is subject to the non-discrimination principle. They thus also have implications for market entry and economic incentives of consumers, (I)FSPs and energy communities involved in DR and renewables self-consumption. The key role of adapting tariff regulation to engage consumers has been discussed in detail in Section 6 of Chapter III. In this subsection, how federal and Flemish law implement relevant EU law on tariff regulation is analyzed consecutively.

#### 2.3.2.1. Federal Approach

549. Under federal law, the determination of the transmission tariff methodology is bound by a range of principles that reflect the requirements of existing EU law. These first include ensuring that TSO is adequately remunerated and incentivized for investments and innovation necessary for performing its tasks in the new market environment.[496] Furthermore, the tariff methodology must refrain from discouraging DR and ensure that active customers and energy communities contribute to the overall system costs in a balanced and adequate manner.[497] As discussed in the previous Chapter, a key challenge to be addressed in the transposition process is how to ensure that active customers and energy communities contribute sufficiently to system costs without compromising the cost-reflective and non-discriminatory nature of tariffs. This issue largely arises from complex network impacts brought by these actors engaged in renewables prosuming. Their use of the grid in the offtake direction may decrease due to renewables self-consumption on the one hand.[498] The system costs incurred by their potential increased grid use in the injection direction for selling their self-generated RES-E should also be reflected in tariffs on the other hand.[499] Such network implications seem to distinguish them from other grid users without generation facilities. An unresolved question in this case is thus whether such entities are subject to the same network charges applied to standard electricity consumption (Lavrijssen et al., 2023). Within the Federal Electricity Law, a provision regulating the tariff methodology is relevant to address this issue. It states that the tariffs for the use of the transmission grid applicable to generation units may differ depending on the technology of these units and the date of their commissioning.[500] Such different treatment in tariffs must be based on differences justified by the TSO in the tariff proposal, which is approved by the CREG.[501]

550. In the Federal Electricity Law, the principles regulating the transmission tariff methodology do not address specifically the introduction of dynamic transmission tariffs. The legislation only states that the structure of tariffs should promote the rational use of energy and infrastructure.[502] The CREG

---

[496] *Belgian Federal Electricity Law*, art. 12, §5, 9° and 20°.

[497] *Belgian Federal Electricity Law*, art. 12, §5, 25°, 28° and 29°.

[498] See Section 3.2 of Chapter III above for more details.

[499] Ibid.

[500] *Belgian Federal Electricity Law*, art. 12, §5, 17°.

[501] Ibid.

[502] *Belgian Federal Electricity Law*, art. 12, §5, 7°.

utilizes this provision as a legal basis for the possibility of incorporating a dynamic component, which varies depending on market electricity prices, into transmission tariffs related to energy taken and injected (CREG, 2022a). Moreover, it allows two categories of power peak tariffs, i.e., tariffs for the monthly peak and tariffs for the annual peak, as tariffs for grid infrastructure management (CREG, 2022a). They aim to encourage grid users to adjust their offtake and injection profiles to optimize the efficient use of the transmission grid (CREG, 2022a). It should be noted that such tariffs differ from the capacity tariffs applied in Flanders. The latter are based on the peak demands of individual consumers, as elaborated later on. In the federal regulatory context, the power peak tariffs are based on the average peak period of using the transmission grid, i.e., the period proposed by the system operator and approved by the CREG, during which the overall network load is statistically highest (CREG, 2022a). By shifting consumers' grid use to non-peak periods, they allow the TSO to acquire flexibility as an alternative to flexibility procurement (CREG, 2022a).

2.3.2.2. Flemish Approach

551. In Flanders, in addition to incorporating the common requirements for tariff setting enshrined in EU law,[503] the Flemish Energy Decree deals with network impacts created by DR and renewables self-consumption, in particular. As explained in Section 6.3 of the previous Chapter, the profound potential of consumers at the distribution grid level is being unlocked. Thus, the distribution grid is expected to integrate more flexibility and generation assets in the years ahead. Recovering reasonable system costs brought by such integration is key to enabling the DSO to take up relevant technical, organizational and regulatory challenges. The potential network impact of these activities has been stressed in the principles for regulating the distribution tariff methodology. Article 4.1.32 of the Decree requires the tariffs to realistically reflect the costs that may result from connecting to and using the distribution grid by distributed RES-E generation installations. During the 2021–2024 tariff period, the VREG has taken actions to tailor tariffs so that grid users involved in renewables self-consumption contribute sufficiently to the distribution system costs. As Table 13 shows, tariffs applied to active customers and energy communities vary depending on their generation capacity and meters.[504]

503 *Flemish Energy Decree*, art. 4.1.32, §1, 1°, 5°, 9°, 15°, 16°, 19° and 20°.
504 *2021–2024 Distribution Tariff Methodology*, 2021.

**Table 13. Distribution tariffs applied to active customers and energy communities**

| Gird users | Applicable distribution tariffs |
|---|---|
| Prosumers (having generation units with a maximum AC capacity less than or equal to 10 kVA) | Injection tariffs have not been applied yet;<br>Offtake tariffs:<br>• For prosumers with a reversing counter, covering three components: (1) periodic distribution tariffs based on net offtake volumes, (2) prosumer tariffs for the unmetered offtake, and (3) minimal contribution to grid costs, i.e., the fixed capacity tariff based on an assumed value;<br>• Prosumers with digital meters: charged based on the electricity they actually take from the grid. 80% of offtake tariffs are capacity tariffs (calculated based on peak capacity, expressed in kW) while the remaining 20% are still volume-based tariffs (the amount of electricity used, expressed in kWh). |
| Active customers or energy communities (having generation units with AC capacity > 10 kVA and having installed digital meters) | Injection tariffs: charged per injected kWh;<br>Offtake tariffs: based on the electricity they actually take from the grid. 80% of offtake tariffs are capacity tariffs while the remaining 20% are volume-based tariffs. |

Source: Author's own elaboration based on 2021–2024 Distribution Tariff Methodology.

552. As can be observed, the existing distribution tariffs applied to consumers and energy communities have implemented EU law's requirements that network charges must account separately for the electricity fed into and consumed from the grid. An exception exists for prosumers having DG units with a maximum AC capacity of ≤ 10 kVA. In the 2021–2024 tariff period, the VREG has not decided on an appropriate level of the injection tariff for prosumers, which will be based on further investigations.[505] In Flemish law, among consumers constituting active customers under EU law, those having DGs with a maximum AC power ≤ 10 kVA are defined as 'prosumers' and viewed as a separate customer group. This is based on the fact that the majority of them were equipped with reversing counters ('terugdraaiende teller').[506] In addition to the need for further investigations, the absence of injection tariffs is also attributed to the unaccomplished deployment of smart meters. As already noted, smart meters are the technical precondition for charging electricity fed into the grid and electricity consumed from the grid separately. For consumers who have not installed digital meters, their traditional meters are only able to log the net amount of electricity purchased from the grid, known as the 'net offtake volume', i.e., the amount of electricity purchased minus the amount

505 *2021–2024 Distribution Tariff Methodology*, section 11.2.4.
506 *Flemish Energy Decree*, art. 1.1.3, 74°/1 and 104°; *2021–2024 Distribution Tariff Methodology*, section 10.2.2.

put on the grid.[507] Thus, applying injection tariffs to them is still technically impossible. Despite this, the VREG has adjusted offtake tariffs to enable these prosumers to adequately contribute to the distribution grid costs incurred by their grid use in the offtake direction.

553. First, in addition to ordinary periodic distribution tariffs for the above net offtake, prosumers with reversing counters are also charged prosumer tariffs to cover the unmetered volume. Their mechanical meters measure the consumption of power taken from the grid but physically reverse as soon as self-produced electricity is injected into the grid in the reverse direction.[508] These meters only display the net offtake volume, as noted. This is an example of 'net metering' explained in Section 3.2.2 of Chapter III. The distribution grid costs cannot be fully recovered with this net offtake volume, as illustrated by a numerical example. If the actual offtake is 75 kWh and the injection is 25 kWh, with the reversing counter, the measured offtake is equal to 50 kWh.[509] When periodic distribution network tariffs are determined purely based on the net offtake value (i.e., 50 kWh rather than the actual offtake volume of 75 kWh in this example), they are not proportional to the actual use of the grid and therefore do not sufficiently cover network costs.[510] Moreover, a discriminatory situation arises where prosumers with reversing counters pay periodic tariffs based only on the net offtake volume, while other grid users pay in full based on their actual offtake.[511] This can lead to cross-subsidization between these prosumers and other grid users, especially those without generation facilities. This is because the uncovered costs stemming from net metering will be passed on to other grid users, as explained in the previous Chapter.

554. To address these issues, for prosumers without smart meters, prosumer tariffs are imposed to reasonably reflect the costs to the distribution system related to the estimated amount of unmetered offtake volume, on top of the periodic distribution tariffs charged based on the foregoing net offtake volume.[512]

555. In addition, with the application of capacity tariffs since 2023 in Flanders, these prosumers must also pay a fixed minimum tariff based on an assumed monthly peak of 2.5 kW.[513] Hence, prosumers with reversing counters are subject to offtake tariffs comprised of three components, as listed in Table 13.

507 *2021–2024 Distribution Tariff Methodology*, section 10.2.2; Claeys et al., 2023.
508 *2021–2024 Distribution Tariff Methodology*, section 10.2.2.1.1.
509 Ibid.
510 Ibid.
511 Ibid.
512 The tariff methodology specifies the tariff structure of the periodic electricity distribution grid tariffs for offtake. For distribution grid users without smart meters, the periodic distribution grid tariffs contain the fixed tariff for grid use (EUR/year), i.e., 'vastnet'. See 2021–2024 Distribution Tariff Methodology, sections 11.2.2 and 11.2.4.
513 *2021–2024 Distribution Tariff Methodology*, section 11.2.2; Claeys et al., 2023.

By contrast, prosumers having smart meters pay offtake tariffs based on their actual offtake from the grid, measured by smart meters, and thus do not apply prosumer tariffs. This is based on the Constitutional Court judgment published in March 2021, which annulled the application of the reversing counter to prosumers with digital meters.[514] Like other grid users, 80% of offtake tariffs are charged in the form of capacity tariffs while the rest 20% are still calculated in a volumetric way, i.e., based on the amount of electricity (kWh) purchased from the grid.[515] Capacity tariffs are not an additional tariff but a different way of charging, which charges users' offtake based on kW-term and calculates tariffs based on mean monthly peak demands, averaged over the last 12 months.[516] The aim of capacity tariffs is to make grid users aware that high peaks in their consumption can entail additional costs to the grid and encourage them to spread consumption and limit their peak demands (i.e., the maximum amount of electricity used by a consumer at the same time) (Desmet et al., 2021).

556. Despite these benefits, capacity tariffs come with some implications for active customers and energy communities. Such capacity-based tariffs lower the marginal cost of the electricity bought from the grid and thus lead to a decrease in the savings attained by renewables self-consumption, though the commodity component, the levies, the costs of implementing PSOs imposed on the DSO, as well as 20% of the network cost all remain volume-based in the electricity bill (Claeys et al., 2023).

557. Active customers and energy communities with generation units having an AC capacity of more than 10 kVA and installed digital meters are subject to both injection and offtake tariffs based on their actual use of the distribution grid. The 2021–2024 Distribution Tariff Methodology does not establish a special method for calculating their tariffs. They are thus subject to offtake and injection tariffs applied to other grid users with generation assets and digital meters. Different from offtake tariffs that are largely capacity-based, injection

514 This judgement, among others, abolished the extension of the system of reversing counters introduced by Art. 42 of the Decree of the 26 APRIL 2019 amending the Energy Decree of 8 May 2009, regarding the rollout of digital meters and amending articles 7.1.1, 7.1.2 and 7.1.5 of the same decree. See *arrest nr. 5/2021 van 14 januari 2021*, 2021.

515 *2021–2024 Distribution Tariff Methodology*, section 11.5.3; Desmet et al., 2021; Claeys et al., 2023.

516 More specifically, digital meters of grid users measure the consumption (in kWh) every 15 minutes. The monthly peak is then determined by the highest average power over the 15-minute intervals of that month. The mean monthly peak demand, which is used for the billing itself, is subsequently determined by averaging over the last 12 months. Capacity tariffs make a minimal contribution to the grid cost. A minimum monthly peak of 2.5 kW is assumed. If the monthly peak demand is less than 2.5 kW, grid users will still be billed the cost equivalent of 2.5 kW. See Claeys et al., 2023; 2021–2024 Distribution Tariff Methodology, section 11.2.2.

tariffs in the 2021–2024 period are volume-based, i.e., based on the amount of active power injected in kWh.[517] The injection tariff structure might be subject to adjustments in the next tariff period to improve more efficient use of the grid.[518]

558. Apart from costs brought to the distribution grid, DR and distributed RES-E may also bring about benefits and cost savings, such as a reduction in grid losses and postponed or avoided network investment.[519] Such benefits must also be reflected in distribution tariffs.[520] For the 2021–2024 tariff period, a specific reduction in tariffs has not been introduced for these grid users. Following the issuance of the 2021–2024 Tariff Methodology, in 2023, the Flemish Energy Decree was amended to transpose EU law on renewables self-consumption. Similar consideration of both costs and benefits in network tariffs is also emphasized in its provisions on energy communities and the sharing and selling of self-generated RES-E. The legislator appears to expect that among the allowed activities of sharing and selling RES-E, three of them can particularly benefit the distribution grid. They are (i) energy activities of energy communities, (ii) electricity sharing between active customers within one building, and (iii) VME sales.[521] Article 4.8.4, §4 of the Energy Decree allows the Flemish Government to request that the VREG examine the relevant remuneration and reductions in grid tariffs that can be provided for the grid users involved in these three activities. Such examination is based on a cost-benefit analysis to investigate to what extent these activities can contribute to the relief of the distribution grid, including the avoided investments and costs in the grid.[522]

559. A study examining, using a cost-benefit analysis, the extent to which activities of energy communities can contribute to relieving the burden on the distribution grid was finished in 2023 (EnergyVille, 2023). This study yields three main findings. First, collective activities where members optimize individual capacity tariffs and collective self-consumption (including those conducted by energy communities) generally do not alter the grid operator's investment needs. This is based on one finding of this study that the offtake peak of individual customers within the collective activity (winter, evening) does not sufficiently coincide with the times when collective activities have maximum PV production (summer, afternoon). Second, specific compositions of collective activities can provide benefits to the distribution network, while these benefits could only be delivered under certain preconditions. For instance, grid losses do decrease

517 *2021–2024 Distribution Tariff Methodology*, section 11.2.3.

518 Ibid.

519 *2021–2024 Distribution Tariff Methodology*, section 11.2.

520 *Flemish Energy Decree*, art. 4.1.32, §1, 17° and 18°.

521 *Flemish Energy Decree*, art. 4.8.4, §4.

522 Ibid.

to a limited extent in later years if PV installations are correctly dimensioned and if there is sufficient flexibility to steer consumption to moments of PV production within the collective activity. The collective activity should also be located on network elements on which the grid operator already experiences congestion problems. Moreover, it must be guaranteed that the collective activity provides structural solutions without exception. Third, this study indicates that collective activities cannot always meet all the preconditions structurally and, therefore, generally do not yield a sustainable benefit for the distribution network.

560. Based on these findings, this study concludes that adjusting grid tariffs for collective activities is not appropriate for the Flemish Region. Other means are therefore suggested to promote collective activities if these activities need to be further facilitated to underscore their environmental or social objectives.

561. In addition to implementing EU law's requirements on tariffs applied to active customers and energy communities, the tariff structure is also adapted to adequately recover the costs incurred by the DSO in fulfilling its increased role entrusted by the CEP. Adaptations mainly cover the following two aspects:

- The introduction of the above-mentioned capacity tariffs: As noted above, such tariffs cover a minimal contribution to grid costs and more accurately reflect the sunk costs of past grid investments in the infrastructure, as well as the services provided by the DSO (Claeys et al., 2023).
- The introduction of a data management tariff:[523] This component covers the costs of the required ICT investments, including the rollout of digital meters and the new role of data manager for the DSO.[524]

562. Lastly, Article 18 of the Electricity Regulation requires NRAs to consider time-differentiated network tariffs in case they have implemented the deployment of smart metering systems. As of 2024, there are no time-differentiated tariffs in Flanders. The VREG has required the DSO to conduct a study into the possible need to introduce time-dependent tariffs at the distribution network level.[525] The possibility of introducing such tariffs will be considered in the tariff methodology applicable from 2025.[526]

523 *2021–2024 Distribution Tariff Methodology*, section 5.6.2.
524 *2021–2024 Distribution Tariff Methodology*, sections 5.6.2, 10.2.1 and 11.2.
525 *2021–2024 Distribution Tariff Methodology*, section 11.2.3.
526 Ibid.

### 2.3.3. *Flexibility Procurement Requirements*

563. Both federal law and Flemish law have incorporated EU law's general requirements on creating non-discriminatory, transparent and market-based procedures for procuring flexibility services and ensuring participation of relevant market participants in the rule-making process.[527] These requirements foster demand-side flexibility by broadening marketplaces and ensuring a level playing field, thereby incentivizing consumers' engagement in DR and renewables self-consumption, either individually or collectively, as addressed in Chapter III. However, some substantive and procedural requirements therein require further clarification during the transposition process. Otherwise, the neutral market facilitator role of both the TSO and the DSO could not be fully attained in practice. A leading example is when the market-based provision of flexibility is considered economically inefficient, system operators can be exempted from the obligation of market-based flexibility procurement.[528] However, how can the economic efficiency of market-based flexibility procurement be assessed? Explicit assessment criteria in this respect are pivotal to safeguard the objectives underlying the general rule of market-based procurement itself. Again, those general rules in EU law are materialized at different levels by federal and Flemish rules. Distinctions are especially evident in terms of specifying exceptions to market-based procurement and securing due process in the development of procurement rules, as discussed below.

#### 2.3.3.1. Consultation Procedures

564. For developing specifications for procuring balancing services and non-frequency ancillary services, federal rules do not detail how the TSO should involve 'all market participants' or 'relevant system users' and thereby secure a 'transparent and participatory process' required by Article 40 of the Electricity Directive. They merely provide that the formulation of relevant procurement rules is subject to public consultation or should consult market players.[529] There are no further rules to guarantee the inclusive participation of all market participants and that their suggestions, comments and concerns were fully considered in the rule-making process. The measures allowing the regulator to monitor and verify the participation of all relevant market players are also absent. Importantly, as noted above, flexibility providers in the distribution

---

527 *Belgian Federal Electricity Law*, art. 8, §1/1 and art. 11, §2; *Flemish Energy Decree*, arts. 4.1.17/4 and 4.1.17/6; *Federal Grid Code*, art. 200, §1; *Electricity code of conduct*, art. 212, §1.

528 *Electricity Directive*, articles 31(7), 32(1) and 40(5).

529 *Belgian Federal Electricity Law*, art. 8, §1/1; *Federal Grid Code*, art. 200, §1; *Electricity code of conduct*, art. 212, §1.

grid also participate in transmission-level electricity markets. Federal law does not clarify whether they are considered 'relevant system users' and should be consulted. If the answer is yes, the market actors to be consulted could be numerous, which might challenge the prevailing approach that the TSO uses to interact with stakeholders.

565. Indeed, the TSO might maintain strong communication with large industrial users and professional stakeholders. However, the traditional methods used to convey information on procurement rules or technical specifications might be inaccessible to stakeholders connected to the distribution grid. As discussed later in Section 3.4, the Irish regulator has identified a deficiency in traditional ways of consulting stakeholders in the context of consumer engagement. Overlooking the disadvantages faced by market players (such as active customers and energy communities) in the distribution grid when engaging in rule-making processes could, in turn, compromise the fairness, neutrality, and proportionality of obligations, remuneration, and penalties created by flexibility procurement rules. For stakeholders from the SME and household sectors, alternatives to the traditional routes of consultation might be needed to enable effective communication and inclusive participation in developing flexibility market arrangements. Considering this, it is essential to first define which market actors are deemed relevant to the TSO's flexibility procurement and, second, to consider how to adapt consultation procedures to secure a participatory rule-making process. The lack of measures in these two respects may partially contribute to barriers for DR to access balancing markets, as noted in Section 2.1.1.2 above, despite the presence of the ToE regime.

566. By contrast, in Flanders, based on principles set out in Articles 4.1.17/4 and 4.1.17/6 of the Flemish Energy Decree, the VREG takes measures to safeguard participatory procedures for developing and amending flexibility procurement specifications and flexibility market processes.[530] Such measures have been further reinforced by the 2023 amendment to the TRDE.[531] A more structured two-step consultation procedure was established, featuring a distinction between the documented stakeholder consultation phase and the formal market consultation phase.[532] This procedure applies to the development of (i) flexibility procurement rules (i.e., for local congestion management, the provision of non-frequency ancillary services and energy for covering grid losses) and (ii) flexibility market processes.[533]

530 *TRDE*, art. 1.2.4, art. 2.3.22, art. 2.3.23 and art. 4.3.63.

531 *Explanatory note of the TRDE*, sections 1.1.2.2 and 1.1.2.3.

532 Ibid.

533 *TRDE*, art. 2.3.22, §3, art. 2.3.23, §3 and art. 4.3.63, §3.

567. This two-step consultation aims to facilitate rule-making transparency and secure the inclusive participation of all relevant market participants.[534] This is achieved through measures that inform stakeholders and enhance the DSO's responsiveness to them.[535] More specifically, when making rules for flexibility procurement and flexibility market processes, the DSO must first hold a stakeholder consultation with the relevant market participants and the TSO, during which the specifications are developed together.[536] This stakeholder consultation should be well documented for monitoring by the VREG, which can verify the participation of the different parties and how their suggestions, comments and concerns were dealt with.[537] In the next step, this jointly elaborated proposal should be consulted in accordance with conditions laid down by Art. 1.2.4, §7 of the TRDE.[538] These conditions include (i) reaching and informing stakeholders of the proposal in the most efficient manner, (ii) allowing stakeholders to formulate comments on the proposal, and (iii) informing stakeholders of how these comments are dealt with by the DSO, including the detailed justification thereof. The DSO's consultation procedure must also be submitted for approval by the VREG (*TRDE*, art. 1.2.4, §7).[539] After consultation, the DSO must submit the proposed procurement rules or market processes, together with a consultation report, to the VREG for approval (*TRDE*, art. 1.2.4, §5).

568. When making rules for procuring non-frequency ancillary services, there is an additional requirement beyond the two-step consultation process mentioned above. The DSO should also explicitly ask the stakeholders about what services they can offer and what benefits they can bring to the grid (*TRDE*, art. 2.3.23, §3). Based on this, in the consultation report, the DSO should explicitly justify which services they consider useful for the grid and which they

534 *Explanatory note of the TRDE*, section 1.1.2.3.

535 As a normative concept, stakeholder responsiveness requires the legitimate interests of stakeholders, which are brought to the attention of bodies and institutions throughout the development and implementation processes, to be reflected in the acts adopted. It covers the promotion of dialogue and provision of participation and feedback mechanisms, as well as safeguards in the form of accountability mechanisms to be put in place, enabling stakeholders to hold the involved bodies and institutions accountable in this respect. See Kohlbacher and Lavrijssen, 2018.

536 *Explanatory note of the TRDE*, section 1.1.2.2; *TRDE*, art. 2.3.22, §3, art. 2.3.23, §3 and art. 4.3.63, §3.

537 *Explanatory note of the TRDE*, section 1.1.2.2.

538 *Explanatory note of the TRDE*, section 1.1.2.2; *TRDE*, art. 2.3.22, §3, art. 2.3.23, §3 and art. 4.3.63, §3.

539 The consultation procedures adapted by the DSO to implement the above two-step consultations were approved by the VREG following the 2023 amendment to the TRDE. See VREG decision on proposed changes to 'Fluvius consultation procedure', annex to BESL-2022-33 [Beslissing van de VREG met betrekking tot voorgestelde wijzigingen aan de 'consultatieprocedures Fluvius', bijlage bij BESL-2022-33], 2023.

do not, taking into account feedback from the stakeholders. The consultation report of 17 January 2022 identified one service, i.e., voltage management.[540]

569. The TRDE does not specifically define the scope of stakeholders to be consulted. In the above-cited Arts. 2.3.22, 2.3.23 and 4.3.63, in addition to 'stakeholders', other terms '*all relevant market participants*' and '*the market participants active on the distribution network*' are also used to represent subjects of consultations. For instance, Art. 2.3.23, §3 provides that '*the electricity DSOs first, in accordance with Article 4.1.17/6 of the Energy Decree, hold a transparent and participatory consultation about the rules with the TSO and all relevant market participants. This consultation consists of a documented stakeholder consultation, followed by consultation with stakeholders in accordance with Art. 1.2.4, §5 and §7.*' It appears that, in this provision, stakeholders include the TSO and all relevant market participants. In the context of Art. 4.3.63, the scope of stakeholders is further specified by stating that '*the market participants active on the distribution network*' include BRPs, access holders and FSPs. Based on these provisions, it can be inferred that, within Flemish law, consumers connected to the distribution grid are not subject to consultations on flexibility procurement and market processes unless they have become market participants (either access holders or FSPs).

570. In specific rule-making processes, the most prominent problems identified by the VREG are insufficient responses to stakeholders' comments. In making flexibility procurement rules for congestion management, the DSO's explanations or comments often do not provide stakeholders with sufficiently clear information and are often limited to vagueness and general statements.[541] For instance, in addition to the consultation report, the DSO also responded to stakeholders' comments in an Excel file. In some places in that file, the DSO referred stakeholders to the consultation report itself, while the feedback there hardly included an answer to the questions or concerns of the market parties.[542] Another example is during making flexibility market processes, Synergrid only noted FEBEG's concerns regarding GDPR, without confirming or refuting these concerns.[543]

571. In addition, some of the DSO's responses increase the difficulty for stakeholders in learning about how the DSO has addressed their concerns. An example concerns the DSO's right to verify the accuracy of data for pools of assets controlled by an aggregator. This right to audit should have a more

---

540 *VREG 2023 Decision on the rules for the purchase of non-frequency-related ancillary services and grid losses*, section II.1.

541 *VREG 2024 Decision on the specifications for flexibility procurement for local congestion management*, section II.3.

542 Ibid.

543 *VREG Decision on Flexibility Market Processes 2.0*, 2024.

visible place in a dedicated discussion of control mechanisms. However, in the DSO's responses to the consultation feedback, a more specific discussion of this right was mentioned as a peripheral remark in the discussion of baseline methodologies.

572. Importantly, when defining deficiencies in the DSO's responses to consultation feedback from stakeholders, the VREG further concretizes the principle of transparency contained in EU-level requirements for flexibility procurement.[544] To date, there is no generally accepted principle of transparency in Belgian administrative law.[545] EU law also lacks a generally accepted definition of the principle of transparency. The VREG interpreted the principle of transparency by adopting public law doctrine, according to which the transparency principle refers to the availability, accessibility and clarity of information about government actions.[546] It may relate to access to specific documents held by the government, while it may also relate to procedures for which it must be clear how they will be carried out or requirements imposed on citizens that must be clearly communicated.[547] This highlights that a clear and complete explanation of procedural and substantive requirements of a specific government action stems from the requirement for ensuring transparency for stakeholders. It can be argued that thorough and clear responses to stakeholders serve as legal safeguards for ensuring transparency. Applying this doctrine to the DSO's flexibility procurement, the VREG determined that the DSO had violated the transparency principle due to its incomplete and unclear responses to stakeholders' concerns and questions. The other two regional independent regulators in Belgium also confirmed the correlation between the rule-maker's clear and thorough responses and compliance with the transparency principle. In their joint comments on the flexibility market processes designed by Synergrid, they emphasized the need for thorough and clear responses to FEBEG's concerns regarding data privacy, in order to ensure transparency (CWaPE et al., 2024).

### 2.3.3.2. Deviation from Market-Based Flexibility Procurement

573. Within EU law, deviation from market-based procurement is allowed in the context of purchasing non-frequency ancillary services and redispatching or grid congestion management.[548] Conditions set out by the Electricity Regulation for allowing non-market-based redispatching are straightforward.

---

[544] The principle of transparency is incorporated into Article 1.2.4, §3 of the TRDE.

[545] *VREG Decision on Flexibility Market Processes 2.0*, section II.2.

[546] Buijze, 2011; *VREG Decision on Flexibility Market Processes 2.0*, section II.2.

[547] Buijze and Widdershoven, 2010; *VREG Decision on Flexibility Market Processes 2.0*, section II.2.

[548] *Electricity Directive*, articles 31(7), 32(1) and 40(5); *Electricity Regulation*, article 13(3).

Within the Electricity Directive, both the TSO and the DSO are allowed to be exempted from market-based procurement of non-frequency ancillary services if the regulatory authority has assessed that the market-based provision of such services is economically inefficient. Aside from considering the economic efficiency of procurement, the conditions for exempting the DSO from market-based procurement of flexibility services for congestion management also include that such procurement would lead to severe market distortions or higher congestion. In applying these conditions, NRAs are faced with questions as to how to ascertain that market-based flexibility procurement is economically inefficient and how to define 'severe market distortions'. Developing criteria for applying these two conditions matters not only to safeguard the level playing field that benefits demand-side flexibility but also to balance the system operator's market facilitator role against other goals, especially the economic efficiency of grid operation and proper market functioning.

574. The Federal Electricity Law requires the CREG to determine in the Code of Conduct the deviation from market-based procurement of non-frequency ancillary services.[549] The Code of Conduct developed by the CREG contains a general rule that ancillary services should be provided at reasonable prices.[550] The justification for the CREG's requirement is that, even if prices are market-based, 'reasonableness' is still expected, which represents the proper functioning of ancillary service markets (CREG, 2022b). However, the Code of Conduct does not specify the criteria under which ancillary service prices are deemed unreasonable and deviations may be triggered.[551]

575. In Flanders, the TRDE specifically materializes criteria for assessing the economic efficiency of market-based flexibility procurement and serious market distortions, under the principles set out in the Flemish Energy Decree.[552] With regard to assessing whether the purchase of flexibility leads to serious market distortions, the marginal cost of market-based flexibility is compared with the marginal cost of reserved technical flexibility, since the latter's remuneration – in accordance with art. 4.1.17/5, §3 of the Energy Decree – is cost-reflective.[553]

---

549 *Belgian Federal Electricity Law*, art. 8, §1/1.

550 *Electricity code of conduct*, art. 208.

551 *Electricity code of conduct*, Title 8.3.

552 *Flemish Energy Decree*, art. 4.1.17/5, §1 and art. 4.1.17/6, §2.

553 The determination of the marginal cost of market-based flexibility should be reflected in the market survey that the DSO will organize. As a result, the marginal cost for a given asset is known in advance. The marginal cost of reserved technical flexibility is determined based on compensation provided in the Flemish Energy Decree. However, this compensation is not known in advance because it is highly dependent on time and technology. It can only be precisely evaluated at the time when local congestion occurs and the subsequent switch-off of specific assets happens. To solve this problem, the VREG proposes a simplified ex-ante

The numerical limit for the ratio of the marginal cost of market-based flexibility and the expected maximum cost of reserved technical flexibility, at which market-based flexibility is considered market-distorting, is set equal to 1.2.[554] The design of this upper limit aims to prevent market-based flexibility from becoming overly expensive relative to reserved technical flexibility, while also considering the degree of margins that commercial flexibility can achieve.[555]

576. The TRDE establishes distinct rules to evaluate the economic inefficiency of market-based flexibility procurement in various contexts. In the local congestion management context, such assessment is conducted by comparing the total expected remuneration for market-based flexibility, on an annual basis, with the avoided accounting costs of the deferred or avoided grid investment.[556] When procuring non-frequency ancillary services, the DSO can request a deviation from market-based procurement ex-ante or ex-post, and the determination of economic inefficiency varies in these two cases as follows (*TRDE*, art. 2.3.23, §8):

- An ex-ante application for derogation for the market-based purchase of non-frequency ancillary services should be submitted before the organization of the actual purchase procedure. The DSO should, after a public consultation, submit an application to VREG to demonstrate that the purchase of the non-frequency ancillary service is economically inefficient.
- An ex-post derogation request is made after the procurement procedure has been actually organized. The economically inefficient procurement is determined based on the results of the procurement. The TRDE lists two criteria: a lack of flexibility providers in the procurement or unreasonable price, while the DSO may demonstrate such economic inefficiency to the VREG based on other contributing factors.

577. In the former case, public consultation plays the role of checking and balancing the relevant decisions of the DSO before the application is submitted for approval. Yet, there are still no criteria for assessing the economic inefficiency of market-based procurement. In the latter case, relatively transparent and objective indicators are put in place, together with the results of the procurement procedure, to support the regulator's assessment of economic inefficiency. However, the TRDE in this context does not elaborate on the factors that the

estimation of the marginal cost for the period under consideration. For more details, see Explanatory note of the TRDE, section 1.1.2.2.

554 *Explanatory note of the TRDE*, section 1.1.2.2; *TRDE*, art. 2.3.22 /1, §2.

555 A value greater than 1 is adopted to recognize that in the case of commercial, market-based flexibility, a margin may be taken, and given the fact that compensation for technical flexibility is, in principle, merely cost-reflective. See Explanatory note of the TRDE, section 1.1.2.2.

556 *Explanatory note of the TRDE*, section 1.1.2.2; *TRDE*, art. 2.3.22 /1, §2.

DSO and the regulator should consider when determining an unreasonable price. There is thus still room for improving transparency and clarity of criteria for assessing whether market-based procurement of ancillary services is economically inefficient.

578. By October 2024, the DSO has not started procuring non-frequency ancillary services and flexibility for local congestion management or redispatching. The VREG has so far only conditionally approved the DSO's specifications for procuring energy to cover grid losses. It again refused to approve specifications for procuring non-frequency ancillary services and those for procuring flexibility for congestion management, as the proposed specifications had not fully met the substantive requirements set out in Articles 2.3.22 and 2.3.23.[557] For the time being, it remains to be seen whether the application of rules on deviations from market-based flexibility procurement would raise new legal issues. Yet, the rejected specifications for procuring flexibility for local congestion management contain some worth-mentioning legal issues.

579. The first issue concerns key features of 'market-based' flexibility procurement. The DSO's proposal for flexibility procurement for local congestion management provides a prominent example showing that the line between market-based and non-market-based ways of accessing flexibility can be blurred. If their distinction is not clarified, the principle for market-based procurement of flexibility can be unduly deviated from.

580. In specifications submitted on 30 June 2023, the DSO submits three types of market products for approval: (i) bilateral flexibility with modulation,[558] (ii) bilateral flexibility with profile,[559] and (iii) multilateral flexibility with

---

557 These flexibility procurement specifications were rejected once in 2022 for gaps in meeting both procedural and substantive requirements set out by the TRDE. The revised proposals for non-frequency ancillary service procurement and for congestion-management flexibility procurement were refused again, respectively, at the end of 2023 and early 2024. The DSO was required to resubmit revised rules for non-frequency ancillary services procurement and those for flexibility procurement for congestion management to the VREG for approval before 30 June and 31 October 2024, respectively. See *VREG 2022 Decision on rules for procuring non-frequency-related ancillary services and grid losses*, 2022, *VREG 2022 Decision on flexibility procurement specifications for local congestion*, 2022, *VREG 2023 Decision on the rules for the purchase of non-frequency-related ancillary services and grid losses*, 2023, *VREG 2024 Decision on the specifications for flexibility procurement for local congestion management*, 2024.

558 This flexibility means that the DSO connects a customer, with a bilateral agreement of a temporary nature, with the right to request in real time a change in offtake or injection capacity within pre-agreed limits. See VREG 2024 Decision on the specifications for flexibility procurement for local congestion management, section I.4.

559 Bilateral flexibility with profile means that the DSO connects a customer with a bilateral agreement of a temporary nature, so that the customer keeps the power within a pre-agreed offtake or injection capacity at certain pre-agreed times. See VREG 2024 Decision on the specifications for flexibility procurement for local congestion management, section I.4.

modulation. The former two kinds of flexibility are obtained through a bilateral agreement made between a customer and the DSO. Multiple flexibility is obtained through an auction, in which interested market participants can voluntarily participate by placing bids, which is thus accessed by a market-based procedure. The DSO prefers bilateral flexibility to multilateral flexibility. Section 4.1.2 of the specifications states that multilateral flexibility is only considered after bilateral flexibility is excluded as an option.[560] In light of this preference, a key question to be addressed is whether prioritizing bilateral flexibility would compromise the principle of market-based flexibility procurement and circumvent the rules governing deviations from that principle. To address this question, one must consider whether bilateral flexibility can be viewed as a market-based approach to procuring flexibility.

581. The VREG analyzed this question in Section II.3 of its 2024 Decision on the specifications for flexibility procurement for local congestion management. It agreed with other stakeholders on this subject and concluded that bilateral flexibility should not be regarded as market-based flexibility procurement for several reasons. First, agreements for bilateral flexibility constitute 'connection agreements', which in many cases do not constitute a free choice, given that the only alternative is to refuse the connection. Market functioning is non-existent in these bilateral flexibility agreements since no other players can bid to offer the requested flexibility; after all, the requested flexibility is not put into the market. Furthermore, there is little to no margin for negotiation in such agreements. For example, the applicant for flexibility (the DSO) determines the price of the requested flexibility. Citing a study of the CEER regarding connection agreements as alternatives when flexibility markets are underdeveloped, the VREG classified bilateral flexibility proposed by the DSO as a separate category from market-based flexibility on the one hand and technical flexibility on the other (CEER, 2023). The possibility to enter into a flexible connection agreement is not provided for in the Flemish energy legislation, thus conflicting with the higher regulations. Aside from lacking the legal basis for allowing access to the bilateral flexibility in question, the VREG also rejected approving it to avoid acting contrary to future new rules on flexible connection agreements introduced by the EU or Flemish law.

582. Once bilateral flexibility is not accessed by market-based procedures, the DSO's proposal of giving priority to it and the accompanying restrictions on (market-based) multilateral flexibility are problematic. In its specifications for congestion-management flexibility procurement, the DSO imposes some

560 *VREG 2024 Decision on the specifications for flexibility procurement for local congestion management*, Section II.3; Fluvius, 2023.

limitations on the use of multiple flexibility and the switch from bilateral flexibility to multilateral flexibility as follows:[561]

- Section 2.6.2 'Concretization of flexibility products' provides that multilateral flexibility is primarily aimed at investment deferral.
- Section 6.2.2 'Channel, mode and frequency of tender publication' states that new tenders can be launched on a continuous basis in acute situations, to replace bilateral flexibility with multilateral flexibility.
- Section 4.4 'Settlement and Compensation' states that bilateral flexibility is replaced by multilateral flexibility when the latter's price is competitive with the compensation for bilateral flexibility.

583. The specifications proposed by the DSO suggest that market-based flexibility procurement is applied only in limited cases, contravening the EU law's requirement to establish it as a general principle. In addition, as rightly pointed out by the VREG, the lack of an availability fee in the case of bilateral flexibility inherently makes the pricing of bilateral flexibility more advantageous than that of multilateral flexibility. It would be easy to avoid switching to market-based flexibility procurement under the standard set out in Section 4.4 of the proposed specifications mentioned above.

584. Another factor contributing to undue deviations from market-based flexibility procurement is that the DSO suggests that the comparison between the economic efficiency of bilateral and multilateral flexibility is based on the marginal cost of the two forms of flexibility. This violates the criterion set by Art. 2.3.22 /1, §2 TRDE for assessing the economic efficiency of flexibility procurement for local congestion management. As noted above, this assessment requires comparison of the total expected remuneration for market-based flexibility on an annual basis *with the avoided accounting costs of the deferred or avoided grid investment*. That is to say, the cost of bilateral and multilateral flexibility should not only be compared in terms of a marginal cost but should also be considered in terms of an absolute cost over the period of investment deferral or postponement, to also provide a correct trade-off with an investment.[562] Breaching this criterion could lead to an incorrect assessment of the economic efficiency of multilateral flexibility, resulting in illegal derogation from market-based congestion management.

585. The DSO's attempt to introduce bilateral flexibility and deal with its relationship with multilateral flexibility highlights two key problems. First,

---

561 *VREG 2024 Decision on the specifications for flexibility procurement for local congestion management*, Section II.3; Fluvius, 2023.

562 *VREG 2024 Decision on the specifications for flexibility procurement for local congestion management*, section II.3.

the principle of market-based flexibility procurement can be violated not only in the organization of the actual purchase procedure but also in the stage of designing flexibility products. The regulator needs to evaluate the nature of specific flexibility products developed by the DSO, especially regarding whether they are procured in a market-based way. Second, if the regulator approves non-market-based flexibility products, the next question concerns specific mechanisms for dealing with the choice and prioritization of market-based and non-market-based flexibility products. The applicable criteria for assessing the economic efficiency of market-based procurement (e.g., those contained in Art. 2.3.22 /1, §2 TRDE) serve as the first legal safeguard for avoiding undue derogation from the principle of procuring flexibility through market-based procedures. The above example shows that concrete mechanisms developed by the DSO can subtly avoid market-based procurement and increase the use of non-market-based flexibility. The second safeguard thus lies in the regulator's approval of the DSO's procurement rules. It should thoroughly examine the misalignment between the DSO's approach to switching to non-market-based flexibility products and the established standards for governing such a switch.

## 3. LEGAL ISSUES IDENTIFIED IN THE TRANSPOSITION PROCESS

586. Under EU law, consumer empowerment is pursued not only by granting energy consumers a range of rights related to their proactive role, but also by providing incentives and instruments to enable the exercise of those rights. This also coincides with the ambitious legislative objective of developing a 'consumer-centred' electricity market. The above Belgian law case study, however, indicates regulatory gaps and challenges in concretizing the rights and obligations of final customers and developing enabling frameworks and ancillary measures. Intractable legal challenges of empowering final customers are also detected in other Member States, as elaborated further below. Some of them could be attributed to weak national transpositions, characterized by the 'copy-out' approach, i.e., a simple literal transposition of EU law without substantiating implementing rules (Haji Bashi et al., 2023; Krug et al., 2023). Bound by the principle of subsidiarity, the supranational framework merely establishes generic principles or broadly worded requirements, refraining from affecting Member States' energy competence while creating sufficient flexibility for regulatory innovation. An example is the right to electricity sharing. Within EU law, there are no detailed requirements for its national transpositions. Yet, as shown above, implementing this right entails manifold legal and regulatory details, such as its definition and applicable obligations. Failing to address them could make this right remain an idea on paper. By the time of writing, very few Member States

had put in place robust implementing frameworks that thoroughly considered and addressed those details, as drawn out later.

587. Apart from poor national transpositions, EU law per se also has some deficiencies and inherent conflicts, leading to challenges or dilemmas in its transposition. They are especially prominent in EU legal provisions addressing the role, rights and obligations as well as the accompanying enabling frameworks. As highlighted in Chapter III, EU law empowers rather than enforces consumers to engage in DR and renewables self-consumption. Its empowerment framework is thus essentially a 'carrot' instead of a 'stick' (Sokołowski, 2020). As with carrots, which can be healthy and fresh, bitten, or unripe (Johnston, 2018; Sokołowski, 2020), the empowerment framework can have problems relating to clarity, certainty and coherence.

588. Along with lessons drawn from the Belgian law case study, this section examines four pillars of EU law on electricity DSM in sequence, using additional examples from ongoing transpositions in other Member States. It also seeks to identify which legal challenges should be addressed in national transpositions and which deficiencies require reflection at the EU level. In the area of electricity DSM, studies and reports have provided empirical data on the compliance level of national law with EU law, including, but not limited to, timeliness and completeness.[563] Instead of simply reporting such data, this section is dedicated to analyzing the prominent legal issues that arise during national transpositions. This section proceeds as follows. Section 3.1 identifies the legal issues in transposing EU law on the role, rights and obligations of final customers and other actors involved in DR and renewables self-consumption. Section 3.2 examines whether sufficient economic incentives are provided for consumers to fulfill their proactive role in facilitating the uptake of RES-E. This evaluation sheds light on regulatory barriers to entering electricity markets and obtaining proper economic incentives. Section 3.3 examines the EU's efforts to provide the required information in shifting the consumers' role. Section 3.4 reflects on Union-level adaptations of network regulation in the context of empowering consumers to support the transition toward a high RES electricity system. Throughout this section, the discussion also examines whether the new amendments adopted in 2023 and 2024 can help address the identified issues or, conversely, give rise to new ones.

[563] The single market scoreboard is an enforcement tool developed by the EC, which covers data on the transposition deficit (the gap between the number of single market directives adopted by the EU and the number of directives transposed by each Member State) and the conformity deficit (the percentage of those directives incorrectly transposed) detected in transposing EU Directives with a transposition deadline on or before 30 November 2022. For other empirical data on the transposition and implementation of EU law on electricity DSM, see e.g., ACER and CEER, 2021; Krug et al., 2023; ACER and CEER, 2023; ACER, 2023.

## 3.1. ROLE, RIGHTS AND OBLIGATIONS

589. This section examines the legal issues involved in giving effect to the rights and obligations associated with the active role of final customers in DR (Section 3.1.1) and renewables prosuming (Section 3.1.2). Given the energy communities' key role in engaging consumers in both DR and renewables self-consumption, their governance frameworks are examined specifically in Section 3.1.3.

### *3.1.1. Entities Involved in DR*

590. The implementation of Union-level frameworks for entitling consumers to engage in both implicit and explicit DR raises different legal issues. In terms of engaging consumers in implicit DR, a major legal problem is linked to the risks and adverse impacts that dynamic price contracts may bring to consumers. The implications of such new offers have legal significance for consumer protection and could enrich consumers' rights and the corresponding obligations imposed on suppliers providing such offers. The potential impacts of applying dynamic price contracts remain to be identified based on empirical evidence. This is why EU law requires Member States to monitor the impact of these contracts on consumers' bills for at least ten years after they become available. Yet, existing empirical data and the energy price crisis already indicate some issues deserving attention.

591. First, aside from the delayed deployment of smart meters, consumers' perceived risks are also found to hinder their adoption of such new offers, especially during exceptionally volatile price periods (Hampton et al., 2022). Furthermore, residential consumers may be more risk-averse than other consumer groups and may be reluctant to enroll in dynamic price contracts (Allcott, 2011b; Bradley et al., 2016; Parrish et al., 2020). However, relevant evidence in this respect is mixed because, on the other hand, high energy prices could also increase the profitability of implicit DR (Parrish et al., 2020). In the context of energy price spikes, either under fixed-price supply contracts or dynamic price contracts, consumers are exposed to increases in electricity bills. It is thus likely that engaging with implicit DR to obtain bill savings based on real-time price changes becomes attractive for customers, which can change the outcomes of weighing up the potential financial savings against relevant risk, convenience and comfort when deciding whether to adjust their electricity use (Parrish et al., 2020; Sridhar et al., 2023). Despite the mixed evidence, there is a need to consider the ability and willingness of different customer groups to enter into dynamic price contracts. The right to shift to such offers may need to be formulated in a more targeted manner to account for distinctions between different customer groups and to better engage and protect them.

592. A lesson drawn from the energy price crisis from mid-2021 is that consumer empowerment is, in some cases, in conflict with consumer protection, as warned by a prior study (Hanke and Lowitzsch, 2020). Consumer protection is emphasized alongside consumer empowerment in the Electricity Directive. However, from a specific legal perspective, the focus is mainly on empowering consumers to shift their roles in the energy transition, while ensuring consumers' access to adequate coping mechanisms to manage potential price rises takes a relatively back seat. In addition to risk-hedging instruments (ACER, 2022), these coping mechanisms should also contain an equal emphasis on consumers' rights to opt for affordable fixed-price and fixed-term contracts. In recent years, suppliers in some Member States have reduced their offers, fixed-price contracts have become scarce, and the choice of offers has become limited (*2024 Amendment to the Electricity Directive*, recital 17). Limited options, together with absent price risk hedging tools, restrict the space for maneuvers available for consumers to deal with wholesale price volatility and soaring prices, placing consumer protection at stake. Facing this problem, there has been a move from emphasizing consumers' right to access dynamic price contracts toward specifying their entitlement to a fixed term, fixed price and dynamic electricity price contract in the 2024 Amendment to the Electricity Directive (*2024 Amendment to the Electricity Directive*, Article 11). Under Article 11 of the amended Electricity Directive, such rights are safeguarded by requiring Member States to ensure that their national regulatory frameworks also enable suppliers to offer fixed-term, fixed-price contracts, in addition to dynamic electricity price contracts. Moreover, all final customers should be able to request a fixed-term, fixed-price electricity contract with a duration of at least one year.

593. Regarding the right to offer explicit DR, EU law aims to increase its accessibility to a wide range of final customers by providing them with more options to engage in explicit DR, such as individually or through intermediaries. Yet, as noted, such accessibility also hinges upon market design allowing for free market entry of medium and small loads and a legal framework fairly assigning rights and obligations to participants engaged in explicit DR and other stakeholders. To date, the efforts introduced by the CEP to adapt market entry conditions are still considered insufficient to enable individual consumer participation (ACER, 2023a; Silva et al., 2023). Legal approaches to mitigating barriers arising from flexibility market design will be discussed specifically in Sections 3.2 and 3.4 below. The consumers' right to cooperate with a third party (i.e., the IFSP) is also restricted by weak and lagging national transpositions in recognizing and defining the role of the IFSP and structuring its relationship with suppliers and BRPs (ACER, 2023a; Sousa and Soares, 2023). At the time of writing (January 2024), 16 Member States have not transposed the EU legal framework for empowering consumers to valorize DR through IFSPs

(ACER, 2023a). As already highlighted in Chapter II, participating in complex and highly formalized electricity markets requires expertise in navigating sophisticated energy regimes, ranging from primary law to network codes and standard contracts for flexibility procurement. Empirical findings suggest that numerous and complex regulations associated with DR even make it difficult for some industrial users to handle (Leinauer et al., 2022). Considering this, the limited possibilities for seeking assistance from the IFSP in practice can even make explicit DR impossible for consumers who suffer from a lack of time and knowledge. These barriers are partially responsible for the untapped potential of demand flexibility from consumers in not only residential but also industrial and commercial sectors within the EU (Scharnhorst et al., 2024).

594. National frameworks materializing the EU-level requirements for regulating the IFSPs' relationship with affected suppliers and BRPs can lead to new legal issues. So far, studies focusing on specific rules adopted by Member States that have already transposed relevant EU law remain very scarce,[564] limiting available data for the legal analysis of this book. Despite this, lessons can be learned from the above case study of the Belgian ToE regime. Several key issues should be considered by legislators or regulators in other Member States.

595. First, the Belgian case study demonstrates the role of a standardized fallback solution in preventing unfair and lengthy bilateral negotiations from disadvantaging IFSPs. Its key role highlights the importance of designing a fair and proportionate standardized mechanism for aligning the conflicting interests of IFSPs and the affected stakeholders (suppliers and BRPs). Care should also be taken to mitigate the potential risks of abuse by involved parties, particularly in the design of the formula that calculates compensation between suppliers and IFSPs. Moreover, another dimension not stressed by EU law but revealed by the ToE regime is that compensation between suppliers and IFSPs can be two-way, depending on the increase or decrease of electricity consumption (Chen and Vandendriessche, 2023b). This should also be specified by specific national law or implementing regulations to fulfill the general requirement of EU law for assigning rights and obligations to DR participants and stakeholders in a clear and transparent manner.

596. Another issue concerns institutional complexity entailed in specific legal arrangements governing the IFSP's relationship with suppliers and BRPs, as indicated by the Belgian ToE regime (Chen and Vandendriessche, 2023b). Such complexity is indeed, to some extent, linked to the nature of regulating interactions among multiple actors. However, complexity, regulatory burdens,

564 This is based on search results for the keywords 'independent flexibility service providers' and 'legal frameworks in EU Member States' in the databases of Google Scholar and Web of Science.

and unreasonable costs existing in dedicated national frameworks can particularly deter small IFSPs and defeat the legislative will to foster greater participation of IFSPs (Chen and Vandendriessche, 2023b). Such concern is even more pronounced given that DR participants face multiple regulatory complexities. On top of the framework devoted to addressing conflicts of interest between IFSPs and suppliers and their BRPs, complexity also arises from general rules for entering different electricity markets, such as those for prequalification in balancing markets (Chen and Vandendriessche, 2023b; Scharnhorst et al., 2024).

597. Belgian law in this area is not an isolated case of creating regulatory complexity. Other empirical research on DR enrollment in recent years also warns that complex regulatory frameworks are becoming regulatory obstacles to DR (Leinauer et al., 2022; Scharnhorst et al., 2024). There is a need to deal more rigorously with the significant trade-off of creating a robust and fair but simplified empowerment framework for IFSPs (Chen and Vandendriessche, 2023b). The complexity of the ToE regime also highlights the need for defining alternatives, such as 'Opt-out' and 'Pass-through' mechanisms, alongside fallback solutions provided by national law. With these alternatives, market players could take simplified solutions by a mutual agreement to counter impacts on suppliers and BRPs (Chen and Vandendriessche, 2023b).

### *3.1.2. Entities Engaged in Renewables Self-Consumption*

598. Within the EU, falling costs of renewables generation technology as well as the energy price crisis of 2021–2022 constitute major drivers for further growth of renewables self-consumption. In 2020, PV panels already met grid parity in some Member States, namely, consumers being able to produce electricity at a cost that is competitive with supplier retail prices (ACER and CEER, 2021). This implies increased profitability of self-consumption and selling surplus electricity in retail markets. The record-high electricity prices in 2022 induced by a pricing mechanism dominated by fossil fuel power plants[565] additionally drove consumers to conduct renewables self-consumption to protect themselves against high prices.[566] However, the delayed transposition of the CEP, as well as regulatory gaps presented in existing implementing rules, could prevent consumers from taking full advantage of these opportunities (ACER and CEER, 2021). This subsection identifies legal challenges of implementing EU-level frameworks for renewables self-consumers and the energy community,

565 For more details of the impact of the PAC pricing mechanism, see Section 5.1.1 of Chapter III.

566 Before the price spikes, mitigating the impact of volatile fossil fuel prices has already been a significant push factor for industrial and residential users to become renewables prosumers. See Woerter et al., 2017; Palm, 2018; Horbach and Rammer, 2018.

respectively. Legal problems that arise in materializing new approaches to selling self-generated RES-E will be discussed separately in Section 3.2 below.

#### 3.1.2.1. Individual Consumers

599. Under EU law, individual consumers are entitled to produce RES-E by becoming either active customers or renewables self-consumers. Respective legal frameworks for active customers and renewables self-consumers have minor variances in terms of defining rights and obligations for consumers, as addressed in Section 3.2 of Chapter III above. Major legal issues relating to their application are examined next.

##### (i) Definitional Issues of 'Active Customer' and 'Renewables Self-Consumer'

600. The first problem is concerned with the Union-level definitions of 'active customers' and 'renewables self-consumers'. Both definitions provided by EU law contain an eligibility criterion that self-consumption activities do not constitute the primary commercial or professional activity (hereinafter the '*non-primary commercial or professional activity criterion*'). That restriction applies to all active customers, while in the definition of renewables self-consumers, it is exclusively set for non-household renewables self-consumers, as detailed in Section 3.2.1 of Chapter III above. Seen from this eligibility criterion, the EU legislator largely intends to distinguish active customers and renewables self-consumers from energy professionals engaged in electricity production, storage and trading, namely 'electricity undertaking' defined by the Electricity Directive. This distinction is significant in terms of regulatory treatment, as PSOs are imposed on electricity undertakings (*Electricity Directive*, Article 9). If there exists conflation between the definitions of 'electricity undertaking' and 'active customer' or 'renewables self-consumer', legal uncertainty regarding the application of PSOs would arise. However, this issue has not been entirely solved by Union-level definitions.

601. The definition of 'electricity undertaking' under EU law excludes final customers and highlights that such undertakings are characterized by fulfilling functions in the electricity sector, including generation, energy storage, supply of electricity, and those who are responsible for the commercial, technical, or maintenance tasks related to those functions.[567] In general, such functions

[567] 'Electricity undertaking' means that '*natural or legal person who carries out at least one of the following functions: generation, transmission, distribution, aggregation, demand response, energy storage, supply or purchase of electricity, and who is responsible for the commercial, technical or maintenance tasks related to those functions, but does not include final customers.*' See Electricity Directive, article 2(57).

can be understood as primary commercial or professional energy activities. Thus, active customers or renewables self-consumers whose participation in production and selling does not constitute primary commercial or professional activities are excluded from electricity undertakings. However, the definition of 'renewables self-consumer' does not prevent household renewables self-consumers from engaging in energy activities as a primary commercial or professional activity.[568] This implies potential overlaps between the notion of a household renewables self-consumer and that of an electricity undertaking, which can be a natural person.

602. The fact that the definition of 'electricity undertaking' excludes 'final customer' cannot prevent such overlaps. This is because when generating RES-E and storing and selling self-produced RES-E, renewables self-consumers are no longer 'final customers' who are customers 'purchasing electricity for own use', as defined by Article 2(3) of the Electricity Directive. It should be noted that even though according to the definition of 'renewable self-consumer', only final customers can constitute renewables self-consumers, it does not mean that renewables self-consumers will maintain the status of final customers in any case. As can be seen from the existing definition of final customers, it only covers two elements: (i) they are electricity buyers, and (ii) they buy electricity to meet own energy demand. While producing, storing and selling RES-E, a final customer has already gone beyond those elements and constitutes a new entity, as shown in Figure 13 below. This new entity may even lose its status as a final customer once it becomes fully self-sufficient and ceases to purchase electricity.

Figure 13. The changing status of active customers and renewables self-consumers

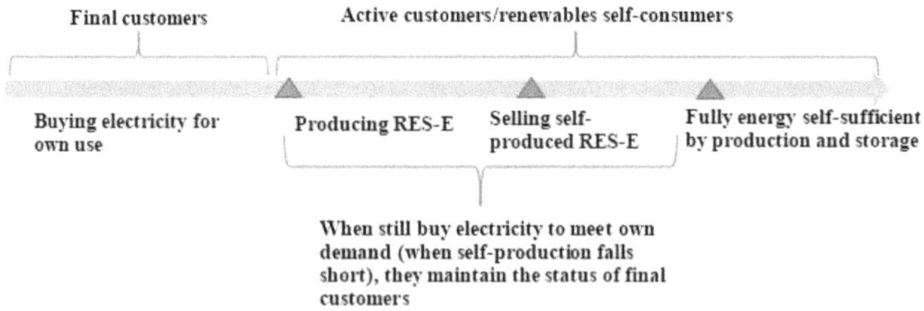


Source: Author's own elaboration.

[568] The restriction that 'those activities do not constitute its primary commercial or professional activity' is only imposed on non-household renewables self-consumers. See REDII, article 2(14).

603. The status of final customers is not static or constant, but instead must be evaluated in specific contexts, which aligns with a general principle derived from the CJEU's case law on general consumer protection law.[569] This principle does not conflict with Article 21(2)(c) of the REDII, which stipulates that renewables self-consumers are entitled '*to maintain their rights and obligations as final consumers*'. This provision cannot be interpreted as meaning that renewables self-consumers maintain the status of final customers in all cases, because the status of final customers can be in flux in practice. Given this, the above-cited Article 21(2)(c) should be understood as meaning that when renewables self-consumers purchase electricity for their own use and thus constitute final customers as defined by EU law, they maintain the relevant rights and obligations applicable to final customers.

604. In summary, the definition of electricity undertakings cannot exclude renewables self-consumers who do not buy electricity and no longer constitute final customers. The dividing lines between electricity undertakings and household renewables self-consumers are blurred, particularly because the latter may lose their customer status while still retaining their status as renewables self-consumers. This implies the need to revisit the definitions of 'renewable self-consumer' and 'electricity undertaking' and refine them. The blurred lines between 'electricity undertaking' and household renewables self-consumers could lead to difficulty in determining the applicability of PSOs. This problem arises from the deficiencies inherent in definitions and potential overlaps between new and preexisting definitions, which were overlooked by EU legislators when introducing new concepts. Considering this, the EU legislator is in a better position to address the conflation between the definitions of 'electricity undertaking' and household renewables self-consumer.

605. The second prominent legal issue related to the definitions of active customers and non-household renewables self-consumers is the difficulty in applying the above-mentioned non-primary commercial or professional activity standard. What are the concrete standards for evaluating whether producing and selling RES-E constitutes the primary commercial or professional activity of an active customer or non-household renewables self-consumer?

606. Moreover, when determining the status of active customers from the residential sector, even more problems arise. As pointed out above in reviewing Flemish law, in reality, the status of household active customers might not be static. Indeed, there are cases in which households do not engage in primary

569 Not all assessment criteria stemming from case law on general consumer law can be applied to the energy sector. Yet, a principle that can be generally applied is that the determination of consumer status is context-specific and it should be made by reference to the position of a certain actor in a particular contract, having regard to the nature and aim of that contract. For more details, see Section 3.2.3.2 of this Chapter below.

commercial or professional activities due to unemployment, for instance. Generating RES-E and consuming it while storing and selling surplus can then become their primary commercial activity (Lavrijssen et al., 2023) although it is still less likely to constitute 'professional activities'. In this context, would they lose the status of active customers (Lavrijssen et al., 2023)? If yes, they would fall outside of the empowerment frameworks for active customers (Lavrijssen et al., 2023). It remains unclear whether, when introducing the concept of active customers, the EU legislator has considered this scenario and already established that consumers, in this case, should no longer enjoy the rights granted to active customers. There thus exists legal uncertainty for some consumers to access self-consumption of RES-E. The application of the definition of household renewables self-consumers would not encounter this problem, since, as noted above, that definition only explicitly applies the non-primary commercial or professional activity criterion to non-household renewables self-consumers.

607. Apparently, the application of the non-primary commercial or professional activity criterion requires further clarification on its connotation and application standards. This should be addressed in national law that concretizes the role and rights of active customers and non-household renewables self-consumers. So far, national law typically circumvents this issue by copying EU law, as exemplified by Flemish law, Walloon law, Irish law, and Austrian law.[570] Several considerations might be useful for elaborating on the non-primary commercial or professional activity criterion, as discussed below.

608. First, further analyzing the EU legislator's intention in applying the non-primary commercial or professional activity criterion is the first step in sorting out its connotation and detailed standards for its application. As already noted, that criterion serves as a restriction. On the face of the definitions of active customers and renewable self-consumers, the restriction applies to all prosumption activities, including the use of self-generated energy. However, in fact, that restriction is primarily set for energy activities that are likely to be converted into commercial or professional activities, including selling self-produced RES-E and generating and storing RES-E for trading purposes. Generating RES-E for consumption purposes and consuming self-produced RES-E are not the subject of that restriction. This is because there is no need to prohibit electricity consumption behavior from constituting non-primary commercial or professional activity. On the one hand, generating RES-E and storing self-produced RES-E to meet own energy demand is generally not regarded

[570] See *Walloon Electricity Decree*, art. 2, 41° bis; *Flemish Energy Decree*, art. 1.1.3, 8°/4; *Renewable Energy Regulations 2022*, Regulation 2; Bundesgesetz über den Ausbau von Energie aus erneuerbaren Quellen (Erneuerbaren-Ausbau-Gesetz – EAG); Gesamte Rechtsvorschrift für Elektrizitätswirtschafts- und -organisationsgesetz 2010.

as a commercial activity. On the other hand, no users make consumption itself their primary professional activity. Therefore, the EU legislator's intention is primarily to prevent three activities involved in renewables prosumption (i.e., selling self-produced RES-E, generating and storing RES-E for electricity sales) from becoming primary commercial or professional activities of active customers and non-household renewables self-consumers. The reason for this has been explained: once these activities become primary commercial or professional activities, active customers and renewables self-consumers could constitute 'electricity undertakings', which can trigger heavy obligations.

609. After clarifying the subject of this restriction, the next step is to elaborate on further standards to apply the non-primary commercial or professional activity restriction. EU law does not prevent the above three activities from becoming commercial or professional activities of active customers or renewables self-consumers. It instead highlights that to maintain the status of active customers or non-household renewables self-consumers, those activities should not become the primary commercial or professional activities of these entities. This implies that, for all commercial or professional activities conducted by active customers or non-household renewables self-consumers, the three renewable prosumption activities – selling self-produced RES-E, generating and storing it for sale – should remain secondary rather than primary roles. In a nutshell, the non-primary nature should be assessed by considering the role of these activities in all activities carried out by active customers or non-household renewables self-consumers. Member States could elaborate on assessment standards on this basis.

610. Among others, such standards should be formulated around revenue sources and devotion of resources (including time, personnel and capitals) of active customers and non-household renewables self-consumers, which offer evidence revealing the actual importance of the above three self-consumption activities, in both revenue generation and resources distribution. More granular standards might be needed, since the detailed evidence for the assessment of the non-core activity nature varies with customers from residential, industrial and commercial sectors. For instance, for active customers or self-consumers from industrial or commercial sectors, the assessment refers to charters or statutes and financial statements (e.g., the income statement, balance sheet, and cash flow statement) as well as examines the time and other resources (including personnel) devoted by them to renewables prosumption. For residential active customers, aside from income proportion and time commitment, the assessment should also consider whether the person depends on the above three renewable prosumption activities as the primary source of livelihood.

611. Overall, assessing whether the above three renewables prosumption activities play a non-primary role among all commercial or professional activities

conducted by active customers or non-household renewable self-consumers can involve complex standards. They can complicate the assessment of the qualification of active customers and non-household renewable self-consumers. Are there other means to ensure compliance with the non-primary commercial or professional activity requirement?

612. In fact, this requirement can be met by highlighting that the primary purpose of renewables prosumption is to meet one's own energy demand, and on this basis, placing restrictions on the distribution of self-produced RES-E for trading purposes.

613. To stress the primary role of consumption in renewables prosumption activities, active consumers and non-household renewable self-consumers must use most of their self-produced RES-E to meet their own demand. Only surplus energy can be stored or sold. In this case, only a small portion of self-produced RES-E is permitted for trading, and active consumers and non-household renewable self-consumers would find it difficult to turn the three commercial prosumption activities (i.e., selling self-produced RES-E, generating and storing it for sale) into primary commercial or professional pursuits.

614. National law could thus translate the non-primary commercial or professional activity requirement into the following standard: final customers' production and other activities involving the disposal *of self-produced electricity must either serve or be subordinate to the consumption purpose*. The primary role of 'consumption' in renewables prosumption is well illustrated by a quote drawn from previous research regarding prosumers: 'They act merely to satisfy their individual needs by consuming the self-produced electricity and selling it only if in excess' (Almeida et al., 2021). The secondary role of selling self-produced RES-E is also reflected in Article 21 (2)(a), which entitles renewables self-consumers to '*sell their excess production of renewable electricity*'. The standard that meeting one's own energy demand should be the primary goal of renewable prosumption, aligning with the EU law's objective of empowering and incentivizing final customers. This approach does not prevent them from managing surplus production – whether through storage or trading – nor does it diminish the additional economic incentives from selling excess self-generated RES-E. At the same time, it provides a more pragmatic way of implementing the non-primary commercial or professional activity requirement.

615. Interestingly, a similar interpretation has already emerged in Ireland, suggesting that EU law facilitates renewables prosumption primarily to increase final customers' energy self-sufficiency. An example is the application of the 'Clean Export Guarantee' tariff. In determining 'deemed' export quantities (i.e., volumes of electricity exported to the grid) of renewables prosumers who

have not installed smart meters,[571] the Irish regulator capped the 'export factor' to 35% of the total generation capacity.[572] It reasons that EU law introducing renewables self-consumption aims to let consumers '*substantially meet their own demand rather than incentivize the export of electricity onto the network*' (CRU, 2021c). Under this interpretation, empowering prosumers to sell self-generated RES-E serves as an additional incentive provided by EU law for renewables prosumption, but not the primary aim.

616. The challenge associated with the second approach to implementing the non-primary commercial or professional activity requirement is how to ensure that only excess RES-E is sold. A straightforward approach is to set upper limits on self-produced RES-E that are permitted to sell, thereby maintaining the qualification of active customers or non-household renewables self-consumers. Such thresholds can take the form of volumes and proportions and may need to vary with customer groups. For instance, the proposal for REDII contained volume-based thresholds. Article 21 of the proposal provided that renewables self-consumers are '*not considered as energy suppliers according to Union or national legislation in relation to the renewable electricity they feed into the grid not exceeding 10 MWh for households and 500 MWh for legal persons on an annual basis*' (*Proposal of the REDII*, 2017). Such volume-based thresholds entail several evident problems, which can explain why they were ultimately not adopted. First, the proposed volumes do not necessarily represent the excess production of all prosumers, especially considering their diverse consumption and production portfolios. Second, facing the diverse and changing status of final customers' production and export volumes, they provide too rigid criteria. Various factors can contribute to such changes, including seasonal variations in RES-E output, shifts in the combinations of production units and storage facilities (such as EVs), or changes within households. As a result, some prosumers are no longer classified as active customers or renewable self-consumers when they are subject to these changes and their surplus electricity for sale exceeds predefined thresholds. Similar problems arise when capping the self-produced RES-E permitted to sell to a particular share of the total generation capacity.

617. Thus, it is not advised to establish too concrete criteria in statutes for assessing whether only surplus production is sold and whether the major share

571 The principle for determining export quantities is that self-consumers with smart meters deployed will only be compensated based on metered export, while 'deemed' export quantities serve as a short-term interim solution for self-consumers who are not in receipt of a smart meter. See CRU, 2021, section 3.2.

572 It capped the share of self-generated RES-E fed into the grid that could receive remuneration. See CRU, 2021, section 3.2.

of self-produced RES-E is for own use. Instead, it can be left to national courts to decide in specific cases whether prosumers indeed use self-produced RES-E primarily to meet their own demand and thereby respect the non-primary commercial or professional activity requirement.

618. To sum up, the above analysis shows that to implement the non-primary commercial or professional activity requirement, the linchpin lies in imposing restrictions on three activities involved in renewables prosumption: selling self-produced RES-E, generating and storing RES-E for electricity sales. It presents two approaches to setting up such restrictions and discusses their respective challenges. The first one entails complex standards for assessing whether the three renewables prosumption activities play a non-primary role among all commercial or professional activities conducted by active customers or non-household renewable self-consumers. Its alternative is to highlight the primary role of consumption in renewables prosumption activities and, correspondingly, the secondary role of other prosumption activities. The non-primary commercial or professional activity criterion can thus be translated into a general requirement that active customers or non-household renewable self-consumers should generate and store RES-E primarily for their own use and only sell self-generated RES-E when there is a surplus. However, Member States should fully consider the disadvantages coming with developing too concrete standards for applying this approach, as stressed above.

619. In addition to residual overlaps with the definition of 'electricity undertaking' and the difficulty in elaborating on the non-primary commercial or professional activity criteria, there is another issue worth noting. That is, the definitions of renewables self-consumers and active customers can also overlap with those of 'producer' and actors involved in electricity 'supply'. Notably, when defining 'producer', 'production' and 'supply', EU law makes no distinction between final customers that produce and sell electricity and actors for whom electricity production and supply constitute primary commercial or professional activities (*Electricity Directive*, Article 2(1)(2) and (38)). One can note that renewables self-consumers and active customers producing or selling RES-E can also constitute producers or suppliers under EU law. A significant legal consequence is that, based on definitions, one cannot conclude that active customers and renewables self-consumers generating and selling RES-E are distinct from suppliers and producers, and thus they are not subject to the existing obligations applied to producers and suppliers set out by EU law and national law. The conflation between these definitions leads to complex legal issues around the applicability of obligations for suppliers and producers, which must be solved by Member States when specifically defining the rights and obligations of renewables self-consumers and active customers. In this book, relevant legal issues and solutions are analyzed by taking the applicability of supplier obligations as an example, which can be found in Section 3.2 below.

### (ii) Relationships with Affected Incumbents

620. Another challenge encountered in supporting the right of final customers to carry out renewables self-consumption is structuring their relationship with suppliers. As explained above in Chapter III, within EU law, properly structuring their relationship aims to prevent a potential risk that suppliers who still maintain contractual relationships with these prosumers but are negatively impacted by their self-consumption place barriers with discriminatory or disproportionate procedures, charges, fees or requirements. In combination with the literature and survey by the Flemish regulator, the above review of Flemish law has explained how suppliers may be affected. Major implications include decreased retail revenues and increased imbalance risks due to consumers sharing or selling electricity. This could also be the case for suppliers in other Member States (Alonso Pedrero and Crespo del Granado, 2023). Furthermore, the impact of renewables self-consumption on suppliers may be country-specific. Additional costs can also arise if suppliers have specific obligations to support the sharing and selling of self-produced RES-E under national law, such as undertaking a separate reconciliation process under Flemish law.

621. The Flemish law case study reveals that to offset the additional costs and burdens associated with enabling renewables self-consumption, suppliers have imposed extra charges and conditions on renewables self-consumers in various forms.[573] Some of them might be disproportionate and unjustified, and restrict consumers' accessibility to renewables self-consumption. Flemish approaches to regulating suppliers' relationships with renewables self-consumers appear rather prudent to avoid overly intervening in suppliers' freedom. They seek to prevent unjustified barriers from suppliers by facilitating the switching of suppliers, secured by ensuring transparency of additional conditions or charges for consumers, coupled with general rules regulating suppliers. Being informed of charges and conditions applied by suppliers, together with the comparison tool developed by the independent regulator, consumers can switch to suppliers with offers that are comparatively conducive to renewables self-consumption. This approach is advisable in the sense that firstly it spares consumers from the demanding task of assessing whether suppliers' additional requirements are justified. Secondly, the regulator also circumvents the tricky issue of monitoring extra prices charged by suppliers. Nonetheless, the above analysis highlights that this approach hinges upon the complete transposition of EU law on switching suppliers, including the required time to cope with requests and switching-related fees. In Member States lacking actions to secure consumers' rights to switch suppliers, consumers cannot switch suppliers who impose unjustified conditions or charges with minimal costs. Moreover, not all customer groups

573 See Section 2.1.2 of this Chapter above.

are covered by the requirement prohibiting switching-related fees. This implies that they face economic losses when terminating contracts with suppliers that impose unjustified conditions or charges. Considering this, NRAs should first specifically monitor the impact of suppliers' conditions and charges on different customer groups involved in renewables self-consumption. Furthermore, a hybrid regulatory approach is recommended to safeguard consumers' entitlement to renewables self-consumption. It can combine general principles governing supply contracts with information-based approaches that harness supplier switching and comparison tools, as well as additional oversight over suppliers' conditions or charges where necessary (for instance, to protect consumers who remain subject to supplier switching fees).

### (iii) Already Fully Empowering All Consumers?

622. In implementing the EU's empowerment frameworks for active customers and renewables self-consumers, a prevalent problem is inadequate national actions to address specific barriers faced by certain customer groups in shifting to renewables self-consumers. Chapter II has elaborated on a variety of factors that lead to consumers' passive role, ranging from financial barriers to constraints of cognitive capacity and resources. It also explained that such disadvantages are reinforced in poverty and vulnerability contexts. So far, the limited cognitive capacity of energy poor or vulnerable customers remains a less-discussed obstacle in terms of ensuring the accessibility of rights and benefits associated with the low-carbon energy transition (DellaValle, 2019; Hanke et al., 2023). Tenants' involvement is limited by access to available space for generating facilities, heavily dependent on landlords, as mentioned in Chapter III. In some cases, poverty also restricts housing choices (DellaValle, 2019; Hanke et al., 2023), making some consumers subject to both tenant dependencies and scarce financial resources. The COVID-19 pandemic, combined with the energy price crisis, has exacerbated the situation of these vulnerable consumer groups.[574] There is thus a discrepancy between one category of consumers who can 'take ownership of and benefit from new technologies' and another category of consumers who are only able to do so to a lesser extent or not at all (Roggenkamp and Diestelmeier, 2020, p 175).

623. This discrepancy implies a more fine-grained way of structuring empowerment frameworks at the national level. National frameworks must contain specific instruments for consumers suffering from unique disadvantages stemming from tenancy, poverty and vulnerability to access the generic right to

[574] For instance, in 2021, about 30% of all German households had no savings or were in debt. The energy crisis increased this number to 60%. The difficult situation of poor or vulnerable consumers is also reported in other Member States. See Ceglia et al., 2022; Haji Bashi et al., 2023; Hanke et al., 2023.

become active customers or renewables self-consumers. Apparently, creating an inclusive framework that fully empowers all consumers must be underpinned by targeted measures. The design of such instruments must be based on a thorough barrier analysis, allowing for an understanding of how various disadvantages stemming from poverty and vulnerability contexts affect consumer behavior and choices, and constrain accessibility to granted rights (Hanke et al., 2023). This reflects the requirement of recognitional justice.[575] It informs rule-makers on the specificities that special instruments should have to successfully empower consumers easily marginalized, constituting the precondition for realizing distributional justice, i.e., equal access to rights to renewables self-consumption (Gajdzik et al., 2023; Hanke and Lowitzsch, 2020). Given the multiple efforts involved, merely copying the general empowerment framework at the Union level would end up leaving out these consumers.

624. The REDII identifies that low-income and vulnerable households and tenants are at high risk of being 'left behind' and stresses their accessibility to renewables self-consumption. However, few Member States have developed targeted regulatory instruments based on the above barrier analysis that identifies these customer groups' constraints, excluding them instead of empowering them (Hanke et al., 2023; Kanellou et al., 2023; Abadeço et al., 2024). In some Member States with measures to address consumers' financial barriers, existing funding instruments are only accessible to high-income earners (Abadeço et al., 2024; Hanke et al., 2023). For consumers who cannot afford the upfront investment in renewables generating installations, even with the help of support schemes, their accessibility to renewables self-consumption has not improved.[576] During the energy price crisis, such injustices are even more pronounced. Consumers successfully shifting toward renewables prosumers benefit from the rising profitability of self-consumption, while those failing to do so are subject to high energy prices.

625. The EU law's goal of leaving no one behind in the energy transition[577] is ambitious, which heavily relies on comprehensive national laws to empower consumers in various vulnerability contexts. Conversely, the national measures

575 See Chapter II for the concept of recognitional justice and its relationship with procedural and distributional justice.

576 For tenants in Germany, balcony power plants (single solar panels) are supported by VAT exemption. However, to take advantage, one needs a balcony and money for up-front costs, and, in the end, the electricity produced is marginal and results in a negative cost and benefit analysis to be a renewables self-consumer. As a result, access to renewables self-consumption is not universal and is mainly seized by higher-income households, exacerbating energy-related injustices. See Hanke et al., 2023.

577 The legislative proposal of the CEP envisages a socially fair clean energy transition wherein the transition to a clean energy system will benefit all Europeans and its transformative impacts on vulnerable members of society are taken into account. This means that all consumers – including those who are vulnerable or energy poor – should feel involved and reap the

adopted so far remain piecemeal, which is similar to a typical approach for addressing energy poverty (Hanke et al., 2023; Kanellou et al., 2023). Such a resolution has long provided short-term financial support to vulnerable and energy-poor households, while refraining from addressing the structural causes of energy vulnerability and exclusion from energy transition benefits (Hanke et al., 2023). Admittedly, the varying ability to engage in renewables self-consumption is inevitable, as it is embedded in heterogeneous socio-technical and socio-spatial contexts.[578] Despite this, national energy law failing to give due account to the inabilities or disadvantages faced by weaker consumer groups can create energy-related injustices. In some cases, beyond uneven accessibility to renewables self-consumption, such injustices are further exacerbated by unfair distribution of burdens or costs. For instance, FIT and other subsidies reserved for some renewables self-consumers in Germany are paid by all end consumers through grid tariffs (Hanke et al., 2023). Consequently, some consumers enjoy the benefits of clean, affordable RES-E, while others, especially low-income tenants, carry a disproportionate share of the burden (Schaefer, 2018; Hanke et al., 2023). It indicates that, being disregarded by energy law, weak consumer groups left behind are also at risk of falling into worse situations (Roggenkamp and Diestelmeier, 2020, p 161; Hoicka et al., 2021).

#### (iv) Active Customers' Rights to Participate in Energy Communities

626. Active customers or renewables self-consumers may face some obstacles in disposing of their energy surplus when participating in energy communities. EU law expressly provides that members or shareholders of CECs and RECs maintain their rights and obligations as final customers or active customers. This implies that within energy communities, (jointly acting) active customers do not lose their right to trade and share RES-E with members or non-members (Giarmanà, 2023; Lavrijssen et al., 2023).[579] Thus, within an energy community, there might exist an internal electricity market and, due to the limited scope, constitute a kind of LEM, namely a 'community-based LEM'.[580]

---

tangible benefits of the sustainable energy transition. See EC, 2016a, 2016b, *European Climate Law*, 2021, recital 2.

578 The ability to offer flexibility is determined by, and embedded in, the combination of a wide variety of social-technical factors, including working patterns and elements of social practices. The same reasoning applies to the ability to engage in renewables self-consumption projects. See Powells and Fell, 2019.

579 The right to energy sharing has been granted to active customers in the 2024 Amendment to the Electricity Directive.

580 Many publications view the LEM as a promising approach to trading or sharing electricity in energy communities. See e.g. Weinhardt et al., 2019; Faia et al., 2021, p 127; Capper et al., 2022.

In this context, energy communities and their members, who constitute renewables self-consumers or active customers, likely compete to offer electricity to other members. Conflicts of interest between them give energy communities incentives to restrict or hinder trading or sharing conducted by members. Energy communities are notably well-placed to do so when they are empowered by national law to operate the distribution grid while only bound by legal unbundling. They can discriminate against members selling or sharing self-produced RES-E by hampering access to the community grid and favoring their affiliates involved in generation and supply activities.[581] Discrimination concerns can be even more pronounced when small-scale energy communities are exempted from unbundling requirements in accordance with EU law.[582] Moreover, if energy communities own or operate market platforms for community-based LEMs, they cannot ensure neutrality in market clearing.

627. Such risks stemming from the competitive relationship between energy communities and consumer members have not received sufficient attention or even been completely overlooked. This is exemplified by some LEM models, which view energy communities as suitable actors to perform the role of market operators of community-based LEMs (REScoop.eu and ClientEarth, 2020; Tushar et al., 2021). Austrian law represents an example of national law that overlooks the need to address potential disadvantages and risks faced by renewables self-consumers or active customers involved in energy communities, thereby exacerbating these risks. It empowers energy communities to control and operate generation units privately owned by their members or shareholders (*Electricity Industry and Organization Act*, §16d(5); Fina and Monsberger, 2022). There is a risk that energy communities can additionally exploit this right to restrict or prevent local trading among their members or shareholders. It is argued that the energy communities' control over members' generation assets serves a fast and simple energy community roll-out (Fina and Fechner, 2021; Fina and Monsberger, 2022). However, the legislation fails to safeguard the rights of renewables prosumers to trade electricity within energy communities.

628. Interactions between energy communities and participating prosumers are becoming increasingly complex as microgrids and LEMs are embedded within energy communities. Member States should take into account their

---

581 Discriminatory behavior mainly includes (i) discriminating against non-affiliated actors in network access, products and market rules definition, offer selection and market clearing, (ii) offering information only to their affiliates engaged in generation and flexibility provision or providing information to them earlier than to competitors, and (iii) strategically withholding network investment to benefit affiliates owning assets offering electricity and flexibility. See Buchmann, 2020; Cabau and Sandberg, 2021, p 114; Rebenaque et al., 2023.

582 Article 35 (4) of the Electricity Directive allows Member States to exempt VIUs that serve less than 100,000 connected customers or small isolated systems from unbundling requirements.

evolving interactions and potential hurdles faced by active customers or renewables self-consumers to share and trade RES-E. Both EU law and national law should pay attention to potential conflicts between respective frameworks for active customers, renewables self-consumers, and energy communities.

#### 3.1.2.2. Energy Communities

629. So far, the development of energy communities is characterized by an imbalance between North-western and, on the other hand, Southern, Eastern, and South-eastern EU Member States (Diestelmeier, 2021, p 124; Palm, 2021; Musolino et al., 2023). This is partially attributed to the fact that, traditionally, most energy communities in the EU are active in North-western Member States, especially Germany, Denmark, and the Netherlands, mainly in the form of renewables cooperatives (Diestelmeier, 2021, p 124; Palm, 2021; Musolino et al., 2023). In comparison, other Member States have limited experience in engaging consumers in renewables self-consumption via energy communities (Diestelmeier, 2021, p 124; Palm, 2021; Musolino et al., 2023). This situation does not necessarily mean that those front-runners have aligned their previous national law for community energy initiatives with existing EU law (REScoop.eu, 2024a). The transposition process in Germany and the Netherlands started comparatively late and was slow, generally exhibiting low-to-average transposition delays (Krug et al., 2023).

630. As set out in Chapter III, supranational frameworks for empowering CECs and RECs stand on three pillars: (i) eligibility criteria, (ii) entitlement to energy activities, and (iii) enabling frameworks addressing barriers. Empowering energy communities to carry out DR and renewables self-consumption faces a common challenge of implementing EU-level eligibility requirements, which will be discussed separately in Section 3.1.3 below. This subsection focuses on major legal issues of entitling and enabling energy communities to carry out renewables self-consumption.

##### (i) Entitlement to Energy Activities

631. Among the rights granted by EU law, those concerning electricity sharing notably pose legal challenges. National transpositions in some Member States, such as Germany, are delayed by definitional issues around electricity sharing (Krug et al., 2023; Lavrijssen et al., 2023). Considering this, legal issues involved in implementing electricity sharing are the major focus here.

632. First, the lack of a clear definition of electricity sharing in national law can lead to legal uncertainties over the rights and obligations of energy communities and members. Before the Electricity Directive was amended in 2024, EU law did not define energy sharing. The 2024 Amendment to the

Electricity Directive defines energy sharing as '*the self-consumption by active customers of renewable energy either: (a) generated or stored offsite or on sites between them by a facility they own, lease or rent in whole or in part; or (b) the right to which has been transferred to them by another active customer for a price or free of charge*.' This definition is limited to energy sharing conducted by active customers. A problem, however, arises as to whether this definition can also apply to energy sharing within energy communities. Article 16(3)(d) of the Electricity Directive indeed specifies that Member States must ensure that '*with regard to consumption of self-generated electricity, citizen energy communities are treated like active customers in accordance with point (e) of Article 15(2)*.' Yet, this provision refers to Article 15(2)(e), which establishes the general requirements governing network charges for the consumption of self-produced electricity, including the separate accounting of electricity fed into and consumed from the grid. It does not mean that with regard to the consumption of self-generated electricity, including electricity sharing, CECs are treated like active customers. Thus, one cannot employ Article 16(3)(d) of the Electricity Directive as a basis for applying the above newly established definition of energy sharing to energy communities. As such, defining energy sharing within energy communities remains a question for Member States.

633. A key issue that Member States must address is clarifying whether energy sharing is considered the sale of electricity. The answer to this question determines whether energy communities sharing electricity constitute suppliers and then apply supplier obligations.

634. If national law, like Flemish law, defines energy sharing as a free exchange of energy, energy communities are not classified as suppliers. As a result, supplier obligations are not applicable. One may doubt this conclusion by employing an EU-level general requirement that consumers participating in energy communities maintain their rights and obligations as final customers. It has been addressed in Section 2 of this Chapter that this general requirement should be understood as consumers do not lose their rights and obligations as final customers, which are established in their specific relationships with suppliers, system operators, flexibility service providers and other market actors. Hence, the participating consumers' rights are determined by their relationship with the energy community, which engages in supply, distribution grid operation and flexibility trading activities. Once electricity sharing is not defined as supply (i.e., the sale of electricity), energy communities that share electricity are not considered to be conducting supply activities. There is no supplier-to-consumer relationship between energy communities and members receiving shared RES-E. Consumer rights stemming from legal regimes governing this relationship are thus not applicable. Correspondingly, the associated obligations imposed on suppliers do not apply to energy communities in this case. The EU-level requirement that energy sharing is 'subject to the community members

retaining their rights and obligations as final customers' can be interpreted as meaning that final customers retain their supply contracts even while participating in energy sharing.

635. Nevertheless, the absence of supplier obligations does not mean that energy communities would not have any obligations toward consumers receiving shared RES-E. In addition to those stemming from electricity sharing agreements, Member States can consider introducing minimum interventions to protect individual consumers involved and ensure the quality of service provided by energy communities. For instance, as mentioned above in Section 2.1.2.3 of this Chapter, Flemish law creates flexibility for such obligations by empowering the government to take measures where necessary. Given that individual consumers may also suffer from the asymmetry of information or bargaining power vis-à-vis energy communities, this arrangement is justified.

636. In comparison, more complex legal issues arise if national law defines electricity sharing as a type of energy transaction, where energy communities and members mutually agree on the price or remuneration for the shared RES-E. In this case, electricity sharing is considered a form of supply. Yet, it is highly contestable whether supplier obligations therefore apply to energy communities, and if so, to what extent such obligations should be applied.[583] As mentioned in the Belgian case study above, the principles of non-discrimination and proportionality are highly relevant to addressing this legal issue. Section 3.2.3.3 below will specifically discuss the applicability of supplier obligations when energy community activities (including electricity sharing and selling electricity to non-members) are classified as electricity supply.[584]

637. In addition to determining the obligations of energy communities when sharing electricity, another legal issue concerns the way EU law specifies the rights of energy communities to share electricity. Article 16(3)(e) of the Electricity Directive and Article 22(2)(b) of the REDII state that CECs and RESs are entitled to share electricity that is produced by the production units owned by the communities. During national transposition, a strict textual interpretation of these two provisions is likely, i.e., potentially treating community ownership of production units as a prerequisite for granting the right to electricity sharing (Giarmanà, 2023). Moreover, within energy communities, aside from production assets, storage facilities might also be used to support electricity sharing. If read literally, this possibility is not incorporated in the above legal provisions that grant the right to electricity sharing. It is unclear whether EU law

583 For divergent perspectives in national decision-making, see e.g. van Soest, 2018; CRU, 2021b; Almeida et al., 2021.

584 This will be discussed in Section 3.2 below since it concerns the determination of energy communities' obligations in electricity trading, i.e., market participation.

is meant to limit assets used for electricity sharing to production units. If Member States replicate the text of EU law, energy communities face uncertainties. Or even worse, some Member States may adopt a narrow interpretation of EU law's wording. They may exclude the possibility of sharing production units' property rights with non-member investors and leasing or renting relevant renewable energy assets (Oberthur et al., 2020). Consequently, non-member investors would be prevented from investing in renewable energy production assets for electricity sharing, which is unfavorable to addressing the barriers that energy communities face in accessing finance. The limited involvement of third-party investment in turn contributes to high minimum investment thresholds, which obstruct the inclusive engagement of low-income or vulnerable consumers, as explained in Section 3.1.3 below. Another risk is excluding the use of storage facilities to exercise this right.

638. Some national legislation changes the wording of EU law to avoid the above legal uncertainties. For instance, the Flemish law entitles CECs to share electricity produced within the energy community without making specific reference to the type of assets for this purpose and the community's ownership (*Flemish Energy Decree*, arts. 4.8.4 and 7.2.1). By contrast, the REC must have ownership rights to the installations it uses to carry out electricity sharing and other energy activities (*Flemish Energy Decree*, art. 4.8.2, §1). Walloon law adopts a different way to reinforce the legal certainty of the entitlement to electricity sharing. As one of the conditions that must be met by electricity sharing within an energy community, the electricity shared should be *produced either by the installations the energy community owns or by the installations over which it has a right of use that can give it the status of producer, or either by the self-generating installations of its members injected into the network and distributed among its participants* (*Walloon Electricity Decree*, art. 35quaterdecies, §1). With this clarification, energy communities can engage non-member investors to develop RES-E production installations and also rent them. Their financial burdens of raising capital can decrease, which is conducive to lowering the energy communities' financial contributions required from members or shareholders and facilitating open participation. A remaining problem, however, is that Walloon law expressly limits installations eligible for electricity sharing to production assets, neglecting storage facilities. This can undermine the implementation of the energy communities' right to share RES-E, especially given the intermittent nature of most renewables used by energy communities.

639. Considering the room for interpretation and the impact on energy communities' economic viability and participation thresholds, the EU legislator should clarify whether electricity generated by production units owned by energy communities is a prerequisite for granting energy communities the right to share electricity. The recent Amendments to the REDII and the Electricity Directive do not solve this problem.

640. One may argue that excluding the possibility of sharing ownership of facilities with third parties and renting renewables assets aims to improve energy communities' autonomy from third parties while avoiding the latter's market logic jeopardizing the delivery of community benefits.[585] The REScoop.eu expresses concerns in this regard that allowing renewables projects owned by third parties will facilitate passive RECs that are mainly driven by professional market actors (REScoop.eu, 2024b). However, EU law has already taken steps to protect energy communities from potential abuse by third parties. These include not granting third parties effective control, requiring RECs to be autonomous, and constraining financial profit-making, as detailed in Chapter III above. The key to avoiding third parties taking advantage of energy communities lies in implementing robust measures to comply with relevant EU-level restrictions. Given this, additional restrictions imposed on third parties cooperating with energy communities to develop assets for sharing RES-E, either through investment or lease, are redundant. They could also unduly restrict energy communities' access to key resources and infrastructure. Moreover, EU law is not intended to prohibit energy communities from cooperating with third parties. This is indicated by recital 71 of the REDII, which stresses that RECs should be autonomous from not only members but also third-party actors, including investors. On these grounds, both the Electricity Directive and the REDII should eliminate redundant elements in provisions defining the entitlement of energy communities to share electricity.

641. Lastly, the 2024 Amendment to the Electricity Directive introduced Article 15a to mainly address active customers' right to energy sharing. Yet, some of the arrangements contained by that legal provision can also be applied to energy sharing within energy communities. For instance, Article 15a(3) specifies the potential roles of a third-party energy sharing organizer that can be appointed by active customers. As indicated by the Flemish case study, a third-party organization that facilitates energy sharing and communicates with other stakeholders can also play a key role in facilitating energy sharing within energy communities, especially those lacking technical expertise. Article 15a(s) could thus provide guidance for enabling energy sharing within energy communities. The newly introduced definition of energy sharing and Article 15a should be restructured to cover energy sharing within energy communities, as they address some common issues equally faced by the latter.

585 The market logic emphasizes the motivation of financial gains and efficiency through the selling of goods and services. When third parties cooperating with energy communities are commercial actors, they may use energy communities to make profits rather than providing economic, environmental or social benefits. For more details about the market logic, see Dudka et al., 2023. Regarding how to ensure that energy communities give priority to providing community benefits rather than profit-making, see Section 3.1.3.1 below of this Chapter.

### (ii) Enabling Frameworks

642. As explained in Chapter III, technical and administrative capacity and financial resources are key prerequisites for energy communities to exercise the rights to renewables prosuming. The Electricity Directive does not require Member States to take measures to facilitate the CEC's capacity and access to finance, while these are critical elements that national enabling frameworks must address under the REDII. So far, aside from some large-scale energy communities initiated top-down through local governments, most energy communities continue to face barriers due to limited resources and capacity (Haji Bashi et al., 2023; Krug et al., 2023). Aside from the delayed national implementation of EU-level requirements regarding financing and capacity building, the EU law's approach to addressing capacity issues of RECs is also worth reflecting on. Legal issues in these two aspects are examined consecutively below.

643. Energy communities' options for accessing finance can be broadly classified into two categories: self-investment and third-party investment (Li and Okur, 2023). Self-investment-based RECs are financed through members' contributions, while they are easily challenged to raise sufficient finance (Candelise and Ruggieri, 2020). It should be highlighted that, in large part, the REC's difficulty in accessing finance stems from its specificities, shaped by eligibility requirements under the REDII. First, the REC's membership is not open to large companies. Nor is its membership open to private SMEs whose participation in the REC constitutes primary commercial or professional activity. This restriction can be translated into national law that limits the amount of resources, including capital, devoted by private companies, as will be explained in Section 3.1.3.2. Moreover, the REDII prescribes that the REC must be effectively controlled by members or shareholders located in the proximity of its renewable energy projects. It can also affect the pool of interested investors since non-local members or shareholders have limited decision-making power in distributing community benefits or financial profits. Despite the possibility of third-party investment, this approach is not easy to access. The REDII requires the REC to be autonomous from traditional market actors cooperating with it through investment. Within national law, this requirement can be translated into restrictions on the size of external financing from traditional undertakings.[586]

644. Given the RECs' disadvantages in raising capital, specific actions to promote their access to finance are instrumental to ensuring the economic

[586] This aims to prevent a risk that non-member investors or partner companies – even an investor member with no decision-making rights – because of the size of the investment, place the economic and financial autonomy of the REC at stake. See REScoop.eu and ClientEarth, 2020.

viability of the RECs established according to the REDII's requirements. Along with national support schemes, EU law requires national enabling frameworks to provide tools to facilitate the REC's access to finance. National rules making available such financing tools, serving as relatively long-term solutions for addressing the REC's financial barriers, remain absent in 16 Member States (Krug et al., 2023).[587]

645. Member States can either develop novel financing instruments, such as revolving funds in Germany and the Netherlands (REScoop.eu, 2024c, 2024d), or enable the REC's access to existing financing tools, such as social lending or crowdfunding.[588] With the latter approach, Member States can apply existing national and EU law concerning the use of general financing tools[589] to the REC. In this sense, compared to the former approach, the latter can be more viable to fill the transposition gap in improving the REC's access to financing tools.

646. Nonetheless, RECs may still face difficulty in applying existing financing instruments. An assessment of REC's accessibility to existing financing tools is needed to identify barriers or disadvantages that deter energy communities from

---

[587] At the time of writing (February 2024), only Austria, the Brussels Region and the Walloon Region of Belgium, Denmark, Germany, Greece, Ireland, Italy, Lithuania, the Netherlands, Portugal, and Spain have taken specific measures to provide energy communities with financing tools. See REScoop.eu, Transposition tracker – Enabling Frameworks & Support Schemes – Austria, available at <https://www.rescoop.eu/policy/austria>, accessed 7 February 2024; REScoop.eu, Transposition tracker – Enabling Frameworks & Support Schemes – Belgium (Brussels), available at <https://www.rescoop.eu/policy/belgium-brussels>, accessed 7 February 2024; REScoop.eu, Transposition tracker – Enabling Frameworks & Support Schemes – Belgium (Wallonia), available at <https://www.rescoop.eu/policy/belgium-wallonia-2>, accessed 7 February 2024; REScoop.eu, Transposition tracker – Enabling Frameworks & Support Schemes – Denmark, available at <https://www.rescoop.eu/policy/denmark>, accessed 7 February 2024; REScoop.eu, Transposition tracker – Enabling Frameworks & Support Schemes – Germany, available at <https://www.rescoop.eu/policy/germany-2>, accessed 7 February 2024; REScoop.eu, Transposition tracker – Enabling Frameworks & Support Schemes – Greece, available at <https://www.rescoop.eu/policy/greece>, accessed 7 February 2024; REScoop.eu, Transposition tracker – Enabling Frameworks & Support Schemes – Ireland, available at <https://www.rescoop.eu/policy/ireland>, accessed 7 February 2024; REScoop.eu, Transposition tracker – Enabling Frameworks & Support Schemes – Italy, available at <https://www.rescoop.eu/policy/italy>, accessed 7 February 2024; REScoop.eu, Transposition tracker – Enabling Frameworks & Support Schemes – Lithuania, available at <https://www.rescoop.eu/policy/lithuania-2>, accessed 7 February 2024; REScoop.eu, Transposition tracker – Enabling Frameworks & Support Schemes – The Netherlands, available at <https://www.rescoop.eu/policy/netherlands>, accessed 7 February 2024; REScoop.eu, Transposition tracker – Enabling Frameworks & Support Schemes – Portugal, available at <https://www.rescoop.eu/policy/portugal>, accessed 7 February 2024; REScoop.eu, Transposition tracker – Enabling Frameworks & Support Schemes – Spain, available at <https://www.rescoop.eu/policy/spain>, accessed 7 February 2024.

[588] This model has the advantage of being able to reach a larger pool of potential investors and thus mobilize a larger amount of equity compared with models that do not rely on an online platform. See Dudka et al., 2023.

[589] See e.g., *Regulation (EU) 2020/1503*, 2020.

using available financing tools, with a specific focus on those stemming from their specificities shaped by EU law's requirements. This assessment could reveal whether existing rules governing financing tools are sufficient or if there is a need to adapt them to promote RECs' access to these general tools.

647. As exemplified by the French case, possible adaptations include specifying the role and obligations of intermediaries or trusted third parties operating relevant financial platforms. Even though many private crowdfunding platforms exist, one actor, *Energie Partagée Investissement*, assumes the central role of helping energy communities organize crowd-equity-raising campaigns and manage the distribution of dividends to investors (Vernay and Sebi, 2020). There is a need for a specific crowdfunding platform, given the complex tasks of representing heterogeneous crowdfunding investors who are directly or indirectly involved in the decision-making or governance of the REC. Generally, the tasks of crowdfunding platforms not only include ensuring investors a follow-up of project developments, but also creating physical and virtual spaces for them to express their expectations (Dudka et al., 2023). The latter task may imply a degree of influence on the RES-E developer's decisions on behalf of numerous investors, although such influence may vary with crowdfunding models and is relatively limited compared to traditional financing, such as venture capital. Compared to commercial renewables projects, this task is more complex in the REC context. Crowdfunding investors may have divergent relationships with the REC and be subject to different restrictions. Some are eligible to be members of the REC in accordance with the REDII, e.g., residential consumers near the renewables project, while others are not eligible for effective control or even membership. For those investors ineligible to be members, their influence on the REC's decision-making is limited by national rules safeguarding the autonomous nature of the REC. The different rights and influences of these investors can complicate the crowdfunding platform's task of communicating the expectations of investors and participating in decision-making regarding the allocation of proceeds.

648. Overall, potential misalignment between prevailing crowdfunding models and the REC's governance framework or needs can be a key factor deterring their accessibility to RECs. Similar problems may arise when RECs utilize other established financing approaches. Hence, in the event that Member States decide not to develop new financing tools, it is vital to assist energy communities in addressing the challenges they encounter when applying existing financing instruments.

649. In addition to obstacles to accessing finance, energy communities can also suffer from a lack of capacity and skills. As shown in Chapter III, the REDII does not require Member States to provide capacity-building support to RECs but to public authorities. Regulatory and capacity-building support should

be provided to public authorities in two aspects: (1) enabling and setting up RECs, and (2) helping authorities to participate in RECs directly. Admittedly, the public authorities' ability to enable RECs should be reinforced, considering that there are several difficulties encountered by local authorities when they want to support RECs (REScoop.eu and ClientEarth, 2020). However, stressing public authorities' direct participation in RECs is likely to raise concerns about fairness.

650. Indeed, public authorities' direct participation can significantly enhance the viability of RECs, as public resources are devoted to the relevant RECs. Such input includes providing additional funding and assets to develop the initiative (e.g., public building rooftops), motivating and involving wider participants (especially those with expertise), and communicating and spreading knowledge (Candelise and Ruggieri, 2020; Musolino et al., 2023). More importantly, once become members or shareholders of energy communities, public authorities can have strong incentives to improve required bureaucratic procedures and even create favorable financing conditions to allow them (Candelise and Ruggieri, 2020; Musolino et al., 2023). However, such tangible benefits become problematic if public authorities do not participate in RECs equally, which leads to unfair distribution of public resources or support. An empirical study presenting comprehensive evidence on energy communities' developments in Italy shows that among 17 energy communities, only 5 have municipalities involved as members or shareholders (Candelise and Ruggieri, 2020). In this case, RECs with public authorities involved can have additional advantages compared to those without direct participation by authorities, especially in terms of capital resources and administrative services. Such advantages can undermine fairness and frustrate the level playing field, notably given that bureaucratic problems and a lack of capital remain major barriers that can cause energy communities to fail (Haji Bashi et al., 2023; Krug et al., 2023). Discriminatory treatment arising from uneven participation of public authorities has also been identified in Italy. When a local authority does not take part in the REC, it could play (at least partially) the role of a barrier (Musolino et al., 2023) or even have fewer incentives to improve the required bureaucratic procedures.

651. Overall, the REDII's requirement for supporting public authorities' direct participation in RECs carries a risk of unfair distribution of public resources among RECs and discriminatory treatment. As shown above, the direct participation of authorities at the regional or local level can bring RECs tangible benefits and some favorable conditions, which may constitute national support or state aid. This is especially the case when the REDII's requirement is fully transposed and public authorities are well equipped to provide comprehensive support to meet RECs' technical, financial and bureaucratic needs. However, in practice, authorities seem to decide their participation arbitrarily,

and the allocation of public support involved in such participation is not subject to existing rules governing national support and state aid or objective criteria. To date, this issue has not received sufficient attention in national transpositions. To address this, national law should provide authorities with capacity-building support, along with objective criteria for determining which RECs are in most need of capacity support, and ensure that public authorities participate in those RECs in a non-discriminatory manner.

652. Aside from advice for national transpositions, there is also room for improving the existing EU-level approach to addressing RECs' capacity issues. In fact, in terms of facilitating the capacity and viability of energy communities, providing capacity support at the community level represents a better alternative to supporting them through the authorities' direct participation. Doing so makes existing rules governing support schemes and state aid applicable to various capacity-building support made available for RECs, helping to avoid the above risk of discrimination and distorting competition.

653. EU law can replace the existing provision that enables public authorities to directly participate, with the general requirement of providing capacity-building support for RECs. In this way, greater flexibility could be created for Member States to choose suitable approaches. Examples of available approaches adopted in Member States are listed below:

- Appointing a specific authority (e.g., the SEAI in Ireland) responsible for creating capacity-building tools[590] or networking;[591]

---

590 After the CEP, the SEAI has developed a particular capacity-building framework to offer detailed guidance to energy communities to enhance their expertise and access to information about the electricity sector. For the sake of offering elaborate and practical guidance, this framework takes the form of soft law. It consists of four documents offering toolkits to energy communities in terms of onshore wind, solar PV, planning and grid connection. Within the guidelines for solar PV and onshore wind, the capacity fostered in project development and delivery is manifold, including technology options, business planning, project development stages and good governance. The guidance is provided in phases, ranging from designing project initiatives, pre-planning, how to access financing, and applying for grid connection and planning permits, to construction and decommissioning. The other two guidelines particularly deal with challenges associated with planning and grid connection, further aggregating detailed and crucial information on respective regimes and how to engage with competent authorities and system operators. For instance, with the grid connection guidelines, energy communities are provided with information and knowledge concerning, for instance, the introduction of the Irish electricity system, connection methods, what constitutes connection costs and network charges, and curtailment. See SEAI, 2021a, 2021b, 2024a, 2024b.

591 The SEAI had started developing the SEC network for developing technical and project management skills of energy communities before the CEP. By registering as an SEC, an energy community could join the nationwide capacity-building network and have access to a wealth of useful community-focused energy-related materials, knowledge and support. See

- Financing independent associations (e.g., Energie Partagée Association and Enercoop in France) with public funds to create a supporting ecosystem for energy communities, whose functions cover, inter alia, technical and operational support as well as knowledge-sharing and networking;[592]
- Granting dedicated grants to address energy communities' capacity issues with national support schemes. For instance, under the Irish national support schemes, the Renewable Electricity Support Scheme, among others, eligible RECs are entitled to receive grants for the cost of professional advice covering all aspects of project delivery (legal, financial and technical) (*State Aid SA.54683*, 2020, Section 2.4). This enables RECs to seek assistance from trusted advisors and intermediaries.

654. The first two approaches serve the same goal of creating an encompassing supportive ecosystem that benefits all energy communities in a given country. They avoid the risk of unequal distribution of public support mentioned above. The EU legislator should grant Member States leeway to decide who is responsible for developing or initiating such supporting ecosystems and whether a diversity of actors will be involved in their development. It should be noted that public authorities are not necessarily the sole key facilitators who can enable the setup and operation of energy communities. For instance, in the Netherlands, beyond public authorities and independent associations, various actors, including large energy incumbents,[593] also compete to provide energy communities with the complementary assets they need (Vernay and Sebi, 2020). Energy communities can benefit more from the supporting ecosystem with diverse input from the public and private sectors. The proactive role of traditional energy companies in the Dutch supportive ecosystem for energy communities challenges a prevailing conception that enabling frameworks should seek to empower energy communities to become autonomous and compete with energy incumbents (Vernay and Sebi, 2020). Existing EU law empowering energy communities appears to build on this notion, which, however, may be subject to change as interactions between energy incumbents and energy communities evolve. Considering the potential that these actors may complement one another in creating value by forming a more symbiotic relationship, capacity-building supporting ecosystems should be open to heterogeneous actors (Vernay and Sebi, 2020).

---

SEAI, 2021a, 2024a. See also <https://www.seai.ie/community-energy/sustainable-energy-communities/> accessed 2 April 2023.

592 Energy community ecosystems include a variety of supporting organizations. The empirical data show that they fulfill four categories of functions: 1) lobbying, 2) networking and knowledge-sharing, 3) technical and commercial support, and 4) financial support. See Vernay and Sebi, 2020.

593 Cooperating with energy communities has become key for energy companies to secure access to local renewable energy production and protect their market shares. See de Bakker et al., 2020; Vernay and Sebi, 2020.

655. The last approach provides capacity support for energy communities with national support schemes. Granting such support is subject to EU law and regulations governing national support schemes and state aid, helping ensure their legality, notably in terms of proportionality, non-discrimination and market compatibility. For instance, in the Irish case, the Renewable Electricity Support Scheme providing such support constitutes state aid and is subject to the EC's assessment under the Guidelines on State Aid for Energy and Environment (*State Aid SA.54683*, 2020, Section 3.3). Hence, allowing Member States to provide capacity support to energy communities via national support schemes is also a better alternative to the existing way of directly engaging public authorities. Member States could also consider combining the first two approaches with the last one, as Ireland has done.

656. To sum up, highlighting the direct participation of public authorities is not the most suitable way of addressing RECs' capacity issues. Given the presence of multiple alternatives, it is plausible to allow Member States to choose specific approaches to reinforcing the capacity of communities. To this end, the REDII should only require Member States to facilitate energy communities' capacity-building without imposing an additional obligation to adopt a specific approach.

### *3.1.3. A Common Challenge of Empowering Energy Communities*

657. EU law empowers the CEC and the REC to enhance consumers' participation in DR and self-consumption of RES-E (*Electricity Directive*, recital 43). However, a precondition for harnessing the community-based approach is fulfilling the eligibility criteria for being such two energy communities, as addressed in Chapter III. The eligibility requirements cover three dimensions: objectives, membership, and operation (i.e., decision-making), distinguishing these two energy communities from traditional energy undertakings. They also serve as justifications for granting rights (e.g., electricity sharing), support, and even possible different or simplified regulatory treatments to energy communities (*REDII*, recital 71). Failing to ensure compliance with such eligibility requirements could lead to abuse of the concept of CECs and RECs (REScoop.eu and ClientEarth, 2020) while frustrating the energy communities' potential to facilitate DR and the use of RES-E. This concern indeed arises in ongoing national transpositions.

658. As shown in Chapter III, most of the eligibility criteria are not specified in dedicated legal provisions that empower these two energy communities, but rather in their definitions. Furthermore, such requirements are broadly worded and open to interpretation, in order to create flexibility and respect Member States' energy competences. To mitigate the risk of abusing these concepts, when empowering the CEC and the REC, national law must first

elaborate on the general eligibility requirements contained in the definitions, making them clear enough to comply with and monitor. As drawn out below, doing so requires a set of legal arrangements dedicated to addressing the eligibility of energy communities and their oversight. In most cases, national legislators may develop legal frameworks based on EU-level definitions (e.g., independent aggregators) without adding further specifications to those definitions. This approach, however, is not suitable for transposing EU law on the CEC and the REC due to the multiple general principles embedded in their definitions. Seen from ongoing transpositions, Member States either fail to realize the need for dedicated efforts to transpose energy communities' definitions or do not take adequate measures.[594]

659. A prevalent problem is that only several eligibility requirements have been further detailed, while others are transposed by simply replicating the wording of EU-level definitions (Palm, 2021; Fina and Monsberger, 2022; Krug et al., 2023).[595] In particular, Eastern EU Member States' transpositions are either lacking or rather weak (Haji Bashi et al., 2023; Krug et al., 2023; REScoop.eu, 2024e). Consequently, energy communities that fit the EU law's definitions are still a marginal phenomenon in these Member States (Krug et al., 2023). Their indifferent attitude toward developing energy communities can be explained by the negative connotations associated with cooperatives and other forms of collective ownership during the socialist period (Krug et al., 2023). This situation highlights that without properly structuring the energy communities' relationship with their members, the community-based approach to engaging consumers might not be widely adopted in Eastern Europe. Lessons drawn from the approaches of other Member States in elaborating relevant governance requirements can be beneficial for Eastern EU Member States.

660. This section examines the legal issues associated with implementing the above three dimensions of eligibility criteria, along with preliminary legal

---

594 The REScoop.eu provides a transposition tracker that assesses the progress of national transposition of the definitions of CECs and RECs, utilizing a traffic light grading system. According to the most recent data at the time of writing (Feb 2024), only Belgium (the Flemish Region, the Walloon Region and the Brussels Region), Denmark, France, Ireland and Italy are graded with green, representing 'good practice' and being pioneering countries of transposing elements contained in definitions of CECs and RECs. 11 Member States still have 'substantial deficiencies' in terms of transposition, including Austria, Bulgaria, Croatia, Estonia, Finland, Hungary, Luxembourg, Malta, Portugal, Romania, Slovakia. 8 Member States have average progress, which are Cyprus, Germany, Greece, Latvia, Lithuania, Slovenia, Spain, and the Netherlands. In the Czech Republic and Sweden, the legislation that touches upon energy communities has not entered into force. See REScoop.eu, Transposition tracker – Definitions, available at <https://www.rescoop.eu/transposition-tracker> accessed 9 February 2024.

595 It is also the case in Belgium, as shown above in Section 2 of this Chapter.

advice to address them. As revealed in the Flemish law case study in Section 2 above, apart from detailed rules for implementing such eligibility requirements, ensuring their compliance after the establishment of energy communities is equally important. Monitoring compliance with eligibility criteria constitutes another pillar of accomplishing energy community empowerment at the national level. This section thus ends with a discussion of regulatory approaches to monitoring energy communities' compliance with eligibility requirements.

3.1.3.1. Primary Purpose

661. The EU law's requirements for the primary purpose of CECs and RECs primarily concern the provision of community benefits, accompanied by a restriction on profit-making. At the initial stage of transposing the CEP, national legislators were suggested to pay special attention to concretizing the concept of three categories of community benefits for better monitoring their compliance (REScoop.eu and ClientEarth, 2020; Diestelmeier, 2021, pp 138–140). The key legal issue is how to identify, measure, and evaluate the provision of community benefits and whether energy communities primarily aim to offer members community benefits rather than financial profits (REScoop.eu and ClientEarth, 2020; Diestelmeier, 2021, p 139; Almeida et al., 2021). Without addressing this issue in national law, there would be a risk that the EU law's ambition to facilitate community benefits remains futile and a hollow concept (Diestelmeier, 2021, p 140). So far, at the national level, the acute legal challenge of lacking transparency in the choice and achievement of three community benefits persists (Diestelmeier, 2021, p 139; Diestelmeier et al., 2023). Based on feedback from the Flemish regulator, the Belgian case study highlighted legal issues arising from the absence of clear definitions of community benefits and detailed criteria for assessing compliance. The REScoop.eu's data show that by February 2024, no Member States have elaborated on three community benefits, while Ireland is the only exception that defines 'societal benefits' (REScoop.eu, 2024f). The existing literature has not provided solutions for defining and implementing community benefits either. This subsection further explores the legal issues involved in materializing the concept of community benefits and assessing the compliance of energy communities. By doing so, it indicates regulatory approaches to further the implementation of community benefits in national law.

662. A review of emerging empirical evidence of energy communities across the EU indicates that the major legal challenge lies in defining 'economic benefits' and dealing with their potential overlaps with 'financial profits'. It is generally straightforward to identify environmental and social benefits, which can be easily distinguished from financial profits. For instance, increasing awareness

about environmental and energy issues, as well as promoting more sustainable lifestyles, can be considered a means of providing environmental benefits.[596] Those engaged in wider community development schemes (e.g., information campaigns or awareness-raising activities to support the use of RES-E) or even wider services (e.g., discounted insurance, banking, internet provision)[597] can be considered to serve environmental and social community benefits. As can be seen from these examples, environmental and social benefits can take diverse forms in practice. When energy communities engage in providing social benefits to the local community beyond their members and shareholders, relevant activities can go far beyond the energy field. Plenty of room should be given to energy communities to create social or environmental benefits when national law seeks to further specify what constitutes such two benefits. This reduces the need for very clearly articulating their connotations within national law. However, a lack of clarification of economic benefits is problematic and notably makes it difficult to prevent CECs and RECs from prioritizing financial profit-making.

663. Economic benefits provided by energy communities typically include returns on investment offered, investments in public infrastructure, and reduced electricity bills (Candelise and Ruggieri, 2020). Returns on investment to members can be provided by sharing RES-E produced by the production units owned or controlled by energy communities, as noted above (Almeida et al., 2021). They also encompass monetary revenues or surpluses generated by energy communities' commercial activities, such as providing energy services (e.g., electricity supply, flexibility, and charging services) for non-members (REScoop.eu and ClientEarth, 2020). One may find that in this case, the financial profits made by energy communities can easily be converted into economic benefits offered to members or shareholders. Energy communities could justify their motive of maximizing financial profits by asserting that these profits are used to offer their members returns on investment and thereby fulfill economic benefits. This possibility explains the reason underlying the difficulty in assessing whether the profit motive of energy communities is subordinate to their primary purpose of providing community benefits. Such difficulty does not simply stem from the fact mentioned by the Flemish regulator that energy communities are also allowed to engage in commercial activities.[598]

---

596 Two RECs called *CommON Light* and *Comunita Energetica e Solidale* in Italy are examples. See Musolino et al., 2023.

597 An example is the REC *Retenergie* in Italy, which redistributes revenues from investments in renewable generation projects across a wider set of activities, including those that do not generate monetary but social benefits for their members. See Candelise and Ruggieri, 2020.

598 See Section 2.1.3 above of this Chapter.

664. Considering that financial profits can translate into economic benefits, the key solution to curbing the profit motive of energy communities is to impose restrictions on the monetary returns distributed to their members or shareholders. Profits distributed to fulfill economic benefits should be limited to 50% of the total margins. At the same time, more than 50% of the total margins must be used to provide environmental or social benefits or other non-monetary economic benefits (such as services related to electricity sharing and energy infrastructure operation). Using this threshold ensures that energy communities are not oriented toward providing financial profits for members or shareholders, but rather aim to provide community benefits required by EU law. In this way, national law could prevent energy communities from falling into a profit-oriented trap. Capping monetary return is also supported by a finding that a high return on equity reveals that an entity is primarily driven by a desire to enable investors to obtain financial returns (Dudka et al., 2023). The ratio of 50% presented here serves as an upper limit. National law can determine a specific ratio by drawing upon established rules for regulating the profit motive of cooperatives or other comparative legal entities. For instance, in Belgium, under the 1962 Royal Decree, to be recognized as a cooperative, the legal entity must limit its dividend to a maximum of 6% return on investment (REScoop.eu and ClientEarth, 2020). Among Member States, Greece and Slovakia are two exceptions that have established rules for governing the profit-making of energy communities.[599] They both constrain the distribution and use of generated profits or surpluses. Slovakian legislation provides that a CEC or a REC can distribute a maximum of 50% of the generated profit among the members (REScoop.eu, 2024g). Greek law prescribes that from the surpluses of each use of the CEC or REC, at least 10% is withheld for the formation of the regular reserve, while at least 70% of the surpluses of each year should remain in the CEC or REC in the form of extraordinary or special reserves.[600] The CEC and the REC can distribute to their members the surpluses of the year, after deducting the reserves as mentioned before, based on a relevant provision in the statutes (REScoop.eu, 2024h).

665. Alternatively, Member States can circumvent the challenge to determine the threshold by limiting the legal forms that energy communities can adopt. This can be done by either identifying several existing legal forms or specifying a single existing legal form (REScoop.eu and ClientEarth, 2020) so that established national law governing their profit motive applies to energy communities.

599 This conclusion is based on a review of data on national transpositions of constraining energy communities' profit-making provided by REScoop.eu by February 2024. See REScoop.eu, 2024d.

600 These extraordinary or special reserves are available, by decision of the general assembly, in accordance with the provisions that regulate the activities a CEC or REC can undertake and the statutes of the community. See REScoop.eu, 2024g.

Some Member States' legislation on cooperatives and other social enterprises often contains rules restricting financial motives (REScoop.eu and ClientEarth, 2020). These rules, for instance, require such legal entities to keep a reserve fund on hand that is non-distributable and dedicated to the common interests of members, accompanied by restrictions on the distribution of surpluses resulting from economic activities (REScoop.eu and ClientEarth, 2020). Despite the merits of mitigating regulatory complexity, limiting available legal forms, especially to a single one, may compromise diversity and disproportionately disrupt existing practices where there are already energy communities in existence (REScoop.eu and ClientEarth, 2020). This trade-off should also be considered by national legislators. Another solution discussed in the literature is adopting concrete provisions that would exclude profit-driven entities from the category of CECs or RECs (Sokołowski, 2020). However, doing so can reduce returns on investment offered to members or shareholders and economic incentives for consumers to engage in energy communities. Participation of commercial actors (including both commercial and industrial customers and energy undertakings) can be notably frustrated, as their motivations are primarily financial, and they typically seek to achieve returns on investment (Dudka et al., 2023; Li and Okur, 2023). Commercial actors act not only as members or shareholders but also as third-party investors, based on different business models and ownership structures (Dudka et al., 2023). Considering this, excluding energy communities' profit-seeking motive may considerably restrict energy communities' access to financing, while lacking capital resources is a typical barrier faced by many energy communities (Watson et al., 2020; Sirr et al., 2023; Haji Bashi et al., 2023).

666. Financial profits are so important that the Austrian legislator even doubts the practicability of excluding financial gain as a primary purpose for energy communities (Fina and Monsberger, 2022). The legislation states that the primary purpose of a REC is not financial gain (*Renewable Energies Expansion Act*, Section 79(2)). Yet, it also states that suggestions for improvement and the need for adaptation shall be evaluated specifically with regard to the practical applicability of the provisions for financial gains (*Renewable Energies Expansion Act*, Section 91(3)). This implies that the legislator doubted that the concepts of CECs and RECs would be widely adopted without the possibility of establishing communities for the primary purpose of gaining profits (Fina and Monsberger, 2022). If proven impractical, the provisions concerning financial gain will perhaps be amended in the future (Fina and Monsberger, 2022), though it is not in line with EU law, which prohibits making profits from being the main aim. This concern suggests that it may not be prudent to prohibit the profit-driven nature of energy communities, which could hinder their widespread adoption.

667. On these grounds, the EU law's general requirement for energy communities' primary purpose should be interpreted as meaning that making financial profits must be secondary to providing community benefits. In other words, CECs and RECs can be driven by profits, but seeking profits cannot be their primary purpose. Hence, national law must clearly define the relationship between the possible aims pursued by energy communities, rather than forbidding financial profit-seeking.

668. To ensure that profit-seeking remains limited to its secondary role, limiting the distribution of profits may not be sufficient. Apart from monetary revenues, sharing RES-E produced by community-owned assets is also an important economic benefit offered to members or shareholders. However, energy communities are likely to sell self-generated RES-E in electricity markets instead of first meeting the energy demand of their members or shareholders. When doing so, energy communities apparently give priority to making financial benefits over providing economic benefits. Such profits resulting from the sale of self-produced electricity to non-members can indeed be subsequently distributed to members or shareholders. However, this situation creates a risk, as discussed above, that economic benefits and financial profits can be easily confused with each other. Hence, when energy communities' proceeds are non-monetary economic benefits that can also be converted to monetary returns, priority should be given to delivering such proceeds in their non-monetary form. This implies the need to regulate the disposal of RES-E produced by assets owned or controlled by energy communities. National law should specify that self-generated RES-E must be first distributed to members or shareholders instead of being sold to non-members. Only when there is a surplus after sharing with members, selling such surplus would not be considered a violation of the primary aim of providing community benefits.

669. Indeed, within EU law, there are no evident restrictions on how CECs and RECs should deal with self-generated electricity. It appears that they have the freedom to decide whether to trade it in electricity markets for financial gains or share it with members or shareholders. However, the above analysis shows that restrictions are embedded in the requirement of prioritizing community benefits and constraining the profit motive of energy communities. They mainly concern the priority given to meeting the electricity demand of members or shareholders, which should be specified by Member States in transpositions.

670. When designing regulatory approaches to reinforce the benefit-oriented nature of CECs and RECs, caution is necessary to avoid disproportionately limiting the activities of energy communities or hindering their access to finance. Many proposed solutions have overlooked this concern. Aside from

the aforementioned example of prohibiting profit motive, some solutions may unduly limit the range of activities of energy communities. For instance, some argued that to ensure energy communities' compliance with the primary aim, the scale of their outside activity should be limited to what does not directly benefit members or shareholders of energy communities – the same concerns as for the site where it is conducted (Sokołowski, 2020). Following this, energy communities may be limited to offering services in geographical proximity – as they should benefit local areas; the development of nationwide charging services for electric vehicles by a given energy community could be challenged on this basis (Sokołowski, 2020). This perspective is problematic, as explained above, because revenues resulting from nationwide economic activities can serve as a category of economic benefit provided to members or shareholders. Activities outside energy communities can thus directly benefit members or shareholders. This fact considerably weakens the justification for restricting the range of economic activities that energy communities can conduct. Instead, what is needed is to properly restrict the distribution of profits when they are used to provide economic benefits. The reason is that if such benefits distributed in monetary terms are too high, energy communities can turn to entities overly focused on profit-making, as set out above.

671. Lastly, how community benefits are defined also has implications for ensuring open and inclusive participation of CECs and RECs. Energy communities typically have minimum investment thresholds to raise the necessary finance, which can constitute entry barriers for energy poor or vulnerable consumers lacking upfront capital, as will be discussed in the following subsection. To lower the entry threshold, various business models and financing approaches have been developed to enhance the engagement of low-income consumers. An example is the Consumer Stock Ownership Plan (CSOP) (Hoicka et al., 2021). With this model, an operating company is authorized to borrow funds for the acquisition of shares in the energy community on behalf of energy poor or vulnerable consumers (Hoicka et al., 2021). These consumers do not have to pay for their membership up front, and the acquisition loan of their share will be repaid by revenues of the investment, e.g., from the sale of the RES-E generated from community-owned assets (Hanke and Lowitzsch, 2020; Hoicka et al., 2021). However, a question arises as to whether using energy communities' revenues to repay the loan for supporting the membership of certain consumers can be viewed as the provision of community benefits. The answer to this question depends on who the beneficiaries are. In principle, such repayment can be considered a form of return on investment, which, as noted above, should be subject to some restrictions. Nevertheless, if such revenues are used to support the participation of energy poor or vulnerable customers, this helps mitigate energy poverty and could be seen as providing social benefits or economic benefits for members or local areas where energy communities operate.

Hence, national legislation also needs to consider this situation in further specifying community benefits, to improve the energy poor or vulnerable consumers' access to both CECs and RECs.

#### 3.1.3.2. Membership

672. EU law governs membership of energy communities in two dimensions. One is the requirement of open and voluntary participation, which restricts the freedom of energy communities in establishing conditions for membership and termination. The other is restrictions on eligibility to be a member or shareholder of the REC.[601] Three legal issues stand out during the transposition process, as elaborated below.

##### (i) Open Participation

673. So far, insufficient efforts have been devoted to ensuring the open participation of energy communities. EU law underlines that open participation is a binding element of constituting a CEC or a REC. The recital of the REDII further specifies that participation in energy communities should be open to all potential members based on objective, transparent and non-discriminatory criteria. This requirement of open participation does not mean that entities failing to engage all eligible potential members will be deprived of the eligibility to be CECs or RECs. Instead, it should be understood that an entity with unjustified or exorbitant entry conditions will not be qualified as a CEC or a REC under EU law (REScoop.eu and ClientEarth, 2020). However, very few Member States have introduced detailed measures for evaluating whether an entity applying to be a CEC or a REC has membership conditions that can unduly restrict open participation.[602]

674. Energy communities typically raise finance by incorporating a minimum financial contribution (e.g., in the form of shares) into their membership criteria. According to empirical data of recent years, entry fees or equity contributions of various energy communities in the Member States range from 85 to 3899 euros (Candelise and Ruggieri, 2020; Hanke and Lowitzsch, 2020; Palm, 2021). Such upfront capital for membership has been reported as a considerable barrier to the participation of energy poor or vulnerable consumers with limited financial means (REScoop.eu and ClientEarth, 2020; Hanke and Lowitzsch, 2020; Palm,

[601] EU law does not restrict eligibility to be a member or shareholder of the CEC, as noted in Chapter III.

[602] Croatia is the only exception. Its legislation prescribes that openness is determined by the CEC in accordance with its 'conditions of participation in CECs'. Those who are denied membership or restricted from leaving may file an objection with the Agency. See REScoop.eu, 2024.

2021; Haji Bashi et al., 2023; Hanke et al., 2023). Considering this, a legal question arises: according to what criteria, can such membership costs be considered excessive and thereby endanger the open nature of a CEC or a REC?

675. This issue is not easy to address because the difficulty of energy communities in accessing finance may justify some demanding financial requirements for membership. Several factors contribute to the difficulty in raising sufficient capital. Compared to commercial actors, energy communities have limited access to credit due to size, lack of collateral and risk assessment (Hanke and Lowitzsch, 2020). Moreover, restrictions imposed by EU law on energy communities' eligibility can also contribute to their difficulty in financing. Constraints on financial profit-making limit the ability of both the CEC and the REC to offer investors high financial returns (Hanke and Lowitzsch, 2020). Limited profitability can particularly reduce the financial attractiveness of energy communities for commercial actors who may invest in energy communities as eligible members or third-party investors. This is because commercial actors are driven by market logic, and their motivations are primarily financial, and they typically seek to achieve some return on investment, as mentioned above (Dudka et al., 2023). In comparison, RECs face even more unfavorable conditions in terms of attracting investment since they are subject to broader restrictions on membership, effective control and autonomy, as explained in Section 3.1.2.2 above.

676. These factors can hinder energy communities from raising sufficient outside capital, and thus they often depend on their members to provide the required equity (Hanke and Lowitzsch, 2020). This is supported by an empirical research investigating 198 RECs in nine Member States, which shows that a majority depend on their members' equity contribution (Doračić et al., 2020; Hanke and Lowitzsch, 2020). Additionally, due to their limited ability to attract commercial actors, energy communities are likely to rely more on members or shareholders from the residential sector to raise finance, and the required contribution from individual members may be high. This is especially true when local authorities are not involved. For energy communities facing these challenges, setting relatively high financial contribution thresholds seems justified. However, such financial requirements may be considered entry barriers from the perspective of energy poor or vulnerable consumers.

677. In this case, the first question that must be addressed by national law is: Would an applicant be considered to have failed to fulfill the condition of open participation due to financial requirements preventing the participation of low-income or vulnerable households? Another related question is how to assess whether the financial requirements for membership are excessive and unduly jeopardize open participation. Should they be assessed merely from the perspective of energy poor or vulnerable customers? If so, such an assessment

can vary depending on the financial means at the disposal of these customer groups. As exemplified by some pilot projects in the Member States, the participation of vulnerable consumers can be hindered even under an inclusive and low-threshold financing approach where the contribution of participating households is small (Doračić et al., 2020; Hanke and Lowitzsch, 2020). Energy communities might thus be compelled to lower membership conditions that block the inclusion of poor or vulnerable households. In this case, a follow-up question is how to ensure that energy communities raise adequate finance, especially given the above disadvantages stemming from eligibility requirements. If the assessment goes beyond the perspectives of poor or vulnerable customers, what other factors should be considered in assessing the proper level of financial contribution for membership? Most national legislation fails to adequately account for the complex issues involved in assessing whether an entity applying to be a CEC or a REC is based on open participation, resulting in a significant transposition gap.[603]

678. To recap, the above analysis indicates that the implementation of open participation is interwoven with the other two issues, namely the inclusion of energy poor or vulnerable customers and energy communities' access to finance. Although the Electricity Directive does not explicitly require Member States to address these two issues, national law should consider their role in ensuring compliance with open participation. By contrast, under the REDII, Member States are obligated to ensure the participation of low-income or vulnerable consumers in the REC and to address barriers for the REC's access to finance. Dedicated measures for improving the REC's access to finance are still scarce, as set out above in Section 3.1.2.2. In addition, most Member States have not taken measures to ensure that RECs are open to energy poor or vulnerable customers.[604] The high costs of buying shares of RECs and the long pay-back time remain the major obstacles for these consumers to join energy communities (Hanke and Lowitzsch, 2020; Palm, 2021). Moreover, buying shares of a REC can be a long-term investment,[605] while as indicated above, consumers experiencing deprivation typically lack the cognitive resources required to make long-term investment decisions. This is another important factor leading to the underrepresentation and passivity of low-income or vulnerable consumers in energy communities (Hanke and Lowitzsch, 2020; Hanke et al., 2023). Such economic and non-economic barriers faced by this customer group are mostly left aside in existing national transpositions (Fina and Fechner, 2021;

603 This conclusion is drawn by a review of country-specific data on how national law implements open participation of CECs and RECs. See REScoop.eu, 2024e.

604 At the time of writing, only Greece, Italy and Spain have taken further steps to address poor or vulnerable consumers' access to RECs. See REScoop.eu, 2024i, 2024j, 2024k.

605 Taking an Italian energy community *Energia Positiva* as an example, its payback time is around ten years, with a rate of return of approximately 9%. See Candelise and Ruggieri, 2020.

Krug et al., 2023). This is indicated by current NECPs and the fact that very few Member States have done a thorough analysis of the barriers to the development of RECs,[606] resulting in a lack of understanding of various restrictions that hinder the involvement of low-income or vulnerable customers (Palm, 2021; Krug et al., 2023).

679. National transpositions in ensuring inclusive participation in the REC can be improved by a hybrid approach (Hanke and Lowitzsch, 2020; REScoop.eu and ClientEarth, 2020). It first consists of national rules dedicated to addressing unique economic and non-economic restrictions or barriers faced by low-income or vulnerable customers in joining the REC. For the sake of recognitional justice, the design of such targeted measures must be based on a barrier assessment that reveals unfavorable conditions stemming from deprivation or vulnerability. The second step concerns actions taken at the energy community level. As addressed above, lowering thresholds for membership is closely linked to addressing the difficulty energy communities face in raising sufficient capital. This finding highlights the importance of transposing the requirement for improving energy communities' access to finance. Alternatively, as suggested by some, national law can provide support or incentives for RECs (Hanke and Lowitzsch, 2020; REScoop.eu and ClientEarth, 2020). Their common aim is to offset required initial monetary investments or other inputs by vulnerable consumers, which is necessary to enable their participation in the first place (Hanke and Lowitzsch, 2020).

(ii) Voluntary Participation

680. Not enough attention has been paid to the trade-offs involved in ensuring voluntary participation.[607] The major problem arises from the requirement of securing the right of members or shareholders to leave the CEC or the REC. Under the legal framework for the CEC, EU law prescribes that in case members or shareholders leave the CEC, Article 12 applies, which governs the cost, efforts and time of switching suppliers or aggregators. This provision implies that national law must ensure that, in principle (*Electricity Directive*, Article 12 (3)), at least for household customers and small enterprises, the CEC is not allowed to charge them any switching-related fees (*Electricity Directive*, Article 12 (2)). In the event that Member States also grant other consumers the right to switch suppliers or aggregators without incurring switching-related fees, other members or shareholders are entitled to leave the CEC freely at any time. However, a legal question arises: could legal arrangements dealing with suppliers and aggregators

606 Conducting a barrier analysis is a requirement of Article 22 of the REDII.

607 This conclusion is drawn by a review of country-specific data on how national law implements voluntary participation of CECs and RECs. See REScoop.eu, 2024e.

switching adequately cover relationships that the CEC could have with its members or shareholders?

681. Members or shareholders may have multiple relationships with energy communities as customers, receiving parties of shared electricity and investors (Roberts, 2020). Leaving the CEC thus implies not only terminating supply contracts or electricity sharing agreements but also withdrawing shares. The literature emphasizes the impact of allowing members to withdraw shares when leaving the energy community without any barriers. It raises concerns about membership volatility, which can undermine the economic viability of energy communities (Oberthur et al., 2020), especially those mainly financed through members' or citizens' contributions.[608] As already noted, the difficulty in accessing financing is a prevalent barrier faced by energy communities. The implications of allowing free termination of membership, accompanied by divestments, for these entities' long-term financial sustainability are not trivial (REScoop.eu and ClientEarth, 2020). Even though not all CECs lack capital resources and are vulnerable to membership volatility, the Electricity Directive's reference to Article 12 leads to a 'one-size-fits-all' approach. It limits the possibility of national law to allow CECs easily suffering from membership volatility to impose proportionate limitations upon membership termination to cover the direct economic loss.[609] Further, Article 12 was designed in the context of supply or energy service contracts to emphasize consumer protection. It is not meant to regulate potential investment relationships between the CEC and its members or shareholders. Employing this provision to address the termination of membership in CECs cannot properly balance the trade-offs between the voluntariness of members and the economic viability of the CEC. Moreover, it is left to Member States to designate existing legal forms that CECs can adopt. Existing laws governing the process of leaving companies, associations, or cooperatives can thus be applied to a CEC that chooses a specific legal form. These laws typically have dealt with the balance required to ensure shareholders' freedom to dissolve investments and counter undue impacts on relevant entities (REScoop.eu and ClientEarth, 2020). However, the Electricity Directive blocks the possibility of applying relevant national law to deal with membership termination. There is a need to amend the present single approach to addressing the termination of the CEC's membership at the EU level.

608 The ownership structure of energy communities founded through the direct financial contribution of citizens is described as the 'full citizen ownership' model in the literature. They are more likely to lack economic sustainability and depend heavily on public financial support, compared to energy communities with diverse members or third-party investors. For examples and analyses of their merits and drawbacks in engaging households and accessing investment, see Candelise and Ruggieri, 2020; Dudka et al., 2023; Vernay et al., 2023.

609 For instance, the legislative proposal in Sweden states that members have a right to cancel their membership in the community and that they have a right to withdraw their shares six months after their membership expires. See REScoop.eu and ClientEarth, 2020.

682. Within the REDII, no provision addresses the termination of the REC's membership. Member States thus have leeway to counteract the impact of membership volatility on the REC by allowing limitations on the freedom of members or shareholders to leave the REC. It should be noted that such limitations also play an important role in safeguarding the autonomy of the REC required by the REDII. Members or shareholders may threaten the financial independence of the REC by dissolving their investment in the community (REScoop.eu and ClientEarth, 2020). One of the approaches to reinforcing the REC's autonomy is to place limitations to ensure that reimbursement in the case of withdrawal of a particular member, or liquidation, from the entity does not place the entity or its purposes at risk (REScoop.eu and ClientEarth, 2020). National law needs to consider the correlation between the termination of governing membership and securing the REC's autonomy from its members or shareholders.

683. Limitations placed on leaving energy communities can include a minimum membership period, notice period or early termination fee, which should be possible as part of the statutes or other internal rules of the energy community (Oberthur et al., 2020). For instance, Luxembourg's draft law states that members or shareholders of RECs are entitled to leave the community, provided they give notice that cannot exceed one year (REScoop.eu and ClientEarth, 2020). The relevant arrangements also include the option for energy communities to commit to buying back a share from a shareholder who wishes to leave, provided the latter has not found a buyer within a reasonable timeframe (Oberthur et al., 2020). For the sake of protecting consumers involved in energy communities, national law should also require energy communities to ensure transparency in the consequences of leaving the entities, including termination fees, notice periods, and rules governing the sale of shares (Oberthur et al., 2020). It is also suggested that national law can allow restrictions upon membership termination based on specific purposes of energy communities and specific contexts. For example, CECs or RECs formed to establish new renewable plants could limit divestments of members or shareholders to some extent during the financing stage (Almeida et al., 2021).

### (iii) Private Undertakings' Membership of the REC

684. The restriction on private undertakings' participation in the REC requires further clarification, as noted in Chapter III. The REDII requires that membership of private undertakings is subject to a requirement that their participation does not constitute their primary commercial or professional activity. As pointed out by the Flemish regulator, without further specifying this principle, it would be difficult to assess compliance (*2022 Report on energy communities, energy sharing*

*and P2P trading*, Section 2.3).[610] Flemish law is an example of simply replicating this broadly worded principle without ancillary rules for assessing the nature of private companies' participation. When an entity applies to become a REC, it is not straightforward to determine whether the private company's involvement constitutes its primary commercial or professional activity.

685. The nature of non-primary activities of a company should be determined by considering their role in all activities or relative to core activities carried out by that entity. To support this assessment, one needs to take a close look at a private company's charters or statutes and analyze its financial statements (e.g., the income statement, balance sheet, and cash flow statement), as well as examine the time and other resources (including personnel) devoted by that company. The statutes show primary commercial or professional activities defined on paper. Revenue sources and the allocation of resources provide evidence of the actual importance of a given activity in both revenue generation and resource distribution. A regulator responsible for approving applications for being a REC needs a case-by-case study of individual companies involved as members or shareholders. In examining the above-mentioned evidence, the regulator also needs a set of criteria for determining whether joining the REC is non-primary for a specific company compared to its core commercial or professional activity. Such criteria may take the form of thresholds for ascertaining the secondary role of a particular activity relative to major ones. For instance, after knowing about the allocation of resources to join a REC, the regulator still needs an objective standard to determine below what ratio, a company's resource allocation to this activity could be considered to serve non-core activities.

686. Simply copying the wording of REDII is insufficient to implement the restriction placed on the private company's membership. There are two approaches to address legal challenges to transpose this restriction. Either Member States elaborate on further requirements and criteria, or EU law improves the wording of that restriction. Member States can do so based on the central considerations discussed above. Yet, EU-level efforts may be even more effective in solving the problem here. This restriction aims to prevent commercial energy companies, even if they are SMEs,[611] from exploiting rights or advantages granted to the REC, and to prevent industrial and commercial users from transitioning into electricity undertakings through the REC

610 See also Section 2.1.3 above of this Chapter.

611 The definition of the REC also limits the membership of companies based on their size. Only companies that are SMEs can become members or shareholders of the REC. See *REDII*, Article 2(16).

framework (*REDII*, recital 70; Almeida et al., 2021). Approaches suitable for this purpose should focus on ensuring that private companies do not assume decisive or significant decision-making powers within RECs (REScoop.eu and ClientEarth, 2020). This general aim can be translated into specific requirements that limit the amount of investment or voting power that private companies can have in a REC (REScoop.eu and ClientEarth, 2020). In comparison, the existing requirement, i.e., limiting a private company's participation via the non-primary commercial or professional activity criterion, is not clear enough and unsuitable to prevent energy undertakings from abusing the REC for their own commercial benefits. There remains a risk that a medium-sized energy company can exert substantial influence in the operation of a REC, even though it does not devote most of its resources and time to activities associated with its membership. On these grounds, the EU legislator may need to reconsider the general approach to limiting membership of private undertakings, making it robust, fit-for-purpose, and pragmatic enough to implement.

#### 3.1.3.3. Operation

687. Eligibility criteria for CECs and RECs also contain general restrictions on their operational decision-making and management. As shown in Chapter III, the aim of governing decision-making of energy communities is to balance the interests or expectations of a variety of stakeholders participating in energy communities or merely cooperating with such entities through investment (Dudka et al., 2023). EU law embeds this balance within the broader context of sustaining the primary aims of the CEC and the REC, specifically in delivering community benefits. This leads to restrictions on influence potentially exerted by large companies, third-party investors and traditional energy undertakings. Among the minimum requirements governing decision-making, 'effective control' and the proximity requirement coupled with it in the REC context raise some noteworthy issues.

688. First, there is a risk that large companies can bypass the existing restrictions on effective control. The eligibility of companies to exercise effective control is limited to small enterprises in the CEC context and SMEs in the REC context. As rightly pointed out by the REScoop.eu, it is possible that large companies can still effectively control energy communities through their subsidiaries or linked enterprises qualified as 'small' or 'medium' enterprises (REScoop.eu and ClientEarth, 2020). To avoid this risk, national standards on effective control should also cover subsidiaries or linked enterprises (REScoop.eu and ClientEarth, 2020). Alternatively, national law can highlight the autonomy of enterprises eligible to be controlling members of the CEC and the REC. Doing so can frustrate the large companies' control of energy communities by controlling their medium or small-sized affiliates. This step is needed since, in some cases,

small enterprises or SMEs are defined without stressing their autonomy.[612] By contrast, the EC's definition of SMEs introduces a standard to characterize their autonomy, e.g., capping one or more minority partnerships with other enterprises to 25% (EC, 2016f). National legislators can refer to existing company law when adding an autonomy requirement for small or medium companies that are eligible to effectively control the CEC or the REC.

689. The EC has indicated that Member States can define what 'effective control' means in the context of governance of energy communities based on their existing statutes on corporate governance (i.e., company law) or tax law (Roberts, 2020). Drawing on existing company law in the Member States, the REScoop.eu distills several cases where certain members or shareholders are considered to exercise effective control in energy communities. They include (1) having majority voting rights in general meetings of the energy community through the amount of capital held (e.g. 51%) or by virtue of an agreement with other members or shareholders; (2) having a decisive influence in the decisions of the REC by virtue of the shares held or its position on the board; and (3) having enough voting power or shares to wield veto power against the other members or shareholders (REScoop.eu and ClientEarth, 2020). As can be seen, central to the concept of effective control is the particular members' ability to exercise 'decisive influence' on the composition, voting behavior or decisions of the energy community, which has been confirmed by other research (Roberts, 2020; Almeida et al., 2021). The Flemish regulator, the VREG, additionally highlights that having property or usage rights to all assets of the energy community or parts thereof should also be considered relevant to exercise such decisive influence (REScoop.eu and ClientEarth, 2020).

690. Clearly, effective control differs from general powers to participate in the decision-making of energy communities. Under the Electricity Directive, the CEC's membership is open to all categories of enterprises, but only small ones are allowed to exercise effective control. The Electricity Directive does not contain other restrictions on companies' decision-making power within the CEC. The legal consequence is that medium-sized and large companies, both within and outside the energy sector, can participate in the decision-making of the CEC, provided their decision-making role does not amount to effective control or direction of the CEC's decision-making (REScoop.eu and ClientEarth, 2020). However, the recital of the Electricity Directive may create confusion. It states that '*the decision-making powers within a citizen energy community should be limited to those members or shareholders that are not engaged in large-scale commercial activity and for which the energy sector does not constitute a primary area of economic activity*'. This implies that not only large energy

612 An example is 'small enterprise' defined by Article 2(7) of the Electricity Directive.

undertakings but also large industrial and commercial consumers should not be involved in the CEC's decision-making. Compared to the legislative text, it extends restrictions on the decision-making powers of these enterprises. Despite adopting binding wording, the recital per se is not binding for Member States. Yet, in national transpositions, recitals play a crucial role in helping to understand the legislative intention and the connotation behind principles or broadly worded legal provisions. This is exemplified by the case of transposing the requirement for autonomy of the REC. The Walloon legislation elaborates on this requirement by drawing on the recital of the REDII that refers to autonomy (*Walloon Electricity Decree*, 2001, art. 35duodecies, §1, 2°; *Walloon government Decision on energy communities*, 2023, art. 11). Considering the recitals' role in guiding national transpositions, the EU legislature should exercise caution when incorporating requirements that go beyond legal provisions into recitals, especially those restricting rights or creating additional obligations. This advice is also based on the fact that requirements in recitals may not undergo thorough analyses of the trade-offs involved in their legal consequences, such as the adverse impacts on the CEC's access to investment from large companies (either within or outside the energy sector).

691. Another legal issue relating to effective control is its implementation in the REC context. The REDII requires that only members or shareholders located within the proximity of the renewable energy project owned or developed by the REC can effectively control the entity. The implementation of the proximity requirement raises two-fold issues. First, how to delimit the scope within which members or shareholders are considered adjacent to project sites? Failing to build objective standards can arbitrarily deprive some members of eligibility to be controlling members.

692. At the national level, such proximity is defined in either a geographical or an electrical sense.[613] Either way has some drawbacks. The geographical proximity approach sets the maximum distance between the REC's members and its renewable energy project. This appears to be a straightforward approach to setting proximity, and it also provides added value by increasing local acceptance of renewable projects, as it grants local people the right to effectively control the REC (REScoop.eu and ClientEarth, 2020). Yet, the geographical extension criterion can be overly restrictive in sparsely populated rural areas (CRU, 2023b). Applying the same maximum distance can lead to divergent consequences in urban and rural areas in terms of the number of members or shareholders in effective control. It is likely that in rural areas with low population density, only a small number of members or shareholders are granted the controlling

[613] The Irish regulator, the CRU, provides an overview of national approaches to defining proximity in its consultation paper seeking stakeholders' views on its proposed approach to setting the proximity requirements for RECs. See CRU, 2023.

position in the REC with a narrowly defined geographical standard (Fina and Fechner, 2021; CRU, 2023b). In this case, it may be challenging for the REC to engage consumers and raise sufficient funding. As noted, losing eligibility to be controlling members implies limited decision-making power over the allocation of the energy community's proceeds, which may affect the incentives of potential members. The smaller the predefined geographical proximity, the wider the impact on the economic incentives for potential members. Moreover, the geographical proximity is often criticized for arbitrariness and the risk of creating lengthy debates (Mauger, 2023). A certain perimeter (e.g., dozens of kilometers)[614] and the geographic scopes delimited by postal code or a local administrative unit (e.g., a county, city or municipality) are generally considered 'local'. Yet, choosing different scopes has different legal consequences in determining the range of members or shareholders eligible to exercise effective control. Then what is the objective criterion for selecting from these scopes?

693. The electrical proximity standard generally reflects grid-related factors, such as the distribution grid or substation. The concern raised by this standard is the likelihood of excluding members physically adjacent to the renewables asset from those in effective control. For instance, the Irish regulator proposed using a physical asset on the distribution system, such as a 38kV substation, to define the proximity (CRU, 2021d). Stakeholders in the consultation process expressed concerns that this electrical boundary is too restrictive and could limit the rights of members or shareholders physically close to the REC's generation assets (CRU, 2021d). This concern is especially evident in the context of a city where several substations exist (CRU, 2021d).

694. Clearly, it is hard to standardize the proximity requirement in a manner that the diversity of situations in practice can be accommodated (CRU, 2023b). Moreover, there is another common dilemma faced by the two approaches to setting proximity. On the one hand, for the sake of clarity of law, the legislator must delimit a specific scope, either in a geographical or an electrical sense. On the other hand, many choices under these two approaches can align with the adjacent nature. What is the objective basis for choosing one but not others that allow a wider range of members in effective control?

695. Furthermore, some Member States have extended the application of the proximity requirement from restricting effective control to membership of the REC (REScoop.eu and ClientEarth, 2020; Palm, 2021; Fina and Monsberger, 2022; Krug et al., 2023). Austria, Spain, Portugal, Italy, Sweden, and the Walloon Region of Belgium are examples of doing so with electrical or geographical

[614] For instance, under German law, at least 75% of the voting rights of a REC must be held by natural persons living in a postcode area that lies entirely or partly within a radius of 50 km around the plant. See Krug et al., 2023.

proximity (REScoop.eu and ClientEarth, 2020; Palm, 2021; Fina and Monsberger, 2022; Krug et al., 2023; *Walloon government Decision on energy communities*, 2023, art. 24). In these Member States, REC participants and generation units must be connected via the low-voltage or medium-voltage grid or located within a specific geographical area. If the boundary of the REC is confined too narrowly, open participation in the REC could be easily undermined. The narrowly defined scope of the REC also prevents economies of scale, exacerbating the difficulty of the REC in raising finance, which is especially the case in rural areas with low population density. Moreover, national legislators are still challenged to seek an objective criterion for determining the local nature of members or shareholders. For instance, in Spain, the REC's participation radius has been recently expanded from 500 m to 2000 m through Royal Decree Law no 18/2022 (Krug et al., 2023). The geographic boundary of limiting membership is much smaller than those adopted by other national legislation, e.g., a radius of 50 km in German law and a municipality in Walloon law (Krug et al., 2023; *Walloon government Decision on energy communities*, 2023, art. 24). It appears that the geographical proximity standard is not consistently established and can vary depending on the legislator's preference.

#### 3.1.3.4. Monitoring Energy Communities' Eligibility

696. Having discussed key considerations for further specifying the eligibility criteria of the CEC and the REC, the next issue to be addressed is how to oversee the compliance of energy communities. Lacking monitoring can lead to a risk that entities that have already claimed themselves as CECs or RECs and exercised relevant rights do not meet the qualifications specified by EU law and national law. So far, several Member States have provided for some sort of oversight of CECs and RECs (*Walloon Electricity Decree*, 2001, art. 35terdecies; *Walloon government Decision on energy communities*, 2023, arts. 14, 16 and 23; REScoop.eu and ClientEarth, 2020). Nevertheless, some of them rely heavily on the notification obligation, i.e., requiring energy communities to report to the regulator their basic attributes, such as activities and composition, as seen in Flemish law and draft law in Luxembourg (REScoop.eu and ClientEarth, 2020). This reporting obligation is considered insufficient since it is not followed by the regulator's oversight of compliance with EU conditions for constituting the CEC or the REC, as indicated by the VREG.[615] Ex-ante monitoring of the establishment of the CEC or the REC is absent, not only in the Flemish Region of Belgium but also in other Member States. In Spain, for example, no regulatory

[615] See Section 2.1.3.2 of this Chapter above.

authority has been given the power to oversee compliance with the definition of a CEC or a REC (Krug et al., 2023). Consequently, there are no operating communities in Spain that correspond precisely to the EU definition of CECs or RECs (Krug et al., 2023). To ensure energy communities function as required by EU law, more systematic approaches are needed to monitor their compliance with eligibility criteria.

697. First, a recognition or application procedure could be introduced to enable the regulator to assess the alignment of applicants with eligibility criteria. To support this ex-ante monitoring, national law can designate a competent authority responsible for assessing whether the applicant can be recognized as a CEC or a REC. This procedure should also include additional obligations for entities applying to become CECs or RECs. For instance, they should submit statutes that contain elements of implementing eligibility requirements for the primary purpose, membership and operation. Based on this, the competent authority verifies whether the conditions for establishing an energy community have been met. To avoid potential abuse of the concept of the CEC or the REC, national legislation should specify that only entities recognized by the designated authority may use the term 'CEC' or 'REC' in their documents, publications or communications.[616] This requirement also aims to protect consumers interested in participating in the CEC or the REC from fraud. Such recognition is significant because most consumers, especially households, lack the time and expertise to verify whether an entity claiming to be a CEC or REC actually constitutes one defined by EU law and national law.

698. Ex-ante monitoring during the establishment of CECs or RECs alone cannot guarantee that the nature of established energy communities remains intact in operation. Thus, follow-up monitoring is required to ensure that energy communities are in a lawful state. This can be supported by an obligation for energy communities to provide data, regarding, for instance, their activities and the delivery of community benefits, and decision-making mechanisms.

699. It should be noted that due to the complexity of assessing compliance with the primary purpose, more fine-grained obligations are necessary for applicants. These first include demonstrating compliance with the primary purpose required by EU law. Merely requiring applicants to report their activities and planning to conduct is insufficient. As pointed out by the Flemish regulator, it is hard to assess whether engaging in certain activities amounts to providing

[616] Art. 14 of the Walloon government Decision on energy communities creates this requirement to prevent entities from falsely claiming to be CECs or RECs without meeting the definitions set out in EU law and national law.

community benefits. To address this challenge, additional steps are needed, as listed in the following:

- Applicants should explain, among the economic, social, and environmental benefits, which category(s) they choose to deliver. This requirement aims to increase transparency in the choice of community benefits and their subsequent monitoring.
- They should also illustrate how they intend to provide the chosen community benefits defined by national law, along with the specific activities they will undertake. In doing so, they should also elaborate on specific approaches they design to ensure compliance with national rules governing the community benefits' relationship with profit-making. Such approaches can serve as detailed baselines for subsequently tracking and monitoring the compliance of energy communities after they are up and running. As discussed above, the distribution of margins serves as a key indicator of the primary aim of energy communities. Thus, national law can also require the applicants' approaches to contain how mechanisms for allocating proceeds implement the restrictions imposed on the distribution of proceeds.

700. To support the assessment of compliance during operation, national law could require energy communities to report how their activities, use of expenses and allocation of proceeds have complied with national requirements for the primary purpose while submitting evidence to the competent regulator. Apart from such external oversight, internal checks may also be conducive to improving the delivery of the primary aim. For instance, in the Walloon Region of Belgium, the energy community's governing body is required to report annually to the members and shareholders on how its activities, actions, and decisions contribute to the achievement of the objectives pursued in terms of ecological, economic or social benefits (*Walloon government Decision on energy communities*, 2023, art. 10). This obligation is required to be incorporated into the statutes of both CECs and RECs (*Walloon government Decision on energy communities*, 2023, art. 10).

701. Lastly, once the established CECs or RECs violate eligibility requirements and fail to restore the lawful state, they should no longer be eligible for rights and national support granted by or pursuant to empowerment frameworks. In Member States governing energy communities' energy sharing with permits, legal consequences of violating eligibility requirements should include withdrawing the admission to electricity sharing. For example, in the Walloon Region of Belgium, no permit for the supply of electricity is required for energy sharing within an energy community, while the Walloon Electricity Decree creates a separate permit-granting procedure for this activity (*Walloon Electricity Decree*, 2001, art. 35quaterdecies, §2 and §3). The implementing law adopted

by the Walloon Government empowers the regulator to withdraw permits for electricity sharing as a penalty for non-compliance with obligations and conditions imposed on energy communities (*Walloon government Decision on energy communities*, 2023, art. 23).

702. Establishing ex-ante and ex-post oversight, as discussed above, represents a strict approach to monitoring energy communities. It can indeed help guarantee compliance with qualification criteria. It, however, can also raise concerns about creating burdensome obligations and lengthy procedures, which can undermine its practicality. As shown above, such comprehensive oversight can create many additional obligations on energy communities and NRAs responsible for recognition and monitoring. Moreover, monitoring the qualification of energy communities also entails an additional duty of verifying the authenticity of data and evidence submitted by these communities. Heavy regulatory burdens also stem from the fact that ex-ante monitoring, in the form of recognition and application procedures, must be accompanied by ex-post monitoring, to ensure the follow-up lawful state of energy communities.

703. An alternative to this comprehensive and strict monitoring is a 'lighter' monitoring regime. It monitors problems that emerge in the initial stage of developing energy communities, for instance, by combining both reporting regimes and complaint-based oversight. Member States can require energy communities to notify the regulator of their establishment and compliance with eligibility criteria, as done by Flemish law. The regulator does not assess the authenticity of reported data and compliance with eligibility criteria, but deals with non-compliance mainly based on complaints from community members or third parties. Furthermore, the aforementioned internal monitoring, by obligating the energy community's governing body to report to its members or shareholders, can also be embedded in this light regime. This approach may be better suited for the early stages of energy community development. It enables a deeper understanding of the practical problems that arise when implementing qualification criteria for energy communities, based on which more targeted and proportionate regulatory tools can be developed.

## 3.2. MARKET-BASED INCENTIVES

704. In addition to granting final customers the right to engage in DR and renewables self-consumption, EU law seeks to enhance economic incentives for these activities. Such incentives are delivered by securing proper market signals, adjusting market design parameters, and expanding approaches to electricity markets, as elaborated in Chapter III. This section begins by examining setbacks in implementing the reinforced measures to reduce price interventions and analyzing relevant responses at the Union level (Section 3.2.1).

It then examines the challenges of reducing market entry barriers resulting from market design parameters and discusses potential solutions (Section 3.2.2). This is followed by an in-depth analysis of the legal issues that arise when facilitating renewables self-consumers to access electricity markets, particularly through P2P electricity trading (Section 3.2.3). It ends with a discussion of the regulatory treatment of energy communities involved in commercial energy activities.

### *3.2.1. Safeguarding Free Price Formation*

705. As addressed in Chapter III above, proper market-based incentives are delivered by free price formation. Price regulation can lower market revenues and discourage consumer engagement in DR and renewables self-consumption, and thus, the CEP steps up efforts to restrict price interventions. Member States are required to transpose rules on free price formation, accompanied by strictly limited derogations, by 31 December 2020 (*Electricity Directive*, Article 71). However, the COVID-19 pandemic and the subsequent energy price crisis of 2021–2022 delayed and set back national actions to phase out price interventions incompatible with existing EU law. Emergency measures protecting final customers from high electricity prices were widely adopted, especially during the price crises (ACER, 2023a), exemplifying how easily established principles of price regulation could be broken free in exceptional situations. Legal challenges of safeguarding compliance with these principles can be well illustrated by national responses to that crisis.

706. At least thirteen Member States had some kind of public intervention in the price setting that predated the energy price crisis for either household, non-household consumers or both (ACER and CEER, 2021; ACER, 2023a). National actions to phase out regulated prices were delayed by the COVID-19 pandemic. Member States reported that the reason for intervening in energy prices is to protect vulnerable energy consumers (ACER and CEER, 2021). However, in 2020, the proportion of vulnerable customers in electricity amounted to a minor share in the majority of Member States, and there were much lower numbers of vulnerable consumers than those falling under price interventions (ACER and CEER, 2021). Moreover, by 2021, only five countries committed to a roadmap for removing retail price intervention (ACER and CEER, 2021).

707. This situation was exacerbated by the historical energy price crisis in the EU between 2021 and 2022.[617] By October 2021, mainly driven by

---

[617] In October 2021, energy commodity prices reached unprecedented high levels across Europe. Gas prices in October 2021 are 400% more expensive than in April 2021. The trend of rising energy prices continued in 2022, following the Russia-Ukraine conflict. In general, retail electricity prices peaked between July 2022 and November 2022 in most Member States.

record-high gas prices, electricity prices had increased by 200% compared to April 2021 (ACER, 2021; EC, 2022a). At least seventeen Member States introduced different types of temporary public price interventions in response to the energy crisis, such as price caps, frozen electricity prices or reimbursements and discounts (ACER, 2023a). In the household market, except for the Netherlands, all Member States had some form of public price intervention, consisting of regulated prices (ACER, 2023a). While energy poor and vulnerable customers were most impacted,[618] other household users were covered by regulated prices (ACER, 2023a). In the non-household market, at least eight Member States had some kind of price intervention implemented in 2022, always consisting of regulated prices, to mitigate the impact on smaller businesses and energy-intensive industries (EC, 2021; ACER, 2023a).

708. In a context of unusually high energy prices, policymakers certainly face a tough dilemma: on the one hand, how to protect end users from undesirable economic consequences, while on the other hand, how to preserve the role and benefits of the price signals to achieve other objectives, such as promoting DR and renewables self-consumption (ACER, 2023a). However, national responses to the crisis seem to give priority to shielding consumers from price rises over striving for acceptable compromises between competing goals. Such compromises are plausible: Member States must ensure consumer protection while allowing for a reasonable exposure to price signals. However, exceptional situations do not mean that the principle of free price formation can be compromised disproportionately, especially considering the presence of available alternatives.

709. The EC provided guidance for Member States to present the pros and cons of available short-term emergency measures,[619] to steer national actions

---

Exceptions to these peaks are observed in Portugal (Apr 2022), and Spain (Mar 2022), while prices peaked later in Bulgaria (Jul – Apr 22), Cyprus (Mar 2023), Lithuania (Jan 2023), and Slovakia (Apr 2023). See ACER, 2021; ACER and CEER, 2021; EC, 2022; ACER, 2023b.

618 Although price spikes affect everyone, the energy poor and the low and lower-middle-income households are most impacted because they spend significantly higher shares of their incomes on energy. Energy poverty has already been exacerbated by the COVID-19 pandemic. During the COVID-19 pandemic, 8 of 21 Member States (where data is available) experienced a year-on-year increase in the energy poverty rate in 2020. See EC, 2021, section 2.2.

619 At the retail level, in addition to regulating retail prices, targeted and temporary measures include direct support to vulnerable end-users, state aid for businesses struggling with excessive energy prices and reduced taxation. At the wholesale level, the options other than directly capping the electricity price include (i) intervening directly in the functioning of the wholesale electricity markets by compensating financially fossil-based electricity generators for part of their extraordinarily high fuel costs so that they reduce their offered price in the wholesale market, and (ii) setting up an aggregator model under which an entity would buy electricity on favorable commercial terms and make it available to certain consumer categories below market price passing onwards the advantages to the consumers, essentially subsidizing the difference between lower retail prices and higher wholesale ones. See EC, 2022.

toward more targeted alternatives with less impact on market functioning (EC, 2021, 2022b, 2022c, 2022a). However, price regulation, which has an immediate positive effect on alleviating consumer pressure, proved to be a preferable instrument from the Member States' perspective. As shown above, during the COVID-19 pandemic and energy price crisis, beyond energy poor and vulnerable customers, other customer groups, notably SMEs, microenterprises and other residential users, also benefited from regulated prices. Such price interventions primarily serve as a general mechanism to mitigate the impact of rising energy prices on customers. They were applied in a way that broke free from restrictions and conditions set out by EU law.[620] The wide presence of these price interventions during exceptional circumstances can undermine market-based incentives that consumers can receive when engaging in DR and renewables self-consumption individually or collectively, and deter private sector investment.[621]

710. The divergence between the Member States and the EU in safeguarding free price formation and its related goals of decarbonization during the crisis highlights a question that did not receive due consideration in EU electricity law. That is, amid extreme price shocks, how to properly govern 'emergency measures' intervening in price setting.[622] Deviating from principles of the legislation or Constitution in extraordinary circumstances or a 'state of exception' has long been a highly debatable subject.[623] The tricky question merits consideration in the energy sector, given the practical difficulty in prohibiting

---

620 EU law only allows retail price regulation for two customer groups, i.e., vulnerable and energy poor households, and microenterprises and household customers, which are neither energy poor nor vulnerable customers, while for the latter, the purpose is limited to establishing effective competition between suppliers and achieving fully effective market-based retail pricing of electricity. See Section 4.1.2 of Chapter III above for more details about restrictions on retail price interventions.

621 Reporting on orders for wind turbines in 2022 showed a year-on-year drop of total wind turbine orders in Europe by 47%. This is partly attributed to 2022's emergency measures, which intervened in wholesale and retail electricity prices, thereby resulting in a slower investment pace than needed to reach EU targets. See ACER, 2023b, sections 4 and 5, annexes 2 and 3.

622 In its assessment of the electricity market design, the ACER highlighted the benefits delivered by the existing electricity market but acknowledged that the electricity market design is, however, not designed for the 'emergency' situation that the EU found itself in during 2021 and 2022. The CEP indeed reinforced legal arrangements for preventing, preparing for and managing electricity crises via the Regulation on risk-preparedness in the electricity sector. However, the electricity crises subject to that Regulation are limited to crises in the security of electricity supply, namely situations where there is a significant electricity shortage or when it is impossible to supply electricity to customers. It does not cover the electricity price crisis not caused by electricity shortage. See *Regulation on risk-preparedness in the electricity sector*, 2019, Articles 1 and 2(9); ACER, 2022.

623 The concept of a state of exception (German: *Ausnahmezustand*) and the exercise of emergency power that transcends the rule of law in the name of the public good have been intensively discussed in Germany, in particular. See e.g. Schmitt, 1921; Agamben, 2008; Kersten, 2016.

Member States from having recourse to such exceptional measures when facing exceptionally high electricity prices. From the EU law perspective, whether and to what extent the free market price is allowed to deviate should be considered in the specific context of price crises. Doing so aims to avoid the potential widespread abuse or misuse of emergency measures and their impact on frustrating the goals whose delivery relies on proper market functioning (e.g., DR and renewables uptake), thereby seeking an acceptable compromise between crisis responses and market functioning. Providing a clear and comprehensive definition of 'extraordinary circumstances' in the energy law sector is quite challenging. To translate lessons learned from the past energy price crisis in a timely manner, what is needed is to define the price crisis and articulate the bounds of EU law for emergency measures in this case. Key legal issues to be addressed are two-fold: (1) defining the exceptional situation, i.e., in which cases, an energy price crisis is considered to occur, and (2) defining, in times of crisis, to what extent price interventions are allowed to extend beyond customer groups allowed by the Electricity Directive and with what conditions.

711. The EU has stepped in to protect the legal order of EU energy law from further devastation. It does so by temporarily extending existing price interventions EU-wide in the case of a price crisis, and on this basis, formalizing such deviations. Unlike the tacit acceptance of national emergency measures that violate EU law, this approach permits new deviations while taking into account the broader interests of the internal electricity market – often overlooked by Member States. As pointed out by the EC when providing an overview of the merits and drawbacks of emergency measures, if not introduced at the EU level, capping prices could '*distort the flow of electricity in the internal market and trigger flows from countries with the cap to those without it without consideration for scarcity consideration*' (EC, 2022c). An EU-level common approach is required to avoid even more profound risks and consequences across the EU that could be brought about by isolated national responses.

712. The EU's actions to re-evaluate and institutionalize permissible deviations from 'market-based supply prices' in the energy price crisis context consist of two steps. First, in 2022, the European Council adopted Council Regulation 1854/2022 to establish an emergency intervention to mitigate the effects of high energy prices through exceptional, targeted and time-limited measures. It can be seen from this Regulation that the legislator acknowledged the difficulty in adopting some non-distortive alternatives, considering that Member States do not all have the same fiscal space to take the necessary measures to protect vulnerable households and companies by providing them with state-financed rebates or subsidies (*Council Regulation (EU) 2022/1854*, recital 57). This may be a significant reason leading the legislator to officially allow extended price interventions to be included in the toolbox of available measures that Member States have at their disposal to support energy consumers.

Article 12 of this Regulation expanded the scope of the public price interventions, allowing Member States to temporarily extend public intervention in price setting for the supply of electricity to SMEs under specific conditions. When applying this derogation, Member States are allowed to set retail electricity prices below cost temporarily and exceptionally for both households and SMEs, subject to certain conditions under Article 13. Table 14 provides an overview of the duration and conditions of new derogations from existing EU law on price regulation.

**Table 14. Temporary emergency price interventions allowed by the EU** *(Council Regulation (EU) 2022/1854*, articles 12, 13, 19 and 22)

| | **Article 12: Intervening in price setting for the supply of electricity to *SMEs*** | **Article 13: *Setting electricity prices below cost* for (1) *SMEs, and (2) household customers and microenterprises which are neither energy poor nor vulnerable customers*** |
|---|---|---|
| **Conditions** | (1) take into account the beneficiary's annual consumption over the last five years and retain an incentive for demand reduction;<br>(2) comply with the conditions set out in Article 5(4) and (7) of the Electricity Directive;<br>(3) when setting electricity prices below cost, comply with the conditions set out in Article 13 of this Regulation. | (1) the measure covers a limited amount of consumption and retains an incentive for demand reduction;<br>(2) no discrimination between suppliers;<br>(3) compensate suppliers for supplying below cost;<br>(4) all suppliers are eligible to provide offers at the price for the supply of electricity which is below cost on the same basis. |
| **Duration** | Temporary interventions are allowed until 31 December 2023 | |
| **Union-level monitoring** | The competent authority of each Member State shall monitor the implementation of the concerned measures taken under Articles 12 and 13;<br>By 31 January 2023 and again by 30 April 2023, Member States shall report to the Commission on any public interventions in the price setting for the supply of electricity referred to in the above two provisions. | |

713. The Council Regulation does not define the energy price crisis, as it is an ad hoc response to a single price crisis. Yet, in the long run, to integrate the lessons of this crisis and avoid the abuse of emergency power, it should be made clear in what cases the EU institutions and Member States may adopt exceptional measures. In the 2024 Amendment to the Electricity Directive, the resilience of the internal electricity market to future price shocks has gained importance. Article 66a was added to the Electricity Directive to ensure affordability during times of price crisis and prevent more household customers from falling into an energy poverty trap (*2024 Amendment to the Electricity Directive*, recital 11). It creates a legal framework for triggering the temporary extension of regulated

prices during an electricity price crisis when wholesale and retail electricity prices increase significantly. This framework contains conditions for allowing Member States to temporarily extend the application of regulated prices and restrictions that must be respected, as outlined in Table 15 below.

**Table 15. The legal framework for triggering deviations from the principle of free supply price formation in the energy price crises**

| | |
|---|---|
| **The precondition for temporary price regulation:** declaring a regional or Union-wide electricity price crisis | • *The implementing powers*: conferred on the Council, acting on a proposal from the Commission;<br>• *The conditions for the electricity price crisis declaration*: the assessment of whether an electricity price crisis exists should be based on a comparison with prices in times of normal market operation;[624]<br>• *Restrictions on this declaration*: (i) specifying its period of validity which may be for a period of up to one year; (ii) the extension of that period is subject to the specific procedure for consecutive periods of up to one year; (iii) ensuring fair competition and trade across all Member States affected by the implementing decision so that the internal market is not unduly distorted. |
| **Restrictions on Member States' temporary targeted public interventions** | • *When temporarily extending the application of regulated prices to SMEs*, public interventions must (i) be limited to at most 70% of the beneficiary's consumption during the same period of the previous year and retain an incentive for demand reduction; (ii) respect the conditions set out in Article 5(4) and (7), mainly regarding ensuring non-discrimination and proportionality and minimizing the effect on market entry and competition; (iii) minimize any negative fragmentation of the internal market; and (iv) comply with conditions for exceptionally and temporarily setting a price for the supply of electricity which is below cost.<br>• *As regards household customers and SMEs, exceptionally and temporarily setting a price for the supply of electricity which is below cost is only allowed when the conditions are fulfilled*: (a) the price set for household customers only applies, at most, to 80% of median household consumption and retains an incentive for demand reduction; (b) there is no discrimination between suppliers; (c) suppliers are compensated for supplying below cost in a transparent and non-discriminatory manner; (d) all suppliers are eligible to provide offers for the price for the supply of electricity which is below cost on the same basis; (e) measures proposed do not distort the internal electricity market. |

Source: Author's own elaboration based on recital 28 and Article 66a of the 2024 Amendment to the Electricity Directive.

---

624 The specific conditions cover (a) the existence of very high average prices in wholesale electricity markets of at least two and a half times the average price during the previous five years, and at least 180 EUR/MWh which is expected to continue for at least six months, the calculation of the average price during the previous five years not taking into account those periods where a regional or Union-wide electricity price crisis was declared; (b) sharp increases in electricity retail prices in the range of 70% occur which are expected to continue for at least three months.

714. For the duration of the validity of the Council's decision declaring a regional or Union-wide electricity price crisis, Article 5 of the Electricity Directive can be deviated from to protect households and SMEs from the price crisis. The newly introduced framework mainly governs the trigger of the above-mentioned 'exceptional circumstance' associated with energy prices and the application of 'emergency measures' in that case. As can be seen from Table 15, it reflects efforts to seek balances between the need for emergency measures and other important interests and objectives, including energy savings[625] and market functioning, while also safeguarding the fundamental principles of EU law, notably non-discrimination and proportionality. Those conditions and restrictions generally aim to reduce ill-designed emergency measures and prevent market functioning from being disproportionately compromised. By doing so, market price signals for DR, renewables self-consumption, and demand reduction can be partially preserved.

715. Overall, energy price regulation is highly politically sensitive. It is not an easy task for Member States to implement strengthened restrictions on price interventions introduced by the CEP. The energy price crisis of 2021–2022 even rolled back the accomplished efforts in this regard. With electricity prices declining and back to 'normal' in 2023, national measures deregulating wholesale and retail prices may be underway to fulfill their obligations under the CEP. Importantly, the energy crisis presents an opportunity for the EU to reflect on a missing element of electricity market design: the capacity to effectively protect consumers from sudden, extraordinary price surges without unduly compromising market principles. The common approach adopted at the Union level is particularly noteworthy. As shown above, it seeks to safeguard the legal order by prudently reassessing deviations in the context of the price crisis and governing the exercise of emergency power by Member States. With ad hoc responses amid the crisis and an ex-post amendment to the legislation built on the lessons learned, the EU helps to avoid the destructive impact of ill-designed price interventions on the adherence to market principles and other decarbonization goals secured by those principles. This is not only of significance for mitigating the impact of the past price crisis, but also for better securing proper market signals and incentives when facing possible future price shocks.

625 The due account of energy savings is reflected in the restriction on the proportion of consumption subject to price interventions and the requirement for retaining an incentive for demand reduction. This aims to prevent creating incentives that encourage increased consumption. See *2024 Amendment to the Electricity Directive*, recital 28.

### 3.2.2. *Electricity Market Design Parameters*

716. The adjustment of market design parameters is rather technical, as shown in Section 4.2 of Chapter III. The ACER has recently given a comprehensive overview of the national implementation of improved market design parameters. There are still some hindering the engagement of individual consumers and those acting via aggregation and energy communities in flexibility procurement for balancing and congestion management (ACER, 2023a). As detailed in Chapter III, EU law merely harmonizes technical parameters of wholesale and balancing markets. Inadequate implementation of Union-level minimum requirements for adapting the market design to final customers' participation is thus one of the factors responsible for market entry barriers. For other flexibility markets, the market principle of removing undue market entry barriers for final customers is translated into a general obligation for system operators to ensure the effective participation of all qualified market participants (*Electricity Directive*, Articles 31, 32 and 40). Such effective market participation is additionally secured by substantive and procedural safeguards: *flexibility procurement rules adopted by the system operator must be objective, transparent and non-discriminatory and subject to regulatory approval, and should be developed in coordination with stakeholders, including relevant system operators and market actors.* The implementation of the participatory rule-making procedure will be separately examined in Section 3.4 below. Here, the major focus is on how to prevent undue market entry barriers by implementing the substantive requirements for flexibility procurement rules.

717. The substantive requirements consist of broad principles, notably transparency and non-discrimination. Despite their fundamental role in EU energy law, their connotation and concrete application criteria in specific contexts have not been specified by EU law. To enable them to become legal safeguards for the above 'effective market participation', NRAs must specify specific requirements stemming from those general principles, against which flexibility procurement rules could be fully assessed and potential market entry barriers could be identified. The technical specifications developed by the Flemish DSO for flexibility procurement demonstrate how a system operator can circumvent regulatory oversight, thereby gaining discretion in designing specific technical parameters for flexibility procurement. Regulatory approval by the VREG indicates how the principle of transparency can be leveraged to ensure effective market participation.

718. In the respective technical specifications for procuring non-frequency ancillary services and flexibility for congestion management, a common problem is that the DSO either failed to completely elaborate on technical parameters

in the specifications submitted for approval or left room to allow tender-specific design, deviations or additions.[626] For instance, the DSO has designed technical specifications for procuring a non-frequency ancillary service, 'voltage management'.[627] Some key parameters of procurement, including the pre-registration conditions for the service and the general operating conditions to qualify for the service, were not exhaustively described in the submitted rules.[628] In addition, the specifications showed that the final elaboration of the bid selection process would be completed by the tender.[629] The same problem also arises in the technical specifications for procuring flexibility for congestion management. The specifications defer the definition of certain parameters, such as response time, control speed, and measurement accuracy, to the tendering phase.[630] Furthermore, the DSO explicitly acknowledged that the specifications are incomplete and intended to refine them through additional market testing.[631] Yet, it does not provide any further elaboration of these market tests, for instance, the purposes of the planned tests and questions to be addressed, the exact approach to market testing and the timing.[632]

719. The above-listed technical parameters have an important impact on which installations can participate in the DSO's flexibility procurement. Defining these parameters during a specific tender or allowing supplements or deviations unique to a tender grants the DSO significant discretion while bypassing the two-step consultation procedures and regulatory approval required by Flemish regulations.[633] This situation can hinder transparency, certainty and predictability of the specifications, which makes it challenging to identify technical parameters that may undermine effective and non-discriminatory market participation.

720. To ensure transparency and prevent potential market hurdles, in its evaluation of the proposed flexibility procurement rules, the VREG interpreted the principle of transparency and elaborated on specific requirements derived

626 *VREG 2023 Decision on the rules for the purchase of non-frequency-related ancillary services and grid losses*, Section II.1.2; *VREG 2024 Decision on the specifications for flexibility procurement for local congestion management*, Section II.3.

627 See Section 2.3.3.1 of this Chapter for more details about the voltage management service.

628 *VREG 2023 Decision on the rules for the purchase of non-frequency-related ancillary services and grid losses*, Section II.1.2.

629 Ibid.

630 Fluvius, 2023; *VREG 2024 Decision on the specifications for flexibility procurement for local congestion management*, Section II.3.

631 *VREG 2024 Decision on the specifications for flexibility procurement for local congestion management*, Section II.3.

632 Fluvius, 2023; *VREG 2024 Decision on the specifications for flexibility procurement for local congestion management*, Section II.3.

633 For more details about the two-step consultation procedures for making flexibility procurement rules established by the TRDE, see Section 2.3.3.1 of this Chapter above.

from that general principle. The regulator applied the general public law doctrine, emphasizing three key elements of that principle: (i) ensuring access to specific procurement rules, (ii) establishing clear procurement procedures, and (iii) effectively communicating requirements to stakeholders.[634] The principle of transparency entails both substantive and procedural requirements, which essentially relate to completeness and clarity of rules and effective communication with stakeholders. Based on these, the VREG established that due to the above missing elements that remain to be defined in the tender or through market tests, not every step in the procurement process is clearly completed. The proposed procurement rules thus did not meet the requirement of transparency.

721. To comply with the transparency principle, the VREG clarified several detailed requirements. First, tender-specific design, supplements or deviations constitute part of flexibility procurement rules and must also be submitted for approval.[635] In other words, the specifications should contain all possible options in terms of conditions for flexibility market participation. Therefore, implementing the transparency requirement implies that the information to be completed, supplemented or adjusted in the tender should also be included in the proposed technical specifications, while the tender should be submitted to VREG for verification.[636] Second, given that some technical parameters are to be specified via market tests, a clear overview of these market tests, including timing, purposes and approaches, should be clearly stated in technical specifications and communicated to stakeholders.[637]

722. The third requirement arising from the principle of transparency is that rule-making should facilitate stakeholders' understanding and ensure effective communication of the rules. This requirement has both procedural and substantive dimensions. Procedurally, it involves stakeholder responsiveness – the DSO must provide clear and comprehensive responses during rule-making processes, as outlined in Section 2.3.3.1 of this chapter. Substantively, the DSO is responsible for formulating procurement rules in a way that ensures effective communication. In the proposed specifications, a problem is that there are additional rules or exceptions to a certain market design element scattered throughout the various sections, which are not cited in the section specifically addressing that element, such as 'penalization'.[638] This hinders effective communication of procurement rules, which can also compromise transparency.

---

634 Lodge and Stirton, 2010, p 352; *VREG 2023 Decision on the rules for the purchase of non-frequency-related ancillary services and grid losses*, Section II.1.2.

635 *VREG 2024 Decision on the specifications for flexibility procurement for local congestion management*, Section II.3.

636 Ibid.

637 Ibid.

638 Ibid.

In specifications that uphold the transparency principle, a market participant seeking to clarify a specific aspect by referencing section titles in the technical specifications should be able to locate all mandatory provisions within the relevant section.

723. The VREG's assessments of the DSO's flexibility procurement rules highlight the role of the law in optimizing market design and lowering market entry barriers. In addition to adapting some technical parameters to consumer participation,[639] the law can also mitigate market entry barriers posed by specific technical parameters by implementing adequate measures to uphold the principle of transparency. As demonstrated above, this approach can minimize the DSO's ability to exercise rule-making discretion and evade scrutiny from both regulators and stakeholders.

724. Overall, technical parameters of flexibility markets are often cited as barriers to market entry for final customers and small aggregators. The Flemish energy regulator suggests another approach to address this persistent challenge, highlighting the crucial role of applying fundamental principles, particularly the principle of transparency.

#### 3.2.3. *Approaches to Accessing Electricity Markets*

725. In addition to the general rule of opening markets to active customers, renewables self-consumers and energy communities, EU law provides specific approaches to allow them to sell self-produced RES-E and seek market-based remuneration, as detailed in Chapter III. Among them, their access to PPAs and P2P electricity trading notably faces legal challenges, as elaborated below.

##### 3.2.3.1. PPAs

726. Member States are required to ensure that active customers, renewables self-consumers and RECs can sell self-generated RES-E via PPAs as required by EU law. So far, few works have addressed legal issues related to PPAs or renewable PPAs.[640] In 2021, the CEER reported that there was still fragmentation

639 The 2024 Amendment to the Electricity Regulation has lowered the minimum bid size to 100 kW. See *2024 Amendment to the Electricity Regulation*, Article 8(3).

640 This is based on search results of the databases Web of Science on 28 March 2024 with the following inclusion criteria: (1) (AB=(power purchase agreement)) AND AB=(law); (2) (AB=(renewables power purchase agreement)) AND AB=(regulatory challenges); (3) (AB=(renewables power purchase agreement)) AND AB=(legal issues); and (4) (AB=(renewables power purchase agreement)) AND AB=(regulatory challenges) AND AB=(EU). The first criterion delivers 19 results, but only one article is concerned with legal issues of implementing PPAs within the EU, which is S Słotwiński, 'The Significance of the "Power Purchase Agreement" for the Development of Local Energy Markets in the Theoretical Perspective of Polish Legal Conditions' (2022) 15 Energies 6691. The second one delivers

across Europe as to the rules surrounding PPAs (CEER, 2021b). France and Germany allowed on-site PPAs where a company would partner with a generator to produce renewable electricity on the company's land to power the company's operations, but physical PPAs[641] were restricted (CEER, 2021b). During the 2021–2022 energy price crisis, renewables PPAs gained increased attention due to their potential to drive investments in RES-E and hedge price risks (ACER, 2022). In response to the price crisis, the EC issued guidance to Member States on good practices for facilitating PPAs (EC, 2022d). The guidance shows that by 2022, only 8 Member States reported on existing barriers and measures to support the uptake of renewables PPAs. For most countries, there was no clear framework for either renewable project developers or consumers to set up direct PPAs (EC, 2022d; Słotwiński, 2022). Moreover, the involvement of small-scale producers and medium and small end users in renewables PPAs remained limited (ACER, 2022; EC, 2022d; Słotwiński, 2022). This implies that PPAs have not been a widely applied approach for renewables self-consumers to sell self-produced RES-E. Several major barriers exist, as noted by Union-level and national authorities (EC, 2022d; CREG, 2024).

727. First, given their customizable feature,[642] they might be less suitable for portfolios of small players (ACER and CEER, 2023a). Small-scale renewable energy projects are facing challenges when entering the corporate PPA market because of a limited portfolio of projects and the limited technical and legal expertise required to negotiate and sign PPAs (EC, 2022d). Even RECs and CECs are often too small to sign economically attractive PPAs with large off-takers (EC, 2022d). One solution would be to pool smaller sellers and open up participation in PPAs to groups of smaller producers (ACER, 2022). However, the inherent customization of PPAs may make it hard to establish a multilateral or standard contract, where all parties agree on the contract specification and who covers the volume risk (ACER and CEER, 2023a). Contractual costs of PPAs may prove prohibitive, which can notably hinder the accessibility to small actors (CREG, 2024).

728. From the perspective of buyers, medium and small consumers notably have difficulty accessing PPAs. The creditworthiness of an off-taker is a major barrier (and a risk factor) across most sectors (EC, 2022d; CREG, 2024). Debt providers to renewables projects continue to require strong credit ratings to

---

5 results, but none of them relate to electricity PPAs within the EU context. No search results were found that match the third and fourth criteria.

641 A physical PPA means that the customer receives the physical delivery of (or title to) the energy through the grid. A financial PPA (also referred to as a virtual PPA and synthetic PPA) allows the buyer to purchase renewable energy virtually – in other words, there is no need to own the title to physical energy. See CEER, 2021. For more details on the taxonomy of PPAs, see Słotwiński, 2022.

642 See Section 4.3.1 of Chapter III for more details about the customizable feature of PPAs.

consider the PPA bankable while most medium and small consumers are not rated by any major credit rating agency (EC, 2022d; CREG, 2024). Moreover, such bilateral arrangements have costly exit clauses (ACER and CEER, 2023a). It can contradict the right of household consumers and small enterprises to switch suppliers without switching-related fees in light of Article 12 of the Electricity Directive. This problem is indicated by the EC's guidance, which suggests that Member States enable flexible contracting for SMEs, including the provision of specific guidance for contract termination fees for small enterprises under Article 12 (EC, 2022d). However, doing so, in turn, undermines the PPAs' advantages of providing long-term commitments and helping producers hedge their investment costs, lowering the attractiveness of PPAs for them.

729. Furthermore, medium and small consumers have limited visibility on their future electricity demand and lower volumes of electricity consumption, which makes managing imbalances more difficult (EC, 2022d). This makes them more hesitant to sign long-term renewables PPAs, especially if there is no clarity on the potential impacts if long-term contracts need to be terminated (EC, 2022d). Long-term contracts offer opportunities for affordable prices, but they also risk locking customers into high prices (ACER and CEER, 2023a). It is also questionable whether long-term PPAs can deliver competitive prices to end users. Competition among producers involved in long-term PPAs is weaker than competition in short-term markets, due to a very limited supply and demand at any given moment, and the absence of cross-border competition.[643] Hence, consumers might, on average, be faced with higher electricity supply costs (ACER and CEER, 2023a).

730. These challenges and paradoxes suggest that it is not an easy task to enable energy communities, active customers and renewables self-consumers to sell self-generated RES-E via PPAs. Actively promoting PPAs also entails some undesired consequences. There is a fear that market power can arise with numerous very long-term contracts (CEER, 2021b). The ACER and CEER warn that the wide roll-out of PPAs also has an impact on market liquidity and transparency. Promoting PPAs means promoting bilateral trading, which means that the MW or MWh covered by these PPAs will inevitably disappear from the volumes in the forward and DA market if those PPAs are physically settled (ACER and CEER, 2023a). On these grounds, the ACER and CEER refrain from actively supporting PPAs and question their suitability for small players. They are thus not in favor of EU-wide obligations for Member States to provide state insurance or guarantees for counterparty risk, even though doing so can facilitate

[643] Facilitating cross-border PPAs would theoretically be welcomed, but this could not be done without the necessary transmission capacity allocation by TSOs to facilitate trading. Capacity allocation in timeframes of 10–20 years is unimaginable in the present and foreseeable future. See ACER and CEER, 2023b.

the access of small off-takers to PPAs.[644] The potential risks of widely applying PPAs and the challenges of engaging small producers and consumers may also explain the wait-and-see approach of some Member States regarding the matter of addressing barriers to PPAs.

731. The 2024 Amendment to the Electricity Regulation introduced a range of rules to facilitate access to the PPA market. Member States must provide financial instruments, such as guarantee schemes, to de-risk PPAs, and allow the participation of projects that reserve part of the electricity for sale through a PPA when designing support schemes for RES-E (*2024 Amendment to the Electricity Regulation*, Article 19a). In parallel, the obligation to provide guarantee schemes is accompanied by a requirement to avoid lowering the liquidity in electricity markets (*2024 Amendment to the Electricity Regulation*, Article 19a). This requirement takes into account the above concerns of ACER and CEER regarding the potential negative impact of promoting PPAs on market liquidity. Yet, it is questionable whether Member States can develop adequate companion measures to mitigate the impact on liquidity in wholesale and forward markets. Amid uncertainties posed by PPAs' rollout and relevant national actions, the EU legislator also introduced follow-up monitoring of the EU-wide rollout of PPAs by requiring the ACER to publish an annual assessment on the PPA market at the Union and Member State level (*2024 Amendment to the Electricity Regulation*, Article 19b (1)). It also requires the EC to draw up specific guidance to steer Member States to solve barriers in the PPA markets (*2024 Amendment to the Electricity Regulation*, Article 19a (10)). This soft-law approach can complement existing Union law, which has not fully addressed barriers to accessing PPAs, such as high contract costs that can easily deter small actors, including renewables self-consumers and RECs.

732. Generally, the 2024 Amendment introduced more granular measures to overcome specific barriers to applying PPAs, including those hindering small actors' access, while taking measures to mitigate the potential risks associated with the wider rollout of such contracts. It may help active customers, renewables self-consumers and energy communities to further harness PPAs to sell self-produced RES-E. Yet, to what extent PPAs backed by these measures are economically attractive for these sellers and end users remains to be seen, given the remaining disadvantages relating to contract termination and affordable prices mentioned above. The role of the EC's guidance and best practices in promoting PPAs and mitigating market liquidity concerns also deserves the attention of future research.

---

644 Providing guarantees aims to address the lack of creditworthiness of an off-taker. By taking over part of the guarantee and thus reducing risk and collateral requirements for private entities, a government could facilitate PPAs between smaller actors. See ACER, 2022.

733. Finally, there is another challenge not mentioned by Union institutions when evaluating further steps to facilitate PPAs. When final customers and energy communities sell electricity directly via physical PPAs, they also assume the role of suppliers. This raises a problem regarding the applicability of supplier obligations, as is the case in P2P electricity trading. The non-discrimination principle must be applied to determine whether provisions governing electricity supply should be equally applied to individual and collective prosumers selling self-produced RES-E. The challenge lies in the absence of well-established criteria for applying the non-discrimination principle, as drawn out in the next subsection. To circumvent supplier obligations, the literature offers the possibility to execute a trilateral agreement with the involvement of an intermediary (Słotwiński, 2022). This solution has been adopted in practice. For instance, in Belgium, offshore project developers entering into physical PPAs are required to work through an intermediary because they do not have a supply license (CREG, 2024). These physical PPAs are 'Merchant PPAs', which involve a utility company (e.g., ENGIE and TotalEnergies) acting as an intermediary between the producer and the industrial customer (CREG, 2024).

#### 3.2.3.2. P2P Electricity Trading

734. Another way for renewables self-consumers to sell surplus self-produced RES-E is through P2P electricity trading. In enabling renewables self-consumers to engage in P2P electricity trading, Member States are confronted with several key issues. Would the peers, both sellers and buyers, retain their consumer status and enjoy the consumer rights granted by European consumer protection law and energy law? Should the selling party of the P2P electricity trading be subject to supplier obligations? How to define the role and obligations of P2P trading platform providers? Are they also subject to supplier obligations? So far, there are no systematic answers to these legal issues (Almeida et al., 2021; Lavrijssen et al., 2023). This contributes to slow large-scale commercial deployment in practice across the EU (Zhou et al., 2023).

735. At the time of writing (March 2024), despite extensive research on the technical aspects of P2P electricity trading,[645] in-depth analyses of the legal issues involved in applying P2P electricity trading across EU Member States remained very scarce.[646] Some existing studies analyze the status, rights, and

645 There are 460 results from the Web of Science database with the inclusion criterion: 'AB=(peer-to-peer electricity trading)'. See e.g. Teotia Falti et al., 2020; Tushar et al., 2021; Schwidtal et al., 2023.

646 On 13 March 2024, the author searched the databases Web of Science with the inclusion criteria: AB=(peer-to-peer electricity trading)) AND AB=(legal issues)) AND AB=(EU). There was only one search result, which concerned the legal issues of processing and protecting personal data in the electricity sector with the advent of innovations such as P2P electricity

obligations of prosumers involved in P2P electricity trading solely through the lens of the CJEU's case law on general consumer protection law. They, however, omit the specific contexts of those case laws and specificities of electricity trading, presenting misleading legal advice as pointed out later on. In discussing the above-listed legal issues, this section will also particularly demonstrate why EU legislation and case law on consumer rights are of limited relevance in determining the legal nature of renewables self-consumers involved in P2P electricity trading.

736. This subsection first examines the consumer status and rights of renewables self-consumers involved in P2P electricity trading in more detail while reviewing existing views on relevant legal issues. A critical review of existing debates will help refine approaches to evaluating the status and rights of renewables self-consumers in the P2P electricity trading context. When self-consumers sell RES-E, their activity constitutes 'supply' defined by EU law. Whether they should be subject to rules governing electricity supply and associated obligations is then discussed. Lastly, this subsection analyzes the legal challenges of regulating digital platforms that support P2P electricity trading.

#### (i) Consumer Status

737. In entitling renewables self-consumers to conduct P2P electricity trading, a key issue is the applicability of consumer rights granted by European general consumer protection law and energy law. This is closely linked to another question as to whether renewables self-consumers involved in P2P trading retain their consumer status. Some argue that the REDII recognizes their consumer nature since when defining P2P trading, it highlights that '*the right to conduct P2P trading shall be without prejudice to the rights and obligations of the parties involved as final customers, producers, suppliers or aggregators*' (*REDII*, Article 2(18); Almeida et al., 2021). Others analyze the consumer status of renewables self-consumers through the lens of the CJEU's case law on consumer rights (Milčiuvienė et al., 2019; Almeida et al., 2021). Both perspectives are problematic.

738. First, the requirement contained in the definition of P2P electricity trading should be interpreted as meaning that when involved parties constitute final customers, rights and obligations set for final customers remain applicable. It remains to be clarified whether the involved renewables self-consumers still qualify as final customers. One can thus not deduce from this requirement

trading. The search results of Google Scholar with the terms 'P2P electricity trading', 'EU' and 'legal issues' show more works regarding legal issues of implementing P2P electricity trading, mainly including those of L de Almeida et al., Lavrijssen, Reins and Ten Caten, Van Soest, which have been reviewed in this book.

that renewables self-consumers maintain their consumer status. True, Article 21 of the REDII explicitly states that renewables self-consumers are entitled to maintain their rights and obligations as final customers. Nevertheless, as addressed above in Sections 2 and 3.1 of this Chapter, this does not mean that renewables self-consumers are always regarded as final customers and enjoy consumer rights in any case. Rather, it entails a step of assessing whether renewables self-consumers still qualify as 'final customers', which is defined by EU law as 'consumers purchasing electricity for own use'. This assessment is necessary since it is conceivable that end users may lose this status when they realize electricity self-sufficiency and no longer buy electricity. Additionally, consumer rights under consumer protection law are not defined in general, abstract terms, but always with respect to a contract.[647] This is not only repeatedly emphasized by case law on consumer protection[648] but also indicated by energy customer rights, which are established in the context of supply and other energy service contracts (see, e.g., *Electricity Directive*, Articles 10 and 13). Hence, the determination of consumer status and consumer rights is context-specific: the certain activity conducted and contracts entered by renewables self-consumers must be considered. The consumer status of renewables self-consumers involved in P2P electricity trading is a question that warrants a dedicated assessment.

739. Second, could the consumer status of renewables self-consumers engaged in P2P electricity trading be determined from the lens of general consumer protection law and its case law? The answer is yes, but not entirely. The existing literature applies the CJEU's rulings on consumer rights to analyze the self-consumers' consumer status and the applicability of consumer rights. For instance, based on an analysis of case C-498/16 against Facebook,[649] Milčiuvienė et al. conclude that 'energy prosumers fall into two main groups for consumer rights protection law' (Milčiuvienė et al., 2019). They argue that according to the ruling of the CJEU, one group of energy prosumers that acts as consumers (the trading activity is only marginal) would enjoy consumer protection, while the other group, which acts for commercial purposes (concerning selling electricity), would lose the consumer protection in relation to contracts that have commercial purposes (Milčiuvienė et al., 2019). However, either for evaluating

647 *Opinion of Advocate General Bobek in Schrems, C-498/16, EU:C:2017:863*, point 29.

648 A consistent line of this Court's case law is that the determination of consumer status must be made by reference to the position of that person in a particular contract, having regard to the nature and aim of that contract. See *Judgment of 3 July 1997, Benincasa, C-269/95, EU:C:1997:337*, paragraph 16.

649 Judgement of 25 January 2018, *Schrems*.

the consumer status of sellers or buyers in P2P electricity trading, the application of the *Schrems* ruling can raise problems.

740. In the *Schrems* case, the court aimed to evaluate the consumer status of a user of the same contract service. At issue was whether the applicant, Mr. *Schrems*, a private Facebook account user, may lose his consumer status when using the Facebook account for carrying out activities such as publishing, lecturing, operating websites, or fund-raising for the enforcement of claims.[650] The court's ruling centers around the assessment of the consumer status of the user of the service supplied by the same contract, given the changing use of that contract service over time (i.e., potentially changing from initially private use to professional use). Simply put, it deals with the position of the user of goods or services under the same supply contract. It is not about assessing whether a person who constitutes a consumer in relation to a supply contract (e.g., the electricity supply contract) still maintains his or her consumer status when entering into another contract of selling different services or goods (e.g., self-produced RES-E). The renewables self-consumer acting as the seller concludes a P2P trading contract for selling surplus production, but not for using services or goods. Apparently, the consumer status issues addressed by the *Schrems* case are different from those to be solved in P2P electricity trading contracts. Misalignment arises when applying the court's ruling on that case to determine the consumer status of the selling party involved in P2P electricity trading.

741. In addition, what the *Schrems* case specifically evaluated is the consumer status within the meaning of Article 15 of Regulation No 44/2001, which aimed to provide special jurisdiction over consumer contracts.[651] It should be highlighted that the special rule of jurisdiction only applies to a specific consumer group deemed to be a weaker party in need of protection, namely the consumer concluding contracts for private purposes (i.e., for purposes falling outside his 'trade or profession').[652] This implies that only natural persons liable to be the economically weaker party than their contractual partners, who are traders or professionals, can enjoy special protection stemming from that provision. Industrial and commercial energy consumers are apparently not consumer groups that Article 15 aims to cover, as they purchase electricity

650 *Judgment of 25 January 2018, Schrems, C-498/16, EU:C:2018:37*, paragraph 25.

651 *Council Regulation (EC) No 44/2001*, Article 15.

652 This is also supported by recital 13 of that Regulation. It states that '*in relation to insurance, consumer contracts and employment, the weaker party should be protected by rules of jurisdiction more favourable to his interests than the general rules provide for.*'

for professional purposes. Similar consumer protection stemming from exceptional jurisdiction arrangements also exists in the Brussels Convention (in Section 4, entitled 'Jurisdiction over consumer contracts', in Title II, consisting of Articles 13 to 15).[653] In the *Gruber* case assessing the consumer status defined by Article 13 of the Brussels Convention, the court highlights that those special arrangements introduced by the provisions of Title II, Section 4, of the Brussels Convention '*only cover private final consumers, not engaged in trade or professional activities*'.[654] They '*derogate from the general rule laid down in the first paragraph of Article 2, and from the rules of special jurisdiction for contracts in general enshrined in Article 5(1) of the Convention, serve to ensure adequate protection for the consumer as the party deemed to be economically weaker and less experienced in legal matters than the other, commercial, party to the contract, who must not therefore be discouraged from suing by being compelled to bring his action before the courts in the Contracting State in which the other party to the contract is domiciled*'.[655]

742. It is clear that neither Regulation No 44/2001 nor the Brussels Convention aims to create generic criteria for assessing the status of all consumers. Instead, they focus on defining which consumers qualify for protection under special jurisdiction rules. The standards contained in these two legal instruments for assessing consumer status and their interpretation by the CJEU[656] could not be generally applied, given the specific purpose they serve. In particular, the court's rulings assessing consumer status within the meaning of those jurisdiction rules are irrelevant when evaluating the consumer status of commercial and industrial renewables self-consumers involved in P2P electricity trading, either as sellers or buyers, as already noted. Summarizing the above analysis, Figure 14 visually depicts which customer groups and in what cases are covered by case law on jurisdiction rules that protect consumers. For the rest of the renewables self-consumers involved in P2P electricity trading, their consumer status remains an unresolved issue.

---

653 *Brussels Convention*, 1968.

654 *Judgment of 21 June 1978, Bertrand, C-150/77, EU:C:1978:137*, paragraph 21; *Judgment of 19 January 1993, Shearson Lehman Hutton, C-89/91, EU:C:1993:15*, paragraphs 19 and 22; *Judgment of 3 July 1997, Benincasa, C-269/95, EU:C:1997:337*, paragraph 15; *Judgment of 11 July 2002, Gabriel, C-96/00, EU:C:2002:436*, paragraph 39; *Judgment of 20 January 2005, Gruber, C-464/01, EU:C:2005:32*, paragraphs 34 and 35.

655 *Judgment of 20 January 2005, Gruber, C-464/01, EU:C:2005:32*, paragraph 34.

656 The Court has inferred that only contracts concluded outside and independently of any trade or professional activity or purpose, solely for the purpose of satisfying an individual's own needs in terms of private consumption, are covered by the special rules laid down by the regulation to protect the consumer as the party deemed to be the weaker party. Such protection is, however, unwarranted in the case of contracts for the purpose of a trade or professional activity. See *Judgment of 20 January 2005, Gruber, C-464/01, EU:C:2005:32*, 2005, paragraph 36.

**Figure 14. Applicability of settled case law on consumer status**

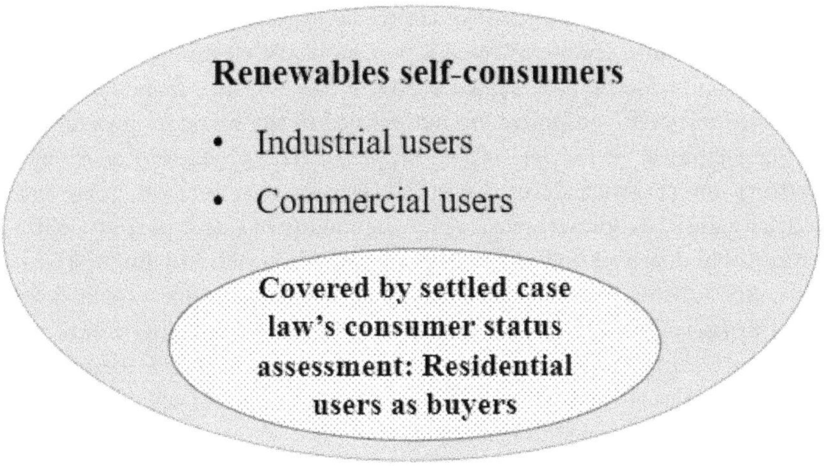


Source: Author's own elaboration.

743. As another well-known case with respect to consumer status, the CJEU's ruling on *Gruber* is also cited by the literature to assess the consumer status of renewables self-consumers in case their P2P contracts constitute the 'dual-purpose' contracts (Milčiuvienė et al., 2019; Almeida et al., 2021). The literature, when doing so, however, circumvents a crucial question as to when P2P contracts may constitute dual-purpose contracts examined in the *Gruber* context (Milčiuvienė et al., 2019; Almeida et al., 2021). This question significantly influences the relevance of the criteria developed by that case for evaluating the consumer status of renewables self-consumers involved in P2P electricity trading.

744. It should be recalled that the dual-purpose contract in *Gruber* is a contract in which an individual uses contract services or goods for both private and professional purposes.[657] Prosumers selling self-generated RES-E do not use goods or services under the P2P trading contracts, and the consumer status assessment principles built by the *Gruber* case are irrelevant. The *Gruber* test is only relevant for evaluating the consumer status of natural persons (but not industrial and commercial users) who purchase electricity, as explained above.[658] The P2P electricity contract could be considered a dual-purpose

657 *Judgment of 20 January 2005, Gruber, C-464/01, EU:C:2005:32*, paragraphs 22, 24, 25 and 27.

658 The question addressed by the court in this case concerns the application of Articles 13 and 14 of the Brussels Convention: whether, and if so, in what circumstances, a contract that has a dual purpose is covered by the special rules of jurisdiction laid down in Articles 13 to 15 of the Brussels Convention. See *Judgment of 20 January 2005, Gruber, C-464/01, EU:C:2005:32*, 2005, paragraph 29.

contract within the meaning of consumer protection law when, for example, a farmer buys electricity for both private use and agricultural business. There is also a possibility that if the resale of electricity proves profitable,[659] renewables self-consumers may choose to resell a portion of the electricity they purchase from peers, in addition to using it for private consumption. It should be noted that renewables self-consumers are not entitled to the resale in question since the right granted by EU law is to sell '*their excess production of renewable electricity*' under Article 21 of the REDII. Despite this, once the buyer resells electricity, the P2P contract comes within the concept of a 'dual-purpose contract' that serves both private and professional or trade purposes, and thus, the *Gruber* test comes in handy. An individual only maintains the consumer status defined by the Brussels Convention if the link between the P2P electricity contract and his or her trade or profession is so slight as to be marginal and, therefore, has only a negligible role in the context of the supply in respect of which the contract was concluded, considered in its entirety.[660]

745. The foregoing analysis demonstrates that the assessment criteria for consumer status established by consumer protection law and its case law can only be applied to households purchasing electricity. Interestingly, prior studies hold divergent opinions on whether these buyers should retain consumer status and enjoy consumer rights. Some claim that household prosumers buying electricity via P2P trading enjoy consumer protection since they conclude contracts to satisfy their own needs in terms of private consumption (Milčiuvienė et al., 2019). The counterargument is that in P2P trading, both parties involved are equal peers and non-professionals (Almeida et al., 2021). The buyer involved is not facing a relatively strong and professional market operator, and he or she is not a relatively weak party compared to their contractual counterparty (Almeida et al., 2021). There is therefore no need to apply general consumer protection law and sector-specific consumer protection rules imposed by energy law (Almeida et al., 2021). The second view differs from the first one mainly based on a consideration of another issue as to whether buyers in P2P electricity trading should be deemed to be on an equal footing with sellers. Two relevant questions come up. Is that truly so that renewables self-consumers are equal peers in P2P electricity trading? Is the presence of the weaker party in a contractual relationship decisive in terms of granting consumer rights in both consumer protection law and energy law?

---

659 This is possible if P2P electricity trading is done at the local level, and various taxes and levies, along with the wholesale electricity costs, can be avoided. Additional cost savings from local trading also stem from the reduced strategic potential of retailers to exploit customers through large differentials between buy and sell prices. See Qiu et al., 2020; Zhou et al., 2023.

660 *Judgment of 20 January 2005, Gruber, C-464/01, EU:C:2005:32*, paragraphs 39–41.

746. To address these questions, it would be helpful to dwell on how settled case law conceptualizes the weaker party in a contractual relationship. The CJEU makes clear that an individual is deemed to be the weaker party as long as he or she concludes the contract outside his or her trade or profession and the other party to the contract carries out business or commercial activities.[661] Once a contract is entered into for that person's trade or professional purposes, he or she must be deemed to be on an equal footing with the other party to the contract, so that the special protection reserved by the above-mentioned jurisdiction rules for consumers is not justified in such a case.[662] Moreover, as lucidly put by the Advocate General and confirmed by the court in the *Benincasa* case, whether an individual in a contract is faced by a party in a position that is objectively superior or superior by reason of the circumstances is not decisive.[663] Consumer protection granted by special rules of jurisdiction under the Brussels Convention only applies when that individual is acting for purposes unrelated to a business activity, that is to say as a '*private final consumer, not engaged in trade or professional activities*' in relation to a given contract.[664] Two findings can be distilled from these rulings. First, in determining whether a party to a certain contract requires protection, an assessment of whether they enter into that contract for private purposes is of paramount importance. Due to the absence of this assessment, the above argument of denying consumer rights of renewables self-consumers involved in P2P trading is not tenable. Second, the court does not restrict the relatively strong party to professionals or undertakings but describes them as operators undertaking commercial activities and contracting with private final customers acting outside of the profession or trade. They also include traders, such as renewables self-consumers selling self-generated RES-E to household customers. On these grounds, it is incorrect to deny the consumer rights of buyers in P2P electricity trading simply because the sellers they face are not energy professionals and thus they are not in a relatively weak position.

747. Furthermore, determining the granting of consumer rights based on the existence of the weaker party in a contractual relationship might not be entirely tenable in the energy law context. Indeed, due to the complexity and highly formalized nature of the energy system, energy consumers, either from industrial or household sectors, might be in a disadvantageous position. The intention of counteracting their disadvantages is reflected in Article 10(3) of the Electricity Directive, which requires suppliers to provide final customers with '*a summary of the key contractual conditions in a prominent manner and in*

---

661 *Judgment of 20 January 2005, Gruber, C-464/01, EU:C:2005:32*, paragraph 34.
662 *Judgment of 20 January 2005, Gruber, C-464/01, EU:C:2005:32*, paragraph 40.
663 *Opinion of Advocate General Ruiz-Jarabo Colomer in Benincasa, C-269/95, EU:C:1997:78*, points 49 to 52; *Judgment of 3 July 1997, Benincasa, C-269/95, EU:C:1997:337*, paragraph 17.
664 *Judgment of 20 January 2005, Gruber, C-464/01, EU:C:2005:32*, paragraph 35.

*concise and simple language.*' The European Parliament introduced this right to mitigate the complexity of electricity supply contracts, which can impede the comparison of offers and put consumers in a disadvantageous position toward suppliers (Pearson, 2020, p 81). The right to speedy and effective complaint-handling procedures is also designed to ensure a high level of consumer protection (*Electricity Directive*, recital 36 and Article 10 (9)). Yet, EU energy law grants consumers another host of rights not merely for consumer protection, but also for enhancing consumer engagement and welfare as well as stimulating competition. For instance, reinforcing consumer rights to switch suppliers (including those related to switching fees, times, and comparison tools) serves multiple objectives. Aside from ensuring consumer protection, the EU legislator also highlights the aims of (1) enriching consumer choices, and (2) improving consumer welfare, consumer engagement, and price and non-price competition among existing suppliers in the market (*Electricity Directive*, recital 22, 33 and 34). Similarly, the existing EU law, which strengthens consumer rights in relation to bills and billing information, also aims to promote both consumer engagement (in DR, particularly, as explained in Chapter III) and protection (*Electricity Directive*, recital 48). Consumers' rights to access consumption data and the prices and service costs associated with their consumption additionally serve to invite competitors to make offers (*Electricity Directive*, recital 56). These rights are contained in Chapter III of the Electricity Directive, which focuses on '*consumer empowerment and protection*'. Consumer protection is not the single objective pursued by energy consumer rights. There is even no evidence showing that the aim of consumer protection is superior to that of consumer empowerment. Hence, the rights that energy consumers enjoy under Chapter III of the Electricity Directive are not created entirely based on the assumption that they are weaker parties than suppliers and other energy service providers. As such, in terms of granting consumer rights, EU energy law differs from general consumer protection law, within which consumer rights are primarily geared toward protecting consumers as the weaker party in contracts. Considering this, one cannot conclude that there is no need to apply consumer rights granted by energy law to renewables self-consumers involved in P2P electricity trading merely because of the non-existence of the 'weaker party'.

748. Having reviewed existing viewpoints on the consumer status of renewables self-consumers and identified flaws therein, the following section refines the approaches to assessing consumer status. Even though, as explained earlier, the criteria for assessing consumer status established by case law in consumer protection law are only applicable in very limited cases, there is a valid general principle. That is, it is not advisable to adopt an approach to the status of consumers that is linked to a general perception of the activities or knowledge of

a given individual.[665] This approach can be easily challenged by the fact that the same actor may be regarded as a consumer in relation to certain transactions and as an economic operator in relation to others. Therefore, the determination of consumer status can be better made by reference to the position of that person in a particular contract, having regard to the nature and aim of that contract. This principle can also be applied to analyze the consumer status of renewables self-consumers involved in P2P electricity trading.

749. Regarding renewables self-consumers as sellers, their consumer status can be determined based on the EU-level definition of 'final customer' and legal provisions that grant energy consumer rights. They conclude P2P electricity trading contracts for selling surplus RES-E, and thus in relation to P2P electricity trading contracts, they are not final customers who 'purchase electricity for own use'. In that contract, they do not use goods or services and thus do not enjoy contractual rights granted to final customers entering into supply contracts.[666] The other party to the P2P trading contract, regardless of their involvement in renewables self-consumption, constitutes the final customer within the meaning of the Electricity Directive since, in terms of that contract, they purchase electricity for own use. Household users who buy electricity for private use also maintain a consumer status within the meaning of the general consumer protection law. Such general consumer protection law includes legislation aimed at protecting consumers in contracts acting for purposes outside their trade, business, craft or profession, including inter alia the Directive on Consumer Rights (*Directive on Consumer Rights*, 2011) and the aforementioned jurisdiction arrangements protecting consumers. Table 16 summarizes the assessment results of consumer status using concepts or criteria of energy law and consumer protection law.

**Table 16. Consumer status of renewables self-consumers engaged in P2P electricity trading**

| | Sellers | Buyers |
|---|---|---|
| **Energy law** | Not final customers | Constitute final customers if electricity purchase serves own use |
| **Consumer protection law and its case law** | Not applicable | For commercial and industrial users: not applicable |
| | | For households purchasing electricity for private use: constitute consumers |

Source: Author's own elaboration.

665 *Opinion of Advocate General Bobek in Schrems, C-498/16, EU:C:2017:863*, point 32.

666 The consumer rights granted to final customers under supply contracts are created by articles 10, 12, 18, and 26, and Annex I of the Electricity Directive.

### (ii) Consumer Rights

750. Renewables self-consumers as buyers in P2P trading may qualify as final customers and consumers within the meaning of EU energy law and consumer protection law, as outlined in Table 16 above. Nevertheless, whether and to what extent they enjoy rights granted to consumers by European consumer protection law and energy law is another complex question worth separate analysis. Prior studies classify consumer rights in these two sectors as 'consumer protection rights' and use the same criteria to determine their applicability, as shown above. However, the foregoing analysis shows that some of the consumer rights granted by EU energy law do not fully align with the concept of 'consumer protection rights'. Moreover, general consumer protection law and EU energy law grant rights to different customer groups. Both jurisdiction arrangements and the Directive on Consumer Rights aim to specifically protect consumers acting outside their trade or profession.[667] This range is smaller than that of final customers enjoying certain rights relating to energy contracts under EU electricity law, which contains all consumers '*purchasing electricity for own use*' (*Electricity Directive*, articles 2(3), 10 to 14 and 26), not merely for '*private use*'. Thus, two separate analyses are needed to examine whether consumer rights laid down by EU energy law and general consumer protection law are applicable.

751. As noted above, as long as households buy electricity for private use, within the meaning of consumer protection law, they are deemed to be the weaker party than the other, commercial party to the P2P electricity contract. They thus enjoy consumer rights granted by consumer protection law. In comparison, within the energy law sector, the analysis involves more complex issues. EU energy law particularly sets out consumer rights in relation to supply contracts and other energy service contracts, such as aggregation. The contestable question of whether those consumer rights apply is closely linked to the nature of contracts concluded for P2P electricity trading. Do they fall within supply contracts or other energy service contracts? As mentioned in Section 2 of this Chapter, the Electricity Directive defines supply as '*the sale, including the resale, of electricity to customers*'. Sellers in P2P electricity trading, according to this definition, also engage in supply; thus, P2P electricity contracts can be classified as a type of supply contract.[668] After identifying the nature of P2P electricity trading contracts, the follow-up question is whether buyers (renewables self-consumers or ordinary consumers) involved can enjoy the full rights granted to final customers contracting with suppliers, especially

---

667 *Council Directive 93/13/EEC*, Article 2; *Directive on Consumer Rights*, Article 2(1).

668 'Supply contract' means '*a contract for the supply of electricity*'. See Article 2(13) of the Electricity Directive.

Articles 10 and 12 of the Electricity Directive and the detailed rights built based on them.

752. As elaborated above, in the supply contract context, EU energy law grants consumer rights for various justifications, broadly categorized as consumer protection and empowerment, as well as facilitating competition. Whether those justifications are still valid in the P2P electricity trading context is highly relevant to determining the applicability of the concerned rights.

753. When assessing the applicability of rights created mainly for consumer protection purposes (e.g., compliant handling), one may consider that an assessment of the existence of the weaker party in a given energy contract is necessary.[669] Yet, as reflected in Chapter III of the Electricity Directive, EU electricity law grants consumer protection to all final customers in electricity supply contracts, without distinguishing between types of suppliers or consumers, and without considering whether final customers face a contractual party in a position that is objectively superior. A possible explanation is that, given the complexity of the energy system and its transactions, EU law considers such sector-specific consumer protection essential to protecting all energy consumers, as noted in the previous subsection. The empirical evidence presented in Chapter II indicates that even certain industrial and commercial users struggle to comprehend the electricity system. Considering general disadvantages faced by energy consumers, EU energy law does not exclude industrial and commercial users from sector-specific protection. The complex and formalized nature of the electricity system underpins the distinct rationale for consumer protection measures in the electricity sector, setting them apart from general consumer protection laws. On these grounds, as long as renewables self-consumers (households or non-households) buy electricity for own use and thereby constitute final customers within the Electricity Directive, consumer rights under supply contracts created by that Directive in principle apply.

754. Beyond consumer protection, final customers under supply contracts have additional consumer rights created for broader purposes. In terms of their application, the foregoing review of existing viewpoints indicates that the assessment of the presence of the weaker party in a contractual relationship is of limited relevance. Once buyers in P2P electricity trading constitute final customers within the meaning of EU electricity law, in principle, they are entitled to the benefit of certain rights created to increase consumer choices, engagement and welfare and enable consumers to benefit from enhanced competition.

---

669 There has not been CJEU's case law that conceptualizes the 'weaker party' in the energy contract. This is based on the search results of the CJEU case database with the inclusion criteria 'Subject-matter = "Energy" AND Text = weaker party'.

Correspondingly, this implies that their contractual partners, the peers as the selling parties, must fulfill the same obligations imposed on suppliers. However, the justifications of consumer protection and welfare are not the sole factors determining the application of supplier obligations. Whether and to what extent those obligations are applicable is also bound by the principles of non-discrimination and proportionality. This intractable question will be dealt with specifically in the next subsection. Furthermore, as will be discussed later, the P2P trading platform provider may also have obligations toward buyers if it has a decisive influence on the delivery of electricity.

755. Aside from these specific considerations, it is worth noting that some obligations imposed on suppliers are intended to address problems inherent in traditional supply contracts. Leading examples include measures that facilitate switching suppliers. The causes driving reinforced EU-level efforts in this respect lie in three barriers inhibiting consumers from switching suppliers (EC, 2016a). One of them is that traditional suppliers typically charge their customers a broad variety of switching-related fees, as a tactic to encourage customer loyalty (EC, 2016d; Pearson, 2020, pp 83–84). Contract law was considered insufficient to govern such charges, and EU energy law reinforced regulatory interventions in conditions for terminating supply contracts. However, the adequacy of contract law in securing customers' freedom to terminate contracts requires reevaluation in the context of P2P electricity trading engaged by renewables self-consumers. It remains uncertain whether renewables self-consumers serving as sellers in P2P electricity trading would adopt the same restrictive practices toward contract termination as traditional suppliers, notably given that they are not energy professionals. Non-negligible distinctions may exist between P2P electricity trading contracts and traditional supply contracts entered into by energy undertakings, although both are classified as supply contracts.[670] On these grounds, Member States may decide not to apply obligations stemming from the standardized supplier switching process to sellers in P2P trading until practical barriers to terminating P2P electricity contracts are widely detected. However, Member States must also assess whether doing so could result in discriminatory treatment of suppliers and sellers in P2P electricity trading.

[670] Such distinctions include that P2P electricity trading may exhibit a feature of achieving differentiated customer preferences. Prosumers involved can independently decide on their energy trading parameters, such as the amount of energy to exchange and the price, as well as determine with whom to exchange the energy and when to do so. This characteristic indicates that consumer inertia – commonly observed in traditional supply contracts and hindering the search for better offers – may be less pronounced in the context of P2P electricity trading. See Morstyn et al., 2018; Sandberg and Davies, 2019, p 62; Tushar et al., 2021.

756. In addition to rules for supply contract termination, legal arrangements for facilitating supplier switching also include rights that enable consumers to actively search for better energy offers by improving their access to information. They are secured by an obligation for Member States to provide impartial and independent supply offer comparison tools, as well as obligations for suppliers to provide user-friendly bills and offers. To stimulate competition and improve consumer welfare, buyers in P2P electricity trading should benefit from these obligations. Again, despite this, extending concerned obligations to renewables self-consumers as sellers in P2P trading is additionally subject to the principles of non-discrimination and proportionality. Yet, Member States may specify that the right to comparison tools also applies to buyers in P2P trading, either ordinary consumers or renewables self-consumers, since this right is not realized by imposing obligations on sellers. The same reasoning also applies to other consumer rights secured by obligations specifically created for Member States, such as the right to develop effective, independent out-of-court dispute settlement mechanisms.

757. A key conclusion from the foregoing discussion is that a fine-grained analysis is necessary to examine whether buyers in P2P electricity trading contracts enjoy the consumer rights granted by general consumer protection law and energy law. Given their correlation with sellers' obligations, the granting of these rights is also balanced against principles of non-discrimination and proportionality. In particular, whether sellers should be subject to the same obligations as suppliers is very much debated, which is the subject of the next subsection. Table 17 summarizes the preliminary findings of assessing the application of consumer rights to buyers in P2P electricity trading based on a detailed categorization of the concerned rights.

**Table 17. Granular approaches to assessing the application of cross-sectorial consumer rights**

| Consumer rights | Buyers in P2P electricity trading | |
|---|---|---|
| | Households | Industrial and commercial consumers |
| Contained in the general consumer protection law | *Apply* when they enter into contracts for private purposes | Not applicable |
| Created by the electricity law for consumer protection purposes | • Consumer protection rights under supply contracts apply generally to all final customers;<br>• For those rights secured by creating obligations for sellers, their application is also considered based on principles of non-discrimination and proportionality;<br>• The platform might be subject to relevant obligations set for sellers. | |

*(continued)*

Table 17 *continued*

| Consumer rights | Buyers in P2P electricity trading | |
|---|---|---|
| | Households | Industrial and commercial consumers |
| Created by the electricity law for multiple purposes | • An evaluation of the presence of the weaker party in a contractual relationship is of limited relevance;<br>• For those rights secured by creating obligations for sellers, their application should also be considered based on principles of non-discrimination and proportionality;<br>• Distinctions between traditional supply contracts and P2P trading contracts should also be considered when determining the application of rights relating to switching fees and times. | |

Source: Author's own elaboration.

### (iii) Selling Parties' Obligations

758. While some buyers in P2P electricity trading retain a consumer status, it does not necessarily lead to the conclusion that they enjoy a comprehensive set of consumer rights granted by energy law, as demonstrated above. One of the major reasons is that such rights must be supported by corresponding obligations for sellers in P2P electricity trading. A lengthy debate arises, notably in terms of whether renewables self-consumers should respect the same obligations for suppliers laid down by energy law when selling RES-E via P2P trading. This debate is largely attributed to the fact that Union-level general obligations for suppliers could be translated into rather detailed and strict obligations at the national level, as exemplified by relevant Flemish law cited in Section 2 of this Chapter. There is a concern that their application could impose significant burdens on renewables self-consumers and discourage P2P electricity trading. This concern serves as a justification for reducing or even exempting obligations potentially applied to renewables self-consumers, as mentioned next. To what extent such concerns are valid, in turn, determines the range of consumer rights that buyers enjoy in P2P electricity trading.

759. In the existing literature, a paradox appears to exist. On the one hand, P2P electricity trading has been viewed as an energy supply paradigm since the current definition of 'supply' is broad enough to cover it (*Electricity Directive*, Article 2 (12); van Soest, 2018). On the other hand, some contend that obligations created for suppliers should not equally apply to renewables self-consumers (Almeida et al., 2021). The reasons referred to in the literature include that, given their non-professional nature, prosumers acting as sellers could hardly ensure a high level of consumer protection to prosumers acting as users (Almeida et al., 2021). It is argued that they could not handle complaints of consumers or other prosumers in a simple, fair and prompt manner because they do not have a complex legal structure that would enable them to do so

(Almeida et al., 2021). This leads to the conclusion that prosumers cannot act in the market as suppliers because their non-professional nature does not allow them to comply with the legal obligations laid down by energy law (Schneiders and Shipworth, 2018; Almeida et al., 2021). The second concern is that requiring renewables self-consumers to respect supplier obligations creates unjustified burdens and imposes a significant constraint and complexity on innovative business models around P2P trading (Poudineh, 2019). Interestingly, recital 42 of the Electricity Directive also takes the same view that the need for consumers who self-generate electricity and sell it to the system to comply with the requirements for suppliers creates administrative burdens and legal barriers for consumers to sell self-generated electricity to the market.[671] Moreover, some put that enforcing the compliance of prosumers with the strict provisions imposed on suppliers would also violate the principle of non-discriminatory treatment to which prosumers are subject according to the REDII (Almeida et al., 2021). However, the concerned literature bases this conclusion on the assumption that renewables self-consumers selling RES-E and suppliers are in different situations, and identical treatment constitutes discrimination. Such an assumption is not supported by a thorough comparability analysis but is based on some general characteristics, such as different capacities to fulfill obligations. As pointed out in Section 3.2.3.3 further below, the same problem exists in determining the obligations of energy communities involved in electricity trading.

760. The above-listed concerns primarily come down to considerations relating to the principles of non-discrimination and proportionality. Before discussing the application of the principle of proportionality, I will first analyze the complex question of whether applying supplier obligations to renewables self-consumers infringes on the non-discrimination principle. For the current analysis, a clarification, however, should be made with regard to PSOs. The existing literature also includes PSOs in the discussion since it seems unclear whether they should also be applied to renewables self-consumers (Almeida et al., 2021). It should be noted that, unlike other Union-level provisions governing supply contracts, PSOs are imposed on electricity undertakings (*Electricity Directive*, Article 9). In general, renewables self-consumers are not subject to PSOs, and the application of PSOs is irrelevant to the analysis at hand. However, as already pointed out in Section 3.1.2.1, Union-level definitions do not entirely avoid potential confusion between the definitions of 'electricity undertaking' and 'renewable self-consumer'. While the definition

671 It states '*legal and commercial barriers exist, including, for example, disproportionate fees for internally consumed electricity, obligations to feed selfgenerated electricity to the energy system, and administrative burdens, such as the need for consumers who self generate electricity and sell it to the system to comply with the requirements for suppliers, etc.*'

of 'electricity undertaking' excludes 'final customer', the line between electricity undertakings and household renewables self-consumers is blurred. There is a need to revisit these definitions and refine them to address the legal uncertainty associated with the applicability of PSOs to renewables self-consumers.

761. Now, I move on to analyze the first question regarding the non-discrimination principle. As mentioned above in Section 3.1 of this Chapter, how to apply the non-discrimination principle is a recurring legal problem when determining the obligations of consumers and energy communities engaged in the same energy activities as traditional energy undertakings. Clear-cut criteria for assessing whether two situations are comparable have not been established. This problem also arises when applying other Union-level provisions, such as those relating to the design of PSOs. In the *Viesgo Infraestructuras Energéticas* case, the referring court requested a preliminary ruling on the interpretation of the requirement of non-discrimination contained in Article 3(2) of the 2009 Electricity Directive since there is a disagreement between itself and a higher jurisdiction as to the existence of 'acte clair'[672] with regard to that requirement.[673] Yet, the CJEU did not carry out the comparability test.[674] It merely cited settled case law in the PSO area[675] which had established that the

672 Opinion of Advocate General Bobek in *Viesgo Infraestructuras Energéticas*, Case C-683/19, EU:C:2021:300, point 30. The acte clair doctrine is a generally accepted principle that obvious legal provisions do not need to be interpreted (clara non sunt interpretanda – 'clear rules are not subject to interpretation'). This principle has been applied by the CJEU in the context of the preliminary reference procedure. This doctrine permits national courts of the last instance to refrain from requesting a preliminary ruling under Article 267(3) TFEU from the CJEU when the point of EU law at issue is indubitably obvious. The lack of 'acte clair' with respect to the non-discrimination requirement in the PSO provision implies that its application is unclear and contestable. See European Parliament, Preliminary reference procedure, available at <https://www.europarl.europa.eu/RegData/etudes/BRIE/2017/608628/EPRS_BRI(2017)608628_EN.pdf> accessed 22 March 2024.

673 Article 3 of the 2009 Electricity Directive concerns 'public service obligations' and consumer protection. It states that '*Having full regard to the relevant provisions of the Treaty, in particular Article 86 thereof, Member States may impose on undertakings operating in the electricity sector, in the general economic interest, public service obligations which may relate to security, including security of supply, regularity, quality and price of supplies and environmental protection, including energy efficiency, energy from renewable sources and climate protection. Such obligations shall be clearly defined, transparent, non-discriminatory, verifiable and shall guarantee equality of access for electricity undertakings of the Community to national consumers. …*'.

674 The Advocate General held that according to case law on PSOs, it is clear that '*the "public service obligation" at issue binds all of the undertakings operating in the same sector equally so as not to adversely affect competition in that sector*' unless different treatment is objectively justified, and '*in practical terms, it is of limited relevance whether the same types of considerations are raised at the level of the assessment of comparability or "downstream" at the level of justifications.*' See *Opinion of Advocate General Bobek in Viesgo Infraestructuras Energéticas, Case C-683/19, EU:C:2021:300*, point 90.

675 The cited case law includes *C-121/15 Association nationale des opérateurs détaillants en énergie (ANODE) v Premier ministre and Others*, paragraph 71; *Judgment of 30 April 2020, Overgas Mrezhi and Balgarska gazova asotsiatsia, C-5/19, EU:C:2020:343*, paragraph 80.

non-discrimination requirement in question should be interpreted as meaning that the Directive '*allows public service obligations to be imposed "on undertakings operating in the electricity sector" in general, not on certain undertakings specifically*' and thus '*the system for designating which undertakings will have public service obligations cannot exclude a priori any of the undertakings operating in the electricity sector. Therefore, any difference in treatment which may arise must be objectively justified*'.[676]

762. Examining the CJEU's case law reveals numerous judgments that touch upon the principle of equality or non-discrimination across various sectors.[677] However, not all judgments provide details on the comparability analysis, as exemplified in the above *Viesgo Infraestructuras Energéticas* case. Moreover, the notion of and the comparability analysis itself have not yet been clearly defined and have changed over time (Castagna, 2023), making it even more challenging to distill normative criteria for the discrimination test. The criteria applied are different even within the same sector, as indicated by judgments in the tax law sector. For instance, in the *Paint Graphos* case, when determining whether tax exemptions granted to cooperatives differentiate between economic operators and create selective advantages, the court held that given '*special characteristics peculiar to cooperative societies,*[678] *'producers' and workers' cooperative societies such as those at issue in the main proceedings cannot, in principle, be regarded as being in a comparable factual and legal situation to that of commercial companies*'.[679] What makes a cooperative society with identified characteristics different is not its impact and behavior in the market but its nature, which is an ontological argument (Castagna, 2023). In other cases, the court highlights that the legally and factually comparable situation must be assessed in the light of the objective pursued by the measure in question.[680] A prominent example is the *Adria-Wien Pipeline and Wietersdorfer & Peggauer Zementwerke*

---

676 *Judgment of 14 October 2021, Viesgo Infraestructuras Energéticas, C-683/19, EU:C:2021:847*, paragraphs 45–53.

677 Using the inclusion criteria 'Text = the principle of non-discrimination' and 'Text = the principle of equality' to search the CJEU case database, there are 3378 and 3936 cases relating to the principle of non-discrimination and the principle of equality, respectively.

678 These special characteristics include that (1) they act in the economic interest of their members and are not managed in the interests of outside investors, (2) their relations with members are not purely commercial but personal and individual, and (3) the members being actively involved in the running of the business and entitled to equitable distribution of the results of economic performance. See *Judgment of 8 September 2011, Paint Graphos and Others, Joined Cases C-78/08 to C-80/08, EU:C:2011:550*, paragraphs 55–61.

679 *Judgment of 8 September 2011, Paint Graphos and Others, Joined Cases C-78/08 to C-80/08, EU:C:2011:550*, paragraph 61.

680 *Case C-75/97 Belgium v Commission [1999] ECR I-3671*, paragraphs 28 to 31; *Case C-143/99 Adria-Wien Pipeline and Wietersdorfer & Peggauer Zementwerke [2001] ECR I-8365*, paragraph 41; *Case C-308/01 GIL Insurance and Others [2004] ECR I-4777*, paragraph 68; *Case C-172/03 Heiser [2005] ECR I-1627*, paragraph 40.

case, in which the court held that even if evident differences existed between undertakings supplying services and undertakings manufacturing goods, they are comparable with regard to the objective of the measure being to tax energy consumption since they are both major consumers of energy (Micheau, 2014). One may find an apparent difference in comparability assessment criteria by comparing judgments of *Paint Graphos* and *Adria-Wien Pipeline and Wietersdorfer & Peggauer Zementwerke*. In the former case, the court concluded that cooperatives and other economic actors are not in a comparable situation, without considering the purpose of the concerned tax measures. However, in the latter case, the objective of a specific tax measure constitutes a major component of evaluating comparability.

763. Further, in terms of the additional criterion of having regard to the objective of the given measure, the court uses different terminologies (Micheau, 2014). In some cases, the court relies on a comparison drawn between undertakings comparable in law and in fact, '*in the light of the objectives pursued by the measure in question*' (Micheau, 2014).[681] In other cases, the comparison is made between two tax treatments for undertakings '*in the light of the objective pursued by the system in question*'.[682] As pointed out by the literature, drawing a comparison in the light of the objective of the tax system (i.e., taxing company profits) or in the light of the objective of the tax measure (i.e., taxing energy consumption) is not the same approach and can result in different outcomes (Micheau, 2014).

764. In the above judgments in the tax law field, the court has established that comparability referred to in the discrimination test amounts to the two actors being in a '*comparable legal and factual situation*'. While repeatedly citing this criterion, the court has not elaborated on in what cases two actors could be considered in a comparable legal situation. When searching for cases on the subject matter 'energy' with the term 'comparable factual and legal situation', the search results of the CJEU case database cover two highly relevant rulings. Although the court did not adopt the exact concept of '*comparable factual and legal situation*' in those rulings, it built relatively thorough discrimination tests and comparability analyses. The comparability analyses therein also echo existing doctrines on the comparability assessment, which help develop clear and pragmatic criteria for discrimination tests in the energy sector.

765. The first case is *Arcelor Atlantique et Lorraine and Others*, in which the court developed criteria for two steps of assessing the breach of the

---

681 See e.g. *Case C-143/99 Adria-Wien Pipeline and Wietersdorfer & Peggauer Zementwerke [2001] ECR I-8365*, paragraph 41; *Judgement of 13 February 2003, Spain v Commission, C-409/00, EU:C:2003:92*, paragraph 47; *Judgement of 6 September 2006, Portugal v Commission, C-88/03, EU:C:2006:511*, paragraph 54.

682 Micheau, 2014; *Case C-308/01 GIL Insurance and Others [2004] ECR I-4777*, paragraph 68.

non-discrimination principle: comparability and objective justification for different treatment.[683] The reference was made by the French Conseil d'État (Council of State) in the course of proceedings concerning the implementation of Directive 2003/87 (hereinafter the 'ETS Directive') in the French legal order.[684] One of the pleas is that the applicant claims that the allowance trading scheme applicable to installations in the steel sector, without including in its scope the aluminum and plastics industries, infringes the principle of equal treatment. The Conseil d'État rejected the pleas in law put forward by the applicants in the main proceedings, with the exception of the plea of breach of the constitutional principle of equal treatment as a result of the different treatment of comparable situations.[685] It referred a question to the CJEU for a preliminary ruling: whether, by excluding the plastics and aluminum sectors from the scope of the ETS Directive, the Community legislature breached the principle of equal treatment with respect to the steel sector.[686]

766. The court first undertook the discrimination test to evaluate whether the steel sector and the plastics and aluminum sectors are in a comparable situation. In doing so, the court confirmed a preexisting doctrine of the comparability test, which highlights that determining the comparability of situations boils down to '*deciding which characteristics are relevant when comparing two situations*' (Bammens, 2011, pp 2–3). The doctrine is that whether their sameness or difference is relevant in the specific context of the measure at issue is of utmost importance for the comparability assessment (Bammens, 2011, p 2). As a result, when two situations are different with regard to aspects that are completely irrelevant, they are not considered different for the

683 The general principle of equal treatment, as a general principle of Community law, requires that '*comparable situations must not be treated differently and different situations must not be treated in the same way unless such treatment is objectively justified*' (see, inter alia, Case 106/83 *Sermide* [1984] ECR 4209, paragraph 28; Joined Cases C-133/93, C-300/93 and C-362/93 *Crispoltoni and Others* [1994] ECR I-4863, paragraphs 50 and 51; and Case C-313/04 *Franz Egenberger* [2006] ECR I-6331, paragraph 33). The principle of equal treatment will not, however, be infringed if the different treatment is justified. Hence, the assessment of whether the differentiation made is supported by objective justification (based on an objective and reasonable criterion) is another key step in examining whether the principle of non-discrimination is violated. See *Arcelor Atlantique et Lorraine and Others (Case C-127/07)*, paragraphs 46 and 47.

684 The applicants in the main proceedings are undertakings in the steel sector. They requested the competent French authorities to repeal Article 1 of Decree No 2004-832 in so far as it made the decree applicable to installations in the steel sector. As their requests remained unanswered, they brought an action before the Conseil d'État for judicial review of the implied decisions rejecting those requests, asking for those authorities to be ordered to effect the repeal in question. In support of their application, they relied on the breach of several constitutional principles, such as the right to property, the freedom to carry on a business, and the principle of equal treatment. See *Arcelor Atlantique et Lorraine and Others (Case C-127/07)*, paragraph 20.

685 *Arcelor Atlantique et Lorraine and Others (Case C-127/07)*, paragraph 21.

686 *Arcelor Atlantique et Lorraine and Others (Case C-127/07)*, paragraph 24.

discrimination test.[687] It is thus likely that a given differentiation may be found discriminatory in one legal area (e.g., tax law) but not in another legal area (e.g., family law), as the aspects determining the comparability of situations may vary among different legal areas.[688]

767. The court applied this doctrine and determined which aspects are relevant and which are not in the context of the ETS Directive. It explicitly states that '*the elements which characterize different situations, and hence their comparability, must in particular be determined and assessed in the light of the subject-matter and purpose of the Community act which makes the distinction in question. The principles and objectives of the field to which the act relates must also be taken into account*'.[689] The analytical approach is rather clear: to examine the existence of comparable characteristics relevant to the discrimination test at hand, the subject matter and purpose of the concerned EU law creating the different treatment at issue, and the principles and objectives of its related field must be considered. Following this criterion, the court analyzed Union-level policy instruments on GHG emissions trading and the legislative proposal of the ETS Directive as well as the recital of that Directive to make clear the objective and subject matter of the concerned legislation and the key principles and aims of the ETS scheme.[690] The court drew three major conclusions.[691] First, the ETS scheme aims to contribute to fulfilling the commitments of the Community. Second, the scheme does not itself reduce those emissions but encourages and promotes the pursuit of the lowest cost of achieving a given amount of emissions reductions. Third, theoretically, the wider the scope of the system, the greater will be the variation in the costs of compliance of individual undertakings, and the greater the potential for lowering costs overall. On this basis, the court held that '*the different sources of greenhouse gas emissions relating to economic activities are in principle in a comparable situation, since all emissions of greenhouse gases are liable to contribute to dangerous interference with the climate system and all*

687 An example might help understand the complex issue of comparability. Two persons who differ in every aspect, save for the color of their shoes, cannot claim equal income tax treatment, since the color of one's shoes is generally irrelevant for income tax purposes. The equality of their shoe color makes them comparable in some regards, but not in the context of income tax. See Bammens, 2011, p 7.

688 The same conclusion also holds true even within the same field: non-residents and residents are considered comparable in the context of income-related tax benefits, while they might not be comparable in the context of person-related tax benefits. See Bammens, 2011, pp 3 and 7.

689 This criterion for the comparability test was further developed based the settled case law, including Case 6/71 *Rheinmühlen Düsseldorf* [1971] ECR 823, paragraph 14; Joined Cases 117/76 and 16/77 *Ruckdeschel and Others* [1977] ECR 1753, paragraph 8; Case C-280/93 *Germany v Council* [1994] ECR I-4973, paragraph 74; and Joined Cases C-364/95 and C-365/95 *T. Port* [1998] ECR I-1023, paragraph 83. See *Arcelor Atlantique et Lorraine and Others (Case C-127/07)*, paragraph 26.

690 *Arcelor Atlantique et Lorraine and Others (Case C-127/07)*, paragraphs 28–33.

691 Ibid.

*sectors of the economy which emit such gases can contribute to the functioning of the allowance trading scheme*'.[692] Apparently, in terms of the discrimination test at issue, the relevant comparable characteristics that different GHG emissions have are their impact on the climate system and the inclusion of all sectors emitting GHG can contribute to implementing the ETS scheme. After searching for relevant aspects, the court further clarified which aspects are irrelevant with respect to the concerned discrimination test. In view in particular of the objectives of the ETS Directive and the functioning of the allowance trading scheme, the quantity of CO2 emitted by each sector and the possible existence of competition between those sectors concerned are not essential aspects.[693]

768. To recap, the decisive criterion of determining comparability is considering the subject matter and purpose of the EU law, which makes the distinction in question, as well as the principles and objectives of the field to which that legal act relates. In the light of the foregoing, the court held that the steel, chemical and non-ferrous metal sectors are, for the purposes of examining the validity of the ETS Directive from the point of view of the principle of equal treatment, in a comparable position while being treated differently.[694]

769. Another example showing how the court solved the confusion involved in the comparability analysis is the *BSEF* case.[695] By its sixth plea, the applicant claims that the Commission Regulation (EU) 2019/2021 ('the contested regulation') prohibiting the use of HFRs (halogenated flame retardants) in the enclosure and stand of electronic displays ('the ban at issue') breaches the principle of equal treatment or non-discrimination, on two grounds.[696] First, the ban at issue discriminates against electronic displays vis-à-vis other categories of products. Second, it discriminates against HFRs vis-à-vis other chemical substances, as HFRs are the only substances banned under the contested regulation. The court rejected the entire sixth plea, which covered these two allegations, based on the above compatibility assessment criterion developed in *Arcelor Atlantique et Lorraine and Others*. Here, the second claim (i.e., the difference in treatment between HFRs and other flame retardants, such as phosphorous flame retardants) is taken as an example to demonstrate how the court concluded that HFRs and other chemicals are not in a comparable situation and thus different treatment is in line with the principle of non-discrimination.

770. The applicant argues that the HFRs present in enclosures and stands are similar to other flame retardants, such as phosphorous flame retardants, as they can create recycling issues. However, the court emphasized that whether they

692 *Arcelor Atlantique et Lorraine and Others (Case C-127/07)*, paragraph 34.
693 *Arcelor Atlantique et Lorraine and Others (Case C-127/07)*, paragraph 36–37.
694 *Arcelor Atlantique et Lorraine and Others (Case C-127/07)*, paragraph 38.
695 *BSEF v EC (Case T-113/20)*, 2022.
696 *BSEF v EC (Case T-113/20)*, paragraphs 1–6.

are comparable must be assessed having regard, in particular, to the objective of the contested regulation, which makes the different treatment in question.[697] By analyzing the impact assessment carried out by the EC with a view to adopting the contested regulation, the court established that the regulation's objective is to increase the recyclability of certain plastic components of electronic displays.[698] The use of HFRs in the enclosure and stand of electronic displays hinders the recyclability of those plastic parts, which are incinerated rather than being dismantled and recycled.[699] As set out in the impact assessment, plastics containing HFRs are not recycled at all.[700] On the contrary, it is clear from the passage quoted by the applicant in its reply that plastics containing phosphorus-based flame retardants are recycled, although the quality of the recycling is slightly inferior to that obtained with plastics that do not contain any flame retardant.[701] Therefore, in terms of the objective of increasing the recyclability of certain plastic components of electronic displays, the situation of HFRs is different from that of other flame retardants that can be recycled.[702] The different treatment created by the ban at issue does not breach the principle of non-discrimination.

771. A two-step criterion for assessing comparability contained in the discrimination test can be drawn from the above two cases: (1) clarifying the subject matter and purpose of the legal act that makes the concerned different treatment and the principles and objectives of the field to which the act relates, and (2) determining comparability having regard to that context. This criterion can help evaluate whether renewables self-consumers, as sellers in P2P electricity trading, are in a comparable situation to suppliers in terms of bearing obligations stemming from sector-specific rules governing supply contracts. When the EU or national legislators intend to treat suppliers and renewables self-consumers differently in a certain legal act, to conduct the comparability test, they must first consider the subject matter of that act while taking into account the principles and objectives of the electricity sector.

772. One may encounter a problem when applying the criterion established by *Arcelor Atlantique et Lorraine and Others* and the case law cited therein in the electricity sector, since Union-level and national electricity (market) legislation typically has multidimensional subject matter and pursues multiple purposes.

---

697 *BSEF v EC (Case T-113/20)*, paragraphs 152–154.

698 *BSEF v EC (Case T-113/20)*, paragraphs 39 and 155.

699 The EC elaborated on this specific issue in the impact assessment, which shows that it is not economically viable for recyclers to determine which specific HFRs are present in plastics; as a result, all plastics containing such substances are incinerated rather than recycled. See *BSEF v EC (Case T-113/20)*, paragraph 155.

700 *BSEF v EC (Case T-113/20)*, paragraph 97.

701 Ibid.

702 *BSEF v EC (Case T-113/20)*, paragraph 154.

In some cases, legal instruments, such as the Electricity Directive and the Electricity Regulation, do not expressly state their purposes, while specific legal provisions pursue different purposes. Similarly, the electricity sector encompasses a variety of principles and objectives, including security of supply, decarbonization, competition enhancement and consumer protection, as exemplified by Article 3 of the Electricity Regulation. Under these circumstances, a remaining question is which subject matter, principle, and objective should be used to conduct the comparability test.

773. The Electricity Directive itself provides a prominent example. The 2024 Amendment to the Electricity Directive treats suppliers and active customers differently by explicitly exempting certain small active customers from supplier obligations.[703] Pursuant to Article 1 of that Directive, its subject matter broadly covers advancing market liberalization and integration, security of supply, decarbonization, and consumer empowerment and protection. The Electricity Directive and the energy field to which the Directive relates also pursue multiple objectives, including advancing decarbonization, ensuring supply security, promoting consumer empowerment (encompassing engagement and welfare enhancement), and fostering competition. Considering different subject matter or purposes can lead to varying results in the comparability analysis, as illustrated below.

- In terms of objectives and subject matter regarding supply security and consumer protection, different actors selling electricity are in a comparable situation since all electricity sellers can contribute to ensuring service quality and realizing consumers' contractual rights.
- In light of the subject matter and objectives of advancing decarbonization or promoting RES-E, sellers delivering RES-E and those offering conventional electricity are in a different situation, as demonstrated in the Judgment on *Essent Belgium* (C-492/14, paragraph 82).[704] It could be argued that active customers selling RES-E are not in an analogous situation to that of suppliers delivering conventional electricity and thus should be treated differently.
- In terms of the subject matter and purpose of empowering final customers to engage in renewables self-consumption, it could be argued that customers selling self-produced RES-E are not in a comparable situation to suppliers selling electricity sourced from the market.

---

703 Article 15a requires Member States to ensure that active customers participating in energy sharing '*are not required to comply with supplier obligations, where renewable energy is shared between households with an installed capacity up to 10,8 kW for single households and up to 50 kW for multi-apartment blocks.*' Moreover, Member States are allowed to adjust these thresholds to reflect national circumstances, with a maximum of 30 kW for single households and a range of 40 kW to 100 kW for multi-apartment blocks.

704 See Section 3.4 below for more details about the *Essent Belgium* case.

774. The criterion for comparability analysis established in *Arcelor Atlantique et Lorraine and Others* and its cited case law is best suited for situations involving a singular subject matter and legal objective. It creates considerable uncertainties in the electricity law context. So far, the CJEU's case law in the energy sector has not solved the deficiency in that criterion. Even so, it can still be argued that the different aspects referred to in the literature, e.g., renewables self-consumers' different capacity levels and different market situations that they deal with, are not relevant aspects of the comparability analysis within the context of electricity legal acts that (potentially) make the distinction. Once again, the decisive criterion is having regard to the subject matter and purpose of the energy legislation or regulation that makes the distinction, as well as the principles and objectives of the energy or electricity sector.

775. Having examined the criterion for the comparability analysis, the next question is how to evaluate whether the different treatment of comparable situations or the identical treatment of different situations is justified.

776. The principle of non-discrimination will not, however, be infringed if the different treatment is objectively justified. The court has further specified criteria for assessing the justification for different treatments. A difference in treatment is justified if it is based on an objective and reasonable criterion, that is, if the difference relates to a legally permitted aim pursued by the legislation in question, and it is proportionate to the aim pursued by the treatment.[705] In the above-cited *Arcelor Atlantique et Lorraine and Others* case, the court provided further details on the criteria for evaluating the validity of the justification for different treatments, as shown below:

- *Being necessary to the aim of the legislation*: (1) the ETS scheme is a novel and complex regime, and the EU legislature is entitled to have recourse to a step-by-step approach and to proceed in the light of the experience gained;[706] (2) excluding the chemical sector in the first stage of implementing the ETS scheme is based on the fact that a large number of installations in that sector, of the order of 34,000, would have considerably increased the administrative complexity of the ETS scheme in its initial stage, undermining

705 *Case 114/76 Bela-Mühle Bergmann [1977] ECR 1211*, paragraph 7; *Case 245/81 Edeka Zentrale [1982] ECR 2745*, paragraphs 11 and 13; *Case C-122/95 Germany v Council [1998] ECR I-973*, paragraphs 68 and 71; *Case C-535/03 Unitymark and North Sea Fishermen's Organisation [2006] ECR I-2689*, paragraphs 53, 63, 68 and 71; *Judgment of 7 September 2016, ANODE, C-121/15, EU:C:2016:637*, paragraph 55; *Essent Belgium (Case C-492/14)*, paragraph 81.

706 *Arcelor Atlantique et Lorraine and Others (Case C-127/07)*, paragraph 57. Regarding the EU legislator's discretion of adopting a step-by-step approach when it is called on to restructure or establish a complex system, see Case 37/83 *Rewe-Zentrale* [1984] ECR 1229, paragraph 20; Case C-63/89 *Assurances du crédit v Council and Commission* [1991] ECR I-1799, paragraph 11; Case C-233/94 *Germany v Parliament and Council* [1997] ECR I-2405, paragraph 43.

administrative feasibility;[707] (3) to serve the legislative aim, the stepwise approach is moreover supported by a review of the measures adopted, inter alia, as regards the sectors covered, at reasonable intervals.[708]

- *Being suitable or appropriate for realizing the legal objective*: from its beginning, that scheme included the largest emitters of CO2 (i.e., the steel sector) who, with a comparatively limited number of fixed installations,[709] were the best suited to start that scheme.
- *Avoiding manifestly inappropriate consequences compared to alternatives*:[710] when exercising its discretion, the Community legislature must, in addition to the principal objective of protecting the environment, fully take into account all the interests involved.[711] In examining the burdens associated with various possible measures, it must be considered that, even if the importance of the objectives pursued is such as to justify even substantial negative economic consequences for certain operators, the Community legislature's exercise of its discretion must not produce results that are manifestly less appropriate than those that would be produced by other measures that were also suitable for those objectives.[712] Applying this principle, the court acknowledged that '*the Community legislature was able to take the view that the advantages of excluding the entire chemical sector at the start of the implementation of the allowance trading scheme outweighed the advantages of including it for attaining the objective of Directive 2003/87*'.[713]

707 *Arcelor Atlantique et Lorraine and Others (Case C-127/07)*, paragraph 53.

708 *Arcelor Atlantique et Lorraine and Others (Case C-127/07)*, paragraph 62.

709 One of the objective criteria that was decisive for determining the scope of the ETS Directive was the level of direct CO2 emissions of a sector. The EU legislator determined the scope based on objective scientific data showing that CO2 emissions in 1990 were 174.8 million tonnes for the steel sector, 26.2 million tonnes for the chemical sector and 16.2 million tonnes for the non-ferrous metal sector. See *Arcelor Atlantique et Lorraine and Others (Case C-127/07)*, paragraph 52.

710 *Arcelor Atlantique et Lorraine and Others (Case C-127/07)*, paragraph 59.

711 On that point, the court cited case law concerning measures relating to agriculture. See Joined Cases C-96/03 and C-97/03 *Tempelman and van Schaijk* [2005] ECR I-1895, paragraph 48, and Case C-504/04 *Agrarproduktion Staebelow* [2006] ECR I-679, paragraph 37.

712 On this point, according to the court's wording, it remains unclear what factors should be considered when assessing the appropriateness of results produced by the difference in treatment. Does it merely refer to the approach's effectiveness in attaining the legal objective, given, after all, substantial negative impacts on certain stakeholders? Or does it mean the appropriateness of the overall results of implementing that different treatment, including both benefits and costs? These two possible interpretations have different legal consequences. In the latter case, whether that unequal treatment will create disproportionate burdens or losses for stakeholders involved matters for the assessment of the validity of the justification for different treatment. Read in conjunction with paragraph 65 of the same judgment, it could be deduced that the former interpretation is what the court means. That is, the advantages or benefits created by the different treatments at issue are the primary concern, and the assessment is about whether the different treatments can ensure their resultant advantages are not manifestly less appropriate than those produced by alternatives.

713 *Arcelor Atlantique et Lorraine and Others (Case C-127/07)*, paragraph 65.

- *Based on objective data*:[714] objective criteria justifying and leading to different treatments must be based on the technical and scientific information available at the time of adoption of the legislation.

777. Different treatment granted to renewables self-consumers could be justified and refrain from breaching the principle of non-discrimination if the above four criteria are satisfied. Any objective justification for discriminatory treatment must relate to a legally permitted aim pursued by the legislation that makes the concerned distinction. An issue pointed out above arises again, i.e., which legal aim should be considered if the legislation in question pursues multiple 'legally permitted' aims, including ensuring security of supply, facilitating competition and advancing the low-carbon energy transition. Could any legally permitted aim of the concerned legislation be invoked to justify the different treatment? This uncertainty arises when facing several legally permitted aims, which is tricky considering that employing different aims can result in different assessments of justifications for the different treatment of comparable situations. The court did not encounter this problem in the *Arcelor Atlantique et Lorraine and Others* case since the ETS Directive's main legal aim is to utilize a well-functioning ETS to cut GHG emissions.

778. This issue can be well illustrated through examples. As mentioned above, in terms of objectives and subject matter regarding supply security and consumer protection, different actors selling electricity are in a comparable situation. Considering different aims results in varying assessments of compatibility with the non-discrimination principle, as shown below.

- Invoking the aim of security of supply: treating renewables self-consumers selling RES-E and suppliers differently may relate to the legal aim of security of supply. This is because reducing or exempting obligations for self-consumers can promote RES-E and self-consumption, enhancing consumers' energy self-sufficiency and contributing to the long-term energy security objective. In this sense, invoking the security of supply objective can help justify preferential treatment for self-consumers and avoid violations of the non-discrimination principle. However, it should be noted that the concept of energy security is multifaceted, extending beyond energy adequacy and source diversification to include requirements and standards for supply service quality.[715] Exempting or simplifying supplier obligations for self-consumers

[714] *Arcelor Atlantique et Lorraine and Others (Case C-127/07)*, paragraph 63.

[715] Energy supply security implicates a wide range of problems. Long-term energy security confronts depletion of oil and gas reserves and the need for sustainable energy consumption, while there is the problem of short-term energy security, which at its narrowest is a question of the quality of supply of electricity or gas. To safeguard such short-term security of supply,

is unrelated to the legal aim of maintaining the quality of supply services and could even hinder the achievement of this objective. A similar problem arises when considering the goal of consumer protection, as explained below. In situations where a legal aim encompasses multiple dimensions that yield different discrimination test outcomes, a critical question arises: which dimension should guide the assessment of justifications for differing treatment of comparable situations or identical treatment of distinct situations?

- Invoking the aim of consumer protection: exempting or reducing supplier obligations for self-consumers would not be justified if the aim of consumer protection is considered. One can hardly associate this exceptional treatment with the goal of consumer protection, since all electricity sellers can contribute to upholding consumer protection. On the contrary, exempting self-consumers from supplier obligations or simplifying such obligations is unnecessary and inappropriate to the aim of consumer protection and can even hinder its implementation. Similar reasoning can be found in settled case law on PSOs. The CJEU established that different treatments based on suppliers' capacity or types can breach the principle of non-discrimination. It held that a difference in treatment on the basis of suppliers' potential capacity bears no relation to the objective of PSOs serving general economic interests.[716] The argument that certain suppliers are more capable of fulfilling obligations[717] is thus not considered a valid justification

ensuring that consumers are provided with the right to be supplied with a certain quality of service has been a key component of energy regulation. See Barton et al., 2010, p 457.

716 The contested national legislation leading to the difference in treatment is Law 24/2013 in Spain. Its Article 45(3) states that the regulated discount covers the difference between the price invoiced to eligible vulnerable consumers and the base price for electricity on the Spanish electricity market. Article 45(4) of that law then describes the regulated discount as a 'public service obligation'. It also states that the financing thereof falls on '*parent companies of groups of companies, or, where applicable, companies which simultaneously carry out production, distribution and retail activities of electricity*' ('the mandatory contribution'). In light of its implementing rules, four companies are to contribute 96.64131% of the costs of the regulated discount: Endesa, SA ('Endesa') (41.612696%), Iberdrola, SA ('Iberdrola') (38.474516%), Gas Natural SDG, SA (14.185142%) and E.ON España, SLU (which later became Viesgo Infraestructuras Energéticas, SL ('Viesgo')) (2.368956%). By contrast, 23 other companies are allocated significantly reduced coefficients, all below 1%. In 2014, E.ON España, SLU (which later became Viesgo) brought administrative law proceedings before the referring court challenging relevant implementing rules. It argued that the arrangements for financing the regulated discount laid down by Law 24/2013 and its implementing rules were incompatible with Article 3(2) of the 2009 Electricity Directive, which, among others, requires PSOs to be non-discriminatory. See *Judgment of 14 October 2021, Viesgo Infraestructuras Energéticas, C-683/19, EU:C:2021:847*, paragraphs 52 and 53; *Opinion of Advocate General Bobek in Viesgo Infraestructuras Energéticas, Case C-683/19, EU:C:2021:300*, points 13–17.

717 The Spanish Government submits that the measure is not discriminatory and, in any event, is objectively justified. The recitals of Royal Decree-Law 9/2013 state that the companies that meet the qualifying characteristics are in a 'unique position' to better cover the cost of the regulated discount since they can shoulder the burden as part of their main business activities in the electricity market. Yet, the CJEU held that '*the differentiation criterion chosen*

for different treatment that exempts others from the PSOs.[718] Applying the reasoning from Judgment on *Viesgo Infraestructuras Energéticas* to the present one: energy consumers are entitled to sector-specific protections, including those related to supply services; differentiating suppliers based on their type or capacity is irrelevant to achieving the objective of delivering such protections. Therefore, in terms of the aim of consumer protection, treating renewables self-consumers and suppliers differently can violate the non-discrimination principle.

779. Another issue is whether a specific legal objective should be consistently applied in both the comparability analysis and the second part of the discrimination test, which evaluates whether justifications legitimize differential treatment of comparable situations or identical treatment of different situations. Equally, assessment results vary depending on whether the same aim is employed for the entire discrimination test.

780. So far, the above uncertainties stemming from applying the criteria derived from the *Arcelor Atlantique et Lorraine and Others* case have neither been resolved in the CJEU's energy case law nor addressed in the literature. Despite the essential role of the non-discrimination principle, studies analyzing its application in the EU energy law context remain very scarce. As of November 2024, a search of the Web of Science databases using the inclusion criteria *AB=(The non-discrimination principle)) AND AB=(energy)) AND AB=(EU)* yields only three results.[719] They either highlight applying this fundamental principle to address legal issues related to regulating electricity interconnectors or merely mention this principle in the context of green public purchasing. None of them explores the concrete criteria for assessing the compatibility with the non-discrimination principle, highlighting a significant research gap. Numerous

---

*by the national legislature is not objectively justified in so far as, in principle, in the light of the objective pursued by that legislature consisting in distributing the cost of the regulated discount among the main commercial activities of the electricity sector, all undertakings which carry on at least one of those main activities should contribute to financing such a cost.*' The Opinion of Advocate General Bobek further detailed why the differentiation criterion at issue is not justified by analyzing its relation to the objective pursued by the PSO per se: '*the "qualifying characteristics" for the mandatory contribution bear no relation to the objective of offering the regulated discount to vulnerable groups of consumers with particular social, consumption, and purchasing power characteristics. Indeed, that objective is not at all affected by the type or number of undertakings that cover the costs arising from that system. In fact, vulnerable consumer groups remain eligible for that system irrespective of who contributes to covering of the costs arising from that system.*' See *Judgment of 14 October 2021, Viesgo Infraestructuras Energéticas, C-683/19, EU:C:2021:847*, paragraph 50; *Opinion of Advocate General Bobek in Viesgo Infraestructuras Energéticas, Case C-683/19, EU:C:2021:300*, points 93–95.

718 *Judgment of 14 October 2021, Viesgo Infraestructuras Energéticas, C-683/19, EU:C:2021:847*, paragraph 53.

719 See <https://www.webofscience.com/wos/woscc/summary/6b87bd22-b231-46f9-a2af-f11e9dcb4917-012925a039/relevance/1>.

future studies are needed to examine whether the court has developed more granular criteria in other fields relevant and comparable to the energy area and to analyze their applicability in determining the regulatory treatment of renewables self-consumers involved in electricity trading.

781. Having discussed multiple issues surrounding applying the non-discrimination principle, now I move on to the challenges of applying the principle of proportionality. First, there exists uncertainty regarding whether the proportionality requirements in Article 21 of the REDII contain the *stricto sensu* test.[720] The third element of the proportionality test, the *stricto sensu* test, requires consideration of the losses to the rights and interests of actors affected by that measure (Tridimas, 1999, p 65; Hannah Kruimer, 2011; Craig, 2018, pp 670–671). As confirmed by the public law doctrine adopted by the VREG, as mentioned in Section 2.1.2.3 above, the test requires weighing competing interests. The balancing exercise assesses whether the costs or limitations caused by a measure (e.g., equally applying supplier obligations) are proportionate to the benefit of the measure. Without an explicit requirement of the *stricto sensu* test, some Member States may not fully consider the potential adverse impacts of applying supplier obligations to self-consumers. The consequential risk of discouraging renewables self-consumption (notably excluding consumers from the household and SME sectors) should be noted by the EU legislature. This risk can be mitigated by incorporating specific requirements for the *stricto sensu* test into the current general requirements of preventing disproportionate procedures, obligations and fees.

782. Another issue concerns potential tensions between the principles of non-discrimination and proportionality. If suppliers and renewable self-consumers

---

[720] The concept of proportionality is most fully developed within German law. In its modern German formulation, the consensus appears to be that proportionality involves three factors, namely suitability, necessity and proportionality *stricto sensu*. The first two elements of the classical German formulation have been found in CJEU's case law, and there are many cases where the judicial analysis begins and ends with a consideration of suitability and necessity. Yet, there has been greater uncertainty as to whether proportionality *stricto sensu* is also an integral part of the proportionality test applied at the Union level, which examines whether the measure was disproportionate to the restrictions thereby involved. There is, it should be acknowledged, little evidence that the CJEU will raise the third limb of proportionality of its own volition. The court, however, addresses the third part of the test when the applicant contesting the legality of the measure puts arguments couched in those terms. In other words, the community courts do accept that this can be regarded as a proper part of the proportionality analysis, but the onus is on the applicant to raise arguments that place the matter before them. See *C-331/88, The Queen v Minister of Agriculture, Fisheries and Food and Secretary of State for Health, ex parte: Fedesa and others [1990] ECR I-4023*, 1990; *C-183/95, Affish BV v Rijksdienst voor de keuring van Vee en Vlees [1997] ECR I 4315*, 1997; *T-13/99 – Pfizer Animal Health v Council [2002] ECR II-3305*, 2002; *C-426/93, Germany v Commission [1995] ECR I-3723*, 1995. While the court is willing to consider the *stricto sensu* proportionality inquiry, the depth of the court's inquiry in this respect differs markedly. See Craig, 2018, pp 656–657, 670.

are considered to be in different situations, exempting self-consumers from supplier obligations or simplifying these obligations aligns with the non-discrimination principle and can address concerns about imposing disproportionate obligations on self-consumers. However, once their comparability is established, while exceptional treatment granted to renewables self-consumers cannot be regarded as 'objectively justified',[721] conflicts with the proportionality principle arise. This situation represents a risk that applying the non-discrimination principle could obstruct exemptions or simplifications of obligations intended to prevent disproportionate obligations or burdens. This risk exists when the above *stricto sensu* test is considered an element of the proportionality principle.

783. If the losses or harm caused to another protectable objective or interest outweighs the benefits brought by that measure, it would fail the *stricto sensu* test. Applying obligations stemming from rules on electricity supply to renewables self-consumers who lack technical and financial capacity or are small in size (notably from SME and residential sectors) may yield disproportionate losses. This brings to the fore the potential contradiction between the principles of non-discrimination and proportionality, as well as the difficult question of reaching compromises between the two principles.

784. The existing EU law has provided two approaches to allow for a space for their possible compromises. That is, revisiting the proportionality of authorization procedures, grid connection procedures and other obligations and adapting them to all small-sized generating facilities having an installed electricity capacity of less than certain thresholds without differentiating operators owning or controlling them, or granting Member States discretion to make such adaptations (e.g., *REDII*, articles 16 and 17; *Electricity Directive*, article 8; *Electricity Regulation*, articles 5 and 12). Applying the same approach means that supplier obligations can be adapted to avoid disproportionate burdens on certain types of small actors selling electricity, rather than adjusting them specifically for renewables self-consumers. Doing so reduces the breach of the principle of non-discrimination, as at least comparable small suppliers and renewables self-consumers are covered by the same adjustment. Nevertheless, it should be noted that this approach cannot entirely prevent violations of the principle of non-discrimination on two grounds. First, the different sizes and portfolios of suppliers are not relevant aspects in determining their differences in terms of the objective and subject matter regarding security of supply and consumer protection, as addressed above. Simplifying obligations for small sellers or even granting them exemptions thus creates discriminatory treatment. Second, avoiding the imposition of obligations disproportionate to the size

[721] This is possible when having regard to specific aims of the energy legislation that create the distinction, notably those regarding consumer protection and supply services, as set out above.

and capacity of certain actors cannot justify different treatment, due to a lack of relation to the aim of consumer protection, as explained above. Hence, the existing approach to seeking compromises is not a silver bullet to solve conflicts between the principles of proportionality and non-discrimination.

785. An alternative way to address conflicting outcomes from applying proportionality and non-discrimination principles is to permit the contractual delegation of obligations or responsibilities. If the discrimination test indicates the need for equal treatment, to reduce breach of the principle of proportionality, the legislation or regulation could be assessed to determine which responsibilities or obligations can be permitted to be outsourced to third parties (REScoop.eu and ClientEarth, 2020). The way EU law applies the balance responsibility is an example of allowing delegation (REScoop.eu and ClientEarth, 2020).

786. To sum up, the determination of specific obligations for renewables self-consumers selling RES-E (including via P2P electricity trading and electricity sharing) relies on the application of fundamental principles, notably the principles of non-discrimination and proportionality. The above analysis highlights two key challenges. First, concrete and granular criteria for applying the non-discrimination principle in the energy sector remain absent. The application of existing criteria developed by the CJEU in energy-related rulings can bring a series of uncertainties. Second, potential conflicts exist between the principles of non-discrimination and proportionality. In some cases, proportionate regulatory treatment may lead to discriminatory outcomes.

### (iv) Platform Regulation

787. A digital trading platform is considered essential for P2P electricity trading, with which potential sellers can connect with potential buyers (Almeida et al., 2021; Lavrijssen et al., 2023). This is a feature distinguishing P2P trading from other transactions. The trading platform also stores information regarding energy consumption, production and contractual agreements among peers (Bukar et al., 2023). Based on the technology employed, in the literature, P2P electricity trading platforms have been classified into decentralized and centralized platforms (Bukar et al., 2023). For instance, blockchain technology can be applied to establish a secure environment for decentralized P2P transactions (Diestelmeier, 2019a; Bukar et al., 2023). There is usually a P2P platform provider (Almeida et al., 2021). In the electricity sector, there have been practical examples that existing market actors, including suppliers,[722]

[722] In this case, existing suppliers offer a P2P trading platform as an additional service, in addition to their core supplier activities. Vandebron in the Netherlands is an example of a retail supplier platform. See Morstyn et al., 2018; van Soest, 2018.

vendors[723] and DSOs,[724] own and provide such platforms (van Soest, 2018). There thus exist triangular relationships between sellers, buyers and platform providers. To enable P2P electricity trading, Member States must be able to regulate such triangular relationships.

788. The literature on the platformization of P2P energy services is emerging, whereas the regulatory framework that applies to these services is still far from focused (Lavrijssen et al., 2023). At the heart of the existing debate are the nature and obligations of P2P electricity trading platforms, which are, among others, linked to the above-discussed consumer rights of buyers in P2P electricity trading. Based on a review of existing legal research on this topic, two issues warrant further examination. First, in what cases is the trading platform also subject to obligations related to consumer rights? Second, to what extent can settled case law on other instances of collaborative platforms be applied to define the nature and obligations of P2P electricity trading platforms? They are discussed consecutively in the following.

789. P2P electricity trading concerns transactions covering both goods, i.e., electricity, and services, i.e., electronic intermediary services. The above subsections have discussed the rights and obligations of sellers and buyers in the electricity transaction layer. Another question is whether, in providing electronic intermediary services to sellers and buyers, the platform provider also bears obligations toward them. Answering this question requires a closer look at the respective contracts that sellers and buyers have with the platform provider. Buyers in P2P electricity trading, whether renewables self-consumers or ordinary customers, who use the electronic intermediary service offered by the platform for private purposes, are considered to have consumer status within the meaning of EU-level general consumer protection law. The platform provider is thus subject to obligations created to protect those consumers. Again, as elaborated above, industrial and commercial users do not purchase electricity and use intermediary services outside trade or profession, they do not constitute consumers in need of protection under general consumer protection law. Sellers also use services provided by the platform but for trade purposes, and thus do not qualify as 'consumers acting outside trade or profession' who can enjoy rights laid down by general consumer protection law. Some argue that, as the platform assumes a professional role and the involved prosumers and consumers are the weaker party, the platform should ensure consumer protection (Almeida et al., 2021). This assertion does not hold since it first disregards the significance of the aim of the contract concluded by

723 An example of this is SonnenCommunity, the platform offered by German battery storage manufacturer Sonnen, which enables the owners of Sonnen battery equipment to trade electricity among themselves. See Morstyn et al., 2018.

724 In the Flemish Region of Belgium, the digital platform is developed by the DSO.

service users when evaluating the consumer status defined in general law on consumer protection. It also fails to analyze the platform provider's obligations in respective contexts of sector-specific law and general consumer protection law, which can be distinct given divergent consumer rights granted in the two sectors.

790. Now, a question comes up: why is energy law also relevant in determining the obligations of digital platform providers? This is linked to the core question around the legal classification of services provided by the P2P trading platform. Are the intermediation services provided by the digital platform to be regarded as an 'information society service'[725] connecting traders, the underlying economic activity, e.g., offering electricity or a combination of both (van Soest, 2018)?[726] Indeed, an intermediation service, which involves connecting sellers and buyers, is, in principle, a separate service from the supply of services or goods.[727] Yet, in some cases, this intermediation service can be regarded as being inherently linked to the supply of services or goods and no longer classified as an information society service. A prominent example is that in the *Uber* Case, the CJEU held that the intermediation service provided by Uber is more than an 'information society service' 'consisting of connecting, by means of a smartphone application, a non-professional driver using his or her own vehicle with a person who wishes to make an urban journey'.[728] On the contrary, the court identified that Uber also exercises decisive influence over the selection of drivers and the conditions under which that service is provided by those drivers.[729] Based on such decisive influences, Uber's intermediation service '*must thus be regarded as forming an integral part of an overall service whose main component is a transport service*,' and be '*classified as "a service in the field of transport"*'.[730] As a result, the EU legislation governing the information society services, including

725 'Information Society service' means any service normally provided for remuneration, at a distance, by electronic means and at the individual request of a recipient of services. See *Directive on Information Society services*, Article 1(1)(b).

726 This is the core issue considered in the *Uber* case. See Judgment of 20 December 2017, *Asociación Profesional Elite Taxi*, C-434/15, EU:C:2017:981, paragraph 15.

727 *Judgment of 20 December 2017, Asociación Profesional Elite Taxi, C-434/15, EU:C:2017:981*, paragraph 34.

728 *Judgment of 20 December 2017, Asociación Profesional Elite Taxi, C-434/15, EU:C:2017:981*, paragraph 37.

729 This is supported by the fact that Uber determines at least the maximum fare by means of the eponymous application, that the company receives that amount from the client before paying part of it to the non professional driver of the vehicle, and that it exercises a certain control over the quality of the vehicles, the drivers and their conduct, which can, in some circumstances, result in their exclusion. See Judgment on *Asociación Profesional Elite Taxi*, paragraph 39.

730 *Judgment of 20 December 2017, Asociación Profesional Elite Taxi, C-434/15, EU:C:2017:981*, paragraph 40.

the Directive on Electronic Commerce,[731] does not apply in this case.[732] The 'decisive influence criterion' is thus drawn from the Uber case: 'If the provider of the platform has a decisive influence on the substantive service that is offered by the supply side of the P2P transaction, it will become subject to the rules that apply to providers of the substantive service' (Hacker, 2018; van Soest, 2018).

791. This criterion can also be applied to P2P electricity trading to determine when the platform provider is considered to be engaging in supply activities and should be subject to the obligations imposed on suppliers by energy law. One may doubt the implications of the *Uber* case for P2P electricity trading, given that P2P electricity trading is characterized by complex layers of transactions covering both goods and services.[733] Indeed, the settled case law concludes that for the purposes of EU law, electricity is considered a good.[734] Therefore, within P2P electricity trading, there exists the provision of both goods between peers and the platform's intermediation services. In that sense, P2P electricity trading is different from the P2P trading discussed in the Uber case, where the underlying economic activity (i.e., transport) facilitated by the platform also involves the provision of services. However, this distinction bears no relation to the application of the criterion stemming from the Uber ruling, as the court sought to identify the legal nature of the platform provider's intermediation activity, rather than the nature of the concerned P2P transaction.[735] In essence, the criterion of decisive control highlights an examination of whether the platform restricts itself to mere intermediation (solely offering the information society service) or implements an 'intermediation plus control' business model (Hacker, 2018). Regardless of whether the platform intermediates services or goods, the nature and obligations of the platform providers can be determined through that test. Considering this, it is questionable whether new legislation is needed to regulate the relationship between the platform and peers.[736]

792. Whether P2P electricity platforms exert a decisive influence on the provision of electricity requires a case-by-case analysis. Due to the large

---

731 Directive 2000/31/EC of the European Parliament and of the Council of 8 June 2000 on certain legal aspects of information society services, in particular electronic commerce, in the Internal Market (hereinafter the 'Directive on electronic commerce').

732 *Judgment of 20 December 2017, Asociación Profesional Elite Taxi, C-434/15, EU:C:2017:981*, paragraph 42.

733 A prior study expresses this concern. See van Soest, 2018.

734 *Judgment of 27 April 1994, Gemeente Almelo, C-393/92, EU: C:1994:171*, paragraph 28; *Judgment of 23 October 1997, Commission v Italy, C-158/94, EU: C:1997:500*, paragraph 17.

735 *Judgment of 20 December 2017, Asociación Profesional Elite Taxi, C-434/15, EU:C:2017:981*, paragraphs 18 and 33.

736 Some claim that new legislation seems necessary to govern their relationship. See Mak, 2022; Lavrijssen et al., 2023.

diversity of different technologies and market schemes applied (Bukar et al., 2023), P2P electricity platforms may vary in terms of the degree of control they exert. The claim of viewing the role of the P2P platform provider primarily as a facilitator rather than an energy supplier (CEER, 2019b) ignores the potential significant impact that the platform could create. For instance, some platforms only register actors on the demand and supply side and facilitate matchmaking (Hacker, 2018). In this case, they merely constitute information society service providers, and the legislation governing information society services[737] applies (Hacker, 2018). However, some models discussed in the literature may allow for a decisive influence of the trading platform. In the centralized P2P market scheme, if the platform also assumes the role of the central coordinator, its tasks include (1) gathering the peers' information and suggesting the energy export and import among the peers, (2) sharing the whole P2P revenue and computing the profits made by each peer according to some predetermined criteria, such as the selling price, and even (3) having direct control over the operational state of peers or directly managing the peers' devices (Bukar et al., 2023). Some of them, especially those related to energy export and import, and managing peers' devices, may be regarded as exerting significant control over electricity delivery, making the platform provider subject to the rules applied to suppliers. Given this, in P2P electricity trading, renewables self-consumers selling RES-E are not the sole party bound by obligations imposed on suppliers.

#### 3.2.3.3. Regulatory Treatment of Energy Communities Involved in Commercial Energy Activities

793. When energy communities participate in electricity markets to sell electricity or flexibility, a question arises as to whether they should be equally subject to rules governing flexibility provision, aggregation and supply. As demonstrated above, addressing this issue hinges upon the specific application of the principles of non-discrimination and proportionality. Future work is still needed to develop the criteria for applying the principle of non-discrimination. Despite this, one finding regarding the comparability test can be applied to help define the obligations of energy communities. Here, the applicability of supplier obligations is taken as an example.

794. Member States must evaluate the applicability of supplier obligations to energy communities in two cases: (i) energy sharing is defined as the sale of electricity, and (ii) when energy communities offer electricity to non-members. In these two cases, electricity sharing within energy communities and electricity trading with a third party constitutes 'supply' defined by EU law. The

[737] See e.g. *Directive on electronic commerce*, 2000; *Directive on Information Society Services*, 2015; *Digital Markets Act*, 2022; *Digital Services Act*, 2022; Lavrijssen et al., 2023.

question arises whether equally applying rules governing electricity supply to energy communities aligns with the principle of non-discrimination.

795. Applying the CJEU's criterion for the comparability test can help resolve the confusion surrounding the assessment of whether energy communities and suppliers are in a comparable situation. Recital 71 of the REDII highlights some specific characteristics of RECs, such as their size, ownership structure and the number of projects, and implies the need to offset disadvantages stemming from these specificities to enable equal competition with other large-scale players. The REScoop.eu, for instance, in its guidance for Member States to transpose EU law on energy communities, employs this recital to justify different regulatory treatment of energy communities (REScoop.eu and ClientEarth, 2020). This is an example of determining different regulatory treatments without a thorough discrimination test. First, not every characteristic is relevant to the discrimination test, since the settled case law highlights that the comparability must be evaluated in the light of the subject matter and purpose of the legal act that makes the concerned distinction, as well as the principles and objectives of the field to which that act relates.

796. In addition to the disadvantages highlighted in recital 71, recital 46 of the Electricity Directive identifies distinctive features that classify energy communities as a new type of entity. These include their membership structures, governance requirements and purposes. These elements indeed distinguish energy communities from other actors. However, it is important to note that they do not necessarily preclude energy communities from being in a comparable situation to other entities. According to the criterion developed by the *Arcelor Atlantique et Lorraine and Others* case, if the subject matter and purpose of the legislation that makes the different treatment is promoting RES-E, for instance, the relevant characteristic for the comparability test is the delivery of RES-E. In light of this subject matter and purpose, all sellers offering RES-E are considered to be in an analogous situation. This implies that energy communities and suppliers are in a comparable situation when both offer RES-E. However, this comparability does not extend to suppliers providing electricity from non-renewable sources. As seen from this example, the disadvantages and features of energy communities mentioned in recitals are not relevant characteristics with respect to the comparability assessment.

797. In practice, Member States might face a situation where some energy communities develop into powerful entities that can compete with suppliers. In Italy, for instance, some energy communities have moved from a paradigm of small, local initiatives to a large and national scale, expanding their member base and developing multiple projects (Candelise and Ruggieri, 2020). This expansion has allowed them to benefit from economies of scale, hire permanent staff, and become more professional in their service provision (Candelise and Ruggieri,

2020). When some energy communities can compete with other suppliers, even traditional energy undertakings, one may find it problematic to define their non-discriminatory treatment based on their specific characteristics. Neither Recital 71 of the RED II nor Recital 46 of the Electricity Directive can substitute for specific discrimination tests. Both the EU and national legislators should reinforce efforts to properly apply the non-discrimination principle and build thorough discrimination tests when introducing different treatments. These efforts include further alignments with existing criteria developed by the CJEU in the energy sector and further work to refine those criteria.

798. As noted above, a thorough discrimination test may suggest that equally applying supplier obligations to energy communities is needed to respect the non-discrimination principle, which may raise conflicts with the principle of proportionality. The possibility of delegating relevant obligations to third parties may help to mitigate such conflicts. When the different treatment aligns with the non-discrimination principle, the design of obligations for energy communities can fully consider how to avoid burdens and obligations that could lead to disproportionate losses to the rights and interests of energy communities.

799. Approaches include developing a different set of rules for these energy communities or simplifying existing rules applied to electricity supply (REScoop.eu and ClientEarth, 2020; CRU, 2021d). Ireland is an example of designing different regulatory treatments for energy communities and other consumers involved in renewables self-consumption. The independent regulator, the CRU, proposed restructuring the existing regulatory framework to better meet the need for overseeing both electricity undertakings and non-commercial actors based on their respective characteristics. The proposed approach contains two key steps. First, the existing framework will be modified to focus on activities rather than market actors (CRU, 2021d). In other words, provisions are set for energy activities, including generating, selling, storing electricity, or even operating the distribution grid. As such, market participants are enabled to choose activities to undertake and develop their projects with a unique design (CRU, 2021d). The second step is that, under this activity-oriented framework, a hybrid approach is presented for each activity to combine the mandatory licensing regime and the voluntary accreditation framework (CRU, 2021d). The accreditation framework is designed for energy communities in situations distinct from those of suppliers or other market actors. Yet, such differences might vanish over time, and reassessment is needed. The CRU highlights several key factors that should be considered in this reassessment, including the number of customers served, maximum installed capacity, and geographic range (CRU, 2021d). These factors are highly relevant to the energy communities' ability to provide energy services and competitiveness. The CRU then presented specific thresholds for each factor, which the regulator can use to determine when energy communities are not eligible for the voluntary accreditation framework (CRU, 2021d).

800. In conclusion, the criteria discussed in the previous subsection could be applied to determine the applicability of supplier obligations to energy communities. Despite some deficiencies, they can help address some present confusion involved in the application of the non-discrimination principle. More attention should be devoted to potential conflicting outcomes of applying the principles of non-discrimination and proportionality, and how to specifically design proportionate obligations for energy communities while upholding a proper level of consumer protection.

## 3.3. INFORMATION PROVISION AND DATA MANAGEMENT

801. Information provision is crucial to inform consumers of the benefits of actively managing their electricity consumption (including through DR and renewables self-consumption) and facilitate the procurement of RES-E. Section 5 of Chapter III has elaborated on specific Union-level legal arrangements for clear, sufficient, efficient, safe and user-friendly information provision. ACER and CEER's market monitoring reports have updated the progress of transposing information provision requirements about consumer bills and smart meter deployment (ACER and CEER, 2023b). In terms of information delivered by electricity bills, in most Member States, consumers have already had access to information items helpful to encourage active energy management, such as those related to the comparison of their current and past energy consumption (ACER and CEER, 2023b). In comparison, some delays exist in facilitating consumers' awareness of shifting to use more RES-E by disclosing the fuel company mix used and the fuel product mix used via electricity bills (ACER and CEER, 2023b). Moreover, in some Member States, there appears to be room for optimizing the display of information items on electricity bills. For instance, electricity bills in Germany and Romania contain 21 and 20 out of 21 information items, respectively (ACER and CEER, 2023b). A high number of items in electricity bills raises concerns about information overload, which can be counterproductive in conveying key information and enabling final customers to fully utilize it, as explained in Chapters II and III above.

802. This section primarily focuses on the prominent legal issues of transposing EU law to promote consumers' access to information. Legal challenges arising from the smart-meter roll-out are first examined in Section 3.3.1, including those related to data management. Section 3.3.2 addresses the remaining legal concerns associated with implementing GO mechanisms.

### *3.3.1. Smart Meter Rollout*

803. Pursuant to the Electricity Directive, in case the deployment of smart metering systems is assessed positively at the national level, at least 80% of final

customers should be equipped with smart meters either within seven years of the date of the positive assessment or by 2024 for those Member States that have initiated the systematic deployment of smart metering systems before 4 July 2019 (*Electricity Directive*, Annex II(3)). At the time of writing, thirteen countries have a smart meter penetration rate of 80% or more (ACER and CEER, 2023b). However, many markets have yet to make smart meters available to their consumers (ACER and CEER, 2023b). Ten Member States still have a roll-out rate below 20%, with some being practically at 0%.[738] In these Member States, the limited availability of smart meters prevents many consumers from accessing accurate and real-time consumption data, hindering them from engaging in implicit DR. Moreover, as explained in Chapter III above, beyond acting as the technical prerequisite for implicit DR, smart meters are a general enabling technology for facilitating consumers' engagement in flexibility provision and renewables self-consumption. For the sake of cost reflectiveness and fair distribution of network costs, EU law requires network charges for active customers and energy communities to account injection and offtake separately. Having smart meters thus typically constitutes a key condition or requirement for selling or sharing self-generated RES-E, as exemplified by Flemish law.[739] The delayed deployment of smart meters can deter consumers from engaging in electricity sharing or trading. There is another risk that some Member States with rather low smart meter penetration allow consumers and energy communities to share or trade self-produced RES-E without separate accounting, leading to unfair allocation of network costs.[740] As evidenced by the existing literature, the deployment of smart metering technologies can also influence the development of energy communities (Haji Bashi et al., 2023).

804. The electricity sector is increasingly digitalized and data-driven (Lavrijssen et al., 2022). This trend has become quite evident over the most recent decade, which is also reflected in and reinforced by the CEP and the subsequent amendments that further adapt the EU's electricity market design, within which digitalization is used as a tool for advancing the low-carbon energy transition (*2024 Amendment to the Electricity Directive*, recital 8). In the literature, the ICT infrastructure has become an essential layer of newly proposed market models to engage consumers further and integrate RES-E

---

738 Some Member States have experienced delays in their plans to develop smart meters: Austria, Slovakia, Romania, Poland, and Cyprus have legal plans to reach an 80% target, but they are still far from this target, while Hungary, Lithuania, and Greece have not set an 80% target yet despite a positive roll-out decision. See ACER, 2023a.

739 See Section 2.1.2 above of this Chapter.

740 Before EU law required separate accounting, some Member States applied net metering to prosumers, undermining the cost reflectiveness of network charges and fair allocation of network costs. The same problem also existed in the Flemish Region. For more details, see Section 2.3.2 of this Chapter above.

and flexibility (see e.g. Jin et al., 2020). It is considered as important as other layers traditionally underlined in market designs, i.e., physical grid, market layer, and control layer.[741] Against this background, access to ICT infrastructure and services is gaining importance in terms of realizing consumers' evolving roles. Care must be taken to address the risk that consumers without access to digital technologies are left behind in the energy transition, which can generate new vulnerabilities and inequalities and increase concerns of an unjust energy transition.[742] Additionally, the digitalization and datafication of the electricity market will not deliver the expected benefits for the energy transition if the rollout of key ICT infrastructure, such as smart meters, does not reach the majority of final consumers (Huhta, 2020b). The adequacy and robustness of existing regimes for ensuring access to essential ICT infrastructure should be evaluated in the context of the rising importance of digitalization in the energy transition. In this regard, there is an argument that access to ICT infrastructure should be stressed more than ever, and a robust regime of guaranteeing consumers' access to ICT infrastructure, like TPA in grid connection, should be developed (Almeida et al., 2021). Doing so can facilitate the energy transition underpinned by the digitalization of energy infrastructure and ensure consumers' fair access to the opportunities and benefits of decarbonization. Yet, a recurring challenge faced by actions to facilitate the rollout of ICT infrastructure remains how to address factors blocking its large-scale deployment, especially those closely tied to tensions with other legislation.

805. The reasons contributing to low rollout rates of smart meters are manifold and country-specific. Aside from key considerations of costs, a regularly mentioned deterrent is data privacy concerns.[743] Households' smart-meter-related data qualify as personal data and thus restrictions stemming from Union data protection law also apply to energy activities engaged by these consumers. They could impede the processing[744] of large smart metering datasets in one

---

741 The control layer is mainly composed of the control functions for the supply side, the demand side, and the grid side. See Jin et al., 2020.

742 Low-income households may struggle with unaffordable energy tariffs or prices due to the implementation of implicit DR. See Almeida et al., 2021; Gantioler et al., 2023.

743 Such concerns were even reinforced by some incidents. For instance, in the Netherlands, there was a huge data theft incident in 2016 involving two million Dutch households' data from two central data registers in the electricity sector, including the 'Connection register' (aansluitingenregister –'C-AR') and the 'End of contract register' (contracteindegegevensregister – 'CER'). Following this, the market parties in the energy sector and the Dutch energy regulator ACM deemed it necessary to establish formal rules to regulate this data exchange in the Information Code Electricity and Gas (ICEG). For more empirical evidence on data privacy concerns in the context of the national rollout of smart meters, see Schallehn and Valogianni, 2022; von Loessl, 2023; Espinosa Apráez, 2023.

744 In light of the GDPR, 'processing' means any operation or set of operations that is performed on personal data or on sets of personal data, whether or not by automated means, such as collection, recording, organization, structuring, storage, adaptation or alteration, retrieval,

go (Huhta, 2020b). For example, smart metering data processing can be lawful with the consent of data subjects (in the present case, the energy consumers), while such consent can be withdrawn at any time (Huhta, 2020; *General Data Protection Regulation*, Article 7). Obtaining voluntary consent from millions of existing customers can significantly increase data processing costs (Huhta, 2020b). The existence of the data subject's right to withdraw consent arbitrarily could even make the situation worse by exposing the electricity system to such a major source of uncertainty (Huhta, 2020b). Moreover, restrictions imposed by data protection law could hinder the application of new technologies that support energy activities in which final customers are empowered to engage. An example is the blockchain technology application in P2P electricity trading (Lavrijssen et al., 2022). The use of this technology can raise incompatibility with EU data protection law, notably the GDPR (Lavrijssen et al., 2022). To ensure the integrity of the data and increase trust, modifications to existing data are very difficult, if not impossible, in blockchain-based P2P electricity trading (Lavrijssen et al., 2022). This can go against data subjects' (energy consumers) rights to be forgotten (erasure) and the right to rectification granted by the GDPR (Almeida et al., 2021; Lavrijssen et al., 2022).

806. These tensions between EU energy law and data protection law stem from the fact that they assign different weights to the exploitation and protection of consumer data. The former emphasizes the use of ICT infrastructure and consumer data to empower and benefit consumers, while the latter is firmly anchored to the concept that the protection of personal data is a fundamental right and that the collection, processing, and transfer of such data is a potential risk or a threat to this right (Huhta, 2020b). Yet, energy law also gives due consideration to the need for data security and protection, while data protection law lays down general conditions for lawful data processing. This interface implies a potential acceptable balance and compromise that can be sought in these two areas of law to allow greater penetration of smart meters and efficient processing of consumer data during market processes of flexibility and self-produced RES-E trading. Such balance and compromise are likely to become even more vital in the years ahead, given the growing importance of ICT infrastructure in enabling the changing role of consumers. How such a compromise can be achieved at the EU and national levels is the major focus of this subsection.

807. At the EU level, the sector-specific approach to addressing the trade-offs associated with consumer data use is a promising way to fully reap the benefits of smart meters and relevant consumer data. Article 23 of the Electricity

consultation, use, disclosure by transmission, dissemination or otherwise making available, alignment or combination, restriction, erasure or destruction. See *General Data Protection Regulation*, article 4(2).

Directive already adopts this approach by setting out specific data protection principles rather than fully relying on the provisions of the GDPR. These independent data protection rules constitute both lex specialis and lex posterior in relation to the GDPR and thus take precedence in the event of a conflict between the two sets of rules (Huhta, 2020b). The specificities of the electricity sector, combined with the objectives of EU energy law, would have warranted a lex specialis approach to data protection in the electricity sector (Huhta, 2020b). With this approach, EU legislators could reconcile the conflicting interests of data use and protection, considering the evolving needs for the energy transition and consumer empowerment, which may not be thoroughly addressed by general rules on data protection. This approach is, in fact, also supported by the GDPR. As will be detailed below, under Article 6 of the GDPR, EU law can set out legal obligations or tasks carried out in the public interest, which could legitimize data processing. This confirms that the electricity legislation could take actions to facilitate smart metering data processing based on its own aims and the public interests it serves in the energy law context. In parallel with special data protection arrangements, an explicit reference to the applicability of the remaining general rules of the GDPR can still be made in the electricity legislation to avoid redundancy.

808. In addition to potential conflicts, when setting out special rules for consumer data processing, care should be taken to address uncertainties arising from the simultaneous application of data protection and electricity legislation (Lavrijssen et al., 2022). One issue in this regard concerns the charges applied to consumers. Article 23(5) of the Electricity Directive stipulates that no additional costs shall be charged to final customers for accessing their data or for requests to make their data available. Yet, the GDPR allows data controllers[745] to charge data subjects a reasonable fee if their data portability requests are excessive, in particular, because of their repetitive character (Lavrijssen et al., 2022). While the Electricity Directive may take precedence, there remains an uncertainty as to whether Article 23(5) can be interpreted to apply to all cases, including excessive requests to provide data to third parties (Lavrijssen et al., 2022). Indeed, the electricity legislation establishes this rule to empower energy consumers. However, it appears that the EU legislator does not fully consider

[745] 'Controller' means the natural or legal person, public authority, agency or other body which, alone or jointly with others, determines the purposes and means of the processing of personal data; where the purposes and means of such processing are determined by Union or Member State law, the controller or the specific criteria for its nomination may be provided for by Union or Member State law. In the context of processing smart metering data, when the DSO is designated to manage and provide smart metering data, it is the controller of the personal data. Once the data (in fact, a copy of the data) was transferred to the requesting eligible parties, such as suppliers or FSPs, to prepare supply contracts or energy service contracts, these players become the controllers of the received data. See Espinosa Apráez, 2023; *General Data Protection Regulation*, Article 4(7).

the administrative burdens on parties responsible for smart metering data management, notably in cases of excessive requests by consumers.[746]

809. At the national level, Member States can advance the deployment of smart meters and data processing by applying broad discretion over the application of legal grounds for lawful data processing under Article 6 of the GDPR. That provision outlines six grounds for lawful data processing. Among them, as noted by the literature cited above, gaining the consent of consumers can induce high transaction costs and uncertainties in processing smart metering data, which is not an optimal way to support the efficient processing of large-scale consumer data. Among the rest five grounds, there are three most relevant to allow the processing of smart metering data: (i) the necessity to perform contracts to which the controller is subject; (ii) the necessity to comply with legal obligations to which the controller is subject; and (iii) the necessity to perform a task carried out in the public interest or the exercise of official authority vested in the controller. System operators, suppliers and FSPs can employ the first ground to process smart metering data in the context of allowing connection of self-produced RES-E, dynamic price contracts,[747] and flexibility trading. Under the second and third grounds, Member States enjoy wide discretion to specify specific legal obligations and tasks that serve public interests, which can legitimize the processing of smart metering data. This implies that Member States have tools at their disposal to facilitate the utilization of smart metering data in response to changing needs. In this process, Member States can enhance alignment between energy law and data protection law, which cannot be realized when applying respective rules in isolation. In specifying grounds relating to legal obligations or tasks, national rules can consider the specific needs and dynamics of the electricity sector, e.g., in terms of types of data and the actors involved in the exchange of data, while evaluating data privacy risks in specific consumer data processing situations and taking tailor-made rules to prevent risks (Espinosa Apráez, 2023). Such preventive measures can include more precise conditions (such as consumers' consent in certain cases) that must be met when invoking legal grounds related to legal obligations or tasks to legitimize data processing (Espinosa Apráez, 2023).

---

746 In the national law context, the task of smart metering data management can be entrusted to system operators. For instance, in the Netherlands, following the Electricity Act 1998, DSOs are legally responsible for installing, operating and collecting the data from smart meters. They are obliged to share smart meter data with suppliers for the purposes of billing, changes of residence and switching of suppliers. It is also the case in the Flemish Region of Belgium. See Section 2.2 of this Chapter above. See also Espinosa Apráez, 2023.

747 In practice, such dynamic pricing requires hourly information on the final customer's consumption and would, therefore, justify the processing of smart metering data. See Huhta, 2020.

810. To achieve alignment between electricity law and data protection law, Member States must take dedicated actions in two dimensions: rule-making and implementation. While the GDPR is directly applied, specific rules are needed to ensure the compliance of smart metering data processing with the GDPR. Such specific rules are designed to specify the aforementioned data processing circumstances in various market processes, including flexibility and self-produced electricity trading, while addressing concrete data privacy concerns identified in these situations (Espinosa Apráez, 2023). An alternative or complementary approach is to require smart metering data managers (e.g., DSOs) to develop codes of conduct that provide practical solutions to problems identified in the data processing activities of particular sectors (European Data Protection Board, 2019; Espinosa Apráez, 2023). Data processing that aligns with energy law objectives while complying with data protection laws would be impossible without cooperation between national data protection authorities and energy regulators. This can be realized by creating a cooperation platform or protocol to strengthen oversight of data processing in the context of the electricity market (Lavrijssen et al., 2022; Espinosa Apráez, 2023).

811. Despite wide national discretion in legitimizing data processing, the application of the above second ground, i.e., the necessity to comply with legal obligations, encounters some problems in Member States. The same problem may exist when applying the third ground, i.e., the necessity to perform a task carried out in the public interest or in the exercise of official authority vested in the controller. The core issue is that setting out obligations that require consumer data processing cannot serve as the legal basis legitimizing data processing, as shown in the Personalised Offer case in the Netherlands.[748]

[748] The background of this case is that in 2018, Dutch DSOs were obliged to share consumer data with suppliers for the preparation of personalized offers under the Information Code Electricity and Gas (ICEG), which is an administrative act or 'generally binding regulation' adopted by the Dutch energy regulator, the Authority for Consumers and Markets (ACM). However, the ACM specified that the ICEG did not provide a lawful basis to process consumers' data under Art. 6(1)(c) of the GDPR (necessity to comply with a legal obligation). Instead, this regulator considered that investigating what could be the appropriate ground for the processing of personal data in this case was beyond its competences, and it was the responsibility of the DSOs to find the appropriate lawful basis to implement the above data sharing obligations. This was subsequently confirmed by a ruling of a Dutch court (the Trade and Industry Appeals Tribunal, in Dutch: College van Beroep voor het Bedrijfsleven) that the Electricity Act 1998 does not allow the introduction of a legal obligation to process (in this case, give access to) personal data in the ICEG. In accordance with the GDPR, a consequence of this ruling is that the ICEG cannot be seen as the basis of a legal obligation to process personal data. That is to say, solely creating obligations or tasks whose accomplishment requires consumer data access cannot legitimize data processing since they per se do not constitute the legal basis referred to in Article 6 of the GDPR. See Espinosa Apráez, 2023; *CBb ruling*, 2020.

812. The Personalised Offer case illustrates that not only must legal obligations be clarified, but also the legal basis for processing consumer data related to these obligations. Otherwise, legal uncertainty would arise regarding whether data can be shared in compliance with the GDPR, which might ultimately hinder data sharing in the electricity market (Espinosa Apráez, 2023). This uncertainty persisted until the CBb ruling annulled the provisions of the ICEG that obliged DSOs to share data from the C-AR and CER with suppliers for the preparation of personalized offers. Before the ruling, the ACM's action of not addressing the legal basis for data processing also left DSOs at a crossroads (Espinosa Apráez, 2023). As pointed out by representatives of the energy market parties, DSOs would either have to comply with the ICEG and share the data with the suppliers, even if they could not invoke another valid ground for personal data processing from the list in Article 6 of the GDPR, risking corrective measures from the Dutch data protection authority; or they would have to refrain from sharing the data with the suppliers to avoid processing data without a basis permitted by the GDPR, risking enforcement actions from the ACM (Espinosa Apráez, 2023; Netbeheer Nederland, 2018). Hence, when applying Article 6 of the GDPR, Member States should specify the legal obligations and tasks that require personal data processing, along with their legal basis, to avoid the foregoing dilemma and uncertainty.

813. Another issue relates to the application of the legal basis relating to the necessity to perform 'tasks carried out in the public interest'. A broad interpretation of 'public interest' could increase the risks of infringing on consumers' rights regarding personal data and lead to increased resistance to smart meter roll-out and the use of relevant data. Traditionally, Member States have had a broad margin of discretion in defining what constitutes a public interest in their national contexts (Huhta, 2020b). Justifications for data processing could be easily established in the context of system operation, for instance. The underlying rationale of the existing market rules is that electricity networks are the very platform on which the markets operate and ensure the security of supply, which is a well-established objective of public interest (Huhta, 2020b). However, as mentioned above, data processing activities encompass a range of activities, including collection, recording, transmission, use, and deletion of personal data. There is a risk that legal grounds based on 'public interest' are formulated too broadly, increasing the misuse of smart-meter-related data and creating detrimental effects on data privacy and security. The principle of proportionality becomes crucial in preventing this risk. When imposing tasks that allow for smart metering data processing, national law should also set out restrictions in specific contexts: the lawfulness of data processing is only established when data processing is limited to what is necessary to achieve the predefined public interest.

814. Aside from data privacy concerns that are blocking the roll-out of smart meters, there is another factor hindering the delivery of the promised benefits of smart meters. That is not enough attention is paid to the subsequent utilization of smart meters. As some Member States increasingly have such enabling technologies in place, it becomes crucial to focus on the extent to which smart meters have been effectively utilized to engage final customers in energy activities and how to enable them to fully leverage these technologies. Some recent empirical evidence shows that even 'engaged' customers may still disassociate themselves from interacting with their smart meter shortly after installation (Hampton et al., 2022). There is therefore a strong case for greater focus on human-technology interactions, providing education and information on the use of smart meters, and allowing for greater customer experiences to benefit from the full potential of smart meters (Darby, 2020; Hampton et al., 2022). This suggests that further actions are needed at both the EU and national levels to fully reap the benefits of smart meter deployment.

### *3.3.2. GOs*

815. In the context of this book, another important mechanism facilitating consumers' access to information is GOs, which can promote consumers' purchase of RES-E. The amount of electricity verified by GOs has increased a hundredfold between 2002 and 2018 (Hamburger, 2019). According to AIB[749] data, the market activity around GOs has been increasing in the recent decade: by the end of 2019, 79% of GOs issued for electricity produced in 2018, and 49% of GOs issued for electricity produced in 2019 were reported as having been canceled (Pototschnig and Conti, 2021). Despite the increasing use of GOs, the lack of regulation on the trade of GOs induces risks of leading to consumer mistrust of the RES-E origin information. As highlighted above in Chapter III, existing EU law has strictly restricted the use of GOs for disclosure purposes (Pototschnig and Conti, 2021). However, it also allows transfers of GOs and underpins cross-border trade of GOs by requiring mutual recognition of such certificates. Moreover, EU law does not prohibit the trading of GOs independently of physical electricity flows. This has resulted in the wide presence of virtual trade of GOs within the EU.[750] A striking example in this respect is that some cross-border GO trade occurred between countries that lacked any interconnector capacities.[751] This means that when consumers

[749] The AIB is the largest issuing body for renewable energy certificates and GOs at the European level. See Pototschnig and Conti, 2021.

[750] In the international trade of GOs, it has been observed that GO export flows exceeded the physical electricity flows. See Hamburger, 2019.

[751] Icelandic GOs can be traded and used for disclosure in mainland Europe even without a physical grid connection. See Hamburger, 2019.

purchase green electricity certified by GOs, they may mistakenly believe they are supporting the production of local renewable energy when that electricity might not even be fed into the European grid (Hast et al., 2015; Wimmers and Madlener, 2024).

816. Despite the existence of a physical grid connection in two Member States trading GOs, confusion could also arise. Danish GOs, for example, can be exported to other European countries and used to disclose the production of green electricity (Wimmers and Madlener, 2024). However, consumers are often unaware of how these redistributions are calculated in the 'residual mixes' (Wimmers and Madlener, 2024). This can create confusion, as consumers in Denmark assume their electricity is mostly renewable, while it is actually generated from fossil fuels due to the purchase of Danish GOs by actors in Germany (Wimmers and Madlener, 2024). A perverse consequence could be that customers wishing to purchase RES-E and probably paying higher prices for this are shown GOs proving RES-E origin, but the supplied electricity is, in effect, generated from non-renewable sources. Although this may provide additional revenues for RES-E generators selling GOs,[752] it hampers the underlying legal aim of conveying accurate and reliable information to consumers. The separation of electricity and the GO trade is also criticized for non-transparency and opportunistic behavior (Wimmers and Madlener, 2024). These issues can further lead to distrust in this system and reduce consumers' voluntary support for RES-E, which could have been promoted by the information disclosure strategy.

817. Moreover, under the Union-level requirement, a GO corresponds strictly to one unit of electricity. Thus, after selling or exporting the GO, the given unit of RES-E cannot be marketed as renewable electricity at the retail level. In this case, the concerned RES-E would be commercialized without its corresponding GO, making consumers unable to verify its RES-E origin. This implies a potential contradiction between the trade of GOs and the legal purpose of GOs because such trade in practice does not contribute to but rather impedes the GOs' primary function of providing viable and trustworthy disclosure (Wimmers and Madlener, 2024). It also sets back the attainment of additional legal objectives such as market transparency and consumer protection. Considering this, EU law needs to provide more clarity on transfers of GOs, which addresses, inter alia, whether the trade of such certificates can be unbundled from the physical electricity transaction. If GOs and physical electricity are allowed to be traded

---

[752] Nevertheless, many empirical studies suggest that the prices of GOs are not enough to provide incentives for RES-E generators or investors and the GO market has not brought a significant increase in generation capacity. The low price of GOs is attributed to the high share of imported Norwegian GOs with low marginal costs. See Hast et al., 2015; Mulder and Zomer, 2016; Dagoumas and Koltsaklis, 2017; Hamburger and Harangozo, 2018; Hamburger, 2019.

separately, the legislation needs to get to grips with the resulting adverse impacts on realizing the GOs' purpose of disclosing RES-E origin.

818. Another challenge is related to the application of requirements governing GOs to renewables self-consumers and energy communities that sell RES-E. Equally, the proper application of principles of non-discrimination and proportionality is essential to determine the applicability of GO requirements. Furthermore, care should be given to potential barriers faced by renewables self-consumers and energy communities in accessing GOs, which can hinder the marketing of such green electricity. A prominent example is that in Flanders, as discussed in Section 2.2.1.2 of this Chapter above, small self-consumers need to install additional meters to obtain GOs. The extra costs associated with proving the renewable origin of self-produced electricity have driven some renewable self-consumers to sell this electricity as 'gray electricity.' This suggests that these self-consumers cannot benefit from the GO mechanism, which increases the public acceptance and competitiveness of RES-E by disclosing its origin. This problem indicates a gap in adapting traditional mechanisms for promoting RES-E, such as GOs, to greater consumer engagement in RES-E production.

## 3.4. NETWORK REGULATION ACCOMMODATING ELECTRICITY DSM

819. Adapting the network segment is an integral component of the EU-level framework for engaging energy consumers in facilitating the penetration of RES-E, as set out in Chapter III above. This section delves into the prominent legal challenges and gaps that arise when Member States attempt to implement the necessary adaptations in network regulation. It starts with common legal issues faced by transmission and distribution grid regulation (Section 3.4.1). Core issues include (i) a complex balance to be sought between competing tariff regulation principles, (ii) greater challenges of ensuring stakeholder responsiveness,[753] as well as (iii) regulatory challenges of facilitating TSO-DSO coordination. Prior to the CEP, TSOs had been more exposed to challenges posed by enabling the engagement of large consumers in market-based flexibility procurement (Anaya et al., 2022). By contrast, DSOs are still in their initial process of fulfilling

[753] As a normative concept, stakeholder responsiveness requires the legitimate interests of stakeholders, which are brought to the attention of bodies and institutions throughout the development and implementation processes, to be reflected in the acts adopted. It covers the promotion of dialogue and provision of participation and feedback mechanisms, as well as safeguards in the form of accountability mechanisms to be put in place, enabling stakeholders to hold the involved bodies and institutions accountable in this respect. See Kohlbacher and Lavrijssen, 2018.

their more proactive role required by the CEP, and few have delivered on desirable changes (Anaya et al., 2022). Legal challenges associated with supporting the DSO's transition are another subject of this section, which relates to incentive regulation and the dilemma of enabling the DSO to act as a neutral market facilitator (Section 3.4.2). Lessons learned from transmission system regulation that can be translated to the distribution level are also discussed.

### *3.4.1. Common Challenges*

820. As can be seen from Chapter III, EU-level principles for network regulation were refined to accommodate system integration of DR and self-generated RES-E. Central to the developments are tariff regulation, stakeholder participation processes, and coordination between the TSO and the DSO. Member States continue to struggle to strike a balance between competing principles rooted in a diverse set of political considerations, including economic efficiency, public acceptance, and sustainability, when developing network-related rules (CEER, 2020b; ACER, 2023a). This is rather pronounced in terms of network charge regulation and flexibility procurement rule-making. The implementation of general network governance principles also heavily relies on concrete regulatory instruments. However, it turns out that in many cases, the theoretical attractions of these instruments in materializing evolving principles were not realized in practice.[754] Potential problems in the general refinements introduced by the CEP, such as benchmarking methods for determining an efficient remuneration level for system operators, are not the focus of this discussion. Instead, a relatively targeted examination is conducted, centered on the application of network governance principles most relevant to facilitating the system integration of DR and self-generated RES-E. Legal issues surrounding network charge regulation are first discussed in Section 3.4.1.1, followed by an assessment of consultation procedures, inter alia, against the normative requirements of good governance and stakeholder responsiveness in Section 3.4.1.2. Lastly, potential challenges associated with reinforcing TSO-DSO coordination are identified in Section 3.4.1.3.

#### 3.4.1.1. Network Charge Regulation

821. Network charge regulation must enable TSOs and DSOs to make sufficient investments to cater to the connection needs of integrating DR and

[754] Reflections on the tariff regulatory reform in the UK (i.e., RIIO) and Germany are examples in this respect. Regulatory gaps are identified when evaluating these regulatory tools against their promises of increasing system operators' income dependence on their performance, stimulating innovation, and providing sufficient incentives. See e.g. Brunekreeft et al., 2021; Thomas, 2023.

self-generated RES-E, while fully exploiting the flexibility from consumers. Moreover, as detailed in Chapter III, network charges are subject to three Union-level principles concerning DR and renewables self-consumption: (1) refraining from discriminating, either positively or negatively, (2) being cost-reflective, proportionate and transparent, and (3) avoiding creating disincentives for self-generation, self-consumption or participation in DR (*Electricity Regulation*, article 18 (1); *REDII*, articles 21(2) and 22(4); *Electricity Directive*, articles 15(1)(2) and 16(1)). This subsection first examines the legal issues that arise from the use of time-differentiated tariffs. It then indicates how several of the foregoing principles are breached by national-level network charge regulation, with a specific focus on a tricky legal issue regarding whether actors involved in DR and renewables self-consumption should be treated differently.

#### (i) Time-Differentiated Tariffs' Diffusion

822. As noted in Chapter I above, time-differentiated tariffs can adjust network use by giving incentives to network users to adapt the timing (i.e., peak shifting) and level off their network use (i.e., peak shedding) to keep network utilization within capacity constraints (Neuteleers et al., 2017; CEER, 2020b). They come into discussion within this book since they are used to incentivize network-beneficial behavior that avoids or defers reinforcements resulting from increasing intermittent renewables production.[755] Article 18(7) of the Electricity Regulation requires Member States that have implemented smart meter deployment to consider time-differentiated network tariffs when fixing or approving transmission tariffs, distribution tariffs, or their methodologies. Based on the most recent data, eight Member States do not apply any type of time differentiation in any of their network tariffs (Bulgaria, Cyprus, Germany, Hungary, Italy, Luxembourg, and Romania) or only for a fraction of network users (the Netherlands) (ACER, 2023a). The remaining Member States (i.e., the vast majority) have embedded a certain time-differentiation in at least one of the network tariff components (ACER, 2023a).

823. Despite the merits of such tariffs in sending appropriate cost signals regarding the cost of network use in congested networks and enabling more cost-reflective network charges, their wider application is subject to a set of concerns. Essentially, these concerns reflect tensions between competing principles for governing network charges, especially between the efficiency of cost signals, fairness and predictability of network tariffs. Recent empirical research on NRAs' perspectives on network charges shows that 100% of NRA

[755] It is one of the DSM mechanisms for altering electricity consumption to achieve more efficient use of the grid and relieve grid constraints caused by the increasing integration of RES-E at both transmission and distribution levels. For more details about this DSM, see Chapter I of this book. See also CEER, 2020.

respondents agree with the use of regulated distribution tariffs as signals to guide the efficient use of the network (Anaya et al., 2022). However, some doubt the time-differentiated tariffs' capability of delivering on their theoretical benefits (ACER, 2023a).

824. The concern first relates to the willingness of network users to react to time-of-use in the network tariff, as pointed out by Italian and Dutch regulators, despite the high penetration of smart meters in such countries (ACER, 2023a). This concern is, among others, linked to network users' negative perception with regard to the fairness of time-differentiated tariffs (Neuteleers et al., 2017). For instance, a survey among Dutch households reveals that dynamic tariffs are less fair than transport and capacity tariffs (Neuteleers et al., 2017). The primary factor contributing to the negative fairness perception and low public acceptance of tariffs with time differentiation is the resultant unfair distribution of benefits and costs between network users (Neuteleers et al., 2017; CEER, 2020b). In particular, differentiating tariffs by time could exclude the least well-off from (minimal) peak use, and network users deem this unfair because it hinders fulfilling basic needs (Neuteleers et al., 2017). This potential disadvantage may make the situation of energy poor or vulnerable customers even worse, giving rise to concerns about consumer protection. Moreover, if a high degree of cost recovery is done through the time-differentiated tariff signal, customers who are unable to respond through the required technology (mainly smart meters) are likely to pay higher network costs (CEER, 2020b). This risk is notably pronounced given that EU law does not mandate consumers to adopt smart meters but instead positions these devices as tools for empowerment. Furthermore, the gradual rollout pace has left some customers without access to smart meters. An unresolved issue in this context is how to avoid unduly disadvantaging those unable to respond to the price signals.

825. The fairness of time-differentiated tariffs can be improved through concrete implementation conditions, including straightforward solutions such as introducing lower rates for vulnerable groups and increasing the predictability of tariffs.[756] However, other conditions are not easy to realize. As mentioned, distributive justice concerns arise from the potential of disadvantaging consumers without automation or technology to respond to time-differentiated tariffs. To mitigate the concerns, NRAs face the challenge of

756 It is found that predictability is important in terms of enhancing consumers' fairness perception, which is notably the case for small customers. Such increased predictability is possible with the assistance of forecasting models and modeling of future congestion, which system operators can use to determine critical periods by network area or point. When peaks are somewhat predictable in advance, there have been some experiments giving consumers notice in advance (e.g., 'tomorrow there will be a peak tariff between 5–6 pm') or formulating a cap on the maximum amount of peak periods (e.g. 'there will be maximum 8 peak hours with peak tariffs every month'). See Neuteleers et al., 2017; CEER, 2020.

thoroughly considering whether such dynamic tariffs should be applied system-wide, and how the costs would be fairly distributed between dynamic and static tariff users (CEER, 2020b). In addition, empirical evidence from the behavioral economics perspective also indicates that consumers' fairness perception and acceptance of time-differentiated tariffs could be enhanced by explaining the arguments for peak pricing in a common language (Neuteleers et al., 2017). They might see peak pricing as more acceptable if, for instance, the revenues are used for something related to what peak pricing is supposed to address (e.g., network capacity, providing batteries, stimulating domestic energy efficiency, etc.) (Neuteleers et al., 2017). Reinforced actions in this respect, in essence, highly depend on more systematic efforts to improve accountability in network governance, which entails a duty to provide an explanation, among others (Kohlbacher and Lavrijssen, 2018). Yet, existing accountability mechanisms remain insufficient, which weakens transparency[757] of network tariffs and stakeholder responsiveness and contributes to low acceptance of tariff design (Kohlbacher and Lavrijssen, 2018).

826. In addition to concerns related to fairness and low public acceptance, the widespread application of time-differentiated tariffs also faces other challenges, particularly increased complexity and uncertainty. The effectiveness of such tariffs, among others, depends on the interaction between the network tariff signals and other behavior-influencing factors (CEER, 2020b). The incentive created by dynamic network tariff signals might be weakened by other factors, for example, dynamic price signals from wholesale markets (CEER, 2020b). Moreover, realizing the benefits of dynamic network tariffs is even more complex when explicit flexibility procurement is applied in parallel. The interaction between both instruments makes the effects of any behavior change in response to tariffs harder to predict (CEER, 2020b). In comparison, the combination of static network tariffs and procured explicit flexibility might be a more reliable way to reduce network costs and further unlock the potential of demand flexibility (CEER, 2020b). Overall, to determine the extent to which time-differentiated tariffs can be used as an effective tool for adjusting network use, NRAs should first seek a clear understanding of the impacts of such tariffs and the alternative instruments at their disposal.

### (ii) Compliance with Network Charge Principles

827. Charges related to transmission and distribution networks can constitute a considerable cost to the network users (ACER, 2023a). The way tariffs are set up

---

[757] Transparency can be interpreted as meaning that network charges should be coherently explained to market participants, and the methodologies for their calculation should be readily accessible and understandable. See REScoop.eu and ClientEarth, 2020.

can provide additional incentives (in addition to those given by energy pricing) for network users to engage in DR and renewables self-consumption (ACER, 2023a). However, attaining the right incentives in practice is challenging. There appears to be no first-best tariff structure that can entirely avoid disadvantaging DR and renewables self-consumption.[758] This is especially the case, considering that tariff design must give due account to other vital aims, such as promoting energy savings and fully recovering rising infrastructure costs.[759] An example is a gradual shift toward capacity-based tariffs at the distribution level,[760] which aims to stimulate more efficient network use and enhance the cost recovery of network services.[761] Yet, capacity tariffs come with some negative implications for active customers and energy communities. As shown in the Flemish case, they can lower the marginal cost of electricity bought from the grid, leading to a decrease in the savings attained through renewable self-consumption.[762] Capacity tariffs also impose strong limits on offtake power flows, which can disincentivize increased demand during periods of excessive production and thereby restrict the use of available DR (Avau et al., 2021).

---

758 Every redistribution of costs is necessarily accompanied in the short term by a group in society that improves and a group that deteriorates. See Avau et al., 2021; Desmet et al., 2021.

759 Different system operator costs show a correlation with different cost drivers. Some costs, such as infrastructure costs, exhibit a strong correlation with capacity usage, while other costs, like network losses, may depend significantly on the energy volume withdrawn from the grid. In the case of capacity tariffs applied in Flanders of Belgium, as mentioned in Section 2 of this Chapter, a minimum monthly peak of 2.5 kW is assumed, i.e., if the monthly peak demand is less than 2.5 kW, households will still be billed the cost equivalent of 2.5 kW, contributing to ensuring full recovery of infrastructure investments. The motivation is that regardless of how much electricity is used in a household, the grid operator still needs to invest in the cable leading to the household, as well as ensure that grid power quality standards are met. See ACER, 2023a; R. Claeys et al., 2023.

760 In the past, distribution tariffs were predominantly volumetric, whereas a shift toward more capacity-based tariffs is currently taking place. See Avau et al., 2021.

761 Capacity-based tariffs are considered preferable in the era of consumers increasingly engaging in renewables self-consumption. Volumetric tariffs could provide strong incentives for renewables self-consumption, which only reduces the costs for renewables self-consumers but increases the costs for other network users not involved in renewables prosuming. This is also empirically confirmed in Australia. In Southeast Queensland, Australia, from 2009 to 2014, the number of households with rooftop solar increased from nearly zero to 25%. The reduction in energy consumption from the network, combined with the volumetric tariff structure, resulted in tariffs increasing by 112% over the five years. That development further increased the incentive to reduce energy consumption from the network, thereby increasing the burden on those unwilling or unable to make similar investments. Potential wealth transfer between consumers with renewables DG and those unable or unwilling to invest in self-consumption entails sensitive (political) considerations, given that volumetric tariffs could be perceived as unfair by ordinary network users relying on electricity supplied by the grid. With the increased self-consumption rate, a concern about relying on volumetric tariffs is that it can end up resulting in spiraling network charges and stranded network assets, known as a 'utility death spiral', as explained in more detail in Section 3.2.1 of Chapter III above. See also Poudineh, 2019; CEER, 2020.

762 See Section 2.3.2 of this Chapter above.

828. Moreover, network charges in some Member States not only deter demand flexibility by distorting price signals but also actively sanction the exploitation of such flexibility due to outdated and inappropriate regulation (Hanny et al., 2022). A prominent example of penalizing the provision of DR is §19(2) of the Electricity Network Fee Ordinance (Stromnetzentgeltverordnung, known as 'StromNEV') of Germany, which grants energy-intensive industrial consumers individual, i.e., reduced, grid charges for keeping their load profiles constant over time (Hanny et al., 2022). While constant load was indeed desirable in a time in which few baseload power plants with large generation capacities were desired to meet a large part of the demand, this is no longer the case in an intermittent RES-based electricity system (Jeddi and Sitzmann, 2019; Hanny et al., 2022). Whenever energy-intensive industrial consumers deviate from constant load in an attempt to flexibly respond to intermittent electricity supply and corresponding price signals, they risk substantially higher electricity costs, due to much higher grid charges, and ultimately, they refrain from supplying flexibility in most cases (Hanny et al., 2022). As a result of this failure, a large part of the existing flexibility potential from large industrial consumers remains unused in Germany.[763] Removing such disincentives calls for a fundamental reconsideration of the regulatory framework of network charges (Hanny et al., 2022), to seek further alignment between the system's flexibility needs and conventional instruments for lowering system costs (e.g., reduced grid charges for industrial users keeping constant load).

829. In addition, the distorted impacts of network charges on price signals for DR also deserve attention. Aside from discouraging DR, they also deviate from some fundamental principles for network charge setting. Some Member States provide exemptions, discounts, or other differentiations in network tariffs to a portion of the consumers (ACER, 2023a). Such differentiations can take several forms: (1) providing explicit exemptions and discounts for some consumers,[764] (2) offering different time-of-use signals for some consumers,[765] and

763 The low supply on balancing markets further underlines this point empirically, as the energy-intensive industry shows reluctance with respect to balancing contractions. See Hanny et al., 2022.

764 For instance, some of the largest industrial consumers are partially exempted from paying the transmission network tariff. Agricultural users in Greece are fully exempted from transmission tariffs. They are also exempted from the capacity and energy charge of distribution tariffs, but not from the small fixed charge of the distribution tariff related to metering, billing, and customer service costs. See ACER, 2023a.

765 By way of example, in Greece, night-time consumption of LV consumers (where separately measured) was partially exempted from paying transmission tariffs until September 2022 and distribution tariffs until May 2023. In France, time-of-use tariffs are embedded both in power and energy-based components for MV consumers; time-of-use tariffs are embedded only in the energy-based component for LV consumers. In the Czech Republic, the charging points for electric vehicles benefit from a peak/off-peak withdrawal charge where the charge

(3) applying different tariff bases for some consumers as an implicit discount.[766] In some instances, these exemptions, discounts or other differentiations have been justified by cost impacts (including consideration of the trade-off between simplicity and cost reflectivity) or could be linked to different capabilities of the consumers' meter (ACER, 2023a). However, in other instances, NRAs have provided no justification, and those differentiations are motivated by non-network-related policy reasons (ACER, 2023a). Typical examples include using network tariffs to support non-network-related policy goals, notably promoting RES-E or supporting specific network users (e.g., agricultural users), without substantiating a corresponding beneficial network impact (ACER, 2023a). In some cases, network charges also cover additional costs, such as non-VAT taxes and levies (ACER, 2023a). Such costs differentiate between particular network user groups while lacking relevance to grid use, which could also interfere with cost signals delivered by network charges, especially when the taxes are linked to the amount of withdrawal or injection (ACER, 2023a).[767]

830. Overall, when discounts or exemptions are offered to certain network users irrespective of such users' cost impacts on the network, they can distort or mitigate cost signals coming from other network tariff design elements and constitute a barrier to DR (ACER, 2023a). Large consumers' incentives might be particularly frustrated, who, in general, may be more interested and capable of reacting to cost signals, and the network impact resulting from changes in their behavior would be more significant (ACER, 2023a).

831. In this context, apart from creating disincentives for DR, network charges also fail to be cost-reflective, as reduced or exempted charges do not accurately reflect the costs incurred by relevant beneficiaries' network connection and use. ACER also notes that differentiations lacking relevance to network use could also discriminate between network users (ACER, 2023a). Such concerns are becoming pronounced, notably considering that some Member States use network charges to support active customers and energy communities. So far, most Member States apply the same network charges (i.e., same values, same tariff basis, same variation of the charge per voltage level, time-of-use and/

is significantly lower in the off-peak period (from 10 p.m. to 6 a.m.) than during the peak period. See ACER, 2023a.

766 In Ireland, for instance, for some consumers the distribution tariff is only energy-based, for other consumers the distribution tariff is energy-based and lump sum, and yet for some other consumers the distribution tariff is energy-based, power-based, and lump sum. In Italy, the distribution tariff for public lighting and public EV charging points has only an energy-based component, while for other consumers it has a power-based and a lump sum component. For more concrete examples in Member States, see ACER, 2023a.

767 More information on the cost recovery of unrelated policy costs (e.g., non-VAT taxes, levies, renewables support schemes, etc.) via network charges in the Member States can be found in Table 45 and Table 46 of ACER's 2023 report on electricity transmission and distribution tariff methodologies in Europe.

or location) for active and non-active customers with seven exceptions.[768] Table 18 provides an overview of different forms of network charges applied to active customers and energy communities.

**Table 18. An overview of different network charges applied to active customers and energy communities[769]**

| Categories of differentiation | Examples in Member States | Based on network cost impact analyses? |
|---|---|---|
| Different connection charges | • **Estonia**: the setting of the connection charge (basis) is different for active customers who sell their self-generated electricity. They must cover the costs associated with reinforcing the grid.<br>• **Malta**: the network charges cover different cost categories: Up to 60A, active customers are charged a lump sum charge to cover metering and administrative costs that non-active customers do not have; over 60A, the charges for connections extended from an existing substation are based on the actual cost and capacity. | No |
| Different withdrawal charges | • **France**: different withdrawal charges apply only for active customers with collective self-consumption;<br>• **Luxembourg**: the amount of withdrawal considered for the calculation of the charge is different for some active customers. RECs benefit from an exemption under certain conditions related to localization and proximity. | France: Yes<br>Luxembourg: No |
| Different injection charges | • **Sweden**: active customers are exempted from paying for the injection charge;<br>• **Slovakia**: network users who both inject into and withdraw from the grid pay costs for access to the grid either based on the injection capacity or based on the withdrawal capacity, depending on which one is higher. | Sweden: Yes<br>Slovakia: No |

832. In these Member States, all NRAs explained that applying different network charges to active customers or energy communities is for network-related reasons, except for Sweden, where the exemption aims to incentivize

[768] ACER's report shows that Belgium also applies different network charges to energy communities: '*for energy communities, different grid fees apply to the quantities of shared electricity depending on the configuration and connection of its members (e.g., in distribution, some transmission tariffs do not apply)*.' Yet, it should be noted that there exists competence allocation in terms of regulating transmission and distribution tariffs between the federal state and the three regions. Three regions are competent for determining network tariffs for energy communities connected to distribution grids within their own territory, and it is thus necessary to examine the network tariffs applied in each region specifically. No one can infer from the ACER's data here whether it represents the whole picture of distribution tariffs for energy communities in three regions or only refers to the situation in one of those regions. Given the evident flaw of the data, it is not listed in Table 18.

[769] This is based on data from ACER, 2023a.

DG (ACER, 2023a). However, as can be seen from Table 18 above, only two of them base their differentiation on a study, pilot project and/or impact assessment which identifies these users' cost impacts on the network. The absence of network cost impact analyses implies that other NRAs may not have sufficient information to evaluate the cost reflectivity and non-discrimination of different network charges applied to active customers and energy communities. This casts doubt over whether the different network charges are indeed cost-reflective and non-discriminatory. Such doubt, however, does not merely exist when active customers and energy communities receive preferential treatment in their network charges compared to other customers. Setting the very same network charges for ordinary customers and those involved in renewables prosuming and DR may not be cost-reflective either if the costs caused by them are remarkably different. In fact, in the majority of Member States applying the same network charges, only three have conducted network cost impact studies or assessments before deciding network charges for network users involved in renewables self-consumption and DR. This implies that NRAs of the remaining 17 Member States cannot determine whether the network cost impact of these network users and other users is about the same. In this case, applying the same network charges can create non-cost-reflective network charges for these users.

833. The potential incompatibility of setting network charges without due account of network cost impacts with the principle of cost-reflectiveness does not appear to be open to doubt. Yet, whether applying identical or different network charges to network users involved in DR and renewables self-consumption, irrespective of their cost impacts on the network, would violate the non-discrimination principle merits a specific examination. This is because the discrimination test entails a two-fold complex assessment: the comparability analysis and the evaluation of whether treating similar situations differently or different situations the same is objectively justified, as detailed in Section 3.2 of this Chapter above. So far, how to apply the non-discrimination principle to determine network charges for consumers involved in renewables self-consumption and DR remains an unresolved legal issue, as noted by the literature on P2P electricity trading (Lavrijssen et al., 2023).

834. ACER takes the view that identifying the cost impact on the network is essential to determining whether the same or different network charges violate the non-discrimination principle. This is why it calls for Member States to conduct a study or assessment to evaluate the network cost impact of active customers and energy communities. Based on the results of such cost analyses, the ACER claims that '*While non-active customers only withdraw from the grid, active customers may also inject. Setting the very same network charges for active and non-active customers cannot be cost-reflective and non-discriminatory if the costs caused by them are remarkably different. The same is true when setting different*

*network charges while the cost impact of the active and non-active customers is about the same, thus any differentiation must be justified based on network-related reasons.*' ACER regards network use (including relevant costs) as the relevant aspect for conducting the non-discrimination test. Furthermore, it appears that only network-related reasons could justify a deviation from the principle of treating comparable situations in the same way and treating incomparable situations differently. In the following, whether ACER's standards hold will be evaluated based on the criteria that Section 3.2 draws out from the CJEU's case law concerning the non-discrimination test.

835. The first question to be addressed is whether network users involved in renewables self-consumption and DR (i.e., active customers, renewables self-consumers and energy communities) are in a comparable situation to that of network users not engaged in these activities. Drawing on the findings of Section 3.2 above, the subject matter and purpose of the concerned legal act that creates the different treatment at issue, as well as the principles and objectives of its related field, must be considered to assess whether the two actors are in a comparable situation. In national law contexts, interestingly, one may note that the results of the comparability test may vary with the specific legislation or regulation that makes differentiations in network charges. If the different charges are set out by a legal instrument devoted to regulating network charges (e.g., the above-mentioned StromNEV in Germany), the objective, subject matter and principles of the concerned act that must be considered for the comparability test may well be mere 'network-related'. They might primarily be concerned with adequately recovering network use costs, incentivizing network-friendly use, or making network charges reflect the actual costs caused by an individual network user (*StromNEV*, 2005, §1; *Electricity Regulation*, Article 18). In light of this, indeed, the network use of concerned grid users is a comparable characteristic relevant to assessing the presence of discrimination stemming from differentiation in network charges. A typical example of relying on network cost impacts to conduct the comparability analysis can be found in the EC's Decision on state aid for baseload consumers granted by StromNEV.[770]

---

[770] The EC's Decision was appealed by Germany and several affected undertakings before the CJEU. The court dismissed those actions challenging the EC's decision regarding whether the exemption in question constitutes state aid. In the case *Covestro Deutschland v Commission*, for instance, the court held that the exemption from network charges for baseload consumers constitutes a measure granted through State resources. The court dismissed the second plea 'no State aid granted through State resources' by applying two factors for identifying the involvement of state resources: first, the existence of a compulsory levy on consumers or customers, normally classified as a 'charge', or more specifically as a 'parafiscal charge', and, second, state control over the administration of the scheme, in particular through State control over the funds or the (third-party) administrators of those funds. The court concluded that the surcharge used to support the implementation of the exemption at issue constitutes state resources. See (*Judgment of the General Court of 6 October 2021, Covestro Deutschland*

836. In that Decision, the EC did not apply the comparability assessment criterion developed by the *Arcelor Atlantique et Lorraine and Others* case and the case law cited therein. Instead, it employed the concept of a '*comparable factual and legal situation*' adopted by *Portugal v Commission* and other case law.[771] While doing so, the EC did not elaborate on its own interpretation of the 'comparable factual and legal situation'. The connotation of this element is not the focus of our present analysis. The key point is based on what objective, subject matter and principles the EC conducted the comparability test. Regardless of containing the foregoing element of the '*comparable factual and legal situation*', one common component shared by the CJEU's case law concerning comparability analyses is that the objective of the concerned legislation that makes different treatments must be considered. The EC confirmed that, for the present decision, the relevant reference framework is the German network charge system, consisting of the German Energy Act 2011 (Energiewirtschaftsgesetz, 'EnWG 2011') and StromNEV, which apply different network charge methodologies for general users and atypical network users.[772] Yet, it did not further specify the objective of the reference system but merely recalled its fundamental principles.[773] Despite this, it can be inferred from its assessment of the relevant distinction that the EC views ensuring that network charges reflect the costs incurred by individual users as the objective of the network charge system at issue. This is because it agreed with Germany on the point that baseload consumers create remarkably different cost impacts on the network compared to general users.[774] Thus, the EC considered '*that the possibility provided for in Paragraph 24 of*

*v Commission, T-745/18, EU:T:2021:644*, paragraphs 95, 113–148; *Judgment of the General Court of 6 October 2021, AZ v Commission, T-196/19, EU:T:2021:646*, 2021; *Judgment of the General Court of 6 October 2021, Infineon Technologies Dresden and Infineon Technologies v Commission, Joined Cases T-233/19 and T-234/19, EU:T:2021:647*, 2021; *Judgment of the General Court of 6 October 2021, Wepa Hygieneprodukte GmbH and Others v Commission, T-238/19, EU:T:2021:648*, 2021; *Commission Decision on SA.34045*, 2018).

771 As explained above, the court did not elaborate on this concept when using it to conduct the comparability test in those judgments. See *Judgement of 6 September 2006, Portugal v Commission, C-88/03, EU:C:2006:511*, paragraph 80; *Judgment of 8 September 2011, Commission v Netherlands, C-279/08 P, ECLI:EU:C:2011:551*, paragraph 62; *Judgment of 21 December 2016, Commission v Hansestadt Lübeck, C-524/14 P, ECLI: EU:C:2016:971*, paragraphs 53–60; *Judgment of 21 December 2016, Commission v Workd Duty Free Group SA, joined cases C 20/15 P and C-21/15 P, ECLI:EU:C:2016:981*, paragraphs 92–94.

772 Paragraph 24 of the EnWG 2011 empowered the federal government to specify by ordinance the methodology for determining the general network charges to be paid. Paragraph 24 of the EnWG made a distinction in this respect between the generality of users and atypical network users which can be charged an individual network charge. The StromNEV implemented this distinction and also contained two sets of methodologies: the methodology applicable to typical network users (Paragraphs 15, 16 and 17 of the StromNEV) and the methodology applicable to atypical network users. See *Commission Decision on SA.34045*, 2018, recitals 17 to 20, 105.

773 *Commission Decision on SA.34045*, 2018, recitals 106–109.

774 Ibid.

*the EnWG 2011 to determine individual network charges for atypical users such as baseload consumers is in line with the principle of cost-causality and non-discrimination*'.[775] The underlying reasoning behind this conclusion is that, in terms of the objective of charging network users for the cost they create to the network, these two groups of network users (i.e., atypical and general users) are not in a comparable situation and must be treated differently. It is interesting to note that although the EnWG is also considered part of the reference framework that created the different treatment, its objective and subject matter, which cover wider dimensions, such as increasing the share of renewables,[776] are not decisive for the comparability analysis. Instead, one can deduce from the EC's assessment that its comparability analysis in fact only considers the objective and principles of the specific network charge regulation implementing the distinction set out by that primary energy legislation.

837. In a similar case where the differentiation is made directly or concretely implemented by a specific network charge regulation, the ACER's assertion mentioned above could hold. That is the network use and the relevant network costs of two groups of network users (involved and not involved in DSM) are decisive for determining their comparability. As long as Member States ignore the network cost impact caused by actors involved in renewables self-consumption and DR, applying either identical or different network charges could risk discriminating between these actors and other network users.

838. By contrast, if a differentiation in network charges directly stems from a national law making general rules for the electricity sector or relevant implementing rules promoting RES-E or flexibility, the network use might not be the (sole) relevant aspect for the comparability test. This instance can be found in the *Essent Belgium* case.[777]

839. The different treatment stems from a free distribution regime in the Flemish Region adopted in 2004. Article 15, in Chapter III of the Electricity Decree, entitled 'Access to the distribution system', provided that '*the system operator shall perform, free of charge, all tasks necessary for the distribution of green electricity, with the exception of connection to the distribution system*'.[778] The Flemish Government was empowered to impose restrictions on the arrangement referred to in this provision.[779] The regional legislation that makes different treatment at issue in the main proceedings concerns two Flemish Government

775 *Commission Decision on SA.34045*, 2018, recital 110.

776 §1 of EnWG prescribes that '*the purpose of the law is to provide the general public with electricity, gas and hydrogen that is as safe, cost-effective, consumer-friendly, efficient, environmentally friendly and greenhouse gas-neutral as possible, which is increasingly based on renewable energies*.'

777 *Essent Belgium (Case C-492/14)*, 2016.

778 *Essent Belgium (Case C-492/14)*, paragraph 24.

779 Ibid.

Decisions. They excluded Essent Belgium from the scheme for free distribution through the distribution system in Flanders, from which it had originally benefited. One of them is the Decision of the Flemish Government promoting the production of electricity from renewable energy sources on 5 March 2004.[780]

840. The court concluded in paragraph 82 of the judgment that '*the regional legislation at issue in the main proceedings applies in the same way to all electricity suppliers using a distribution system that is located in the region concerned, it nevertheless does not lead to any exemption from the fees for the distribution of electricity delivered by those suppliers except where that electricity is green electricity fed directly into such a system or into a distribution system located in the Member State to which that region belongs, and therefore results in electricity suppliers being treated differently, depending in particular, as Essent Belgium complains in the main proceedings, on the origin of the green electricity being marketed by those suppliers.*' In this ruling, the court did not elaborate on the comparability test, but established that the objective of the regional legislation, which makes a difference in the network charges at issue, is to promote the production of green electricity. The cited 82 paragraph implies that, having regard, in particular, to the objective of promoting green electricity, all suppliers delivering green electricity are in a comparable situation. As such, delivering green electricity or not (instead of the suppliers' cost impact on the network) is the comparable characteristic relevant to the discrimination test in question. Exemptions from distribution charges should, in principle, apply equally to suppliers offering green electricity, regardless of their specific impact on the distribution grid. Likewise, in light of the objective of promoting RES-E, suppliers delivering green electricity and those offering conventional electricity are in a different situation. Treating them differently (e.g., by exempting the former from distribution network charges) is thus in line with the principle of non-discrimination. In this case, although these two groups of network users may be similar in terms of network cost impact, they are not comparable in the context of promoting RES-E and thus cannot apply identical exemptions.[781]

---

780 Article 18 of this Decision provided: '*§1. In accordance with the second paragraph of Article 15 of the [Electricity Decree], free distribution, as referred to in the first paragraph of Article 15 of that Decree, is restricted to the electricity supplied to end-users connected to a distribution system in the Flemish Region which is produced from a renewable energy source, as provided for in Article 15, in a generating installation which feeds its electricity directly into a distribution system in Belgium. §2. Suppliers of electricity, as referred to in §1, shall not charge in the final account of the end-users of that electricity any fee for the cost of its distribution, as referred to in the first paragraph of Article 15 of the [Electricity Decree]*'. See Judgment on *Essent Belgium*, paragraphs 29 and 30.

781 It should be recalled that 'when two situations are only identical with regard to aspects that are completely irrelevant, they are not comparable for the purpose of the non-discrimination test.' For more details about identifying which aspects are relevant and which are not for the comparability test, see Section 3.2 of this Chapter above. See also Bammens, 2011, p 7.

841. To recap, the 'network-related' factor is not always the relevant aspect for assessing the existence of discrimination in different network charges. This finding calls into question the ACER's view above, which builds an absolute link between network use and comparability, although, indeed, granting exemptions or reductions without considering the costs caused by concerned network users to the system compromises the cost-reflectiveness of network charges. The comparability test in the *Essent Belgium* ruling implies that if network charges discounts or exemptions are granted to active customers or energy communities by national legislation aimed at promoting RES-E or flexibility, despite not being motivated by network-related reasons, they may not constitute discrimination. The decisive factor alone is whether these grid users and others are in a comparable situation in light of the objective and subject matter of the specific promotional law.

842. Based on the above analysis, Table 19 summarizes different discrimination assessment results determined by different aspects relevant to the comparability analysis. They essentially vary with the objective(s) of the concerned legal act(s) from which the concerned different treatment stems. Such objectives might not be merely related to network use. In this sense, non-cost-reflective differentiation in network charges may not infringe on the principle of non-discrimination.

**Table 19. Discrimination assessment results that vary with specific contexts**

| Which legislation makes the concerned differentiation in network charges? | The objective and subject matter of the legislation that makes the distinction | Relevant aspects for comparability tests | Consequences of exemptions or reductions granted to network users involved in DR and renewables self-consumption disregarding network cost impacts |
|---|---|---|---|
| National law regulating network charges | Adequately recovering costs actually caused by network users to the network | Cost impacts caused by network users | In principle, constitute discrimination[782] |
| Primary legislation on energy or electricity, and concretely implemented by network charge regulations | Which legal act should be considered is uncertain | Vary with different legal acts considered for the comparability test | Depend on which legal act is invoked for the discrimination test |

*(continued)*

[782] The examination of the justification for different treatments is temporarily deferred and will be dealt with specifically later on.

Table 19 *continued*

| Which legislation makes the concerned differentiation in network charges? | The objective and subject matter of the legislation that makes the distinction | Relevant aspects for comparability tests | Consequences of exemptions or reductions granted to network users involved in DR and renewables self-consumption disregarding network cost impacts |
|---|---|---|---|
| • Primary legislation on energy or electricity, and concretely implemented by specific law for promoting RES-E or flexibility;<br>or<br>• Specific law for promoting RES-E or flexibility | Promoting RES-E or flexibility (based on the judgment of *Essent Belgium*) | Whether network users engage in RES-E production or flexibility provision | Do not constitute discrimination |

Source: Author's own elaboration.

843. As indicated in Table 19, as helpful as they are, the comparability assessment criterion derived from the *Arcelor Atlantique et Lorraine and Others* case and related case law encounters problems again. Notably, in the second scenario, where the different network charge is set out by primary energy or electricity law and concretely implemented by a network charge regulation, a question remains as to which one's purpose and subject matter should be considered for the comparability test. As shown above, if the former's purpose is considered, one may arrive at contrary comparability test results, since network use and relevant costs are no longer the decisive factors for determining the comparability of network users. In the Commission Decision on SA.34045, the EC circumvented two key issues. First, the German Energy Act creates the general rule for the concerned distinction, but why was not this legislation with a broader range of purposes considered for the comparability analysis purpose? Second, how to deal with a situation where referring to the purposes of two involved legal acts creates different comparability assessment results? The core issue to be addressed lies in determining the objective criterion for selecting one legal act over another to conduct the comparability test when multiple legal acts create the distinction in question, and their respective purposes lead to divergent comparability analysis results. Furthermore, an unresolved issue remains how to deal with the situation where the chosen legal instrument explicitly serves multiple subject matters and purposes, or where a general objective is not established while specific provisions target distinct purposes, as highlighted in Section 3.2.3.2 above.

844. Assessing the existence of different treatments of comparable situations is not the only component of the discrimination test. As noted in preceding sections of this Chapter, both treating comparable network users differently and different users in the same way could breach the principle of non-discrimination, unless such treatment is objectively justified. Section 3.2 above has already elaborated on the criteria for assessing such objective justifications by reviewing the CJEU's settled case law. The principle is that the difference is objectively justified when it relates to a legally permitted aim pursued by the legislation in question, and it is proportionate to the aim pursued by the different treatment. Relevant criteria detailing this general principle also apply when assessing if network charges for renewables prosumers and DR providers comply with the principle of non-discrimination.

845. Moreover, a review of case law on network charge matters shows that there are additional considerations in assessing the valid justifications for distinction. Such extra elements must be considered, notably because network charge exemptions or reductions and other forms of differentiation may constitute PSOs and state aid. In these cases, either EU law specifies particular deviations from non-discriminatory TPA[783] or settled case law has developed more sophisticated criteria for assessing objective justifications for permitting differences in treatment. Furthermore, as set out later, the CJEU's case law on network charges also provides additional guidance on conducting the proportionality test contained in the general criterion for assessing the objective justification. These also constitute key components of assessing justifications for different treatment in network charge, complementing the aforementioned general criteria derived from the *Arcelor Atlantique et Lorraine and Others* case and the relevant case law, as detailed next.

846. It is very likely that Member States grant network charge exemptions or reductions to renewables prosumers and DR providers by imposing a PSO on TSOs or DSOs. The above-cited ruling on *Essent Belgium* serves as an example of extra conditions that should be considered when justifying different treatment of comparable situations. In that case, the court confirmed that the Flemish DSOs had a PSO since they were required, under the regional legislation at issue, to distribute free of charge green electricity fed

783 Discriminating network users in terms of network charges also induces infringement of the non-discriminatory TPA enshrined in Article 6 of the Electricity Directive. Settled case law also confirms that Member States are prohibited from organizing access to the network in a discriminatory manner, and this prohibition relates generally to all discrimination, including, therefore, any discrimination in terms of the cost of using the system. See *Judgment of 7 June 2005, VEMW and Others, C-17/03, EU:C:2005:362*, paragraphs 36, 45 and 46; *Judgments of 14 April 2005, AEM and AEM Torino, C-128/03 and C-129/03, EU:C:2005:224*, paragraph 59.

directly into those systems or into the distribution systems in Belgium.[784] Hence, regard must also be given to Article 3(2) and (8) of the 2003 Electricity Directive concerning the PSOs that the Member States can impose on undertakings in the electricity sector.[785] Article 3(8) of the 2003 Electricity Directive conditionally allowed a deviation from the non-discriminatory TPA for the sake of implementing the PSO: *non-discriminatory TPA to the transmission and distribution systems can be deviated when its application would obstruct the performance, in law or in fact, of the PSOs thus imposed on electricity undertakings.*[786] In the case of *Citiworks*, the CJEU had the opportunity to specify the conditions for applying such exceptions to avoid the abuse of exceptions that would undermine the TPA as the fundamental principle of the internal electricity market.[787] The condition is that '*in order to be able to derogate in this way from the requirements of Article 20 of Directive 2003/54,*[788] *Member States must, inter alia, ascertain whether the performance by the system operators of their public service obligations cannot be achieved by other means which do not impact adversely on the right of access to the systems*'.[789] That is to say, only when alternatives for implementing PSOs without violating non-discriminatory TPA do not exist, deviations from equal TPA are legally permitted. In the *Essent Belgium* case, the court held that excluding the applicant from the concerned distribution fee exemptions violates the non-discriminatory TPA principle, as the above condition for deviating from it was not satisfied. The reasoning is '*that there were, moreover, other methods – such as, for example, the grant of green certificates – which do contribute in a certain and effective way to the pursuit of the objective of increasing green electricity production, notably without undermining the introduction of third-party free access to distribution systems*'.[790]

---

784 *Essent Belgium (Case C-492/14)*, paragraph 49.

785 Ibid.

786 *Essent Belgium (Case C-492/14)*, paragraph 91.

787 Open TPA to transmission and distribution systems established by the Electricity Directive constitutes one of the essential measures that the Member States are required to implement in order to bring about the completion of the internal market in electricity, as confirmed in the *Judgment of the Court of 9 October 2008, Sabatauskas and Others, C-239/07*, paragraph 33 and the case-law cited. In accordance with the established interpretation of EU law, exceptions should always be interpreted narrowly to avoid undermining the objectives of the rules themselves. See, e.g. C-72/83 *Campus Oil Limited and others v Minister for Industry and Energy and others* [1984] ECR 2727, para 37; C-54/99 *Association Eglise de scientologie de Paris and Scientology International Reserves Trust v The Prime Minister* [2000] ECR I-1335 para 17; C-503/99 *Commission v Belgium* [2002] ECR I-4809, para 47; C-13/78 *Joh. Eggers Sohn & Co. v Freie Hansestadt Bremen* [1978] ECR I-1935, para 30; C-159/94 *Commission v France* [1997] ECR I-5815, paras 53–55; C-157/94 *Commission v Netherlands* [1997] ECR I-5699, para 37; C-159/94 *Commission v France* [1997] ECR I-5815, paras 53–55. See also Hancher and Larouche, 2011, p 743; Huhta, 2020b.

788 Article 20 of the 2003 Electricity Directive is about TPA.

789 *Judgment of 22 May 2008, citiworks, C-439/06, EU:C:2008:298*, paragraph 60; *Essent Belgium (Case C-492/14)*, paragraph 91.

790 *Essent Belgium (Case C-492/14)*, paragraphs 108, 109 and 116.

847. It should be noted that the condition for deviating from non-discriminatory TPA developed by the *citiworks* ruling is still applicable since the deviation set out by Article 3(8) of the 2003 Electricity Directive was preserved by Article 9(5) of the existing Electricity Directive. Hence, when legislators or NRAs justify differentiated network charges for renewable prosumers and DR providers, they must do more than ensure the distinction pursues a legally permitted objective and is proportionate. In light of the legal provisions on PSOs and related case law, they must also ensure that the conditions for derogating from the non-discriminatory TPA principle are met. In addition, when network charge exemptions or reductions constitute PSOs and state aid simultaneously, other requirements become relevant to assess compatibility with the principle of non-discrimination, as drawn out later on.

848. Aside from assessing conformity with the principle of non-discrimination in the concrete context of TPA, the court also further complemented the criteria developed in the judgment of *Arcelor Atlantique and Lorraine and Others* for examining whether the different treatment at issue is proportionate to the aim pursued by the treatment. The criteria detailed in the *Essent Belgium* case are primarily concerned with two elements[791] of the proportionality test, i.e., the appropriateness and necessity of the differentiation in distribution fee exemptions at issue in terms of attaining the aim (in that case, i.e., promoting RES-E production).[792] The assessment rests on two dimensions: one is examining the concerned differentiation in network charges itself to identify whether it has specific measures in place to ensure goal achievement.[793] The other is looking at the consequences of implementing that scheme, namely, the effectiveness of contributing to the given objective.[794] Before this two-fold assessment, the court first clarified that in the context of the 2001 Renewable Electricity Directive,[795] the national renewables support scheme must, in principle, lead to an increase in the national production of green electricity.[796] Furthermore, they must be able to '*favor directly the production of green electricity, rather than solely its*

---

791 In the ruling on *Arcelor Atlantique and Lorraine and Others*, as addressed in Section 3.2 above of this Chapter, the proportionality test for assessing valid justifications for different treatment concerns three aspects: (i) the distinction is necessary to the aim of the legislation, (ii) such treatment being suitable or appropriate for realizing the legal objective, and (iii) the implementation of difference in treatment avoiding manifestly inappropriate consequences compared to alternatives. In the case of *Essent Belgium*, the court only examined the former two aspects. These two cases represent examples of uncertainty regarding which elements the proportionality test should cover. See Craig, 2018, pp 656–657, 670.

792 *Essent Belgium (Case C-492/14)*, paragraph 104.

793 *Essent Belgium (Case C-492/14)*, paragraph 113.

794 *Essent Belgium (Case C-492/14)*, paragraph 114.

795 Directive 2001/77/EC of the European Parliament and of the Council of 27 September 2001 on the promotion of electricity produced from renewable energy sources in the internal electricity market (hereinafter the '2001 Renewable Electricity Directive').

796 *Essent Belgium (Case C-492/14)*, paragraph 106.

*consumption'.*[797] This is supported, '*in particular, by the fact that the green nature of the electricity relates only to its method of production and that, accordingly, it is primarily at the production stage that the environmental objectives in terms of the reduction of greenhouse gases can actually be pursued'.*[798] Therefore, the court highlighted that to be suitable and necessary to the aim of promoting RES-E, the free distribution scheme at issue must directly favor RES-E producers. Having made clear this, the court evaluated the proportionality of that scheme as follows:

- Examining the specific provisions of the free distribution scheme that create distinction at issue, the court concluded that that support mechanism itself '*offers no certainty that the economic advantage thus obtained for suppliers will ultimately actually and essentially be required to benefit producers of green electricity, particularly the smallest local generating installations which the Flemish Region claims to have wanted to support, which are not both producers and suppliers'.*[799]
- From the dimension of evaluating the results of this scheme, the court held that the benefit that green electricity producers may derive from the economic advantage given to suppliers will depend on various factors specific to the markets.[800]

849. In view of the indirect, uncertain and risky nature of any support that might flow for the green electricity producer himself from the free distribution scheme at issue, the court concluded that the different treatment stemming from the free distribution scheme is not proportionate to the aim of promoting RES-E production, and cannot objectively justify the different treatment.[801]

850. Several detailed criteria can be distilled from the ruling on *Essent Belgium*. First, as regards the proportionality test for assessing valid justifications for different treatments, both the measures of the concerned scheme that make the distinction and the potential results of implementing that scheme should

---

797 *Essent Belgium (Case C-492/14)*, paragraph 105.

798 Ibid.

799 *Essent Belgium (Case C-492/14)*, paragraph 113.

800 Such factors include, for example, electricity prices on the market, supply and demand, or the balance of power between the operators involved, and the extent to which suppliers will be prepared to allow producers to benefit from that advantage. See Judgment on *Essent Belgium*, paragraph 114.

801 The court states that '*the genuine ability of that scheme to achieve the legitimate objective pursued in the present case (which is to create an effective incentive for operators to produce more green electricity notwithstanding the additional costs of production, thus contributing to the Member States' achievement of the indicative production targets imposed on them under Article 3 of Directive 2001/77) has not been established.*' See Judgment on *Essent Belgium*, paragraph 115.

be analyzed. Second, they must be analyzed against a criterion: whether the difference in treatment at issue is capable of substantially contributing to the attainment of the concerned legitimate objective in a certain and direct manner. The court has held that such a substantial contribution cannot be established if the contribution is risky, uncertain and indirect, and depends on an additional set of conditions (e.g., in the present case, those listed in paragraph 114 of the judgment[802]).

851. In assessing whether different network charges for renewables prosumers and DR providers are objectively justified, in addition to the criteria referred to in the ruling on *Arcelor Atlantique and Lorraine and Others*, the above-mentioned standards elaborated by the *Essent Belgium* case relating to appropriateness and necessity of the distinction should also be considered. Nevertheless, relying solely on criteria distilled from these rulings is insufficient to address the legal issues involved in evaluating the validity of justifications for different treatments. Examining the above-mentioned Commission Decision on SA.34045, one may find a question: in case a differentiation in network charges stems from a specific national law (e.g., EnWG 2011) with a wide set of objectives, such as promoting RES-E, and is implemented by a specific network charge regulation (e.g., StromNEV), which of them should be considered to determine 'the aim pursued by that treatment'?

852. In the Commission Decision on SA.34045, the EC did not base the assessment on the aim of the EnWG 2011 but instead on that of the StromNEV. As a result, the legal objectives of ensuring the security of supply and promoting RES-E put forward by Germany were not regarded by the EC as motivations justifying different treatment at issue (i.e., granting the full network charge exemption to baseload consumers). Given that only the system of network charges is considered, those motivations external to network charges do not relate to its objective and thus fail to justify the different treatment. The EC's reasoning is closely linked to the potential that entirely exempting baseload consumers from network charges constitutes state aid.[803] Such full exemption constitutes state

---

802 See footnote 800 above.

803 The EC cited settled case law to clarify that the exemption at issue does not constitute a PSO aimed to perform a service in the interest of the society but may constitute state aid. Therefore, the abovementioned deviation from non-discriminatory TPA contained in the legal provision for PSOs and the condition for this deviation are not applicable in this case. More specifically, in its 'Altmark' ruling, the CJEU has clarified that the following four criteria must all be met for compensation for a service of general economic interest not to constitute state aid under Art. 107(1) TFEU: (1) the recipient undertaking must actually have PSOs to discharge and the obligations must be clearly defined; (2) the parameters on the basis of which the compensation is calculated must be established in advance in an objective and transparent manner, to avoid it conferring an economic advantage which may favor the recipient undertaking over competing undertakings; (3) the compensation cannot exceed what is necessary to cover all or part of the costs incurred in the discharge of PSOs, taking

aid to the extent that the advantage granted is selective.[804] As such, assessing the presence of a selective advantage essentially amounts to a discrimination test.[805] In settled case law on state aid in relation to charges, there exists a

---

into account the relevant receipts and a reasonable profit for discharging those obligations; (4) where the undertaking which is to discharge PSOs, in a specific case, is not chosen pursuant to a public procurement procedure which would allow for the selection of the tenderer capable of providing those services at the least cost to the community, the level of compensation needed must be determined on the basis of an analysis of the costs which a typical undertaking, well run and adequately provided with the necessary means, would have incurred in discharging those obligations, taking into account the relevant receipts and a reasonable profit for discharging the obligations. It is observed that those four cumulative conditions are not fulfilled in the present case. First, the German legislation does not identify any service of general economic interest that would consist of stable consumption, and it does not entrust baseload consumers with any PSO. Second, the law does not specify any parameters for calculating costs to avoid overcompensation. Third, the full exemption necessarily leads to overcompensation as it exceeds what compensation would have been necessary to cover the extra costs related to the alleged PSO. This is supported by the fact that for many of the baseload consumers, having a consumption reaching 7,000 hours of full use and exceeding 10 GWh simply corresponds to their normal consumption profile and does not imply any particular costs. Finally, the undertakings were not chosen pursuant to a public procurement procedure and the exemption has not been determined on the basis of an analysis of the costs which a typical undertaking, well run and adequately provided with the necessary means, would have incurred in discharging those obligations, taking into account the relevant receipts and a reasonable profit for discharging the obligations. Germany, on the other hand, indicated that it was hard to quantify the value that a stable load had for the network. See *Judgment of 24 July 2003, Altmark Trans and Regierungspräsidium Magdeburg, C-280/00, EU:C:2003:415*, paragraphs 87–93; *Commission Decision on SA.34045*, recitals 87 and 88; section 5.1.2.

804 Article 107(1) TFEU introduces four cumulative criteria that constitute the concept of State aid by providing that '*save as otherwise provided in the Treaties, any aid granted by a Member State or through State resources in any form whatsoever which distorts or threatens to distort competition by favouring certain undertakings or the production of certain goods shall, in so far as it affects trade between Member States, be incompatible with the internal market.*' When interpreting this provision, the CJEU has consistently emphasized that classification of a national measure as 'State aid' for the purposes of Article 107(1) TFEU requires that all the conditions set out in that provision are fulfilled: (1) there must be an intervention by the State or through State resources, (2) the intervention must be liable to affect trade between Member States, (3) it must confer a selective advantage on the recipient, and (4) it must distort or threaten to distort competition. See Commission Decision on SA.34045, recitals 102 and 171; Judgment on *Altmark Trans and Regierungspräsidium Magdeburg*, paragraph 74; Case C-128/16 P *Commission v Spain and Others* [2018] ECLI:EU:C:2018:591, paragraph 35; Case C-657/15 P *Viasat Broadcasting UK v TV2/Danmark* [2017] ECLI:EU:C:2017:837, paragraph 32; Case C-20/15 P *Commission v World Duty Free Group* [2016] ECLI:EU:C:2016:981, paragraph 53; Case C-262/12 *Vent De Colère and Others* [2013] ECLI:EU:C:2013:851, paragraph 15; Case C-399/08 P *Commission v Deutsche Post* [2010] ECR I-7831, ECLI:EU:C:2010:481, paragraph 38; Case C-206/06 *Essent Netwerk Noord and Others* [2008] ECR I-5497, ECLI:EU:C:2008:413, paragraphs 63–64. See also Iliopoulos, 2021, pp 157–158.

805 The EC reasoned that '*in order to establish that an advantage is selective, the Commission has to demonstrate that a measure differentiates between economic operators who are, in light of the objective of the reference system identified, in a comparable factual and legal situation and that such a differentiation cannot be justified by the nature or the general scheme of the reference system.*' See Commission Decision on SA.34045.

particular standard for evaluating when the concerned distinction would not be considered to constitute a selective advantage or discrimination. That is, '*the concept of aid does not encompass measures creating different treatment of undertakings in relation to charges where that difference is attributable to the nature and general scheme of the system of charges in question*'.[806]

853. This standard implies that when different network charges may constitute state aid, the specific network charge system, rather than the primary energy legislation (although the latter sets out general rules for the concerned differentiation), is the focus of assessing whether the different treatment is objectively justified. As exemplified in the Commission Decision on SA.34045, in this context, likely, the nature and general scheme of the network charge system are solely related to network use.[807]

854. As such, when renewables prosumers and DR providers are considered in a comparable situation to that of other network users, reducing or exempting network charges for them can violate the principle of non-discrimination if such differentiation is set out by a network charge regulation and lacks relevance to the nature and general scheme of that system of charges. The EC may therefore raise doubts as to whether the special charges for these network users involved in DSM activities could be declared lawful state aid and compatible with the internal market.

855. There are, however, some cases where non-network-related reasons can also justify different network charges and prevent them from falling within the concept of 'selective advantage'. That is, if such differentiation in network charges merely stems from the general legislation governing the energy sector or is implemented by national law dedicated to facilitating RES-E or flexibility, such national law may be deemed to be '*the system of charges in question*'. The nature and general scheme of the charging system are then likely linked to broader energy legislative objectives, such as promoting RES-E, which can be used for

806 *Judgment of 29 April 2004, Netherlands v Commission, C-159/01, EU:C:2004:246*, paragraph 42; *Judgment of 8 September 2011, Commission v Netherlands, C-279/08 P, ECLI:EU:C:2011:551*, paragraph 62.

807 In that Decision, the EC considered that the possibility provided in Paragraph 24 of the EnWG 2011 to determine individual network charges for atypical users such as baseload consumers is in line with the principles of cost-causality and non-discrimination, as elaborated above. It confirmed that this arrangement must be regarded as an integral part of the reference system, as it serves as a corrective to take into account the network costs actually caused by atypical network users such as baseload consumers. The concept of individual network costs attributable to a given network user and the arrangement for correcting atypical users' non-cost-reflective network charges under the published network charges between 2011 and 2013 are viewed as the nature and the general scheme of the network charge system, which are essentially concerned with network-related considerations. See Commission Decision on SA.34045, recitals 110, 115, 116, 118 and 119.

supporting the lawfulness of the different treatment (i.e., without violating the principle of non-discrimination and constituting state aid). Table 20 provides a summary of assessment results of reasons for justifying different network charges when the distinction may constitute state aid.

**Table 20. The assessment of valid justifications supporting lawful different treatment when lower network charges may constitute state aid**

| Where do different network charges stem from? | What is '*the system of charges*' referred to in the exception to the concept of state aid? | Valid justification for the distinction |
|---|---|---|
| • The general legislation on energy or electricity matters, implemented by a network charge regulation; Or<br>• Merely from a network charge regulation | The network charge regulation | (Primarily) network-related reasons, and generally, other motivations such as promoting RES-E are not considered |
| • The general legislation on energy or electricity matters, implemented by measures for promoting RES-E or flexibility; Or<br>• Merely from the general energy legislation; Or<br>• Merely from specific regulations promoting RES-E or flexibility | The general legislation or specific legal acts for promoting RES-E or flexibility | Justifications are not network-related but include promoting RES-E and the security of supply |

Source: Author's own elaboration.

856. To sum up, granting different network charges in the form of exemptions or discounts may be concretely implemented as a PSO or constitute state aid. The above analysis demonstrates that, aside from the general criteria for the non-discrimination test, EU law and its case law on these two subjects create more sophisticated criteria. To ensure compatibility with the principle of non-discrimination and state aid rules, Member States should fully consider these criteria when relevant network charges are applied in the form of PSOs and may constitute state aid.[808] Both the comparability test and the assessment of justifications for distinction require the identification of the aim of the legislation that makes the different treatment. By taking some examples, the above analysis shows that differentiation in network charges that lacks relevance to

[808] For more details about the four cumulative criteria that must all be met for compensation for a service of general economic interest not to constitute State aid, see Judgment on *Altmark Trans and Regierungspräsidium Magdeburg*, paragraphs 87–93.

network-related reasons (notably the network service used[809] and cost impacts on the network) is not necessarily at odds with the principle of non-discrimination. The discrimination test results may vary depending on the context, particularly on whether a national network charge regulation is involved in creating the concerned differentiation in network charges.

857. True, non-network-related motivations may justify different network charges for network users involved in renewables self-consumption or DR. However, such different treatments, if unrelated to network usage or incurred costs, could still violate the requirement of designing cost-reflective network charges. To align with the principles of non-discrimination and cost-reflectiveness while preventing distorting price signals from network charges, it is recommended to avoid using network charges as a tool for incentivizing renewables prosumers and DR providers when their activities do not yield corresponding beneficial network impacts.[810]

---

[809] It follows from Article 14(1) of the Regulation on access to natural gas transmission networks that transmission system users, similar or not, should be treated equally when using the same services. It seems that the use of network services is also a relevant aspect of the comparability test in terms of the objective of the network access regime. See *Regulation (EC) No 715/2009*, Article 14; Hannah Kruimer, 2011.

[810] This is also the advice of the network cost impact analysis of the Flemish Region. The 2021 amendment to the Flemish Energy Decree allows the Flemish Government to ask the VREG to examine the relevant remuneration and reductions in grid tariffs that can be provided for energy communities based on the benefits their activities can bring to the grid. A study examining, using a cost-benefit analysis, the extent to which activities of energy communities can contribute to relieving the burden on the distribution grid was finished in 2023. This study has three main findings. First, collective activities where members optimize individual capacity tariffs and collective self-consumption (including those conducted by energy communities) generally do not create a change in the grid operator's investment needs. This is based on one finding of this study that the offtake peak of individual customers within the collective activity (winter, evening) does not sufficiently coincide with the times when collective activities have maximum PV production (summer, afternoon). Second, specific compositions of collective activities can provide benefits to the distribution network, but these benefits could only be delivered under certain preconditions. For instance, grid losses do decrease to a limited extent in later years if PV installations are correctly dimensioned and if there is sufficient flexibility to steer consumption to moments of PV production within the collective activity. The collective activity should also be located on network elements on which the grid operator already experiences congestion problems. Moreover, it must be guaranteed that the collective activity provides structural solutions without exception. Third, this study indicates that collective activities cannot always structurally meet all the preconditions and thus, in general, do not realize a sustainable benefit for the distribution network. Based on these findings, this study concludes that an adjustment in grid tariffs for collective activities is not appropriate for the Flemish Region. Other means than grid tariffs are therefore suggested to promote collective activities if such activities need to be further facilitated to underscore their environmental or social objectives. See *Flemish Energy Decree*, art. 4.8.4, §4; EnergyVille, 2023.

### 3.4.1.2. Rule-Making Procedures

858. Both the TSO and the DSO must ensure the participation of all market participants when establishing flexibility procurement rules, technical requirements for participating in flexibility markets they organize, and specifications for flexibility procured for different purposes,[811] as listed in Section 6 of Chapter III above. Apart from the inclusiveness requirement, EU law additionally requires TSOs and DSOs to ensure the effective participation of all market participants in developing specifications for non-frequency ancillary services and flexibility for congestion management.[812] The requirements of EU law seem rather straightforward. However, these principles regarding due process are not easy to comply with in practice. Their implementation requires multiple safeguards, especially considering that electricity undertakings and large industrial consumers are no longer the sole stakeholders involved in rule-making processes.

859. The CEP reinforces regulatory impetus and widens avenues for prompting consumers to offer flexibility to the system. A common challenge faced by TSOs and DSOs is how to realize the participatory, inclusive and effective rule-making process required by EU law with growing market participants offering flexibility. This challenge is even more pronounced, considering that consumers connected to the distribution grid are also becoming stakeholders in the flexibility market rules, which are small in size and vastly distributed. Engaging with them entails increasing complexity and transaction costs.

860. Moreover, effective participation in relevant rule-making processes typically requires some know-how, especially regarding technical parameters of flexibility products, the design of flexibility markets, and, more importantly, the positive or negative consequences of adopting different technical requirements or standards. Small consumers – particularly SMEs and households – often lack the experience and expertise to navigate the highly formalized electricity system, both in terms of market participation and relevant rule-making processes. They are vulnerable to under- and misrepresentation in relevant consultations. It is hard for these players to identify potential market access barriers stemming from the proposed flexibility service specifications, procurement rules and market participation technical requirements. Such insufficient representation, in turn, undermines the effectiveness of the participatory process in terms of identifying and addressing unjustified market entry barriers or restrictions, as well as ensuring wider market participation by various demand flexibility

811 *Electricity Directive*, articles 31(6)(8), 32(2) and 40(4)(6).

812 *Electricity Directive*, articles 32(2) and 40(6).

providers. This problem may be partially responsible for the fact that market design parameters (particularly those of balancing markets) persistently hinder the market participation of small individual consumers and small-scale IFSPs, as shown in Sections 2 and 3.2 of this Chapter above.

861. A key takeaway is that substantive legal issues often stem from shortcomings in the underlying rule-making process. This also applies to the drafting of rules relating to flexibility markets organized by TSOs and DSOs. These rules are highly technical and set out key conditions for entering markets or exert significant influence over potential market actors' incentives to bid on flexibility markets. Market entry barriers or restrictions can easily arise when some stakeholders' legitimate interests are insufficiently represented and impartially weighed, due to the difficulty in understanding and providing substantial input in the development of relevant rules. As exemplified by balancing market rules and the ToE regime examined above,[813] technical rules (e.g., prequalification) and data exchange measures could be rather demanding and complex. They are blamed for creating disproportionate requirements, as is the case in Belgium and other Member States.[814] A recurring concern is whether the TSO has made a thorough trade-off and sought to pursue a balance between safety considerations and improving market entry conditions. This concern is amplified by the lack of transparency in how the TSO handles input from stakeholders and weighs their priorities and preferences against other key considerations arising from its core tasks of system operation.

862. Despite being subject to approval by independent regulators, non-negligible discretion may remain with system operators regarding the development of draft measures for balancing markets, other flexibility procurement, and market participation.[815] This potentially considerable residual discretion stems from technical expertise, which amounts to epistemic authority.[816] Without robust safeguards to ensure the TSO responds to stakeholders' input, it becomes challenging to guarantee that the rules it drafts devote sufficient effort to seeking a proper balance between competing goals. The potential inaction in optimizing flexibility market design highlights a key legal issue that must be considered by Member States when transposing the generic Union-level principles for rule-making processes. That is, to what level the responsiveness to stakeholder input should be achieved, and whether legal and other accountability mechanisms should be put in place to ensure such stakeholder responsiveness. This general

813 See Sections 2 and 3.2 of this Chapter above.

814 Ibid.

815 System operators and the ENTSO-E's power in influencing network rule-making stems from their technical expertise. See Kohlbacher and Lavrijssen, 2018.

816 Epistemic authority as regards technical issues concerning the electricity grid can result in significant factual influence over the network code development process. See Kohlbacher and Lavrijssen, 2018.

question can be translated into specific questions, including the extent to which system operators should consider and reflect stakeholders' legitimate interests in the draft rules.[817] These issues matter because if the legitimate interests of new actors (renewables self-consumers, active customers, and energy communities) are crowded out in the rule-making process, the flexibility market design will not be adaptable to their participation.

863. Indeed, market entry barriers could be mitigated by reinforcing the regulator's role in reviewing whether system operators have taken enough measures to create proportionate and streamlined rules. However, without the relevant market participants' adequate input, the regulator could not identify well whether the proposed rules would impose disproportionate burdens on them. Compared to solely reinforcing regulatory oversight, it is preferable to elaborate on how system operators should make dialogue and deliberation processes accessible to all market participants and provide feedback mechanisms, accompanied by monitoring over the TSOs' performance in this respect. Flemish law provides an example of adopting this approach, as shown in Section 2.3.3.1 above of this Chapter.

864. In addition to potential room for elaborating on system operators' obligations to ensure effective and participatory rule-making processes, further instruments are needed to address the disadvantages faced by certain stakeholders. With a metaphor of 'picking up the carrot in the basket', Section 3.1 of this Chapter highlights that granting rights is not the sole step of consumer empowerment. Certain consumer groups face specific barriers to exercising their rights, including both substantive rights to engage in DR and renewables self-consumption, as well as procedural rights to provide input in the development of relevant rules. Empowering them should thus also contain the provision of instruments for overcoming their obstacles, which also applies to the participation process of making rules for flexibility procurement. Member States need to develop instruments to adequately support the engagement of various market participants in flexibility provision, while avoiding the risk of lengthy legal procedures.

865. The dilemma between the efficient and inclusive rule-making process is a recurrent issue. The key solution lies in reducing complexity and providing the necessary support when structuring the voice of stakeholders. The Flemish case study above demonstrates that appointing intermediaries is a promising

[817] Stakeholder responsiveness in rule-making processes is clearly related to the principle of good administration. Good administration and its sub-principles are established as general principles of EU law, which grant individuals rights also vis-à-vis Member States when implementing and enforcing EU law. It requires giving due consideration to stakeholder input, weighing the interests of all parties impartially, and reflecting their input in network rules. See Hofmann, 2017, p 228; Kohlbacher and Lavrijssen, 2018.

approach to reducing transaction costs and complexity when engaging with massive market participants. Likewise, introducing intermediaries in the flexibility market rule-making process might also be helpful. Stakeholder committees, already operating in other jurisdictions such as Australia and the UK (in the form of the 'Customer Forum'), play a similar role in representing massive stakeholders to interact with system operators (Kohlbacher and Lavrijssen, 2018; Havyatt, 2022). They do so by gathering information on consumer perspectives and priorities and structuring dialogue among heterogeneous stakeholders (Kohlbacher and Lavrijssen, 2018; Havyatt, 2022). More importantly, they could also be formalized, serving as a tool for empowering stakeholders in respect of understanding proposed rules and enabling stakeholders to pose questions and pass judgments (Kohlbacher and Lavrijssen, 2018). The realization of this role depends on a set of design elements, such as the composition of these committees, which may include energy professionals providing technical support and consultation (Havyatt, 2022). By facilitating the accessibility of rule-making processes to stakeholders, such stakeholder committees also help to reinforce a social accountability mechanism (Kohlbacher and Lavrijssen, 2018). Complementing the existing legal and political accountability in drawing up network-related rules, such social accountability can contribute to improving the responsiveness of flexibility rule-making to stakeholder input (Kohlbacher and Lavrijssen, 2018).

866. Moreover, conventional consultation processes may have other regulatory gaps in fully engaging new actors that are empowered to provide flexibility, especially households and energy communities. The Irish regulator, CRU, has already identified such gaps. It noted that national regulators and system operators have maintained strong communication with industry and professional stakeholders (CRU, 2021d). However, the traditional methods used to convey information on proposed market arrangements and consult stakeholders may be inaccessible for non-industry market participants, notably including energy communities and active consumers from commercial and residential sectors (CRU, 2021d). These stakeholders may not have the resources to participate in the traditional routes of consultation processes (CRU, 2021d). Better alternatives for effective communication, resting on improvements on two fronts, information dissemination and public discussions (Hanke et al., 2023), are vital to effectively engaging them in flexibility market rule drafting. Recognizing this need, the CRU implemented various consultation mechanisms to engage stakeholders when developing rules for active customers and energy communities. In addition to the information displayed on its webpage, it adopted webinars, radio interviews, print media editorials, short video blogs, and social media to engage stakeholders (CRU, 2021d). In particular, two webinars were hosted to disclose general information and updates to a wide audience, and learn about feedback from active customers from non-industrial

sectors and energy communities (CRU, 2021d). The regulator viewed webinars as a better alternative for engaging stakeholders who are large in number and lack resources to participate in traditional consultations, and thereby are liable to be underrepresented.

867. The Irish regulator's attempts demonstrate the potential room for improving existing rule-making processes to ensure sufficient input from stakeholders interested in DR and renewables self-consumption. A revisit and adaptation of rule-making processes are imperative in the interest of ensuring adequate representation of the interests of consumers, whether acting individually or collectively, given that prevailing consultation processes may not be accessible to these market participants. System operators' rule-making processes relating to flexibility procurement are a key component. Member States should consider how to ensure that system operators take into account the disadvantages faced by these market participants in effectively participating in flexibility market rule-making procedures. To secure adequate representation of these stakeholders, system operators should also be able to innovate the way they communicate proposed rules and interact with impacted stakeholders to learn about their concerns regarding relevant rules.

#### 3.4.1.3. The Application of Flexible Connection Agreements

868. The 2024 Amendment to the Electricity Directive introduced a framework for flexible connection agreements. In areas where electricity grids have limited or no network capacity for new connections, TSOs and DSOs should be able to offer to network users the possibility of establishing a flexible connection agreement, i.e., "*a set of agreed conditions for connecting electrical capacity to the grid that includes conditions to limit and control the electricity injection to and withdrawal from the transmission network or distribution network*" (*Electricity Directive*, Article 2(24c)). Article 6a of the Electricity Directive provides that the regulatory authority should develop frameworks for such flexible connections, ensuring that: (i) they do not delay the network reinforcements, (ii) conversion to a firm connection agreement is ensured, once the network is ready, and (iii) flexible connections are enabled as a permanent solution for areas where network reinforcement is not the most efficient solution.

869. A question worth further investigation is concerned with the relationship between market-based flexibility procurement and flexible connection agreements. Why does the amendment introduce flexible connection agreements, given that EU law has already specified the market-based way for congestion management? Would their application undermine the market-based way for congestion management enshrined by Article 32 of the Electricity Directive and Article 13 of the Electricity Regulation?

870. The amendment to the Electricity Directive does not clarify the relationship between flexible connection agreements and market-based flexibility procurement. Neither does it specify if such agreements constitute non-market-based redispatching, such as curtailment referred to in Article 13 of the Electricity Regulation. Clarifying the role of flexible connection agreements in congestion management requires a specific examination of Article 6a of the amendment to the Electricity Directive, in conjunction with recital 15. As noted above, the legislation positions these agreements as a tool for grid bottlenecks that are caused by capacity shortages due to a lack of investment or long lead times for reinforcement. They target structural or long-term grid congestion, serving as an alternative to network reinforcements, which are explicitly defined as the structural solutions in Recital 15 of the amendment. Their primary purpose is to serve as substitutes for structural solutions for grid congestion, either on a temporary or permanent basis, which explains why they have been introduced by EU law as a distinct regulatory instrument, working in parallel with flexibility markets. Their introduction also implies that the legislator does not consider flexibility markets suitable for delivering such structural substitutes, although, as pointed out later, the EU legislator should clarify this.

871. Moreover, under Article 6a, the use of flexible connection agreements is not contingent on the inefficiency or failure of market-based flexibility procurement, i.e., cases where '*the regulatory authorities have established that the procurement of such services is not economically efficient or would lead to severe market distortions or increased congestion*'. This suggests that, unlike non-market-based redispatching, they are not designed to deviate from market-based flexibility procurement. Several features may distinguish flexible connection agreements from non-market-based redispatching, as shown in Table 21. Non-market-based redispatching is used as a last resort when market-based options are exhausted or bring suboptimal results. Flexible connection agreements may also involve curtailment-like elements while they are based on contractual arrangements, which define in advance when and how the user's injection and withdrawal can be limited.

**Table 21. Comparisons of grid congestion solutions mandated by EU law**

| | Purposes/features/conditions |
|---|---|
| Market-based flexibility markets (under Article 32 of the Electricity Directive; Article 13 of the Electricity Regulation) | • Alleviating the need to upgrade or replace electricity capacity and supporting the efficient and secure operation of the distribution system;<br>• Serving as a principle unless the regulatory authorities have established that the procurement of such services is not economically efficient or that such procurement would lead to severe market distortions or to higher congestion. |

*(continued)*

Table 21 *continued*

| | Purposes/features/conditions |
|---|---|
| Non-market-based redispatching (under Article 13 of the Electricity Regulation) | Only used where:<br>(a) no market-based alternative is available;<br>(b) market-based resources are exhausted;<br>(c) liquidity in flexibility markets is too low to ensure effective competition; or<br>(d) the current grid situation leads to congestion in such a regular and predictable way that market-based redispatching would lead to regular strategic bidding which would increase the level of internal congestion. |
| Flexible connection agreements (under Articles 2(24c) and 6a of the amended Electricity Directive) | • Serving as a temporary solution where network capacity is limited or unavailable and where network reinforcement is planned; Becoming a permanent solution where network development is not the most efficient solution;<br>• Limitations and controls on grid connection are ex-ante agreed and predictable; grid users know in advance the flexibility conditions (e.g., maximum injection, the agreed duration of the flexible connection agreement, and the applicable network charges). |

872. Although, as noted above, under Article 6a, flexible connection agreements are not intended as an exception to market-based flexibility procurement, their introduction raises a risk that they could undermine the principle of market-based congestion management. So far, EU law has not elaborated on the criteria for assessing the economic efficiency of flexibility procurement. With the introduction of flexible connection agreements, national regulators are likely to define these criteria by referencing the costs associated with these agreements. In practice, if flexible connection agreements or similar instruments[818] prove to be more economically efficient than flexibility procurement, the latter may be deemed economically inefficient, potentially justifying a deviation from market-based congestion management. The economic efficiency of flexible connection agreements may be particularly evident in two situations: (i) during the early stage of developing

818 An example is the 'Fall-Back Flex' product in Flanders. In the process of amending the proposed specifications for market-based flexibility procurement for congestion management, formal consultations took place between the VREG and Fluvius on October 23, 2024, and December 12, 2024, in response to several specific connection requests. During these consultations, the societal need for flexible connections as an alternative to refusing a connection was raised. This led to the consideration of including a temporary market product for a flexible connection in the market tests for the market-based procurement of flexibility services for local congestion management. In 2025, the Flemish Utility Regulator approved the Flemish DSO's proposal for 'Fall-Back Flex' procurement. Acting as a temporary solution for providing flexible grid access, this product will expire once either (a) the necessary grid investments are completed or (b) EU law on flexible connection agreements is transposed and implemented. See Decision on the 'Fall-back flex', 2025, Sections I and II.

distribution-level flexibility markets, where market liquidity is low,[819] and (ii) where frequently-recurring congestion requires continuous procurement, as in cases of structural congestion.[820] In these circumstances, national regulators and system operators may rely on flexible connection agreements as a common congestion management practice, by invoking both Article 6a and the derogations provided under Article 32 of the Electricity Directive. Hence, within the current EU legal framework, the application of flexible connection agreements can undermine market-based congestion management as a general principle.

873. It appears that the EU legislator did not realize this risk when introducing flexible connection agreements, reflected in two aspects. First, the above-cited Article 6a does not expressly deal with the relationship between these agreements and market-based flexibility procurement, whilst it only highlights the general rule of not delaying the network reinforcements. Second, no adaptations to Article 32 of the Electricity Directive and Article 13 of the Electricity Regulation were made to prevent the aforementioned risk of circumventing the principle of market-based congestion management. Flexible connection agreements now co-exist with flexibility markets, both offering solutions when grid capacity is limited and network development is pending. It remains unclear how national regulators should choose between them to pursue a desirable balance between the market-based principle and cost-efficient network operation. Considering this, the EU legislator should refine minimum requirements for implementing market-based congestion management in the context of using flexible connection agreements. EU law is better placed to address the involved trade-off, given that national regulators may not give due account to competing EU-level principles concerning flexibility procurement and grid investment, which can lead to sub-optimal results.

874. A possible way to reduce deviation from the principle of market-based congestion management is to further define the role of flexible connection agreements and market-based flexibility procurement. For instance, a possible interpretation is that flexible connection agreements are intended to address structural (long-term) congestion where capacity is insufficient and reinforcement is pending or not efficient, while market-based flexibility procurement is

819 Flexibility markets at the distribution level are liable to encounter low market liquidity due to limited market participation of local resources and their relatively small scale. See Pressmair et al., 2021.

820 See Article 2(6) of the Electricity Regulation for the definition of 'structural congestion'.

geared toward operational (short-term) congestion management.[821] However, there is no evidence that the EU legislator intends to position market-based flexibility procurement solely as a tool for operational congestion management. Furthermore, EU law does not provide a legal definition of operational or short-term congestion. The EU legislator needs to thoroughly consider the regulatory impact of existing congestion management solutions on transmission and distribution grid operation and other important goals (notably developing flexibility markets and consumer engagement), and determine in which cases, market-based approach should remain to be the principle. This process may take place with new definitions and adaptations of existing provisions on flexible connection agreements and congestion management, including those governing tariffs.

#### 3.4.1.4. TSO-DSO Coordination Mechanisms

875. TSO-DSO coordination is instrumental in ensuring wider market participation of DR and self-generated RES-E, as well as achieving system operators' coordinated access to these DERs, as addressed in Chapter III above. A market-based coordination approach increasingly comes into discussion, which aims to enhance the coordination of existing and emerging markets for flexibility. Coordinating or even restructuring market models is gaining importance also because DSOs are involved in procuring flexibility services, and some of them may do so through launching local markets. The advent of distribution-level flexibility markets raises several questions that need to be addressed. First, how are such markets to co-exist and coordinate with ancillary service (balancing and non-frequency) and congestion management markets organized at the transmission level? Second, given the potential trend of developing local markets for encouraging prosumers to trade self-generated electricity (Butenko, 2016; Rosen and Madlener, 2016; Olivella-Rosell et al., 2018; Faia et al., 2021, p 127), should the design of market models for TSO-DSO coordination cater to this trend? If so, how can it be made possible?

876. In the field of adjusting electricity market structures, the discussion from the technical and economic perspectives has been intense (see e.g. Burger et al., 2019; Papalexopoulos et al., 2020). However, its legal aspects and compatibility of the proposed market models with existing EU energy law have

---

821 CEER distinguishes between structural congestion (predictable, long-term) and sporadic congestion (unpredictable, short-term). It also argues that market-based approaches may have advantages for more dynamic problems that occur for limited time periods. See CEER, 2020a, Sections 3.2 and 4.6.

not received due attention. In this subsection, the focus will be on identifying preliminary legal issues or challenges based on a review of the general literature on market models designed to facilitate TSO-DSO coordination. The core legal question centers around how to adjust and reallocate the role, obligations and responsibilities of TSOs and DSOs to enable optimal co-existence of multi-level electricity markets.

877. The market-based approach to TSO-DSO coordination warrants attention at both the EU and national levels, not only due to its multiple potential benefits but also the resultant legal issues in several dimensions. As pointed out later, such issues range from impacting market integration to the potential for restructuring the rights and obligations of system operators and actors trading DR and self-produced RES-E. So far, EU law has not devoted attention to reforming market models toward favoring TSO-DSO coordination and other core legal aims, notably creating a 'customer-centred electricity market'. In the literature, there has not been an agreement on a common European market model for coordinating flexibility service procurement (Ringelstein et al., 2022). Moreover, despite the potential multiple benefits, flexibility markets at the distribution level are still in their infancy (Li, 2015; Papalexopoulos et al., 2020). The implementation of such markets is riddled with market and technical challenges, which are inter alia related to the governance of DSOs (Papalexopoulos et al., 2020). Considering the potential implications for internal market integration created by reshaping market architecture, there is a need to establish a minimum common understanding of the means for such adjustment and to what extent the centralized approach to organizing energy and flexibility markets should be deviated from. This calls for proportionate EU-level impetus and guidance to adjust relevant market models, with due regard to the principle of subsidiarity. Aside from Union-level actions, in the interest of better transposing and implementing EU law on empowering consumers and developing system flexibility, Member States also need to give due attention to adapting market structures and corresponding roles and obligations of TSOs and DSOs.

878. In the existing literature, most TSO-DSO coordination mechanisms based on market models can be categorized along this spectrum: (i) centralized approaches that include integrated optimization of the entire system by the TSO, (ii) decoupled approaches that include separate flexibility procurement by the TSO and the DSO with minimum interaction between them, and (iii) TSO-DSO market-based cooperation that requires intensive interactions between them (Kristov et al., 2016; Caramanis et al., 2016; Hartnett et al., 2021, p 280; Vagropoulos et al., 2022). Within these three major approaches, a number of more detailed market models have been proposed (Gerard et al., 2018; IRENA, 2020), as Figure 15 shows.

**Figure 15. Market models for TSO-DSO coordination**

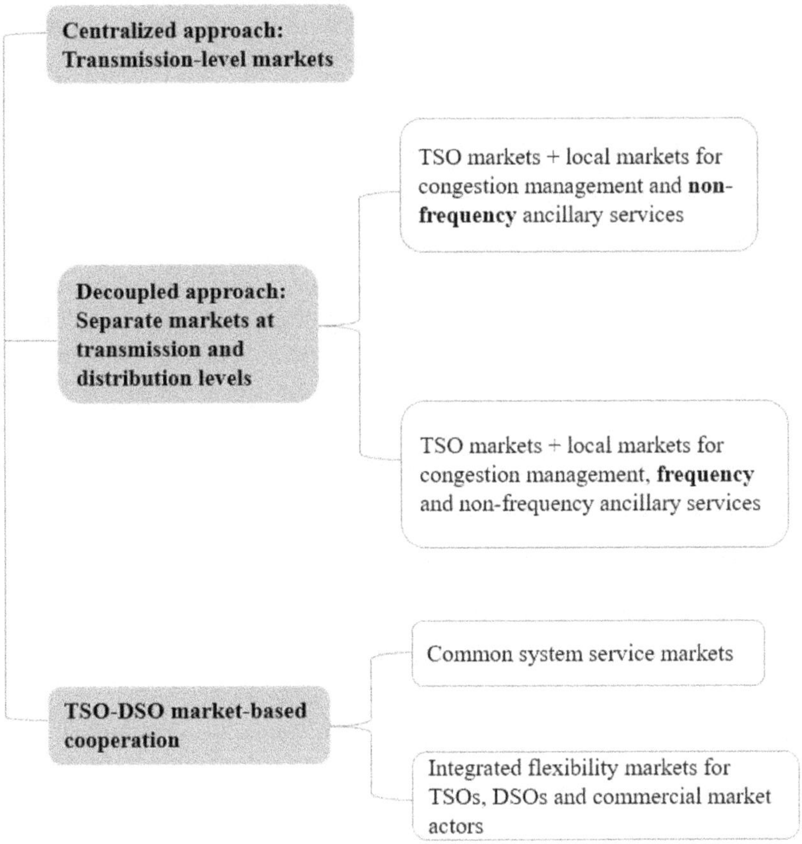


Source: Author's own elaboration.

879. The first approach more or less continues the existing top-down market architecture (Hartnett et al., 2021, p 280). It reflects the current situation in some European countries where few DSOs have started procuring flexibility services, and the TSO is the major buyer. As such, there are only central market platforms for flexibility services from both transmission and distribution levels (IRENA, 2020). The TSO is responsible for performing dispatch and prequalification of these resources, considering the network constraints of both the distribution and transmission networks (Givisiez et al., 2020; IRENA, 2020). In comparison with the TSO, the role of the DSO is rather limited. It does not procure flexibility services for its own use but only provides the TSO with necessary data, checks for constraints in the distribution grid, and assists in technical validation in the implementation of system prequalification (Givisiez et al., 2020; IRENA, 2020). This market set-up, which serves centralized

procurement by the TSO, accompanied by limited responsibilities of DSOs and cost allocation solutions, has been applied in balancing markets, as discussed in Section 6.1.4 of Chapter III. Such a TSO-managed model substantially simplifies the TSO-DSO coordination process and minimizes tensions arising from the simultaneous use of flexibility services by the TSO and the DSO (Givisiez et al., 2020). However, its evident disadvantage is that it fails to fit and facilitate a more proactive role of the DSO under existing EU law (IRENA, 2020), namely, utilizing flexibility services to manage the distribution network actively and being a neutral market facilitator.

880. Under the second approach, a bottom-up pathway is adopted, which features the set-up of separate flexibility markets at the distribution level (Hartnett et al., 2021; Vagropoulos et al., 2022). DSOs are envisioned to organize and operate local flexibility markets for their own use. Another distinct character lies in DSOs having the priority to use demand flexibility connected to their own networks (Givisiez et al., 2020; IRENA, 2020). The TSO could only acquire remaining local flexibility from the DSO after all flexibility needs of the latter have been satisfied (Givisiez et al., 2020; IRENA, 2020; Vagropoulos et al., 2022). Specific processes of sequential clearing of DSO and TSO markets for this purpose are thus presented (Papavasiliou and Mezghani, 2018; Vagropoulos et al., 2022). As one of the steps therein, the DSO may aggregate and transfer the unused local flexibility bids to the TSO market while ensuring that only bids respecting distribution grid constraints are offered (Gerard et al., 2018; Papavasiliou and Mezghani, 2018; IRENA, 2020; Vagropoulos et al., 2022).

881. According to the different goals served, the second approach contains two possible markets at the distribution level: (i) local congestion and non-frequency ancillary service markets, and (ii) markets for local balancing.[822] For the former case, EU law has explicitly provided three cases where the DSO is allowed to access certain categories of flexibility: (i) procuring the energy it uses to cover energy losses in its system, (ii) procuring non-frequency ancillary services for efficient network operation, and (iii) using flexibility services for the local congestion relieving purpose (*Electricity Directive*, articles 31(5)(6)(7) and 32 (1)). For the latter case, however, there has not been an explicit legal basis under EU law that allows the reallocation of balancing responsibility between TSOs and DSOs. Nor is there clear permission for allowing DSOs to procure frequency ancillary services for the so-called 'local balancing' within EU law, which may lead to incompatibility with existing unbundling rules. Similar concerns also exist in the literature on creating LEMs.

822 In the second model, in addition to the priority to access local flexibility, the DSO will play a new role of balancing the distribution grid according to a schedule defined upfront between the TSO and the DSO. Hence, the DSO procures local flexible resources to resolve both local congestion and local balancing. See IRENA, 2020; Hartnett et al., 2021, p 280.

Relevant legal challenges of enabling the DSO's active role while complying with unbundling rules are discussed in more detail in Section 3.4.2.1 below.

882. Apart from potential conflicts with EU law, several problems or risks are worth noting if separate flexibility markets are built at the distribution level. One aspect is that smaller-sized DSOs may lack the necessary market liquidity to procure flexibility services in their networks, raising concerns about market power.[823] Low liquidity of such local markets would also considerably increase the flexibility procurement costs of the DSO.[824] Some studies also indicate that small DSOs may find it difficult to operate local markets due to a lack of expertise in this area (Johansson et al., 2020). Moreover, the relatively wide role of DSOs, especially aggregating the non-cleared offers to TSOs, may breach strict unbundling rules in some Member States, which prohibit DSOs from engaging in aggregation.[825] This again highlights questions regarding the contested future role of the DSO and how to support the DSO's transition to a proactive system operator, as elaborated on later in Section 3.4.2.1.

883. The common feature of the first two approaches is that they only require limited interactions between TSOs and DSOs. Coordinated access to flexibility services is approached by establishing different priorities for accessing relevant resources and diminishing tensions. By contrast, the common market models discussed within the third approach take the TSO-DSO coordination a step further. They require a higher degree of collaboration between TSOs and DSOs rather than merely avoiding tensions in accessing flexibility. The first relevant model is a common flexibility market jointly operated by the TSO and the DSO for accessing and allocating flexible resources connected to the transmission and distribution grid (IRENA, 2020). Neither the TSO nor the DSO has priority to access flexibility sources. Instead, the common market is cleared jointly by TSO and DSO, through which flexibility services are allocated to the system operator with the highest need (IRENA, 2020). Such a joint marketplace has the potential to reduce the total procurement cost from the system perspective[826]

---

823 There may be only one or two actors that can offer services to DSOs. See IRENA, 2020; Johansson et al., 2020; Vagropoulos et al., 2022.

824 This is why DSOs are allowed to procure flexibility from markets beyond their local ones. See VREG, 2020; Flemish Energy Decree, art. 4.1.6, §1.

825 While EU law does not exclude the possibility of the DSO performing aggregation-related activities, in Belgium, the Flemish Energy Decree prohibits the DSO and its operating companies from undertaking any activities related to acting as aggregators or FSPs. See Flemish Energy Decree, art. 4.1.8/1.

826 The joint market framework can prevent undesired price coupling that can occur in the case of separate markets, thereby lowering the procurement cost as a whole. In the case of two separate system service markets where demand-side flexibility can participate, they will prefer the one with higher prices. In practice, the transmission-level market will typically have higher prices, as bids from final customers are cleared alongside those from generators. Consequently, consumers will either refuse to participate in DSO markets or increase the offer

and lower transaction costs faced by small consumers participating in transmission-level markets. However, harvesting these benefits hinges upon establishing fair cost allocation schemes between TSOs and DSOs and realigning specific market procedures for prequalification, activation and settlement, which consider the technical characteristics of both system operators (Roos, 2017).

884. The second model under the common-market approach is a hybrid one that integrates flexibility markets for commercial parties and system operators. It allows both system operators (i.e., the regulated monopolies) and commercial market actors (e.g., BRPs) to participate in the common market.[827] The presence of both monopolies and market players necessitates the introduction of an independent market operator to ensure the fair allocation of flexibility sources and a level playing field, particularly for commercial market actors (IRENA, 2020). The independent market operator is responsible for allocating resources to the highest bidder (based on competition between system operators and commercial market players), data management and settlement of the market (IRENA, 2020). In addition to the greater complexity involved in this model (Roos, 2017), it raises potential concerns that overlap with ID markets (IRENA, 2020). Under EU law, the ID market has become the primary marketplace for market actors to address imbalances according to EU law (*Electricity Regulation*, recital 13 and Article 7 (2)(b); Webster, 2021, p 697). This overlap may hinder the development and liquidity of ID markets (IRENA, 2020). There is a need to consider the co-existence of the two markets in specific market design, by, for instance, enabling them to complement each other or offering different services in different timeframes (IRENA, 2020).

885. Several key findings can be drawn from the foregoing review of proposed market models for TSO-DSO coordination in academic and non-academic literature. First, different market-based coordination approaches, especially those wholly or partially deviating from the present centralized model, directly affect the roles and responsibilities across grid operators, independent market operators and market actors engaged in DR and renewables self-consumption (Hartnett et al., 2021, p 279; Ringelstein et al., 2022).

886. Second, these approaches differ in terms of the degree to which they enhance interaction between the TSO and the DSO. Some market designs

prices according to their lost opportunity cost. This may reduce the liquidity of a separate DSO market or considerably increase the costs for the DSO. On the joint market, on the contrary, the participants will not know beforehand how the offers will be allocated between TSOs and DSOs and help avoid high-price offers occurring in separate TSO and DSO markets. See Roos, 2017.

827 There are many stakeholders beyond TSOs and DSOs who want to access demand-side flexibility for various purposes, including IFSPs, suppliers and BRPs. See IRENA, 2020; Hartnett et al., 2021, p 280.

merely focus on reducing potential tensions between them by building separate markets at both transmission and distribution levels, establishing priority access to flexibility services and sequential market clearing. Others seek greater collaboration among these entities through a common market setting, beyond merely avoiding conflicts.

887. Third, each of the three market-based approaches to TSO-DSO coordination has its own merits and drawbacks, including incompatibility with existing EU law and national law, limited market liquidity or increased complexity. Addressing these in a detailed market design also influences the roles and responsibilities of the involved parties. For example, allowing multiple DSOs instead of individual DSOs to operate local markets may help mitigate inadequate market liquidity (IRENA, 2020). This implies the need to define the scope of local markets further, realign prequalification and procurement specifications reflecting the needs of involved DSOs and obligations of DSOs, and allow DERs located in their grids to participate in such joint local markets. Moreover, to better ensure fair access to DERs by all involved DSOs, an independent market operator can also be introduced in this case.

888. Another noteworthy issue is whether the DSO's priority access to flexibility aligns with EU law. As mentioned above, some market models propose granting the DSO priority to access flexibility services from its own grid. Demand-side flexibility, thus, will be required to first participate in the flexibility procurement organized by the DSO, and only the unused flexibility will be allowed to bid on flexibility markets (for grid balancing and congestion management) operated by the TSO. Within EU law, there is no legal basis for granting DSOs priority access to flexibility sources. Moreover, EU law does not establish a priority ranking of congestion management in the distribution grid and system balancing. There is no explicit requirement that solving local distribution issues (e.g., congestion) must take precedence over broader transmission-level concerns. Moreover, guaranteeing free market entry based on market actors' assessment of the economic and financial viability of their operations is one of the fundamental principles of EU electricity law, as stipulated in Article 3 of the Electricity Regulation. Requiring flexibility services to be offered first in distribution-level procurement can hinder flexibility providers from basing their market entry decisions on the assessment of the economic viability of operating in different flexibility markets, thereby violating the principle of free market entry. Doing so can also limit consumers' opportunities to access potentially higher remuneration available through TSO-level flexibility procurement.

889. From an economic perspective, such priority access is also questionable, as it may limit resources available to the TSO and BRPs requesting flexibility, and can increase the costs of procuring flexibility for these FRPs. It remains unclear

whether the benefits gained by the DSO with priority access to flexibility can outweigh the losses incurred by other stakeholders, and whether such priority access can reduce the overall flexibility procurement cost for the entire system.

890. Overall, the co-existence of flexibility markets at distribution and transmission levels cannot be approached by granting DSOs privileged access to local flexibility. One potential approach to ensuring the coexistence and coordination of multi-level markets is to allow flexibility providers to respond to price signals that allocate flexibility to where it is most valued or required.

891. Lastly, some proposed market models for TSO-DSO coordination serve the sole purpose of enhancing coordination in accessing flexibility services. Contemplating in this way somewhat makes them overlook other legal objectives and the potential impact on the multi-level market structures (Hartnett et al., 2021, p 280). For instance, a prominent question is whether the presence of distribution-level flexibility markets, coupled with local markets for electricity, retail markets and existing flexibility and wholesale markets at the transmission level would considerably increase the complexity of the multi-level market architecture. The follow-up problems include increased coordination costs (between grid operators and involved market actors) and transaction costs, as well as potentially overlapping market designs. Moreover, assisting final customers to participate in more markets could be particularly challenging for DSOs.[828] A possible solution worth considering is integrating local markets for trading flexibility and energy. The exact design of such local markets has not yet been defined, and one aspect is the trade product itself (Schumann et al., 2022). Greater co-benefits could be achieved if market models for coordinating system operators' access to flexibility services are considered in conjunction with flexibility requests from other market actors and the role of local energy trading in maximizing consumers' market participation.

[828] To further increase the market liquidity of these markets and facilitate market participation of DR and self-generated RES-E, relevant consumers or FSPs may be allowed to engage in these markets simultaneously. The resulting problems include settlement issues, double payments and aligning timeframes between markets, requiring higher efforts from TSOs and DSOs as well as substantial changes in existing market processes. In Belgium, for instance, from the TSO's perspective, the proposal of allowing a delivery point to simultaneously participate in the balancing and DA/ID markets (referred to as 'combo activation') during the same imbalance settlement period is too complex to implement. Similar tasks may be more challenging for DSOs that have recently begun adapting to their active role under EU law. In particular, smaller DSOs are found to have difficulty in delivering smarter and decarbonized grids in the regions they operate. This may create the need for more granular regulatory approaches to manage the challenges faced by smaller DSOs when integrating DR and DG. See TSO 2019 Study, sections 6 and 9.3; Johansson et al., 2020; Papalexopoulos et al., 2020; Pereira et al., 2020; Vagropoulos et al., 2022. For a more detailed discussion of DSOs' path dependence and challenges faced in the transition, see Section 3.4.2 below of this Chapter.

892. In brief, reforming market models to enhance TSO-DSO coordination involves a range of legal issues that extend beyond the coordination itself. The choice of market models is also subject to several factors: (i) a limited set of permitted activities of TSOs and DSOs under unbundling rules, (ii) the potential need for developing local energy markets to better serve the consumer-centric market objective, and (iii) the increased complexity and resultant impacts on market participation. Moreover, whether specific models create disproportionate burdens on smaller-sized DSOs should also be taken into account. These considerations will, in turn, reshape the role, obligations, and responsibilities of TSOs and DSOs, which deserve future research.

### *3.4.2. Distribution Network Regulation*

893. As shown in Chapter III above, changes in the role and tasks of DSOs introduced by EU law are revolutionary. In addition to dealing with increasing connection requests from consumers engaged in renewables self-consumption and DR, they must be able to utilize flexibility services and assist those connected to their grid to participate in other electricity markets. The latter task serves as a key step in fostering markets for flexibility services from actors involved in DR and renewables self-consumption and broadening their revenue streams. The DSO's fulfillment of relevant obligations is of significance not only for efficient and safe system operation but also for ensuring sufficient market-based incentives, which is the second building block of the framework for engaging customers in facilitating RES-E uptake. The DSO must be proactive enough to organize flexibility procurement and develop associated market rules, while also leveling the playing field of flexibility procurement by inter alia respecting unbundling rules. Relevant requirements can boil down to requiring the DSO to become a 'neutral market facilitator', as elaborated in Section 6.3.2 of Chapter III. As discussed later, with the advent of diverse market models that accommodate the DSO's proactive role, a dilemma can arise when the DSO seeks to fulfill its neutral market facilitator role. This issue will be discussed in Section 3.4.2.1 below. It is followed by Section 3.4.2.2, which focuses on another challenge related to regulatory tools for supporting the DSO in addressing the challenges of utilizing flexibility.

#### 3.4.2.1. The Dilemma Coming with the Expanding Role of DSOs

894. Before the CEP introduced relevant reforms to change the DSO's role, it was pointed out that there is a tension between the greater role of DSOs in the energy transition and the limited leeway and instruments at their disposal allowed by law (Edens and Lavrijssen, 2019). The CEP has further clarified the role of the DSO as a neutral market facilitator. However, it seems far from clear how to deal with potential conflicts between such an active role and its neutrality.

This is confirmed by a 2022 study that conducted two parallel surveys of DSOs and their NRAs across Member States.[829] It shows significant disagreement in the answers to questions about the future of the DSO between and within their sample of NRAs and DSOs (Anaya et al., 2022). This disagreement is further deepened when it comes to how far the DSO's role in further market integration of DR and self-generated RES-E can exactly reach (Anaya et al., 2022). One could better understand the reason behind this divergence by considering the ongoing active discussion of multiple potential roles that the DSO can assume in market models designed to maximize consumer engagement. On the one hand, both EU law and national law for regulating monopolistic activities tend to clearly delimit and tightly monitor activities that grid operators are allowed to perform, serving the need for unbundling and economic regulation. On the other hand, centered around the aim of further engaging consumers, innovative market models under discussion highlight the DSO's role as a market facilitator without giving due regard to the compatibility of its expanding role with existing restrictions on the DSO, as exemplified by the above-reviewed literature on TSO-DSO coordination. Pronounced tensions arise between innovative market models and the restrictions imposed by existing energy law on the DSO to secure its neutrality and non-discrimination. Such tensions not only exist in the case of adapting market models to enhance TSO-DSO coordination but also in the novel proposition of LEMs. Given that the LEM's market design elements can further manifest the tensions stemming from the DSO's role as a neutral market facilitator, this section will take them as an example to explain the dilemma inherent in that role.

895. What kinds of tasks can be assigned to the DSO are actively discussed in the general literature on LEMs. Multiple roles assigned to the DSO include the network operator, the FRP and the LMO, who can aggregate local offers and bid on upper-level markets on behalf of consumers and prosumers (see e.g. Villar et al., 2018; Farrokhseresht et al., 2020). However, the potential conflicts of simultaneously performing these roles with the EU law principles of regulating DSOs are largely neglected.

896. Firstly, when claiming that the DSO can engage in aggregating DERs and selling them on wholesale and balancing markets, the relevant literature blurs the boundary between regulated activities and commercial activities (Agrell et al., 2013; Buchmann, 2020; Schittekatte and Meeus, 2020). This gives rise to contradictions with legal unbundling, which, in principle, requires a separation between network operation and commercial activities (*Electricity Directive*, Article 35). At present, the legally permissible market activity of the DSO under

[829] It received 39 responses from DSOs and 12 responses from NRAs, covering, respectively, 40% and 78% of customers in those countries. See Anaya et al., 2022.

EU law primarily refers to procuring flexibility for efficient, reliable and secure operation, congestion management and loss reduction, as noted in the previous subsection (*Electricity Directive*, Articles 31 and 32). This occurs within the context of transitioning the DSO's role to facilitate active network management (*Electricity Directive*, recital 61). Member States are granted the flexibility to allow DSOs to perform activities other than those provided by the Electricity Directive and the Electricity Regulation, but subject to the criteria that such activities are necessary for the DSOs to fulfill their obligations in the two legal acts (*Electricity Directive*, Article 31(10)). Hence, bound by unbundling, within existing EU law, the DSO's market participation is only allowed when it serves its obligations under EU electricity law. Such obligations are set to ensure efficient and secure network operation and non-discriminatory network access (ranging from flexibility procurement, and data management to redispatching) as well as dispatch. Wider DSO tasks envisioned by some LEM models, such as aggregating and selling DERs, go beyond the DSOs' obligations defined by EU law, and this derogation is not applicable.

897. There is, however, another exception to legal unbundling. Its reasoning might be used to support a legal approach to deviating from unbundling restrictions for the sake of creating a market that accommodates the integration of renewables. That is the exception of allowing the DSO to conditionally own, develop, manage or operate energy storage facilities, as laid down in Article 36 of the Electricity Directive. The rationale behind this exception is that if DSOs are not in the position to pick up activities that are necessary for the facilitation of the energy transition and that are not offered by other market parties, this may hamper the transition to a low-carbon energy system (Lavrijssen, 2017). To avoid this problem, in the Netherlands, it was proposed that the DSO may be granted a temporary task to develop potentially competitive non-core activities in case these are important for the future development of the smart grid and other market parties cannot sufficiently deliver these services yet (Lavrijssen, 2017). However, there indeed exists a risk that if DSOs do too much, they can distort competition in potentially competitive activities (Lavrijssen, 2017). Therefore, a set of restrictions and conditions must be imposed on DSOs when they are allowed to assume the role of fostering the development of markets for low-carbon technologies. It seems that the existing Electricity Directive has chosen to follow the Dutch approach with its Article 36 (Lavrijssen, 2017).

898. While this exception is limited to storage facilities, it implies that the EU legislator has considered deviating from legal unbundling conditionally as a possible way to satisfy the practical need for a more active role of the DSO in the energy transition context. This deviation could potentially be broadened in the future to allow the DSOs a greater role in market operations and to foster consumers' participation across multi-level electricity markets. Despite

this, the accompanying conditions and restrictions would also be applicable in that case, to minimize the potential impact on competitive segments. Among other things, the NRAs must first establish that other commercial actors cannot deliver relevant services (such as aggregating bids unused in LEMs or operating LEMs) at a reasonable cost and in a timely manner. In this respect, it is noteworthy that numerous studies have emphasized the benefits of appointing third-party entities as independent market operators.[830] The presence of such entities in practice could block the application of the derogation in question. In addition to the concern of exceeding legally permitted core tasks, entrusting the task of operating local market platforms to the DSO could also increase discrimination risks, as detailed later.

899. There is a similar risk of contradicting unbundling when the DSO is responsible for balancing the distribution grid by procuring frequency ancillary services on LEMs. To implement unbundling, in what cases the TSO and the DSO are permitted to be buyers of energy and flexibility depends on the explicit permission of EU law. Current EU law only provides three cases where the DSO is allowed to access certain categories of system services, as noted in the previous subsection (*Electricity Directive*, articles 31(5)(6)(7) and 32(1)). So far, within EU law, there has been no explicit permission to allow the DSO to procure frequency ancillary services for the so-called 'local balancing'. This should also be read in conjunction with the system balancing responsibility expressly reserved to the TSO.[831] Under EU law, there is no legal basis to support the DSO's wider procurement activities for local balancing purposes. Hence, a LEM tasked with providing balancing services for the DSO entails a risk of violating unbundling, which should be considered when determining the aims and transactional objects of LEMs.

900. The application of LEMs can also provoke new discrimination risks, closely linked to the involvement of the DSO in LEMs. Prior studies have already identified several discrimination concerns arising from the involvement of the DSO that is only bound by legal unbundling[832] in the local market for flexibility (Buchmann, 2020; Rebenaque et al., 2023). Based on their findings and the literature on the implications of limited unbundling, Table 22 summarizes

[830] They favor a third-party LMO on the grounds of ensuring transparency and neutrality in the development of market rules and clearing markets. See Ramos et al., 2016; Burger et al., 2019; Schittekatte and Meeus, 2020; Buchmann, 2020.

[831] Recital 13 of the Electricity Regulation clearly states that the TSO is responsible for addressing residual imbalances remaining after the end of the ID market and for organizing the balancing market. The TSO is clearly allowed to operate the balancing market under Article 40 of the Electricity Directive.

[832] Under the Electricity Directive, DSOs are merely bound by legal unbundling rather than full ownership unbundling. See *Electricity Directive*, article 35.

three sources of discrimination potential and the corresponding discriminatory behavior of the DSO.

**Table 22. Discrimination concerns relating to the DSO's involvement in LEMs**

| Sources of discrimination | Discriminatory behavior |
|---|---|
| Owning or operating local market platforms | Discriminating against non-affiliated market participants in network access, products and market rules definition, offers selection and market clearing (Buchmann, 2020; Rebenaque et al., 2023) |
| Information advantages: holding information (e.g., maintenance programs for generation projects and load forecasts, expected levels of congestion, and the timing of congestion alleviating measures) that is commercially important to consumers and prosumers offering electricity and flexibility (Cabau and Sandberg, 2021, p 114) | Offering information only to its affiliates engaged in generation and flexibility provision or providing it to them earlier than to competitors (Buchmann, 2020) |
| Network investment decisions | Strategically withholding network investment to benefit affiliates owning assets offering electricity and flexibility (*Electricity Directive*, recital 67; Buchmann, 2020) |

Source: Author's own elaboration.

901. When the DSO owns or operates a local market platform, non-affiliates are subject to its potential discriminatory behavior in network access and market participation, as shown above. Moreover, when opening the LEM to other FPRs, including retailers and BRPs, allowing the DSO to operate the market platform can also undermine the neutrality of market clearing, given conflicts of interest in accessing local flexibility.

902. The last two discrimination risks are not exclusive to the DSO's involvement in local electricity or flexibility trading, but may also exist in traditional retail markets without the application of ownership unbundling.[833] This is exemplified by the fact that the risk of strategic network investment withholding has been recognized by the EU legislator since 2009 (*2009 Electricity Directive*, recital 9). Nevertheless, the DSO's discriminatory information sharing can exacerbate market power issues that may be encountered in developing LEMs. As a result of such information provision, the flexibility service branch of a VIU can accurately determine the grid status or potential congestion.

833 The debate on the transmission grid level shows that the incentive for strategic network investment withholding and strategic information sharing cannot be sufficiently addressed by legal unbundling. See e.g. Lowe et al., 2007; Buchmann, 2020.

It is thus well placed to consciously aggravate (expected) congestion by strategically changing its bids on wholesale markets and then being paid in the local congestion market to solve the problem it created itself (Schittekatte and Meeus, 2020). This can increase the risk of gaming between existing markets and LEMs. In addition, economic withholding[834] within a LEM becomes more likely due to discriminately sharing information about the location of system constraints. The affiliates involved in flexibility provision may be prompted to use relevant information to overcharge for their services (Kouzelis et al., 2015; Farrokhseresht et al., 2020).

903. Several governance models have been proposed to mitigate concerns about discrimination caused by the DSO on the LEM. Among them, building a common flexibility platform (CFP) is considered superior to other methods in terms of adequately dealing with the three discrimination concerns while avoiding the negative impacts of ownership unbundling, such as increased coordination costs (Buchmann, 2020). These advantages are achieved by its inclusive stakeholder-based decision-making, based on which the platform can reinforce checks of the DSO's decisions and thus ensure neutrality for all market participants (Buchmann, 2020). This approach, however, is not without challenges. Notably, it is questionable whether network investment withholding can be identified and prevented by market stakeholders, given the presence of information asymmetry. Revealing unlawful behavior in this respect might be viable in very limited cases, such as in a LEM jointly operated by several DSOs having network expertise. The above discrimination concerns can be even more pronounced when certain small DSOs are exempted from unbundling requirements in accordance with EU law.[835]

904. In the context of applying legal unbundling and exempting small DSOs from unbundling obligations, it is paramount to uphold the other three pillars built by EU law for eliminating discriminatory behavior by system operators.[836] Reinforced regulatory oversight is recommended for implementing access regulation measures, including general and specific non-discrimination obligations for system operators (e.g., when procuring ancillary services), as

---

834 The exercise of market power in electricity markets is divided into two broad strategies that a generator can use to artificially increase electricity market prices: economic withholding and capacity withholding. In capacity withholding, a strategic market participant can influence the market price by withdrawing its cheaper units. In the economic withholding, a strategic market player can maximize its revenue mainly due to system constraints. DERs participating in LEMs can have market power despite their small size, as the market size is still smaller, and location matters for economic withholding. See Farrokhseresht et al., 2020.

835 Article 35(4) of the Electricity Directive allows Member States to exempt VIUs which serve less than 100,000 connected customers or small isolated systems from unbundling requirements.

836 For a more detailed analysis of the four pillars, see Hannah Kruimer, 2011.

well as designing fair network codes. For instance, detailed mechanisms for implementing EU-level requirements of ensuring a 'transparent and participatory process' can play an instrumental role in preventing biased flexibility procurement rules (Electricity Directive, articles 31(6) and 32(2)). A leading example in this regard is a structured two-step consultation procedure introduced in Flemish regulations, covering the documented stakeholder consultation phase and the formal market consultation phase (*TRDE*, art. 1.2.4, art. 2.3.22, art. 2.3.23 and art. 4.3.63).

#### 3.4.2.2. How to Support the Move to a More Active DSO?

905. The move toward more active DSOs remains a work in progress for both DSOs and their NRAs (Anaya et al., 2022). Based on recent empirical data, most DSOs are in the early stage of adapting to a more active role in flexibility procurement (Givisiez et al., 2020; Johansson et al., 2020). Empirical research looking at how the transition of the DSO is progressing reports that challenges faced by DSOs cover organizational, technical and regulatory dimensions (Anaya et al., 2022). The degree to which flexibility will be utilized in the electricity system will, among others, depend on the DSOs' confidence in and the credibility of different flexibility resources, depending on factors such as their availability and predictability, combined with proper incentives and framework conditions (Sæle et al., 2023). This highlights that while dealing with other enablers and barriers (i.e., those from the perspective of consumers), challenges from the perspective of the DSO must be identified and addressed properly, to make flexibility procurement a pragmatic alternative to network expansion (Sæle et al., 2023).

906. An interesting finding from empirical research reveals significant disagreement between surveyed DSOs and NRAs on the major barriers that prevent DSOs from assuming a more proactive role (Anaya et al., 2022). NRAs viewed the lack of local flexibility providers as the prime barrier to fulfilling the DSO's obligations to utilize flexibility.[837] Other barriers identified by NRAs can be summarized as concerns that the DSO lacks capacity on two fronts: (1) operation, tech and asset management, and (2) organizational and business models (Pereira et al., 2018; Anaya et al., 2022). Approximately 20% of responding NRAs acknowledged that tariffs also pose a barrier (Anaya et al., 2022). Interestingly, DSOs have contrary views on the barriers they face. Over half of the responding DSOs attribute the current barriers to the tariff structure, while the second-largest barriers mainly relate to the regulatory

[837] Congestion and reactive power services are localized and might not generate sufficient liquidity for market-based options. See Anaya et al., 2022.

framework.[838] The primary concern about grid tariffs reflects the DSOs' desire for additional returns or incentives to address the higher perceived technical and regulatory risks associated with their new role and obligations.[839] As a result of the divergence between NRAs and DSOs in terms of major barriers to shifting to active DSOs, they are not fully aligned on how that transition should be supported (Anaya et al., 2022). Even so, a common ground still exists that incentives or support are vital to enable the DSO to adapt capacity and business models to flexibility use tasks and accept the risks associated with utilizing flexibility solutions (Anaya et al., 2022). This indicates the future path for reinforcing regulatory support for the DSO. Two directions worth considering are discussed.

907. First, actions that enable DSOs to accept and manage risks or uncertainties associated with flexibility utilization are crucial. Empirical data suggests that DSOs have the inertia associated with their traditional business culture, which challenges the adoption of innovative technologies and hinders the possibility for disruptive ideas to be considered (Pereira et al., 2018). Such inertia may be attributed to their passive role in the traditional energy regime, which also contributes to the low willingness to use flexibility solutions and accept associated risks or uncertainties. Network regulation can solve this problem by providing continued support for demonstration projects and piloting of flexibility solutions, which would build DSOs' experience, reduce uncertainties of the operational flexibility characteristics, and thereby contribute to de-risking flexibility solutions (Sæle et al., 2023). Parallel changes in incentive regulation may also be needed to support such experimentation that enables risk-taking, which is one of the lessons learned from incentive regulation at the transmission level (Brunekreeft et al., 2021).

908. Second, another lesson learned from supporting experimentation at the transmission level is that sufficient incentives are needed to engage network users in relevant experiments or pilots. Innovation activities by the grid operators frequently require grid users also to be actively involved in developing and testing innovations (Brunekreeft et al., 2021). However, grid users are currently not sufficiently incentivized to participate in experiments of this type (Brunekreeft et al., 2021). For instance, in Germany, the experimentation clause

838 Other significant barriers mentioned by DSOs include the lack of regulations and guidance, the existence of regulatory obstacles, and the lack of government support. See Anaya et al., 2022.

839 DSOs may be averse to accepting smaller security margins in operation or taking the risk that flexibility resources may not always be available and respond when called for during grid operation. This implies that grid operators must deal with new types of operational risks, and more generally, that DSOs need to rely on flexibility provided by third parties. It involves more interactions with grid users and with grid operation, and it changes the risk picture. See Anaya et al., 2022; Sæle et al., 2023.

in SINTEG-V[840] creates compensation for disadvantages (Brunekreeft et al., 2021). Yet, stakeholders responsible for pilot projects at the transmission level state that grid users lack incentives to participate beyond the compensation for disadvantages (Brunekreeft et al., 2021). To address this issue, the regulator could consider introducing a dedicated experimentation budget for grid operators (Brunekreeft et al., 2021). They could then have a budget that is defined ex-ante for third parties participating in an experiment, for example, to compensate for disadvantages and generally incentivize participation (Brunekreeft et al., 2021).

## 4. INTERIM CONCLUSION

909. This chapter critically examines challenges and gaps in the EU-level legal pathways of empowering energy consumers. These challenges and gaps are revealed by contrasting EU law and its implementing rules with legal principles and essential attributes of the law (mainly clarity, certainty and consistency) (Fuller, 1964), as well as legal objectives reflecting the core tasks of electricity DSM. The main findings and conclusions of this chapter are presented along the building blocks of EU law on electricity DSM.

### 4.1. GIVING EFFECT TO RIGHTS AND OBLIGATIONS

910. Legal challenges of implementing the framework that entitles consumers to engage in DR and renewables self-consumption can be summarized in three dimensions. First, there exist definitional issues in eligibility requirements for constituting new actors entitled to engage in DR and renewables self-consumption. As shown in the previous chapter, the eligibility for constituting an 'active customer', 'renewables self-consumer', 'citizen energy community' and 'renewable energy community' who enjoy rights granted by respective legal frameworks is specified in definitions of these actors. This chapter found that the relevant EU-level definitions entail a range of legal issues, while Member States have not entirely resolved or even circumvented them by replicating the wording of EU law in their national transpositions.

911. Section 3.1.2 above provided a detailed discussion of the legal issues related to the definitions of 'active customer' and 'renewables self-consumer', which should be addressed by EU and national legislators, respectively.

840 Ordinance on creating a legal framework for gathering experience as part of the "Smart Energy Showcases –Digital Agenda for the Energy Transition" [Verordnung zur Schaffung eines rechtlichen Rahmens zur Sammlung von Erfahrungen im Förderprogramm "Schaufenster intelligente Energie – Digitale Agenda für die Energiewende"].

912. First, there exist potential overlaps between the definition of a household renewables self-consumer and that of an electricity undertaking. The blurred lines between 'electricity undertaking' and household renewables self-consumer could lead to legal uncertainty in determining the applicability of PSOs. This problem essentially arises from the deficiencies in definitions and potential overlaps between new and preexisting definitions, which EU legislators overlooked when introducing new concepts. Considering this, the EU legislator is in a better position to address the conflation between the definitions of 'electricity undertaking' and household renewables self-consumer.

913. Second, the application of the non-primary commercial or professional activity criterion requires further clarification on its connotation and application standards. This should be addressed in national law that concretizes the role and rights of active customers and renewables self-consumers. The above analysis demonstrates that to implement the non-primary commercial or professional activity requirement, the linchpin lies in imposing restrictions on three activities involved in renewables prosumption, namely selling self-produced RES-E, generating and storing RES-E for electricity sales. The analysis presents two approaches to setting up such restrictions while discussing their respective merits and drawbacks. The first one entails complex standards for assessing whether the three renewables prosumption activities play a non-primary role among all commercial or professional activities conducted by active customers or non-household renewable self-consumers. Its alternative is to highlight the primary role of consumption in renewables prosumption activities and, correspondingly, the secondary role of other prosumption activities. The non-primary commercial or professional activity criterion can be translated into a general requirement that active customers or non-household renewable self-consumers should generate and store RES-E primarily for own use and only sell self-generated RES-E when there is a surplus. The conducted analysis further recommends that Member States should fully consider the disadvantages of developing too concrete standards for applying this approach.

914. Section 3.1.3 points out that there are even more legal issues relating to definitions of the CEC and the REC, which contain eligibility criteria around their primary purpose, membership and operation. Seen from the ongoing national transpositions, Member States either fail to consider the legal issues arising from the direct application of these broadly worded criteria and the need for detailed rules for their application, or do not make adequate efforts to transpose them.

915. Regarding the primary purpose of energy communities, the key legal issue is how to identify and measure the provision of community benefits, and whether the primary purpose of energy communities is to provide community benefits rather than financial profits. The analysis in Section 3.1.3 highlights that

among the three community benefits, special attention should be paid to the lack of a clear definition of 'economic benefits' and the resultant overlaps with 'financial profits'. The potential overlap between economic benefits and financial profits is mainly responsible for the difficulty in assessing whether the energy communities' profit motive is subordinate to the main purpose of providing community benefits. It concludes that the key solution for constraining the profit motive of energy communities is to introduce restrictions on the disposal of both monetary and non-monetary proceeds of energy communities. First, more than 50% of the total profits must be used to provide environmental or social benefits or other non-monetary economic benefits (such as services related to electricity sharing and energy infrastructure operation). Second, when energy communities' proceeds are non-monetary economic benefits that can also be converted into monetary returns, priority should be given to delivering such proceeds in their original form, e.g., sharing self-generated RES-E with members instead of selling to non-members, unless there is a surplus after sharing.

916. Regarding conditions for membership, it is also challenging to safeguard open and voluntary participation, as its application is interwoven with other vital goals and requirements for energy communities. The analysis in this chapter shows that safeguarding open participation faces a trade-off between keeping the financial contribution threshold low (to notably ensure accessibility to low-income households or vulnerable consumers as required by the REDII) and ensuring the energy community's ability to raise adequate finance. To transpose this seemingly straightforward requirement, national implementing rules need to elaborate inter alia on how to assess whether the membership fee is excessive and unduly jeopardizes open participation. Such rules remain absent in most countries. Furthermore, drawing on empirical data, this chapter's analysis calls for special attention to the strong link between relying heavily on members' financial contributions and the energy communities' general difficulty in accessing (third-party) investment and financing. Such difficulty, among others, results from a set of restrictions relating to profit-making, autonomy and effective control. A legal challenge underlying the foregoing trade-off is that applying other eligibility criteria may defeat compliance with open participation, which is especially the case for the REC, which is subject to stricter eligibility requirements. A finding is thus that ensuring open participation is far more than merely requiring a low membership barrier. Bearing in mind the aforementioned trade-off, lowering the financial threshold for participating in energy communities should be accompanied by other measures that enhance the economic viability of these communities. Conversely, if a Member State is considering phasing out public financial support for energy communities, a strict requirement for lowering membership fees is not advisable, given its negative implications for access to finance.

917. Similarly, in applying the eligibility criterion for voluntary participation, this chapter's analysis also highlights the correlation between membership termination and the autonomy required by the REDII for the REC. Securing the members' high-level freedom to leave the REC could undermine its autonomy since members or shareholders may threaten the financial independence of the REC by freely dissolving their investment in the community. Regarding the termination of CEC membership, the conducted analysis demonstrates that the cross-reference to Article 12 overlooks multiple relationships between the CEC and its members, as well as the adverse impacts of membership volatility on the financial sustainability of the energy community. The current method of regulating membership termination at the CEC leads to a 'one-size-fits-all' approach, which limits the ways that can be adopted to balance members' freedom to leave the CEC with the community's financial sustainability.

918. Regarding the eligibility requirements for energy communities' operational decision-making, as revealed in Section 3.1.3.3, there is a risk that large companies may circumvent the restriction on effective control. Moreover, the EU legislator should remove restrictions on the decision-making power within the CEC. They exceed the minimum requirements of legal provisions and can lead to misinterpretations in national transpositions. Additional legal issues have been identified regarding the proximity requirement in conjunction with effective control in the context of the REC. Having discussed different ways of defining proximity presented in the literature and national rule-making processes, it is found that it is challenging to standardize proximity requirements in a manner that accommodates the diversity of situations in practice.

919. Apart from a range of legal challenges in implementing the eligibility requirements for energy communities, another intractable problem is how to monitor their compliance in practice to prevent abuse of the concepts of CEC and REC. Section 3.1.3.4 elaborated on the approaches to carrying out ex-ante and ex-post regulatory oversight, as well as the corresponding obligations for energy communities in demonstrating a lawful state, while discussing the role of energy regulators. These approaches were developed based on previous discussions about potential ways to concretize eligibility criteria, especially for improving compliance with the energy communities' primary purpose of offering community benefits. However, whether these theoretical solutions can function well in practice is another issue. Section 3.1.3.4 argues that applying an ex-ante recognition or application procedure in the establishment of energy communities and the subsequent monitoring during their operation can be rather burdensome for energy communities, inducing non-trivial regulatory complexity. It thus highlights the need for due attention to administrative feasibility and proportionality concerns raised by such a 'strict' approach to scrutinizing energy communities' compliance with EU-level definitions, while

proposing a relatively 'light' regime, which might be preferable in the initial stage of fostering energy communities.

920. From the discussion so far, it can be concluded that while energy communities are a rather promising way of further empowering consumers to engage in DR and renewables use, realizing their role encounters a variety of issues when put into practice. The rights to become active customers, renewables self-consumers, and participate in energy communities remain difficult for consumers to exercise. This chapter suggests that some of the legal barriers can be attributed to EU legislation itself, while others are caused by weak transposition and implementation that fail to address the complex legal issues involved in the broadly worded EU law. The exercise of the granted rights is also contingent upon the availability of tools and safeguards provided by enabling frameworks. Sections 3.1.2.1 and 3.1.2.2, respectively, have identified deficiencies in the enabling frameworks for active customers, renewables self-consumers and energy communities, particularly regarding engaging marginalized energy poor and vulnerable consumers and solving capacity and financial barriers faced by energy communities.

921. A review of national transpositions reveals that Member States have not taken sufficient action to ensure the accessibility of renewables self-consumption to low-income or vulnerable customers. Such actions should not only solve financial barriers but also cognitive constraints, which require systematic but not short-term and fragmented responses. This poses a long-term challenge for Member States.

922. As regards enablers provided for energy communities, this chapter identifies gaps and issues of solving financial barriers and providing capacity support. Most Member States have not taken robust measures to identify the barriers to accessing finance faced by energy communities, including the use of existing financing tools. The analysis highlights that if Member States decide not to develop new financing tools, it is crucial to address the challenges encountered by energy communities when applying existing financing instruments. In terms of helping energy communities improve capacity, the existing approach taken by the REDII is problematic. It is concluded that the direct participation of public authorities is not the most suitable way of addressing the RECs' capacity issues. Given the presence of multiple alternatives already adopted at the national level, it is plausible to allow Member States to choose specific approaches to reinforcing communities' capacity. To this end, the REDII should only require Member States to facilitate energy communities' capacity-building without imposing an additional obligation to adopt a specific approach. A soft law approach disseminating best practices in Member States can be applied to underpin the implementation of this general requirement.

923. To enable final customers to exercise the rights granted by EU law, as highlighted, it is important to deal with their relationships with other stakeholders involved in DR and renewables self-consumption, including traditional and emerging actors. The ToE regime in Belgium serves as an example of how conflicting interests between IFSPs and affected suppliers and BRPs can be reconciled by encouraging negotiated solutions while providing standardized arrangements as a fallback. An important lesson is that, given the potential institutional complexity brought by standardized mechanisms for dealing with their relationship, allowing negotiated solutions is pivotal, such as opt-out and pass-through mechanisms recognized by Belgian law. Despite this, care should be given to the institutional complexity of such standardized arrangements, which, as highlighted in the Belgian law case, can undermine the practicability of this standardized framework.

924. As shown in Sections 2 and 3.1.2.1, suppliers are also affected when consumers engage in renewables self-consumption (including P2P electricity trading and electricity sharing), and they may impose disproportionate conditions or charges on involved consumers. The Flemish legal approach, which combines information disclosure and supplier switching, represents a less intrusive way of preventing suppliers from applying unjustified charges or conditions. This approach heavily relies on measures that facilitate fast and cost-efficient supplier switching, as well as user-friendly information provided by comparison tools. Moreover, considering that not all customer groups are covered by the requirement of not charging switching-related fees, some consumers face economic losses when switching suppliers with disproportionate conditions or charges for renewables self-consumption. A hybrid regulatory approach is recommended to safeguard consumers' entitlement to renewables self-consumption. It can integrate general principles governing supply contracts, information-based approaches that leverage supplier switching and comparison tools, and additional oversight of supplier conditions or charges to protect consumers who are subject to supplier switching fees.

925. Another emerging risk worth noting is that when participating in energy communities, individual and jointly acting prosumers' rights to trade or share electricity may be affected by energy communities. The energy community has incentives to impede these members' activities since they compete with the community to meet the energy demands of other members. When operating market platforms or grids (including distribution grids and microgrids) within communities, energy communities are better positioned to restrict the electricity exchange conducted by participating prosumers. Some national legislation overlooks the increased risks of discrimination and anti-competitive practices, for instance, by allowing energy communities to control members' generation assets. The relationship between participating prosumers and energy communities in the context of embedding LEMs and microgrids within energy communities

adds a new dimension to the relationships that members can have with energy communities. The added dimension may reshape measures governing the relationship between energy communities and their members.

## 4.2. MARKET ENTRY AND ECONOMIC INCENTIVES

926. EU law's efforts to facilitate the market entry of DR and self-generated RES-E and provide them with proper price signals have encountered several setbacks in recent years. First, it is hard to safeguard free price formation during crisis times. Section 3.2.1 analyzes the lessons learned from the past energy price crisis and EU-level responses during and after the crisis. It concludes that to balance the need for protecting consumers from exceptional price shocks and preserving the role of price signals in incentivizing consumers, the linchpin lies in creating rules to govern 'emergency measures' that interfere with price setting during extraordinary circumstances.

927. Smaller-sized aggregators and individual consumers are still hindered by the technical parameters of wholesale markets and flexibility markets organized by system operators. Technical specifications of electricity markets have long been blamed, which serve as a stumbling block for genuinely transitioning toward a consumer-centric electricity market. In the literature, it is commonly suggested that market design be simplified to avoid requiring consumers to be 'experts' in energy when engaging them in electricity markets. This argument is rather straightforward, but the challenge lies in determining to what extent the electricity market design should be simplified.

928. From a legal perspective, an intriguing question is how the law can play a role in reducing market entry barriers created by technical parameters of electricity markets. Based on discussions in Sections 2 and 3.2.1, it can be concluded that the law can incrementally adapt the market design to consumer participation via three legal safeguards. The first action is harmonizing market design parameters (e.g., minimum bid sizes) and adjusting these requirements gradually, as has been done by the Balancing Regulation, the Electricity Regulation and the 2024 Amendment to the Electricity Regulation. The second and third safeguards ensure that the design of detailed market design parameters reflects the need to engage final customers. They contain procedural and substantive requirements for market rules, procurement rules or technical specifications, i.e., participatory rule-making processes, and transparent and non-discriminatory rules. The role of the first safeguard is limited, given the EU's restricted competence in harmonizing technical parameters of electricity markets. The latter two safeguards will play a more instrumental role in adapting electricity market design to consumer engagement.

929. As shown by the Flemish law case study, the second and third safeguards can help lower undesirable discretion that system operators may have over designing technical parameters and identify and address market entry barriers that exist in proposed market rules or flexibility procurement rules. However, Sections 2 and 3.2.1 emphasize that to enable these two safeguards to function effectively, detailed implementing rules are required at the Member State level, grounded in a more nuanced interpretation of the broad principles of non-discrimination and transparency.

930. Under the existing EU law, final customers have wider routes to sell their self-generated RES-E, while their access to renewables PPAs and P2P electricity trading remains limited. Section 3.2.3.1 indicates that, acting as either sellers or buyers, medium and small renewables prosumers (including self-consumers and energy communities) face some barriers to concluding renewables PPAs. Opening up participation in PPAs to smaller prosumers by pooling them can be hindered by the inherently customized nature of PPAs. Multiple unfavorable conditions faced by buyers also impede prosumers from utilizing renewables PPAs to deal with surplus self-produced RES-E. They mainly include costly exit clauses of such bilateral agreements, which can contradict consumers' right to switch suppliers, the difficulty of managing imbalances, and the risk of getting locked in at a high price.

931. In comparison, enabling renewables self-consumers to carry out P2P electricity trading involves even more complex legal issues. They are mainly concerned with (i) the consumer status of self-consumers and consumers involved in P2P electricity trading, (ii) consumer rights of renewables self-consumers as buyers in P2P trading contracts, (iii) the selling party's obligations, and (iv) the role and obligations of the P2P trading platform provider. So far, neither implementing rules in Member States nor the literature has provided systematic solutions to these issues. Section 3.2.3.2 conducted an in-depth analysis of these issues, identifying misleading views presented in prior studies.

932. Regarding the question of whether renewables self-consumers involved in P2P electricity trading retain consumer status, the legal analysis in Section 3.2.3.2 highlights that the determination of consumer status and consumer rights is always context-specific. It indicates that to assess the consumer status and relevant rights, certain activities conducted and contracts entered into by renewables self-consumers must be considered. This conclusion is pivotal to understanding Article 21(2)(c). This provision cannot be interpreted as meaning that renewables self-consumers maintain the status of final customers in all cases, considering that the status of final customers can be in flux in practice. Instead, it should be understood as meaning that when renewables self-consumers purchase electricity for their own use and thus constitute final customers as

defined by EU law, they maintain the relevant rights and obligations applicable to final customers.

933. Another finding is that the consumer status of renewables self-consumers engaged in P2P electricity trading could not be entirely determined from the lens of the EU's general consumer protection law and its case law. Assessment criteria for consumer status established by consumer protection law and its case law can only be applied to households purchasing electricity, but not to industrial and commercial users. Additionally, the existing literature considers the presence of the weaker party in a contractual relationship to be a decisive factor in granting consumer rights. The analysis conducted above suggests that this argument is not entirely tenable in the context of energy law. This is because, under EU energy law, consumer rights are granted for various justifications, which can be broadly classified into consumer protection and empowerment, as well as driving competition.

934. In existing debates, a divergence also exists regarding whether a weak party exists in P2P electricity trading involving prosumers and household consumers. By reviewing how the CJEU's settled case law on consumer protection law conceptualizes the weaker party in a contractual relationship, the analysis concludes that it is incorrect to deny consumers' rights in P2P electricity trading simply because the sellers they face are not energy professionals. Within the context of consumer protection law, when assessing whether a party to a specific contract requires protection, it is of paramount importance to determine whether they enter into that contract for private purposes. Second, the court does not restrict the relatively strong party to professionals or undertakings but describes them as operators undertaking commercial activities and contracting with private final customers acting outside of profession or trade. They also include traders, either legal persons or natural persons, such as renewables self-consumers selling self-generated RES-E to household customers.

935. Having examined existing viewpoints on the consumer status of renewables self-consumers and identified issues therein, Section 3.2.3 refined the approaches to assessing consumer status as follows. This approach is based on a principle distilled from the CJEU's case law, namely that the determination of consumer status can be better made by reference to the position of that consumer in a particular contract, taking into account the nature and purpose of that contract.

- Regarding renewables self-consumers as sellers, their consumer status can be determined based on the EU-level definition of 'final customer' and legal provisions that grant energy consumer rights. When they conclude P2P electricity trading contracts for selling surplus RES-E, they are not final customers who 'purchase electricity for own use'.

- The other party to the P2P trading contract, regardless of whether it is involved in renewables self-consumption, constitutes the final customer within the meaning of the Electricity Directive, as it purchases electricity for its own use under that contract. Household users buying electricity for private use also maintain consumer status within the meaning of the EU's general consumer protection law.

936. Regarding examining whether buyers in P2P electricity trading enjoy consumer rights, a general conclusion is that a fine-grained analysis is needed. Three conclusions are presented based on this granular analysis: (i) the applicability of consumer rights should be evaluated in respective contexts of general consumer protection law and energy law; (ii) the applicability of consumer rights varies with different customer groups, and (iii) a separate examination is required given that some consumer rights granted by energy law are not merely for consumer protection. Table 17 above summarizes the preliminary findings of assessing the applicability of consumer rights based on the detailed categorization of the concerned rights. Another finding worth highlighting is that, given that buyers' rights are supported by sellers' obligations, the granting of these rights is also balanced against principles of non-discrimination and proportionality.

937. This chapter then discussed the contestable issue of whether renewables self-consumers should respect the same obligations for suppliers laid down by energy law when selling RES-E (including via P2P trading). After reviewing existing views on this subject, the analysis indicates that relevant debates essentially concern the application of the principles of non-discrimination and proportionality. How to apply the non-discrimination principle is a notably complex legal problem that recurs when determining the obligations of consumers and energy communities engaged in the same energy activities as producers and suppliers. Legal challenges in this respect stem from the confusion that easily emerges when conducting the comparability analysis contained in the discrimination test. The long-term absence of applicable standards for applying the non-discrimination principle is, inter alia, attributed to the nuanced variations in standards applied by the CJEU in different cases, as indicated by the set of examples given above.

938. There is a multitude of the CJEU's judgments touching upon the principle of equality or non-discrimination across different sectors. In its judgments on the subject matter of 'energy', the court built relatively thorough discrimination tests and comparability analyses in the case of *Arcelor Atlantique et Lorraine and Others* and the *BSEF* case. A two-step criterion for assessing comparability contained in the discrimination test can be drawn from the rulings of these two cases and the case law cited therein: (i) considering the subject matter and purpose of the legislation which makes the distinction in question as well

as the principles and objectives of the field to which that legal act relates, and (ii) determining comparability having regard to that context.

939. The principle of non-discrimination will not be infringed if the different treatment is objectively justified. The CJEU's rulings were analyzed to identify criteria for objective justifications that legitimize different treatments. The overall standard is that a difference in treatment is justified if it is based on an objective and reasonable criterion, that is, if the difference relates to a legally permitted aim pursued by the legislation in question, and it is proportionate to the aim pursued by the treatment. Four detailed criteria under that general standard were distilled from the ruling on *Arcelor Atlantique et Lorraine and Others:* (i) necessity for achieving the legislation's aim, (ii) suitability or appropriateness for realizing the legal aim, (iii) avoidance of manifestly inappropriate consequences compared to alternatives, and (iv) reliance on objective data. Different treatment granted to renewables self-consumers could be justified and refrain from breaching the principle of non-discrimination if those four criteria are satisfied. The analysis shows that promoting RES-E could be a valid justification for treating renewables self-consumers selling RES-E and suppliers differently, given that it may be a legally permitted aim pursued by the legislation that makes the distinction. However, such different treatment, in the form of either obligation exemption or simplification, must be in line with the other three criteria, especially '*avoiding manifestly inappropriate consequences compared to alternatives*'. Satisfying the four criteria cumulatively implies that the legislator or regulator must conduct a detailed assessment if they seek to treat suppliers and renewables self-consumers differently.

940. While helpful, the criteria for applying the non-discrimination principle established by the CJEU's case law in the energy field have some limitations. They are best suited for situations involving a singular subject matter and legal objective. As shown above, at either the EU or national level, electricity market legislation tends to encompass multiple subject matters and purposes. The electricity sector also encompasses a range of principles and objectives, including security of supply, decarbonization, and consumer protection. In some cases, the electricity legislation does not specify legal objectives, and legal provisions pursue different purposes. By giving examples, Section 3.2.3.2 demonstrates that applying the criteria for the discrimination test derived from *Arcelor Atlantique et Lorraine and Others* and related case law can create a set of uncertain assessment outcomes regarding (i) comparability of renewables self-consumers and suppliers, and (ii) whether the concerned different treatment of comparable situations and identical treatment of different situations can be objectively justified.

941. As regards the application of proportionality, there are two significant problems. First, there exists uncertainty regarding whether the proportionality

requirements in Article 21 of the REDII contain the *stricto sensu* test. This uncertainty stems from the fact that EU law does not specify the connotation of the principle of proportionality, while the CJEU does not consistently conduct the *stricto sensu* test when applying the principle of proportionality. Without an explicit requirement of the *stricto sensu* test, some Member States may not fully consider the potential adverse impacts of applying supplier obligations to self-consumers. It is thus highlighted that the consequential risk of discouraging renewables self-consumption (notably excluding consumers from the household and SME sectors) should be noted by the EU legislature. This risk can be mitigated by incorporating specific requirements for the *stricto sensu* test into the current general requirements of preventing disproportionate procedures, obligations and fees.

942. In addition, the conducted analysis identified potential tensions between the principles of non-discrimination and proportionality. Applying the non-discrimination principle can fail the proportionality *stricto sensu* test, creating disproportionate obligations. Section 3.2.3.2 discussed two approaches adopted by existing EU energy law to seek compromises between the two principles, along with their limitations. Ensuring coherence between these two principles is a crucial question that requires further exploration, following the clarification of specific criteria for their application.

943. Lastly, there are ongoing discussions regarding the nature and obligations of P2P electricity trading platforms. Following a review of existing legal research surrounding this debate, two issues deserving further examination were identified: (i) in what cases the trading platform is also bound by obligations created to protect consumers, and (ii) to what extent settled case law on other instances of collaborative platforms can be applied to define the nature and obligations of P2P electricity trading platforms.

944. For the first question, a closer look at the respective contracts that sellers and buyers have with the platform provider is needed. Several conclusions can be drawn from the conducted analysis:

- Buyers in P2P electricity trading, either renewables self-consumers or ordinary customers, provided that they use the electronic intermediary service offered by the platform for private purposes, have consumer status within the meaning of EU-level general consumer protection law. The platform provider is thus subject to obligations created to protect those consumers. Again, as elaborated above, industrial and commercial users do not purchase electricity and use intermediary services outside trade or profession. They thus do not constitute consumers in need of protection under general consumer protection law.

- Sellers also use services provided by the platform but for trade purposes, and thus do not qualify as 'consumers acting outside trade or profession' who can enjoy rights laid down by the EU's general consumer protection law.

945. The application of obligations set out by energy law is linked to the core question around the legal classification of services provided by the P2P trading platform. The analysis in Section 3.2.3.2 shows that the criterion of decisive control drawn from the CJEU's ruling on the *Uber* case can be applied to assess whether the intermediation service provided by the digital platform is regarded as an 'information society service' connecting traders, or the underlying economic activity, namely offering electricity, or a combination of both. It also suggests that whether the platform exercises decisive influence over the provision of electricity requires a case-by-case analysis.

946. Section 3.2 lastly discussed the regulatory treatment of energy communities involved in electricity and flexibility trading. It concludes that the criteria derived from the CJEU's case law related to energy matters could be applied to determine the applicability of supplier obligations to energy communities. Despite some deficiencies, they can help address some present confusion involved in the application of the non-discrimination principle. Legislators at both the EU and national levels should reinforce efforts to properly apply the principle of non-discrimination. Neither Recital 71 of the REDII nor Recital 46 of the Electricity Directive can replace a thorough discrimination test when treating energy communities and other market actors differently. The analysis also emphasizes the need for greater attention to the potentially conflicting outcomes of applying the principles of non-discrimination and proportionality, as well as specific approaches to designing proportionate obligations for energy communities while maintaining a proper level of consumer protection.

## 4.3. INFORMATION ACCESS AND DATA MANAGEMENT

947. Given the essential role of ICT infrastructure in emerging business and market models that facilitate consumer empowerment, section 3.3 highlights the risk that consumers who have not accessed digital technologies will be left behind in the energy transition, potentially generating new vulnerabilities and inequalities and increasing concerns about an unjust energy transition. Moreover, Section 3.3 analyzed tensions between the efficient use of smart-meter-related data and secure data management. Drawing on existing academic research, it concludes that by incorporating specific data protection rules into electricity legislation, EU legislators could reconcile the conflicting interests of data use and protection, considering the evolving needs for the energy transition and

consumer empowerment, which may not be thoroughly addressed by general data protection rules.

948. Moreover, Section 3.3 discussed legal concerns of applying legal grounds for lawful data processing under Article 6 of the GDPR. Under the second and third grounds, Member States enjoy broad discretion to specify specific legal obligations and tasks that serve public interests, which can legitimize the processing of smart metering data. By taking the Personalized Offer case in the Netherlands as an example, it was shown that setting out obligations that require consumer data processing cannot serve as the legal basis for legitimizing data processing. Both the legal obligations to process consumer data and their underlying legal basis must be clearly defined. Another issue relates to the application of the legal basis relating to the necessity to perform 'tasks carried out in the public interest'. A broad interpretation of 'public interest' could increase the risk of infringing on consumers' rights regarding personal data, which may hinder the roll-out of smart meters and the use of relevant data. When imposing tasks that allow for smart metering data processing, national law should also place restrictions in specific contexts: the lawfulness of data processing is only established when data processing is limited to what is necessary to achieve the predefined public interest.

949. Section 3.3 lastly examined whether existing EU law for GOs has already fully enabled their role as a tool for conveying accurate and reliable information to consumers and facilitating consumers' choice of RES-E. It indicates that the separation of electricity and the GO trade may lead to distrust in this system and reduce consumers' voluntary support for RES-E, which the information disclosure strategy could have promoted. Another prominent issue concerns the rights and obligations of individual and collective self-consumers associated with GOs. The proper application of principles of non-discrimination and proportionality is essential to determine the applicability of GO requirements to energy communities and renewables self-consumers offering RES-E. Furthermore, care should be given to potential barriers faced by renewables self-consumers and energy communities in accessing GOs, which can hinder the market participation of green electricity from them.

## 4.4. NETWORK REGULATION ACCOMMODATING DSM

950. This chapter finally discussed the legal challenges and gaps that arise when Member States implement the required adaptations in network operation and regulation, including common legal issues faced by transmission and distribution grid regulation, as well as specific legal challenges associated with supporting the DSO's transition.

951. Common challenges are mainly concerned with network charges, rule-making procedures of flexibility procurement and TSO-DSO cooperation. While time-differentiated tariffs provide system operators with a tool to manage grid congestion caused by the growing penetration of demand-side resources, Section 3.4.1 discussed several legal concerns raised by the diffusion of such network tariffs. Essentially, these concerns reflect tensions between competing principles for governing network charges, especially between the efficiency of cost signals, fairness and predictability of network tariffs. Moreover, the wide application of time-differentiated tariffs also faces other challenges, especially increased complexity and uncertainties when dynamic price contracts are also applied. The conducted analysis highlights that to ascertain the extent to which time-differentiated tariffs could be used as an appropriate tool for calling on flexibility, NRAs should first seek a clear understanding of the impacts of such tariffs and alternative instruments.

952. In Section 3.4.1, network charge regulation was examined against EU-level principles governing network charges and the requirement of avoiding disadvantaging DR and renewables self-consumption. The analysis therein notably delved into a debatable question as to whether discounts or exemptions offered to actors involved in DR and renewables self-consumption contradict the principles of non-discrimination and cost-reflectiveness. This question warrants a specific examination, given that Member States are applying different tariffs to these players, as shown in Table 18 in Section 3.4.1, while their compatibility with EU law remains unclear. The lack of specific criteria for applying the non-discrimination principle, again, comes to the fore.

953. Starting with relevant views of the ACER, the analysis examined whether network use (including the relevant cost impact on the network) is decisive in determining the violation of the non-discrimination principle. Taking the CJEU's judgment on *Essent Belgium* as an example, it indicated that, in light of the legal objective of promoting RES-E, whether actors supply RES-E is the decisive factor that must be considered in the comparability test. In that judgment, the court consistently applied the standard for the comparability analysis developed in the *Arcelor Atlantique et Lorraine and Others* case, which highlights considering the subject matter and purpose of the legislation that makes the distinction at issue. Under the legal objective of promoting green electricity, the delivery of green electricity, rather than the 'network-related' factor, is the relevant aspect for assessing the existence of discrimination in different network charges.

954. The analysis in Section 3.4 further pointed out that the criteria developed by *Arcelor Atlantique et Lorraine and Others* and related case law are not granular enough to contend with complex and diverse situations in the real world. The case in the Commission Decision on SA.34045 is a typical example,

in which both primary legislation and its implementing rules were involved in making different network charges. They cover different subject matters and serve different purposes. This situation raises a question about which aim should be considered when conducting the discrimination test, including assessments of comparability and justifications for different treatments. As shown above, referring to the different aims of the involved rules that make the distinction can lead to divergent results in the discrimination test. Combining findings of Sections 3.2 and 3.4, applying the criteria adopted by the *Arcelor Atlantique et Lorraine and Others* case and related case law can lead to uncertain results in two scenarios: (i) where the legal act that makes the distinction address multiple subject matters and objectives, and (ii) where the different treatment arises from two or more legal acts with different subject matters and legal aims.

955. Overall, energy consumers' wider economic activities resulting from their greater role in facilitating RES-E uptake induce an intractable question faced by both market and network realms. That is how to determine their regulatory treatment, including rights, obligations, (network) charges and taxes. The legal analysis of this chapter shows that the CJEU's rulings in the energy sector have not yet provided clear-cut and granular answers to this question. Future work is needed to examine whether, in other areas relevant and comparable to the energy sector, the court has refined the above criteria and clarified how to analyze comparability and assess justifications for different treatments in the two scenarios mentioned above. If more granular standards exist, their applicability in the specific context of determining the regulatory treatment of individual and collective prosumers is another issue to be explored. These indicate a path for future research.

956. Additionally, a review of case law on network charge matters also underlines that there are additional considerations in assessing the valid justifications for different treatments. Different network charges in the form of exemptions or discounts may be implemented as a PSO or constitute state aid. The above analysis shows that, aside from general criteria for the non-discrimination test, EU law and its case law on PSOs and state aid create more sophisticated criteria. Such extra elements must be considered when assessing whether network charges applied to network users involved in DR and renewables self-consumption violate the non-discrimination principle.

957. To recap, there exist non-network-related motivations that may justify discounts, reductions or even partial exemptions of network charges for network users involved in renewables self-consumption or DR. However, relevant preferential treatment, which is not based on the cost impact caused by these network users on the network, could still contravene the requirement of ensuring the cost-reflectiveness of network charges. To ensure compatibility with the principles of non-discrimination and cost-reflectiveness, the advice is to avoid

using network charges as a tool for incentivizing renewables prosumers and DR providers when their activities do not bring corresponding beneficial network impacts.

958. System operators are also challenged to comply with EU-level requirements for inclusive and participatory rule-making processes of flexibility procurement. Section 3.4.1.2 explained the correlation between flexibility market entry barriers and the lack of robust safeguards to ensure that system operators respond to stakeholders' input. Drawing on reflections in some Member States, it highlights that conventional consultation processes cannot fully involve new actors providing flexibility, especially households and energy communities. To secure adequate representation for these stakeholders, who are small in size and lack expertise in the energy system, system operators should be able to innovate the way they communicate proposed rules and interact with them to learn about their concerns regarding relevant rules. Moreover, stakeholder committees represent a promising approach to representing a wide range of stakeholders and engaging with system operators, thereby helping to resolve the dilemma between an efficient and inclusive rule-making process in the context of engaging consumers.

959. Applying flexible connection agreements raises a significant issue regarding how to safeguard compliance with the principle of market-based congestion management when such agreements or similar instruments can provide (economically efficient) alternatives to flexibility markets. Flexible connection agreements defined by EU law are a non-market instrument. Monitoring and mitigating their impact on market-based congestion management of transmission and distribution systems remains a prominent issue. As analyzed in Section 3.4.1.3, there is another question equally worth noting under existing EU law: are there situations, such as structural congestion, in which flexible connection agreements should take precedence over market-based flexibility procurement? Addressing this issue requires a reassessment of the situations in which the market-first principle is applied in congestion management. These questions and uncertainties arise in national transpositions, while the EU law is better positioned to address them, as demonstrated above.

960. Section 3.4.1.4 discussed the regulatory challenges of realizing TSO-DSO cooperation in enabling market participation of DR and self-produced RES-E. They were identified based on a review of market models designed to mitigate conflicts between system operators when accessing flexibility. It concludes that the choice of market models should notably consider a limited set of permitted activities of TSOs and DSOs under unbundling rules, the increased complexity, and the resultant impacts on market participation. Moreover, whether certain models create disproportionate burdens on smaller-sized DSOs should also be taken into account.

961. In terms of realizing the required transition of distribution networks, there are some specific legal challenges associated with the specificities of DSOs and consumers connected to the distribution grid. Section 3.4.2.1 analyzed a dilemma in the DSO's role as a neutral market facilitator under EU law. With the rise of new market models facilitating local trading and TSO-DSO cooperation, tensions between potential roles that can be played by the DSO and the restrictions imposed by existing energy law on the DSO are becoming more pronounced. By examining the example of local electricity trading, the analysis above demonstrates how the potential roles of the DSO may conflict with legal unbundling and introduce discrimination risks. This analysis can inform theoretical market models to help them align with EU energy law. In addition, there is potential to extend the existing deviation from legal unbundling to create a market that accommodates the integration of renewables. As regards discrimination risks arising from a more active role of the DSO, after reviewing the pros and cons of solutions presented in the literature, it is concluded that upholding the other three pillars built by EU law for eliminating discriminatory behavior and ensuring participatory rule-making of flexibility procurement play an instrumental role in mitigating discrimination concerns.

962. The empirical evidence indicates that DSOs encounter organizational, technical, and regulatory challenges in adapting their capacity and business models to leverage flexibility and accept the associated risks. Section 3.4.2.2 specifically discussed the role of demonstration projects and experimentation in supporting the DSO's gradual transition, based on lessons learned from supporting experimentation at the transmission level. Beyond compensation for disadvantages, grid users should be incentivized to participate in pilot programs.

# CHAPTER V
# CONCLUSIONS

963. This book is devoted to exploring how the law translates consumer empowerment into specific electricity DSM measures in the context of facilitating RES-E uptake. EU law stands out as a representative example of advancing convergent development of electricity DSM and RES-E. The EU law case study also demonstrates how consumer empowerment shapes the development of electricity market legislation and renewable energy promotional laws. Based on the findings of the previous chapters, which address the core tasks of electricity DSM and their translation into EU law, this Chapter concludes the book by answering the guiding research question. This is followed by general lessons and policy implications that can be drawn from the EU law case study. This Chapter ends with suggestions for further research.

## 1. THE EU'S EFFORTS TO EMPOWER ENERGY CONSUMERS: REMAINING GAPS AND CHALLENGES

964. A general finding of this research is that EU law has room for improvement, while a greater challenge lies in its implementation. National laws and regulations have not adequately addressed the complex legal issues involved in the EU's general definitions, rights and obligations of final customers as well as enabling instruments. Given this, in the following, conclusions and recommendations will be presented separately for EU law and its national transpositions.

### 1.1. LIMITATIONS AND GAPS IN EU LAW

965. As shown in Chapter III, EU law empowers energy consumers by taking measures to address economic and non-economic barriers to engaging consumers in supporting the system integration and use of RES-E. This is reflected in the four pillars of the EU legal framework for electricity DSM. They seek to define the rights and obligations relating to the consumers' active role, enable and incentivize consumers to engage in energy activities that favor greater

uptake of RES-E, while providing options, choices and tools for prompting consumers. In parallel with adjusting electricity consumption behavior, EU law also adapts the electricity system to accommodate the active engagement of consumers who are relatively small and unprofessional compared to traditional actors. Such adaptations include changes in electricity market design, system planning and operation, and the role and obligations of traditional actors engaging with final customers, notably system operators and suppliers. In this regard, it represents a two-way approach to empowering consumers, which entails changes on both sides of end users and the electricity system. Moreover, EU law for electricity DSM can be defined as 'carrots', as it steers electricity consumption by empowering consumers and providing enablers and incentives rather than applying a command-and-control approach. Together with the two-way changes, the EU's approach avoids overly burdening consumers when involving them in the low-carbon energy transition and prevents unfair allocation of responsibility between consumers and the electricity system. The above analysis reveals substantial room for further adaptation of the electricity system.

966. Chapter II also shows that different customer groups, especially end users from residential, commercial and public sectors, face different behavioral constraints in changing their electricity consumption patterns. In theory, targeted measures are needed to enhance these consumers' agency and competence in supporting the uptake of RES-E. Such measures must be based on a comprehensive understanding of the various aspects of their decision-making regarding energy matters. EU law largely circumvents this step by harnessing the assistance of actors engaged in providing energy services to enhance the agency and competence of different customers. Instead of shifting all consumers to become 'experts' of the energy system, a more pragmatic approach suitable for upscaling is to create additional points of contact that connect consumers and the formalized electricity system. Traditionally, suppliers have long been the major point of contact (Poudineh, 2019). Now, EU law recognizes and fosters more intermediaries (e.g., IFSPs and energy communities) to engage consumers in DR and renewables use. Its actions can be summarized into two aspects: (i) creating dedicated legal frameworks for these new intermediaries and empowering consumers to cooperate with them, and (ii) lowering their barriers to engaging consumers, performing energy activities and entering electricity markets. Open and voluntary membership of energy communities and the possibility of contracting with professional energy service providers imply greater potential to engage consumers with different priorities, load features and different levels of willingness and capacity. At the same time, individual consumers are also empowered to act on their own. As such, consumer

empowerment under EU law is characterized by more choices and opportunities to participate in the transition toward a high-renewables electricity system. It particularly echoes and advances energy democracy with available choices as its essence (Sokołowski, 2020). Indeed, consumer empowerment existed in EU energy law before the introduction of the legal framework for electricity DSM. Looking back at the EU's first three energy legislative packages, widening consumer choices by, for example, granting them more rights under supply contracts has historically been used to intensify electricity market competition. Consumer empowerment has thus been a key component of market liberalization. As indicated by specific electricity DSM measures, consumer empowerment in the EU now brings co-benefits in facilitating both sustainability and competition.

967. It should be noted that within the EU law context, the EU's limited competence in the energy sector and the principle of subsidiarity prevent EU-level legislation from adopting a highly granular approach to engaging different customer groups. Equally, bound by limited rule-making competence, EU law typically adopts broad wording. It also only lists elements of enabling frameworks, including prerequisites and tools that must be solved and provided to enable consumers or energy communities to exercise rights. By doing so, sufficient flexibility is left to Member States to design specific enabling frameworks. Analyses in Chapters III and IV have highlighted the role of enabling frameworks in supporting energy consumers to exercise their rights. Since the elaboration of enabling frameworks is left to Member States, achievement of consumer empowerment is, among others, contingent upon the adequacy and robustness of national enabling frameworks.

968. This research recommends the following concrete changes to improve the existing EU legal framework for electricity DSM:

- As shown in Section 3.1.2 of Chapter IV, the blurred lines between 'electricity undertaking' and household renewables self-consumers could lead to legal uncertainty in determining the applicability of PSOs. The EU legislator should address the conflation between the definitions of 'electricity undertaking' and household renewables self-consumer.
- Without an explicit requirement of the proportionality *stricto sensu* test, some Member States may not fully consider the potential adverse impacts of applying supplier obligations to self-consumers. Section 3.2.3 of Chapter IV argues that there is a need to incorporate specific requirements for the *stricto sensu* test into the general requirements of protecting renewables self-consumers from disproportionate procedures, obligations and fees.

- Section 3.1.3 of Chapter IV points out that the current method of regulating membership termination in the CEC leads to a 'one-size-fits-all' approach. That method is to be amended to create more flexibility for national law to address trade-offs between the voluntariness of members and the economic viability of the CEC.
- The REDII's requirement for supporting public authorities' direct participation in RECs carries a risk of unfair distribution of public resources among RECs and discriminatory treatment. Section 3.1.2 of Chapter IV suggests that EU law should replace the existing provision of enabling public authorities to directly participate with the general requirement of providing capacity-building support for RECs.
- Restricting a private company's participation in RECs through the non-primary commercial or professional activity criterion is not clear enough. It is unsuitable to prevent energy undertakings from abusing the REC for their own commercial benefits, as demonstrated by Section 3.1.3 of Chapter IV. The EU legislator should reconsider the general approach to limiting membership of private undertakings to make it robust, fit-for-purpose, and pragmatic enough to implement.
- Section 3.1.2 of Chapter IV recommends two modifications to the existing EU energy law on energy sharing. First, to address legal uncertainty and the negative impact on the economic viability and participation thresholds of energy communities, the EU legislator should clarify whether the energy communities' ownership right to production units is a condition for granting them the right to energy sharing. Second, the new definition and legal provision for energy sharing should be restructured to govern energy sharing within energy communities.
- EU law should give priority to the GO's primary function of disclosing RES-E origin and only permit GO transfers together with the physical transfer of electricity, as highlighted in Section 3.3.2 of Chapter IV.
- Recitals of the EU legislation provide important guidance for national transpositions. However, as noted in Sections 3.1.3.3 and 3.2.3.3 of Chapter IV, some of them risk causing misinterpretation of legal provisions by extending restrictions beyond the EU law's minimum requirements or by suggesting differential treatment of market actors without thorough discrimination tests. These issues in the recitals should be addressed, and the EU legislator should exercise greater caution in formulating recitals.
- The application of flexible connection agreements may undermine compliance with the principle of market-based congestion management. The EU legislator should further clarify, in the event that such agreements can provide more economically efficient alternatives to flexibility procurement, whether the market-first principle of congestion management should still be respected.

## 1.2. CHALLENGES OF IMPLEMENTING EU LAW

969. Union-level consumer empowerment frameworks entail some legal issues that must be addressed by national law. Some of them arise from broadly worded definitions and empowerment frameworks for the sake of respecting national rule-making competence and discretion, while others are deficiencies or gaps existing in empowerment frameworks per se. Chapter IV analyzed which of them should be paid special attention during national transpositions. Particularly, EU legal frameworks for renewables self-consumers, active customers and energy communities provide striking examples of complex legal issues covered in seemingly straightforward definitions and requirements. Chapter IV unfolded these complex legal issues, mainly regarding (i) eligibility requirements contained in definitions, and (ii) the relationships that consumers involved in DR and renewables self-consumption have with suppliers and energy communities. It also explained how failing to solve them in national rules could frustrate the effectiveness of Union-level empowerment frameworks. On this basis, the analysis highlights that translating Union-level empowerment frameworks into national law essentially requires addressing those issues, rather than 'literal transposition', i.e., replicating the rights that EU law grants to consumers and energy communities.

970. A key legal issue often overlooked in the transposition of empowerment frameworks is how to monitor compliance with the eligibility requirements outlined in the definitions of active customers, renewable self-consumers, and energy communities. Chapter IV discussed the pros and cons of possible regulatory approaches and stressed due account to administrative feasibility and the principle of proportionality when designing specific regulatory oversight.

971. This research also highlights gaps in materializing enabling frameworks at the national level. Typical examples include (i) the lack of targeted instruments for consumers suffering from unique disadvantages stemming from the tenancy, poverty and vulnerability to access the right to become renewables self-consumers, (ii) the absence of national law providing financing tools for RECs, which easily have disadvantages in raising capitals particularly due to restrictions imposed by strict eligibility requirements, (iii) the neglected dimension of how to provide two-fold capacity-building support to public authorities in enabling and setting up RECs and in helping authorities direct participation in RECs. Based on recent empirical data about the barriers faced by individual consumers and energy communities in financial and competence dimensions, the above chapters demonstrate that the EU's consumer empowerment is indeed undermined by weak and delayed national actions to implement elements of enabling frameworks.

972. In terms of properly incentivizing consumers to participate in DR and renewables use, the remaining legal challenges are mainly concerned with safeguarding free price formation, adapting electricity market design and specifying concrete rights and obligations of prosumers and consumers involved in RES-E trading. Chapter IV discussed lessons learned from the past energy price crisis and examined new legal arrangements that balance the need to protect consumers from price shocks and prevent market prices from undue intervention during emergencies.

973. Adapting technical parameters of electricity markets (including flexibility markets organized by system operators) to allow greater participation of consumers is a gradual process. In addition to harmonizing electricity market design parameters, EU law provides two other legal safeguards, e.g., procedural and substantive requirements for market rule-making (including flexibility procurement rules and technical specifications) to mitigate market entry barriers stemming from specific market design elements. By taking examples in Member States, notably Flanders in Belgium and Ireland, this book highlights that for these two safeguards to function effectively, detailed implementing rules are required at the Member State level, grounded in a more nuanced interpretation of the broad principles of non-discrimination and transparency. These two legal safeguards are vital for advancing the ambitious goal of establishing a consumer-centric electricity market.

974. Broadening routes to electricity markets is another important measure to incentivize consumers to engage in renewables self-consumption. Section 3.2 of Chapter IV demonstrates that the accessibility of renewable PPAs and P2P electricity trading hinges on the resolution of a set of complex legal issues. Renewables PPAs and P2P electricity trading are not novel for traditional market players, especially energy undertakings engaged in production and electricity supply. However, Chapter IV indicates that when renewables self-consumers apply these approaches to trade self-produced RES-E, complex legal issues arise regarding the role, rights and obligations of sellers and buyers in the trading. One of the core issues is whether a renewables self-consumer selling electricity constitutes a supplier and is thus subject to supplier obligations, and correspondingly, whether its contractual counterparty maintains the role of final customer and enjoys associated rights.

975. Based on an analysis of the different philosophies and aims underlying the rights granted to consumers under EU energy law and general consumer protection law, this book demonstrates that the role, rights, and obligations of renewables self-consumers involved in PPAs and P2P electricity trading should be analyzed separately in the context of these two legislative frameworks. Critically reviewing prior studies, the analysis therein first explained why the consumer status of renewables self-consumers engaged in those transactions

cannot be determined entirely from the lens of the EU's general consumer protection law and its case law. On this basis, it presented analysis results on the consumer status of both sellers and buyers in electricity transactions involving renewables self-consumers within the context of EU energy law and general consumer protection law. The analysis then proposed a granular approach to assessing the applicability of consumer rights granted by general consumer protection law and energy law at the EU level. The granularity is inter alia reflected in an emphasis that consumer rights under EU electricity law serve broader purposes in addition to consumer protection, which leads to different results in assessing the applicability of consumer rights. For those rights secured by imposing obligations for sellers, their application should also be determined based on principles of non-discrimination and proportionality. A follow-up legal issue is to determine the selling party's obligations. Drawing on the CJEU's judgments on the subject matter of energy, Chapter IV distilled more detailed criteria for applying the non-discrimination principle, including for assessing comparability and justifications that can legitimize different treatments.

976. A two-step criterion for assessing comparability contained in the discrimination test can be drawn from the rulings of *Arcelor Atlantique et Lorraine and Others and* the related case law. Different treatment does not violate the non-discrimination principle if objective justifications relate to and are proportionate to a legally permitted aim pursued by the legislation that creates the concerned distinction. A key finding is that the legal purpose of the legislation that creates the different treatment plays an essential role in assessing comparability and justifications legitimizing the different treatment.

977. However, the analyses in Sections 3.2 and 3.4 of Chapter IV demonstrate that the criteria adopted by the *Arcelor Atlantique et Lorraine and Others* case and related case law are not clear and granular enough to determine the regulatory treatment of individual and collective self-consumers involved in electricity trading. Their application can lead to uncertain results in two scenarios: (i) in case the legal act that makes the distinction addresses multiple subject matters and objectives, and (ii) in case the different treatment follows from two or more legal acts that each have different subject matters and legal aims. To date, the CJEU's rulings in the energy sector have not addressed these issues. Nor have they been noticed in the literature. Future research should explore whether courts have refined these criteria in other fields relevant and comparable to the energy sector, and whether such refinements could be applied to the energy sector, particularly to address the regulatory treatment of individual and collective self-consumers.

978. Regarding the application of the principle of proportionality, this book identified potential tensions between the principles of non-discrimination

and proportionality. Applying the non-discrimination principle can fail the proportionality *stricto sensu* test, creating disproportionate obligations. It discussed two approaches adopted by existing EU energy law to seek compromises between these two principles and their limitations. Ensuring coherence between these two principles is a crucial question that requires further exploration.

979. In P2P electricity trading, an additional legal issue arises regarding the triangular relationships among sellers, buyers, and trading platform providers. The core issue lies in defining the obligations of the platform provider toward the involved renewables self-consumers and consumers. Section 3.2 of Chapter IV shows that a criterion developed by the CJEU's case law on other P2P trading can be applied: whether the platform assumes a decisive role in offering electricity determines whether its service is merely classified as an information society service or should be defined as a supply of electricity. However, such a decisive role should be evaluated in different P2P electricity market models.

980. In addition to economic incentives, desirable changes in electricity consumption are stimulated by conveying information about opportunities for saving bills and the environmental impacts of different energy sources. Section 3.3 of Chapter IV highlights the increasing need to ensure accessibility to key ICT infrastructure, notably smart meters, while discussing further national actions required to enable the safe and efficient use of smart-meter-related data, built upon the interplay between EU energy law and data protection law.

981. The last building block of EU law on electricity DSM is adapting network operation and its regulation to specifically accommodate consumers' engagement in DR and renewables self-consumption. Section 3.4 of Chapter IV first identified common challenges of realizing adaptations of transmission and distribution systems, summarized as follows.

- Legal concerns and drawbacks of applying time-differentiated tariffs: Those concerns reflect tensions between competing principles for governing network charges, especially between the efficiency of cost signals, fairness and predictability of network tariffs. Moreover, the wide application of time-differentiated tariffs also faces other challenges, especially increased complexity and uncertainties when dynamic price contracts are applied simultaneously. To ascertain the extent to which time-differentiated tariffs can be used as an effective tool for efficient network operation, NRAs are advised to first understand the costs and benefits of such tariffs and the alternative instruments.
- Acute challenges of designing cost-reflective and non-discriminatory network tariffs for network users involved in DR and renewables

self-consumption: Network charge regulation was examined against EU-level principles governing network charges and the requirement of avoiding disadvantaging DR and renewables self-consumption. The CJEU's rulings on network charges provide additional details on the criteria for applying the non-discrimination principle. Despite this, my analysis demonstrated a need for a more in-depth examination of and improvement to existing criteria for the discrimination test. It requires research on extensive CJEU case law relating to the principles of non-discrimination and equality, beyond the energy sector, combined with consideration of their application in diverse contexts of consumer engagement. To ensure compatibility with both the principles of non-discrimination and cost-reflectiveness, this book suggests avoiding using network charges to incentivize renewables prosumers and DR providers when their activities do not bring corresponding beneficial network impacts.
- Challenges of ensuring system operators' responses to stakeholders' input in making rules for flexibility procurement: Conventional consultation processes cannot fully engage new actors providing flexibility, especially households and energy communities. To secure adequate representation for these stakeholders, who are small in size and inexperienced, NRAs should ensure that system operators innovate the way they communicate proposed rules and interact with impacted stakeholders. This is key to further improving flexibility market rules to accommodate more involvement of consumers.
- Challenges raised by approaches to coordinating flexibility procurement of TSOs and DSOs: First, some market models grant more roles to DSOs, leading to misalignment with unbundling rules. Second, when considering adjustments to the market design to enhance TSO-DSO cooperation, care should be taken to account for the potential complexity of multi-level market structures and the resultant barriers to consumers' participation in multiple markets. Additionally, whether certain models create disproportionate burdens on smaller-sized DSOs should also be taken into account.

982. The transition of distribution networks faces unique challenges tied to the characteristics of the DSO and the existing regulatory framework. With the rise of new market models facilitating local trading and TSO-DSO cooperation, tensions between the potential roles that can be performed by the DSO and the restrictions imposed on the DSO are becoming more pronounced. A more active role of the DSO can also increase discrimination concerns. This book demonstrates that other legal safeguards for mitigating discrimination risks become crucial. Enhanced regulatory oversight is recommended to support the implementation of procedural requirements for establishing flexibility procurement rules and ensure the DSO's compliance with non-discrimination obligations in network code design and flexibility procurement.

983. To support DSOs in accepting and managing the risks associated with utilizing flexibility, national law should further facilitate the application of demonstration projects and experimentation. Lessons could be learned from supporting experimentation at the transmission level, especially in terms of incentivizing the DSO and grid users to conduct relevant pilots.

984. In conclusion, the EU law for electricity DSM has not entirely addressed the challenges of empowering energy consumers to facilitate the uptake of RES-E. In creating and applying a legal framework for electricity DSM, a range of legal issues arises, which remain to be addressed at either the EU or national level. Among others, this research highlights that the sensible application of fundamental principles of EU energy law, notably non-discrimination, proportionality and transparency, plays an essential role in addressing the remaining legal challenges. As rightly pointed out by prior studies, 'ensuring an effective enforcement of existing rules by regulators could still be a more pressing need than creating a detailed and harmonised regulatory framework' (Rumpf and Bjørnebye, 2019).

## 2. LESSONS AND IMPLICATIONS

985. Empowering consumers to play a proactive role in promoting RES-E requires a two-fold change in their electricity consumption behavior: adjusting demand to match variable RES-E production and increasing the share of RES-E in consumption. By doing so, final customers, who had long been passive actors in the traditional energy regime, could proactively contribute to advancing deep decarbonization and sustainability of the electricity system. Adapting electricity demand should be an integral part of a whole-system approach to transitioning to a sustainable electricity system with high penetration of RES-E. Demand-side oriented approaches to developing RES-E, as an important category of electricity DSM, have, however, not received the attention it deserves in many jurisdictions until the recent decade. Against this background, this book examines the EU, one of the pioneers in energy consumer empowerment, with a specific focus on how to develop a legal framework for electricity DSM and the legal issues that arise in this process. This section draws out general lessons and implications from the EU law case study, which could provide insights for other jurisdictions facing a need to engage consumers in promoting RES-E.

986. First, to realize the benefits of electricity DSM in steering electricity consumption behavior to favor system integration and the use of RES-E, a legal framework must incorporate the core tasks of electricity DSM. Such core tasks, as shown in Chapters II and III, encompass both addressing barriers

that hinder consumers from actively adjusting their electricity consumption and providing enablers. In addition to the intensively discussed obstacles of lacking economic incentives and information, special attention should be paid to identifying and tackling complex behavioral barriers. Ignoring consumers' behavioral and decision-making biases and constraints shaped by different customer groups' features, needs and priorities can defeat efforts to empower consumers with incentives and information. Providing proper incentives and information while improving consumers' agency and competence to make rational choices and decisions represents the pillars of electricity DSM. They aim to empower and enable consumers to benefit from the energy transition while respecting their autonomy and ensuring transparency of interventions. EU law is a representative example of developing electricity DSM by complementary pillars and 'boosting' consumers instead of 'nudging' them. It demonstrates how to realize such 'boosts' with law: by defining the role, rights and obligations of consumers and entities assisting them, accompanied by measures providing enabling instruments and incentives to exercise those rights.

987. Essentially, these legal approaches mirror the EU's overarching pathway of consumer empowerment, i.e., embedding long-term changes in consumer behavior in the transition to a sustainable electricity system and even seeking to address the deeper socio-cultural roots of consumers' inactivity and passivity (Silva, 2022). This pathway is chosen under the EU's ambitious policy goal of letting 'citizens take ownership of the energy transition' and the legal objective of creating a 'consumer-centred electricity market'. Among others, whether energy consumers are envisioned to play a central role in facilitating RES-E also shapes the specific way of translating electricity DSM mechanisms into law. This should be considered when assessing the extent to which EU law on electricity DSM can be transplanted into other jurisdictions, which may have different objectives for consumer empowerment. In addition, as highlighted, the EU's legal approach to empowering energy consumers heavily relies on its internal electricity market. Jurisdictions without competitive electricity markets may need to consider alternatives for incentivizing consumers.

988. Second, the EU law case study demonstrates that developing electricity DSM with law can give rise to a set of complex legal issues. Failing to address them will constitute legal barriers to realizing the consumers' greater role in facilitating RES-E uptake. Prominent examples include creating legal definitions that clearly distinguish prosumers from other traditional actors involved in the production and supply of RES-E, as well as monitoring compliance with eligibility criteria set for new actors, including active customers, renewables self-consumers, and energy communities. In addition, prosumers' engagement in RES-E production and trading also raises an acute legal issue regarding how to set up non-discriminatory and proportionate obligations and network

charges for them. Their regulatory treatment (including rights and obligations, i.e., whether they are comparable to producers and suppliers defined under EU electricity law and subject to the same obligations as the latter) can significantly impact their incentives to engage in renewables self-consumption and the level playing field. On the one hand, treating prosumers (including energy communities) differently may risk creating special advantages relative to other market actors also involved in production and supply. On the other hand, subjecting prosumers to the same obligations as producers and suppliers may create disproportionate obligations and undue administrative burdens, impeding their market entry. Both risks can be regarded as hampering the level playing field and free competition within the context of the EU electricity market legislation. The conducted analysis reveals that resolving this dilemma necessitates detailed criteria for applying the non-discrimination principle across the diverse contexts of consumer involvement in market and network realms.

989. Another leading example concerns energy communities. This book suggests that, while promising, developing a community-based approach to empower consumers is not straightforward. It demonstrates that to enable energy communities to effectively involve consumers, the legal framework must be able to properly structure the relationship between energy communities and participating consumers, and avoid such entities being exploited by electricity undertakings to generate profits. These lead to a range of restrictions on two types of energy communities developed by EU law, such as those relating to their membership, primary aims and operation. They serve as legal safeguards to ensure that energy communities are committed to facilitating consumers' engagement in activities that promote RES-E uptake. In addition to their impacts on the financial viability of energy communities and accessibility to low-income consumers, the main challenges also lie in their implementation and compliance. These challenges imply a risk that the community-based approach might be either misused or remain a futile concept.

990. Lastly, EU law on electricity DSM showcases typical legal challenges faced by a legal framework that is subject to rule-making competence allocation. For jurisdictions with similar competence allocation between national and regional or local institutions, EU law presents the core principles and elements that are suited to be tackled by the primary legislation for electricity DSM. The case study of EU law in this book also demonstrates how definitional issues, deficiencies, and one-size-fits-all approaches in primary legislation for electricity DSM can impact its effective implementation. It also discusses legal safeguards or implementing mechanisms (including hard law and soft law) that should be in place to apply those general principles and elements. In developing multi-level legal frameworks for electricity DSM, respective legal issues identified at the EU and national levels should be considered.

# 3. SUGGESTIONS FOR FURTHER RESEARCH

991. This book examines the EU's legal approaches to empowering energy consumers to facilitate RES-E uptake. The focus is limited to adjustments of electricity consumption behavior. Consumer behavior, in a broad sense, including network use and the operation of storage facilities, can also be adapted to support system integration and the use of RES-E. As shown above in Section 3.4 of Chapter IV, dynamic tariffs that adjust network use behavior can conflict with dynamic price contracts that flex electricity consumption. This implies that measures facilitating flexible network use may defeat the efficiency of those stimulating flexible electricity consumption. Potential tensions should be considered in future research focusing on adapting consumer behavior beyond electricity use.

992. Second, this research also highlights the limitations of the law in improving consumers' decision-making competences and helping overcome cognitive or motivational biases. The legal framework on electricity DSM provides pivotal norms for steering desirable consumer behavior. Nevertheless, on some occasions, soft law and policies are better positioned to provide other awareness-raising and behavior-changing strategies. This book provides examples of how soft law approaches can complement electricity DSM law, such as in creating effective data exchange mechanisms and overcoming barriers to using renewable PPAs. The potential for soft law and policies to complement the legal framework for electricity DSM to further empower energy consumers is an important issue that warrants further research.

993. Third, improving consumers' market participation is a key approach upon which EU law relies to incentivize them to engage in DR and renewables self-consumption. The CEP introduced the objective of creating a consumer-centred electricity market, which can serve as a further driving force for future reforms of the EU's electricity market design. To achieve this ambitious aim, there will be continued efforts to adapt electricity markets to facilitate wider market participation by consumers, particularly small ones currently facing unfavorable conditions for participating in wholesale markets and flexibility markets organized by system operators. In addition to incrementally adapting technical parameters of existing markets, adjusting market models is another way that has received attention in the most recent decade. There are ongoing discussions around shifting away from the prevailing centralized market models to decentralized local market settings. Legal issues raised by LEMs, including those relating to embedding such markets within energy communities and integrating them into the existing electricity market sequence, merit a specific examination.

994. The development of LEMs should also be considered with the need for coordinating flexibility procurement of TSOs and DSOs. There is a need to seek the potential synergy between LEM market design and market-based approaches to facilitating TSO-DSO cooperation (i.e., coordinating their flexibility procurement). The proposed market models in the two areas have some overlaps and potential conflicts, as shown above in Chapter IV. These two streams of market design are intertwined but not subcategories of each other, as they serve different primary goals. The TSO-DSO cooperation market design hardly considers whether the market is local or not. While it also considers how to ease consumers' market participation, its main goal is to meet the flexibility needs of system operators in a coordinated way and reduce the overall costs of flexibility procurement from a system-wide perspective. LEMs consider TSO-DSO cooperation mainly because it is an inevitable issue when integrating LEMs into the existing electricity market sequence. However, TSO-DSO coordination is not the core concern or starting point of LEM initiatives. LEMs and market models for TSO-DSO cooperation thus can have overlaps in answering the question 'how to adapt the existing electricity market design to deep decarbonization and greater consumer engagement'. Overall, their tensions and conflicts lie in the fact that they serve different legal objectives under EU law and give priority to economic efficiency in system operation and consumer engagement respectively.

995. Now, theoretical market models and pilots for TSO-DSO cooperation and local trading co-exist. Proceeding with market reform based on the coexistence of market design initiatives in these two areas would increase the complexity of multi-level market coordination and integration. Aside from the overlaps and resultant regulatory fragmentation, these market models hardly give due consideration to the multiple legal objectives pursued by EU electricity law and the potential co-benefits. Thus, it is time to classify, organize, and review the existing market models in these two areas, identify their potential overlaps and conflicts, and ultimately seek their (maximum) synergy. This can be another path for future research.

996. Fourth, clarifying specific criteria for applying the fundamental principles of EU energy law is the linchpin to addressing significant legal challenges in the context of empowering energy consumers. As shown in this book, determining the regulatory treatment (including rights, obligations, charges and taxes) of individual and collective prosumers relies on the concrete application of the principles of non-discrimination and proportionality. Furthermore, the principles of non-discrimination and transparency are crucial legal safeguards, ensuring system operators' responsiveness to stakeholders in flexibility-related rule-making and market operations while facilitating the ongoing adaptation

of electricity and flexibility market design to enhance consumer engagement. Further research is urgently needed to explore the specific application standards of these principles.

997. Finally, national transpositions and implementation of existing EU law on electricity DSM are still ongoing. Moreover, the examination of relevant EU law is also based on empirical data about energy activities carried out by final customers, IFSPs and energy communities, some of which are limited. For instance, research on the inclusion and participation of vulnerable consumers in community energy, notably in RECs, is scarce (Hanke and Lowitzsch, 2020). The lack of empirical evidence in this respect restricts legal research assessing the inclusiveness of RECs. Considering these situations, this book does not mark the end of examining existing legal approaches, but instead paves the way for future research. In addition, new legal issues will arise with new amendments to the Electricity Directive, the Electricity Regulation and the RED entering into force. Within the context of these amendments, future research can advance legal research on electricity DSM based on this book.

# BIBLIOGRAPHY


2 APRIL 2021. – Decree amending the Energy Decree of 8 May 2009 partially transposing Directive (EU) 2018/2001 of the European Parliament and of the Council of 11 December 2018 on the promotion of the use of energy from renewable sources and transposing Directive (EU) 2019/944 of the European Parliament and of the Council of 5 June 2019 on common rules for the internal market in electricity and amending Directive 2012/27/EU [2 APRIL 2021. – Decreet tot wijziging van het Energiedecreet van 8 mei 2009 tot gedeeltelijke omzetting van richtlijn (EU) 2018/2001 van het Europees Parlement en de Raad van 11 december 2018 ter bevordering van het gebruik van energie uit hernieuwbare bronnen en tot omzetting van richtlijn (EU) 2019/944 van het Europees Parlement en de Raad van 5 juni 2019 betreffende gemeenschappelijke regels voor de interne markt voor elektriciteit en tot wijziging vanRichtlijn 2012/27/EU], 2021.

3 JUNE 2024. – Royal Decree establishing the competitive tender procedure, the conditions and the procedure for awarding the domain concessions and the general conditions for the use of the plots for the construction and operation of an installation for the production of electricity from renewable energy sources in the maritime areas under the jurisdiction of Belgium [3 JUNI 2024. – Koninklijk besluit tot vaststelling van de concurrerende inschrijvingsprocedure, de voorwaarden en de procedure tot toekenning van de domeinconcessies en de algemene voorwaarden voor het gebruik van de kavels voor de bouw en exploitatie van een installatie voor de productie van elektriciteit uit hernieuwbare energiebronnen in de zeegebieden onder de rechtsbevoegdheid van België], 2024.

9 DECEMBER 2021. – Royal Decree determining minimum requirements to be met by gas and electricity invoices and billing information [9 DECEMBER 2021. – Koninklijk besluit tot bepaling van de minimumvereisten waaraan de facturen en factureringsinformatie voor gas en elektriciteit moeten voldoen], 2021.

16 JULY 2002. – Royal Decree on the establishment of mechanisms for the promotion of electricity generated from renewable energy sources [and compensation of offshore domain concession holders in case of unavailability of the Modular Offshore Grid] [16 JULI 2002. – Koninklijk besluit betreffende de instelling van mechanismen voor de bevordering van elektriciteit opgewekt uit hernieuwbare energiebronnen [en de vergoeding van de houders van een offshore domeinconcessie in geval van onbeschikbaarheid van het Modular Offshore Grid]], 2002.

17 FEBRUARY 2023. – Ministerial decree organising calls for the year 2023 for the submission of aid applications for medium-sized solar installations and small and medium-sized wind turbines [17 FEBRUARI 2023. – Ministerieel besluit houdende de organisatie van calls voor het jaar 2023 voor het indienen van steunaanvragen

voor middelgrote installaties op basis van zonne-energie en kleine en middelgrote windturbines], 2023.

17 JULY 2020. – Decree of the Flemish Government amending the Energy Decree of 19 November 2010, regarding the maximum roll-out of digital meters [17 JULI 2020. – Besluit van de Vlaamse Regering tot wijziging van het Energiebesluit van 19 november 2010, wat betreft de maximale uitrol van digitale meters], 2020.

20 DECEMBER 2007. – Royal Decree on the procedure for elaboration, approval and publication of the plan on development of the electricity transmission network [20 DECEMBER 2007. – Koninklijk besluit betreffende de procedure voor uitwerking, goedkeuring en bekendmaking van het plan inzake ontwikkeling van het transmissienet voor elektriciteit], 2007.

22 APRIL 2019. – Royal decree on technical regulations for the management of the electricity transmission network and access to it [22 APRIL 2019. – Koninklijk besluit houdende een technisch reglement voor het beheer van het transmissienet van elektriciteit en de toegang ertoe], 2019.

30 JULY 2013. – Royal Decree on the establishment of a system for granting guarantees of origin for electricity generated from renewable energy sources [30 JULI 2013. – Koninklijk besluit betreffende de instelling van een systeem voor de toekenning van garanties van oorsprong voor elektriciteit opgewekt uit hernieuwbare energiebronnen], 2013.

2019 Study on the Transfer of Energy in DA-ID Markets, 2019.

2024 Report on Energy Communities, Energy Sharing and Sales [Rapport 7/05/2024 Energiegemeenschappen, energiedelen en energie verkopen] (No. RAPP-2024-10), 2024.

Abadeço, M., Rodrigues, M.J., Ferrão, P., Luz, G., Freitas, S., Brito, M.C., 2024. Solar Self-Consumption and Urban Energy Vulnerability: Case Study in Lisbon. Sustainability 16. https://doi.org/10.3390/su16156635.

Abdalla, O., Awlad-Thani, M., Al-Wardi, M., Al-Qaidi, K., Al-Farsi, S., Al-Balushi, I., Al-Mahdhoori, S., 2009. Key Performance Indicators of a Transmission System. Omar H. Abdalla.

Abraham-Dukuma, M., 2020. Sovereignty, trade, and legislation: The evolution of energy law in a changing climate. Energy Research & Social Science 59, 101305. https://doi.org/10.1016/j.erss.2019.101305.

ACER, 2023a. ACER Demand response and other distributed energy resources: what barriers are holding them back? 2023 Market Monitoring Report.

ACER, 2023b. Assessment of emergency measures in electricity markets: 2023 Market Monitoring Report.

ACER, 2022. ACER's Final Assessment of the EU Wholesale Electricity Market Design.

ACER, 2021. High Energy Prices.

ACER, CEER, 2023a. ACER-CEER Reaction to the European Commission's public consultation on electricity market design.

ACER, CEER, 2023b. Energy Retail and Consumer Protection 2023 Market Monitoring Report.

ACER, CEER, 2021. ACER Annual Report on the Results of Monitoring the Internal Electricity and Natural Gas Markets in 2020 – Energy Retail Markets and Consumer Protection Volume.

ACER, CEER, 2015. Joint ACER-CEER response to European Commission's Consultation on a new Energy Market Design.

Ackermann, T., Andersson, G., Söder, L., 2001. Distributed generation: a definition. Electric Power Systems Research 57, 195–204. https://doi.org/10.1016/S0378-7796(01)00101-8.

Adamkovič, M., Martončik, M., 2017. A Review of Consequences of Poverty on Economic Decision-Making: A Hypothesized Model of a Cognitive Mechanism. Frontiers in Psychology 8, 1784. https://doi.org/10.3389/fpsyg.2017.01784.

Agamben, G., 2008. State of Exception. University of Chicago Press.

Agrell, P.J., Bogetoft, P., Mikkers, M., 2013. Smart-grid investments, regulation and organization. Energy Policy 52, 656–666. https://doi.org/10.1016/j.enpol.2012.10.026.

Ajodhia, V., Hakvoort, R., 2005. Economic regulation of quality in electricity distribution networks. Utilities Policy 13, 211–221. https://doi.org/10.1016/j.jup.2004.07.008.

Akkoord 'De consument in de vrije elektriciteits- en gasmarkt,' 2022.

Akorede, M.F., Hizam, H., Pouresmaeil, E., 2010. Distributed energy resources and benefits to the environment. Renewable and Sustainable Energy Reviews 14, 724–734. https://doi.org/10.1016/j.rser.2009.10.025.

Alcázar-Ortega, M., Calpe, C., Theisen, T., Carbonell-Carretero, J.F., 2015. Methodology for the identification, evaluation and prioritization of market handicaps which prevent the implementation of Demand Response: Application to European electricity markets. Energy Policy 86, 529–543. https://doi.org/10.1016/j.enpol.2015.08.006.

Alexiadis, P., Cave, M., 2012. Regulation and competition law in telecommunications and other network industries, in: Baldwin, R., Cave, M., Lodge, M. (Eds.), The Oxford Handbook of Regulation. Oxford University Press, p. 515.

Allcott, H., 2011a. Social norms and energy conservation. Journal of Public Economics 95, 1082–1095. https://doi.org/10.1016/j.jpubeco.2011.03.003.

Allcott, H., 2011b. Rethinking real-time electricity pricing. Resource and Energy Economics 33, 820–842. https://doi.org/10.1016/j.reseneeco.2011.06.003.

Allcott, H., Mullainathan, S., 2010. Behavior and Energy Policy. Science 327, 1204–1205. https://doi.org/10.1126/science.1180775.

Almeida, L. de, Klausmann, N., Soest, H. van, Cappelli, V., 2021. Peer-to-Peer Trading and Energy Community in the Electricity Market – Analysing the Literature on Law and Regulation and Looking Ahead to Future Challenges (Robert Schuman Centre for Advanced Studies Research Paper No. RSCAS 2021/35). Florence School of Regulation.

Alonso Pedrero, R., Crespo del Granado, P., 2023. Assessing the impact of energy communities on retailers' balancing positions in the power market. Energy 283, 128384. https://doi.org/10.1016/j.energy.2023.128384.

Althaher, S., Mancarella, P., Mutale, J., 2015. Automated Demand Response From Home Energy Management System Under Dynamic Pricing and Power and Comfort Constraints. IEEE Transactions on Smart Grid 6, 1874–1883. https://doi.org/10.1109/TSG.2014.2388357.

Anaya, K.L., Giulietti, M., Pollitt, M.G., 2022. Where next for the electricity distribution system operator? Evidence from a survey of European DSOs and National Regulatory Authorities. Competition and Regulation in Network Industries 23, 245–269. https://doi.org/10.1177/17835917221139828.

Anaya, K.L., Pollitt, M.G., 2017. Going smarter in the connection of distributed generation. Energy Policy 105, 608–617. https://doi.org/10.1016/j.enpol.2017.01.036.

Anderson, C.J., 2003. The psychology of doing nothing: Forms of decision avoidance result from reason and emotion. Psychological Bulletin 129, 139.

Annala, S., Lukkarinen, J., Primmer, E., Honkapuro, S., Ollikka, K., Sunila, K., Ahonen, T., 2018a. Regulation as an enabler of demand response in electricity markets and power systems. Journal of Cleaner Production 195, 1139–1148. https://doi.org/10.1016/j.jclepro.2018.05.276.

Annala, S., Mendes, G., Honkapuro, S., Matos, L., Klein, L., 2018b. Comparison of Opportunities and Challenges in Demand Response Pilots in Finland and Portugal. Presented at the 15th International Conference on the European Energy Market, pp. 1–5. https://doi.org/10.1109/EEM.2018.8469894.

APRIL 12, 2001. - Decree on the organization of the regional electricity market [12 APRIL 2001. - Decreet betreffende de organisatie van de gewestelijke elektriciteitsmarkt], 2001.

Armstrong, M., Sappington, D.E.M., 2006. Regulation, Competition and Liberalization. Journal of Economic Literature 44, 325–366. https://doi.org/10.1257/jel.44.2.325.

Arrest nr. 5/2021 van 14 januari 2021, 2021.

Arrest nr. 56/2016, 2016.

Auffhammer, M., Wang, M., Xie, L., Xu, J., 2021. Renewable Electricity Development in China: Policies, Performance, and Challenges. Review of Environmental Economics and Policy 15, 323–339. https://doi.org/10.1086/715624.

Autorité de la concurrence, 2013. Opinion n ° 13-A-25 of 20 December 2013 concerning demand response in the electricity sector [Avis n° 13-A-25 du 20 décembre 2013 concernant l'effacement de consommation dans le secteur de l'électricité].

Avau, M., Govaerts, N., Delarue, E., 2021. Impact of distribution tariffs on prosumer demand response. Energy Policy 151, 112116. https://doi.org/10.1016/j.enpol.2020.112116.

Azarova, V., Cohen, J., Friedl, C., Reichl, J., 2019. Designing local renewable energy communities to increase social acceptance: Evidence from a choice experiment in Austria, Germany, Italy, and Switzerland. Energy Policy 132, 1176–1183. https://doi.org/10.1016/j.enpol.2019.06.067.

Baker, B., Trémolet, S., 2000. Regulation of quality of infrastructure services in developing countries.

Balcombe, P., Rigby, D., Azapagic, A., 2014. Investigating the importance of motivations and barriers related to microgeneration uptake in the UK. Applied Energy 130, 403–418. https://doi.org/10.1016/j.apenergy.2014.05.047.

Baldwin, R., Cave, M., Lodge, M., 2012. Understanding Regulation: Theory, Strategy, and Practice, 2nd ed. Oxford University Press.

Balta-Ozkan, N., Davidson, R., Bicket, M., Whitmarsh, L., 2013. Social barriers to the adoption of smart homes. Energy Policy 63, 363–374. https://doi.org/10.1016/j.enpol.2013.08.043.

Bammens, N., 2011. The Principle of Non-discrimination in International and European Tax Law (PhD Dissertation). Katholieke Universiteit Leuven.

Banet, C., 2012. Tradable green certificates schemes under EU law: the influence of EU law on national support schemes for renewable electricity generation. University of Oslo.

Barbero, M., Igualada, L., Corchero, C., 2018. Overview of the Regulation on Aggregator Agents in Europe, in: 2018 15th International Conference on the European Energy Market (EEM). pp. 1–5. https://doi.org/10.1109/EEM.2018.8470015.

Barton, B., Redgwell, C., Rønne, A., Zillman, D.N., Barton, B., Redgwell, C., Rønne, A., Zillman, D.N. (Eds.), 2010. Energy Security in the Twenty-First Century, in: Energy Security: Managing Risk in a Dynamic Legal and Regulatory Environment. Oxford University Press, p. 0. https://doi.org/10.1093/acprof:oso/9780199271610.003.0019.

Barzantny, K., Betz, R., Betzenbichler, W., Butzengeiger, S., Diekmann, J., 2004. The EU Emissions Trading Scheme – Issues and Challenges. Intereconomics 39, 116–131.

Battisti, R., 2019. Fotovoltaico e autoconsumo collettivo nei condomini austriaci.

Bauknecht, D., Brunekreeft, G., 2008. Distributed Generation and the Regulation of Electricity Networks, in: Sioshansi, F.P. (Ed.), Competitive Electricity Markets: Design, Implementation, Performance. Elsevier, p. 469.

Bauknecht, D., Voß, J.-P., 2009. Network Regulation, in: Praetorius, B. (Ed.), Innovation for Sustainable Electricity Systems: Exploring the Dynamics of Energy Transitions. Physica-Verlag, p. 195.

Bedggood, R., Russell-Bennett, R., McAndrew, R., Glavas, C., Dulleck, U., 2023. Challenging the social-power paradigm: Moving beyond consumer empowerment to an energy ecosystem of shared value. Energy Policy 173, 113405. https://doi.org/10.1016/j.enpol.2022.113405.

Belgian Constitution, n.d.

Bijlage 2 bij BESL-2023-07 Toelichtende nota, 2023.

Billinton, R., Pan, Z., 2004. Historic performance-based distribution system risk assessment. IEEE Transactions on Power Delivery 19, 1759–1765. https://doi.org/10.1109/TPWRD.2004.832404.

Biresselioglu, M.E., Demir, M.H., Solak, B., Savas, Z.F., Kollmann, A., Kirchler, B., Ozcureci, B., 2024. Empowering energy citizenship: Exploring dimensions and drivers in citizen engagement during the energy transition. Energy Reports 11, 1894–1909. https://doi.org/10.1016/j.egyr.2024.01.040.

Bjarghov, S., Löschenbrand, M., Ibn Saif, A.U.N., Alonso Pedrero, R., Pfeiffer, C., Khadem, S.K., Rabelhofer, M., Revheim, F., Farahmand, H., 2021. Developments and Challenges in Local Electricity Markets: A Comprehensive Review. IEEE Access 9, 58910–58943. https://doi.org/10.1109/ACCESS.2021.3071830.

Blasch, J., Filippini, M., Kumar, N., 2019. Boundedly rational consumers, energy and investment literacy, and the display of information on household appliances. Resource and Energy Economics 56, 39–58. https://doi.org/10.1016/j.reseneeco.2017.06.001.

Boasson, E.L., 2021. Europeanization of renewables support, in: Boasson, E.L., Leiren, M.D., Wettestad, J. (Eds.), Edition Comparative Renewables Policy: Political, Organizational and European Fields. Routledge, p. 58.

Boasson, E.L., 2019. Constitutionalization and Entrepreneurship: Explaining Increased EU Steering of Renewables Support Schemes. Politics and Governance 7, 70–80.

Bohne, E., 2011. Conflicts between national regulatory cultures and EU energy regulations. Utilities Policy 19, 255–269. https://doi.org/10.1016/j.jup.2011.05.003.

Bollinger, B., Gillingham, K., 2012. Peer effects in the diffusion of solar photovoltaic panels. Marketing Science 31, 900–912. https://doi.org/10.1287/mksc.1120.0727.

Bolton, R., Foxon, T.J., 2011. Governing Infrastructure Networks for a Low Carbon Economy: Co-Evolution of Technologies and Institutions in UK Electricity Distribution Networks. Competition and Regulation in Network Industries 12, 2–26. https://doi.org/10.1177/178359171101200101.

Boon, F.P., Dieperink, C., 2014. Local civil society based renewable energy organisations in the Netherlands: Exploring the factors that stimulate their emergence and development. Energy Policy 69, 297–307. https://doi.org/10.1016/j.enpol.2014.01.046.

Borenstein, S., Bushnell, J.B., Wolak, F.A., 2002. Measuring Market Inefficiencies in California's Restructured Wholesale Electricity Market. American Economic Review 92, 1376–1405. https://doi.org/10.1257/000282802762024557.

Borne, O., Korte, K., Perez, Y., Petit, M., Purkus, A., 2018. Barriers to entry in frequency-regulation services markets: Review of the status quo and options for improvements. Renewable and Sustainable Energy Reviews 81, 605–614. https://doi.org/10.1016/j.rser.2017.08.052.

Bouffard, F., Kirschen, D.S., 2008. Centralised and distributed electricity systems. Energy Policy 36, 4504–4508. https://doi.org/10.1016/j.enpol.2008.09.060.

Bouzarovski, S., Petrova, S., 2015. A global perspective on domestic energy deprivation: Overcoming the energy poverty–fuel poverty binary. Energy Research & Social Science 10, 31–40. https://doi.org/10.1016/j.erss.2015.06.007.

Bovens, L., 2010. Nudges and Cultural Variance: a Note on Selinger and Whyte. Knowledge, Technology & Policy 23, 483–486. https://doi.org/10.1007/s12130-010-9128-2.

Božič, D., Pantoš, M., 2013. Assessment of investment efficiency in a power system under performance-based regulation. Energy 51, 330–338. https://doi.org/10.1016/j.energy.2012.11.038.

Bradley, P., Coke, A., Leach, M., 2016. Financial incentive approaches for reducing peak electricity demand, experience from pilot trials with a UK energy provider. Energy Policy 98, 108–120. https://doi.org/10.1016/j.enpol.2016.07.022.

Bradley, P., Leach, M., Torriti, J., 2013. A review of the costs and benefits of demand response for electricity in the UK. Energy Policy 52, 312–327. https://doi.org/10.1016/j.enpol.2012.09.039.

Bray, R., Woodman, B., 2018. Unlocking Local Energy Markets. University of Exeter, Energy Policy Group.

Bribosia, H., 2008. The Main Institutional Innovations of the Lisbon Treaty, in: Griller, S., Ziller, J. (Eds.), The Lisbon Treaty: EU Constitutionalism without a Constitutional Treaty? Springer, p. 78.

Brown, M.A., 2001. Market failures and barriers as a basis for clean energy policies. Energy Policy 29, 1197–1207. https://doi.org/10.1016/S0301-4215(01)00067-2.

Bruck, M., Sandborn, P., Goudarzi, N., 2018. A Levelized Cost of Energy (LCOE) model for wind farms that include Power Purchase Agreements (PPAs). Renewable Energy 122, 131–139. https://doi.org/10.1016/j.renene.2017.12.100.

Brunekreeft, G., 2013. On the Role of International Benchmarking of Electricity Transmission System Operators Facing Significant Investment Requirements. Competition and Regulation in Network Industries 14, 2–23. https://doi.org/10.1177/178359171301400101.

Brunekreeft, G., Buchmann, M., Kusznir, J., Meyer, R., 2021. Further developing incentives for digitalisation and innovation in incentive regulation for TSOs.

Bruninx, K., Pandžić, H., Le Cadre, H., Delarue, E., 2020. On the Interaction Between Aggregators, Electricity Markets and Residential Demand Response Providers. IEEE Transactions on Power Systems 35, 840–853. https://doi.org/10.1109/TPWRS.2019.2943670.

Buchmann, M., 2020. How decentralization drives a change of the institutional framework on the distribution grid level in the electricity sector – The case of local congestion markets. Energy Policy 145, 111725. https://doi.org/10.1016/j.enpol.2020.111725.

Buijze, A.W.G.J., 2011. Waarom het transparantiebeginsel maar niet transparant wil worden. Nederlands Tijdschrift voor Europees Recht 7, 240–248.

Buijze, A.W.G.J., Widdershoven, R.J.G.M., 2010. De Awb en EU-recht: het transparantiebeginsel, in: Ouden, W. den, Polak, J.E.M. (Eds.), Bestuursrecht Harmoniseren: 15 Jaar Awb. Boom Juridische uitgevers, pp. 589–607.

Bukar, A.L., Hamza, M.F., Ayub, S., Abobaker, A.K., Modu, B., Mohseni, S., Brent, A.C., Ogbonnaya, C., Mustapha, K., Idakwo, H.O., 2023. Peer-to-peer electricity trading: A systematic review on current developments and perspectives. Renewable Energy Focus 44, 317–333. https://doi.org/10.1016/j.ref.2023.01.008.

Burger, S.P., Jenkins, J.D., Batlle, C., Pérez-Arriaga, I.J., 2019. Restructuring Revisited Part 2: Coordination in Electricity Distribution Systems. The Energy Journal 40, 55–76. https://doi.org/10.5547/01956574.40.3.jjen.

Burke, M.J., Stephens, J.C., 2018. Political power and renewable energy futures: A critical review. Energy Research & Social Science 35, 78–93. https://doi.org/10.1016/j.erss.2017.10.018.

Burns, P., Riechmann, C., 2004. Regulatory instruments and investment behaviour. Utilities Policy 12, 211–219. https://doi.org/10.1016/j.jup.2004.07.002.

Busch, C., 2016. The future of pre-contractual information duties: From behavioural insights to big data, in: Twigg-Flesner, C. (Ed.), Research Handbook on EU Consumer and Contract Law. Cheltenham.

Butenko, A., 2016. User-Centered Innovation and Regulatory Framework: Energy Prosumers' Market Access in EU Regulation (No. TILEC Discussion Paper No. 2016-015).

C8/05 Data exchanges between Grid Operators and Market Parties in the context of energy transfer [C8/05 Gegevensuitwisselingen tussen Netbeheerders en Marktpartijen in het kader van de energieoverdracht], 2018.

C-121/15 Association nationale des opérateurs détaillants en énergie (ANODE) v Premier ministre and Others, 2016.

C-183/95, Affish BV v Rijksdienst voor de keuring van Vee en Vlees [1997] ECR I 4315, 1997.

C-265/08 Federutility and Others v Autorità per l'energia elettrica e il gas, 2010.

C-331/88, The Queen v Minister of Agriculture, Fisheries and Food and Secretary of State for Health, ex parte: Fedesa and others [1990] ECR I-4023, 1990.

C-426/93, Germany v Commission [1995] ECR I-3723, 1995.

Cabau, E., Kovács, K., 2021. National Regulatory Authorities, in: Jones, C., Kettlewell, W.-J. (Eds.), EU Energy Law Volume I: The Internal Energy Market. CLAEYS & CASTEELS, p. 265.

Cabau, E., Sandberg, L., 2021. Unbundling of Transmission System Operators, in: Jones, C., Kettlewell, W.-J. (Eds.), EU Energy Law Volume I: The Internal Energy Market. CLAEYS & CASTEELS, pp. 113–114.

Cagno, E., Worrell, E., Trianni, A., Pugliese, G., 2013. A novel approach for barriers to industrial energy efficiency. Renewable and Sustainable Energy Reviews 19, 290–308. https://doi.org/10.1016/j.rser.2012.11.007.

Calliess, C., Hey, C., 2013. Multilevel Energy Policy in the EU: Paving the Way for Renewables? Journal for European Environmental & Planning Law 10, 87–131. https://doi.org/10.1163/18760104-01002002.

Calver, P., Simcock, N., 2021a. Demand response and energy justice: A critical overview of ethical risks and opportunities within digital, decentralised, and decarbonised futures. Energy Policy 151, 112198. https://doi.org/10.1016/j.enpol.2021.112198.

Calver, P., Simcock, N., 2021b. Demand response and energy justice: A critical overview of ethical risks and opportunities within digital, decentralised, and decarbonised futures. Energy Policy 151, 112198. https://doi.org/10.1016/j.enpol.2021.112198.

Cambini, C., Croce, A., Fumagalli, E., 2014. Output-based incentive regulation in electricity distribution: Evidence from Italy. Energy Economics 45, 205–216. https://doi.org/10.1016/j.eneco.2014.07.002.

Candelise, C., Ruggieri, G., 2020. Status and Evolution of the Community Energy Sector in Italy. Energies 13. https://doi.org/10.3390/en13081888.

Capellán-Pérez, I., Campos-Celador, Á., Terés-Zubiaga, J., 2018. Renewable Energy Cooperatives as an instrument towards the energy transition in Spain. Energy Policy 123, 215–229. https://doi.org/10.1016/j.enpol.2018.08.064.

Capper, T., Gorbatcheva, A., Mustafa, M.A., Bahloul, M., Schwidtal, J.M., Chitchyan, R., Andoni, M., Robu, V., Montakhabi, M., Scott, I.J., Francis, C., Mbavarira, T., Espana, J.M., Kiesling, L., 2022. Peer-to-peer, community self-consumption, and transactive energy: A systematic literature review of local energy market models. Renewable and Sustainable Energy Reviews 162, 112403. https://doi.org/10.1016/j.rser.2022.112403.

Caramanis, M., Ntakou, E., Hogan, W.W., Chakrabortty, A., Schoene, J., 2016. Co-Optimization of Power and Reserves in Dynamic T&D Power Markets With Nondispatchable Renewable Generation and Distributed Energy Resources. Proceedings of the IEEE 104, 807–836. https://doi.org/10.1109/JPROC.2016.2520758.

Caramizaru, Elena, Uihlein, A., 2020. Energy communities: an overview of energy and social innovation (No. EUR 30083 EN). Publications Office of the European Union, Luxembourg.

Caramizaru, E, Uihlein, A., 2020. Energy communities: an overview of energy and social innovation (Scientific analysis or review, Policy assessment No. KJ-NA-30083-EN-N (online)). Publications Office of the European Union, Luxembourg (Luxembourg). https://doi.org/10.2760/180576 (online).

Cardell, J., Tabors, R., 1997. Operation and Control in a Competitive Market: Distributed Generation in a Restructured Industry. The Energy Journal 18, 111–136. https://doi.org/10.5547/ISSN0195-6574-EJ-Vol18-NoSI-6.

Cardoso, C.A., Torriti, J., Lorincz, M., 2020. Making demand side response happen: A review of barriers in commercial and public organisations. Energy Research & Social Science 64, 101443. https://doi.org/10.1016/j.erss.2020.101443.

Case 114/76 Bela-Mühle Bergmann [1977] ECR 1211, 1977.

Case 245/81 Edeka Zentrale [1982] ECR 2745, 1982.
Case C-75/97 Belgium v Commission [1999] ECR I-3671, 1999.
Case C-122/95 Germany v Council [1998] ECR I-973, 1998.
Case C-143/99 Adria-Wien Pipeline and Wietersdorfer & Peggauer Zementwerke [2001] ECR I-8365, 2001.
Case C-172/03 Heiser [2005] ECR I-1627, 2005.
Case C-308/01 GIL Insurance and Others [2004] ECR I-4777, 2004.
Case C-535/03 Unitymark and North Sea Fishermen's Organisation [2006] ECR I-2689, 2006.
Castagna, S., 2023. Comparing Comparability: A Study of EU, ISDS, and WTO Tax 'Like' Cases. Intertax 51, 487–505. https://doi.org/10.54648/TAXI2023045.
CEER, 2023. CEER Paper on Alternative Connection Agreement.
CEER, 2021a. Status Review of Renewable Support Schemes in Europe for 2018 and 2019.
CEER, 2021b. Long-Term Generation Investment Signals in a Market with High Shares of Renewables (No. C21- FP-49- 03).
CEER, 2020a. CEER Paper on DSO Procedures of Procurement of Flexibility.
CEER, 2020b. CEER Paper on Electricity Distribution Tariffs Supporting the Energy Transition (No. C19- DS-55- 04).
CEER, 2019a. Implementing Technology that Benefits Consumers in the Clean Energy for All Europeans Package Selected Case Studies.
CEER, 2019b. Consultation on Dynamic Regulation to Enable Digitalisation of the Energy System Conclusions Paper (No. C19- DSG- 09- 03).
CEER, 2015. The Future Role of DSOs.
CEER, 2013. Status Review on the Transposition of Unbundling Requirements for DSOs and Closed Distribution System Operators.
CEER, 2012. Fifth CEER benchmarking report on the quality of electricity supply.
Ceglia, F., Marrasso, E., Samanta, S., Sasso, M., 2022. Addressing Energy Poverty in the Energy Community: Assessment of Energy, Environmental, Economic, and Social Benefits for an Italian Residential Case Study. Sustainability 14. https://doi.org/10.3390/su142215077.
Chen, T., Vandendriessche, F., 2023a. Evolution of the EU legal framework for promoting RES-E: A market compatible paradigm shift? Utilities Policy 83, 101608. https://doi.org/10.1016/j.jup.2023.101608.
Chen, T., Vandendriessche, F., 2023b. Enabling independent flexibility service providers to participate in electricity markets: A legal analysis of the Belgium case. Utilities Policy 81, 101496. https://doi.org/10.1016/j.jup.2023.101496.
Clark W. Gellings, John H. Chamberlin, 1993. Demand-side management: concepts and methods, second. ed. Fairmont Press.
Cohen, J., Moeltner, K., Reichl, J., Schmidthaler, M., 2016. An Empirical Analysis of Local Opposition to New Transmission Lines Across the EU-27. The Energy Journal 37, 59–82. https://doi.org/10.5547/01956574.37.3.jcoh.
Colmenar-Santos, A., Reino-Rio, C., Borge-Diez, D., Collado-Fernández, E., 2016. Distributed generation: A review of factors that can contribute most to achieve a scenario of DG units embedded in the new distribution networks. Renewable and Sustainable Energy Reviews 59, 1130–1148. https://doi.org/10.1016/j.rser.2016.01.023.

Commission Decision (EU) 2019/56 of 28 May 2018 on aid scheme SA.34045 (2013/c) (ex 2012/NN) implemented by Germany for baseload consumers under Paragraph 19 StromNEV, 2018.

Commission of the European Communities, 2001. European Governance: A White Paper.

Commission of the European Communities, 1985. Completing the Internal Market: White Paper from the Commission to the European Council.

Commission Regulation (EU) 2016/1388 of 17 August 2016 establishing a Network Code on Demand Connection, 2016.

Commission Regulation (EU) 2017/1485 of 2 August 2017 establishing a guideline on electricity transmission system operation, 2017.

Commission Regulation (EU) 2017/2195 of 23 November 2017 establishing a guideline on electricity balancing, 2017.

Connolly, D., Lund, H., Mathiesen, B.V., 2016. Smart Energy Europe: The technical and economic impact of one potential 100% renewable energy scenario for the European Union. Renewable and Sustainable Energy Reviews 60, 1634–1653. https://doi.org/10.1016/j.rser.2016.02.025.

Consolidated version of the Treaty on European Union [2016] OJ C 202/13, 2016.

Consolidated Version of the Treaty on the Functioning of the European Union [2012] OJ C 326/47, 2012.

Consolidated Versions of the Treaty Establishing the European Community (2002/C 325/01), 2002.

Convention of 27 September 1968 on Jurisdiction and the Enforcement of Judgments in Civil and Commercial Matters, 1968.

Cooremans, C., 2012. Investment in energy efficiency: do the characteristics of investments matter? Energy Efficiency 5, 497–518. https://doi.org/10.1007/s12053-012-9154-x.

Cooremans, C., 2011. Make it strategic! Financial investment logic is not enough. Energy Efficiency 4, 473–492. https://doi.org/10.1007/s12053-011-9125-7.

Corr, P., Plagnol, A., 2019. Behavioral economics: The basics, 1st ed. Routledge.

Correlje, A.F., Vries, L.J.D., 2008. Hybrid Electricity Markets: The Problem of Explaining Different Patterns of Restructuring, in: Sioshani, F. (Ed.), Competitive Electricity Markets: Design Implementation Performance. Elsevier, p. 65.

Cossent, R., Gómez, T., Frías, P., 2009. Towards a future with large penetration of distributed generation: Is the current regulation of electricity distribution ready? Regulatory recommendations under a European perspective. Energy Policy 37, 1145–1155. https://doi.org/10.1016/j.enpol.2008.11.011.

Council Directive 93/13/EEC of 5 April 1993 on unfair terms in consumer contracts, 1993.

Council Regulation (EC) No 44/2001 of 22 December 2000 on jurisdiction and the recognition and enforcement of judgments in civil and commercial matters, 2001.

Council Regulation (EU) 2022/1854 of 6 October 2022 on an emergency intervention to address high energy prices, 2022.

Craig, P., 2018. EU Administrative Law. Oxford University Press.

Creamer, E., Eadson, W., van Veelen, B., Pinker, A., Tingey, M., Braunholtz-Speight, T., Markantoni, M., Foden, M., Lacey-Barnacle, M., 2018. Community energy:

Entanglements of community, state, and private sector. Geography Compass 12, e12378. https://doi.org/10.1111/gec3.12378.
CREG, 2024. Studie (F)2782 11 april 2024 Power Purchase Agreements: Stand van zaken en evaluatie.
CREG, 2022a. CREG Decision (Z)1109/11 establishing the tariff methodology for the electricity transmission network and electricity networks with a transmission function for the regulatory period 2024–2027 Article 12, §§2, 5, 8 and 9 of the Act of 29 April 1999 on the organisation of the electricity market [Besluit (Z)1109/11 tot vaststelling van de tariefmethodologie voor het elektriciteitstransmissienet en voor de elektriciteitsnetten met een transmissiefunctie voor de regulatoire periode 2024–2027 Artikel 12, §§2, 5, 8 en 9 van de wet van 29 april 1999 betreffende de organisatie van de elektriciteitsmarkt].
CREG, 2022b. Decision (B)2409 laying down the code of conduct on the conditions for connection and access to the transmission system and the methods for calculating or fixing the conditions relating to the provision of ancillary services and access to cross-border infrastructure, including the procedures for allocating capacity and congestion management, and approving in that context Elia's proposal for connection procedures to the transmission system [Beslissing (B)2409 tot vaststelling van de gedragscode houdende de voorwaarden voor de aansluiting op en de toegang tot het transmissienet en houdende de methoden voor het berekenen of vastleggen van de voorwaarden inzake de verstrekking van ondersteunende diensten en de toegang tot de grensoverschrijdende infrastructuur, inclusief de procedures voor de toewijzing van capaciteit en congestiebeheer, en tot goedkeuring in dat kader van het voorstel van Elia van aansluitingsprocedures op het transmissienet].
CREG, 2021a. Annual Report 2020.
CREG, 2021b. Decision (B) 2195 on the proposal of the Elia Transmission Belgium SA/NV concerning the rules organizing the transfer of energy Article 19bis, §2 of the Law of 29 April 1999 on the organisation of the electricity market [Beslissing (B) 2195 over het voorstel van de nv Elia Transmission Belgium betreffende de regels die de energieoverdracht organiseren Artikel 19bis, §2 van de wet van 29 april 1999 betreffende de organisatie van de elektriciteitsmarkt].
CREG Decision (B) 1677/3 implementing Article 19bis, §§3 to 5 of the Law of 29 April 1999 on the organisation of the electricity market to enable the ToE [Beslissing (B) 1677/3 houdende uitvoering van artikel 19bis, §§3 tot 5 van de wet van 29 april 1999 betreffende de organisatie van de elektriciteitsmarkt, om de energieoverdracht mogelijk te maken], 2020.
Crossley, P., 2017. The Role of Renewable Energy Law and Policy in Meeting the EU's Energy Security (No. Legal Studies Research Paper No. 17/83).
CRU, 2023a. Proximity Requirements for Renewable Energy Communities Consultation paper.
CRU, 2023b. Proximity Requirements for Renewable Energy Communities Decision Paper.
CRU, 2021a. 2021 Roadmap for the Clean Energy Package's Electricity and Renewables Directives.
CRU, 2021b. Conclusions and Next Steps on Energy Community and Active Consumer Development.

CRU, 2021c. Remuneration of Renewables Self-consumers for exported electricity: Interim Clean Export Guarantee.

CRU, 2021d. Conclusions from Consultation CRU/21028 on Energy Communities and Active Consumers.

Curtin, J., McInerney, C., Gallachóir, B.Ó., Salm, S., 2019. Energizing local communities – What motivates Irish citizens to invest in distributed renewables? Energy Research & Social Science 48, 177–188. https://doi.org/10.1016/j.erss.2018.08.020.

Curtis, M., 2017. Demand side response aggregators: How they decide customer suitability, in: 14th International Conference on the European Energy Market (EEM). pp. 1–6. https://doi.org/10.1109/EEM.2017.7981909.

CWaPE, Brugel, VREG, 2024. Joint note with comments from regional regulators regarding document release 2 [Gezamenlijke nota met commentaar van de regionale regulatoren met betrekking tot document release 2].

Dagoumas, A.S., Koltsaklis, N.E., 2017. Price Signal of Tradable Guarantees of Origin for Hedging Risk of Renewable Energy Sources Investments. International Journal of Energy Economics and Policy 7, 59.

Darby, S.J., 2020. Demand response and smart technology in theory and practice: Customer experiences and system actors. Energy Policy 143, 111573. https://doi.org/10.1016/j.enpol.2020.111573.

de Bakker, M., Lagendijk, A., Wiering, M., 2020. Cooperatives, incumbency, or market hybridity: New alliances in the Dutch energy provision. Energy Research & Social Science 61, 101345. https://doi.org/10.1016/j.erss.2019.101345.

de Joode, J., Jansen, J.C., van der Welle, A.J., Scheepers, M.J.J., 2009. Increasing penetration of renewable and distributed electricity generation and the need for different network regulation. Energy Policy 37, 2907–2915. https://doi.org/10.1016/j.enpol.2009.03.014.

De Vos, M., 2020. The European Court of Justice and the march towards substantive equality in European Union anti-discrimination law. International Journal of Discrimination and the Law 20, 62–87. https://doi.org/10.1177/1358229120927947.

Decision of the Flemish Government containing general provisions on energy policy [Besluit van de Vlaamse Regering houdende algemene bepalingen over het energiebeleid], 2010.

Decision of the Flemish Utility Regulator on the 'Fall-back flex' [Beslissing van Vlaamse Nutsregulator met betrekking tot een productfiche "Fall-Back Flex" bij de specificaties voor de aankoop van flexibiliteitsdiensten, voor het beheer van lokale congestie of redispatching, voorgelegd door de elektriciteitsdistributienetbeheerders, zoals vermeld in artikel 4.1.17/4, §1 Energiedecreet en artikel 2.3.22, §2 Technisch Reglement voor de Distributie van Elektriciteit in het Vlaamse Gewest], BESL-2025-06, 2025.

Decision of the VREG of 3/12/2019 regarding the determination of the amount and method of collection of the fee for the use of the VREG platform for transactions involving guarantees of origin [Beslissing van de VREG van 3/12/2019 met betrekking tot het vaststellen van bedrag en wijze van inning van de retributie voor het gebruik van het VREG-platform voor transacties betreffende garanties van oorsprong], 2019.

Decision of the VREG of 13/08/2019 regarding the refusal of Swedish Guarantees of Origin [Beslissing van de VREG van 13/08/2019 met betrekking tot de weigering van Zweedse Garanties van Oorsprong], 2019.

Decision of the VREG of 26 April 2011 regarding the detailed rules for the use of guarantees of origin amended by decision of the VREG on 25 October 2011, on 19 February 2014, on 13 April 2016, and on October 3, 2017 [Beslissing van de Vlaamse Regulator van de Elektriciteits- en Gasmarkt van 26 april 2011 met betrekking tot de nadere regels bij het gebruik van garanties van oorsprong gewijzigd bij beslissing van de VREG op 25 oktober 2011, op 19 februari 2014, op 13 april 2016, en op 3 oktober 2017], 2011.

Decision of the VREG on the rules for the purchase of non-frequency-related ancillary services and grid losses submitted by the electricity distribution system operators, as referred to in Article 4.1.17/6, §1 Energy Decree and Article 2.3.23 TRDE in the Flemish Region [Beslissing van de VREG met betrekking tot de regels voor de aankoop van de niet-frequentiegerelateerde ondersteunende diensten en netverliezen, voorgelegd door de elektriciteitsdistributienetbeheerders, zoals vermeld in artikel 4.1.17/6, §1 Energiedecreet en artikel 2.3.23 Technisch Reglement voor de Distributie van Elektriciteit in het Vlaamse Gewest], 2022.

Decision of the VREG on the rules for the purchase of non-frequency-related ancillary services and grid losses submitted by the electricity distribution system operators, as referred to in Article 4.1.17/6, §1 of the Energy Decree and Article 2.3.23 Technical Regulations for the Distribution of Electricity in the Flemish Region [Beslissing van de VREG met betrekking tot de regels voor de aankoop van de niet-frequentiegerelateerde ondersteunende diensten en netverliezen, voorgelegd door de elektriciteitsdistributienetbeheerders, zoals vermeld in artikel 4.1.17/6, §1 van het Energiedecreet en artikel 2.3.23 Technisch Reglement voor de Distributie van Elektriciteit in het Vlaamse Gewest], 2023.

Decision of the VREG regarding the approval of the FSP-DNB contract, the rules for the market processes for flexibility ("Market Guide Flexibility"), the technical regulation C8/01 and the technical regulation C8/06, as submitted by Synergrid on behalf and on behalf of the Flemish distribution system operators [Beslissing van de VREG met betrekking tot de goedkeuring van het contract FSP-DNB, de regels voor de marktprocessen voor flexibiliteit ("Marktgids flexibiliteit"), het technisch voorschrift C8/01 en het technisch voorschrift C8/06, zoals voorgelegd door Synergrid in naam en voor rekening van de Vlaamse distributienetbeheerders], 2024.

Decision of the VREG regarding the approval of the proposal of the electricity distribution system operators regarding the protocol on energy sharing, peer-to-peer trading of green electricity and sale of green electricity in apartment buildings or multifunctional buildings (protocol version 3.1) [Beslissing van de VREG met betrekking tot de goedkeuring van het voorstel van de elektriciteitsdistributienetbeheerders betreffende het protocol inzake energiedelen, peer-to-peerhandel van groene stroom en verkoop van groene stroom in appartementsgebouwen of multifunctionele gebouwen (protocolversie 3.1)], 2023.

Decision of the VREG regarding the approval of the proposal of the electricity distribution system operators regarding the protocol on energy sharing, peer-to-peer trading of green power and sale of green power in apartment buildings or multifunctional buildings (protocol version 3.2), and the deviation from the consultation obligation from art. 4.3.64, §7 and art. 4.3.66, §6 in conjunction with art. 1.2.4 TRDE [Beslissing van de VREG met betrekking tot de goedkeuring van het voorstel van de elektriciteitsdistributienetbeheerders betreffende het protocol inzake energiedelen, peer-to-peerhandel van groene stroom en verkoop van groene stroom in appartementsgebouwen of multifunctionele gebouwen (protocolversie 3.2), en de afwijking van de consultatieplicht uit art. 4.3.64, §7 en art. 4.3.66, §6 juncto art. 1.2.4 TRDE], 2024.

Decision of the VREG regarding the specifications for the purchase of flexibility services, for the management of local congestion or redispatching, submitted by the electricity distribution system operators, as mentioned in Article 4.1.17/4, §1 Energy Decree and Article 2.3.22, §2 Technical Regulation for the Distribution of Electricity in the Flemish Region, 2024.

Decision of the VREG regarding the specifications for the purchase of flexibility services, for the management of local congestion or redispatching, submitted by the electricity distribution system operators, as mentioned in Article 4.1.17/4, §1 Energy Decree and Article 2.3.22 TRDE in the Flemish Region [Beslissing van de VREG met betrekking tot de specificaties voor de aankoop van flexibiliteitsdiensten, voor het beheer van lokale congestie of redispatching, voorgelegd door de elektriciteitsdistributienetbeheerders, zoals vermeld in artikel 4.1.17/4, §1 Energiedecreet en artikel 2.3.22 TRDE in het Vlaamse Gewest], 2022.

Decree of 8 May 2009 laying down general provisions on energy policy [8 MEI 2009. - Decreet houdende algemene bepalingen betreffende het energiebeleid], 2009.

DellaValle, N., 2019. People's decisions matter: understanding and addressing energy poverty with behavioral economics. Energy and Buildings 204, 109515. https://doi.org/10.1016/j.enbuild.2019.109515.

Delta-EE, smartEn, 2020. EU Market Monitor for Demand side Flexibility 2020.

Delta-EE, smartEn, 2019. EU Market Monitor for Demand side Flexibility 2019.

Department of the Environment of Ireland, 2022. Micro-generation Support Scheme (MSS) Final Scheme Design.

Desmet, J., Claeys, R., Cleenwerck, R., Greve, G.D., Vanhove, T., 2021. Onderzoek naar de impact van het capaciteitstarief (Onderzoek i.o.v. het Vlaams Energie- en Klimaatagentschap). Universiteit Gent.

Devine-Wright, P., 2013. Explaining "NIMBY" Objections to a Power Line: The Role of Personal, Place Attachment and Project-Related Factors. Environment and Behavior 45, 761–781. https://doi.org/10.1177/0013916512440435.

D'hulst, R., Labeeuw, W., Beusen, B., Claessens, S., Deconinck, G., Vanthournout, K., 2015. Demand response flexibility and flexibility potential of residential smart appliances: Experiences from large pilot test in Belgium. Applied Energy 155, 79–90. https://doi.org/10.1016/j.apenergy.2015.05.101.

Di Silvestre, M.L., Ippolito, M.G., Sanseverino, E.R., Sciumè, G., Vasile, A., 2021. Energy self-consumers and renewable energy communities in Italy: New actors of the electric power systems. Renewable and Sustainable Energy Reviews 151, 111565. https://doi.org/10.1016/j.rser.2021.111565.

Didden, M.H., D'haeseleer, W.D., 2003. Demand Side Management in a competitive European market: Who should be responsible for its implementation? Energy Policy 31, 1307–1314. https://doi.org/10.1016/S0301-4215(02)00189-1.

Diestelmeier, L., 2021a. Regulating residential prosumers, in: Roggenkamp, M.M., Graaf, K.J.D., Fleming, R.C. (Eds.), Energy Law, Climate Change and the Environment. Edward Elgar.

Diestelmeier, L., 2021b. Citizen Energy Communities as a Vehicle for a Just Energy Transition in the EU – Challenges for the Transposition. Oil, Gas & Energy Law Intelligence 1, 1–12.

Diestelmeier, L., 2021c. The Role of Energy Communities in Facilitating Sustainable Energy Democracy: Legal Challenges, in: Fleming, R., Huhta, K., Reins, L. (Eds.), Sustainable Energy Democracy and the Law. Brill.

Diestelmeier, L., 2019a. Changing power: Shifting the role of electricity consumers with blockchain technology – Policy implications for EU electricity law. Energy Policy 128, 189–196. https://doi.org/10.1016/j.enpol.2018.12.065.

Diestelmeier, L., 2019b. Unlocking Flexibility with Law (PhD Dissertation). University of Groningen.

Diestelmeier, L., Hanak, M., Krishnan, D.P., 2023. Developing an empirical legal methodology for exploring the concept of "community benefits" in the context of "energy communities" under EU law. Presented at the 3rd International Conference: New Pathways for a Just and Inclusive Energy Transition, Groningen.

Directive 96/92/EC of the European Parliament and of the Council of 19 December 1996 concerning common rules for the internal market in electricity, 1996.

Directive 2000/31/EC of the European Parliament and of the Council of 8 June 2000 on certain legal aspects of information society services, in particular electronic commerce, in the Internal Market, 2000.

Directive 2001/77/EC of the European Parliament and of the Council of 27 September 2001 on the promotion of electricity produced from renewable energy sources in the internal electricity Market [2001] OJ L 283/33, 2001.

Directive 2003/54/EC of the European Parliament and of the Council of 26 June 2003 concerning common rules for the internal market in electricity and repealing Directive 96/92/EC, 2003.

Directive 2009/28/EC of the European Parliament and of the Council of 23 April 2009 on the promotion of the use of energy from renewable sources and amending and subsequently repealing Directives 2001/77/EC and 2003/30/EC [2009] OJ L 140/16, 2009.

Directive 2009/72/EC of the European Parliament and of the Council of 13 July 2009 concerning common rules for the internal market in electricity and repealing Directive 2003/54/EC, 2009.

Directive 2011/83/EU of the European Parliament and of the Councile of 25 October 2011 on consumer rights, amending Council Directive 93/13/EEC and Directive 1999/44/EC of the European Parliament and of the Council and repealing Council Directive 85/577/EEC and Directive 97/7/EC of the European Parliament and of the Council, 2011.

Directive 2012/27/EU of the European Parliament and of the Council of 25 October 2012 on energy efficiency, amending Directives 2009/125/EC and 2010/30/EU and repealing Directives 2004/8/EC and 2006/32/EC, 2012.

Directive (EU) 2015/1535 of the European Parliament and the Council of 9 September 2015 laying down a procedure for the provision of information in the field of technical regulations and of rules on Information Society services, 2015.

Directive (EU) 2018/2001 of the European Parliament and of the Council of 11 December 2018 on the promotion of the use of energy from renewable sources, 2018.

Directive (EU) 2019/944 of the European Parliament and of the Council of 5 June 2019 on common rules for the internal market for electricity and amending Directive 2012/27/EU, 2019.

Directive (EU) 2023/2413 of the European Parliament and of the Council of 18 October 2023 amending Directive (EU) 2018/2001, Regulation (EU) 2018/1999 and Directive 98/70/EC as regards the promotion of energy from renewable sources, and repealing Council Directive (EU) 2015/652, 2023.

Directive (EU) 2024/1711 of the European Parliament and of the Council of 13 June 2024 amending Directives (EU) 2018/2001 and (EU) 2019/944 as regards improving the Union's electricity market design, 2024.

Doračić, B., Knoefel, J., Naber, N., 2020. Prosumers for the Energy Union: mainstreaming active participation of citizens in the energy transition – Review and characterisation of collective renewable energy prosumer initiatives, (Deliverable N°2.1). Horizon 2020 (H2020-LCE-2017) Grant Agreement N°764056.

Dorian Frieden, Josh Roberts, Andrej Gubina, 2019. Collective self-consumption and energy communities: Overview of emerging regulatory approaches in Europe (Working paper).

Drexler, A., Fischer, G., Schoar, A., 2014. Keeping It Simple: Financial Literacy and Rules of Thumb. American Economic Journal: Applied Economics 6, 1–31. https://doi.org/10.1257/app.6.2.1.

Dudjak, V., Neves, D., Alskaif, T., Khadem, S., Pena-Bello, A., Saggese, P., Bowler, B., Andoni, M., Bertolini, M., Zhou, Y., Lormeteau, B., Mustafa, M.A., Wang, Y., Francis, C., Zobiri, F., Parra, D., Papaemmanouil, A., 2021. Impact of local energy markets integration in power systems layer: A comprehensive review. Applied Energy 301, 117434. https://doi.org/10.1016/j.apenergy.2021.117434.

Dudka, A., Moratal, N., Bauwens, T., 2023. A typology of community-based energy citizenship: An analysis of the ownership structure and institutional logics of 164 energy communities in France. Energy Policy 178, 113588. https://doi.org/10.1016/j.enpol.2023.113588.

Dütschke, E., Paetz, A.-G., 2013. Dynamic electricity pricing – Which programs do consumers prefer? Energy Policy 59, 226–234. https://doi.org/10.1016/j.enpol.2013.03.025.

EC, 2022a. Communication from the Commission to the European Parliament, the European Council, the Council, the European Economic and Social Committee and the Committee of the Regions, Security of supply and affordable energy prices: Options for immediate measures and preparing for next winter, COM(2022) 138 final.

EC, 2022b. Communication from the Commission on Temporary Crisis Framework for State Aid measures to support the economy following the aggression against Ukraine by Russia, COM(2022)1890 final.

EC, 2022c. Annex to the Communication from the Commission to the European Parliament, the European Council, the Council, the European Economic and Social Committee and the Committee of the Regions, Security of supply and affordable energy prices: Options for immediate measures and preparing for next winter.
EC, 2022d. Commission Staff Working Document Guidance to Member States on good practices to speed up permit granting procedures for renewable energy projects and on facilitating Power Purchase Agreements Accompanying the document Commission Recommendation on speeding up permit-granting procedures for renewable energy projects and facilitating Power Purchase Agreements.
EC, 2021. Communication from the Commission to the European Parliament, the European Council, the Council, the European Economic and Social Committee and the Committee of the Regions, Tackling rising energy prices: a toolbox for action and support, COM(2021) 660 final.
EC, 2016a. Commission Staff Working Document Impact Assessment Accompanying the document Proposal for a Directive of the European Parliament and of the Council on common rules for the internal market in electricity (recast) Proposal for a Regulation of the European Parliament and of the Council on the electricity market (recast) Proposal for a Regulation of the European Parliament and of the Council establishing a European Union Agency for the Cooperation of Energy Regulators (recast) Proposal for a Regulation of the European Parliament and of the Council on risk preparedness in the electricity sector, SWD/2016/0410 final.
EC, 2016b. Proposal for a Directive of the European Parliament and of the Council on common rules for the internal market in electricity.
EC, 2016c. Communication from the Commission to the European Parliament, the Council, the European Economic and Social Committee, the Committee of the Regions and the European Investment Bank: Clean Energy For All Europeans.
EC, 2016d. Communication from the Commission to the European Parliament, the Council, the European Economic and Social Committee, the Committee of the Regions and the European Investment Bank: Clean Energy For All Europeans, COM(2016) 860 final.
EC, 2016e. Annex Action to boost the clean energy transition to the COM(2016) 860 final.
EC, 2016f. User guide to the SME Definition.
EC, 2015a. Delivering a new deal for energy consumers. COM(2015) 339 final.
EC, 2015b. Energy Union Package-Communication from the Commission to the European Parliament, the Council, the European Economic and Social Committee, the Committee of the Regions and the European Investment Bank: A Framework Strategy for a Resilient Energy Union with a Forward-Looking Climate Change Policy.
EC, 2014a. COMMUNICATION FROM THE COMMISSION Guidelines on State aid for environmental protection and energy 2014–2020.
EC, 2014b. Commission staff working document, Energy Prices and Costs Report.
EC, 2012a. A European consumer agenda – Boosting confidence and growth. COM(2012) 225 final.
EC, 2012b. Commission Recommendation of 9 March 2012 on preparations for the roll-out of smart metering systems.
EC, 2001. Community guidelines on State aid for environmental protection (2001/C 37/03).

Edens, M.G., Lavrijssen, S.A.C.M., 2019. Balancing public values during the energy transition – How can German and Dutch DSOs safeguard sustainability? Energy Policy 128, 57–65. https://doi.org/10.1016/j.enpol.2018.12.048.

Ehricke, U., Hackländer, D., Bausch, A., Schwenker, B., 2009. European Energy Policy on the Basis of the New Provisions in the Treaty of Lisbon, in: Handbook Utility Management. Springer, p. 742.

Eid, C., Bollinger, L.A., Koirala, B., Scholten, D., Facchinetti, E., Lilliestam, J., Hakvoort, R., 2016. Market integration of local energy systems: Is local energy management compatible with European regulation for retail competition? Energy 114, 913–922. https://doi.org/10.1016/j.energy.2016.08.072.

Eid, C., Reneses Guillén, J., Frías Marín, P., Hakvoort, R., 2014. The economic effect of electricity net-metering with solar PV: Consequences for network cost recovery, cross subsidies and policy objectives. Energy Policy 75, 244–254. https://doi.org/10.1016/j.enpol.2014.09.011.

El Gohary, F., Nyström, S., Reitsma, L., Bartusch, C., 2021. Identifying Challenges in Engaging Users to Increase Self-Consumption of Electricity in Microgrids. Energies 14. https://doi.org/10.3390/en14051257.

Electricity and gas market report 2022 [Marktrapport elektriciteit en gas 2022] (No. RAPP-2023-13), 2023.

Electricity code of conduct [Gedragscode Elektriciteit], 2022.

Electricity Industry and Organization Act [Elektrizitaetswirtschafts- und Organisationsgesetz], 2010.

Element Energy, 2012. Demand Side Response in the Non-Domestic sector' Final report For Ofgem.

Emami, H., Sadri, J.A., 2012. Congestion management of transmission lines in the market environment. International Research Journal of Applied and Basic Sciences 3, 2572.

EnergyVille, 2023. Cost-benefit analysis regarding the contributions to the relief of the Flemish electricity distribution network of renewable energy communities, citizen energy communities, persons involved in the sale of green electricity in accordance with Article 7.2.3 of the Energy Decree or the active consumers in a building, and analysis of the resulting relevant compensations [Kosten-batenanalyse betreffende de bijdragen aan de ontlasting van het Vlaamse elektriciteitsdistributienet van hernieuwbareenergiegemeenschappen, energiegemeenschappen van burgers, betrokken personen van de verkoop van groene stroom conform artikel 7.2.3 Energiedecreet of de actieve afnemers in een gebouw, en analyse van de resulterende relevante vergoedingen].

Espinosa Apráez, B., 2023. The challenges of sharing data at the intersection of EU data protection and electricity market legislation: lessons from the Netherlands. Journal of Energy & Natural Resources Law 41, 403–429. https://doi.org/10.1080/02646811.2022.2143673.

Eurelectric, 2013. Active Distribution System Management: a Key Tool for the Smooth Integration of Distributed Generation.

European Data Protection Board, 2019. Guidelines 1/2019 on Codes of Conduct and Monitoring Bodies under Regulation 2016/679 (EDPB 2019) Version 2.0 9.

European Smart Grids Task Force Expert Group 3, 2019. Final Report: Demand Side Flexibility Perceived barriers and proposed recommendations.
EUROPEAN UNION (RENEWABLE ENERGY) REGULATIONS 2022, 2022.
Faia, R., Lezama, F., Corchado, J.M., 2021. Local electricity markets – practical implementations, in: Pinto, T., Vale, Z., Widergren, S. (Eds.), Local Electricity Market. Elsevier, p. 127.
Farhangi, H., 2010. The path of the smart grid. IEEE Power and Energy Magazine 8, 18–28. https://doi.org/10.1109/MPE.2009.934876.
Farrokhseresht, M., Slootweg, H., Gibescu, M., 2020. Strategic bidding of distributed energy resources in coupled local and central markets. Sustainable Energy, Grids and Networks 24, 100390. https://doi.org/10.1016/j.segan.2020.100390.
Faruqui, A., Hajos, A., Hledik, R.M., Newell, S.A., 2010. Fostering economic demand response in the Midwest ISO. Energy 35, 1544–1552. https://doi.org/10.1016/j.energy.2009.09.014.
Faruqui, A., Palmer, J., 2011. Dynamic pricing and its discontents. Regulation 34, 16.
Fawcett, T., Rosenow, J., Bertoldi, P., 2019. Energy efficiency obligation schemes: their future in the EU. Energy Efficiency 12, 57–71. https://doi.org/10.1007/s12053-018-9657-1.
Fehr, E., Rangel, A., 2011. Neuroeconomic Foundations of Economic Choice--Recent Advances. Journal of Economic Perspectives 25, 3–30. https://doi.org/10.1257/jep.25.4.3.
Feldman, Y., Perez, O., 2009. How Law Changes the Environmental Mind: An Experimental Study of the Effect of Legal Norms on Moral Perceptions and Civic Enforcement. Journal of Law and Society 36, 501–535. https://doi.org/10.1111/j.1467-6478.2009.00481.x.
Fell, M., Nicolson, M., Huebner, G., Shipworth, D., 2015. Is it time? Consumers and time of use tariffs. UCL Energy Institute. https://doi.org/10.13140/2.1.2466.1288.
FERC, n.d. Electric Power Markets [WWW Document]. URL https://www.ferc.gov/electric-power-markets (accessed 8.2.24).
Fernández, J.M.R., Payán, M.B., Santos, J.M.R., García, Á.L.T., 2016. Renewable generation versus demand-side management. A comparison for the Spanish market. Energy Policy 96, 458–470. https://doi.org/10.1016/j.enpol.2016.06.014.
Fernandez, R., 2021. Community Renewable Energy Projects: The Future of the Sustainable Energy Transition? The International Spectator 56, 87–104. https://doi.org/10.1080/03932729.2021.1959755.
Fina, B., Fechner, H., 2021. Transposition of European Guidelines for Energy Communities into Austrian Law: A Comparison and Discussion of Issues and Positive Aspects. Energies 14. https://doi.org/10.3390/en14133922.
Fina, B., Monsberger, C., 2022. Legislation for renewable energy communities and citizen energy communities in Austria: changes from the legislative draft to the finally enacted law. The Journal of World Energy Law & Business 15, 237–244. https://doi.org/10.1093/jwelb/jwac008.
Fleiß, E., Hatzl, S., Seebauer, S., Posch, A., 2017. Money, not morale: The impact of desires and beliefs on private investment in photovoltaic citizen participation initiatives. Journal of Cleaner Production 141, 920–927. https://doi.org/10.1016/j.jclepro.2016.09.123.
Flexibility Market Processes 2.0 [MARKTGIDS FLEXIBILITEIT 2.0], 2023.

Fluvius, 2023a. Wil je een groenestroomteller laten plaatsen? [WWW Document]. URL https://www.fluvius.be/nl/groene-energie/grote-productie-installatie/plaatsen-groenestroomteller?app-refresh=1733851569772> accessed 10 December 2024 (accessed 12.10.24).

Fluvius, 2023b. Specifications for the market-based purchase of flexibility services for local congestion management [Specificaties voor de marktgebaseerde aankoop van flexibiliteitsdiensten voor het beheer van lokale congestie].

Forouli, A., Bakirtzis, E.A., Papazoglou, G., Oureilidis, K., Gkountis, V., Candido, L., Ferrer, E.D., Biskas, P., 2021. Assessment of Demand Side Flexibility in European Electricity Markets: A Country Level Review. Energies 14. https://doi.org/10.3390/en14082324.

Fraser, R., 1994. Price, quality and regulation: An analysis of price capping and the reliability of electricity supply. Energy Economics 16, 175–183. https://doi.org/10.1016/0140-9883(94)90031-0.

Freixas, X., Guesnerie, R., Tirole, J., 1985. Planning under Incomplete Information and the Ratchet Effect. The Review of Economic Studies 52, 173–191. https://doi.org/10.2307/2297615.

Frías, P., Gómez, T., Cossent, R., Rivier, J., 2009. Improvements in current European network regulation to facilitate the integration of distributed generation. International Journal of Electrical Power & Energy Systems 31, 445–451. https://doi.org/10.1016/j.ijepes.2009.03.001.

Friedl, C., Reichl, J., 2016. Realizing energy infrastructure projects – A qualitative empirical analysis of local practices to address social acceptance. Energy Policy 89, 184–193. https://doi.org/10.1016/j.enpol.2015.11.027.

Friis, F., Haunstrup Christensen, T., 2016. The challenge of time shifting energy demand practices: Insights from Denmark. Energy Research & Social Science 19, 124–133. https://doi.org/10.1016/j.erss.2016.05.017.

Fuller, L.L., 1964. The Morality of Law. Yale University Press.

Funcke, S., Bauknecht, D., 2016. Typology of centralised and decentralised visions for electricity infrastructure. Utilities Policy 40, 67–74. https://doi.org/10.1016/j.jup.2016.03.005.

Gabrielli, P., Aboutalebi, R., Sansavini, G., 2022. Mitigating financial risk of corporate power purchase agreements via portfolio optimization. Energy Economics 109, 105980. https://doi.org/10.1016/j.eneco.2022.105980.

Gajdzik, B., Jaciow, M., Wolniak, R., Wolny, R., Grebski, W.W., 2023. Energy Behaviors of Prosumers in Example of Polish Households. Energies 16. https://doi.org/10.3390/en16073186.

Galligan, D.J., 1996. Due Process and Fair Procedures: A Study of Administrative Procedures. Clarendon Press.

Gamel, J., Menrad, K., Decker, T., 2016. Is it really all about the return on investment? Exploring private wind energy investors' preferences. Energy Research & Social Science 14, 22–32. https://doi.org/10.1016/j.erss.2016.01.004.

Gantioler, S., Balest, J., Tomasi, S., Voltolini, F., DellaValle, N., 2023. Transformative disruptiveness or transition? Revealing digitalization and deep decarbonization pathways in the Italian smart electricity meter roll-out. Energy Research & Social Science 106, 103309. https://doi.org/10.1016/j.erss.2023.103309.

Gedragscode voor de bescherming van de zelfstandigen en de kmo's in de elektriciteits- en gasmarkt, 2023.

Geels, F.W., 2010. Ontologies, socio-technical transitions (to sustainability), and the multi-level perspective. Research Policy 39, 495–510. https://doi.org/10.1016/j.respol.2010.01.022.

Gerard, H., Rivero Puente, E.I., Six, D., 2018. Coordination between transmission and distribution system operators in the electricity sector: A conceptual framework. Utilities Policy 50, 40–48. https://doi.org/10.1016/j.jup.2017.09.011.

Ghiassi-Farrokhfal, Y., Ketter, W., Collins, J., 2021. Making green power purchase agreements more predictable and reliable for companies. Decision Support Systems 144, 113514. https://doi.org/10.1016/j.dss.2021.113514.

Ghisellini, F., Chang, B.Y., 2018. Behavioral Economics: Moving Forward. Palgrave Macmillan Cham.

Giannakis, D., Jamasb, T., Pollitt, M., 2005. Benchmarking and incentive regulation of quality of service: an application to the UK electricity distribution networks. Energy Policy 33, 2256–2271. https://doi.org/10.1016/j.enpol.2004.04.021.

Giarmanà, E., 2023. Managing renewable electricity within collective self-consumption schemes: A systematic private law approach. Renewable and Sustainable Energy Reviews 188, 113896. https://doi.org/10.1016/j.rser.2023.113896.

Gigerenzer, G., Gaissmaier, W., 2011. Heuristic Decision Making. Annual review of psychology 62, 451–82. https://doi.org/10.1146/annurev-psych-120709-145346.

Gils, H.C., 2014. Assessment of the theoretical demand response potential in Europe. Energy 67, 1–18. https://doi.org/10.1016/j.energy.2014.02.019.

Gimeno, J.Á., Llera, E., Scarpellini, S., 2018. Investment Determinants in Self-Consumption Facilities: Characterization and Qualitative Analysis in Spain. Energies 11. https://doi.org/10.3390/en11082178.

Givisiez, A.G., Petrou, K., Ochoa, L.F., 2020. A Review on TSO-DSO Coordination Models and Solution Techniques. Electric Power Systems Research 189, 106659. https://doi.org/10.1016/j.epsr.2020.106659.

Gkarakis, K., Dagoumas, A., 2016. Assessment of the implementation of Guarantees of Origin (GOs) in Europe.

Goldthau, A., 2014. Rethinking the governance of energy infrastructure: Scale, decentralization and polycentrism. Energy Research & Social Science 1, 134–140. https://doi.org/10.1016/j.erss.2014.02.009.

Good, N., Ellis, K.A., Mancarella, P., 2017. Review and classification of barriers and enablers of demand response in the smart grid. Renewable and Sustainable Energy Reviews 72, 57–72. https://doi.org/10.1016/j.rser.2017.01.043.

Goulden, M., Spence, A., 2015. Caught in the middle: The role of the Facilities Manager in organisational energy use. Energy Policy 85, 280–287. https://doi.org/10.1016/j.enpol.2015.06.014.

Graaf, T.V. de, Laes, E., Verbruggen, A., 2019. Energy Governance in Belgium, in: Michèle Knodt, Jörg Kemmerzell (Eds.), Handbook of Energy Governance in Europe. Springer.

Gräper, F., Schoser, C., Stamati, M., 2021. Network regulation and third party access, in: Jones, C., Kettlewell, W.-J. (Eds.), EU Energy Law Volume I: The Internal Energy Market. CLAEYS & CASTEELS, p. 3.

Graziano, M., Gillingham, K., 2015. Spatial patterns of solar photovoltaic system adoption: The influence of neighbors and the built environment ‡. Journal of Economic Geography 15, 815–839. https://doi.org/10.1093/jeg/lbu036.

Graziano, M., Gillingham, K., 2014. Spatial patterns of solar photovoltaic system adoption: The influence of neighbors and the built environment ‡. Journal of Economic Geography 15, 815–839. https://doi.org/10.1093/jeg/lbu036.

Gruber, A., Biedermann, F., Roon, S. von, 2014. The Merit Order of Demand Response in Industry. Presented at the 9th Conference on energy economics and technology, Dresden, Germany.

Grüne-Yanoff, T., Hertwig, R., 2016. Nudge Versus Boost: How Coherent are Policy and Theory? Minds and Machines 26, 149–183. https://doi.org/10.1007/s11023-015-9367-9.

Gui, E.M., MacGill, I., 2018. Typology of future clean energy communities: An exploratory structure, opportunities, and challenges. Energy Research & Social Science 35, 94–107. https://doi.org/10.1016/j.erss.2017.10.019.

Gurba, B., 2021. Public service obligations and the EU energy market legislation, in: Jones, C., Kettlewell, W.-J. (Eds.), EU Energy Law Volume I: The Internal Energy Market. CLAEYS & CASTEELS, p. 540.

GWEC, 2022. Global Wind Report 2022.

GWEC, 2013. Global Wind Report 2013.

Haas, R., Panzer, C., Resch, G., Ragwitz, M., Reece, G., Held, A., 2011. A historical review of promotion strategies for electricity from renewable energy sources in EU countries. Renewable and Sustainable Energy Reviews 15, 1003–1034. https://doi.org/10.1016/j.rser.2010.11.015.

Hacker, P., 2018. UberPop, UberBlack, and the Regulation of Digital Platforms after the Asociación Profesional Elite Taxi Judgment of the CJEU. Judgment of the Court (Grand Chamber) 20 December 2017, Asociación Profesional Elite Taxi (C-434/15), European Review of Contract Law 14, 80–96. https://doi.org/10.1515/ercl-2018-1005.

Hadush, S.Y., Meeus, L., 2018. DSO-TSO cooperation issues and solutions for distribution grid congestion management. Energy Policy 120, 610–621. https://doi.org/10.1016/j.enpol.2018.05.065.

Haji Bashi, M., De Tommasi, L., Le Cam, A., Relaño, L.S., Lyons, P., Mundó, J., Pandelieva-Dimova, I., Schapp, H., Loth-Babut, K., Egger, C., Camps, M., Cassidy, B., Angelov, G., Stancioff, C.E., 2023. A review and mapping exercise of energy community regulatory challenges in European member states based on a survey of collective energy actors. Renewable and Sustainable Energy Reviews 172, 113055. https://doi.org/10.1016/j.rser.2022.113055.

Haley, B., Gaede, J., Winfield, M., Love, P., 2020. From utility demand side management to low-carbon transitions: Opportunities and challenges for energy efficiency governance in a new era. Energy Research & Social Science 59, 101312. https://doi.org/10.1016/j.erss.2019.101312.

Hamburger, Á., 2019. Is guarantee of origin really an effective energy policy tool in Europe? A critical approach. Society and Economy 41, 487–507. https://doi.org/10.1556/204.2019.41.4.6.

Hamburger, Á., Harangozo, G., 2018. Factors Affecting the Evolution of Renewable Electricity Generating Capacities: A Panel Data Analysis of European Countries. International Journal of Energy Economics and Policy 8, 161.

Hampton, H., Foley, A., Rio, D.F.D., Smyth, B., Laverty, D., Caulfield, B., 2022. Customer engagement strategies in retail electricity markets: A comprehensive and comparative review. Energy Research & Social Science 90, 102611. https://doi.org/10.1016/j.erss.2022.102611.

Hancher, L., Larouche, P., 2011. The Coming of Age of EU Regulation of Network Industries and Services of General Economic Interest, in: Craig, P., Búrca, G.D. (Eds.), The Evolution of EU Law. Oxford University Press, p. 575.

Haney, A.B., Pollitt, M.G., 2011. Exploring the determinants of "best practice" benchmarking in electricity network regulation. Energy Policy 39, 7739–7746. https://doi.org/10.1016/j.enpol.2011.09.018.

Hanke, F., Grossmann, K., Sandmann, L., 2023. Excluded despite their support – The perspectives of energy-poor households on their participation in the German energy transition narrative. Energy Research & Social Science 104, 103259. https://doi.org/10.1016/j.erss.2023.103259.

Hanke, F., Lowitzsch, J., 2020. Empowering Vulnerable Consumers to Join Renewable Energy Communities – Towards an Inclusive Design of the Clean Energy Package. Energies 13. https://doi.org/10.3390/en13071615.

Hannah Kruimer, H.T., 2011. Non-Discriminatory Energy System Operation: What Does it Mean? Competition and Regulation in Network Industries 12, 260–286. https://doi.org/10.1177/178359171101200304.

Hanny, L., Wagner, J., Buhl, H.U., Heffron, R., Körner, M.-F., Schöpf, M., Weibelzahl, M., 2022. On the progress in flexibility and grid charges in light of the energy transition: The case of Germany. Energy Policy 165, 112882. https://doi.org/10.1016/j.enpol.2022.112882.

Hansson, M., Carlsson, F., 2012. The Potential of Renewable Energy in the Swedish Distribution Networks: A Case Study in Souther Sweden. Presented at the 13th Wind Integration Workshop.

Haraldsdóttir, K., 2014. The Limits of EU Competence to Regulate Conditions for Exploitation of Energy Resources: Analysis of Article 194(2) TFEU. European Energy and Environmental Law Review 208–218.

Hartnett, S., Morris, J., Vlachos, I., 2021. EW Flex: A decentralized flexibility marketplace fostering TSO-DSO cooperation, in: Dagoumas, A. (Ed.), Mathematical Modelling of Contemporary Electricity Markets. Elsevier.

Hast, A., Syri, S., Jokiniemi, J., Huuskonen, M., Cross, S., 2015. Review of green electricity products in the United Kingdom, Germany and Finland. Renewable and Sustainable Energy Reviews 42, 1370–1384. https://doi.org/10.1016/j.rser.2014.10.104.

Haushofer, J., Fehr, E., 2014. On the psychology of poverty. Science 344, 862–867. https://doi.org/10.1126/science.1232491.

Hausman, D.M., Welch, B., 2010. Debate: To Nudge or Not to Nudge. Journal of Political Philosophy 18, 123–136. https://doi.org/10.1111/j.1467-9760.2009.00351.x.

Havyatt, D., 2022. Toward consumer-centric energy network regulation: Australia's experience. Utilities Policy 78, 101404. https://doi.org/10.1016/j.jup.2022.101404.

Heffron, R.J., Talus, K., 2016. The evolution of energy law and energy jurisprudence: Insights for energy analysts and researchers. Energy Research & Social Science 19, 1–10. https://doi.org/10.1016/j.erss.2016.05.004.

Helm, D.R., 2012. European Energy Policy, in: Jones, E., Menon, A., Weatherill, S. (Eds.), The Oxford Handbook of the European Union. Oxford University Press, p. 559.

Herbes, C., Rilling, B., MacDonald, S., Boutin, N., Bigerna, S., 2020. Are voluntary markets effective in replacing state-led support for the expansion of renewables? – A comparative analysis of voluntary green electricity markets in the UK, Germany, France and Italy. Energy Policy 141, 111473. https://doi.org/10.1016/j.enpol.2020.111473.

Hermann, A., Jensen, T.V., Østergaard, J., Kazempour, J., 2022. A complementarity model for electric power transmission-distribution coordination under uncertainty. European Journal of Operational Research 299, 313–329. https://doi.org/10.1016/j.ejor.2021.08.018.

Hertwig, R., Grüne-Yanoff, T., 2017. Nudging and Boosting: Steering or Empowering Good Decisions. Perspect Psychol Sci 12, 973–986. https://doi.org/10.1177/1745691617702496.

Hicks, J., Ison, N., 2018. An exploration of the boundaries of 'community' in community renewable energy projects: Navigating between motivations and context. Energy Policy 113, 523–534. https://doi.org/10.1016/j.enpol.2017.10.031.

Hobman, E.V., Frederiks, E.R., Stenner, K., Meikle, S., 2016. Uptake and usage of cost-reflective electricity pricing: Insights from psychology and behavioural economics. Renewable and Sustainable Energy Reviews 57, 455–467. https://doi.org/10.1016/j.rser.2015.12.144.

Hoecke, M.V., 2011. Legal doctrine: which method(s) for what kind of discipline?, in: Hoecke, M.V. (Ed.), Methodologies of Legal Research: What Kind of Method for What Kind of Discipline? Hart Publishing, pp. 1–18.

Hofmann, H.C.H., 2017. General Principles of EU law and EU Administrative Law, in: Barnard, C., Peers, S. (Eds.), European Union Law. Oxford University Press.

Hoggett, R., 2017. People, Demand and Governance in Future Energy Systems (No. EPG Working Paper: EPG1701).

Hoicka, C.E., Lowitzsch, J., Brisbois, M.C., Kumar, A., Ramirez Camargo, L., 2021. Implementing a just renewable energy transition: Policy advice for transposing the new European rules for renewable energy communities. Energy Policy 156, 112435. https://doi.org/10.1016/j.enpol.2021.112435.

Horbach, J., Jacob, J., 2018. The relevance of personal characteristics and gender diversity for (eco-)innovation activities at the firm-level: Results from a linked employer–employee database in Germany. Business Strategy and the Environment 27, 924–934. https://doi.org/10.1002/bse.2042.

Horbach, J., Rammer, C., 2018. Energy transition in Germany and regional spill-overs: The diffusion of renewable energy in firms. Energy Policy 121, 404–414. https://doi.org/10.1016/j.enpol.2018.06.042.

Horstink, L., Luz, G., Soares, M., 2017. Review and Characterisation of Collective Renewable Energy Prosumer Initiatives, PROSEU-Prosumers for the Energy Union: Mainstreaming Active Participation of Citizens in the Energy Transition (Deliverable N°2.1); Horizon 2020 (H2020- LCE-2017) Grant Agreement N°764056.

Howes, T., Hodson, P., Jones, C., Steen, H.V., 2010. "Trading" renewable energy and types of national support schemes, in: EU Energy Law Volume III Book One: Renewable Energy Law and Policy in the European Union. CLAEYS & CASTEELS, pp. 110–111.

Hu, Z., Kim, J., Wang, J., Byrne, J., 2015. Review of dynamic pricing programs in the U.S. and Europe: Status quo and policy recommendations. Renewable and Sustainable Energy Reviews 42, 743–751. https://doi.org/10.1016/j.rser.2014.10.078.

Huang, Y., Söder, L., 2017a. Assessing the impact of incentive regulation on distribution network investment considering distributed generation integration. International Journal of Electrical Power & Energy Systems 89, 126–135. https://doi.org/10.1016/j.ijepes.2017.01.018.

Huang, Y., Söder, L., 2017b. Evaluation of economic regulation in distribution systems with distributed generation. Energy 126, 192–201. https://doi.org/10.1016/j.energy.2017.03.019.

Huhta, K., 2021. THE SCOPE OF STATE SOVEREIGNTY UNDER ARTICLE 194(2) TFEU AND THE EVOLUTION OF EU COMPETENCES IN THE ENERGY SECTOR. International and Comparative Law Quarterly 70, 991–1010. https://doi.org/10.1017/S0020589321000269.

Huhta, K., 2020a. Trust in the invisible hand? The roles of the State and the markets in EU energy law. The Journal of World Energy Law & Business 13, 1–11. https://doi.org/10.1093/jwelb/jwaa003.

Huhta, K., 2020b. Smartening up while keeping safe? Advances in smart metering and data protection under EU law. Journal of Energy & Natural Resources Law 38, 5–22. https://doi.org/10.1080/02646811.2019.1622244.

Huybrechts, B., 2013. Social enterprise, social innovation and alternative economies: insights from fair trade and renewable energy, in: Zademach, H.-M., Hillebrand, S. (Eds.), Alternative Economies and Spaces. New Perspectives for a Sustainable Economy. Transcript Verlag, p. 113.

IEA, 2023. Renewables 2023: Analysis and forecast to 2028.

IEA, 2021. Renewable electricity growth is accelerating faster than ever worldwide, supporting the emergence of the new global energy economy.

IEA, 2016. Re-powering Markets: Market design and regulation during the transition to low-carbon power systems [WWW Document]. URL https://iea.blob.core.windows.net/assets/4452f4ea-59d0-497b-8736-069b4cb39851/REPOWERINGMARKETS.pdf.

Ikäheimo, J., Evens, C., Kärkkäinen, S., 2010. DER Aggregator Business: the Finnish Case (No. RESEARCH REPORT VTT-R-06961-09).

Iliopoulos, T., 2021. The Law of Support Schemes for Renewable Energy Sources: Towards a New Legal Framework in the EU (PhD Dissertation). Hasselt University.

Inês, C., Guilherme, P.L., Esther, M.-G., Swantje, G., Stephen, H., Lars, H., 2020. Regulatory challenges and opportunities for collective renewable energy prosumers in the EU. Energy Policy 138, 111212. https://doi.org/10.1016/j.enpol.2019.111212.

Ioannidou, M., 2018. Effective Paths for Consumer Empowerment and Protection in Retail Energy Markets. Journal of Consumer Policy 41, 135–157. https://doi.org/10.1007/s10603-018-9372-5.

IRENA, 2023a. Renewable capacity statistics 2023.

IRENA, 2023b. Record Growth in Renewables Achieved Despite Energy Crisis.

IRENA, 2020. Co-operation between transmission and distribution system operators: Innovation Landscape Brief.

IRENA, 2019. Demand-side flexibility for power sector transformation.

Jacobs, D., 2012. Renewable Energy Policy Convergence in the EU: The Evolution of Feed-in Tariffs in Germany, Spain and France. Routledge.

Jager, D., Rathmann, M., Klessmann, C., Coenraads, R., Colamonico, C., Buttazzoni, M., 2008. Policy instrument design to reduce financing costs in renewable energy technology projects.

Jamasb, T., Mota, R., Newbery, D., Pollitt, M., 2004. Electricity Sector Reform in Developing Countries: A Survey of Empirical Evidence on Determinants and Performance (No. Cambridge Working Papers in Economics CWPE 0439).

Jamasb, T., Pollitt, M., 2008. Liberalisation and R&D in network industries: The case of the electricity industry. Research Policy 37, 995–1008. https://doi.org/10.1016/j.respol.2008.04.010.

Jamasb, T., Pollitt, M., 2007. Incentive regulation of electricity distribution networks: Lessons of experience from Britain. Energy Policy 35, 6163–6187. https://doi.org/10.1016/j.enpol.2007.06.022.

Jeddi, S., Sitzmann, A., 2019. Netzentgeltsystematik in Deutschland – Status-Quo, Alternativen und europäische Erfahrungen. Zeitschrift für Energiewirtschaft 43, 245–267. https://doi.org/10.1007/s12398-019-00265-6.

Jin, X., Wu, Q., Jia, H., 2020. Local flexibility markets: Literature review on concepts, models and clearing methods. Applied Energy 261, 114387. https://doi.org/10.1016/j.apenergy.2019.114387.

Johansson, P., Vendel, M., Nuur, C., 2020. Integrating distributed energy resources in electricity distribution systems: An explorative study of challenges facing DSOs in Sweden. Utilities Policy 67, 101117. https://doi.org/10.1016/j.jup.2020.101117.

Johnston, J.S., 2018. Regulatory Carrots and Sticks in Climate Policy: Some Political Economic Observations. Texas A&M Law Review 6, 107–146.

Jolls, C., Sunstein, C.R., 2005. Debiasing through Law (No. National Bureau of Economic Research Working Paper 11738).

Jones, B.R., Sovacool, B.K., Sidortsov, R.V., 2015. Making the Ethical and Philosophical Case for "Energy Justice." Environmental Ethics 37, 145.

Jones, C., 2019. EU Energy Law: Volume II EU Competition Law and Energy Markets, Fifth. ed. CLAEYS & CASTEELS.

Jones, C., Kettlewell, W.-J., 2021. Unbundling of Distribution System Operators, in: Jones, C., Kettlewell, W.-J. (Eds.), EU Energy Law Volume I: The Internal Energy Market. CLAEYS & CASTEELS, p. 217.

Jörgens, H., Öller, E., Solorio, I., 2017. Conclusions: patterns of Europeanization and policy change in the renewable energy policy domain, in: Solorio, I., Jörgens, H. (Eds.), A Guide to EU Renewable Energy Policy Comparing Europeanization and Domestic Policy Change in EU Member States. Edward Elgar, p. 289.

Joskow, P., 2006. Incentive Regulation in Theory and Practice: Electricity Distribution and Transmission Networks. Cambridge Working Papers in Economics 0607.

Joskow, P., Kahn, E., 2001. A quantitative analysis of pricing behavior in California's wholesale electricity market during summer 2000, in: 2001 Power Engineering Society Summer Meeting. Conference Proceedings (Cat. No.01CH37262). pp. 392–394 vol.1. https://doi.org/10.1109/PESS.2001.970049.

Joskow, P.L., 2008. Lessons Learned From Electricity Market Liberalization. The Energy Journal 29, 9–42. https://doi.org/10.5547/ISSN0195-6574-EJ-Vol29-NoSI2-3.

Joskow, P.L., 2007. Supply security in competitive electricity and natural gas markets, in: Robinson, C. (Ed.), Utility Regulation in Competitive Markets. Edward Elgar.

Judgement of 6 September 2006, Portugal v Commission, C-88/03, EU:C:2006:511, 2006.

Judgement of 13 February 2003, Spain v Commission, C-409/00, EU:C:2003:92, 2003.

Judgment of 3 July 1997, Benincasa, C-269/95, EU:C:1997:337, 1997.

Judgment of 7 June 2005, VEMW and Others, C-17/03, EU:C:2005:362, 2005.

Judgment of 7 September 2016, ANODE, C-121/15, EU:C:2016:637, 2016.

Judgment of 8 September 2011, Commission v Netherlands, C-279/08 P, ECLI:EU:C:2011:551, 2011.

Judgment of 8 September 2011, Paint Graphos and Others, Joined Cases C-78/08 to C-80/08, EU:C:2011:550, 2011.

Judgment of 11 July 2002, Gabriel, C-96/00, EU:C:2002:436, 2002.

Judgment of 14 October 2021, Viesgo Infraestructuras Energéticas, C-683/19, EU:C:2021:847, 2021.

Judgment of 16 December 2008, Arcelor Atlantique et Lorraine and Others, Case C-127/07, EU:C:2008:728, 2008.

Judgment of 16 March 2022, Bromine Science Environnemental Forum (BSEF) v European Commission, T-113/20, EU:T:2022:142, 2022.

Judgment of 19 January 1993, Shearson Lehman Hutton, C-89/91, EU:C:1993:15, 1993.

Judgment of 20 December 2017, Asociación Profesional Elite Taxi, C-434/15, EU:C:2017:981, 2017.

Judgment of 20 January 2005, Gruber, C-464/01, EU:C:2005:32, 2005.

Judgment of 21 December 2016, Commission v Hansestadt Lübeck, C-524/14 P, ECLI:EU:C:2016:971, 2016.

Judgment of 21 December 2016, Commission v Workd Duty Free Group SA, joined cases C 20/15 P and C-21/15 P, ECLI:EU:C:2016:981, 2016.

Judgment of 21 June 1978, Bertrand, C-150/77, EU:C:1978:137, 1978.

Judgment of 22 May 2008, citiworks, C-439/06, EU:C:2008:298, 2008.

Judgment of 23 October 1997, Commission v Italy, C-158/94, EU: C:1997:500, 1997.

Judgment of 24 July 2003, Altmark Trans and Regierungspräsidium Magdeburg, C-280/00, EU:C:2003:415, 2003.

Judgment of 25 January 2018, Schrems, C-498/16, EU:C:2018:37, 2018.

Judgment of 27 April 1994, Gemeente Almelo, C-393/92, EU: C:1994:171, 1994.

Judgment of 29 April 2004, Netherlands v Commission, C-159/01, EU:C:2004:246, 2004.

Judgment of 29 September 2016, Essent Belgium NV v Vlaams Gewest and Others, C-492/14, EU:C:2016:732, 2016.

Judgment of 30 April 2020, Overgas Mrezhi and Balgarska gazova asotsiatsia, C-5/19, EU:C:2020:343, 2020.

Judgment of the Court of 9 October 2008, Sabatauskas and Others, C-239/07, 2008.

Judgment of the General Court of 6 October 2021, AZ v Commission, T-196/19, EU:T:2021:646, 2021.

Judgment of the General Court of 6 October 2021, Covestro Deutschland v Commission, T-745/18, EU:T:2021:644, 2021.

Judgment of the General Court of 6 October 2021, Infineon Technologies Dresden and Infineon Technologies v Commission, Joined Cases T-233/19 and T-234/19, EU:T:2021:647, 2021.

Judgment of the General Court of 6 October 2021, Wepa Hygieneprodukte GmbH and Others v Commission, T-238/19, EU:T:2021:648, 2021.

Judgments of 14 April 2005, AEM and AEM Torino, C-128/03 and C-129/03, EU:C:2005:224, 2005.

Julian, C., 2021. Creating Local Energy Economies: Lessons from Germany.

Jung, J.Y., Mellers, B.A., 2016. American attitudes toward nudges. Judgment and Decision Making 11, 62–74. https://doi.org/10.1017/S1930297500007592.

Kahn, A.E., Cramton, P.C., Porter, R.H., Tabors, R.D., 2001. Uniform Pricing or Pay-as-Bid Pricing: A Dilemma for California and Beyond. The Electricity Journal 14, 70–79. https://doi.org/10.1016/S1040-6190(01)00216-0.

Kahneman, D., 2003a. Maps of bounded rationality: Psychology for behavioral economics. American Economic Review. https://doi.org/10.1257/000282803322655392.

Kahneman, D., 2003b. A perspective on judgment and choice: Mapping bounded rationality. American Psychologist 58, 697–720. https://doi.org/10.1037/0003-066X.58.9.697.

Kahneman, D., Knetsch, J.L., Thaler, R.H., 1991. Anomalies: The Endowment Effect, Loss Aversion, and Status Quo Bias. Journal of Economic Perspectives 5, 193–206. https://doi.org/10.1257/jep.5.1.193.

Kahneman, D., Tversky, A., 1984. Choices, values, and frames. American Psychologist 39, 341–350. https://doi.org/10.1037/0003-066X.39.4.341.

Kahneman, D., Tversky, A., 1979. Prospect Theory: An Analysis of Decision under Risk. Econometrica 47, 263–291. https://doi.org/10.2307/1914185.

Kahrl, F., Williams, J., Jianhua, D., Junfeng, H., 2011. Challenges to China's transition to a low carbon electricity system. Energy Policy 39, 4032–4041. https://doi.org/10.1016/j.enpol.2011.01.031.

Kalkbrenner, B.J., Roosen, J., 2016. Citizens' willingness to participate in local renewable energy projects: The role of community and trust in Germany. Energy Research & Social Science 13, 60–70. https://doi.org/10.1016/j.erss.2015.12.006.

Kanellou, E., Hinsch, A., Vorkapić, V., Torres, A.-D., Konstantopoulos, G., Matsagkos, N., Doukas, H., 2023. Lessons Learnt and Policy Implications from Implementing the POWERPOOR Approach to Alleviate Energy Poverty. Sustainability 15. https://doi.org/10.3390/su15118854.

Kantamneni, A., Winkler, R., Gauchia, L., Pearce, J.M., 2016. Emerging economic viability of grid defection in a northern climate using solar hybrid systems. Energy Policy 95, 378–389. https://doi.org/10.1016/j.enpol.2016.05.013.

Kara, G., Tomasgard, A., Farahmand, H., 2022. Characterizing flexibility in power markets and systems. Utilities Policy 75, 101349. https://doi.org/10.1016/j.jup.2022.101349

Karki, R., Hu, P., Billinton, R., 2009. Adequacy criteria and methods for wind power transmission planning, in: 2009 IEEE Power & Energy Society General Meeting. Presented at the 2009 IEEE Power & Energy Society General Meeting, pp. 1–7. https://doi.org/10.1109/PES.2009.5275810.

Karteris, M., Papadopoulos, A.M., 2012. Residential photovoltaic systems in Greece and in other European countries: a comparison and an overview. Advances in Building Energy Research 6, 141–158. https://doi.org/10.1080/17512549.2012.672005.

Kaushal, A., Van Hertem, D., 2019. An Overview of Ancillary Services and HVDC Systems in European Context. Energies 12. https://doi.org/10.3390/en12183481

Kelsey, N., Meckling, J., 2018. Who wins in renewable energy? Evidence from Europe and the United States. Energy Research & Social Science 37, 65–73. https://doi.org/10.1016/j.erss.2017.08.003.

Kersten, J., 2016. Ausnahmezustand? Juristische Schulung 56, 193.

Khalilpour, R., Vassallo, A., 2015. Leaving the grid: An ambition or a real choice? Energy Policy 82, 207–221. https://doi.org/10.1016/j.enpol.2015.03.005.

Kim, J.-H., Shcherbakova, A., 2011. Common failures of demand response. Energy 36, 873.

Kitzing, L., Mitchell, C., Morthorst, P.E., 2012. Renewable energy policies in Europe: Converging or diverging? Energy Policy 51, 192–201. https://doi.org/10.1016/j.enpol.2012.08.064.

Klobasa, M., Angerer, G., Lüllmann, A., Schleich, J., Buber, T., 2014. Load Management as a Way of Covering Peak Demand in Southern Germany (No. No. 040/04-S-2014/EN).

Knieps, G., 2013. Renewable Energy, Efficient Electricity Networks, and Sector-Specific Market Power Regulation, in: Sioshansi, F.P. (Ed.), Evolution of Global Electricity Markets: New Paradigms, New Challenges, New Approaches. Elsevier, p. 147.

Kobus, J., Nasrallah, A.I., Guidera, J., 2021. The role of corporate renewable power purchase agreements in supporting US wind and solar deployment. Center on Global Energy Policy.

Kohlbacher, T., Lavrijssen, S., 2018. Good Governance in the Development of Network Codes for the EU Internal Electricity Market. 'Good Governance in the Development of Network Codes for the EU Internal Electricity Market' (2018) 2 Review of European Administrative Law 2, 27.

Koliou, E., Muhaimin, T., Hakvoort, R., Kremers, R., 2015. Complexity of demand response integration in European electricity markets, in: 12th International Conference on the European Energy Market. Lisbon.

Kotilainen, K., Valta, J., Valta, J., Kojo, M., Ruostetsaari, I., 2021. From energy consumers to prosumers – How do policies influence the transition?, in: Aalto, P. (Ed.), Electrification Accelerating the Energy Transition. Elsevier.

Kouzelis, K., Bak-Jensen, B., Pillai, J.R., 2015. The geographical aspect of flexibility in distribution grids, in: 2015 IEEE Power & Energy Society Innovative Smart Grid Technologies Conference (ISGT). Presented at the 2015 IEEE Power & Energy Society Innovative Smart Grid Technologies Conference (ISGT), pp. 1–5. https://doi.org/10.1109/ISGT.2015.7131888.

Kowalska-Pyzalska, A., 2018. What makes consumers adopt to innovative energy services in the energy market? A review of incentives and barriers. Renewable and Sustainable Energy Reviews 82, 3570–3581. https://doi.org/10.1016/j.rser.2017.10.103.

Kristov, L., Martini, P.D., Taft, J.D., 2016. A Tale of Two Visions: Designing a Decentralized Transactive Electric System. IEEE Power and Energy Magazine 14, 63–69. https://doi.org/10.1109/MPE.2016.2524964.

Krug, M., Di Nucci, M.R., Schwarz, L., Alonso, I., Azevedo, I., Bastiani, M., Dyląg, A., Laes, E., Hinsch, A., Klāvs, G., Kudreņickis, I., Maleki, P., Massa, G., Meynaerts, E., Pappa, S., Standal, K., 2023. Implementing European Union Provisions and Enabling Frameworks for Renewable Energy Communities in Nine Countries: Progress, Delays, and Gaps. Sustainability 15. https://doi.org/10.3390/su15118861.

Kuiken, D., Más, H.F., 2019. Integrating demand side management into EU electricity distribution system operation: A Dutch example. Energy Policy 129, 153–160. https://doi.org/10.1016/j.enpol.2019.01.066.

Kumar, A., Srivastava, S.C., Singh, S.N., 2004. A zonal congestion management approach using real and reactive power rescheduling. IEEE Transactions on Power Systems 19, 554–562. https://doi.org/10.1109/TPWRS.2003.821448.

Kunze, C., Becker, S., 2015. Collective ownership in renewable energy and opportunities for sustainable degrowth. Sustainability Science 10. https://doi.org/10.1007/s11625-015-0301-0.

Kuzemko, C., Mitchell, C., Lockwood, M., Hoggett, R., 2017. Policies, politics and demand side innovations: The untold story of Germany's energy transition. Energy Research & Social Science 28, 58–67. https://doi.org/10.1016/j.erss.2017.03.013.

Kyoto Protocol to the United Nations Framework Convention on Climate Change, 1997.

Laes, E., Bombaerts, G., 2022. Energy Communities and the Tensions Between Neoliberalism and Communitarianism. Science and Engineering Ethics 28, 3. https://doi.org/10.1007/s11948-021-00359-w.

Lambrecht, A., Tucker, C., 2012. Paying with Money or Effort: Pricing When Customers Anticipate Hassle. Journal of Marketing Research 49, 66–82. https://doi.org/10.1509/jmr.09.0530.

Lamprinos, I., Hatziargyriou, N.D., Kokos, I., Dimeas, A.D., 2016. Making Demand Response a Reality in Europe: Policy, Regulations, and Deployment Status. IEEE Communications Magazine 54, 108–113. https://doi.org/10.1109/MCOM.2016.1600323CM.

Lashmar, N., Wade, B., Molyneaux, L., Ashworth, P., 2022. Motivations, barriers, and enablers for demand response programs: A commercial and industrial consumer perspective. Energy Research & Social Science 90, 102667. https://doi.org/10.1016/j.erss.2022.102667

Lauber, V., Schenner, E., 2011. The struggle over support schemes for renewable electricity in the European Union: a discursive-institutionalist analysis. Environmental Politics 20, 508–527. https://doi.org/10.1080/09644016.2011.589578.

Lavrijssen, S., Espinosa Apráez, B., ten Caten, T., 2022. The Legal Complexities of Processing and Protecting Personal Data in the Electricity Sector. Energies 15. https://doi.org/10.3390/en15031088.

Lavrijssen, S., Reins, L., Caten, T. ten, 2023. Realizing Peer-to-Peer Trading in the Electricity Market in the EU and its Member States, in: Bellantuono, G., Godden, L., Mostert, H., Wiseman, H., Zhang, H. (Eds.), Handbook of Energy Law in the Low-Carbon Transition. De Gruyter, Berlin, Boston, pp. 513–530. https://doi.org/doi:10.1515/9783110752403-039.

Lavrijssen, S.A.C.M., 2017. Power to the Energy Consumers. European Energy and Environmental Law Review 172–187.

Law of 29 April 1999 on the organisation of the electricity market [29 APRIL 1999 Wet van betreffende de organisatie van de elektriciteitsmarkt], 1999.

Laws, N.D., Epps, B.P., Peterson, S.O., Laser, M.S., Wanjiru, G.K., 2017. On the utility death spiral and the impact of utility rate structures on the adoption of residential solar photovoltaics and energy storage. Applied Energy 185, 627–641. https://doi.org/10.1016/j.apenergy.2016.10.123.

Lee, Z.E., Zhang, K.M., 2023. Regulated peer-to-peer energy markets for harnessing decentralized demand flexibility. Applied Energy 336, 120672. https://doi.org/10.1016/j.apenergy.2023.120672.

Leinauer, C., Schott, P., Fridgen, G., Keller, R., Ollig, P., Weibelzahl, M., 2022. Obstacles to demand response: Why industrial companies do not adapt their power consumption to volatile power generation. Energy Policy 165, 112876. https://doi.org/10.1016/j.enpol.2022.112876.

Lennon, B., Dunphy, N.P., Sanvicente, E., 2019. Community acceptability and the energy transition: a citizens' perspective. Energy, Sustainability and Society 9, 35. https://doi.org/10.1186/s13705-019-0218-z.

Leuffen, D., Rittberger, B., Schimmelfennig, F., 2013. Differentiated integration: explaining variation in the European Union. Palgrave Macmillan.

Levin, T., Botterud, A., 2015. Electricity market design for generator revenue sufficiency with increased variable generation. Energy Policy 87, 392–406. https://doi.org/10.1016/j.enpol.2015.09.012.

Li, D., Jayaweera, S., Lavrova, O., Jordan, R., 2011. Load Management for Price-based Demand Response Scheduling – a Block Scheduling Model. Renewable Energy and Power Quality Journal. https://doi.org/10.24084/repqj09.431.

Li, N., 2015. A market mechanism for electric distribution networks. Presented at the 2015 54th IEEE Conference on Decision and Control, Osaka, p. 2282. https://doi.org/10.1109/CDC.2015.7402546.

Li, N., Okur, Ö., 2023. Economic analysis of energy communities: Investment options and cost allocation. Applied Energy 336, 120706. https://doi.org/10.1016/j.apenergy.2023.120706.

Lin, B., Chen, J., Wesseh, P.K., 2022. Peak-valley tariffs and solar prosumers: Why renewable energy policies should target local electricity markets. Energy Policy 165, 112984. https://doi.org/10.1016/j.enpol.2022.112984.

Lind, L., Cossent, R., Chaves-Ávila, J.P., Gómez San Román, T., 2019. Transmission and distribution coordination in power systems with high shares of distributed energy resources providing balancing and congestion management services. WIREs Energy and Environment 8, e357. https://doi.org/10.1002/wene.357.

Llorca, M., Orea, L., Pollitt, M.G., 2016. Efficiency and environmental factors in the US electricity transmission industry. Energy Economics 55, 234–246. https://doi.org/10.1016/j.eneco.2016.02.004.

Lockwood, M., 2016. Creating protective space for innovation in electricity distribution networks in Great Britain: The politics of institutional change. Environmental Innovation and Societal Transitions 18, 111–127. https://doi.org/10.1016/j.eist.2015.05.007.

Lockwood, M., Mitchell, C., Hoggett, R., 2020. Incumbent lobbying as a barrier to forward-looking regulation: The case of demand-side response in the GB capacity market for electricity. Energy Policy 140, 111426. https://doi.org/10.1016/j.enpol.2020.111426.

Lodge, M., Stirton, L., 2010. Accountability in the Regulatory State, in: Baldwin, R., Cave, M., Lodge, M. (Eds.), The Oxford Handbook of Regulation. Oxford University Press.

Loewenstein, G., Thaler, R.H., 1989. Anomalies: Intertemporal Choice. Journal of Economic Perspectives 3, 181–193. https://doi.org/10.1257/jep.3.4.181.

Louis, J.-V., 2009. Community law Fifty years on, in: Cruz, J.B., Montero, C.C. (Eds.), European Integration from Rome to Berlin: 1957–2007 History, Law and Politics. Peter Lang, p. 66.

Lowe, P., Pucinskaite, I., Webster, W., Lindberg, P., 2007. Effective unbundling of energy transmission networks: lessons from the Energy Sector Inquiry. Competition Policy Newsletter 1, 23.

Lowitzsch, J., Hoicka, C.E., van Tulder, F.J., 2020. Renewable energy communities under the 2019 European Clean Energy Package – Governance model for the energy clusters of the future? Renewable and Sustainable Energy Reviews 122, 109489. https://doi.org/10.1016/j.rser.2019.109489.

Lund, P., Cherian, S., 2005. A Cell Controller for Autonomous Operation of a 60 kV Distribution Area. International Journal of Distributed Energy Resources 1.

Luttrell, C., Quiroz, S., Scrutton, C., Bird, K., 2009. Understanding and operationalising empowerment (Working Paper No. 308). Overseas Development Institute.

Määttä, S., 2021. Rethinking collaborative action and citizen empowerment: Characterising a Whole-of-Society approach to the energy transition. Energy Research & Social Science 81, 102277. https://doi.org/10.1016/j.erss.2021.102277.

Maher, I., Stefan, O., 2019. Delegation of powers and the rule of law: Energy justice in EU energy regulation. Energy Policy 128, 84–93. https://doi.org/10.1016/j.enpol.2018.12.046.

Mak, V., 2022. De "prosument" in de platformeconomie: Startpunt voor herijking van het privaat recht. Nederlands Juristenblad 97, 1978.

Mani, A., Mullainathan, S., Shafir, E., Zhao, J., 2013. Poverty Impedes Cognitive Function. Science 341, 976–980. https://doi.org/10.1126/science.1238041.

Manuel de Villena, M., Gautier, A., Ernst, D., Glavic, M., Fonteneau, R., 2021. Modelling and assessing the impact of the DSO remuneration strategy on its interaction with electricity users. International Journal of Electrical Power & Energy Systems 126, 106585. https://doi.org/10.1016/j.ijepes.2020.106585.

MARCH 17, 2022. – Ordinance amending the ordinance of 19 July 2001 on the organization of the electricity market in the Brussels-Capital Region, the ordinance of 1 April 2004 on the organization of the gas market in the Brussels-Capital Region, on road charges for gas and electricity and amending the ordinance of 19 July 2001 on the organization of the electricity market in the Brussels-Capital Region and the ordinance of 12 December 1991 establishing budget funds with a view to the transposition of Directive 2018/2001 and Directive 2019/944 [17 MAART 2022. – Ordonnantie tot wijziging van de ordonnantie van 19 juli 2001 betreffende de organisatie van de elektriciteitsmarkt in het Brussels Hoofdstedelijk Gewest, de ordonnantie van 1 april 2004 betreffende de organisatie van de gasmarkt in het Brussels Hoofdstedelijk Gewest, betreffende wegenisretributies inzake gas en elektriciteit en houdende wijziging van de ordonnantie van 19 juli 2001 betreffende de organisatie van de elektriciteitsmarkt in het Brussels Hoofdstedelijk Gewest en de ordonnantie van 12 december 1991 houdende oprichting van begrotingsfondsen met het oog op de omzetting van richtlijn 2018/2001 en richtlijn 2019/944], 2022.

MARCH 17, 2023. – Decision of the Walloon Government on energy communities and energy sharing [17 MAART 2023. – Besluit van de Waalse Regering over energiegemeenschappen en het delen van energie], 2023.

Marinova, Y., 2021. Implementation of the Third Internal Energy Market Package, in: Jones, C., Kettlewell, W.-J. (Eds.), EU Energy Law Volume I: The Internal Energy Market. CLAEYS & CASTEELS, pp. 774–775.

Märkle-Huß, J., Feuerriegel, S., Neumann, D., 2018. Large-scale demand response and its implications for spot prices, load and policies: Insights from the German-Austrian electricity market. Applied Energy 210, 1290–1298. https://doi.org/10.1016/j.apenergy.2017.08.039.

Masini, A., Menichetti, E., 2013. Investment decisions in the renewable energy sector: An analysis of non-financial drivers. Technological Forecasting and Social Change 80, 510–524. https://doi.org/10.1016/j.techfore.2012.08.003.

Mateo, C., Frías, P., Cossent, R., Sonvilla, P., Barth, B., 2017. Overcoming the barriers that hamper a large-scale integration of solar photovoltaic power generation in European distribution grids. Solar Energy 153, 574–583. https://doi.org/10.1016/j.solener.2017.06.008.

Mauger, R., 2023. Defining microgrids: from technology to law. Journal of Energy & Natural Resources Law 41, 287–304. https://doi.org/10.1080/02646811.2022.2124742.

MAY 5, 2022. – Decree amending several provisions on energy as part of the partial transposition of Directives 2019/944/EU of 5 June 2019 on common rules for the internal market in electricity and 2018/2001/EU of 11 December 2018 on the promotion of the use of energy from renewable sources and with a view to adapting the principles on tariff methodology [5 MEI 2022. – Decreet tot wijziging van verscheidene bepalingen inzake energie in het kader van de gedeeltelijke omzetting van richtlijnen 2019/944/EU van 5 juni 2019 betreffende gemeenschappelijke regels voor de interne markt voor elektriciteit en 2018/2001/EU van 11 december 2018 ter bevordering van het gebruik van energie uit hernieuwbare bronnen en met het oog op de aanpassing van de beginselen betreffende de tariefmethodologie], 2022.

McDonald, J., 2008. Adaptive intelligent power systems: Active distribution networks. Energy Policy 36, 4346–4351. https://doi.org/10.1016/j.enpol.2008.09.038.

McHarg, A., 2012. Evolution and Revolution in British Energy Network Regulation: From RPI-X to RIIO, in: Roggenkamp, M.M., Barrera-Hernández, L., Zillman, D.N., Guayo, I. del (Eds.), Energy Networks and the Law: Innovative Solutions in Changing Markets. Oxford University Press. https://doi.org/10.1093/acprof:oso/9780199645039.001.0001.

Mehigan, L., Deane, J.P., Gallachóir, B.P.Ó., Bertsch, V., 2018. A review of the role of distributed generation (DG) in future electricity systems. Energy 163, 822–836. https://doi.org/10.1016/j.energy.2018.08.022.

Mendicino, L., Menniti, D., Pinnarelli, A., Sorrentino, N., 2019. Corporate power purchase agreement: Formulation of the related levelized cost of energy and its application to a real life case study. Applied Energy 253, 113577. https://doi.org/10.1016/j.apenergy.2019.113577.

Meyer, N.I., 2003. European schemes for promoting renewables in liberalised markets. Energy Policy 31, 665–676. https://doi.org/10.1016/S0301-4215(02)00151-9.

Michaelis, A., Hanny, L., Körner, M.-F., Strüker, J., Weibelzahl, M., 2024. Consumer-centric electricity markets: Six design principles. Renewable and Sustainable Energy Reviews 191, 113817. https://doi.org/10.1016/j.rser.2023.113817.

Micheau, C., 2014. Tax selectivity in European law of State aid – Legal assessment and alternative approaches (No. Law Working Paper Series Paper number 2014-06). University of Luxembourg.

MIIT, 2019. Guidelines of electricity DSM in the industrial sector [工业和信息化部关于印发《工业领域电力需求侧管理工作指南》的通知].

Milčiuvienė, S., Kiršienė, J., Doheijo, E., Urbonas, R., Milčius, D., 2019. The Role of Renewable Energy Prosumers in Implementing Energy Justice Theory. Sustainability 11. https://doi.org/10.3390/su11195286.

Ministerial Decree approving the 2024–2034 federal development plan of the electricity transmission network, in accordance with Article 11 of the Royal Decree of 20 December 2007 on the procedure for elaboration, approval and publication of the plan for development of the electricity transmission network [Ministerieel besluit tot goedkeuring van het federaal ontwikkelingsplan 2024–2034 van het transmissienet voor elektriciteit, overeenkomstig artikel 11 van het koninklijk besluit van 20 december 2007 betreffende de procedure voor uitwerking, goedkeuring en bekendmaking van het plan inzake ontwikkeling van het transmissienet voor elektriciteit], 2023.

Ministerie van Economische Zaken en Klimaat, 2022. Memorie van Toelichting wetsvoorstel Energiewet – versie RvS.

Miskinis, V., Norvaisa, E., Galinis, A., Konstantinaviciute, I., 2011. Trends of distributed generation development in Lithuania. Energy Policy 39, 4656–4663. https://doi.org/10.1016/j.enpol.2011.05.022.

Mitchell, C., Woodman, B., 2012. Regulation and sustainable energy system, in: Baldwin, R., Cave, M.E., Lodge, M. (Eds.), The Oxford Handbook of Regulation. Oxford University Press, p. 582.

Morstyn, T., Farrell, N., Darby, S.J., McCulloch, M.D., 2018. Using peer-to-peer energy-trading platforms to incentivize prosumers to form federated power plants. Nature Energy 3, 94–101. https://doi.org/10.1038/s41560-017-0075-y.

Mould, R., Baker, K.J., 2017. Documenting fuel poverty from the householders' perspective. Energy Research & Social Science 31, 21–31. https://doi.org/10.1016/j.erss.2017.06.004.

Moura, P.S., de Almeida, A.T., 2010. The role of demand-side management in the grid integration of wind power. Applied Energy 87, 2581–2588. https://doi.org/10.1016/j.apenergy.2010.03.019

Mulder, M., 2016. Economic Regulation of Energy Networks, in: Beaulieu, A., Wilde, J. de, Scherpen, J.M.A. (Eds.), Smart Grids from a Global Perspective: Bridging Old and New Energy Systems. Springer Cham.

Mulder, M., Zomer, S.P.E., 2016. Contribution of green labels in electricity retail markets to fostering renewable energy. Energy Policy 99, 100–109. https://doi.org/10.1016/j.enpol.2016.09.040.

Müller, S., Rode, J., 2013a. The adoption of photovoltaic systems in Wiesbaden, Germany. Economics of Innovation and New Technology 22, 519–535. https://doi.org/10.1080/10438599.2013.804333.

Müller, S., Rode, J., 2013b. The adoption of photovoltaic systems in Wiesbaden, Germany. Economics of Innovation and New Technology 22, 519–535. https://doi.org/10.1080/10438599.2013.804333.

Musolino, M., Maggio, G., D'Aleo, E., Nicita, A., 2023. Three case studies to explore relevant features of emerging renewable energy communities in Italy. Renewable Energy 210, 540–555. https://doi.org/10.1016/j.renene.2023.04.094.

Navarro-Espinosa, A., Ochoa, L.F., 2016. Probabilistic Impact Assessment of Low Carbon Technologies in LV Distribution Systems. IEEE Transactions on Power Systems 31, 2192–2203. https://doi.org/10.1109/TPWRS.2015.2448663.

NDRC, 2018. Notice of the NDRC and the NEA on printing and distributing the action plan for clean energy consumption (2018–2020) [国家发展改革委、国家能源局关于印发《清洁能源消纳行动计划(2018–2020年)》的通知].

NDRC, 2017. Measures for electricity DSM [电力需求侧管理办法].

NDRC, NEA, 2022. 14th Five-Year Plan for the Modern Energy System ["十四五"现代能源体系规划].

NEA, 2018. Brief of NEA on 2017 national renewable energy power development monitoring and evaluation.

Nepal, R., Jamasb, T., 2015. Incentive regulation and utility benchmarking for electricity network security. Economic Analysis and Policy 48, 117–127. https://doi.org/10.1016/j.eap.2015.11.001.

Netbeheer Nederland, 2018. Zienswijze Netbeheer Nederland Op Ontwerp Codebesluit Dataveiligheid [WWW Document]. URL www.acm.nl/nl/publicaties/zienswijze-netbeheer-nederland-op-ontwerp-codebesluit-dataveiligheid (accessed 6.18.24).

Neuhoff, K., Wolter, S., Schwenen, S., 2016. Power Markets with Renewables: New Perspectives for the European Target Model. The Energy Journal 37. https://doi.org/10.5547/01956574.37.2.kneu.

Neuteleers, S., Mulder, M., Hindriks, F., 2017. Assessing fairness of dynamic grid tariffs. Energy Policy 108, 111–120. https://doi.org/10.1016/j.enpol.2017.05.028.

Newbery, D., 2002. Problems of Liberalising the Electricity Industry. European Economic Review 46, 919–927. https://doi.org/10.1016/S0014-2921(01)00225-2.

Newbery, D., Pollitt, M.G., Ritz, R.A., Strielkowski, W., 2018. Market design for a high-renewables European electricity system. Renewable and Sustainable Energy Reviews 91, 695–707. https://doi.org/10.1016/j.rser.2018.04.025.

Ngan, H.W., 2010. Electricity regulation and electricity market reforms in China. Energy Policy 38, 2142–2148. https://doi.org/10.1016/j.enpol.2009.06.044.

Nicolson, M., Huebner, G., Shipworth, D., 2017. Are consumers willing to switch to smart time of use electricity tariffs? The importance of loss-aversion and electric vehicle ownership. Energy Research & Social Science 23, 82–96. https://doi.org/10.1016/j.erss.2016.12.001.

Nolan, J.M., Schultz, P.W., Cialdini, R.B., Goldstein, N.J., Griskevicius, V., 2008. Normative Social Influence is Underdetected. Pers Soc Psychol Bull 34, 913–923. https://doi.org/10.1177/0146167208316691.

Nolan, S., O'Malley, M., 2015. Challenges and barriers to demand response deployment and evaluation. Applied Energy 152, 1–10. https://doi.org/10.1016/j.apenergy.2015.04.083.

Nolting, L., Schuller, V., Gaumnitz, F., Praktiknjo, A., 2019. Incentivizing timely investments in electrical grids: Analysis of the amendment of the German distribution grid regulation. Energy Policy 132, 754–763. https://doi.org/10.1016/j.enpol.2019.06.027.

Nyborg, S., Røpke, I., 2013. Constructing users in the smart grid – insights from the Danish eFlex project. Energy Efficiency 6, 655–670. https://doi.org/10.1007/s12053-013-9210-1.

Nykamp, S., Andor, M., Hurink, J.L., 2012. 'Standard' incentive regulation hinders the integration of renewable energy generation. Energy Policy 47, 222–237. https://doi.org/10.1016/j.enpol.2012.04.061.

Oberthur, S., Söebech, Ó., Derde, H., Jackers, K., Vanhoenacker, J., Vermeir, T., Vandorpe, W., Haverbeke, D., 2020. Legislative options and obstacles for energy communities in Belgium: Summary of key issues identified & recommendations (ROLECS project Task 2.3.1). VUB.

Ocker, F., 2017. Design and performance of European balancing power auctions, in: 2017 14th International Conference on the European Energy Market (EEM). Presented at the 2017 14th International Conference on the European Energy Market (EEM), pp. 1–6. https://doi.org/10.1109/EEM.2017.7981861.

O'Connell, N., Pinson, P., Madsen, H., O'Malley, M., 2014. Benefits and challenges of electrical demand response: A critical review. Renewable and Sustainable Energy Reviews 39, 686–699. https://doi.org/10.1016/j.rser.2014.07.098.

OCTOBER 23, 2022. – Law amending the Act of 29 April 1999 on the organization of the electricity market and transposing Directive (EU) 2019/944 of the European Parliament and of the Council of 5 June 2019 on common rules for internal electricity market and amending Directive 2012/27/EU [23 OKTOBER 2022. – Wet tot wijziging van de wet van 29 april 1999 betreffende de organisatie van de elektriciteitsmarkt en tot omzetting van de Richtlijn (EU) 2019/944 van het Europees Parlement en de Raad van 5 juni 2019 betreffende gemeenschappelijke regels voor de interne markt voor elektriciteit en tot wijziging van Richtlijn 2012/27/EU], 2022.

OFGEM, 2010. RIIO, A New Way to Regulate Energy Networks: Final Decision.

OFGEM, 2001. Information and incentives project, Incentive schemes: Final proposals.

Olivella-Rosell, P., Bullich-Massagué, E., Aragüés-Peñalba, M., Sumper, A., Ottesen, S.Ø., Vidal-Clos, J.-A., Villafáfila-Robles, R., 2018. Optimization problem for meeting distribution system operator requests in local flexibility markets with distributed energy resources. Applied Energy 210, 881–895. https://doi.org/10.1016/j.apenergy.2017.08.136.

Oliver, G., Sophia, P., Daphne, V., 2017. Innovation incentives for distribution systems operators – a must in the new energy market development. CIRED 1, 2791–2794. https://doi.org/10.1049/oap-cired.2017.0064.

Olsthoorn, M., Schleich, J., Klobasa, M., 2015. Barriers to electricity load shift in companies: A survey-based exploration of the end-user perspective. Energy Policy 76, 32–42. https://doi.org/10.1016/j.enpol.2014.11.015.

Opinion of Advocate General Bobek in Schrems, C-498/16, EU:C:2017:863, 2017.

Opinion of Advocate General Bobek in Viesgo Infraestructuras Energéticas, Case C-683/19, EU:C:2021:300, 2021.

Opinion of Advocate General Ruiz-Jarabo Colomer in Benincasa, C-269/95, EU:C:1997:78, 1997.

Overbeeke, F. van, Roberts, V., 2002. Active networks as facilitators for embedded generation. Cogeneration and On-Site Power Production 3, 37.

Pablo-Romero, M.P., Sánchez-Braza, A., Galyan, A., 2021. Renewable energy use for electricity generation in transition economies: Evolution, targets and promotion policies. Renewable and Sustainable Energy Reviews 138, 110481. https://doi.org/10.1016/j.rser.2020.110481.

Paddock, L., Youngblood, C., 2012. Demand Response and Infrastructure Development in the United States, in: Roggenkamp, M.M., Barrera-Hernández, L., Zillman,

D.N., del Guayo, I. (Eds.), Energy Networks and the Law: Innovative Solutions in Changing Markets. Oxford University Press, p. 0. https://doi.org/10.1093/acprof:oso/9780199645039.003.0009.

Paetz, A.-G., Dütschke, E., Fichtner, W., 2012. Smart Homes as a Means to Sustainable Energy Consumption: A Study of Consumer Perceptions. Journal of Consumer Policy 35, 23–41. https://doi.org/10.1007/s10603-011-9177-2.

Palensky, P., Dietrich, D., 2011. Demand Side Management: Demand Response, Intelligent Energy Systems, and Smart Loads. IEEE Transactions on Industrial Informatics 7, 381–388. https://doi.org/10.1109/TII.2011.2158841.

Palm, A., 2017. Peer effects in residential solar photovoltaics adoption – A mixed methods study of Swedish users. Energy Research & Social Science 26, 1–10. https://doi.org/10.1016/j.erss.2017.01.008.

Palm, J., 2021. The Transposition of Energy Communities into Swedish Regulations: Overview and Critique of Emerging Regulations. Energies 14. https://doi.org/10.3390/en14164982.

Palm, J., 2018. Household installation of solar panels – Motives and barriers in a 10-year perspective. Energy Policy 113, 1–8. https://doi.org/10.1016/j.enpol.2017.10.047.

Papalexopoulos, A., Frowd, R., Birbas, A., 2020. On the development of organized nodal local energy markets and a framework for the TSO-DSO coordination. Electric Power Systems Research 189, 106810. https://doi.org/10.1016/j.epsr.2020.106810.

Papavasiliou, A., Mezghani, I., 2018. Coordination Schemes for the Integration of Transmission and Distribution System Operations, in: 2018 Power Systems Computation Conference (PSCC). Presented at the 2018 Power Systems Computation Conference (PSCC), pp. 1–7. https://doi.org/10.23919/PSCC.2018.8443022.

Papsch, J., 2020. Renewable energies in the electricity market, in: Jones, C., Ermacora, F. (Eds.), EU Energy Law Volume XII: Electricity Market Design in the European Union – The New Legal Framework for Decarbonising Europe's Electricity Market. CLAEYS & CASTEELS, p. 39.

Parag, Y., Sovacool, B.K., 2016. Electricity market design for the prosumer era. Nature Energy 1, 16032. https://doi.org/10.1038/nenergy.2016.32.

Paris Agreement, 2015.

Park, C., Heo, W., 2020. Review of the changing electricity industry value chain in the ICT convergence era. Journal of Cleaner Production 258, 120743. https://doi.org/10.1016/j.jclepro.2020.120743.

Parrish, B., Heptonstall, P., Gross, R., Sovacool, B.K., 2020. A systematic review of motivations, enablers and barriers for consumer engagement with residential demand response. Energy Policy 138, 111221. https://doi.org/10.1016/j.enpol.2019.111221.

Paterakis, N.G., Erdinç, O., Catalão, J.P.S., 2017. An overview of Demand Response: Key-elements and international experience. Renewable and Sustainable Energy Reviews 69, 871–891. https://doi.org/10.1016/j.rser.2016.11.167.

Paul Craig, 2006. EU Administrative Law. Oxford University Press.

Paulus, M., Borggrefe, F., 2011. The potential of demand-side management in energy-intensive industries for electricity markets in Germany. Applied Energy 88, 432–441. https://doi.org/10.1016/j.apenergy.2010.03.017.

Pearson, I., 2020. The role of consumers and innovation, in: Jones, C., Ermacora, F. (Eds.), EU Energy Law Volume XII: Electricity Market Design in the European Union – The New Legal Framework for Decarbonising Europe's Electricity Market. CLAEYS & CASTEELS.

Peng, D., Poudineh, R., 2019. Electricity market design under increasing renewable energy penetration: Misalignments observed in the European Union. Utilities Policy 61, 100970. https://doi.org/10.1016/j.jup.2019.100970.

Pepermans, G., Driesen, J., Haeseldonckx, D., Belmans, R., D'haeseleer, W., 2005. Distributed generation: definition, benefits and issues. Energy Policy 33, 787–798. https://doi.org/10.1016/j.enpol.2003.10.004.

Pereira, G.I., Pereira da Silva, P., Cerqueira, P.A., 2020. Electricity distribution incumbents' adaptation toward decarbonized and smarter grids: Evidence on the role market, regulatory, investment, and firm-level factors. Energy Policy 142, 111477. https://doi.org/10.1016/j.enpol.2020.111477.

Pereira, G.I., Specht, J.M., Silva, P.P., Madlener, R., 2018. Technology, business model, and market design adaptation toward smart electricity distribution: Insights for policy making. Energy Policy 121, 426–440. https://doi.org/10.1016/j.enpol.2018.06.018.

Pesendorfer, W., 2006. Behavioral Economics Comes of Age: A Review Essay on *Advances in Behavioral Economics*. Journal of Economic Literature 44, 712–721. https://doi.org/10.1257/jel.44.3.712.

Piris, J.-C., 2010. The Lisbon Treaty: A Legal and Political Analysis. Cambridge University Press.

Pollitt, M.G., Haney, A.B., 2013. Dismantling a Competitive Electricity Sector: The U.K.'s Electricity Market Reform. The Electricity Journal 26, 8–15. https://doi.org/10.1016/j.tej.2013.11.001.

Popelier, P., 2011. Governance and Better Regulation: Dealing with the Legitimacy Paradox. European Public Law 555–569.

Poplavskaya, K., Lago, J., de Vries, L., 2020. Effect of market design on strategic bidding behavior: Model-based analysis of European electricity balancing markets. Applied Energy 270, 115130. https://doi.org/10.1016/j.apenergy.2020.115130.

Poplavskaya, K., Lago, J., Strömer, S., de Vries, L., 2021. Making the most of short-term flexibility in the balancing market: Opportunities and challenges of voluntary bids in the new balancing market design. Energy Policy 158, 112522. https://doi.org/10.1016/j.enpol.2021.112522.

Poplavskaya, K., Vries, L. de, 2019. Distributed energy resources and the organized balancing market: A symbiosis yet? Case of three European balancing markets. Energy Policy 126, 264–276. https://doi.org/10.1016/j.enpol.2018.11.009.

Poplavskaya, K., Vries, L. de, 2018. A (not so) Independent Aggregator in the Balancing Market Theory, Policy and Reality Check, in: 2018 15th International Conference on the European Energy Market (EEM). Presented at the 2018 15th International Conference on the European Energy Market (EEM), pp. 1–6. https://doi.org/10.1109/EEM.2018.8469981.

Porto, F.D., Rangone, N., 2015. Behavioural Sciences in Practices: Lessons for EU Policymakers, in: Alemanno, A., Sibony, A.-L. (Eds.), Nudge and the Law: A European Perspective. Hart Publishing.

Pototschnig, A., Conti, I., 2021. Upgrading Guarantees of Origin to Promote the Achievement of the EU Renewable Energy Target at Least Cost (Research Project Report). Florence School of Regulation.

Potter, J., Stuart, E., Cappers, P., 2018. Barriers and Opportunities to Broader Adoption of Integrated Demand Side Management at Electric Utilities. Energy Analysis and Environmental Impacts Division Lawrence Berkeley National Laboratory.

Poudineh, R., 2019. Liberalized retail electricity markets: What we have learned after two decades of experience? (No. Oxford Institute for Energy Studies Paper: EL 38).

Pound, R., 1912. The Scope and Purpose of Sociological Jurisprudence. [Concluded.] III. Sociological Jurisprudence. Harvard Law Review 25, 489–516. https://doi.org/10.2307/1324775.

Powells, G., Fell, M.J., 2019. Flexibility capital and flexibility justice in smart energy systems. Energy Research & Social Science 54, 56–59. https://doi.org/10.1016/j.erss.2019.03.015.

Pressmair, G., Kapassa, E., Casado-Mansilla, D., Borges, C.E., Themistocleous, M., 2021. Overcoming barriers for the adoption of Local Energy and Flexibility Markets: A user-centric and hybrid model. Journal of Cleaner Production 317, 128323. https://doi.org/10.1016/j.jclepro.2021.128323.

Prettico, G., Flammini, M.G., Andreadou, N., Vitiello, S., Fulli, G., Masera, M., 2019. Distribution System Operators Observatory 2018 (No. JRC113926).

Proposal for a DIRECTIVE OF THE EUROPEAN PARLIAMENT AND OF THE COUNCIL on the promotion of the use of energy from renewable sources, 2017.

Protocol on Sharing and Selling Self-generated RES-E – version 3.2 [Protocol energiedelen, persoon-aan-persoonverkoop en verkoop in gebouwen – versie 3.2], 2024.

Qiu, D., Ye, Y., Papadaskalopoulos, D., 2020. Exploring the effects of local energy markets on electricity retailers and customers. Electric Power Systems Research 189, 106761. https://doi.org/10.1016/j.epsr.2020.106761.

Quan, H., Srinivasan, D., Khambadkone, A.M., Khosravi, A., 2015. A computational framework for uncertainty integration in stochastic unit commitment with intermittent renewable energy sources. Applied Energy 152, 71–82. https://doi.org/10.1016/j.apenergy.2015.04.103.

Quint, R., Dangelmaier, L., Green, I., Edelson, D., Ganugula, V., Kaneshiro, R., Pigeon, J., Quaintance, B., Riesz, J., Stringer, N., 2019. Transformation of the Grid: The Impact of Distributed Energy Resources on Bulk Power Systems. IEEE Power and Energy Magazine 17, 35–45. https://doi.org/10.1109/MPE.2019.2933071.

R. Claeys, R. Cleenwerck, J. Knockaert, J. Desmet, 2023. Volumetric or capacity-based grid tariffs: a case study for residential consumers in Flanders, in: 27th International Conference on Electricity Distribution (CIRED 2023). Presented at the 27th International Conference on Electricity Distribution (CIRED 2023), pp. 1430–1434. https://doi.org/10.1049/icp.2023.0761.

Raadal, H.L., Dotzauer, E., Hanssen, O.J., Kildal, H.P., 2012. The interaction between Electricity Disclosure and Tradable Green Certificates. Energy Policy 42, 419–428. https://doi.org/10.1016/j.enpol.2011.12.006.

Raadal, H.L., Nyland, C.A., Hanssen, O.J., 2009. Calculation of Residual Electricity Mixes when Accounting for the EECS (European Electricity Certificate System) – the Need for a Harmonised System. Energies 2, 477–489. https://doi.org/10.3390/en20300477.

Ragwitz, M., del Río González, P., Resch, G., 2009. Assessing the advantages and drawbacks of government trading of guarantees of origin for renewable electricity in Europe. Energy Policy 37, 300–307. https://doi.org/10.1016/j.enpol.2008.07.032.

Raineau, L., 2022. Rethinking path dependence, technical innovation and social practices in a renewable energy future. Energy Research & Social Science 84, 102411. https://doi.org/10.1016/j.erss.2021.102411.

Ramos, A., De Jonghe, C., Gómez, V., Belmans, R., 2016. Realizing the smart grid's potential: Defining local markets for flexibility. Utilities Policy 40, 26–35. https://doi.org/10.1016/j.jup.2016.03.006.

Rebenaque, O., Schmitt, C., Schumann, K., Dronne, T., Roques, F., 2023. Success of local flexibility market implementation: A review of current projects. Utilities Policy 80, 101491. https://doi.org/10.1016/j.jup.2023.101491.

Rebours, Y.G., Kirschen, D.S., Trotignon, M., Rossignol, S., 2007. A Survey of Frequency and Voltage Control Ancillary Services – Part I: Technical Features. IEEE Transactions on Power Systems 22, 350–357. https://doi.org/10.1109/TPWRS.2006.888963.

Regulation (EC) No 715/2009 of the European Parliament and of the Council of 13 July 2009 on conditions for access to the natural gas transmission networks and repealing Regulation (EC) No 1775/2005, 2009.

Regulation (EU) 2016/679 of the European Parliament and of the Council of 27 April 2016 on the protection of natural persons with regard to the processing of personal data and on the free movement of such data, and repealing Directive 95/46/EC [2016] OJ L 119/1, 2016.

Regulation (EU) 2018/1725 of the European Parliament and of the Council of 23 October 2018 on the protection of natural persons with regard to the processing of personal data by the Union institutions, bodies, offices and agencies and on the free movement of such data, and repealing Regulation (EC) No 45/2001 and Decision No 1247/2002/EC [2018] OJ L 295/39, 2018.

Regulation (EU) 2018/1999 of the European Parliament and of the Council of 11 December 2018 on the Governance of the Energy Union and Climate Action, amending Regulations (EC) No 663/2009 and (EC) No 715/2009 of the European Parliament and of the Council, Directives 94/22/EC, 98/70/EC, 2009/31/EC, 2009/73/EC, 2010/31/EU, 2012/27/EU and 2013/30/EU of the European Parliament and of the Council, Council Directives 2009/119/EC and (EU) 2015/652 and repealing Regulation (EU) No 525/2013 of the European Parliament and of the Council, 2018.

Regulation (EU) 2019/941 of the European Parliament and of the Council of 5 June 2019 on risk-preparedness in the electricity sector and repealing Directive 2005/89/EC, 2019.

Regulation (EU) 2019/943 of the European Parliament and of the Council of 5 June 2019 on the internal market for electricity [2019] OJ L 158/54.

Regulation (EU) 2020/1503 of the European Parliament and of the Council of 7 October 2020 on European crowdfunding service providers for business, and amending Regulation (EU) 2017/1129 and Directive (EU) 2019/1937, 2020.

Regulation (EU) 2021/1119 of the European Parliament and of the Council of 30 June 2021 establishing the framework for achieving climate neutrality and amending Regulations (EC) No 401/2009 and (EU) 2018/1999, 2021.

Regulation (EU) 2022/1925 of the European Parliament and of the Council of 14 September 2022 on contestable and fair markets in the digital sector and amending Directives (EU) 2019/1937 and (EU) 2020/1828, 2022.

Regulation (EU) 2022/2065 of the European Parliament and of the Council of 19 October 2022 on a Single Market For Digital Services and amending Directive 2000/31/EC, 2022.

Regulation (EU) 2024/1747 of the European Parliament and of the Council of 13 June 2024 amending Regulations (EU) 2019/942 and (EU) 2019/943 as regards improving the Union's electricity market design, 2024.

Regulation (EU) No 1227/2011 of the European Parliament and of the Council of 25 October 2011 on wholesale energy market integrity and transparency, 2011.

Reijula, S., Hertwig, R., 2022. Self-nudging and the citizen choice architect. Behavioural Public Policy 6, 119–149. https://doi.org/10.1017/bpp.2020.5.

Reisch, L.A., Sunstein, C.R., Gwozdz, W., 2017. Viewpoint: Beyond carrots and sticks: Europeans support health nudges. Food Policy 69, 1–10. https://doi.org/10.1016/j.foodpol.2017.01.007.

Renewable Energies Expansion Act [Bundesgesetz über den Ausbau von Energie aus erneuerbaren Quellen (Erneuerbaren-Ausbau-Gesetz – EAG)], 2021.

Report on Energy communities, energy sharing and peer-to-peer trading of green power in 2022 [Rapport Energiegemeenschappen, energiedelen en peer-to-peerhandel van groene stroom in 2022] (RAPP-2022-23), 2022.

Resch, G., Gephart, M., Steinhilber, S., Klessmann, C., Rio, P. del, Ragwitz, M., 2013. Coordination or harmonization? Feasible pathways for a European RES strategy beyond 2020. Energy & Environment 24, 147–169. https://doi.org/10.1260/0958-305X.24.1-2.147.

REScoop.eu, 2024a. Transposition tracker – Enabling Frameworks & Support Schemes [WWW Document]. URL https://www.rescoop.eu/transposition-tracker-support-schemes (accessed 2.7.24).

REScoop.eu, 2024b. Transposition tracker – Definitions – Portugal [WWW Document]. URL https://www.rescoop.eu/policy/portugal-rec-cec-definitions (accessed 2.7.24).

REScoop.eu, 2024c. Transposition tracker – Enabling Frameworks & Support Schemes – The Netherlands [WWW Document]. URL https://www.rescoop.eu/policy/netherlands (accessed 2.7.24).

REScoop.eu, 2024d. Transposition tracker – Enabling Frameworks & Support Schemes – Germany [WWW Document]. URL https://www.rescoop.eu/policy/germany-2 (accessed 2.7.24).

REScoop.eu, 2024e. Transposition tracker – Definitions [WWW Document]. URL https://www.rescoop.eu/transposition-tracker (accessed 2.9.24).

REScoop.eu, 2024f. Transposition tracker – Definitions -Ireland [WWW Document]. URL https://www.rescoop.eu/policy/ireland-rec-cec-definitions (accessed 2.9.24).

REScoop.eu, 2024g. Transposition tracker – Definitions – Slovakia [WWW Document]. URL https://www.rescoop.eu/policy/slovakia (accessed 2.8.24).

REScoop.eu, 2024h. Transposition tracker – Definitions – Greece [WWW Document]. URL https://www.rescoop.eu/policy/greece-rec-cec-definitions (accessed 2.8.24).

REScoop.eu, 2024i. Transposition tracker – Definitions – Croatia [WWW Document]. URL https://www.rescoop.eu/policy/greece-rec-cec-definitions (accessed 2.8.24).

RESCoop.eu, 2024j. Transposition tracker – Enabling Frameworks & Support Schemes – Greece [WWW Document]. URL https://www.rescoop.eu/policy/greece (accessed 2.8.24).

RESCoop.eu, 2024k. Transposition tracker – Enabling Frameworks & Support Schemes – Italy [WWW Document]. URL https://www.rescoop.eu/policy/italy (accessed 2.8.24).

RESCoop.eu, 2024l. Transposition tracker – Enabling Frameworks & Support Schemes – Spain [WWW Document]. URL https://www.rescoop.eu/policy/spain (accessed 2.8.24).

RESCoop.eu, ClientEarth, 2020. Energy Communities under the Clean Energy Package: Transposition Guidance.

Rikkonen, P., Tapio, P., Rintamäki, H., 2019. Visions for small-scale renewable energy production on Finnish farms – A Delphi study on the opportunities for new business. Energy Policy 129, 939–948. https://doi.org/10.1016/j.enpol.2019.03.004.

Ringelstein, J., Vogt, M., Khavari, A.M., Ciavarella, R., Di Somma, M., Graditi, G., 2022. A methodology for improved TSO-DSO coordination in grid operation planning. Electric Power Systems Research 211, 108445. https://doi.org/10.1016/j.epsr.2022.108445.

Roberts, J., 2020. Power to the people? Implications of the Clean Energy Package for the role of community ownership in Europe's energy transition. Review of European, Comparative & International Environmental Law 29, 232–244. https://doi.org/10.1111/reel.12346.

Robilant, A.D., 2006. Genealogies of Soft Law. The American Journal of Comparative Law 54, 499–554. https://doi.org/10.1093/ajcl/54.3.499.

Roggenkamp, M., Diestelmeier, L., 2020. Energy Market Reforms in the EU: A New Focus on Energy Consumers, Energy Poverty, and Energy (in)Justice?, in: Guayo, I. del, Godden, L., Zillman, D.D., Montoya, M.F., González, J.J. (Eds.), Energy Justice and Energy Law. Oxford University Press, p. 160.

Roos, A., 2017. Designing a joint market for procurement of transmission and distribution system services from demand flexibility. Renewable Energy Focus 21, 16–24. https://doi.org/10.1016/j.ref.2017.06.004.

Rosen, C., Madlener, R., 2016. Regulatory Options for Local Reserve Energy Markets: Implications for Prosumers, Utilities, and other Stakeholders. The Energy Journal 37, 39–50. https://doi.org/10.5547/01956574.37.SI2.cros.

Rosenow, J., 2012. Energy savings obligations in the UK – A history of change. Energy Policy 49, 373–382. https://doi.org/10.1016/j.enpol.2012.06.052.

Rowlands, I.H., 2005. The European directive on renewable electricity: conflicts and compromises. Energy Policy 33, 965–974. https://doi.org/10.1016/j.enpol.2003.10.019.

Ruester, S., Schwenen, S., Batlle, C., Pérez-Arriaga, I., 2014. From distribution networks to smart distribution systems: Rethinking the regulation of European electricity DSOs. Utilities Policy 31, 229–237. https://doi.org/10.1016/j.jup.2014.03.007.

Ruggiero, S., Varho, V., Rikkonen, P., 2015. Transition to distributed energy generation in Finland: Prospects and barriers. Energy Policy 86, 433–443. https://doi.org/10.1016/j.enpol.2015.07.024.

Rules on the organization of transfer of energy [Regels voor de organisatie van de Energieoverdracht], 2021.

Ruling of 14 January 2020, cases 18/2783 and 18/2846, NJB 2020/245, ECLI:NL:CBB:2020:3, 2020.

Rumpf, J., Bjørnebye, H., 2019. Just how much is enough? EU regulation of capacity and reliability margins on electricity interconnectors. Journal of Energy & Natural Resources Law 37, 67–91. https://doi.org/10.1080/02646811.2018.1471802.

Rumpf, J., Hancher, L., 2021. Baltic Cable AB v Energimarknadsinspektionen (C-454/18): The CJEU Decides on Congestion Income Regulation of Single Electricity Interconnector Companies and Applies Classic Remedies for Modern Issues. European Law Review 46.

Ruotsalainen, J., Karjalainen, J., Child, M., Heinonen, S., 2017. Culture, values, lifestyles, and power in energy futures: A critical peer-to-peer vision for renewable energy. Energy Research & Social Science 34, 231–239. https://doi.org/10.1016/j.erss.2017.08.001.

Sæle, H., Sperstad, I.B., Wang Hoiem, K., Mathiesen, V., 2023. Understanding barriers to utilising flexibility in operation and planning of the electricity distribution system – Classification frameworks with applications to Norway. Energy Policy 180, 113618. https://doi.org/10.1016/j.enpol.2023.113618.

Salies, E., 2013. Real-time pricing when some consumers resist in saving electricity. Energy Policy 59, 843–849. https://doi.org/10.1016/j.enpol.2013.04.050.

Samenwerkingsovereenkomst Elia – DNB, 2021.

Samuelson, W., Zeckhauser, R., 1988. Status quo bias in decision making. Journal of Risk and Uncertainty 1, 7–59. https://doi.org/10.1007/BF00055564.

Sandberg, L., Davies, L., 2019. The relevant geographic market – Electricity, in: Jones, C. (Ed.), EU Energy Law: Volume II EU Competition Law and Energy Markets. CLAEYS & CASTEELS.

Santos Silva, M., 2022. Nudging and Other Behaviourally Based Policies as Enablers for Environmental Sustainability. Laws 11. https://doi.org/10.3390/laws11010009.

Schaefer, T., 2018. EEG-Umlage: Umverteilung von unten nach oben (No. IW-Kurzbericht No. 67/2018). Institut der deutschen Wirtschaft.

Schallehn, F., Valogianni, K., 2022. Sustainability awareness and smart meter privacy concerns: The cases of US and Germany. Energy Policy 161, 112756. https://doi.org/10.1016/j.enpol.2021.112756.

Scharnhorst, L., Sloot, D., Lehmann, N., Ardone, A., Fichtner, W., 2024. Barriers to demand response in the commercial and industrial sectors – An empirical investigation. Renewable and Sustainable Energy Reviews 190, 114067. https://doi.org/10.1016/j.rser.2023.114067.

Schittekatte, T., Meeus, L., 2020. Flexibility markets: Q&A with project pioneers. Utilities Policy 63, 101017. https://doi.org/10.1016/j.jup.2020.101017.

Schittekatte, T., Reif, V., Meeus, L., 2020. The EU Electricity Network Codes.

Schively, C., 2007. Understanding the NIMBY and LULU Phenomena: Reassessing Our Knowledge Base and Informing Future Research. Journal of Planning Literature 21, 255–266. https://doi.org/10.1177/0885412206295845.

Schleich, J., 2009. Barriers to energy efficiency: A comparison across the German commercial and services sector. Ecological Economics 68, 2150–2159. https://doi.org/10.1016/j.ecolecon.2009.02.008.

Schleich, J., Gruber, E., 2008. Beyond case studies: Barriers to energy efficiency in commerce and the services sector. Energy Economics 30, 449–464. https://doi.org/10.1016/j.eneco.2006.08.004.

Schleicher-Tappeser, R., 2012. How renewables will change electricity markets in the next five years. Energy Policy 48, 64–75. https://doi.org/10.1016/j.enpol.2012.04.042.

Schmid, E., Knopf, B., Pechan, A., 2016. Putting an energy system transformation into practice: The case of the German Energiewende. Energy Research & Social Science 11, 263–275. https://doi.org/10.1016/j.erss.2015.11.002.

Schmitt, C., 1921. Die Diktatur.

Schneiders, A., Shipworth, D., 2018. Energy Cooperatives: A Missing Piece of the Peer-to-Peer Energy Regulation Puzzle? University College London (UCL) Energy Institute.

Schoser, C., Sandberg, L., 2021. The regulation on cross-border electricity exchanges: substantive rules, in: Jones, C., Kettlewell, W.-J. (Eds.), EU Energy Law Volume I: The Internal Energy Market. CLAEYS & CASTEELS, pp. 503–506.

Schumann, K., Zocher, J., Cramer, W., Ulbig, A., 2022. Impact of preference-based electricity products on local energy markets. Electric Power Systems Research 212, 108492. https://doi.org/10.1016/j.epsr.2022.108492.

Schwidtal, J.M., Piccini, P., Troncia, M., Chitchyan, R., Montakhabi, M., Francis, C., Gorbatcheva, A., Capper, T., Mustafa, M.A., Andoni, M., Robu, V., Bahloul, M., Scott, I.J., Mbavarira, T., España, J.M., Kiesling, L., 2023. Emerging business models in local energy markets: A systematic review of peer-to-peer, community self-consumption, and transactive energy models. Renewable and Sustainable Energy Reviews 179, 113273. https://doi.org/10.1016/j.rser.2023.113273.

Scott, C., 2009. Governing Without Law or Governing Without Government? New-ish Governance and the Legitimacy of the EU. European Law Journal 15, 160–173. https://doi.org/10.1111/j.1468-0386.2008.00456.x.

Scott, C., 2001. Analysing regulatory space: fragmented resources and institutional design. Public Law 283–305.

SEAI, 2024a. Community Energy Resource Toolkit-Solar PV.

SEAI, 2024b. Community Energy Resource Toolkit-The Planning Process.

SEAI, 2021a. Community Energy Resource Toolkit-Onshore Wind.

SEAI, 2021b. Community Energy Resource Toolkit-Grid Connection.

SEDC, 2017. Explicit Demand Response in Europe Mapping the Markets 2017.

SEDC, 2014. Mapping Demand Response in Europe Today.

Shafie-khah, M., Siano, P., Aghaei, J., Masoum, M.A.S., Li, F., Catalão, J.P.S., 2019. Comprehensive Review of the Recent Advances in Industrial and Commercial DR. IEEE Transactions on Industrial Informatics 15, 3757–3771. https://doi.org/10.1109/TII.2019.2909276.

Shafir, E., 2017. Decisions in poverty contexts. Current Opinion in Psychology 18, 131–136. https://doi.org/10.1016/j.copsyc.2017.08.026.

Shah, A.K., Zhao, J., Mullainathan, S., Shafir, E., 2018. Money in the Mental Lives of the Poor. Social Cognition 36, 4–19. https://doi.org/10.1521/soco.2018.36.1.4.

Shaw, R., Attree, M., Jackson, T., 2010. Developing electricity distribution networks and their regulation to support sustainable energy. Energy Policy 38, 5927–5937. https://doi.org/10.1016/j.enpol.2010.05.046.

Shen, B., Ghatikar, G., Lei, Z., Li, J., Wikler, G., Martin, P., 2014. The role of regulatory reforms, market changes, and technology development to make demand response a viable resource in meeting energy challenges. Applied Energy 130, 814–823. https://doi.org/10.1016/j.apenergy.2013.12.069.

Shleifer, A., 1985. A theory of yardstick competition. Rand Journal of Economics 16, 319.

Shoreh, M.H., Siano, P., Shafie-khah, M., Loia, V., Catalão, J.P.S., 2016. A survey of industrial applications of Demand Response. Electric Power Systems Research 141, 31–49. https://doi.org/10.1016/j.epsr.2016.07.008.

Shuttleworth, G., 2005. Benchmarking of electricity networks: Practical problems with its use for regulation. Utilities Policy 13, 310–317. https://doi.org/10.1016/j.jup.2005.01.002.

Silva, C., Faria, P., Vale, Z., 2023. Demand Response Implementation: Overview of Europe and United States Status. Energies 16. https://doi.org/10.3390/en16104043.

Silva, J., Sumaili, J., R. J. Bessa, L. Seca, M. A. Matos, Miranda, V., Caujolle, M., Goncer, B., Sebastian-Viana, M., 2018. Estimating the Active and Reactive Power Flexibility Area at the TSO-DSO Interface. IEEE Transactions on Power Systems 33, 4741–4750. https://doi.org/10.1109/TPWRS.2018.2805765.

Silva, N., Pinto, C.M., Bernardo, A.M., Carrapatoso, A., Pestana, R., Dias, S., 2012. The interaction between DSO and TSO to increase DG penetration – The Portuguese example, in: CIRED 2012 Workshop: Integration of Renewables into the Distribution Grid. Presented at the CIRED 2012 Workshop: Integration of Renewables into the Distribution Grid, pp. 1–4. https://doi.org/10.1049/cp.2012.0885.

Simon, H.A., 1955. A Behavioral Model of Rational Choice. The Quarterly Journal of Economics 69, 99–118. https://doi.org/10.2307/1884852.

Simshauser, P., 2016. Distribution network prices and solar PV: Resolving rate instability and wealth transfers through demand tariffs. Energy Economics 54, 108–122. https://doi.org/10.1016/j.eneco.2015.11.011.

Sioshansi, F.P., Pfaffenberger, W., 2006. Electricity Market Reform: An International Perspective. Elsevier.

Sirr, G., Power, B., Ryan, G., Eakins, J., O'Connor, E., le Maitre, J., 2023. An analysis of the factors affecting Irish citizens' willingness to invest in wind energy projects. Energy Policy 173, 113364. https://doi.org/10.1016/j.enpol.2022.113364.

Słotwiński, S., 2022. The Significance of the "Power Purchase Agreement" for the Development of Local Energy Markets in the Theoretical Perspective of Polish Legal Conditions. Energies 15. https://doi.org/10.3390/en15186691.

smartEn Map, 2018. European Balancing Markets Edition 2018.

Smits, J.M., 2017. What is Legal Doctrine? On the Aims and Methods of Legal-Dogmatic Research, in: Gestel, R. van, Hans-W. Micklitz, Rubin, E.L. (Eds.), Rethinking Legal Scholarship: A Transatlantic Dialogue. Cambridge University Press.

Soares, T., Carvalho, L., Morais, H., Bessa, R.J., Abreu, T., Lambert, E., 2020. Reactive power provision by the DSO to the TSO considering renewable energy sources uncertainty. Sustainable Energy, Grids and Networks 22, 100333. https://doi.org/10.1016/j.segan.2020.100333.

Sokołowski, M.M., 2020. Renewable and citizen energy communities in the European Union: how (not) to regulate community energy in national laws and policies. Journal of Energy & Natural Resources Law 38, 289–304. https://doi.org/10.1080/02646811.2020.1759247.

Solomon, B.D., Krishna, K., 2011. The coming sustainable energy transition: History, strategies, and outlook. Energy Policy 39, 7422–7431. https://doi.org/10.1016/j.enpol.2011.09.009.

Sorrell, S., 2015. Reducing energy demand: A review of issues, challenges and approaches. Renewable and Sustainable Energy Reviews 47, 74–82. https://doi.org/10.1016/j.rser.2015.03.002.

Sorrell, S., O'Malley, E., Schleich, J., 2004. The Economics of Energy Efficiency. Edward Elgar.

Sotkiewicz, P.M., Vignolo, J.M., 2007. Towards a Cost Causation-Based Tariff for Distribution Networks With DG. IEEE Transactions on Power Systems 22, 1051–1060. https://doi.org/10.1109/TPWRS.2007.901284.

Sousa, J., Soares, I., 2023. Benefits and barriers concerning demand response stakeholder value chain: A systematic literature review. Energy 280, 128065. https://doi.org/10.1016/j.energy.2023.128065.

Sousa, T., Soares, T., Pinson, P., Moret, F., Baroche, T., Sorin, E., 2019. Peer-to-peer and community-based markets: A comprehensive review. Renewable and Sustainable Energy Reviews 104, 367–378. https://doi.org/10.1016/j.rser.2019.01.036.

Sovacool, B.K., 2013. Energy policymaking in Denmark: Implications for global energy security and sustainability. Energy Policy 61, 829–839. https://doi.org/10.1016/j.enpol.2013.06.106.

Sovacool, B.K., Dworkin, M.H., 2015. Energy justice: Conceptual insights and practical applications. Applied Energy 142, 435–444. https://doi.org/10.1016/j.apenergy.2015.01.002.

Sovacool, B.K., Heffron, R.J., McCauley, D., Goldthau, A., 2016. Energy decisions reframed as justice and ethical concerns. Nature Energy 1, 16024. https://doi.org/10.1038/nenergy.2016.24.

Sovacool, B.K., Hook, A., Sareen, S., Geels, F.W., 2021. Global sustainability, innovation and governance dynamics of national smart electricity meter transitions. Global Environmental Change 68, 102272. https://doi.org/10.1016/j.gloenvcha.2021.102272.

Sovacool, B.K., Kivimaa, P., Hielscher, S., Jenkins, K., 2017. Vulnerability and resistance in the United Kingdom's smart meter transition. Energy Policy 109, 767–781. https://doi.org/10.1016/j.enpol.2017.07.037.

Spears, D., 2011. Economic Decision-Making in Poverty Depletes Behavioral Control. The B.E. Journal of Economic Analysis & Policy 11. https://doi.org/10.2202/1935-1682.2973.

Special Law of 8 August 1980 on the Reform of Institution [8 AUGUSTUS 1980. – Bijzondere wet tot hervorming der instellingen], n.d.

Sridhar, A., Honkapuro, S., Ruiz, F., Stoklasa, J., Annala, S., Wolff, A., Rautiainen, A., 2023. Toward residential flexibility – Consumer willingness to enroll household loads in demand response. Applied Energy 342, 121204. https://doi.org/10.1016/j.apenergy.2023.121204.

Standing Committee of the National People's Congress, 1997. Energy Conservation Law of the People's Republic of China [中华人民共和国节约能源法].

State Aid SA.54683 (2020/N) – Ireland: Renewable Electricity Support Scheme (RESS), COM(2020) 4795 final, 2020.

Stede, J., Arnold, K., Dufter, C., Holtz, G., von Roon, S., Richstein, J.C., 2020. The role of aggregators in facilitating industrial demand response: Evidence from Germany. Energy Policy 147, 111893. https://doi.org/10.1016/j.enpol.2020.111893.

Steurer, M., Miller, M., Fahl, U., Hufendiek, K., 2015. Enabling demand side integration – assessment of appropriate information and communication technology infrastructures, their costs and possible impacts on the electricity system.

Stötzer, M., Hauer, I., Richter, M., Styczynski, Z.A., 2015. Potential of demand side integration to maximize use of renewable energy sources in Germany. Applied Energy 146, 344–352. https://doi.org/10.1016/j.apenergy.2015.02.015.

Strbac, G., 2008. Demand side management: Benefits and challenges. Energy Policy 36, 4419–4426. https://doi.org/10.1016/j.enpol.2008.09.030.

Streimikiene, D., Baležentis, T., Volkov, A., Morkūnas, M., Žičkienė, A., Streimikis, J., 2021. Barriers and Drivers of Renewable Energy Penetration in Rural Areas. Energies 14. https://doi.org/10.3390/en14206452.

Study (F)160503-CDC-1459 on the resources to be applied to facilitate participation in demand flexibility on the electricity markets in Belgium [Studie (F)160503-CDC-1459 over 'de middelen die moeten worden toegepast om de deelname aan de flexibiliteit van de vraag op de elektriciteitsmarkten in België te faciliteren'], 2016.

Su, W., Liu, M., Zeng, S., Štreimikienė, D., Baležentis, T., Ališauskaitė-Šeškienė, I., 2018. Valuating renewable microgeneration technologies in Lithuanian households: A study on willingness to pay. Journal of Cleaner Production 191, 318–329. https://doi.org/10.1016/j.jclepro.2018.04.199.

Sunstein, C.R., 2002. Risk and Reason, Safety, Law, and the Environment. Cambridge University Press.

Sunstein, C.R., 1990. After the Rights Revolution: Reconceiving the Regulatory State. Harvard University Press.

SWECO, 2015. Study on the effective integration of Distributed Energy Resources for providing flexibility to the electricity system: Final report to The European Commission.

T-13/99 – Pfizer Animal Health v Council [2002] ECR II-3305, 2002.

Talus, K., 2016. Introduction to EU Energy Law. Oxford University Press. https://doi.org/10.1093/acprof:oso/9780198791812.001.0001.

Talus, K., 2013. EU Energy Law and Policy: A Critical Account. Oxford University Press. https://doi.org/10.1093/acprof:oso/9780199686391.001.0001.

Tariff methodology for distribution electricity and natural gas during the regulatory period 2021–2024 [Tariefmethodologie voor distributie elektriciteit en aardgas gedurende de reguleringsperiode 2021–2024], 2021.

Technical Regulations for Distribution of Electricity in the Flemish Region [Technisch Reglement voor de Distributie van Elektriciteit in het Vlaamse Gewest], 2023.

Teotia Falti, Mathuria Parul, Bhakar Rohit, 2020. Peer-to-peer local electricity market platform pricing strategies for prosumers. IET Generation, Transmission & Distribution 14, 4388–4397. https://doi.org/10.1049/iet-gtd.2019.0578.

Ter-Martirosyan, A., 2003. The effects of incentive regulation on quality of service in electricity markets. Department of Economics, George Washington University.

Ter-Martirosyan, A., Kwoka, J., 2010. Incentive regulation, service quality, and standards in U.S. electricity distribution. Journal of Regulatory Economics 38, 258–273. https://doi.org/10.1007/s11149-010-9126-z.

Terms and Conditions for balancing service providers for manual Frequency Restoration Reserve (mFRR), 2020.

Tews, K., 2015. Europeanization of Energy and Climate Policy: The Struggle Between Competing Ideas of Coordinating Energy Transitions. The Journal of Environment & Development 24, 267–291. https://doi.org/10.1177/1070496515591578.

Thaler, R., 1981. Some empirical evidence on dynamic inconsistency. Economics Letters 8, 201–207. https://doi.org/10.1016/0165-1765(81)90067-7.

Thaler, R.H., Sunstein, C.R., 2021. Nudge: The Final Edition. Penguin Press.

Thaler, R.H., Sunstein, C.R., 2008. Nudge: improving decisions about health, wealth, and happiness. Yale University Press.

Thomas, S., 2023. A perspective on the RIIO formula: Old wine in new bottles. Utilities Policy 80, 101450. https://doi.org/10.1016/j.jup.2022.101450.

Tierney, S., Schatzki, T., Mukerji, R., 2010. Uniform-Pricing versus Pay-as-Bid in Wholesale Electricity Markets: Does it Make a Difference?

Torriti, J., Hassan, M.G., Leach, M., 2010. Demand response experience in Europe: Policies, programmes and implementation. Energy 35, 1575–1583. https://doi.org/10.1016/j.energy.2009.05.021.

Tridimas, T., 1999. Proportionality in Community Law: Searching for the Appropriate Standard of Scrutiny, in: Ellis, E. (Ed.), The Principle of Proportionality in the Laws of Europe. Hart Publishing.

Tushar, W., Yuen, C., Saha, T.K., Morstyn, T., Chapman, A.C., Alam, M.J.E., Hanif, S., Poor, H.V., 2021. Peer-to-peer energy systems for connected communities: A review of recent advances and emerging challenges. Applied Energy 282, 116131. https://doi.org/10.1016/j.apenergy.2020.116131.

Tversky, A., Kahneman, D., 1974. Judgment under Uncertainty: Heuristics and Biases. Science 185, 1124–1131. https://doi.org/10.1126/science.185.4157.1124.

Tversky, A., Kahneman, D., 1973. Availability: A heuristic for judging frequency and probability. Cognitive Psychology 5, 207–232. https://doi.org/10.1016/0010-0285(73)90033-9.

United Nations Framework Convention on Climate Change, 1992.

Vagropoulos, S.I., Biskas, P.N., Bakirtzis, A.G., 2022. Market-based TSO-DSO coordination for enhanced flexibility services provision. Electric Power Systems Research 208, 107883. https://doi.org/10.1016/j.epsr.2022.107883.

Vallés, M., Reneses, J., Cossent, R., Frías, P., 2016. Regulatory and market barriers to the realization of demand response in electricity distribution networks: A European perspective. Electric Power Systems Research 140, 689–698. https://doi.org/10.1016/j.epsr.2016.04.026.

van der Welle, A.J., de Joode, J., 2011. Regulatory road maps for the integration of intermittent electricity generation: Methodology development and the case of The Netherlands. Energy Policy 39, 5829–5839. https://doi.org/10.1016/j.enpol.2011.06.017.

van Soest, H., 2018. Peer-to-peer electricity trading: A review of the legal context. Competition and Regulation in Network Industries 19, 180–199. https://doi.org/10.1177/1783591719834902.

Vandendriessche, F., Bogaert, P.V., 2023. De bevoegde regelgevers voor het energierecht, in: Vandendriessche, F. (Ed.), Energierecht in België En Vlaanderen 2023. Intersentia, p. 17.

Vandorpe, W., Callaerts, R., 2018. De federale regulering van flexibiliteit en opslag van elektriciteit: een lichte voorsprong op Europa, in: Deketelaere, K., Delvaux, B. (Eds.), Jaarboek Energierecht 2017. Intersentia.

Vandorpe, W., Callaerts, R., 2017. Flexibiliteit en demand side management juridisch bekeken. Ex umbra in solem?, in: Deketelaere, K., Delvaux, B. (Eds.), Jaarboek Energierecht 2016. Intersentia, p. 221.

Varho, V., Rikkonen, P., Rasi, S., 2016. Futures of distributed small-scale renewable energy in Finland – A Delphi study of the opportunities and obstacles up to 2025. Technological Forecasting and Social Change 104, 30–37. https://doi.org/10.1016/j.techfore.2015.12.001.

Verbong, G., Geels, F., 2007. The ongoing energy transition: Lessons from a socio-technical, multi-level analysis of the Dutch electricity system (1960–2004). Energy Policy 35, 1025–1037. https://doi.org/10.1016/j.enpol.2006.02.010.

Vernay, A.-L., Sebi, C., 2020. Energy communities and their ecosystems: A comparison of France and the Netherlands. Technological Forecasting and Social Change 158, 120123. https://doi.org/10.1016/j.techfore.2020.120123.

Vernay, A.-L., Sebi, C., Arroyo, F., 2023. Energy community business models and their impact on the energy transition: Lessons learnt from France. Energy Policy 175, 113473. https://doi.org/10.1016/j.enpol.2023.113473.

Verordnung über die Anreizregulierung der Energieversorgungsnetze, 2007.

Verordnung über die Entgelte für den Zugang zu Elektrizitätsversorgungsnetzen, 2005.

Verpoorten, K., De Jonghe, C., Belmans, R., 2016. Market barriers for harmonised demand-response in balancing reserves: Cross-country comparison, in: 2016 13th International Conference on the European Energy Market (EEM). pp. 1–5. https://doi.org/10.1109/EEM.2016.7521327.

Verzijlbergh, R.A., Vries, L.J.D., Lukszo, Z., 2014. Renewable Energy Sources and Responsive Demand. Do We Need Congestion Management in the Distribution Grid? IEEE Transactions on Power Systems 29, 2119–2128. https://doi.org/10.1109/TPWRS.2014.2300941.

Veum, K., Bauknecht, D., 2019. How to reach the EU renewables target by 2030? An analysis of the governance framework. Energy Policy 127, 299–307. https://doi.org/10.1016/j.enpol.2018.12.013.

Villar, J., Bessa, R., Matos, M., 2018. Flexibility products and markets: Literature review. Electric Power Systems Research 154, 329–340. https://doi.org/10.1016/j.epsr.2017.09.005.

Vogelsang, I., 2005. Electricity Transmission Pricing and Performance-Based Regulation. The Energy Journal 27. https://doi.org/10.2307/23297035.

von Loessl, V., 2023. Smart meter-related data privacy concerns and dynamic electricity tariffs: Evidence from a stated choice experiment. Energy Policy 180, 113645. https://doi.org/10.1016/j.enpol.2023.113645.

VREG, 2024. Electricity and gas market report 2023 [Marktrapport elektriciteit en gas 2023] (No. RAPP-2024-13).

VREG, 2022a. Beslissing van de VREG met betrekking tot de oplegging van een administratieve geldboete, conform artikel 13.3.2 Energiedecreet, aan de opdrachthoudende vereniging FLUVIUS ANTWERPEN wegens de niet-naleving van de artikelen 7.2.1, §1 en 7.2.2, §2 Energiedecreet evenals de artikelen 4.3.64 en 4.3.65 TRDE.

VREG, 2022b. Beslissing van de VREG met betrekking tot de oplegging van een administratieve geldboete, conform artikel 13.3.2 Energiedecreet, aan de opdrachthoudende vereniging FLUVIUS LIMBURG wegens de niet-naleving van de artikelen 7.2.1, §1 en 7.2.2, §2 Energiedecreet evenals de artikelen 4.3.64 en 4.3.65 TRDE.

VREG, 2022c. Beslissing van de VREG met betrekking tot de oplegging van een administratieve geldboete, conform artikel 13.3.2 Energiedecreet, aan de opdrachthoudende vereniging FLUVIUS WEST wegens de niet-naleving van de artikelen 7.2.1, §1 en 7.2.2, §2 Energiedecreet evenals de artikelen 4.3.64 en 4.3.65 TRDE.

VREG, 2022d. Beslissing van de VREG met betrekking tot de oplegging van een administratieve geldboete, conform artikel 13.3.2 Energiedecreet, aan de opdrachthoudende vereniging GASELWEST wegens de niet-naleving van de artikelen 7.2.1, §1 en 7.2.2, §2 Energiedecreet evenals de artikelen 4.3.64 en 4.3.65 TRDE.

VREG, 2022e. Beslissing van de VREG met betrekking tot de oplegging van een administratieve geldboete, conform artikel 13.3.2 Energiedecreet, aan de opdrachthoudende vereniging IMEWO wegens de nietnaleving van de artikelen 7.2.1, §1 en 7.2.2, §2 Energiedecreet evenals de artikelen 4.3.64 en 4.3.65 TRDE.

VREG, 2022f. Beslissing van de VREG met betrekking tot de oplegging van een administratieve geldboete, conform artikel 13.3.2 Energiedecreet, aan de opdrachthoudende vereniging INTERGEM wegens de nietnaleving van de artikelen 7.2.1, §1 en 7.2.2, §2 Energiedecreet evenals de artikelen 4.3.64 en 4.3.65 TRDE.

VREG, 2022g. Beslissing van de VREG met betrekking tot de oplegging van een administratieve geldboete, conform artikel 13.3.2 Energiedecreet, aan de opdrachthoudende vereniging IVEKA wegens de nietnaleving van de artikelen 7.2.1, §1 en 7.2.2, §2 Energiedecreet evenals de artikelen 4.3.64 en 4.3.65 TRDE.

VREG, 2022h. Beslissing van de VREG met betrekking tot de oplegging van een administratieve geldboete, conform artikel 13.3.2 Energiedecreet, aan de opdrachthoudende vereniging IVERLEK wegens de nietnaleving van de artikelen 7.2.1, §1 en 7.2.2, §2 Energiedecreet evenals de artikelen 4.3.64 en 4.3.65 TRDE.

VREG, 2022i. Beslissing van de VREG met betrekking tot de oplegging van een administratieve geldboete, conform artikel 13.3.2 Energiedecreet, aan de opdrachthoudende vereniging PBE wegens de nietnaleving van de artikelen 7.2.1, §1 en 7.2.2, §2 Energiedecreet evenals de artikelen 4.3.64 en 4.3.65 TRDE.

VREG, 2022j. Beslissing van de VREG met betrekking tot de oplegging van een administratieve geldboete, conform artikel 13.3.2 Energiedecreet, aan de opdrachthoudende vereniging SIBELGAS wegens de nietnaleving van de artikelen 7.2.1, §1 en 7.2.2, §2 Energiedecreet evenals de artikelen 4.3.64 en 4.3.65 TRDE.

VREG, 2020. Advies van de VREG van 27/11/2020 met betrekking tot het voorontwerp van decreet tot wijziging van het Energiedecreet van 8 mei 2009 tot gedeeltelijke omzetting van richtlijn (EU) 2018/2001 van het Europees Parlement en de Raad van 11 december 2018 ter bevordering van het gebruik van energie uit hernieuwbare bronnen en tot omzetting van richtlijn (EU) 2019/944 van het Europees Parlement en de Raad van 5 juni 2019 betreffende gemeenschappelijke regels voor de interne markt voor elektriciteit en tot wijziging van Richtlijn 2012/27/EU.

VREG decision on proposed changes to 'Fluvius consultation procedure', annex to BESL-2022-33 [Beslissing van de VREG met betrekking tot voorgestelde wijzigingen aan de 'consultatieprocedures Fluvius', bijlage bij BESL-2022-33], 2023.

VREG Decision on the approval of the proposal of the electricity distribution system operators concerning the protocol on energy sharing and peer-to-peer trading of green electricity (third protocol version) [Beslissing van de VREG met betrekking tot de goedkeuring van het voorstel van de elektriciteitsdistributienetbeheerders betreffende het protocol inzake energiedelen en peer-to-peerhandel van groene stroom (derde protocolversie)], 2022.

Wagner, O., Berlo, K., 2015. The wave of remunicipalisation of energy networks and supply in Germany: the establishment of 72 new municipal power utilities, in: Lindström, T.L. (Ed.), First Fuel Now: ECEEE 2015 Summer Study. European Council for an Energy Efficient Economy, p. 559.

Walker, G., Day, R., 2012. Fuel poverty as injustice: Integrating distribution, recognition and procedure in the struggle for affordable warmth. Energy Policy 49, 69–75. https://doi.org/10.1016/j.enpol.2012.01.044.

Walker, G., Devine-Wright, P., 2008. Community renewable energy: What should it mean? Energy Policy 36, 497–500. https://doi.org/10.1016/j.enpol.2007.10.019.

Walker, G., Simcock, N., Day, R., 2016. Necessary energy uses and a minimum standard of living in the United Kingdom: Energy justice or escalating expectations? Energy Research & Social Science 18, 129–138. https://doi.org/10.1016/j.erss.2016.02.007.

Warren, P., 2015. Demand-Side Management Policy: Mechanisms for Success and Failure (PhD Dissertation). University College London.

Warren, P., 2014. A review of demand-side management policy in the UK. Renewable and Sustainable Energy Reviews 29, 941–951. https://doi.org/10.1016/j.rser.2013.09.009.

Watson, C., Boyle, E., Mullally, G., Gallachóir, B.Ó., 2020. Responding to the Energy Transition in Ireland: The Experience and Capacity of Communities (No. Report No.337). Environmental Protection Agency.

Weber, C., Just, S., 2012. Strategic Behavior in the German Balancing Energy Mechanism: Incentives, Evidence, Costs and Solutions. Journal of Regulatory Economics 48. https://doi.org/10.1007/s11149-015-9270-6.

Webster, W., 2021. Security of supply, in: Jones, C., Kettlewell, W.-J. (Eds.), EU Energy Law Volume I: The Internal Energy Market. CLAEYS & CASTEELS.

Weck, M.H.J., van Hooff, J., van Sark, W.G.J.H.M., 2017. Review of barriers to the introduction of residential demand response: a case study in the Netherlands. International Journal of Energy Research 41, 790–816. https://doi.org/10.1002/er.3683.

Weinhardt, C., Mengelkamp, E., Cramer, W., Hambridge, S., Hobert, A., Kremers, E., Otter, W., Pinson, P., Tiefenbeck, V., Zade, M., 2019. How far along are Local Energy Markets in the DACH+ Region? A Comparative Market Engineering Approach, in: Proceedings of the Tenth ACM International Conference on Future Energy Systems, E-Energy' 19. Association for Computing Machinery, New York, NY, USA, pp. 544–549. https://doi.org/10.1145/3307772.3335318.

Willems, B., Zhou, J., 2020. The Clean Energy Package and Demand Response: Setting Correct Incentives. Energies 13. https://doi.org/10.3390/en13215672.

Wimmers, A., Madlener, R., 2024. The European Market for Guarantees of Origin for Green Electricity: A Scenario-Based Evaluation of Trading under Uncertainty. Energies 17. https://doi.org/10.3390/en17010104.

Woerter, M., Stucki, T., Arvanitis, S., Rammer, C., Peneder, M., 2017. The adoption of green energy technologies: The role of policies in Austria, Germany, and Switzerland. International Journal of Green Energy 14, 1192–1208. https://doi.org/10.1080/15435075.2017.1381612.

Wohlfarth, K., Klingler, A.-L., Eichhammer, W., 2020. The flexibility deployment of the service sector – A demand response modelling approach coupled with evidence from a market research survey. Energy Strategy Reviews 28, 100460. https://doi.org/10.1016/j.esr.2020.100460.

Wolsink, M., 2007. Wind power implementation: The nature of public attitudes: Equity and fairness instead of 'backyard motives.' Renewable and Sustainable Energy Reviews 11, 1188–1207. https://doi.org/10.1016/j.rser.2005.10.005.

Woodman, B., Baker, P., 2008. Regulatory frameworks for decentralised energy. Energy Policy 36, 4527–4531. https://doi.org/10.1016/j.enpol.2008.09.017

Wüstenhagen, R., Bilharz, M., 2006. Green energy market development in Germany: effective public policy and emerging customer demand. Energy Policy 34, 1681–1696. https://doi.org/10.1016/j.enpol.2004.07.013.

Wüstenhagen, R., Menichetti, E., 2012. Strategic choices for renewable energy investment: Conceptual framework and opportunities for further research. Energy Policy 40, 1–10. https://doi.org/10.1016/j.enpol.2011.06.050.

Yildiz, Ö., Rommel, J., Debor, S., Holstenkamp, L., Mey, F., Müller, J.R., Radtke, J., Rognli, J., 2015. Renewable energy cooperatives as gatekeepers or facilitators? Recent developments in Germany and a multidisciplinary research agenda. Energy Research & Social Science 6, 59–73. https://doi.org/10.1016/j.erss.2014.12.001.

Yousefi, A., Nguyen, T.T., Zareipour, H., Malik, O.P., 2012. Congestion management using demand response and FACTS devices. International Journal of Electrical Power & Energy Systems 37, 78–85. https://doi.org/10.1016/j.ijepes.2011.12.008.

Yuan, Z., Hesamzadeh, M.R., 2017. Hierarchical coordination of TSO-DSO economic dispatch considering large-scale integration of distributed energy resources. Applied Energy 195, 600–615. https://doi.org/10.1016/j.apenergy.2017.03.042.

Zegers, A., Brunner, H., 2014. TSO-DSO interaction: An Overview of current interaction between transmission and distribution system operators and an assessment of their cooperation in Smart Grids (ISGAN Discussion Paper).

Zehir, M.A., Batman, A., Sonmez, M.A., Font, A., Tsiamitros, D., Stimoniaris, D., Kollatou, T., Bagriyanik, M., Ozdemir, A., Dialynas, E., 2017. Impacts of microgrids with renewables on secondary distribution networks. Applied Energy 201, 308–319. https://doi.org/10.1016/j.apenergy.2016.12.138.

Zhang, Y., 2016. Statistics of curtailing wind power generation from 2011 to 2015. Wind Energy 2, 34.

Zhou, Q., Bialek, J.W., 2007. Generation curtailment to manage voltage constraints in distribution networks. Generation, Transmission & Distribution, IET 1, 492–498. https://doi.org/10.1049/iet-gtd:20060246.

Zhou, S., Matisoff, D.C., Kingsley, G.A., Brown, M.A., 2019. Understanding renewable energy policy adoption and evolution in Europe: The impact of coercion, normative emulation, competition, and learning. Energy Research & Social Science 51, 1–11. https://doi.org/10.1016/j.erss.2018.12.011.

Zhou, Y., Wu, J., Gan, W., 2023. P2P energy trading via public power networks: Practical challenges, emerging solutions, and the way forward. Frontiers in Energy 17, 189–197. https://doi.org/10.1007/s11708-023-0873-9.

www.ingramcontent.com/pod-product-compliance
Ingram Content Group UK Ltd.
Pitfield, Milton Keynes, MK11 3LW, UK
UKHW051906290926
8980IPUK00018B/1798

9 781839 706172